FRANZ LISZT AND HIS WORLD

Franz Liszt

AND HIS WORLD

EDITED BY CHRISTOPHER H. GIBBS
AND DANA GOOLEY

PRINCETON UNIVERSITY PRESS
PRINCETON AND OXFORD

Copyright © 2006 by Princeton University Press

Published by Princeton University Press, 41 William Street,
Princeton, New Jersey 08540
In the United Kingdom: Princeton University Press,
3 Market Place, Woodstock, Oxfordshire OX20 1SY

All Rights Reserved

For permissions information, see page xiii.

Library of Congress Control Number 2006925776

ISBN-13: 978-0-691-12901-3 (cloth)
ISBN-10: 0-691-12901-0 (cloth)
ISBN-13: 978-0-691-12902-0 (paperback)
ISBN-10: 0-691-12902-9 (paperback)

British Library Cataloging-in-Publication Data is available

This publication has been produced by the Bard College Publications Office:

Ginger Shore, Director

Francie Soosman, Cover design

Natalie Kelly, Design

Text edited by Paul De Angelis and Erin Clermont

Music typeset by Don Giller

This publication has been underwritten in part by a grant from
Furthermore: a program of the J. M. Kaplan Fund.

Printed on acid-free paper. ∞

pup.princeton.edu

Printed in the United States of America

1 3 5 7 9 10 8 6 4 2

This volume is dedicated to

Ruth and David E. Schwab II

Bard College Class of 1952

on the occasion of their 75th birthdays;

we thank them for their love of music

and loyalty to the Bard Music Festival.

Contents

Contents

PART IV
REFLECTIONS ON FRANZ LISZT

Acknowledgments

The volumes in the Bard Music Festival series published each year by Princeton University Press follow an unusually accelerated production schedule and is only possible given the professionalism and dedication of many individuals. We are most grateful to the authors and contributors to this volume who have understood the timetable, accommodated it, and often made helpful suggestions of how to shape the book.

Ginger Shore, director of the Bard Publications Office, has overseen this series with committed concern and helpful support. Paul De Angelis, who also has many years experience, provided critical feedback for this book at every stage of the process and gave a fresh perspective to editors who sometimes can no longer see the forest for the trees. Irene Zedlacher, executive director of the Bard Music Festival, generously took time to read the entire book and provided further comment. Natalie Kelly and Don Giller provided the design and music typeset. Our final thanks go to Leon Botstein, founder of the Festival and originator of these books, who inspires with his vision and by his intellectual example.

Permissions and Credits

Front cover image: *Franz Liszt*. Oil painting by Ary Scheffer (1795–1858). Reproduced by permission of Klassik Stiftung Weimar.

"Liszt, Italy, and the Republic of the Imagination": figure 1, Giovanni Paolo Panini's *Roma Antica* is reproduced by permission of the Staatsgalerie, Stuttgart; figure 2, Raphael's *Sposalizio* is reproduced by permission of the Ministero per i Beni e le Attività Culturali; Soprintendenza per il Patrimonio Storico Artistico ed Etnoantropologico per le Province di Milano, Bergamo, Como, Lecco, Lodi, Pavia, Sondria, Varese; figure 3, Michelangelo's *Il penseroso* is reproduced by permission of the Soprintendenza Speciale per il Polo Museale fiorentino (Ufficio Permessi e Concessioni, Florence); figure 4, Salvatore Rosa's *Self-Portrait*, is reproduced by permission of the National Gallery, London; figure 5, Henri Lehmann's *Portrait of Liszt*, is reproduced by permission of the Mairie de Paris, Direction des Affaires Culturelles; figure 6 is from the Goethe- und Schiller-Archiv, 601 I 17 and is reproduced by permission of Klassik Stiftung Weimar.

"Prophet and Populace in Liszt's 'Beethoven' Cantatas": figure 1, *The Artists' Concert*, from *Illustrirte Zeitung* 116, is reproduced courtesy of the Bildarchiv, Deutsches Historisches Museum, Berlin; figure 2 is reproduced by permission of Beethoven-Haus, Bonn; figure 3 is reproduced from *Festgabe zu der am 12ten August 1845 stattfindenden Inauguration des Beethoven Monuments*, by H. K. Breidenstein (Bonn: 1845)

"'Just Two Words. Enormous Success'": all figures reproduced by permission of the Archiv, Bibliothek und Sammlungen der Gesellschaft der Musikfreunde, Vienna; translation by Charles Suttoni of Franz Grillparzer's "Clara Wieck und Beethoven (f-moll Sonate)" quoted from Franz Liszt, *An Arist's Journey: Lettres d'un bachelier ès musique 1835–1841*, is reprinted with permission of University of Chicago Press.

"Publishing Paraphrases and Creating Collectors": all figures reproduced by permission of the Sächsisches Staatsarchiv Leipzig.

"From the Biographer's Workshop": Questionnaire No. 10/1875 is reproduced with the kind permission of the Goethe- und Schiller-Archiv, Weimar.

"A Mirror to the Nineteenth Century": figures 1 and 3 are reproduced from *Die Mode: Menschen und Moden im Neunzehnten Jahrhundert, 1790–1817*, by Max von Boehn and Oskar Fischel (Munich: 1908); figures 5, 7, and 8 are from *Die Mode: Menschen und Moden im Neunzehnten Jahrhundert, 1818–1842*, by Max von Boehn and Oskar Fischel (Munich: 1907); figures 4 and 6 are from *Die Mode: Menschen und Moden im Neunzehnten Jahrhundert, 1843–1878,* by Max von Boehn and Oskar Fischel (Munich: 1908); figure 2 is from Norbert Stern, *Mode und Kultur,* vol. 1 (Dresden: 1915); figures 9 and 10 are from Ernst Burger, *Franz Liszt: A Chronicle of His Life in Pictures and Documents* (Princeton, N.J.: Princeton University Press, 1989); and figure 11 is from Ernst Burger, *Franz Liszt in der Photographie seiner Zeit: 260 Portraits, 1843–1886* (Munich: Hirmer Verlag, 2003).

Preface

Viewing Franz Liszt's career as a whole, one is continually struck by the sheer range of his activities and the diversity of his affiliations. As a young boy in Vienna during the early 1820s, he absorbed the legacy of Czerny, Salieri, and Beethoven. When he died in 1886, his example was being carried forward by such radicals as Strauss, Debussy, and Busoni. His achievements in pianism, composition, teaching, and institution building are of lasting significance. He promoted musical Classicism alongside musical Romanticism. He cultivated deep and sustained social networks in Paris, Vienna, Weimar, Rome, Budapest, and elsewhere. The number of people he knew and influenced probably exceeds that of any other figure in the history of music. His personal life has been a source of fascination for nearly two centuries. Cast simultaneously as a saintly figure of extraordinary generosity who took minor religious orders in mid-life, and as a satanic virtuoso notorious for his vanity, love affairs, and habitual indulgence in tobacco and alcohol, the contradictions are striking. If it seems too much of a cliché to say he was the first rock star among pianists (a portrayal presented in Ken Russell's film *Lisztomania*), one finds in Liszt nonetheless an uneasy and confounding juxtaposition of spiritual fervor with a 19th-century expression of "drugs, sex, and rock 'n' roll."

Out of this extraordinary variety, how does one condense a unified, embracing image or interpretive angle? With Liszt, most historians and critics throw up their hands at the thought of reconciling the contradictions into a coherent whole, preferring to regard them as evidence of a historical era ridden with inconsistencies. As his first biographer pointed out in 1835, and as Leon Botstein reasserts in the title to his concluding essay in this volume, Liszt bears the imprint of his world more completely than any artist of the 19th century. Understanding Liszt, then, demands that we understand also the world that formed him and continued to shape him well beyond his youth.

Over the past twenty years scholars have shown an impressive determination to organize and clean up Liszt's shop, which was left messy by a huge output of letters and music, by the geographical and linguistic dispersion of his papers, and by an enduring capacity for mythmaking on the part of his admirers as well as his detractors. In his imposing three-volume biography, the most complete work of its kind, Alan Walker has produced an engaging narrative and important reference. In the recent edition of the *New Grove Dictionary of Music and Musicians,* Rena Charnin Mueller and Mária Eckhardt have updated the list of works with meticulous and patient researches into Liszt's manuscripts and first editions. Long-needed critical editions of his works and writings are well under way. The difficulty of negotiating Liszt's correspondence has been alleviated considerably by Charles Suttoni's bibliographic explorations and by new editions of letters to individual correspondents such as Anna Liszt, Olga von Meyerdorff, Marie d'Agoult, and Agnes Street-Klindworth. Two large documentary collections compiled by Adrian Williams, one of letters, the other of observations and reminiscences by Liszt and his contemporaries, offer English readers a textured, close-up view of his life and circumstances. All of these projects have put Liszt's legacy on a far more solid foundation and made it much easier for the curious to find reliable information and documentation than was possible even as recently as 1985.

A disadvantage of these preoccupations is that they have tended to isolate Liszt studies in a hermetic world, relatively out of touch with the larger field of musicology, not to mention other disciplines. The resulting loss of intellectual vitality has found poor compensation in the defensive or even righteous tone that one characteristically finds in liner notes and biographies. "Once unfairly attacked in his lifetime," Graham Robb wrote in his 1995 biography of Balzac, "the writer will forever be unfairly defended, even to his detriment, and even when the court has long since been empty. Balzac has suffered more than any other novelist from this kind of critical defense." The words could be transferred directly to Liszt: he is defended to his detriment. He is a complex and elusive subject who can make us rethink some of the basic hierarchies of traditional historiography and analysis. His music alone confounds boundaries between national styles, between genres, between work and performer, between "authentic" and "revised" versions, between "pure" classical form and "poetic" program. Approaching him thus requires an openness to non-traditional, flexible, self-aware models of understanding. The values of an older generation of musicology—favoring structural integrity and consistency in the music, and ascetic artistic commitment in the life—tend to work against Liszt. So too does the hagiographic tone adopted by so many of his commentators and biographers, which all too clearly replicates the cultish admiration of his own audiences, colleagues, and students. The values of more recent musicology and cultural studies—

with their embrace of plurality and boundary-crossing, of performance, self-fashioning, and associative meaning—should be working in his favor. Jim Samson's embrace of these methods, combined with the best in traditional scholarship, has borne fruit in his recent, magnificent book on the *Transcendental Etudes*, entitled *Virtuosity and the Musical Work*.

The essays in this volume all concern Liszt without isolating him in the spotlight. They strive instead for a "dual focus," taking full measure of the specialized literature and in some cases adding new archival research, but placing this information in broader historical and critical perspective than has been usual in Liszt studies. The most common second focus is the public culture of the 19th century, the domain where he arguably had the deepest and most lasting impact. Ryan Minor highlights the power of choral music in defining national and cultural communities. Comparing Liszt's two relatively unknown "Beethoven" cantatas, written decades apart, he traces the evolution of Beethoven's symbolic status for the broader public, of which Liszt considered himself something of a curator. James Deaville's research into the archives of publisher Friedrich Hofmeister sheds new light on how Liszt, as represented in his published works, circulated in the commercial and material culture of the 19th century. His essay here provides uncommonly concrete evidence of the intimate links between virtuosos and sheet music publishing in the 1840s and beyond. Dana Gooley's essay reconstructs the critique of instrumental virtuosos that developed in the early 19th century— which was founded on a social and ethical perspective as much as it was an aesthetic one—and offers explanations for how Liszt escaped it. Leon Botstein's concluding contribution takes a long-range view of Liszt in relation to public musical culture, demonstrating multiple ways in which he adapted the older, more aristocratic values of Viennese Classicism, which he inherited as a boy, to the contexts of urban modernity of mid-19th-century musical culture, where audiences were larger, less communally educated, and immersed in a culture of fiction reading that reconstructed their experiences of time and imagination.

The two essays engaging most directly with Liszt's musical language, which remains the least developed area of Liszt scholarship as a whole, are Susan Youens's essay on the Heine songs, and Rainer Kleinertz's study of the symphonic poem *Orpheus* in relation to Wagner's *Tristan und Isolde*. While Liszt's songs are generally agreed to be among his best compositions and have recently been treated with survey-like commentary, they have received remarkably little critical or interpretive attention. Youens's essay raises the bar. Combining acute insights on Liszt's compositional strategies with an informed view of Heine, she argues that

Liszt's progressivism in the songs is more than a merely musical project, but an extension of Heine's own progressive program for poetry. Kleinertz's essay on Liszt and Wagner, without engaging the vexed old question of who influenced whom, identifies *Orpheus* as a key link between the two composers. He fills a significant gap in music analysis: a vocabulary for discussing phrase relationships that are not organized by closure or classical periodicity.

Liszt lived or spent significant periods of time in an astonishing variety of places—Vienna, Paris, Geneva, Venice, Weimar, Budapest, and Rome—and each left an imprint on his outlook and music. Two essays here explore Liszt in relationship to specific locales. Anna Celenza provides a new angle on Liszt's years of pilgrimage (1835–39) by showing how invested he was in a Romantic construct of Italy as a "republic of the imagination." Her essay, with its eye for literary detail, reminds us that no matter how "real" the Italian journey was, his travel essays and evocative compositions filter his voyages through the prism of Romantic fantasy. Christopher Gibbs's richly documented essay places Liszt's 1838 triumphs in Vienna, which were decisive for his career, within the context of that city's broader concert life. Comparing Liszt with other major virtuosos in the city, notably Sigismond Thalberg and Clara Wieck, it offers new perspective on the distinct physiognomy of Liszt's concert strategies and corrects a number of errors long perpetuated in biographies.

The nineteenth century was a century of the monumental biography: Spitta on Bach, Abert on Mozart, Thayer on Beethoven, to mention some examples from music. The earlier efforts of Lina Ramann and Peter Raabe notwithstanding, tradition has only caught up with Liszt in recent times, with the work of Alan Walker, complementing significant biographical explorations by Bernard Gavoty, Serge Gut, Klára Hamburger, Emmerich Karl Horvath, and Dezsö Legány. Liszt's contemporaries had to make do with shorter biographies written to meet tight deadlines. Three documents presented in Part II put the biographical enterprise into historical context and assist us in reimagining how Liszt might have appeared to his contemporaries. Each of these documents was produced by a confidant of Liszt and took shape from its author's background and priorities. Joseph d'Ortigue's 1835 study from the French press accents Liszt as a product of modern intellectual and spiritual culture—"performing Zeitgeist" as Benjamin Walton puts it in his introduction. Berlin critic Ludwig Rellstab's biographical sketch from 1842, intended as a pamphlet to accompany Liszt's German tours and prefaced here by Allan Keiler, pays closer attention to the virtuoso's advocacy of German masters and his charity efforts. Rena Mueller's presentation of Ramann's written questionnaires to Liszt documents the methods of his first major biographer. Liszt's written responses provide unusual glimpses into how he sought to be presented and remembered while suggesting that he was not entirely at ease with her modern philological methods. Liszt is given another chance to speak directly in Part II through a translation of one of his own writings. The issue of the true authorship of much of what was published under his name has vexed the Liszt literature since his own time, but about the contribution presented here there can be little question. The final installment of Liszt's humanitarian essay "On the Situation of Artists and on Their Condition in Society," a rare example of a text that survives in his own hand, is a brief but fully representative sample of the heady, somewhat chaotic mix of philosophy, spirituality, and Romantic inspiration that engulfed the young artist in the early 1830s.

Part III, "Criticism and Reception," offers some key 19th-century documents concerning Liszt and his circle that have not been accessible, or only incompletely so, in English. Although Belgian critic François-Joseph Fétis was initially little inclined toward the Romantic young virtuoso, in his 1841 review of Liszt's *Transcendental Etudes,* introduced here by Peter Bloom, he found himself at last won over. José Antonio Bowen's selection of reviews of Liszt playing and conducting at the Bonn Beethoven festival of 1845 isolate a crucial historical moment where the values of performance and the values associated with Beethoven were being transformed by the younger generation of musicians. Of Heinrich Heine's three incomparably entertaining and perceptive essays on Liszt, only one has been fully available in English translation (in Charles Suttoni's *An Artist's Journey*). Here we offer the other two, the second of which, as Rainer Kleinertz explains, has a complicated genesis shedding new light on the relationship between Liszt and Heine. The two published versions of this essay are presented here on facing pages to clarify how Heine changed his views and his strategies of articulation. Felix Draeseke's defense of Liszt's symphonic poems, introduced by James Deaville, gives voice to the progressive party in the so-called War of the Romantics, thus balancing out the better-known conservative manifesto signed by Joseph Joachim and Johannes Brahms.

Two worlds of Liszt not prominently featured in this book, although inevitably touched upon at various points, are his relationship to the Hungarian nation, which played an especially significant role during the last third of his life, and his religious faith, a lifelong preoccupation that also bloomed in his later years. The lack of emphasis upon these two areas in no way reflects the editors' convictions about the importance of these subjects. Readers interested in Liszt's connections with Hungary will find thorough coverage in Deszö Legány's two-volume *Liszt and His Country*. Paul Merrick's book *Revolution and Religion in the Music of Franz Liszt* touches upon many of the key issues in Liszt's religious music.

Liszt's achievements as pianist, composer, and teacher all evince a commitment to immediacy and efficacy of communication. In performance he promoted audience engagement by expressing the sense of the music in his facial expressions and body language. In his numerous piano transcriptions he would unhesitatingly violate the letter of Schubert's and Beethoven's scores if in doing so it would help convey to listeners the spirit of the original. In the symphonic poems Liszt articulated feelings and ideas—such as heroism, lament, passion, and love—in a direct, no-nonsense manner, so as not to interfere with the elevated themes, characters, or causes he wanted to convey. This set his symphonic music apart from Wagner, who was inclined to invest his works with metaphysical or symbolic weight, and from Brahms, where musical ideas were invented with constructive and developmental possibilities in mind. Liszt resisted esotericism and devoted himself to effective communication in protest of the inertia of urban modernity, where music was fast becoming commodified as entertainment and luxury, and thereby risked becoming trivial and marginal. Whether arguing (early on) that artists ought to be the focal point of social regeneration, or trying (later on) to revitalize the music of the weakening Catholic church through an infusion of modern music resources, he strove to close the gap between artists and contemporary audiences. In today's world, where the task of generating audience sympathy for classical music is largely assigned to professional agents and marketers, Liszt serves as an example of where we may want to go.

PART I

ESSAYS

Liszt, Italy, and the Republic

of the Imagination

ANNA HARWELL CELENZA

Liszt's first encounter with Italy has been told time and again in various guises: as a romance, a travelogue, and a *Bildungsroman*.[1] Italy's breathtaking beauty has been credited with luring him over the Alps. As Chateaubriand once said, "Nothing is comparable to the beauty of the Roman horizon, to the sweet inclination of the plains as they meet the soft and flowing contours of the hills."[2] Such sensual descriptions attracted many visitors to Italy, but there was more to Liszt's travels than scenic diversion. When he journeyed south in 1837, he joined a steady stream of artists, aristocrats, writers, and musicians who for centuries had made the long and difficult trip. Like these travelers, Liszt was drawn by Italy's reputation as the cradle of European culture, by the beauty of its art, and by the mystery of its past. Although it is true that he was in the middle of a scandalous relationship with Marie d'Agoult when he journeyed south with her, this was old news; their first child had already been born, in 1835. Liszt was escaping more than mere gossip when he left Paris. He was on a quest to discover his creative essence, a new artistic identity. Liszt had a "premeditated master plan" concerning the future course of his career, and during the second half of the 1830s he planned on "distinguishing himself" in intellectual pursuits that were accorded more prestige than mere performing—namely composition and literature.[3] Italy offered beauty and comfort; but more important, it held the promise of an intellectually rich escape.

The image of Italy as a destination for the cultured and well educated took shape in the mid-eighteenth century. Painters such as Canaletto captured the beauty of Italian cities and landscapes, and archaeological excavations across the peninsula fueled a growing interest in antiquity. Scholars like Johann Joachim Winckelmann in Germany and Comte Anne-Claude-Philippe de Caylus in France pondered Italy's ancient past. Their studies drew countless travelers from across Europe, and the Grand Tour became a required activity in the education of every "European gentleman." Rome, in particular, served as a living textbook—the undisputed capital of the visual arts (figure 1).[4] Some scholars have described Liszt's first journey to Italy as his own Grand Tour.[5] This description is valid as far as it goes, since it is clear that Liszt sought an education of sorts as he traveled. But self-enlightenment was not at the core of his motivation. Simply put, Liszt traveled to Italy to escape his own past. Troubled by the music politics he had recently experienced in Paris, he sought refuge, and Italy seemed the perfect sanctuary.

Scholars have mapped every step of Liszt's journey, from the moment he first crossed the Alps to his twilight days in Tivoli late in life. My goal is somewhat different. Instead of describing "Liszt in Italy," I reflect on the image of Italy he alluded to in his music, specifically the second volume of his *Années de pèlerinage* (Years of pilgrimage)—*Deuxième Année: Italie* (Second year: Italy).[6] Liszt published this work in 1858, three years after *Première Année: Suisse* (First year: Switzerland), appeared.[7] The first volume consists of nine pieces, all of which are related to impressions of nature and scenic Swiss locales. In contrast, the Italy volume contains seven pieces directly related to the visual arts and poetry of early-modern Italy:

"Sposalizio" (a painting by Raphael)
"Il penseroso" (a sculpture by Michelangelo)
"Canzonetta del Salvator Rosa"
"Sonetto 47 del Petrarca"
"Sonetto 104 del Petrarca"
"Sonetto 123 del Petrarca"
"Après une lecture du Dante (Fantasia quasi Sonata)"

In addition to revealing the art and literary works Liszt encountered in Italy, year two of *Années de pèlerinage* roughly replicates the itinerary he followed, from Milan and Venice to Florence and Rome.[8] By the time he crossed the Alps, these cities had become reputed havens for political and social exiles. The end of the Napoleonic era marked a new chapter in the region's history. Humbled politically, Italy had become a cultural refuge, "the Paradise of Exiles" as Shelley described it in 1824.[9] Lord Byron had much to do with the creation of this image. In the final installment (Canto IV) of *Childe Harold's Pilgrimage* (published in 1818), Byron blended the popular image of the poet as rebel and bearer of freedom with that of the social outcast and solitary wanderer. Italy offered self-exiles like Liszt a new start—a chance to face up to his mission as a "poet" in the Romantic sense of the word and define his artistic identity as an expatriate in a foreign land.

Various pieces in the first two volumes of *Années de pèlerinage* are framed by quotations from Cantos III and IV of *Childe Harold's Pilgrimage*. Like Byron, Liszt consciously created a public image of himself as a lone pilgrim, an intellectual "poet" whose travels across Switzerland served as the scenic prelude to a full artistic awakening in Italy. Liszt presented this Byronic image of himself to Parisian readers through a series of articles (commonly referred to as *Lettres d'un bachelier ès musique*) published in *Revue et Gazette musicale de Paris* and *L'Artiste* during his years abroad. The authorship of these articles has been a topic of debate for nearly a century. Although Liszt's name appeared as the sole author, even he acknowledged that d'Agoult sometimes contributed to their production. To date, Rainer Kleinertz has given the most even-handed assessment of

Figure 1. Giovanni Paolo Panini, *Roma Antica,* or *Views of Ancient Rome with the Artist Finishing a Copy of the Aldobrini Wedding.* Stuttgart, Staatsgallerie.

the Liszt-d'Agoult authorship issue. In the commentary to his edition of Liszt's complete writings, Kleinertz describes d'Agoult's contributions to various article drafts written between 1837 and 1841 and, in so doing, convincingly demonstrates that the overall structure and content of the articles should be attributed primarily to Liszt.[10] Charles Suttoni expressed a similar opinion in his own study of Liszt's literary works, claiming that they were the result of "an active and fluid literary partnership" where "Liszt's ideas" were at times "expressed in d'Agoult's words."[11] Despite their authorship, Liszt's articles drew attention to his travel experiences and intellectual inquiries—they also highlighted many of the literary and artistic influences that later defined his *Années de pèlerinage*.

In recent years, scholars interested in Liszt's *Années de pèlerinage* have concentrated on purely musical aspects, namely the composition's genesis and form.[12] My approach is markedly different. Focusing on the extra-musical origins of the Italy volume, I describe in detail the cultural and historical circumstances that informed Liszt's reception of Italian art and literature. As I hope to demonstrate, the literary and artistic sources Liszt encountered during his travels across Italy profoundly influenced his self-image as a composer and his creation of *Années de pèlerinage*. In Liszt's mind, Italy became part of an ideal landscape that I call the Republic of the Imagination. This term is closely tied to George Sand's descriptions of a "republic of music" and "holy colony of artists" in her letters to Liszt.[13] When Sand coined these ideas in the early 1830s, their political resonance was especially strong, and my use of the phrase Republic of the Imagination makes reference to this.[14] Sand's ideas clearly influenced Liszt's perception of Italy; his Republic of the Imagination was a state of mind, an imaginary place where artists, writers, and musicians interacted freely, unbound by political or historical ties. Specifically, it was a creative space where Liszt interacted with an imagined community of artists derived from early-modern Italian art and literature.

Like many northern travelers before him—including Goethe, Byron, and Heine—Liszt toured Switzerland before venturing on to Italy.[15] Sand wrote to him at this time, describing the "divine" inspiration she knew he would find there. Encouraging him to forget about music politics in Paris, she recommended he join the "holy colony of artists" and pledge allegiance to the metaphorical "republic" of music—a land that would be revealed to him via the wondrous beauty of nature.[16] Liszt attempted to follow her advice, but as he explained in a response published in the *Revue et Gazette musicale* in December 1835, he was unable "to fathom the treasures of the snow" as she had. "The wall-nettles, bindweeds, and harts' tongues" that had whispered "harmonious secrets" in her ear, remained silent in his presence. Liszt was at a loss, and he described his state of mind in great detail:

> The republic of music, already established by a leap of your young imagination, is still only a dream for me. . . . I blush with shame and confusion when I reflect seriously on my life and pit your dreams against my realities: . . . your noble presentiments, your beautiful illusions about the social effects of the art to which I have dedicated my life, against the gloomy discouragement that sometimes seizes me when I compare the impotence of the *effort* with the eagerness of the *desire*, the nothingness of the *work* with the limitlessness of the *idea*;—those miracles of understanding and regeneration wrought by the thrice-blessed lyre of ancient times, against the sad and sterile role to which it is seemingly confined today.[17]

Liszt's self-doubt was exacerbated by the fact that Sigismond Thalberg had recently descended on Paris and was being hailed as "le premier pianiste du monde."[18] Intent on confronting this new "mysterious rival," Liszt postponed his travel plans to Italy and returned to Paris.[19] On 8 January 1837, he published a mean-spirited review of Thalberg's music in the *Revue et Gazette musicale*. This article angered many of Liszt's colleagues, especially the critic François-Joseph Fétis, who later came to Thalberg's defense in an article of his own.[20] Reactions such as this turned Liszt into something of a pariah in Parisian musical politics, and he soon took up his pen again—this time in the guise of a persecuted artist. In an article addressed "To a Poet-Voyager" (i.e., George Sand), Liszt expressed his desire to escape.[21] Using language strikingly similar to that found in Madame de Staël's novel *Corinne ou Italie*, he lamented Italy's political misfortune and explained why it was the perfect refuge for "those exiles from heaven," like himself, "who suffer and sing" all in the name of "poetry":

> Italy! Italy! The foreigner's steel has scattered your noblest children far and wide. They wander among the nations, their brows branded with a sacred curse. Yet no matter how implacable your oppressors might be, you will not be forsaken, because you were and will always be the land of choice for those men who have no brothers among men, for those children of God, those exiles from heaven who suffer and sing and whom the world calls "poets."
> Yes, the inspired man—philosopher, artist, or poet—will always be tormented by a secret misfortune, a burning hope in your regard. Italy's misfortune will always be the misfortune of noble souls, and

all of them will exclaim, along with Goethe's mysterious child: DAHIN! DAHIN![22]

Liszt had chosen Italy as his destination, and in a later article he described, in language clearly influenced by Byron's *Childe Harold*, his destiny as a vagabond artist:

> It behooves an artist more than anyone else to pitch a tent for only an hour and not to build anything like a permanent residence. Isn't he always a stranger among men? Isn't his homeland somewhere else? Whatever he does, wherever he goes, he always feels himself an exile. . . . What then can he do to escape his vague sadness and undefined regrets? He must sing and move on, pass through the crowd, scattering his works to it without caring where they land, without listening to the clamor with which people stifle them, and without paying attention to the contemptible laurels with which they crown him. What a sad and great destiny to be an artist![23]

These are the sentiments of a man in crisis. "I have just spent the past six months living a life of shabby squabbles and virtually sterile endeavors," Liszt lamented. "Day by day, hour by hour, I endured the silent tortures of the perpetual misunderstanding that . . . exists between the public and the artist."[24] Liszt felt isolated, unsure of the future. As Dana Gooley explains, the Parisian public had not fully embraced his approach to virtuosity, which was "aimed at the sensibilities of the *literati*, the *artistes*." Liszt, according to Gooley, had asked his audiences "to listen in new ways," and this had "presented a challenge to his general acceptance."[25] He believed that his approach to music was in need of more public support, a stronger sense of community. These were things that the visual arts had already achieved, and Liszt looked to them with envy:

> Among all the progressive ideas I *dream* about, there is one that should be easy to implement and that came to me a few days ago when, strolling silently through the galleries of the Louvre, I was able to survey, one after the other, the profoundly poetic brushstrokes of Scheffer, the gorgeous colors of Delacroix, the pure lines of Flandrin, of Lehmann, and the vigorous scenes of Brascassat. I asked myself: Why isn't music invited to participate in these annual festivals? . . . How is it that composers do not bring the finest flowers of their calling here as do the painters, their brothers?[26]

Liszt had recently attended the Paris "Salon," a government-sponsored exhibit of works by contemporary French artists, and he dreamed of a similar opportunity for music. Most of the artists named in Liszt's article were living together in Rome at the French Academy; the paintings they had sent back to Paris revealed the intellectual bond they shared. In Rome, these artists worked closely with one another; they shared studio space, models, and creative ideas. They read the same books, visited the same ancient sites, and often contemplated similar historic and literary themes in their art.[27] Living together as a group of expatriates, they had been deemed by the French government to be the best in their field. Liszt revered these artists, and in Italy he hoped to find a similar artistic community for himself.[28]

Liszt and d'Agoult departed for Italy the first week of May 1837. As they journeyed south, they visited friends—George Sand in Nohant, and Lamartine at his country home, Saint-Pont—and traveled through Switzerland again as a prelude to Italy. On 17 August they reached their first stop in Italy—Baveno on the shore of Lake Maggiore—but quickly moved on. Liszt was eager to experience life in the major cities. He read voraciously and sought out noted musical figures as he traveled from one capital to the next. Certain key experiences connected with Liszt's travels deserve to be highlighted, since they shaped his writing of the "Italy" volume of *Années de pèlerinage* and the formation of his Republic of the Imagination.

Shortly after his arrival in Italy, Liszt wrote three articles in quick succession that reveal much about his state of mind at the time. The first, addressed "To Adolphe Pictet," begins with the query: "Where am I going? What will I become?"[29] In response to these questions, Liszt described the "metaphysical fund" of ideas he had recently gained in the company of George Sand. With her his "activities and diversions" had been simple: "reading the works of some indigenous thinker or profound poet (Montaigne or Dante, Hoffmann or Shakespeare)." Literature fueled Liszt's imagination, and he composed regularly, looking to the piano as an inextricable part of his creative voice: "My piano is to me what a ship is to the sailor, what a steed is to the Arab, and perhaps more because even now my piano is myself, my speech, my life."[30] According to Liszt, creating music was an act of communication, a cooperative effort. Great artists never worked in isolation—the input of many could be heard in a single composition: "Certain authors, when speaking of their works, say my book, my commentary, my account, etc. . . . They would do better to say our book, our commentary, our account, etc., seeing that there is usually more of other people's work than their own therein."[31]

Liszt elaborated on this idea of communal inspiration in his next article, "To Louis de Ronchaud."[32] Here Lamartine, "the happy poet of the age," served as his role model. Although Chateaubriand "gloriously established a new literature in France," it was Lamartine who had "the gift of knowing just how far innovation can go." Lamartine appealed to those "basically subjective readers who love to find themselves reflected in everything and thus can easily inject their own stories into the harmonious framework of his divine poetry."[33] This was clearly shown in his *Méditations poétiques*, published in 1820. Liszt greatly revered this collection. For the first time in French literature, Lamartine presented poetry not as an art of pure form (wherein the message was secondary to the formal poetic structure) but as a mode of earnest communication. In these works Lamartine appeared to speak plaintively from the heart about his personal reflections on art, nature, and love. One poem in particular, "Philosophie," must have appealed to Liszt as he traveled across Italy. In this work Lamartine mixed a desire to escape "to the shores of the Arno" with an evocation of Petrarch and Dante. Like Byron, Lamartine took on the guise of an itinerant poet reflecting on life's purpose and the inevitable passage of time.

Lamartine's evocation of Petrarch and Dante in the opening stanza of "Philosophie" can be read as a commentary of sorts—a poetic reaction to the works of his Italian predecessors. As literary historian Robert Hollander explains, an outpouring of Dante commentaries swept across Europe during the early decades of the nineteenth century. Many of Liszt's French colleagues, most notably Lamartine, Lamennais, Hugo, and Sand, looked to Dante as the Romantic poet of the great damned souls: "What Dante knew best how to portray, for these and other illustrious figures, was the passion of suffering."[34] This image of Dante excited Liszt, and he soon began writing his own commentaries. For example, in an article written in September–October 1837, he compared Dante's depiction of Beatrice in the *Divine Comedy* to his own conception of "woman sublime":

I must confess that I have always been terribly disturbed by one thing in that immense, incomparable poem, and that is the fact that the poet has conceived Beatrice, not as the ideal of love, but as the ideal of learning. I do not like to see a scholarly theologian's spirit inhabiting that beautiful, transfigured body, explaining dogma, refuting heresy, and expounding on the mysteries. It is certainly not because of her reasoning and her powers of demonstration that a woman reigns over a man's heart. It is certainly not for her to *prove* God to him, but to give him a sense of God through love and thus lead him to heavenly matters. It is in her emotions, not in her knowledge, that her power lies. A loving woman is sublime; she is man's true guardian angel. A pedantic woman is a contradiction in terms, a dissonance; she does not occupy her proper place in the hierarchy of beings.[35]

Liszt's excursus reveals much about his concept of women at the time.[36] His woman sublime was the ideal muse, a figure clearly derived from Goethe's *Faust*. Liszt deeply respected d'Agoult's mind and her talents as a writer, but if he ever conceived of her as his muse, it was not for these intellectual attributes.[37] As he clearly explained, he sought a woman of undying devotion, "that beautiful, transfigured body" who could give him a sense of the divine through love. Liszt's woman sublime, as we shall see, was a philosophical ideal, an inspirational muse, not the object of physical, earthly love. She had little to do with real-life experiences. Instead, she was an amalgam of the women Liszt encountered in Italian literature and painting, and as such she played a crucial role in year two of *Années de pèlerinage*.

Milan: "Sposalizio"

Liszt went to Italy in search of inspiration, and as he visited the major cities, he sought out people he thought might share his creative interests. Chief among Liszt's colleagues in Milan was Gioacchino Rossini, who had recently established a series of Friday night musicales in his home. As Rossini himself explained in a letter written during the height of Liszt's participation, these soirées served as an open door to the elite of Milan's musical society: "My musical evenings make something of a sensation. . . . Dilletantes, singers, maestri, all sing in the choruses; I have about 40 choral voices, not counting all the solo parts. . . . The most distinguished people are admitted to my soirées; Olympe does the honors successfully, and we carry things off well."[38]

Among the many choral works performed at these events was Rossini's *Il pianto delle muse in morte di Lord Byron*. Ricordi had published this *canzone con coro* in 1825, along with a virtuosic paraphrase for solo piano arranged by Rossini himself.[39] Rossini's homage to Byron drew little interest from his Italian compatriots, but it intrigued Liszt. As he explained in an article written in early 1838, Rossini was the only Italian composer who showed any real appreciation for literature. Unfortunately, he was also a slave to public opinion and consequently never realized his musico-poetic aspirations.[40] The musical community Liszt found in Milan welcomed him, but it did not provide the intellectual stimulation he sought. Consequently, he turned to literature and art for inspiration. He visited the Milan cathedral, remembering that Madame de Staël had defined music as "the architecture of sound," and explored the treasures of the Brera.[41] Liszt was struck by numerous paintings in Milan, but only one became part of his *Années de pèlerinage*: Raphael's image of the *Sposalizio*—the Betrothal of the Virgin Mary and Joseph (figure 2).

Raphael's painting is based on a parable recounted by Saint Jerome in the apocryphal "Protevangelium" and in Jacobus of Voragine's thirteenth-century *Legenda Aurea* (The Golden Legend). Liszt would have known the story; it tells of the day when Mary came of age to wed. The high priest ordered all the unmarried male descendants of David to bring a wooden rod to the Temple of Jerusalem. When they arrived, the Holy Spirit descended in the form of a dove and caused Joseph's rod to blossom, a sign that he had been chosen to become Mary's husband.

It is easy to see why this painting appealed to Liszt. The Virgin's clothes and stance give her the appearance of a classical muse. She is woman sublime—the "beautiful, transfigured body" that Liszt had evoked earlier when contemplating Dante's *Divine Comedy*. In contrast, Joseph appears as a mere mortal, with downcast eyes and bare, deformed feet. He is the chosen one, the recipient of God's blessing and Mary's devotion. Borrowing language from Liszt's own description of ideal love in relation to Dante's Beatrice and woman sublime, one can interpret the scene in Raphael's painting as a metaphor for divine inspiration: as the Virgin accepts Joseph's ring, she "gives him a sense of God through love and thus leads him to heavenly matters." Raphael's figures do not appear in the real world; they reside in an ideal, utopian landscape. Nonetheless, symbols of the real world do exist: a Bramante-inspired temple anchors the scene, its open door framing the vanishing point and leading the eye upward into the infinite sky beyond. Inscribed above the door is Raphael's signature (RAPHAEL URBINAS MDIIII), a reminder to viewers that what they see is neither reality nor fantasy, but an artwork. To nineteenth-century viewers, Raphael's *Sposalizio* was a vision of inspiration personified, a testament to the artistic link between man's spiritual present and the historic past.[42]

Figure 2. Raphael, *Sposalizio*. Milan, Brera Museum.

Venice

Liszt's interest in art persisted as he made his way to Venice in March 1838. According to d'Agoult, the city captivated him immediately: "He was absorbed by its canals, its bridges, and the play of the light across its unique architecture."[43] Liszt visited the Piazza San Marco, La Fenice, the art galleries, churches, and the Doge's Palace. He sought out every tourist highlight, and even hired as his guide a gondolier named Cornelio, who claimed to have shown Byron the same sights years before. Venice sparked Liszt's imagination, as is clearly shown in the essays he wrote shortly after his arrival. In an article "To Heinrich Heine," Liszt described his new state of mind through a Byronic evocation of the city's "poetic desolation":

> Have you ever been to Venice? Have you ever glided on the sleepy waters in a black gondola down the length of the Grand Canal or along the banks of the Giudecca? Have you felt the weight of centuries crushing down on your helpless thoughts? Have you breathed that turgid, heavy air that presses you and thrusts you down into inconceivable languor? Have you seen the moon cast its pale rays on the leaden domes of old Saint Mark's? Did your ear, uneasy about the deathly silence, ever seek out some sound, just as the eye seeks out the light in the darkness of the dungeon? Yes, no doubt about it. Then you are familiar perhaps with the most poetic desolation in the world.[44]

Much has been written about Liszt's first visit to Venice—especially his learning of the disastrous floods in Hungary and his consequential departure for Vienna.[45] What has not been thoroughly discussed, however, is the manner in which Liszt later reflected on his trip to Austria and the circumstances that preceded his departure. Liszt's purported sudden desire to come to the rescue of his homeland, Hungary, was intimately tied to his experiences in Italy: his interest in Byron, his search for art's role in society, and his longing for a new form of intellectual community. In a two-part article "To Lambert Massart," written in the summer of 1838, Liszt explained, albeit in a coded manner, how his experiences in Italy and success in Vienna had led to a transformation of his artistic identity.[46] Although both parts of the article were written after Liszt returned from Vienna, the text itself is arranged in a "before and after" format. Part one describes Liszt's state of mind before learning of the floods in Hungary; part two gives a description of his experiences in Vienna and his new artistic identity.

At first glance, part one of the article appears to be just another description of Milan's music scene. But what begins as a routine account of a soirée in the home of Julia Pahlen-Samoyloff soon digresses into a dream sequence.[47] Leaving the chaos of "reality" in the Milanese ballroom, Liszt ventures into an unknown landscape, a fantastical realm that is clearly located in his Republic of the Imagination:

> I left the ballroom and went in search of a secluded, unoccupied corner where I could be alone . . . I sat down in a huge armchair whose black carvings and Gothic forms carried my imagination to a past age, while the scent of the exotic flowers conjured up images of distant climes. I do not know if my imagination . . . caused me to see a startling, supernatural apparition. All I know for certain is that I very quickly lost all sense of reality, all feeling for time and place, and that I suddenly found myself wandering all alone in an unknown land on a deserted beach beside a stormy sea.[48]

Trapped in the middle of this desolate landscape, Liszt discovers that he is not alone. Ahead of him is "a pensive figure . . . walking along the sand."

> He was still young, although his face was pale, his look intense, and his cheeks haggard. He stared at the horizon with an indescribable expression of anxiety and hope. A magnetic force drew me after him. . . . The farther I went, the more it seemed to me that my existence was linked to his, that his breath animated my life, that he held the secret of my destiny, and that we, he and I, had to merge with and transform each other. . . . "Oh, whoever you are," I cried, ". . . [you], who has fascinated and taken complete possession of me, tell me, who are you? Where do you come from? Where are you going? What is the reason for your journey? What are you seeking? Where do you rest? . . . Are you a condemned man under an irrevocable sentence? Are you a pilgrim filled with hope eagerly traveling to a peaceful, holy place?"[49]

In the past, scholars have avoided identifying this pensive figure. I propose that he is none other than Childe Harold himself, as he appeared in the early stanzas of Canto I:

> And now Childe Harold was sore sick at heart,
> And from his fellow bacchanals would flee;
> 'Tis said, at times the sullen tear would start,

But Pride congeal'd the drop within his e'e:
Apart he stalked in joyless reverie,
And from his native land resolved to go,
And visit scorching climes beyond the sea;
With pleasure drug'd he almost long'd for woe,
And e'en for change of scene would seek the shades below.[50]

Liszt's apparition holds "an oddly shaped musical instrument whose bright, metallic finish shone like a mirror in the rays of the setting sun." This is further proof that the stranger is Childe Harold, for he too carried a harp when he first set sail on his pilgrimage:

But when the sun was sinking in the sea
He seized his harp, which he at times could string,
And strike albeit with untaught melody,
When deem'd he no strange ear was listening:
And now his finger o'er it he did fling,
And tun'd his farewell in the dim twilight.
While flew the vessel on her snowy wing,
And fleeting shores receded from his sight,
Thus to the elements he pour'd his last "Good night."[51]

The stranger in Liszt's dream tries to bid him "Adieu," but Liszt refuses to leave. As the stranger describes the circumstances that have instigated his pilgrimage, we realize that they are startlingly similar to Liszt's own:

I come from a distant land that I can no longer remember. . . . For a long, long time . . . I was disgusted by an earth so empty of blessings, so full of tears. I quickened my steps. I walked, walked ceaselessly, looking toward the distant horizon for my unknown homeland.

So far it has all been in vain. I yearn, I sense the future, but nothing is apparent yet. I do not know if after all this time I am coming to the end of my journey. The force that drives me is silent; it tells me nothing of my path.

At times the breeze coming over the water carries ineffable harmonies to me; I listen to them rapturously, but as soon as I think they are coming nearer, they are smothered by the discordant din of human strife. . . .

If it is a malevolent force that harasses and torments me, why these divine dreams, these inexpressible, voluptuous floods of desire? If it is a beneficent power that is drawing me to it, why does it leave me in anguish and doubt, with the pangs of a hope that is always alive yet always thwarted?[52]

Liszt awakens from the dream and quickly makes his way home—all his friends can see that he has been visited by "that Demon of inspiration." With the memory of his encounter fresh in his mind, Liszt sits down at the piano, where he enters the Republic of the Imagination once again. Like Childe Harold, he is a pilgrim wandering in search of a homeland; and at the piano, he discovers another traveler on a similar quest, Schubert's "Wanderer":

"Der Wanderer" came to mind, and that song, so sad and so poetic, affected me more than it ever had before. I seemed to sense a tenuous and secret analogy between Schubert's music and the music I had heard in my dream.[53]

Liszt's description of his encounters with Childe Harold and the Wanderer serves to explain his state of mind before traveling to Vienna. As he claims in part two of the article, he supposedly found part one "lying forgotten on the writing table" when he returned to Venice in June 1838. Part two is presented as having been written a month or so later as an extended postscript—the purpose being to explain what had happened to Liszt since that fateful night in Milan.

In the opening of part two, Liszt describes how he "was badly shaken" by news of the disaster in Hungary: "The surge of emotions revealed to me the meaning of the word 'homeland.' I was suddenly transported back to the past, and in my heart I found the treasury of memories from my childhood intact." No longer a rootless wanderer like poor Childe Harold, Liszt "exclaimed his patriotic zeal" and reveled in the thought that he, too, was "a son" of Hungary. But as much as this article is a proclamation of Liszt's allegiance to Hungary, it is also a public rebuke of France. Throughout part two, Liszt makes a point of separating his new identity from the "time of burning fever, misdirected energy, and vigorous, mad vitality on French soil."[54] Parisian music politics no longer concerned him. Liszt claimed to have found a new sense of purpose in Vienna, and at the end of the article, he included a final reference to Byron. Upon bidding his reader "Adieu" Liszt claimed to be "rushing to get the whole package in the post" in order to refrain from giving "a parenthetical account of a voyage to Constantinople."[55] Liszt had not yet traveled to Constantinople, but Childe Harold had, in Canto II of his *Pilgrimage*.

Florence: *Il Penseroso* and "Canzonetta del Salvator Rosa"

Liszt spent the winter of 1838–39 in Florence, and while there toured various art galleries and churches in search of creative inspiration. Upon visiting the tombs of Lorenzo de' Medici, Duke of Urbino (1492–1519) and Giuliano de' Medici, Duke of Nemours (1479–1516) in the Medici Chapel in the Church of San Lorenzo, Liszt was struck by Michelangelo's visual depiction of the contemplative man versus the man of action.[56] The Medici Chapel consists of two large wall tombs facing each other across a high, domed room. One was designed for Giuliano de' Medici (the son of Lorenzo the Magnificent), the other for Giuliano's nephew, Lorenzo de' Medici (the grandson of Lorenzo the Magnificent). Michelangelo conceived of the two tombs as representing opposite types: Giuliano symbolized the active, extroverted personality; Lorenzo, the contemplative, introspective one. As we know from Liszt's *Années de pèlerinage*, he was most strongly drawn to Michelangelo's image of Lorenzo, *Il penseroso* (figure 3).[57]

Michelangelo created *Il penseroso* as a man deep in thought, removed from the world of earthly goods and concerns. This is clearly indicated by Lorenzo's gestures: his helmet and furrowed brow shadow his features. His left elbow rests on a closed cashbox, the index finger of his hand covering his mouth in a gesture of silence. To further strengthen the symbolism, Michelangelo adorned Lorenzo's cashbox with a bat—a popular symbol for melancholia.[58] This final trait, perhaps more than any other, confirms the artist's interest in Neoplatonism. According to Panofsky, "among all his contemporaries," Michelangelo was the only one who adopted key aspects of Neoplatonism as "a metaphysical justification of his own self."[59] Early-modern Neoplatonists such as Marsilio Ficino (1433–99) and Pico della Mirandola (1463–94), contemporaries of Michelangelo, argued that melancholy could be interpreted as a sign of intellectual prowess, even genius. They recalled Aristotle's remark that all geniuses are melancholy, and were largely responsible for developing the modern concept of genius that later pervaded nineteenth-century literature.[60]

Upon seeing Michelangelo's tombs for the Medici dukes, Michelangelo's contemporary, Giovan Battista Strozzi the Elder (1505–71), composed a sonnet in praise of the female figure *Notte* (Night) who rests in front of the "active man" Giuliano de' Medici:

Figure 3. Michelangelo, *Il penseroso*. Florence, Medici Chapel.

La Notte, che tu vedi in sì dolci atti	The Night that in such a graceful attitude you see
dormir, fu da un Angelo scolpita	sleeping, was sculpted by an Angel
in questo sasso, e perchè dorme ha vita:	in this stone, and since she sleeps, she must have life;
Destala, se nol credi, e parleratti.	wake her, if you don't believe it, and she'll speak to you.

In response to Strozzi (a man whose politics Michelangelo disdained) Michelangelo wrote a quatrain, full of bitterness, which made a veiled reference to the recent collapse of the Florentine republic:

Caro m'e il sonno, e più l'esser di sasso	Dear to me is sleep; and more dear to be made of stone
Mentre che'l danno e la vergogna dura.	As long as there exists injustice and shame.
Non veder, non sentir m'è gran ventura;	Not to see and not to hear is a great blessing to me;
Però non mi destar, deh! parla basso!	Therefore, do not disturb me! Speak softly![61]

Liszt clearly understood the message of this quatrain; the story of Strozzi, Michelangelo, and the Florentine republic was told time and again in nineteenth-century guidebooks.[62] When Liszt published his *Années de pèlerinage* in 1858, he borrowed the quatrain originally associated with Michelangelo's figure *Notte* and attached it to *Il penseroso* instead. By doing so, he altered, ever so slightly, the iconology of Michelangelo's statue—in Liszt's version the figure of "contemplative man" is enhanced by a shade of rebelliousness.[63]

The theme of rebelliousness also played a role in Liszt's interest in the works of Salvator Rosa (1615–73), one of the most original artists of the seventeenth century. Rosa's works ranged from landscapes characterized by wild and mountainous beauty to macabre subjects and erudite philosophical allegories. In addition to his work as a painter, Rosa was a well-known poet of satire; a close relationship exists between his visual and literary works. Liszt probably first learned of Rosa through Parisian friends such as Berlioz and Alexander Dumas, père.[64] Rosa was a popular figure in French literature during the 1830s, and in Florence, Liszt would have learned even more about Rosa's fiery temperament, immense ambition, and intellectual prowess.[65] Rosa had been part of a Florentine circle of intellectuals that included poets, historians, painters, scientists, and philosophers.

His house was the meeting place for the Accademia dei Percossi, where members regularly read tributes to Rosa's paintings and took part in theatrical performances. In 1830s Florence Rosa enjoyed a keen reception, most notably among the English community there. Myths and legends clustered around him, and it was widely believed that he had taken part in a popular uprising against the Spanish in Naples. These legends were immortalized in 1824 by Lady Morgan's biography, *The Life and Times of Salvator Rosa*.[66] Although there is no direct evidence that Liszt actually read this work, he no doubt was aware of the Rosa legend it had generated. Rosa had become an exemplar of the ideal artist: a noble exile and enemy of tyranny, whose wild genius was expressed in art and poetry and untrammeled by academic rules. According to Lady Morgan, Rosa was also a musician,[67] and his activities as a composer strongly defined his artistic identity: "Music, the true language of passion, which speaks so powerfully, and yet so mysteriously . . . appears to have engrossed his undivided attention." She even went so far as to claim that Rosa had discovered "a novel style of composition, expressively called *la musica parlante*" (spoken music) that proved to be "Il cantar che nel animo si sente" (the singing that one feels in the soul).[68] Most important, Morgan defined music as Rosa's primary means of artistic escape: "In his wayward and original mood . . . he betook himself to that school where no master lays down the law" and in so doing "felt proud and elated in the consciousness of the career he had struck out for himself, which left him free and unshackled in his high calling."[69]

In addition to learning of Rosa's supposed talents as a musician, Liszt would have become familiar with reproductions of the artist's famous self-portrait (figure 4).[70] Liszt's good friend in Florence, the artist Henri Lehmann, knew this painting well, and I propose he looked to it as a model when designing his famous portrait of Liszt (figure 5).[71] The parallels between these two paintings are clearly more than coincidence. The stances of Rosa and Liszt are similar, and the faces in both portraits are almost identical, from the shape and size of the eyes, nose, and chin to the play of light and shadow across their features. Rosa's self-portrait strikingly illustrates his confidence as both an artist and an intellectual. Wearing a scholar's cap and gown and a dark, forbidding expression, he points to a Latin inscription: "Keep silent, unless your speech is more profitable than silence."[72] Lehmann captured a similar mood in his portrait of Liszt. Concentrating on the composer's lithe figure and penetrating gaze, he created a haunting portrait that exudes an air of confidence and mystery. A similar sense of confidence is expressed in the text of the "canzonetta" that Liszt transcribed for his *Années de pèlerinage*, believing mistakenly that it was a musical work by Rosa:

Vado ben spesso cangiando loco	Often I change my location,
Ma non si mai cangiar desio.	But I shall never change my desire.
Sempre l'istesso sarà il mio fuoco	The fire within me will always be
E sarò sempre l'istesso anch'io.	the same
	And I myself will also always be
	the same.

Figure 4. Salvatore Rosa, *Self-Portrait*. London, National Gallery.

More than a half-century has passed since Frank Walker revealed that this canzonetta was composed by Giovanni Battista Bononcini (1672–1750), not Rosa.[73] But in Liszt's day, "Vado ben spesso" was firmly tied to the artistic identity of Salvator Rosa. Both Charles Burney and Lady Morgan published the aria in their studies of Rosa.[74] In Morgan's description of

Figure 5. Henri Lehmann, *Portrait of Liszt*. Paris, Musée Carnavalet.

the piece, the "desire" and "flame" referred to in the text were "construed as a vehement mixture of Romantic ideals," not "the perennial common-places of Italian courtly love."[75]

Liszt further reflected on the arts in a series of articles he wrote while living in Florence. This series can be divided into two separate groups: topical travelogues, published in the arts magazine *L'Artiste*, reflecting contemporary Italy; and philosophical articles rooted in Liszt's Republic of the Imagination that appeared in the *Revue et Gazette musicale*. Of the various discussions presented in this latter group of articles, the most fas-cinating with respect to Liszt's ideas concerning the role of the artist and the development of artistic communities are "The *Perseus* of Benvenuto Cellini" and "The *Saint Cecilia* of Raphael." Liszt wrote his article on Cellini's work in November 1838.[76] He had obviously been reading Cellini's autobiography, and it appears he was especially intrigued by Cellini's account of how he had endured as an artist, despite public persecution. Liszt begins his article much like a novel, a sign that he is entering his Republic of the Imagination. It is two o'clock in the morning on a crisp September night. Liszt leaves a ball at the palace of Prince Poniatowski and "walks aimlessly along the Arno." Quite by accident, he comes across Cellini's *Perseus*, and the statue makes an "incomparably strong impres-sion" on him: "I was detained by an invisible force. It seemed as if a mysterious voice was speaking, as if the statue's spirit was talking to me." Liszt tells the story of Perseus, which he considers to be "one of the beau-tiful myths of Greek poetry." Perseus is a hero who prevailed in the "struggle between good and evil." He is a man of genius who "seeks to unite himself with beauty, the poet's eternal lover."[77]

Once the story is laid out, Liszt discusses Cellini's interpretation of the Perseus story and describes the regenerative effect literature can have on all the arts, generation after generation:

> When initially assuming its most abstract form, art reveals itself in words. Poetry lends its language to art; it symbolizes art. In Perseus, antiquity gives us a profound, perfect allegory. It is the first stage, the first step, in the development of an idea. . . . In modern times and in the hands of a great artist, art takes on a perceptible form, it becomes plastic. The casting furnace is lit, the metal liquefies, it runs into the mold, and Perseus emerges fully armed, holding Medusa's head aloft in his hand, the emblem of his victory.[78]

Liszt then moves on to a discussion of Berlioz's place in this artistic con-tinuum. Inspired by Cellini, who was inspired by Perseus, Berlioz composed his masterful opera in 1838. Layer upon layer, the tradition continues. An imagined community of artists, separated by time but united in thought and spirit, work together for the sake of art.

The other important article Liszt wrote in Florence, "The *Saint Cecilia* of Raphael," was the result of a brief trip he took to Bologna in December 1838.[79] The official purpose of this trip was to give a series of concerts, but as he explained in his article, the first item on his agenda was to visit the city's museum: "I hurried right through three galleries . . . as I was anxious to see the *Saint Cecilia*."[80] D'Agoult had seen the painting a few months earlier, finding it to be "less laudable" than what she had expected.[81] Liszt's reaction was markedly different:

> I do not know by what secret magic that painting made an immediate and twofold impression on my soul: first as a ravishing portrayal of the most noble and ideal qualities of the human form, a marvel of grace, purity, and harmony; and at the same instant and with no strain of the imagination, I also saw it as an admirable and perfect symbol of the art to which we have dedicated our lives.[82]

Like the Virgin in Raphael's *Sposalizio*, Saint Cecilia appeared to Liszt as woman sublime. She also stood as "a symbol of music at the height of its power," of "art in its most spiritual and holy form. . . . Like the inspiration that sometimes fills an artist's heart," Raphael's personification of music was "pure, true, full of insight, and unalloyed with mundane matters."[83] Most important, it served as a font of inspiration for untold numbers of viewers:

> Like all works of genius, his painting stirs the mind and excites the imagination of all those who ponder it. Each of us sees it in his own way and, depending upon his own makeup, discovers a novel form of beauty there, something new to admire and praise. That is precisely what makes genius immortal, what makes it eternally young, fertile, and stirring.[84]

Liszt saw in Raphael's art the power of creative suggestion, an intellectual link from one artist to the next across time. So it should come as no surprise that as he continued his journey across Italy, his appreciation for literature and the visual arts began to manifest itself in his activities as a composer.

Rome: The Petrarch Sonnets and
"Après une lecture du Dante"

That Liszt was thinking about various works of art as creative fodder is evident from a journal entry made in February 1839, shortly after his arrival in Rome.[85]

> If I feel within me the strength of life, I will attempt a symphonic composition based on Dante, then another on Faust—within three years time—meanwhile, I will make three "sketches": *The Triumph of Death* (Orcagna), *The Comedy of Death* (Holbein), and a *Fragment dantesque*. *Il Pensieroso* [*sic*] bewitches me as well.[86]

As the above entry reveals, Liszt had mapped out plans for six separate programmatic compositions: the two symphonic pieces became his "Faust" and "Dante" symphonies, the "Triumph" and "Comedy" served as inspiration for his *Totentanz* Concerto, and "Il penseroso" and the "Fragment dantesque" became the second and last pieces in the Italy volume of *Années de pèlerinage*. As Rena Mueller explains, the genesis of the Italy volume is extremely complex.[87] Early drafts of all the movements can be found in various sketchbooks and manuscripts, which indicate that Liszt worked on each movement separately and only later decided on the volume's overall layout.[88] In addition, it appears Liszt made a sketch for each movement, if not a complete draft, during the winter months of 1838–39.[89]

Rome was the culmination of Liszt's Italian pilgrimage. During his five months there, from February through June 1839, he visited St. Peter's, the Sistine Chapel, and the Vatican Museum. But the most important aspect of his stay in the capital was his interaction with artists at the French Academy. Liszt became something of an honorary fellow at the Academy, thanks to the influence of its director, Jean-August Ingres. Ingres was an accomplished violinist, and he spent countless evenings with Liszt performing chamber music, most notably that of Beethoven, at the Villa Medici. During the day, Ingres took Liszt and the *pensionnaires* at the French Academy on personal tours of Rome's art galleries and museums.[90] Liszt spoke about this newfound artistic fellowship in an article addressed "To Hector Berlioz."[91] Here he described his friendship with Ingres as "one of the luckiest encounters" of his life.[92] Ingres possessed an unrivaled knowledge of Rome's art treasures. "His glowing words gave new life to all those masterpieces," wrote Liszt. "His eloquence transported us to bygone centuries."[93] Liszt even went so far as to describe Ingres's explanations of art as intellectual masterpieces in their own right: "It was the genius of modern times evoking the genius of antiquity."[94] In Rome, Liszt finally found the intellectual community he had been seeking—it was rooted in the city's culture and expatriate artists. As Liszt explained to Berlioz, Ingres strengthened his desire to increase his understanding of art, and in so doing broadened his exploration of the Republic of the Imagination:

> The beauty in this special land became evident to me in its purest and most sublime form. Art in all its splendor disclosed itself to my eyes. It revealed its universality and unity to me. Day by day my feelings and thoughts gave me deeper insight into the hidden relationship that unites all works of genius. Raphael and Michelangelo increased my understanding of Mozart and Beethoven; Giovanni Pisano, Fra Beato, and Il Francia explained Allegri, Marcello, and Palestrina to me. Titian and Rossini appeared to me like twin stars shining with the same light. The Colosseum and the *Campo Santo* are not as foreign as one thinks to the Eroica Symphony and the Requiem. Dante has found his pictorial expression in Orcagna and Michelangelo, and someday perhaps he will find his musical expression in the Beethoven of the future.[95]

Was Liszt thinking of himself when he referred to the "Beethoven of the future"? I would wager yes, because a few weeks later he described his personal artistic goals to d'Agoult in less ambiguous prose: "Maybe I am a would-be genius; that is something that only time can tell. . . . My mission, as I see it, is to be the first to introduce poetry into the music of the piano with some degree of style."[96]

Ideas such as this were likely the impetus behind Liszt's setting of three Petrarch sonnets (nos. 47, 104, and 123) in 1839. He first set the sonnets as songs for high tenor voice, then transcribed them for piano shortly thereafter.[97] Together, the three sonnets describe the various states of artistic inspiration and emotional turmoil brought on by Petrarch's contemplation of woman sublime, the chaste, unattainable Laura. Sonnet 47 begins with a description of the exact moment when "two bright eyes" enthralled the poet's soul and bound him fast. The final six lines then praise the inspiration that grew out of this encounter: "Blest be those sonnets, sources of my fame; / And blest that thought—Oh! Never to remove! / Which turns to her alone, from her alone which came."[98] Sonnet 104 reveals how contemplation of the ideal can release a range of desolate emotions: "I feed on grief, I laugh with sob-racked breast / And death and life alike to me are bleak: / My Lady, thus I am because of you."[99] Finally, in Sonnet 123, the vision of woman sublime returns to soothe the poet's desire for inspiration: "I saw angelic grace in earthly spheres, / And heavenly beauty paralleled of none, / Which now I joy and grieve to think upon, / Since now all else dream, shadow, smoke appears."[100]

Liszt included his heavily revised piano transcriptions of the above three sonnets in *Années de pèlerinage*, and I propose that they are among his earliest attempts "to introduce poetry into the music of the piano with some degree of style."[101] These pieces are not love songs as much as they are Liszt's musical commentary on Petrarch. Liszt presents Petrarch's Laura as woman sublime—indeed, he even added her name to the song text of Sonnet 104, in case there was any doubt. Like Raphael's *Sposalizio* and *Saint Cecilia,* she is a chaste, unobtainable figure who blesses the artist-poet with divine inspiration.[102] This practice of evoking women from the past was nothing new. Liszt's literary heroes, Byron, Lamartine, and Madame de Staël had each done the same in the works they wrote about Italy.[103] Aesthetic commentary via works of art was a common practice in Liszt's Republic of the Imagination, and this is perhaps most evident in the final piece of year two of his *Années de pèlerinage*, "Après une lecture du Dante (Fantasia quasi Sonata)."

Although Liszt showed an interest in Dante's *Divine Comedy* as early as 1832, it appears he waited until February 1839 to begin writing music inspired by the work.[104] Liszt never published a program for this piece, but a look at the evolution of its title reveals much about his compositional approach. He first referred to the music in February 1839 as "a *Fragment dantesque*," and it was premiered under this title in December at a concert in Vienna.[105] Liszt considered publishing the composition in 1840, but these plans never came to fruition. By 1849, he was working on the piece again. The earliest extant manuscript source dates from this period and bears the title "Paralipomènes à la Divina Commedia: Fantasie Symphonique pour Piano" (figure 6). The term "Paralipomènes" refers to supplementary items originally omitted from the body of a work. Thus Liszt was composing a piece that expanded upon Dante's *Divine Comedy*, much in the way that Byron had done in the *Prophesy of Dante* (1821).[106] Sometime later, Liszt crossed out "paralipomènes" and replaced it with the word *prolegomènes* (preliminary discourses). This title, like the previous one, implies that Liszt was conceiving of his work as a commentary. Finally, around 1853, Liszt settled on the title we know today: "Après une lecture du Dante (Fantasia quasi Sonata)." The first half of the title is a subtle reference to a poem by Victor Hugo; the second half is an allusion to the genre title adopted by Beethoven for his two piano sonatas, op. 27.

The poem by Victor Hugo, titled "Après une lecture de Dante" (after a reading of Dante), is a poetic commentary on Dante's depiction of hell.

Figure 6. Franz Liszt, page showing various early titles for "Après une lecture du Dante (Fantasia quasi Sonata)." Weimar, Goethe- und Schiller-Archiv, MS I 17.

It is part of a collection of fifty-one poems (many of which are commentaries on artists and poets, such as Dürer and Virgil) published under the title *Les Voix intérieures* (Interior voices). When Liszt published his musical commentary on Dante, titled "Après une lecture du Dante" (after a reading of *the* Dante, i.e., *The Divine Comedy*), he purposely referenced Hugo's poem without citing it directly. Liszt wanted audiences to recognize that, like Hugo, he was offering them his personal response to Dante's work. His musical commentary on Dante was one of his "voix intérieures"—a product of his travels across the Republic of the Imagination.

How did Liszt's experiences in Italy influence his creation of the *Années de pèlerinage*? Ultimately, they provided him with a program—an artistic philosophy from which he could draw. Looking at the titles of the various movements in *Deuxième Année: Italie* of *Années de pèlerinage*, one quickly realizes that the community Liszt encountered in Italy, via literature and art, provided him with creative role models. With the help of Byron, Michelangelo, and Rosa Liszt found his identity as an artist. Like Childe Harold, he became a pilgrim in search of a homeland. Like *Il penseroso*, he sought a life of contemplation free from the politics of contemporary society. Raphael and Petrarch offered images of woman sublime. Dante served as an "interior voice," the intellectual culmination of his travels.

Although Liszt titled the second album of his *Années de pèlerinage* "Italy," the music more accurately reflects his Republic of the Imagination. Perhaps he realized this as well, for in 1859, one year after the publication of *Années de pèlerinage, Deuxième Année: Italie*, he released a "supplement" to the volume, which is notably different in character. It comprises three pieces based on contemporary folk songs and opera arias: "Gondoliera," "Canzone," and "Tarantella"; the supplement symbolizes the contemporary, "real-life" music Liszt encountered in Italy—opera arias by Rossini and folk songs sung by Cornelio, Liszt's Venetian gondolier.[107]

Liszt added a third volume to his *Années de pèlerinage* in 1883, and it too included pieces inspired by Italy. But discussion of that music will have to wait. By the time the *Troisième Année* was published, much had changed: Liszt had become an *abbé*; Italy had become a unified nation; and a new community of intellectuals had taken up residence in his Republic of the Imagination.

NOTES

1. The earliest accounts set Liszt's travels in the context of a romance: Marie d'Agoult, *Mémoires 1833–1854*, ed. Daniel Ollivier (Paris: 1927); and Lina Ramann, *Franz Liszt als Künstler und Mensch* (Leipzig, 1880–94); Sharon Winklhofer, in "Liszt, Marie d'Agoult, and the 'Dante' Sonata," *19th-Century Music* 1 (1976): 15–32, follows this approach as well. Later writers have tended to describe Liszt's journey in the context of a travelogue: Alan Walker, *Franz Liszt: The Virtuoso Years 1811–1847* (Ithaca, N.Y.:1987, rev. ed.), pp. 244–84; Charles Suttoni, ed., *An Artist's Journey: Franz Liszt* (Chicago: 1989); and Luciano Chiappari's series: *Liszt a Firenze, Pisa e Lucca* (Pisa: 1989); *Liszt a Como e Milano* (Pisa: 1997); *Liszt francescano tra Umbria e Marche* (Grottammare: 2000), or as a Bildungsroman: Cesare Simeone Motta, *Liszt Viaggiatore Europeo: Il soggiorno svizzero e italiano di Franz Liszt e Marie d'Agoult (1835–39)* (Moncalieri: 2000).

2. Chateaubriand's "Lettre à Fontanes sur la campagne romaine," dated 10 January 1804, was published in *Mercure de France*, 3 March 1804.

3. Dana Gooley, *The Virtuoso Liszt* (Cambridge, Eng.: 2004), pp. 22–23.

4. Wheelock Whitney, "Introduction," in *The Lure of Rome: Some Northern Artists in Italy in the Nineteenth Century*, exhibition catalogue, Hazlitt, Gooden & Fox Gallery (London), October–November 1979, p. 7.

5. See especially Motta, whose primary thesis in *Liszt Viaggiatore Europeo* is that as Liszt and d'Agoult traveled across Italy, Liszt began to see his time there as a period of enlightenment typical of the Grand Tour experience.

6. Italy served as the inspirational push behind many of Liszt's works—the tone poem *Tasso*, the incomplete opera *Sarandapale, Totentanz, Réminiscences de la Scala*, and *Venezia e Napoli*, for example, but none give as complete an overview of Liszt's intellectual pursuits as *Années de pèlerinage: Deuxième Année, Italie.*

7. As Dolores Pesce, "Expressive Resonance in Liszt's Piano Music," in *Nineteenth-Century Piano Music*, ed. R. Larry Todd (New York: 1990), pp. 358–59, explains, the contents of this volume "relate at least in part to an earlier collection that appeared in 1842, the *Album d'un Voyager* (Album of a traveler)," which Liszt began writing during a trip to Switzerland in 1835–36. "The *Album* consists of three parts: *Impressions and poésies*, seven titled pieces that became the core of *Année 1*; *Fleurs mélodiques des Alpes*, nine untitled pieces based on Swiss folk songs or popular art songs (two reappearing in *Année 1*); and *Paraphrases*, three arrangements of Swiss folk airs." It should be noted that if Liszt withdrew this publication before publishing *Années de pèlerinage*, one reason may be that in its revised version, this set of pieces inspired by Switzerland presented a markedly different program.

8. Many have mistakenly claimed that as Liszt traveled across Italy, he followed the path previously laid out by Goethe. Although it is true that Liszt visited many of the same locales, he did not follow his predecessor's itinerary.

9. Percy Bysshe Shelley, "Julian and Maddalo" in *Posthumous Poems* (London: 1824), lines 55–57: "How beautiful is sunset, when the glow / Of Heaven descends upon a land like thee, / Thou Paradise of exiles, Italy!" For discussions of this period in Italy's history, see Christopher Duggan, *A Concise History of Italy* (Cambridge, Eng.: 1994). For discussions of the effects of Italian politics on nineteenth-century English literature, see Maura O'Connor, *The Romance of Italy and the English Political Imagination* (London: 1998); Daryl S. Ogden, "Byron, Italy, and the Poetics of Liberal Imperialism," *Keats-Shelley Journal* 49 (2000): 114–38.

10. Franz Liszt, *Sämtliche Schriften*, ed. Rainer Kleinertz (Wiesbaden: 2000), vol. 1, pp. 455–503.

11. Charles Suttoni, *An Artist's Journey* (Chicago: 1989), p. 244. For the most recent discussion of this topic, see Alan Walker, "Liszt the Writer: On Music and Musicians,"

Reflections on Liszt (Ithaca, N.Y.: 2005), pp. 217–38. In truth, the authorship of these articles is of little consequence to my investigation, since, despite their origins, they nonetheless present a reliable description of Liszt's reactions to art and literature as he traveled through Italy.

12. See especially Pesce, "Expressive Resonance in Liszt's Piano Music," 355–75; Andrew J. Fowler, "Franz Liszt's *Années de pèlerinage* as megacycle," *Journal of the American Liszt Society* 40 (1996): 113–29; William J. Hughes, Jr. "Liszt's *Première Année de Pèlerinage: Suisse*: A Comparative Study of Early and Revised Versions," D.M.A. diss., Eastman School of Music, 1985; Karen Wilson, "A Historical Study and Stylistic Analysis of Franz Liszt's *Années de pèlerinage*," Ph.D. diss., University of North Carolina, 1977, and Martin Zenck, "Die Poetik und Struktur in Franz Liszt's Tondichtung *Après une lecture du Dante* im Zusammenhang der 'Correspondance de Liszt et de la Comtesse d'Agoult,'" in *Musik und Szene: Festschrift für Werner Braun zum 75. Geburtstag* (Saarbrücken: 2001), pp. 575–95.

13. George Sand, "Lettre d'un Voyageur," *Revue des deux mondes*, 1 September 1835. Another source for my use of the phrase "Republic of the Imagination" comes from the title of an article by Azar Nafisi that appeared in the *Book World* section of the *Washington Post* on 5 December 2004. In this article, Nafisi defines her own encounters with the Republic of the Imagination—her private escape, via masterpieces of Western literature, from the political and intellectual oppression of life in Iran. I had the pleasure of discussing the Republic of the Imagination with Dr. Nafisi on several occasions at the American Academy in Rome in Summer 2005, and I am sincerely grateful for her insight into the topic.

14. I thank Dana Gooley and Christopher Gibbs for the various discussions we had concerning the politically charged atmosphere Liszt experienced in Paris. Liszt was a supporter of the 1830 revolution in France, which alas brought a monarchy. A significant line of thought about Romanticism claims that when its participants became disillusioned by political failures such as the 1830 French revolution, they waged their own philosophical battles in the realm of fantasy. This is an apt description that can be applied to both Sand and Liszt.

15. For a daily account of Liszt's tour through Switzerland, see Mária P. Eckhardt, "Diary of a Wayfarer: The Wanderings of Franz Liszt and Marie d'Agoult in Switzerland June–July 1835," *Journal of the American Liszt Society* 11 (June 1982): 11–17; and 12 (December 1982): 182–83.

16. Sand, "Lettre d'un Voyageur."

17. Liszt, *Sämtliche Schriften*, vol. 1, p. 78; Suttoni, *An Artist's Journey*, pp. 4–5.

18. *Ménestrel* 3, no. 15 (13 March 1836). As Dana Gooley explains in *The Virtuoso Liszt*, "Three aspects of Thalberg's reception were particularly troublesome for Liszt." First, the praise from Parisian audiences was unanimous for Thalberg, but not for Liszt. Second, Thalberg was revered even though he "was not in any sense a literary or philosophical *artiste*," which was the way that Liszt wanted to be envisioned. Third, Thalberg was praised for his talents as a composer in addition to his abilities as a performer, something that Liszt could not yet claim (pp. 23–24).

19. Gooley, *The Virtuoso Liszt*, p. 27.

20. Berlioz was also distressed by Liszt's attack on Thalberg; he was acting editor of the *Revue et Gazette musicale de Paris* when Liszt submitted the review, and he added a notice to the article dissociating the journal from Liszt's personal opinions.

21. *Revue et Gazette musicale*, 12 February 1836.

22. Liszt, *Sämtliche Schriften*, vol. 1, p. 90; Suttoni, *An Artist's Journey*, pp. 14–15. The final line is a reference to Mignon's song from Goethe's *Wilhelm Meister*: "Kennst du das Land, wo die Zitronen blühn? . . . Dahin! Dahin! Möcht' ich mit dir, o mein Geliebter, ziehn." (Do you know the land, where the lemons bloom? . . . There! There! Do I wish to move, with you, o my beloved.)

23. Liszt, *Sämtliche Schriften*, vol. 1, p. 100; Suttoni, *An Artist's Journey*, pp. 28–29.

24. Liszt, *Sämtliche Schriften*, vol. 1, p. 104; Suttoni, *An Artist's Journey*, pp. 30–31.

25. Gooley, *The Virtuoso Liszt*, p. 19.

26. Liszt, *Sämtliche Schriften*, vol. 1, p. 108; Suttoni, *An Artist's Journey*, pp. 34–35.

27. For an excellent overview of the French Academy at this time see the exhibition catalogue *Maestà di Roma da Napoleone all'unità d'Italia: Da Ingres a Degas: Artisti francesi a Roma* (Rome, 7 March–29 June 2003).

28. Liszt described this desire for artistic interaction in rather poetic terms: "Somewhere, far away in a land that I know, there is a limpid spring that lovingly bathes the roots of a lone palm tree. The palm tree raises its fronds above the spring, sheltering it from the sun's rays. I want to rest in that shade—a touching symbol of the holy and indestructible affection that supplants all earthly concerns and will doubtless flourish in heaven." Liszt, *Sämtliche Schriften*, vol. 1, p. 112; Suttoni, *An Artist's Journey*, p. 38.

29. *Revue et Gazette musicale*, 11 February 1838. Liszt first met Adolphe Pictet de Rochemont (1799–1875) during his first trip to Geneva. On that occasion, Pictet accompanied Liszt, d'Agoult, and Sand on a trip to Chamonix. Pictet published an account of this trip in *Une Course à Chamonix* (Paris: 1838). Liszt's queries are strikingly familiar with those found in Letter 53 of Senancour's *Obermann*.

30. Liszt, *Sämtliche Schriften*, vol. 1, pp. 114–18; Suttoni, *An Artist's Journey*, pp. 41–45.

31. Liszt, *Sämtliche Schriften*, vol. 1, p. 122; Suttoni, *An Artist's Journey*, p. 47. Liszt is referring to a passage he read in Blaise Pascal's *Pensées* (1660). H. F. Stewart, editor of *Pascal's Pensées* (London: 1950), p. 504, claims that Pascal got this idea from Jacques-Bénigne Bossuet (1627–1704).

32. *Revue et Gazette musicale*, 25 March 1838. Louis de Ronchaud (1816–87) was a young writer, later an art historian, whom Liszt and d'Agoult met in Geneva. In later years, he became d'Agoult's literary executor, and he edited her posthumous *Mes Souvenirs 1806–1833* (Paris: 1877).

33. Liszt, *Sämtliche Schriften*, vol. 1, p. 133; Suttoni, *An Artist's Journey*, pp. 56–57.

34. Robert Hollander, "Dante and His Commentators," in *The Cambridge Companion to Dante*, ed. Rachel Jacoff (Cambridge, Eng.: 1993), p. 232.

35. "Lake Como—To Louis de Ronchaud" *Revue et Gazette musicale* (22 July 1838). Liszt, *Sämtliche Schriften*, vol. 1, p. 162; Suttoni, *An Artist's Journey*, p. 67. Sharon Winklhofer, "Liszt, Marie d'Agoult, and the 'Dante' Sonata," attributes this passage to d'Agoult alone, claiming that Liszt showed little interest in Dante at this time (p. 24), but she gives no evidence to support this assumption.

36. This description of women also explains why Liszt often referred to Sand as "he" instead of "she" in his personal correspondence and articles.

37. In her article "Liszt, Marie d'Agoult, and the 'Dante' Sonata," Winklhofer successfully destroyed the myth Lina Ramann perpetuated concerning the origins of Liszt's "Dante" Sonata. But she also started a new myth by asserting that Dante provided Liszt with "a model for his relationship with Marie d'Agoult" and that as "the Dante-Beatrice roles proved impossible to uphold" Liszt's concept of Dante changed. There is no direct evidence that Liszt ever looked to d'Agoult as his Beatrice—all the sources presented by Winklhofer came from d'Agoult's memoires. I propose that it was d'Agoult who looked to Beatrice and Dante as the paradigm for her relationship with Liszt. This appears to be the way Liszt himself saw the situation. As Walker explains in *Franz Liszt: The Virtuoso Years*, after their breakup, it was Marie who kept referring to the Beatrice-Dante model. Liszt was noticeably less enamored with this model: "Bah, Dante! Bah, Beatrice! The Dantes create the Beatrices, and the real ones die at eighteen!" (p. 246).

38. Suttoni, *An Artist's Journey*, p. 83. Liszt often performed at these soirees. As Suttoni mentions, Liszt and the tenor Adolphe Nourrit performed at Rossini's with great success on 12 January 1838 (p. 72).

39. The plate numbers for these works are 2116 for the tenor and chorus version and 9115 for the piano transcription. I thank Francesco Izzo for assisting me in tracking down the publication dates for these works. Although they are difficult to come by today, they would have been readily available to Liszt when he was in Milan. A copy of the piano transcription, which originally belonged to Gelasii Caietani, can now be found in the Vatican Library (Racc. Gen. Musica. II 262 [int. 1–6]). The Rossini piece is bound together with a collection of piano transcriptions dating from the same period. Curiously, the back cover of the Rossini transcription contains a pencil sketch of a woman (in typical 1830s Italian fashion) and a man in profile whose appearance is strikingly similar to that of Rossini.

40. "La Scala: To Maurice Schlesinger," *Revue et Gazette musicale,* 27 May 1838: "Everything in the sphere of art corresponding to the feelings immortally exemplified by Hamlet, Faust, Childe Harold, René, Obermann, and Lélia is for the Italians a foreign, barbaric tongue that they reject in horror. . . . Rossini, that great master who possessed a fully strung lyre, scarcely sounded anything but the melodic string for them. He treated them like spoiled children, entertaining them as they wanted to be entertained." Liszt, *Sämtliche Schriften*, vol. 1, p. 158; Suttoni, *An Artist's Journey*, pp. 76–77. Liszt also paid homage to Rossini at this time by transcribing for piano solo his *William Tell* Overture and a collection of his songs and duets entitled *Soirées musicales*.

41. In a later article about Milan ("To Lambert Massart") that appeared in the *Revue et Gazette musicale* on 2 September 1838, Liszt mentioned "Madame de Staël's definition that 'music is the architecture of sounds.'" Liszt, *Sämtliche Schriften*, vol. 1, p. 185; Suttoni, *An Artist's Journey*, p. 90.

42. Elizabeth Way, "Raphael as a Musical Model: Liszt's 'Sposalizio'," *Journal of the American Liszt Society* 40 (1996): pp. 103–12; and Joan Backus, "Liszt's 'Sposalizio'": A Study in Musical Perspective," *19th-Century Music* 12, no. 2 (1988): 173–83, propose that Raphael's *Sposalizio* and the Liszt piece share similar compositional designs.

43. Marie d'Agoult, *Mémoires 1833–1854,* (Paris: 1927), p. 131.

44. "To Heinrich Heine," *Revue et Gazette musicale,* 8 July 1838; Liszt, *Sämtliche Schriften*, vol. 1, p. 176; Suttoni, *An Artist's Journey*, p. 106. The article begins with a quote from Canto IV of *Childe Harold's Pilgrimage*: "I stood in Venice, on the Bridge of Sighs." And sigh Liszt most certainly did as he responded to what he believed to be a gratuitous attack from a close friend and colleague. In particular, Liszt was troubled by Heine's accusation that he was "unsettled" philosophically. Much like Byron, Liszt prefaced the description of Venice with references to some of the city's most famous landmarks and historic figures: the bronze horses of St. Mark's—"the winged lion of St. Mark, still atop his African column and still gazing toward the sea"—and the medieval doges Enrico Dandolo (d. 1205) and Marino Faliero (ca. 1278–1355). Faliero, a corrupt commander of the Venetian forces who was elected doge in 1354 and committed murder in an attempt to become prince, was an especially popular literary character at the time. Both Byron and Dasimir Delavigne made him the subject of tragedies. He was also the central character in a tale by E. T. A. Hoffmann and an opera by Donizetti that premiered in 1835.

45. Liszt remained in Vienna 10 April–26 May. For a detailed description of this trip see the chapter by Christopher Gibbs, "Just Two Words. Enormous Success," included in this volume. Press reports of Liszt's Vienna concerts are given in Dezső Legány, *Franz Liszt: Unbekannte Presse und Briefe aus Wien 1822–1886* (Budapest: 1984), pp. 22–58.

46. Liszt mentioned this article in a letter to his mother in late July 1838: "Tell Massart that I have written a letter addressed to him for the *Revue et Gazette musicale*. He

will have it very soon." Liszt, *Briefe an seine Mutter*, ed. La Mara (Leipzig: 1918), pp. 48–49. In his collection of Liszt's articles, Suttoni separates the two parts of this letter and inserts the article "To Heinrich Heine" between them, since part I discusses "Milan" and part II discusses "Venice." This might seem practical in terms of creating a chronological trave-logue of Liszt's time in Italy, but it completely destroys the "before-and-after effect" that I think Liszt was intending to present in this article.

47. Julia Pahlen-Samoyloff (1803–1875), a Russian noblewoman living in Milan, hosted numerous music soirées. Liszt became good friends with her during his time in Milan, and he dedicated the Ricordi edition of his (Rossini) *Soirées musicales* to her.

48. Liszt, *Sämtliche Schriften*, vol. 1, p. 190; Suttoni, *An Artist's Journey*, p. 95. Suttoni claims that this dream sequence is a reference to Heine, but it is clearly connected to Liszt's reading of Byron's *Childe Harold's Pilgrimage*.

49. Liszt, *Sämtliche Schriften*, vol. 1, p. 192; Suttoni, *An Artist's Journey*, pp. 95–96.

50. Byron, *Childe Harold's Pilgrimage*, Canto I, ll. 46–54, p. 24.

51. Ibid., ll. 109–17.

52. Liszt, *Sämtliche Schriften*, vol. 1, p. 194; Suttoni, *An Artist's Journey*, p. 97.

53. Liszt, *Sämtliche Schriften*, vol. 1, p. 194; Suttoni, *An Artist's Journey*, p. 98.

54. Liszt, *Sämtliche Schriften*, vol. 1, p. 196; Suttoni, *An Artist's Journey*, p. 139.

55. Liszt, *Sämtliche Schriften*, vol. 1, p. 204; Suttoni, *An Artist's Journey*, p. 144.

56. On 26 November 1838 d'Agoult wrote to Adolphe Pictet that she and Liszt were visiting the Medici Chapel often in order to study Michelangelo's statues. Robert Bory, *Une Retraite romantique en Suisse: Liszt et la Comtesse d'Agoult* (Lucerne: 1930), pp. 148–49.

57. Lorenzo de' Medici, duke of Urbino, ruled Florence from 1513 until his untimely death in 1519. He was an avid patron of arts and letters and the dedicatee of Niccolò Machiavelli's *The Prince* (1515).

58. The bat serves as the emblematic animal in Dürer's famous engraving, *Melancholia I*.

59. Erwin Panofsky, *Studies in Iconology: Humanistic Themes in the Art of the Renaissance* (New York: 1939), p. 180. Since the appearance of Panofsky's work on Michelangelo, some scholars have challenged his ideas, claiming that artists such as Michelangelo would not have drawn on philosophical sources to such a great degree. For a comprehensive look at the reception of Panofsky's work in the last half-century, see Carl Landauer, "Erwin Panofsky and the Renascence of the Renaissance," *Renaissance Quarterly* 47, no. 2 (1994): 255ff.

60. Panofsky, *Studies in Iconology*, p. 209.

61. *The Poetry of Michelangelo: An Annotated Translation*, trans. J. Saslow (New Haven, Conn.: 1991), p. 419. For the original Italian, see Michelangelo Buonarroti, *Rime* (Milan: 1975).

62. According to Rena Mueller, in "Liszt's 'Tasso' Sketchbook: Studies in Sources and Revision," Ph.D diss., New York University, 1986, there are two citations on pages 19 and 20 in Liszt's *Poetisches Album* (Weimar: Goethe- und Schiller-Archiv, MS 142) labeled "Strozzi's Inschrift zur Michel Angelos Nacht" and "Michel Angelos Antwort" which date from the 1840s (pp. 157–58).

63. It should be noted that in the 1860s Liszt composed a work called "La Notte," which is an expanded version (with additional Hungarian material) of "Il Penseroso."

64. Rosa was the primary character in "Signor Formica," a short story by E. T. A Hoffmann. Berlioz's librettists Wailly and Barbier incorporated elements of this story into the carnival scene in *Benvenuto Cellini*. Rosa also made an appearance, albeit fictive, in chap-ter 30 of *Le Corricolo* by Alexander Dumas, père. For a detailed study of Rosa's reception in France, see James S. Patty, *Salvator Rosa in French Literature: From the Bizarre to the Sublime* (Lexington, Ky.: 2005). For information concerning the publication of Hoffmann's "Signor Formica" in the *Revue et Gazette musicale* see: James Haar, "The *Conte Musical* and Early Music," in *La Renaissance et sa musique au XIXe siècle*, ed. Philippe Vendrix (Tours: 2004),

p. 187; and Katherine Ellis, *Music Criticism in Nineteenth-Century France: Revue et Gazette musicale de Paris 1834–1880* (Cambridge, Eng.: 1995), App. 3.

65. Helen Langdon, "Salvator Rosa," *Grove Dictionary of Art*, ed. Jane Turner (London: 1996).

66. Lady (Sydney) Morgan, *The Life and Times of Salvator Rosa*, 2 vols. (London: 1824).

67. As Margaret Murata, "Dr. Burney Bought a Music Book," *Journal of Musicology* 17, no. 1 (1999): 82, explains: "Musical notation in Rosa's hand can be seen in two paintings attributed to him," one of which Liszt might have seen in Italy: "an allegorical representation of *La Musica*" that "holds a texted vocal part (Rome: Galleria Nazionale d'Arte Antica)." In addition, Michael Mahoney, *The Drawings of Salvator Rosa*, 2 vols. (New York: 1977), notes at least three drawings preserved on sheets of lined music paper (vol.1, p. 289).

68. Morgan, *Life and Times of Salvator Rosa*, vol.1, pp. 73, 76.

69. Ibid., pp. 95, 99.

70. For a recent study on the reception of this painting, see W. Rowarth: "Salvator Rosa's Self-portraits: Some Problems of Identity and Meaning," *The Seventeenth Century*, vol. 4 of *The Cambridge Guide to the Arts in Britain*, ed. B. Ford (Cambridge, Eng.: 1989), pp. 117–48.

71. In addition to his talents as a painter, Lehmann was an avid scholar of seventeenth-century art with close ties to the French Academy in Rome. He painted portraits of both d'Agoult and Liszt during their stay in Florence, and like Liszt he was fascinated by the art and poetry of Salvator Rosa. Liszt and d'Agoult formed a close friendship with Lehmann, and in later years the relationship between Lehmann and d'Agoult grew ever more intimate. For a detailed study of their friendship as revealed in their correspondence, see Solange Joubert, *Une Correspondance romantique: Madame d'Agoult, Liszt, Henri Lehmann* (Paris: 1947).

72. Michael Howard, "Henri Lehmann," *Grove Dictionary of Art*, ed. Jane Turner (London: 1996), vol. 19, p. 93.

73. Frank Walker, "Salvator Rosa and Music," *Monthly Musical Record* 79 and 80 (1949 and 1950).

74. Burney purchased a seventeenth-century music manuscript during his travels in Italy that he believed was by Salvator Rosa. As Murata in "Dr. Burney Bought a Music Book," explains: "Burney made good of the 'music book by Salvator Rosa' when he came to write of the seventeenth-century Italian cantata for his *General History*" (p. 77). For the chapter "Of Cantatas, or Narrative Chamber Music" he transcribed what he claimed were nine excerpts of Rosa's music, including "Vado ben spesso."

75. Ibid., p. 88. Liszt interpreted the text in a similar manner; in *Années de pèlerinage* he indicated that the "Canzonetta del Salvator Rosa" should be played "andante marziale." Unfortunately, many modern-day pianists ignore this indication.

76. The article was published in the *Revue et Gazette musicale*, 13 January 1839.

77. Liszt, *Sämtliche Schriften*, vol. 1, p. 270; Suttoni, *An Artist's Journey*, p. 153.

78. Liszt, *Sämtliche Schriften*, vol. 1, pp. 270-72; Suttoni, *An Artist's Journey*, p. 154.

79. In a letter in to Pierre Erard dated 1 February 1839, Liszt commented on his visit to Bologna: "Since you last received news from me I've spent eight days in Bologna and three months in Florence. I won't tell you about *Saint Cecilia*, the Medici *Venus*, or the *Fates* of Michelangelo—not because I haven't studied and admired these masterpieces as best I could, but because it would require of me, and you too, far more leisure time than we have right now. We'll save it for our future dinners." Marc Pincherle, *Musiciens peints par eux-mêmes: Lettres de compositeurs écrites en français (1771–1910)* (Paris: 1939), p. 96.

80. Liszt, *Sämtliche Schriften*, vol. 1, p. 296; Suttoni, *An Artist's Journey*, p. 162. The article was published in *Revue et Gazette musicale* on 14 April 1839.

81. D'Agoult passed through Bologna in October 1838 and recorded the visit in her diary: "Nice day. Arrival in Bologna. First Impression, disappointment. . . . Saint Cecilia less laudable than I expected. I'm beginning to think that Raphael's reputation is a bit overrated." D'Agoult, *Mémoires*, p. 158.

82. Liszt, *Sämtliche Schriften*, vol. 1, p. 296; Suttoni, *An Artist's Journey*, p. 163.

83. Ibid.

84. Liszt, *Sämtliche Schriften*, vol. 1, p. 300; Suttoni, *An Artist's Journey*, p. 166.

85. Liszt and d'Agoult had just arrived in Rome, after passing through Pisa and Siena. In Pisa Liszt visited the Campo Santo and studied the thirteenth-century fresco *Trionfo della Morte*, believed at that time to be a work by Orcagna. For a thorough description of Liszt's reaction to this artwork and its connection to the program for his *Totentanz*, see Anna Celenza, "Death Transfigured: The Origins and Evolution of Franz Liszt's *Totentanz*," in *Nineteenth-Century Music: Selected Proceedings of the Tenth International Conference* (Aldershot, Eng.: 2002), pp. 125–54.

86. Franz Liszt, *Journal des Zÿi*, in d'Agoult, *Mémoires*, p. 180.

87. Through a comprehensive study of the numerous manuscript sources, Rena Mueller, "Liszt's 'Tasso' Sketchbook," traces the evolution of the work, from the origins of the various movements in 1838–39 to the final published version (pp. 143–58).

88. As Mueller explains in "Liszt's 'Tasso' Sketchbook," this practice is made evident by a draft inventory for the volume found in Liszt's *Ce qu'on entend* sketchbook (Weimar: Goethe- und Schiller-Archiv, MS N1), probably dating from 1847, which shows a selection of pieces that differs greatly from the final version (p. 149).

89. An article by Fétis, published in the *Revue et Gazette musicale* on 9 May 1841 (see Peter Bloom's "Fétis's Review of the Transcendental Etudes" in this volume), indicates that by that date Liszt already had plans for publishing the Swiss and Italian volumes of *Années de pèlerinage*. Also, Mueller explains that an inventory of Liszt's works, written in his own hand (found in Weimar: Goethe- und Schiller-Archiv, MS B20), suggests that by June 1848 he had finished the compilation of both volumes, which he referred to as "*Années de pèlerinage*—Childe H?" and that in a letter written to Czerny in 1852, Liszt explained that he was going to reissue the *Album d'un voyageur* (an early version of the Swiss volume) in a greatly revised form as part of "*Années de pèlerinage*, Suite de Compositions pour le piano—Suisse et Italie" (pp. 142, 147–49).

90. It should be noted that in addition to their shared interest in music, Liszt and Ingres shared a similar reverence for Raphael's images of the Virgin Mary. Like Liszt, Ingres interpreted Raphael's images as metaphors for divine inspiration (as shown in his *Vow of Louis XIII* [1824] in the Montaubon Cathedral). Indeed, this was a common interpretation of Raphael's work among artists at the French Academy. For a detailed study of Raphael reception among Liszt's French contemporaries, see Carl Goldstein, "French Identity in the Realm of Raphael," in *The Cambridge Companion to Raphael* (Cambridge, Eng.: 2005), pp. 237–60.

91. *Revue et Gazette musicale* (24 October 1839).

92. Liszt, *Sämtliche Schriften*, vol. 1, p. 306; Suttoni, *An Artist's Journey*, p. 186.

93. Liszt, *Sämtliche Schriften*, vol. 1, p. 306; Suttoni, *An Artist's Journey*, p. 187.

94. Ibid.

95. Ibid.

96. D'Agoult, *Mémoires*, pp. 164–65.

97. For an overview of Liszt's various settings of these sonnets, for both voice and piano and solo piano, see Monika Hennemann, "Liszt's Lieder," in *The Cambridge Companion to Liszt*, ed. Kenneth Hamilton (Cambridge, Eng.: 2005), pp. 195, 199–201, 203–205.

98. Sonnet 47, ll. 12–14, in *Petrarch: Selected Sonnets, Odes and Letters*, ed. Thomas Goddard Bergin (New Haven, Conn.: 1966), p. 40.

99. Ibid., p. 64. Sonnet 104, ll. 12–14.

100. Ibid., 69. Sonnet 123, ll 1–4.

101. D'Agoult, *Mémoires*, p. 165. It should be noted that Liszt's first step in this process appears to have taken place the year before, in 1838, when he began transcribing a number of Schubert songs—most notably "Der Wanderer," which played a prominent role in his first description of the Republic of the Imagination discussed above.

102. Liszt made reference to such an interpretation in 1880 in a letter to Giuseppe Ferrazzi: "As for my 3 Petrarch Sonnets . . . piano transcriptions of them were brought out long ago by Schott; but I hesitate to publish the second original version for voice, for to express the feeling that I tried to breathe into the musical notation of these Sonnets would call for some poetic singer, enamored of an ideal of love . . . *rarae aves in terries.*" *Franz Liszt: Selected Letters*, ed. Adrian Williams (Oxford, Eng.: 1998), p. 852.

103. See Chloe Chard, "Emma Hamilton and Corrine," in *The Impact of Italy: The Grand Tour and Beyond*, ed. Clare Hornsby (London: 2000), pp. 147–69. Chard discusses in detail the ways in which Byron (*Childe Harold's Pilgrimage*), Lamartine (*Dernier chant du pèlerinage d'Harold*), and de Staël (*Corinne ou Italie*) place female characters in various forms of affiliation with antiquity in their literary works, often using them as metaphors for inspiration or for a revival of the past.

104. Winklhofer, "Liszt, Marie d'Agoult, and the 'Dante' Sonata," claims that d'Agoult was largely responsible for piquing Liszt's interest in Dante, yet Auguste Boissier, *Liszt pédagogue: Leçons de piano donnée par Liszt à Mademoiselle Valérie Boissier* (Paris: 1837), p. 53, claims that as early as 21 February 1832, Liszt discussed the *Inferno* with her in one of her lessons. And as early as 1836, Liszt's close friend George Sand regularly described his appearance as "Dantesque" in her articles. See, for example, *Lettre d'un Voyageur à Charles Didier* in *Oeuvres Autobiographiques*, ed. Georges Lubin, 2 vols. (Paris: 1927), vol. 2, p. 915. As Winklhofer explains, d'Agoult and Balzac began seeing the resemblance themselves shortly thereafter (p. 25).

105. For information concerning the various stages of composition see Mueller, "Liszt's 'Tasso' Sketchbook," pp. 150–54, which offers a correction of Winklhofer, "Liszt, Marie d'Agoult, and the 'Dante' Sonata," pp. 30–32. Liszt apparently did not begin working on the piece in earnest for several months. On 26 September 1839 d'Agoult wrote to Henri Lehmann: "Le bravo suonatore began a *Fragment dantesque* this morning that is sending him to the very Devil. He is so consumed by it that he won't go on to Naples." Joubert, *Une correspondance romantique*, p. 33. In a description of concerts in Vienna at that time, the *Allgemeine musikalische Zeitung* referred to the work as *Fragment nach Dante*. "Wien, Musikalische Chronik des vierten Vierteljahres 1839," *AMZ* series 1, vol. 42 (1840; repr. Amsterdam, 1966), pp. 91–92.

106. Published as a companion to *Marino Faliero, Doge of Venice: A Historical Tragedy in Five Acts*, and viewed as a parallel to the *Lament of Tasso* (a work that Liszt looked to when composing his symphonic poem *Tasso*), Byron's *Prophesy of Dante* (London: 1821) focuses on Dante's years of exile from his native Florence and gives to him a vision of the future of Italy. It is a commentary of sorts presented in the guise of a poetic work.

107. For Liszt's interaction with Italian folk music, see Rossana Dalmonte, "Liszt and Italian Folklore," *Revista de musicologia* 16, no. 3 (1993): 1832–49. These pieces had been published previously as part of Liszt's *Venezia e Napoli* (1840). Liszt later used the theme from "Gondoliera" yet again in his symphonic poem *Tasso*. As Reeves Shulstad, "Liszt's Symphonic Poems and Symphonies," *Cambridge Companion to Liszt*, explains: "Liszt claims to have heard gondoliers in Venice singing . . . the first lines of Tasso's *Gerusalemme liberata*" (p. 207).

Heine, Liszt, and the Song of the Future

SUSAN YOUENS

For years, one commentator after another has pointed out that much of what is best in Liszt is encapsulated in his songs and that this repertory deserves more attention than it has received to date. Despite the efforts both of Liszt scholars and performers to make people aware of the works beyond such chestnuts as "Kling' leise, mein Lied" and "Es muß ein Wunderbares sein" (these works, however, deserve their status as favorites), one could still drop the names of certain Liszt songs to musicians, even to cognoscenti of Romantic music, without a glimmer of recognition.[1] There are, happily, exceptions: Liszt's affinity for Victor Hugo's poetry led to such marvelous *mélodies* as "Oh! quand je dors," "S'il est un charmant gazon," "Enfant, si j'étais roi," and "Comment, disaient-ils," and these are rightly beloved of singers. A few of the extended songs so characteristic of this composer have made their way into the recital-canon of those performers with the skill to master their formidable challenges. Most notably, there are the three Petrarch sonnets on which Liszt lavished such care (the turn to Petrarch more than makes up for his first song in Italian, "Angiolin del biondo crin," to an anodyne poem by Césare Bocella), the three songs on texts from Schiller's *Wilhelm Tell* ("Der Fischerknabe," "Der Hirt," "Der Alpenjäger"), and his compatriot Nikolaus Lenau's "Die drei Zigeuner," but others—for example, the dramatic "Jeanne d'arc au bûcher"—are seldom heard. While there is a more or less complete recording of the songs from 1987, including different versions, the set is extremely difficult to find.[2] And scholarship has much more to say about both the better- and lesser-known works.[3]

Liszt's songs attest to his intermittent commitment to the genre over a span of forty-plus years and to his habit of revising songs in order to find new music in them. Here too, one encounters Liszt the cosmopolite, who drew his song texts not only from the German and Hungarian sources one would expect from a native of the Austro-Hungarian empire, but from Italian, British, French, and Russian literature. Within these pages, the denizens of literature's Mount Olympus—Goethe, Schiller, Heine, Hugo, Tennyson, Tolstoy, Petrarch—rub shoulders with poetasters from Liszt's aristocratic milieu, such as the so-called Princess von Hohenlohe (Carolyne von Sayn-Wittgenstein's daughter Marie, who married Prince Constantine von Hohenlohe in 1859), and third-rate versifiers on the order of Rudolfo Coronini, Ludwig von Biegeleben, and Schubert's friend Franz von Schober. The music for words by this motley crew is similarly variegated, running the gamut from French salon-style at its most refined to virtuosic demands for both pianist and singer to austere explorations of the land beyond tonality. No "Sunday pianist," no amateur singer, should or could tackle Liszt's first version of "Der Fischerknabe" (The Fisher Lad), while other Liszt songs, less physically demanding than this one, are conceptually complex, a challenge to the mind rather than fingers and throats. One imagines Liszt asking himself, "How many different things can song be and do?" and then demonstrating to the world different guises of this genre. Those who disdained the virtuoso could not similarly disdain works that strike so deep.

That is, if they bothered to look at them. Both the nineteenth-century's schizophrenia regarding song composition and Liszt's estimation of the genre are on display in a letter he wrote to Wagner on 28 October 1849: "Another string for your bow," Liszt tells Wagner, would be to give the public an anthology of songs. "For works of this sort, signed with your name, it would not be difficult for me to find a publisher and arrange for a decent payment, and surely you would not scorn taking the path that Mozart, Beethoven, Schubert, and Rossini did not disdain."[4] I have retained Liszt's multiple negatives in my translation because they are so revelatory of song's second-class citizenship in the nineteenth-century musical world. In order to make his case to Wagner, Liszt had to point out that song was an honorable enterprise because the likes of Mozart and Beethoven had engaged in it, but awareness that many people disdained song composition is the readily apparent subtext of his words. Songs were, of course, a highly successful commodity for sale to the music-loving bourgeoisie, even if they failed to command as much respect at music's highest tiers as symphonies, chamber music, and opera. Hence Liszt's generous offer to pave his friend's path, if not to fame and fortune, at least to name recognition and some extra cash by this avenue, though both men knew that titans did not make colossal reputations by means of song.

And yet, Liszt's praise of Schubert came from the heart: he knew that this composer and his own contemporary Schumann had taken the genre seriously, had elevated the Lied to new heights. They had shown that songs and cycles could break new ground, and for their visionary endeavors, both men found the poetry of Heinrich Heine especially useful. They understood the radicalism of Heine's poetic project and created futuristic tonal realizations of his bitterness and terseness. In fact, Heine was the poet of choice for composers in the 1820s, '30s, and '40s who wanted to do radical things with song, since he poured new wine into the old bottles of folklike strophes, including sentiments barred from the verse of his day; even George Eliot, who admired Heine greatly, was shocked by some of the "coarser" poems and called for their removal, out of reach of "immature minds."[5] When the Viennese composer Johann Vesque von Püttlingen published settings of the entirety of Heine's *Die Heimkehr* in 1851, Eduard Hanslick took him gently to task in a review that year for choosing "uncomposable poems," and the young Franz Lachner, a friend of Schubert's in his last years, made of poems such as "Wasserfahrt" remarkable experiments in music depicting extreme psychological states.[6] The importance to Liszt of his many-faceted engagement with Schubert's and Schumann's songs cannot be overestimated: he introduced Schubert's songs to such great singers as the tenor Adolphe Nourrit; he accompanied him and other singers in performances of this repertory; and he transcribed songs by both men, including arrangements of all six of Schubert's Heine songs for publication in 1840 in the dead composer's own city of Vienna.[7] Throughout his life, Liszt conducted a conversation from inside his own music with those composers who most mattered to him. The allusions to Schubert and Schumann I have found in the songs discussed in this chapter are the result of his keen interest in the musical world around him: a song by Liszt is not just the result of grappling with a poet's words but of relationships forged in tone and rhythm with other musicians.[8] For him, influence was not a matter of anxiety, *pace* Harold Bloom, but of a singular form of collaboration with great musical minds.

Most of Liszt's songs—in his old age, all of them—are not directed to the same public who worshipped at the altar of star performers like himself, their seemingly superhuman skills offering audiences access to a rapturous sense of liberation.[9] In songs, he could, for example, fashion endings that peer around the tonal corner into whatever realm might lie beyond Romantic-saturated chromaticism; these "conclusions" are question marks in music. The indeterminate endings of the late songs become increasingly a matter of mourning as well: an elderly man, acquainted with grief, more and more depressed as death drew near, concocts a bitter new vocabulary of music. "Hurling a lance into the boundless realm of future" (Liszt's famous phrase) was not always an optimistic enterprise; not only was the future ultimately unguessable, but the composer looks back at bygone certainty with regret. Ghosts of tonality waft through these songs, and we sense their imminent disappearance in company with their creator.[10] The journey from his earliest songs in 1839 to this acid-etched tonal language, shot through with silences and extreme dissonance, is a long one, and the compound of curiosity and courage required to probe what might come next, after his departure from this life, is revelatory of his character from the start. Long before Liszt's last years, Heine half-praised, half-mocked the musician he knew personally when he wrote in 1837:

> Heaven knows in what spiritual stall he will find his next hobbyhorse! But this tireless thirsting after light and divinity remains ever praise-worthy, a testament to his sense for what is holy, for things religious. That such a restless mind, driven to distraction by all the troubles and dogmas of the day, who feels the need to encumber himself with all of humanity's demands, *who gladly sticks his nose into all the pots in which the good God is cooking the future*: that Franz Liszt could not be merely a nice, biddable pianist for contented merchants in their sleeping caps is clearly understood.[11]

Heine was no hagiographer of anyone or anything, and Liszt's "tinsel" (Schumann's term for his contemporary's virtuosic glitz and glitter) soon drew fire from him.[12] And, of course, the writer's death in 1856 meant that he never encountered the songs in which Liszt "cooked the future" in his last years. One wonders what he might have thought of them.

As Rena Charnin Mueller has demonstrated, Liszt seems never to have considered a song "finished," but rather made a habit of revisiting poems he had previously set in order to create new tonal possibilities for them.[13] The five versions of Heine's "Ich weiß nicht, was soll es bedeuten" (or "Die Loreley") are a spectacular instance of this propensity, but there are many others.[14] In this regard, he comes close to out-Schuberting Schubert, who also returned to prior poetry on numerous occasions in order that he might wrestle with it some more (the different musical guises he creates for Mignon, from *Lied im Volkston* to quasi-operatic style are the best-known specimens). As a result of Liszt's incessant tinkering, with pages inserted into manuscripts over a period of years and a bewildering variety of versions, the sources are complex; in fact, "the qualitative difference between an *Urschrift* and an *Abschrift* was often rendered meaningless," Mueller writes, and the composer's close association with his copyists renders an already complex source-world even more so.[15]

To avoid the Scylla of list making and the Charybdis of chronological trekking through an oeuvre (since the chronology is so difficult to determine, those rocks would be very sharp indeed), I have chosen instead to focus on three of Liszt's songs to texts by Heine, whose poems have been set to music more often than any other poet. From the moment his poems appeared on the scene in the 1820s, composers by the hundreds gravitated to these bite-size, biting poems by someone who could make words jump through hoops as only true writers can. But his *Buch der Lieder* might as well have been bound in barbed wire, such were its traps for the unwary. "My malicious-sentimental poems," Heine once called them, and one notes which adjective came first.[16] Heine's surfaces are not to be trusted, and only conceptually complex music can do justice to his depths, even when a composer chooses, as the best ones do on occasion, to point the words in another direction by means of music or even quarrel with the poet outright. Liszt may not have hit a home run with Heine's poetry every time—both he and Schumann suppress the poet's mockery of "pure" Romantic poetry in "Du bist wie eine Blume," the insistence by certain critics that a poem be "schön und hold und rein" (beautiful and gentle and pure)—but several of his Heine Lieder belong on the short list of truly great settings of this poet.

A Ruptured Friendship, a Collaboration for the Ages: Liszt and Heine

No Lisztian or Germanist could fail to be fascinated by the conjunction in song and in life of two giants of the era. For those who come after, the history of their friendship is all the more convoluted because of the legends besetting the perception of both men: the myth of Liszt as a meretricious virtuoso who only intermittently achieved greatness and the myth of Heine as a mendacious creature obsessed with money and prone to malicious slander. Poet and musician met in Paris in 1831 and were, for a few years, quite companionable, singing each other's praises to all and sundry. Heine, Liszt wrote, was "the most spiritual and Parisian of Germans," and Heine heaped his own brand of ambivalent praise on Liszt's head.[17] But the poet soon came to prefer Chopin's brand of pianism ("he comes from the country of Mozart, of Raphael, of Goethe; his true birthplace is the land of Poetry") to the heaven-storming virtuosity of Liszt at the keyboard, although Chopin's aristocratic elitism did not meet with his entire approval either. In his "Confidential Letter" about the Thalberg-Liszt controversy in the *Revue et Gazette musicale de Paris* of 4 February 1838, Heine lauds the two pianists for their awe-inspiring technical dexterity (he hymns Liszt as "possessed, tempestuous, volcanic, and as fiery as a titan") but confesses that "despite my friendship for Liszt, his music does not affect my sensibilities in an agreeable way."[18] One can trace the step-by-step souring of Liszt's and Heine's association through various stages, from their divergent views about the excommunicated revolutionary priest Félicité de Lamennais (who once wrote, "There is something satanic about that man [Heine]") to the three versions of Heine's "Musikalische Saison von 1844" with their varying degrees of anti-Lisztian mockery to a final rupture triggered by the revolutionary outbreaks of 1848–49.[19] From his "Matratzengruft," the mattress-grave on which the paralyzed poet lay dying by degrees from 1848 to 1856, Heine heaped coals of fire on Liszt's transformation into a "Stadtmusikus" in Weimar and the composer's supposed betrayal of the republican ideals of 1830.[20] Because this poet was so memorably witty whenever he attacked anyone or anything, it is the acidulous invocations of Liszt in the later poems that have dictated the tone of scholarly comment on the subject, as Rainer Kleinertz has observed in his study of their fraught friendship.[21] Lines such as "Es fiel der Freiheit letzte Schanz', / Und Ungarn blutet sich zu Tode— / Doch unversehrt blieb Ritter Franz, / Sein Säbel auch—er liegt in der Kommode" (Freedom's last bulwark fell, and Hungary bled to death—but Knight Franz was not harmed; his saber, too, lies in the chest of drawers) from the poem "Im Oktober 1849" spell the end of an association that was once so promising.[22]

In particular, I join company with everyone else who has ever paid serious attention to Liszt's songs in praising "Vergiftet sind meine Lieder" as one of the finest Lieder, not just in this composer's oeuvre but in the whole of nineteenth-century song. First published in 1844, the Lied was subsequently revised in a process that began in 1849 and culminated in the Schlesinger and Kahnt editions of 1859 and 1860; it is this later version I will be discussing.[23] Earlier commentators have described this work as "one of the most terrible hate-songs ever written" or as "one of the finest settings of anger . . . on a par with Wolf's greatest songs," but these are overly reductive summations of what is actually a complex brew of accusation, vulnerability, helplessness, lamentation, even fear, all of it remarkably raw.[24] The initial phrase of the song, after all, is one Liszt also used in his "Vallée d'Obermann" in the first volume of the *Années de pèlerinage* and that is a work *about* lament; like the song, it too concludes in the major mode, a signifier of reluctant resignation at the last minute to inalterable circumstance (Examples 1 and 2).[25]

Liszt was perhaps the first composer to discover the fifty-first poem in the *Lyrisches Intermezzo* for song. His other Heine texts, including "Du bist wie eine Blume" and "Die Loreley," were already the stuff of music by other men and women, but not this unstable compound of vulnerability and Vesuvian lava.[26] There was a "safe Heine," misunderstood as a tender

Example 1. Beginning, "Vergiftet sind meine Lieder."

Example 2. Beginning, "Vallée d'Obermann."

sentimentalist, who served a horde of composers as fodder for syrupy parlor songs (many of the 415 settings of "Du bist wie eine Blume" are cases in point), and an unsafe Heine, who couched his assaults on the Romantic poetic project in the form of witty-savage-sharp deconstructions of bourgeois codes of desire.[27] This poem is what one might call semi-unsafe: one could construe it as a lament for lost love, one of thousands in the storehouse of lyric verse, but its accusatory anguish goes far beyond the likes of "Was will die einsame Träne," a best-seller with nineteenth-century composers. On the surface of "Vergiftet sind meine Lieder," a lover accuses the beloved of having poisoned him, whether by venereal infection (the verb *gießen* bespeaks fluids, and poisoned fluids suggest sex and disease), emotional ruin, or the corruption of innocence we do not know. The phrase "many serpents" seems a latter-day variation on Medusa's snaky coiffeur, especially from *this* poet, one of whose missions was to make myth modern. Both here and elsewhere, snakes wind their way throughout his poems ("Ich sah die Schlang', die dir am Herzen frißt," the persona laments in "Ich grolle nicht"), with their multiple symbolic resonances of the serpent in Eden, of pubic hair transposed to Medusa's head, of death-dealing, slithering creatures. The words "blossoming life" imply that the speaker is in the springtime of his days, and hence this cry of anguish might have been impelled by sexual awakening in adolescence or young manhood, by the end of the first serious affair, with despair and disillusionment the result. Read in one way, the poem exudes a young poet's shock at the realities of desire rather than chivalrous love on the printed page, love of the sort that had impelled so many prior poems and songs over the centuries. Here, one remembers Heine's debt to the poet of the Schubert song cycles, Wilhelm Müller, whose poem "Blümlein Vergißmein" (Little Forget-me Flower) from *Die schöne Müllerin*—Schubert omitted it from his cycle—tells of the same archetypal experience so tersely evoked in "Vergiftet sind meine Lieder."

LI.	No. 51
Vergiftet sind meine Lieder;—	Poisoned are my songs—
Wie könnt' es anders seyn?	how could it be otherwise?
Du hast mir ja Gift gegossen	You poured poison
In's blühende Leben hinein.	into blossoming life.
Vergiftet sind meine Lieder;—	Poisoned are my songs—
Wie könnt' es anders seyn?	how could it be otherwise?
Ich trage im Herzen viel Schlangen,	I bear many serpents in my heart,[29]
Und dich, Geliebte mein.[28]	and you, my beloved.

Read in another way, this poem exemplifies the conflict between the Ideal and the Real that would be Heine's lifelong dilemma. "O dieser Streit wird enden nimmermehr, / Stets wird die Wahrheit hadern mit dem Schönen" (Oh, this battle will never end—the Beautiful will incessantly wrangle with the Real), he writes in "Es träumte mir von einer Sommernacht" (I dreamed of a summer night), one of his last poems inspired by "die Mouche," the Muse of his final months of existence.[30] Viewed in this fashion, "Vergiftet sind meine Lieder" is a Janus-faced creation. The "Geliebte mein" can be understood as both the Romantic muse—the figure of the Ideal—who has poisoned *his* art of real life and as the Real who poisons the Ideal. No matter which way the poet turns, he cannot win, cannot void the poison. But I wonder whether Liszt would have seen such esoteric nuances of a poet's predicament in this poem or whether he perhaps saw in it something more personal: a reflection of his disintegrating relationship with Marie d'Agoult, which came to an end in April and May of 1844, the same year in which he composed the first version of this song. "I am very sad and deeply grieved," he wrote her on 11 April, "I am counting one by one all the sorrows I have caused you, and neither anything nor anyone will ever be able to save me from myself. I no longer want either to speak to you, or see you, still less write to you. Didn't you tell me I was a play-actor? Yes, like those who would play the dying athlete after drinking hemlock."[31] He too speaks of poison. In another brief letter written that same month, he wrote, "I have given you everything I had: heart, head, and arms. I shan't make you account for anything."[32] Someone who could write these words, it seems to me, would find in "Vergiftet sind meine Lieder" an eerily exact mirror of his own agony. Whatever the dangers of the biographical fallacy, it seems obvious that composers are occasionally attracted to particular poems because the words speak to exigencies in their own lives. The connections may be veiled or circuitous, but it stands to reason that some poems become personal.

Liszt was evidently struck by Heine's first syntactical twist in this poem: the poeticizing inversion of the first statement, not "Meine Lieder sind vergiftet" but "Vergiftet sind meine Lieder." The word *vergiftet* (poisoned) is the first word we read/see/hear: the poem is poisoned from the start. In the forty-seventh poem from the same cycle, "Sie haben mich gequälet," the poet multiplies the sources of poison—"They poisoned my bread, they poured poison in my glass, one with her love, one with her hate"— but here, the poisoner is in the singular.[33] "How could it be otherwise?" the speaker asks twice, a doubled hint that it was never otherwise. This much repetition in so small a poem commands attention. Not only is it an *aide-mémoire* ("This you may not forget," the poet bids us), but the effect is litany-like, the persona telling his beads of helpless anguish. That he loved the shadowy beloved is evident in accusations that may be, *are*, as strong as he can make them but lack any hint that she has acted maliciously ("I shan't make you account for anything"). The bitter, fearful question "What will become of me, now that I and my songs are poisoned?" lurks in the offing, around the next corner of the poem.

In his revisions of "Vergiftet sind meine Lieder," Liszt experimented with adding or deleting the customary piano introduction, the traditional means of establishing the basic musical materials, tonality, mood, and atmosphere of a Lied. For art songs in folklike style of a sort fashionable throughout the nineteenth century, composers often dispensed with piano introductions or made them minimal, but no one in his right mind would describe "Vergiftet sind meine Lieder" as "volkstümlich." In the original tenor version of the song, there is no piano prelude, and the effect is of an unpremeditated outburst that seems to come from nowhere, a volcanic eruption exploding without warning through the psyche's thin crust. It is a marvelously effective way to begin, but Liszt, as he so often did, reconsidered the matter. The result of his tinkering is reminiscent of those

Schubert personae who think or feel something wordlessly in the piano introduction before adding language to the enterprise in the body of the song. "Morgengruss" from *Die schöne Müllerin* is one example, with its miller lad who mentally rehearses his ardent, worshipful "wake-up call" to the miller maid, then sees her, puts an end to his inner rehearsal *sans mots*, and launches into one of the sweetest greetings ever created. In the piano introduction found in a French edition of "Vergiftet sind meine Lieder," circa 1870 (Example 3), Liszt's persona also rehearses the first line of the poem in his mind but as the rawest of outbursts: no sweetness here.

(Die rechte Hand ist Pausen.)

Example 3. Piano introduction, "Vergiftet sind meine Lieder," French edition, ca. 1870.

Dissonant, accented, fortissimo seventh chords—instrumental screams— precede the preliminary wordless statement of the initial vocal phrase in the left hand (the right hand is silent). The massive repeated dissonances of a major seventh (F and E), struck over and over before "resolving" to still more dissonance, make pain palpable before a single word is sung.[34] It is, I think, impossible to say which is better, the version with or without piano introduction, as each brings lamentation to sounding life with unforgettable power.

This marvelous oddity of a song is formally organized by repetitions of the initial theme with and without words: one circles back to the same lament over and over in a mini-rondo of obsessive grief. For the recurring declamatory declaration "My songs are poisoned," Liszt makes a distantly Bachian "weeping" descending line, filled with desire-laden appoggiaturas, into something both accusatory and anguished (see Example 1). The word *vergiftet* is separated from the remainder of the poet's first line by two eighth-note rests in which the plosive double -*t* sounds ("-tet") echo in unmistakable emphasis and the singer draws breath for the snakelike sibilance at the start of "sind." It has been a truism of commentary on this composer's German songs to critique his prosody as flawed, but the shaping and bending of word stresses for interpretive purposes could not be more brilliantly executed than it is here. The vocal line is doubled in the piano only at the crucial words "[Ver]-giftet" and "Lieder," the piano accompaniment otherwise restricted to harmonically mysterious thirds, their context not yet clear. Both "meine" and "Lieder" are emphasized ("MY songs" and "My SONGS," the persona cries): the adjective is trebly heightened by the absence of the piano, by the appoggiatura, and by the dotted rhythmic pattern, while the word *Lieder* is invested with as much poignancy as Liszt could give it in such a wracked environment. The bottommost pole of the lamenting descent, it culminates with the first tonic chord of the song, even if we cannot identify it as such just yet. "Poison—self—song" constitute hammer strokes down a slippery slope into an interior hell made audible.

Questions always pose a dual conundrum for composers: Is the question real or rhetorical, and what constitutes a "questioning" gesture in music? *This* question sounds more than once, and Liszt takes full advantage of the opportunity thus afforded him to inflect it differently when it reappears. After the loud proclamation of poisoned song, Liszt directs that the first statement of the words, "Wie könnt' es anders sein?" be sung softly. When forte lament is followed by piano question, the effect is one of retreat within the mind; irrefutable, grim truths cut deeper when said or sung so quietly. The questioning word *wie* is emphasized by its placement on the downbeat without competition from the piano, followed by a phrase that curls upward in true questioning fashion. As the singer sustains the verb of being, *sein,* after the arpeggiated staccato completion of the chord below (the dominant of C-sharp minor) has dropped off the face of the earth, we hear doubt as well as existential solitude. "To be" hangs in midair.

And no wonder—where are we tonally? In both beginnings of the song, with and without piano introduction, Liszt hints that we stumble across this lava flow *in medias res,* that subterranean depths boiled and seethed in the persona's mind before we arrived on the scene. Consequently, context, or rather contexts plural, must be reconstructed in retrospect in this world where everything is warped, tonality included. We can hear that the declaration "Vergiftet sind meine Lieder" could be either C-sharp minor with leanings to E major or some nether world in between, with the pitches of the eventual tonic triad (C♯–E– G♯) emphasized. But the skeletal progression could also sketch an incomplete dominant seventh of E, followed by the submediant—motion we might hear as "deceptive" if only we knew definitively where we were. One key is poisoning another without the incursion of a single chromatic pitch. Part of what the musical question does is clarify matters (albeit only for a moment), stating the dominant of C-sharp minor. How could it be otherwise? The tragic option is all that is left.

And yet, the persona cannot accept it and answers his own question in a manner emblematic of Liszt's originality as a song composer. The first inversion harmonies that slide downward for the question in mm. 3–4 are now reversed and climb upward in maximal tension ("pesante," "heavy," Liszt directs the pianist performing these flowing triplets) as the *j'accuse* is leveled: "Du hast mir ja Gift gegossen," in which E major is "poisoned" with its Neapolitan, the F-natural premonitory of the Picardy third E♯ at song's end. Liszt chose to separate the poet's third and fourth lines, syntactically a single declarative statement ("Du hast mir ja Gift gegossen / ins blühende Leben hinein") in order to establish a contrast between the poisoned E major of the accusation and the wistful invocation of "blossoming life." After the arpeggiated dominant seventh harmony of E major in the first half of measure 7, the piano disappears momentarily. The words "blühende Leben" are unsupported by a backdrop of instrumental sound; they are a wraith, a memory, a wistful tendril of melody. The tritone leap to the fermata-prolonged accented syllable of "Le-[ben]" is palpable in its longing, the singer reluctant to leave the word. The prolonged D♯—leading tone of E major—does not resolve upward to E, but falls back down again to the supertonic of E (Example 4.). "Resolution" does not really happen, or rather it does so in a thoroughly ironic sense:

Example 4. "Vergiftet sind meine Lieder."

we "resolve" to an even more desperate return of the initial proclamation in the piano, beginning not with the original C♯ pitch but with tripled Es. Liszt, I believe, learned from Schubert how to make the piano part the conveyer of an artfully shaped simulacrum of stream of consciousness thought processes in advance of words and in the aftermath of words. Because the invocation of a blossoming life now in ruins stops short of resolution to its tonic at both scale ends of the spectrum, Liszt bids the pianist hammer away fortissimo on multiple E pitches in mm. 8–9; here is E, but not "tonic" as the persona would wish it to be, as it had once been.

In other words, the brief mention of life impels another upsurge of feeling. The flames of helpless pain mount higher and higher as we go through this song, and each repetition of the declaration/question pair in lines 1 and 2 of the poem is varied to tell of misery grown hotter still. Now it is the word *anders* that stabs deepest, in a harmonic pun: the word is repeated and reharmonized, but it leads to the same half-cadence in C-sharp minor as before. Something is both made "other" and yet cannot change. This in its turn unleashes another fit of wordless anguish in the piano corridor to the final lines of Heine's terse poem, a remarkable passage because inherited musical emblems of great tension are voiced in a significant manner; we do not necessarily "hear" the effect, but those who see the score realize the physical convolutions briefly required of the pianist. Against the faster-and-faster reiterated G♯ octaves in the right hand, the left hand rises chromatically (one thinks of Schubert's "Gruppe aus dem Tartarus," in which a mass of nameless souls are driven toward Eternity through hollow, rocky corridors of chromaticism). Unless one redistributes the pitches between the hands, especially in mm. 17–18 while still managing to accent the lower voices as Liszt indicates, the two hands must be thoroughly entangled to play these four bars before the "Allegro molto." We see as well as hear the sheer tortuousness of this experience, the collision of forces within the mind.

Where this headlong rush toward explosion brings us is a tritone away from the starting point, from piano to fortissimo, from G♯ to D, in a mere four measures. Borrowing from Schubert's and others' recourse to tremolandi to tell of senses reeling under the impact of strong emotion ("Es schwindelt mir, es brennt mein Eingeweide," Mignon and the Harper cry out to tremolando chromaticism in Schubert's great B-minor duet setting), Liszt's persona three times in a row traverses the tetrachord from A to D, each time with the pitch C♯ accented in mid-measure. Harping on the tonic to come, Liszt makes the *soi-disant* "leading tone" more of a force to be reckoned with than its point of resolution. The conjunction of the right-hand tremolo and the reiterated bass pitch C♯, savagely emphasized, creates the simultaneity of an augmented triad, not used in its customary fashion as the result of passing motion. Liszt, as R. Larry Todd and others have observed, is the great liberator of the augmented triad in the nineteenth century (Example 5).[35] Now E in yet another manifestation becomes a grinding sforzando dissonance scraping against the tremolo F–A ostinato when the singer's words "[Her]-zen viel Schlangen"

Example 5. "Vergiftet sind meine Lieder."

are doubled in the piano, perhaps something else Liszt learned from Schubert, who uses this sort of doubling powerfully and infrequently ("Der Atlas," another Heine song, is the case *par excellence*).

But in this crescendo-accelerando of a song, the most shattering effects happen as we approach the end. The designation of "du" (you) as his lover ("Geliebte mein") impels the transformation of F into E♯ as the accusatory address in the familiar, "und DICH," is sustained over a harshly dissonant ninth chord (V⁹/C-sharp major). One does not, of course, *hear* the singer's re-spelled pitch as different, but seeing the transformation on the word *you* adds to the experience of what is perhaps the most crashing, crushing dissonance in all of Liszt. That something twists and writhes, its very substance changed in mid-word, is spelled out for us in the notation, and the same writhing serpents-cum-augmented triad (F–A–C♯) we heard before is outlined in the singer's final phrase. What began on a singularly tentative D minor ends on C-sharp major, and seldom has the major mode, even as skeletally adumbrated as here, sounded this bitter. "Gift," "dich," "[Ge]-*lieb*-[te]: we now understand that they are one and the same. This is the first truly final-sounding tonic cadence in the song thus far: that she is Beloved and Poison alike is a certainty, says this cadence, its resolution assigned to the voice alone. The culmination of this *"j'accuse"* of a song is nearly naked, the piano stripped away at the beginning and end of the phrase. When I hear the completed cadence and the last sung word, I always involuntarily recall Wilhelm Müller's "Mein!" in *Die schöne Müllerin*, in which a youth sings of a "Geliebte" who is finally "mein." The result soon after is the poisoning of his songs and the ending of his life.

The way in which Liszt elides the end of the texted body with the postlude in the piano is another of the many marvels of this song, a new twist on the relationship between song and instrumental aftermath. For the fourth and fifth times, we hear "Vergiftet sind meine Lieder"—without words, but by this juncture, we hardly need them. C♯ is the central pitch by dint of repetition, while major mode is made dubious by the A♮s. A♮ only sinks to the "dominant" pitch G♯ on the fourth and last beat of the final measure, which sounds remarkably unfinal, and no wonder: Liszt yet again sounds the augmented triad of the allegro molto passage, only "resolving" on the fourth beat of the last bar to a Picardy third like no other. This is an ending that trails off as if in exhaustion—who could sustain such intense emotion for long without being drained by it? From the agitated and very loud beginning of the postlude, it sinks down an octave lower, and then lower still. The tonic chord in major mode at the end is—perhaps—the sounding emblem of an exceedingly tentative acceptance of reality, a fragile resignation susceptible to renewed onslaughts of pain (Example 6). When the pianist lifts his or her hands at the close, I always see members of the audience shift uneasily, wondering if this is really the end, if it is time to applaud.

It is always shocking to realize that Schubert's futuristic Heine songs were composed in the 1820s, and similar awe is appropriate for this radical Lied, first composed when Wagner was barely under way with his Germanic operas of the 1840s. "Vergiftet sind meine Lieder" is a work that shreds conventions like so much paper. One searches amid the roiling chromatic convolutions for a hillock or two of firm tonal ground and finds it only twice, both times predominantly for the voice alone: the uncompleted approach to E major at the words "ins blühende Leben hinein" and the anguished cadence that designates the beloved as poison. Here, every

Example 6. "Vergiftet sind meine Lieder."

component of song is under maximum stress. If the lava of this Lied is kept tightly in check both by repeated passages and other, less obvious compositional devices, we are meant, I believe, to hear the nearness of the breaking point. Poem and song alike are brief because control can only be exerted over molten magma for so long and no longer. For Liszt, Heine's words were the medium through which to experiment magnificently with the questioning of received categories in song. Tonal certainty, firm rhythmic ground underfoot (those recitative-like phrases by their very nature render rhythm fluid), meter, song form—all are subjected to an incandescent probing. That the song is so brief only adds to its power. Like a thunderbolt from the blue, like some sort of violent assault, it is over almost before we know it, leaving us dazed and gasping for air.

To Endure the Unbearable: "Anfangs wollt' ich fast verzagen"

Seven years after the first version of "Vergiftet sind meine Lieder," Liszt turned to another text by Heine: "Anfangs wollt ich fast verzagen."[36] Unlike the poisoned lamentation, this tiny poem had already been famously set to music by Schumann and less famously by Franz Lachner as well as a few minor composers.[37] Neither poem was among those most colonized by composers; "Vergiftet sind meine Lieder" was such strong stuff that few were bold enough to tackle it, and "Anfangs wollt ich fast verzagen" is epigrammatic to a degree.

VIII.	VIII.
(*From the* Junge Leiden: Lieder *section of the* Buch der Lieder)	(from the *Young Sorrows: Songs* section of the *Book of Songs*)
Anfangs wollt' ich fast verzagen,	At first, I almost wanted to give up,
Und ich glaubt' ich trüg' es nie,	and I thought I could never bear it,
Und ich hab' es doch getragen,—	and yet I have borne it,—
Aber fragt mich nur nicht: wie?[38]	But don't ask me "How?"

Heine first published this poem in his 1822 *Gedichte* with the subtitle, "An Carl v. U. / Ins Stammbuch" (To Carl von U., in his family album). In the so-called Arbeitsexemplar of the *Gedichte* with corrections both by Heine and an editor named Friedrich Merckel, the dedicatee's last name is completed as "Unzer," and this clue led scholars to a school chum of Heine's from his Düsseldorf days, one Gustav Friedrich von Untzer; Heine may have written the first version of this poem as an inscription in his friend's album before leaving Düsseldorf in July 1816, although why he altered Untzer's name is anyone's guess (to shield his identity?). Untzer fought as a volunteer against Napoleon's armies and was severely wounded at Waterloo, "the crowning carnage," as Byron dubbed it.[39] "Next to a battle lost, the greatest misery is a battle gained," said Wellington when he surveyed the vast expanse of dead, dying, and wounded in the wake of the engagement.[40] Knowing this, "it" suddenly becomes specific, even if these origins are lost in the transference to a wider world of undefined miseries.

With the word *fast* (almost, nearly) in the first line, Heine acknowledges a friend's will to survive even in the direst physical distress, when the wish to let go is a hair's breadth away.

But in Liszt, we do not know what the almost unbearable grief is: "it" expands exponentially, the mind ranging among the myriad possibilities of causation. Liszt, I would speculate, realized that the poem achieves maximal power on its own, not as part of a cycle that provides context and partial explanation, but as a rootless entity in which the very inability to define "it" is crucial. Here, utmost compression joins forces with a simulation of immediacy, of thought unfurling on the spot, produced by the two inner lines that each begin with the connective "und." Three declarative statements make up "Anfangs wollt' ich fast verzagen," the last one split into two parts: a declaration of "fact" and a complex variation on the act of questioning. The poem ends with an order in the imperative *not* to ask the question "How?" and yet Heine in the final version pins a question mark to the poem's tail. This is the classic formulation by which "Don't think of X" makes thinking of X irresistible. Among the most forward-looking of Heine's early poems, this work seems like the artful arrangement of terse prose that just happens to rhyme. If this small artifact can be linked to the tradition of the epigrammatic fragment-poem beloved of the Romantics and to an even longer tradition of album inscriptions, it is nevertheless amazingly modern in its slice of pure psychology and its universality. One reads this poem and involuntarily recollects ordeals from one's own past that were, somehow, survived.

Liszt's second version of this song makes clear that whatever "it" may be, the persona is still enduring it, and it is a staggering load even now. This approach is very unlike Schumann's in his op. 24 Heine *Liederkreis*, where the song—only eleven measures long—is couched between "Berg' und Burgen" (which ends with a stark, eerily exposed 4–3 suspension above the tonic pitch A) and the last song, "Mit Myrthen und Rosen," in D major. "Anfangs wollt' ich fast verzagen" "ends" on a half-cadence in D minor, at the "close" of a unique chorale, followed by a memorial to bygone poems/songs in the final song. Schumann takes note of the "und" connectives that convey us through the tiny poem and makes his solemn block chords unstoppable, inexorable. Above the Baroque-style "walking bass" in the left hand and the pseudo-chorale for all the miserable of this earth in the right hand, the singer doubles the chorale's topmost voice an octave higher—and neither tessitura is that of conventional chorales, which tend to happen in the congregational middle register, suitable for untrained voices in a church. As John Finson has pointed out, Schumann cites the melody of the Lutheran chorale "Wer nur den lieben Gott läßt walten" at the beginning of the latterday song, but he removes it from congregational contexts into the realm of individual suffering.[41] The piano's register is lower than that of most chorales, the singer's higher. Indeed, the vocal line is centered almost entirely in the "passagio," the hinge in most tenor and soprano voices between the comfort of medium range and the breakthrough to the high register (Example 7). Like everything else in this miniature masterpiece, the positioning of both piano and voice seems multivalent. The huge tension of whatever trial has been overcome is evident in the way the singer inhabits the passagio for much of this song, and yet there is something proclamatory about it as well, the singer wishing to soar above suffering, to proclaim its end to the heavens. This is truly a "chorale" with a difference.

Why does Schumann avail himself of olden-style hymnody and engage in counterpoint for a setting of *this* poem? Is he perhaps suggesting in this manner that the speaker's faith has kept him from despair? If so, the suggestion is fraught with equivocation. One notes the piling on of dissonance and chromaticism both harmonic and linear at the two places where doubt is most evident (mm. 5–6, "und ich glaubt', ich trüg' es nie," and mm. 9–10,

Example 7. "Anfangs wollt' ich fast verzagen."

"aber fragt mich nur nicht, wie?"). Schumann momentarily emphasizes harmonies suggesting the relative major (F major) when the persona speaks of having borne "it" (mm. 7–8, "und ich hab' es doch getragen"), but then turns back to the regnant D minor of death, suffering, and requiem at the end. "Have I really borne it, or can it come back to afflict me once more?" his persona seems to ask and then refuses to return to the beginning. Not until he can transform D minor into D major does he resume the thread of the cycle.

Liszt's setting is very different conceptually from Schumann's. What seems to have fascinated Liszt was the notion of just barely holding on while the sands of hope, reason, and certainty continually shift underfoot. The battle against "giving up" is ongoing, Liszt tells us in the piano introduction before a word is sung, and it is a desperate battle, constantly on the verge of defeat. He, in fact, suggests by song's end that agony on this scale may be unconquerable, that life drags us down to defeat no matter how heroic our efforts. If one looks at the voice leading in mm. 1–2, one sees slippage by descending semitones first in the alto voice, then the tenor, and finally the soprano, which lowers the third degree in F-sharp major to A-natural. The gloomy end of the endeavor is already prophesied in the second bar. Attempting to overcome the sinking motion, the topmost voice vaults upward a fifth to the downbeat of m. 3, but the chromatic descent continues in the tenor voice and immediately ensues in the soprano as well from its new, higher vantage point. The composer marshals every means at his command to convey tenuousness; the meter, for example, is not symmetrical duple meter, with its inherent "foursquareness," but triple meter. The same rhythmic pattern of two quarter notes, an eighth-note rest, and an eighth note is repeated in mm. 1–3, and each measure is slurred as a single unit. The result is that the final eighth-note chord both is and is not an anacrusis to what follows, although the non-legato markings negate the effect in sound of the slurs we see on the page. "Schwankend" (tottering, staggering), Liszt directs the pianist and then shreds the four bars into fragmentary gasping bits in advance of the singer doing likewise. If tonic and dominant are duly present and accounted for, they lack the ability to sound resolute, to define a key solidly and securely, surrounded as they are by lines that keep coming unmoored. And yet, we maintain the desperate grasp on the tonic F♯ in the bass, the anchor to which this persona clings (Example 8). Every aspect of this song is in service to a concept whereby we hold on tenaciously to something that is surrounded, indeed invaded, by quicksand.

"At the beginning," the persona says: that is, "in the past." Liszt sets the terse recounting of the past when the persona thought he could not

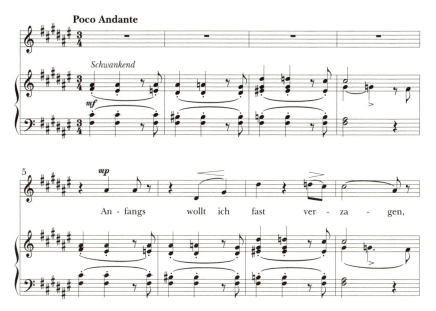

Example 8. "Anfangs wollt' ich fast verzagen."

bear it in F-sharp major (only a rare and extreme key would do), which serves as a large-scale "leading tone" to the G major tonality introduced in measure 14 at the words "und ich hab' es doch getragen." It seems only right that both keys should be in major mode. After all, if one wishes to enact in music the repeated erosion of hope, life, tranquility, and brightness by despair, this is the way to do it: begin with major mode and wear it down, press a chromatic weight on it. In this three-part singularity of a formal structure, G major then suffers the same fate as virtually every other phrase in this work and sinks down a semitone to the starting point of F-sharp major/minor. This highly unusual key scheme for a song is a grim tonal pun for the cognoscenti to relish: what I thought I could not bear *leads* to the fact that I bore it anyway. Or rather, I am still bearing it: the passage in mm. 14–22 is a transposed, forte marcato (a proclamation), slightly varied version of the preceding strains. The same quicksand is at work a half-step higher; for example, the chromatic slippage at the word *doch* and the catch-in-the-throat break before the verb *getragen* repeat the prior break in measure 7 between the crucial adverb *fast* and *verzagen*. Unlike Schumann, who was clearly struck by the poem's coupling of brevity and power and sought to replicate it in his music, Liszt's persona repeats the third line of text and then prolongs the prohibited but irresistible question through an entire additional section of the song. Schumann repeats only the words "nicht, wie?" before stopping short of closure in D minor with a half-cadence and a bar of silence. If the possibility of asking again still reverberates in the hush at song's end, this persona refuses to succumb to the temptation. The final song follows on its heels and answers the question "wie?" in what passes for optimistic mode in Schumann's Heine: with myrtles and roses, with the memory of what is bygone preserved in art. That is how one survives travail. But for Liszt's darker persona, *plus ça change, plus c'est la même chose*. His "Anfangs wollt' ich fast verzagen" is post-traumatic stress disorder in tones and rhythm. Nor is alleviation in sight anywhere on the horizon, as we discover in the final section of the song.

This virtuoso pianist who could turn the page almost solid black with notes to be played at warp speed banishes the piano altogether for particularly crucial phrases in his songs, and he does so here for the first invocation of Heine's last line, "Aber fragt mich nur nicht, wie?" (Both Schumann and Liszt use the version of the poem in which "nicht" and "wie" are more strongly separated by a colon rather than a comma.) In Liszt's hands, "wie?" becomes "where?" by the end of this skeletal phrase, with its hinge between a rapidly vanishing G major and the return of F-sharp major. The chromatic sinking motion we see and hear so often as linear melody is transferred here to the tonal level and brings us back to the beginning via economical mystification. The repetition of Heine's third line, "ich hab' es doch getragen" (Liszt eliminates the connective "und" as no longer necessary), in mm. 18–22 is still organized around an ostinato pitch, but the anchor tone is no longer tonic. What begins as the fifth scale degree in an extraordinarily tenuous key becomes something else as the outermost voices converge in contrary motion in the piano, the right hand sinking, the left hand rising around the omnipresent pitch (Example 9). What we have here is a cramped, constricted, incomplete, varied latter-

Example 9. "Anfangs wollt' ich fast verzagen," mm. 18–22.

day echo of the famous "omnibus" passage near the end of Schubert's "Der Wegweiser," the twentieth song in *Winterreise*, when the winter wanderer sees a signpost in the mind, designating something too dreadful to reveal. When Liszt's passage culminates in a diminished seventh harmony on G♯, we are for a certainty exiting G major, but where are we? Only at the end can we look back and realize that this phrase presages the F-sharp minor in which the song ends, reversing the traditional Picardy cadence: major mode cedes to minor at the close. When the singer skeletonizes the diminished seventh chord for the first statement of the poem's last line, the piano falls silent—until the end, when it loudly *(sf)* doubles the pitch D. Liszt knew how to make the interrogatory word *wie* insistent, how to underscore the mystery of endurance. When the dominant pitch C♯ of F-sharp major/minor sounds in both the bass line and the piano's inner voice while the singer is still brooding on D, we hear another dissonant manifestation of the pain "it" caused, whatever "it" was.

We glimpse the futuristic Schubert again toward the end, when the initial music returns varied in suggestive ways. Now, the third degree of major mode (A♯) slips down to A♮ immediately, where earlier it had hung on for a little over a measure before sinking. The inner voice is activated by a written-out "trill," and the ostinato pitch C♯—again, not the tonic—is made elegiac by chiming tones in the treble, requiring the left hand to cross over the right hand. Although these hand-crossing chimes are admittedly a standard pianistic figure in Liszt, it will recall to some the slow movement of Schubert's late B-flat Piano Sonata (D960), with its similar chimes in the returned A section, and the andantino slow movement (in F-sharp minor!) of the A Major Sonata (D959) from September 1828, whose returned A section also activates elegy with more motion in the subordinate voices and "passing bell" tones. At the end, in the stark piano postlude, Liszt finally reveals the meaning of the song's persistent smaller-scale sinking figures by extending them into a full-scale lamentatio tetrachord in the bass (Example 10). Nothing is secure in this world, not even misery: the conjunction of the descending bass and the raised fourth degree in the antepenultimate measure (m. 38) produces an enharmonic ghostly visitant: the former dominant of G major strayed out of its bounds and then ceding to F-sharp tonic six-four and root-position chords. There is no dominant seventh of F-sharp here, we notice, and its omission and replacement are chilling. One last fragmentary veiled attempt to assert without words that "I have borne it" is defeated.

I always wonder whether Liszt might have had Schumann's burden of mental disease and Heine's agony on the mattress-grave in mind when he composed the two versions of this song. Certainly there is no shortage

Example 10. "Anfangs wollt' ich fast verzagen."

of misery past, present, and future to which one can attach this song, and the applicability of these words to suffering humanity extends far beyond Heine's eight-year martyrdom on the rue d'Amsterdam or Schumann's terrible travails. Like most mortal fools who long for a *lieto fine* not always or often or ultimately available, I prefer Schumann's nugget of dark grandeur in which overcoming predominates over succumbing, but one must give Liszt the palm for the sort of "Wahrheit bis zur Grausamkeit" one also finds in "Vergiftet sind meine Lieder." These may not be pretty songs, but they are beautiful in the only sense that really matters.

Romantic Desire and Altered Endings:
"Ein Fichtenbaum steht einsam"

Like all those drawn to Liszt's songs, I find the multiple versions and incessant tinkering fascinating and therefore wish to conclude the present enterprise by taking a brief look at Liszt's two settings of "Ein Fichtenbaum steht einsam," begun in 1845 and first published in 1860. The thirty-third poem in the *Lyrical Intermezzo* cycle was one of the Heine poems considered safe for nineteenth-century consumption, set to music by composers both well-known today (Fanny Mendelssohn, Balakirev, Grieg, Loewe, Rimsky-Korsakov, Rachmaninov, Karl Stenhammar—this poem, somewhat comically, was beloved by composers in northern climes) and little-known (Jakob Rosenhain, Vesque von Püttlingen, Mary Francis Allitsen, Agathe Backer-Gröndahl—although the settings are worth renewed attention).[42] And no wonder: entire disquisitions on the nature of Romantic desire are encapsulated in these eight lines. On the surface of the poem, Heine tells of Man and Woman, as unlike as possible, their longing for one another increased by the vast distances separating them.

Lyrisches Intermezzo, XXXIII. Lyrical Intermezzo, no. 33

Ein Fichtenbaum steht einsam A fir tree stands alone,
Im Norden auf kahler Höh'. in the north on the bare heights.
Ihn schläfert; mit weißer Decke It sleeps; with a white mantle
Umhüllen ihn Eis und Schnee. ice and snow envelop it.

Er träumt von einer Palme, It dreams of a palm tree
Die, fern im Morgenland, that, far away in the Orient,
Einsam und schweigend trauert alone and mute, mourns
Auf brennender Felsenwand.[43] by the burning rocky wall.

The poem began with music, so it seems only right that it should go on to impel much more music in its afterlife. On 26 February 1822, Heine attended the performance of the opera *Aucassin und Nicolette,* based on the medieval French tale, with a libretto by Johann Ferdinand Koreff (1783–1851) and music by Georg Abraham Schneider (1770–1839).[44] In the first of his *Briefe aus Berlin,* dated 16 March 1822, Heine wrote that he was delighted by Koreff's colorful fairy tale, especially the contrast between "the serious West and the merry Orient," which "stirred in me the spirit of blossoming Romanticism."[45] The amateur librettist's palm tree mourns the beloved who lingers far away in anodyne lines that were certainly no competition for Heine, but provide us with a striking example of the third-rate giving birth to the first-rate: "Wohl trauert verwittwet die Palme, / Ihr weilt der Geliebte so fern" (The widowed palm tree mourns; her beloved tarries so far away).[46] Did Heine's readers, one wonders, understand the adjective "serious" in the Berlin letters as a pejorative, even mocking term, translatable as "Church-haunted," "anti-sensual," while the Orient is its commendable sensualist antipode? One remembers Heine's encomium to Goethe's *West-östliche Divan* in *Die romantische Schule:* a "magic book . . . a *salaam* sent by the Occident to the Orient," the younger poet called it. "Here, Goethe put the most intoxicating enjoyment of life into verse so light, so right, so airy, so ethereal that one is amazed that such a thing was possible in the German language," and its influence was immediate; "our poets now celebrated the Orient in song."[47] For much of his life, Heine called for an art predicated on the sensuality he located mostly in ancient Greece, a sensuality unlike Christianity's hatred of the flesh (he made an occasional exception for the Madonna's traditional depiction as female beauty incarnate).

While the "spirit of blossoming Romanticism" was a frequent visitor to Heine's writing desk, he was no undiluted Romantic, and his love-hate relationship with the literary world from which he came is encoded in this poem. Here the German Romantic poet, symbolized by the evergreen tree, (was he tweaking pretensions to immortality?) is isolated on his wintry peak; Heine took note of the Romantics who surveyed time, space, and history from their mountaintop vantage points and surrounds *his* poet with wintry death. Sunk in Romantic sleep, the tree persona dreams of the Oriental "ferne Geliebte," who mourns for him in her far-off land. (In English translation, one loses what German readers see immediately: the masculine-phallic fir tree, the feminine-exotic palm.) What a clever variation on Petrarchan fire and ice, on the distant beloved, on the Norse and Oriental preoccupations of the latter-day Romantics! Passion and poetry now exist only in the grief-stricken reveries of lovers separated by leagues and light years; geography and dreams are two degrees of distance. The palm tree, one notes, is silent: this is what happens to Muses so far removed from the poets they love. For all the beauty of these images, neither the sensual nor the real is possible in such a Romantic-poetic world.

What does Liszt make of this exercise in ambivalent beauty? He understood, I believe, the artistic dilemma at the core of Heine's words. Poets' longing for unattainable beauty, for dreams rather than reality, is futile, Heine tells us, and Liszt makes of this futility something circular in each version. In fact, the motif repeated throughout the piano introduction and piano postlude of the second version echoes back and forth between the left and right hands in circular fashion, its semitones echoing in roundelay fashion between registers (Example 11); this could go on, we realize, for a singularly unblessed, dreary eternity. Unlike those songs whose endings open out into indeterminacy, both versions wend their way back to some form of the austere, minor-mode, chromatically haunted strains of the beginning after a brief interlude of "luxe, calme, et volupté."[48] In the first version, the dream music sounds as if imported from "Widmung" (which Liszt, of course, transcribed for piano), the repeated harmonies of the earlier song's midsection rendered ethereal in the treble register. There is even a counter-melody of the sort Schumann cultivated. The second time around, Liszt sings of the palm tree to Loreley-like harp strains; although the circumstances of modulation are different, the enharmonic change from A♭ (a cadence on A-flat minor in mm. 15–16 of Liszt's song) to the third degree G♯ in E major reminds one of "Widmung" yet again, at a far remove (Example 12). The interludes are so beautiful that we understand why one would yearn for such as this, but even as we bask in mellifluous loveliness, it begins to morph into that which will carry the persona back to the start of it all.

Example 11a. Introduction, "Ein Fichtenbaum steht einsam," first version, mm. 1–9.

Example 11b. "Ein Fichtenbaum steht einsam," second version, opening, mm. 1–5.

The two versions of this song follow a progression evident elsewhere in Liszt, a sea change to greater introversion in the later incarnation. It is clear that Liszt used the same musical material for his two versions, especially at the beginning and ending sections, with their figures that emphasize the leading tone-to-tonic pitches and 6–5 in C minor, but they

Example 12a. "Ein Fichtenbaum steht einsam," first version, mm. 21–34.

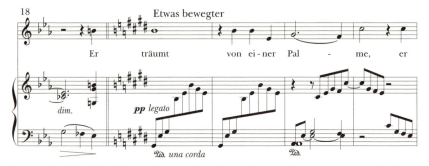

Example 12b. "Ein Fichtenbaum steht einsam," second version, mm. 18–22.

are differently shaped by the older man. In the first version, the "langsam-düster" mood is due in part to the heaviness of the Neapolitan harmony in measure 3, the first fully delineated root-position chord in the song and one very unconventionally treated. One of the organizing principles for the first section is a slow chromatic crawl upward from F to C in the top-most voice of the piano part and the voice, the upper end of the tension-laden maneuver made even more dramatic by octave leaps down-ward ("umhüllen ihn Eis und Schnee"). The transition from this dramatic invocation of ice and snow to the dream of exotic climes is Lisztian mys-tery in a nutshell: unharmonized F♯s and E♭s rise upward, with the final E♭ sustained by a fermata. Where are we tonally at this point? It is diffi-cult to say. From a chromatically clouded C minor, we have gone to brief emphasis on dark and stormy E-flat minor harmonies, barely tonicized before we leave them, and from thence to midair. The effect when pure, diatonic A-flat major chords appear is extraordinary, although this too shifts and changes. The naming of the palm tree brings us to short-lived arrival at a distant "Morgenland" on F-sharp major, a tritone away from the "umhüllt" C minor of the fir tree—as far away as possible. I always like to think that Liszt probably reveled in the tonal symbolism by which a tra-ditional key of mourning is opposed by a key Schubert had earlier associated in his songs with visionary spirit worlds ("Schwestergruß" to words by Franz von Bruchmann, "Auf den Tod einer Nachtigall," "Pilgerweise," "Totengräberweise").

Perhaps most notably, Liszt ends the two versions in very different ways. In the first, we hear a loud lamentatio chromatic tetrachord descend-ing from F down to low C (this reverses the chromatic motion between the same pitches in the first section of the song), with the right hand tolling on repeated Gs and a Picardy third at the close to seal the antique deal (Example 13a). Whenever I hear this ending, I involuntarily recall the piano postlude at the close of Schubert's "Ihr Bild," after the persona's declaration of peripeteia, "And ah, I cannot believe that I have lost you!" ("you" is really the persona himself—this is a variation on the Narcissus myth). A similar lamentatio tetrachord, likewise very loud, makes the close of the earlier song unforgettable, and the final measures of Liszt's song are perhaps among the many echoes of that famous rendition of Heine. But Liszt rethought the matter when he returned to "Ein Fichtenbaum steht einsam." Clearly bothered on occasion by the brevity of Heine's poems, Liszt repeats most of the poet's second stanza, and he makes the first setting of the crucial verb *trauert* the enharmonic hinge by which to begin his return to C minor at song's end. Liszt fashions burning grief at rocky walls as the juxtaposition of ostinato Cs (the obdurate wall) and complex layers of descending chromatic voices (incendiary emotion), to be performed accelerando and crescendo. Mourning catches fire quickly, Liszt tells us, but it runs into an impasse after a mere four bars: unisono A♭s that no longer transform into G♯s so that we might immerse ourselves in E-major dream worlds. Instead, we are returned to the ring-like figure from the introduction, bringing us back to the mournful dilemma at the start of it all. Liszt's emancipation of the augmented triad is once again on display at the close, where the collusion and doubling of the voice-leading strands produce not the firm conclusion provided by authentic and plagal cadences, but the augmented triad on the mediant (in first inversion, such that 5–1 appears in the bass and the leading tone-to-tonic pitches in the inner voice) as the penultimate sonority. As we listen to the fermata-prolonged, unfinal-sounding final tonic chord, we wait for the wheel of futility to start up again (Example 13b).

I realize, somewhat guiltily, that I am misrepresenting Liszt's songs to a certain degree by focusing on such a small sample of his most concentrated, reticent creations. Even "Vergiftet sind meine Lieder" can be so described when placed next to virtuosity on the scale of "Der Fischerknabe" in its first incarnation—a thrilling thing to hear when the best performers take it in hand. The "siren song" of female sexuality and the power of music to act on the human psyche find their concomitant in stratospheric strains, Liszt's mermaid proclaiming, "Lieb' Knabe, bist mein!" (Darling boy, you are mine), in tones of such icy triumph as to send chills down the spine. But I have chosen my examples in the interest of propaganda on Liszt's behalf. Imagining the future of music was a province of serious composers for much of the century, and Liszt is one of the major players in this great game. Like Schubert's "Die Stadt," "Vergiftet sind meine Lieder" will, I believe, always retain its ability to make the listener feel shock and awe for all the *right* reasons. W. H. Auden once said that even the greatest poets could expect to create only a few truly great poems; by that reckoning, had Liszt composed nothing but "Vergiftet sind meine Lieder," he would, I believe, still deserve a place in the pantheon of the very best nineteenth-century song composers.

Example 13a. "Ein Fichtenbaum steht einsam," first version, mm. 50–57.

Example 13b. "Ein Fichtenbaum steht einsam," second version, mm. 40–47.

NOTES

I am grateful to Anna Harwell Celenza and Rena Charnin Mueller for their help with this chapter.

1. "Kling leise, mein Lied" (S301/1 and 301/2 and LW N42, text by Johannes Nordmann) and "Es muß ein Wunderbares sein" (LW N49, text by Otto von Redwitz). The "S" numbers refer to Humphrey Searle, "Franz Liszt: Works" in vol. 1 of *The New Grove Press Early Romantic Masters: Chopin, Schumann, Liszt*, ed. Sharon Winklhofer (London: 1985); the LW numbers are from the most recent Liszt catalogue by Rena Charnin Mueller and Mária Eckhardt, "Franz Liszt: Works" in vol. 14 of *The New Grove Dictionary of Music and Musicians*, ed. Stanley Sadie, 2nd ed. (London: 2001), vol. 14, pp. 853–59.

2. The set of four CDs entitled *Franz Liszt—Lieder: Intégrale* on the French label Adda (1987) showcases the singers Donna Brown, soprano; Gabriele Schreckenbach, contralto; Ernest Haefliger and Guy de Mey, tenors; and Philippe Huttenlocher, baritone, accompanied by Cyril Huvé on an 1850 Erard piano. Dietrich Fischer-Dieskau, one of the twentieth-century's foremost singers, recorded many of Liszt's songs, and his performances have recently been reissued on CDs.

3. The secondary sources include: Eduard Reuss, *Liszts Lieder* (Leipzig: 1907); Joseph Wenz, "Franz Liszt als Liederkomponist," Ph.D. diss., University of Frankfurt, 1921; Ben Arnold, "Songs and Melodramas" in *The Liszt Companion*, ed. Ben Arnold (Westport, Conn.: 2002), pp. 403–38; Suzanne Montu-Berthon, "Un Liszt Méconnu: Mélodies et Lieder," *La Revue musicale*, nos. 342–44 (1981): 7–197, and nos. 345–46 (1981): 6–56; Ben Arnold, "Visions and Revisions: Looking into Liszt's 'Lieder,'" in *Liszt and the Birth of Modern Europe: Music as a Mirror of Political, Religious, Social, and Aesthetic Transformations*, ed. Michael Saffle and Rossana Dalmonte (Hillsdale, N.Y.: 1997); William Dart, "Revisions and Reworkings in the Lieder of Franz Liszt," *Studies in Music* 9 (Australia) (1975); Martin Cooper, "Liszt as a Song Writer," *Music & Letters* 19 (1938); Christopher Headington, "The Songs," in *Franz Liszt: The Man and His Music,* ed. Alan Walker (London: 1970), pp. 221–47; Philip Friedheim, "First Version, Second Version, Alternative Version: Some Remarks on the Music of Liszt," *The Music Review* 44 (1983): 194–202; W. J. Dart, "Revisions and Reworkings in the Lieder of Franz Liszt," SMA 9 (1975): 41–53; Klára Hamburger, "Liszt and French Romanticism: His Lieder on Poems by Victor Hugo and Alfred de Musset," in *Liszt the Progressive*, ed. Hans Kagebeck and Johan Lagerfelt (Lewiston, Me.: 2001); Alan Walker, "Liszt and the Lied," *Reflections on Liszt*, (Ithaca, N.Y.: 2005) chap. 7; and Rena Charnin Mueller, "The Lieder of Liszt" in *The Cambridge Companion to the Lied*, ed. James Parsons (Cambridge, Eng.: 2004), pp. 168–84.

4. See Hanjo Kesting, ed., *Franz Liszt—Richard Wagner Briefwechsel* (Frankfurt: 1988), p. 93.

5. George Eliot, "German Wit: Heinrich Heine" in *Essays of George Eliot*, ed. Thomas Pinney (New York: 1963), p. 224. Eliot's article—one of the earliest lengthy discussions of Heine in the English language—was originally commissioned by John Chapman for *Westminster Review* 65 (January 1856): 1–33.

6. Eduard Hanslick, "Aesthetische Reflexionen über Hoven's Komposition der Heine'schen 'Heimkehr'" in *Sämtliche Schriften: Historisch-kritische Ausgabe*, vol. 1, part 2: *Aufsätze und Rezensionen 1849–1854,* ed. Dietmar Strauß (Vienna: 1993), pp. 160–68. Lachner's setting of Heine's "Wasserfahrt" (recently recorded by Christoph Prégardien and Andreas Staier) comes from his song cycle *Sängerfahrt,* op. 33, composed in 1831 and consisting of sixteen songs all on texts by Heine.

7. A particularly fascinating discussion of Liszt's engagement with one Schubert Lied is found in Christopher Gibbs, "The Presence of *Erlkönig*: Reception and Reworkings of

a Schubert Lied," Ph.D. diss., Columbia University, 1992. See also Thomas Kabisch, *Liszt und Schubert* (Munich: 1984).

8. Anna Harwell Celenza points out Liszt's desire for a music community that would support a progressive attitude to the arts in "Imagined Communities Made Real: The Impact of Robert Schumann's *Neue Zeitschrift für Musik* on the Formation of Music Communities in the Mid-Nineteenth Century," *Journal of Musicological Research* 24, no. 1 (2005): 20–22.

9. We owe a number of Liszt's finest songs to the illustrious performers with whom he worked. During his Weimar years, from 1848 to 1861, Liszt was closely associated with such stellar singers as Rosa von Milde (née Agthe, 1827–1906) and her husband, Feodor von Milde (1821–99), the lyric tenor Franz von Götze (1814–88), and the soprano Emilie Genast (nicknamed "Mici," 1833–1905), for whom Liszt formed a deep attachment. Devoted to Liszt's songs, these renowned singers performed them both at Liszt's hilltop home and in concerts in Berlin, Karlsruhe, Aachen, and elsewhere. When Liszt's *Gesammelte Lieder* appeared in 1860, Liszt asked the editor of the collection, Franz Brendel, to send a copy to Götze because the singer had, the composer felt, "a special claim to them." See La Mara, ed., *Franz Liszts Briefe*, vol. 1 (Leipzig: 1893), p. 132.

10. Two examples are "Einst" (S332, LW N73), composed in 1878 to a poem by the explorer-poet Friedrich von Bodenstedt (1819–92) and published in 1879, also "Die tote Nachtigall" to a poem by Philip Kaufmann in its quietly startling second version (S291/2, LW N17), composed in the 1870s and first published in Liszt's Leipzig song anthology of 1879.

11. This passage (with my italics) comes from the "Zehnter Brief" of Heine's "Über die französische Bühne;" see Heinrich Heine, *Säkularausgabe*, vol. 7: *Über Frankreich 1831–1837, Berichte über Kunst und Politik*, ed. Fritz Mende (Berlin: 1970), p. 287.

12. Valuable recent accounts of Liszt's virtuosity include Dana Gooley, *The Virtuoso Liszt* (Cambridge, Eng.: 2004), with chapters on "Liszt, Thalberg, and the Parisian publics" and "Anatomy of 'Lisztomania': The Berlin Episode"; and Lawrence Kramer, "Franz Liszt and the Virtuoso Public Sphere: Sight and Sound in the Rise of Mass Entertainment" in *Musical Meaning: Toward a Critical History* (Berkeley and Los Angeles: 2002), pp. 68-99. The term "Lisztomania" was, of course, coined by Heine.

13. Rena Charnin Mueller, "Reevaluating the Liszt Chronology: The Case of *Anfangs wollt ich fast verzagen*," in *19th-Century Music* 12, no. 2 (Fall 1988): 132–47.

14. Only three are for solo voice: S73/1, LW N5 was composed in 1841, published in 1843; the second version, S273/2, was composed between 1854 and 1859, published in 1856 and 1860; the third version for voice and orchestra (S369) was composed in 1860, published in 1862.

15. Mueller, "Reevaluating the Liszt Chronology," p. 134.

16. The phrase "my little malicious-sentimental poems" invokes the *Lyrisches Intermezzo* and comes from a letter Heine wrote to Karl Immermann on 24 December 1822. See Heinrich Heine, *Säkularausgabe*, vol. 20: *Briefe 1815–1831*, ed. Fritz Eisner (Berlin: 1970), p. 61.

17. The quotation can be found in Liszt, "De la situation des artistes, et de leur condition dans la société," from *Sämtliche Schriften*, ed. Detlef Altenburg, vol. 1, *Frühe Schriften*, ed. Rainer Kleinertz (Wiesbaden: 1998), p. 26.

18. See Heinrich Heine, *Säkularausgabe*, vol. 18: *De la France*, ed. Fritz Mende (Berlin: 1977), pp. 189–92.

19. Lamennais never actually met Heine. See Félicité de Lamennais, *Correspondance générale*, ed. Louis Le Guillou (Paris: 1971), vol. 6, p. 816; Heinrich Heine, *Säkularausgabe*, vol. 10: *Pariser Berichte 1840–1848*, ed. Lucienne Netter (Berlin: 1979), pp. 230–33.

20. There was not enough known in Heine's day about diseases of the central nervous system for later neurologists to ascertain the cause of his hideously prolonged dying with any certainty. Physicians have proposed various possibilities, from Lou Gehrig's disease to a cerebrospinal syphilis that somehow spared his mental faculties to the very end,

but no one really knows. The most exhaustive study of the subject is Henner Montanus, *Der kranke Heine* (Stuttgart: 1995), with its fascinating study of what the poet's portraits reveal and of Heine's erotic life and sexuality. Montanus concludes that encephalitis disseminata (a leading candidate) cannot explain all of Heine's symptoms, unless one postulates a second illness concurrent with it. Whatever central nervous system disease was at work, a tubercular infection was what killed him in the end.

21. Rainer Kleinertz, "'Wie sehr ich auch Liszt liebe, so wirkt doch seine Musik nicht angenehm auf mein Gemüt': Freundschaft und Entfremdung zwischen Heine und Liszt," *Heine-Jahrbuch* 37 (1998): 107–39.

22. Heinrich Heine, *Säkularausgabe,* vol. 3: *Gedichte 1845–1856,* ed. Helmut Brandt and Renate Francke (Berlin: 1986), p. 101. Even after the parting of the ways, Liszt—tolerant and literarily curious to the end of his days—paid heed to Heine's doings. If a drop or two of acid falls on the page, that is understandable in light of Heine's attacks on him. In a letter of 23 March 1875, Liszt tells Olga von Meyendorff of spending several hours with Anton Rubinstein, who "very ingeniously explained to me Chopin's first sonata (in B-flat minor [*sic!*—this was Chopin's second sonata]) by Heine's *Tragödie*. I'll tell you about this soon." See Franz Liszt, *The Letters of Franz Liszt to Olga von Meyendorff 1871–1886 in the Mildred Bliss Collection at Dumbarton Oaks,* trans. William Tyler, notes by Edward N. Waters (Washington, D.C.: 1979), p. 187. Waters identifies the work by Heine as the *Tragödien, nebst einem lyrischen Intermezzo* but it seems more likely to me that the reference is to the trilogy of poems collectively entitled "Tragödie" ("Entflieh mit mir und sey mein Weib," "Es fiel ein Reif in der Frühlingsnacht," and "Auf ihrem Grab da steht eine Linde") at the end of this poet's *Neue Gedichte*. The "Tragödie" poems were on the Heine "bestseller" list for composers, including Rubinstein, who set them to music as his op. 57, no. 6. How interesting that Rubinstein resorts to the still-living model of Beethoven's *An die ferne Geliebte* for his single large "song as mini-cycle," with piano interludes carrying us seamlessly from stage to stage.

23. I am grateful to Rena Charnin Mueller for sending me information regarding the extant manuscripts of "Vergiftet sind meine Lieder" from her forthcoming Liszt catalogue. It is fascinating material: with regard to the earliest manuscript of this song from 1844, Mueller tells me that the final measures have the right hand *descending* in octaves after the final invocation of the words "und dich, Geliebte mein!" instead of the "rumble up" that he finally settles on in the printed edition. In a later manuscript on paper he used when he was composing and revising songs in 1849 and which then sat until the 1850s and the Schlesinger and Kahnt editions of 1856, 1859, and 1860, one finds both the tenor version on the recto side of the folio and a transposition for baritone in G-sharp minor with two additional measures of piano introduction. It is Mueller's discovery that transposition opened up new vistas for Liszt when reworking his songs; see her article "Sketches, Drafts, and Revisions: Liszt at Work," in *Wissenschaftliche Arbeiten aus dem Burgenland: Die Projekte der Liszt-Forschung,* ed. Deflef Altenburg and Gerhard J. Winkler. (Eisenstadt:1991), pp. 23–34.

24. See Gerald Abraham, *The Concise Oxford History of Music* (New York: 1979), pp. 771–72, and Arnold, "Songs and Melodramas," p. 423.

25. I am grateful to Dana Gooley for pointing out the kinship between "Vergiftet sind meine Lieder" and "Vallée d'Obermann." The piano composition was inspired by Etienne Pivert de Sénancour's quasi-Byronic epistolary novel *Obermann,* whose protagonist laments at length from his lonely Alpine valley.

26. In Günter Metzner, *Heine in der Musik: Bibliographie der Heine-Vertonungen,* vol. 10 (Tutzing: 1992), pp. 332–34, one finds twenty-eight settings in all.

27. One example of an "unsafe" poem, "Der bleiche, herbstliche Halbmond" (no. 28 in *Die Heimkehr*), with its dysfunctional family (a Bible-thumping parson's widow, a son

bent on a brigand's life, and a daughter who declares her intent to give her body to the wealthy aristocrat who desires her), was only appropriated for song by Vesque von Püttlingen and four Kleinmeister. Secondary sources on desire, marriage, and sexuality as they appear both in German literature and in society include Paul Kluckhohn's classic *Die Auffassung der Liebe in der Literatur des 18. Jahrhunderts und in der deutschen Romantik* (Tübingen: 1966, 3rd ed.); Isabel V. Hull, *Sexuality, State, and Civil Society in Germany, 1700–1815* (Ithaca, N.Y.: 1996); Niklas Luhmann, *Love as Passion: The Codification of Intimacy*, trans. Jeremy Gaines and Doris L. Jones (Cambridge, Mass.: 1986); Peter Borscheid, "Romantic Love or Material Interest: Choosing Partners in Nineteenth-Century Germany," *Journal of Family History* 11 (1986): 57–68; Josef Ehmer, *Heiratsverhalten, Sozialstruktur, ökonomischer Wandel: England und Mitteleuropa in der Formationsperiode des Kapitalismus* (Göttingen: 1991); and Ute Frevert, *"Mann und Weib, und Weib und Mann": Geschlechter-Differenzen in der Moderne* (Munich: 1995).

28. Heinrich Heine, *Säkularausgabe*, vol. 1: *Gedichte 1812–1827*, ed. Hans Böhm (Berlin: 1979), p. 84.

29. *Tragen* can also mean "endure" and "support"; both meanings are operative here as well.

30. Heinrich Heine, *Säkularausgabe*, vol. 3, p. 299.

31. See Franz Liszt, *Selected Letters*, trans. and ed. Adrian Williams (Oxford: 1998), p. 211. See also Franz Liszt, *Correspondance Franz Liszt, Marie d'Agoult*, ed. Serge Gut and Jacqueline Bellas (Paris: 2001) for much more about the Liszt-d'Agoult "affaire."

32. Ibid., p. 212.

33. Heine, *Säkularausgabe*, vol. 1, p. 82.

34. In Peter Raabe, ed., *Franz Liszts Musikalische Werke: Einstimmige Lieder und Gesänge*, vol. 2 (Leipzig: 1921), p. xiii, one finds the introduction from the French edition.

35. R. Larry Todd, "The 'Unwelcome Guest' Regaled: Franz Liszt and the Augmented Triad" *19th-Century Music* 12, no. 2 (Fall 1988): 101, 103. Todd derives his striking title from Carl Friedrich Weitzmann's treatise *Der übermässige Dreiklang* (Berlin: 1853); Weitzmann called for the emancipation of the augmented triad.

36. "Anfangs wollt' ich fast verzagen" (S311, LW N48) was first composed and revised in 1849, copied by Liszt's copyist August Conradi before September 1849, and revised again over the course of the next ten years. A French edition from 1880 has a new ending.

37. See Günter Metzner, *Heine in der Musik*, vol. 9 (Tutzing: 1992), pp. 250–51.

38. Heine, *Säkularausgabe*, vol. 1, p. 35.

39. Cited in Andrew Roberts, *Waterloo, June 18, 1815: The Battle for Modern Europe* (New York: 2005), p. 14.

40. Ibid., opposite p. 97.

41. See Jon W. Finson, "The Intentional Tourist: Romantic Irony in the Eichendorf *Liederkreis* of Robert Schumann" in *Schumann and His World*, ed. R. Larry Todd (Princeton, N.J.: 1994), pp. 166–67.

42. See Metzner, *Heine in der Musik*, vol. 10, pp. 13–25.

43. Heine, *Säkularausgabe*, vol. 1, p. 76.

44. It was Heinrich Uhlendahl in his *Fünf Kapitel über Heinrich Heine und E. T. A. Hoffmann* (Berlin: 1919), p. 81, who first identified the genesis of "Ein Fichtenbaum steht einsam."

45. Heinrich Heine, "Zweite Briefe" from the *Briefe aus Berlin* in *Säkularausgabe*, vol. 4: *Tragödien: Frühe Prosa 1820–1831*, ed. Karl Wolfgang Becker (Berlin: 1981), p. 132.

46. See Johann Ferdinand Koreff, *Aucassin und Nicolette* (Berlin: 1822).

47. Heinrich Heine, *Die romantische Schule* in *Säkularausgabe*, vol. 8: *Über Deutschland, 1833–1836*, ed. Renate Francke (Berlin: 1971), p. 41.

48. I have cited Baudelaire's "L'Invitation au voyage" deliberately: in "Le Thyrse" of 1863, Baudelaire wrote, "Dear Liszt, through the mist, beyond the rivers, above the cities where pianos sing your glory, where the printing press translates your wisdom, wherever you may be, in the splendors of the Eternal City or in the haze of dreamy countries consoled by Gambrinus, improvising songs of delectation or of ineffable sorrow, or confiding to paper your abstruse meditations, singer of everlasting Delight and Anguish, philosopher, poet and artist, I greet you in immortality!" By "songs," Baudelaire most likely meant music *"tout entière,"* but it is tempting to appropriate the reference literally.

The Battle Against Instrumental Virtuosity

in the Early Nineteenth Century

DANA GOOLEY

Ah, this virtuosity!—so many bad things have been said about it! So
many people have attacked it in the name of art, with a capital *A!*
Do you remember that absurd, impious battle declared against the
concertos, even those of Beethoven and Mozart?
—Camille Saint-Saëns, *Au courant de la vie*

When Eduard Hanslick published his compendious history of Viennese
concert life in 1869, he mapped that history in four phases, each with its
own "book": the "patriarchal period" (1750–1800), "associations of dilettantes" (1800–30), the "virtuoso era" (1830–48), and "associations of artists"
(1848–68). Hanslick's outline celebrates his present-day musical culture
with a double teleology: the "artists" of book four have displaced the
"dilettantes" of book two, representing a triumph of professional musicianship over amateurism. The other teleology is implied in the subtitle
of book four, "musical renaissance," which figures the virtuoso era as a
dark age. "Vormärz Vienna," Hanslick writes, "was dominated by an immense
cult of virtuosity, Italian opera, dance music, the concerts of Saphir, and
the legs of Fanny Ellsler. It is understandable that gradually, in this effem-
inizing, indolent atmosphere, serious lovers of art were unsatisfied."[1]
Virtuosity, not accidentally, holds the first position in this list of decadent
attractions. So attached were Viennese audiences to virtuosity that they
could not even appreciate new orchestral music without it. Berlioz and
Félicien David, Hanslick claimed, had some success, but "it was foremost
the virtuoso element in the works of these two Frenchmen that attracted
our public. They are specifically virtuosos of instrumentation."[2]

This triumph of artists over virtuosos and amateurs bears a strong note of historical inevitability. The virtuoso era, as Hanslick presents it, was a passing phase, an oversaturated indulgence in sensuality and enthusiasm that exhausted audiences and thereby produced in them the desire for its antithesis—noble and serious music: "The public had not only become tired of the astonishing achievements of external bravura—it had also become saturated and worn out by its own enthusiasm."[3] The end of the wild days, Hanslick concludes, was the year 1846, when a prominent Viennese critic claimed audiences were tired of superficial virtuosity. In fact, various writers had already been "reporting" this for years. "All of Germany is tired of concerts!" announced the author of an article called "Virtuoso Nonsense" in 1843.[4] When critics described the waning taste for virtuosity, as they did repeatedly (and repetitively) in the 1830s and '40s, they were often enough trying to impose symphonic taste—to give readers the feeling they should not like virtuosity. Concealing values as observations, they ensured that a preference for serious symphonic works would appear to have emerged spontaneously and naturally—democrat-ically—from "the public." But ultimately, symphonic taste did not emerge so naturally. It was advanced by an elite class of critics and professional performers, in a battle with the public's inclinations that came to its cli-max precisely in the peak years of Liszt's virtuoso career, 1838–47.[5]

Much of the battle against virtuosity, including Hanslick's, was carried out on a manifestly aesthetic plane. It dwelled on questions such as what is beautiful, moving, "truthful," or profound in compositions and concerts. The dichotomy-ridden debates—whether too much instrumental brilliance distracts from the discursive logic of a composition, whether double-notes and octaves give an attractive, superficial sheen to fundamentally vapid musical ideas, whether virtuosity loses expression in pursuit of astonishment, and so forth—are familiar enough. Rather than revisit such binaries, I pro-pose to examine here their social, ethical, and political subtexts, which can help explain the extremely fervent and moralistic tone of much anti-virtuosity rhetoric. These subtexts sometimes came to the foreground because opponents of instrumental virtuosity were engaged in social and professional competition. They came principally from a small class of com-posers, performers, critics, and teachers whose tastes hardly corresponded to those of the majority. Preserving and expanding the domain of their inter-ests meant demanding deep changes in the distribution of social power, in the public's attitude toward musical experience and amateur music-making, and in the relationship of the state to musical institutions.

Essays explicitly addressing such issues are rare in nineteenth-century periodicals. Indeed, a lack of critical reflectiveness may have been crucial to the successful spread of anti-virtuosity sentiment. By the time Hanslick was writing his history, journalists of serious aesthetic persuasion had hammered away at oppositions like substance vs. surface, inner vs. outer, and fidelity vs. egotism to the point where audiences had adopted them as "normal" or "natural." Perhaps it is here—in the repetitive, mechanical rehearsals of phrases such as "excessive ornament" and "superficial virtuosity"—that the most important, permanent work was done. But around 1840, as Lisztomania was reaching its climax, a number of extended essays on virtuosity appeared in periodicals from the central and northern German orbit of Leipzig and Berlin. Sometimes cast in the form of a Socratic dialogue, these polemics open a window onto the values—social and ethical as well as aesthetic—that were at stake in the battle against virtuosity, before its vocabulary hardened into rigid and formulaic binary oppositions. In my discussion of these essays I will highlight two recurring issues: first, the figure of the amateur or dilettante, who was positioned between the lay listener and the trained professional; and second, a preoccupation with the solo virtuoso as a positive or negative model of selfhood. The latter part of my essay measures Liszt's concert activities against the backdrop of these concerns, with a particular emphasis on how he managed to escape the darts of even starkly anti-virtuosity critics.

The battle against virtuosity was neither a centralized movement nor a particularly self-conscious one. It proceeded at different tempos in different places—earlier and more vehement in London, Leipzig, and Berlin than in Paris, Vienna, or St. Petersburg—and its targets ranged from major virtuosos to audiences, publishers, and teachers. In all its forms, it was integrally related to the rise of the symphony and its attendant musical values, a complex process whose first stirrings are apparent in London's concert life of the 1780s and '90s. Although the ideology of "absolute music" is often credited with dignifying the symphony and lifting instrumental music from its traditionally subordinate position to vocal music, that was an issue largely confined to philosophy. The most effective and concrete strategy for advancing the virtues of the symphony was to profile it against other *instrumental* music—variations, potpourris, fantasies, and concertos—not deemed "serious" or "symphonic."[6] Advocates of the symphony (above all Mozart and Haydn, but somewhat later Beethoven as well) thus built and reinforced an ideologically charged binary opposition positioning serious or "symphonic" music against insignificant, "dilettantish" instrumental music. This was the basic shape of Schumann's critique of virtuoso showpieces, and as we have already seen, Hanslick projected the opposition into an inevitable historical process.

An early, unambiguous antagonism between virtuosity and "serious" musical values is found in the founding charter of the Philharmonic Society of London, an orchestra of free-standing professionals formed in 1813 under the leadership of William Crotch. No contemporary institution in Europe, the German states included, was more zealous in advancing the cause of the symphony in its concert programming. In its first charter, the Foundation Book, the Philharmonic directly linked its advocacy of symphonic works to the exclusion of soloistic virtuosity. Concert programs, one statute stipulated, would consist of "the best and most approved instrumental music, consisting of Full Pieces, Concertantes for not less than three principal instruments, Sextetts, Quintetts and Trios; *excluding* Concertos, Solos and Duets; and requiring that vocal music, when introduced, shall have full orchestral accompaniments, and shall be subjected to the same restrictions," i.e., no solos or duets.[7] This categorical ban on vocal and instrumental solos was an extreme gesture, imitated neither in the immediate nor the long-term future of orchestral institutions. In London as elsewhere, solos and arias had for decades been a normal and accepted feature of all orchestra-centered concerts, including those of the Philharmonic's immediate antecedent, the Professional Concert.[8] Now they were anathema.

The aesthetic background of the Philharmonic's devotion to the symphony was articulated by Crotch himself in a series of lectures delivered in 1818.[9] But the principal aim of the ban on virtuoso solos was not aesthetic: it was aimed at reforming the *presentational* aspect of instrumental concerts. Concertos were not objectionable because they failed to meet the criterion of "the best and most approved instrumental pieces," but because their presentation conflicted with the strictly egalitarian social ideals of the Philharmonic Society. The Philharmonic built these ideals into its statutes: demonstrations of self-interest were rigorously policed by a strict attendance policy and by a rule denying extra payment to members who played *concertato* parts or led a section. Performances would embody such egalitarianism by excluding pieces that openly elevated a single performer above the group, or section leaders among their sections. Even the very top players, the First Prospectus stipulated, must come in the spirit of "reciprocal gratification . . . no distinctions of rank as to stations in the Orchestra are allowed to exist."[10] One sympathizer at the *Morning Chronicle* admired such performed equality, witnessed in the spectacle of "celebrated leaders playing the subordinate parts."[11] Quality music would be a social leveler, a supersensible ideal before which all distinctions in the social body would properly disappear. The presentational form of the symphony, in which no individual or section is singled out for very long, was the perfect embodiment of the egalitarian political ideal. Without any performer or leader to focus the listener's attention, the music could not seem to "belong" to any individual.

Through the symphony, then, the Philharmonic was advancing an aggressively new, and at least implicitly political, conception of what an orchestra might mean. In the eighteenth century and well into the nineteenth, the favorite metaphors for the orchestra had been authoritarian and military ones—with orchestral leaders cast hierarchically as "generals"—reflecting the aristocratic circumstances under which most permanent orchestras operated.[12] Founding members of the Philharmonic, by contrast, submitted themselves only to laws they had determined for themselves; indeed, in the Foundation Book the undersigned swore to "reciprocally engage strictly to obey all its laws."[13] The newly conceived orchestra—not only its internal organziation but also its presentation— would incarnate professional autonomy and democratic process. As an admiring writer at London's *Spectator* put it, this orchestra had "the merit . . . to disown any dependence upon fashionable control or patronage and assert the ability of musical professors to manage the affairs of a musical society."[14] It is important to note that the Philharmonic's ban on virtuoso solos not only helped challenge the aristocratic model, but the free-market model as well. The recent heros of London's entrepreneurial concert scene— people like C. P. E. Bach and Carl Abel, Ignaz Pleyel and J. P. Salomon—had all featured themselves as composer-virtuosos in concertos and bravura rondos, and their popularity derived partly from such individualism. The idealistic Philharmonic rejected both the financial motive and the individualism: all members would strive to integrate themselves into a larger, transcendental whole or body, mirroring the elevated status accorded to the symphony.

London's Philharmonic Society was unable to follow through on its high-minded principles. The rule eliminating distinctions within the orchestra was changed within a matter of weeks. From 1818 solo concertos were found regularly on programs, and the rules of equal payment frequently contravened to accommodate major virtuosos passing through London. Yet in their extremity, the first statutes lay bare the ideals that other musicians would work to realize in the course of the nineteenth century. In two significant ways the Philharmonic's ban on concertos and arias anticipates the essays on virtuosity that I analyze below. First, it was organized by a small but inspired and enthusiastic class of musical professionals to advance a "symphonic" musical taste against the tastes of the general public and the prevailing customs of concert life. Second, it was an attempt to rethink the terms of presentation in musical performance, particularly the relationship of individual and collective, in light of symphonic values. Specialist music journals such as the *Quarterly Musical Magazine and Review* (1818–28) and the *Harmonicon* (1823–33) soon emerged to help disseminate the Philharmonic's agenda, but at least early on, it first pursued its mission in practice—in real concert activity—rather than speculatively or in public discourse.

Starting in the 1820s and increasing into the 1830s, the vast growth of music periodicals and other forms of music journalism quickly made criticism a powerful force in the battle against virtuosity.[15] A brief look at parallel circumstances in Berlin will illustrate this change. In 1819, Carl Möser, principal violinist at the Prussian court, started a series of orchestral concerts that regularly featured large-scale symphonies by Beethoven, Mozart, and Haydn, and in this respect stood in the European vanguard. At first, Möser programmed these symphonies alongside arias and virtuoso solos, in keeping with the normative conventions of public concerts. But soon A. B. Marx, the most important critic in Berlin and a passionate proselytizer for Beethoven, intervened. In his new journal, the *Berliner allgemeine musikalische Zeitung* (1824–30), he prompted Möser to purify his programs by ridding them of singers and virtuoso solos. Möser briefly experimented with some remarkably "pure" symphonic programs, though he soon had to retreat and restore at least some convention. Marx's aggressive campaigning for serious symphonic repertory had a palpable effect on musical audiences in Berlin. In 1828 Bernhard Romberg, who himself had an orchestral series in which he regularly featured himself in virtuoso solos of his own composition, had lost so much ground to Möser he was forced to cancel his series altogether.[16]

Contemplating Virtuosity

The essay-length critiques of virtuosity I will discuss here (see table below) emerged almost exclusively in the German-speaking milieu, with a particularly large representation in the *Neue Zeitschrift für Musik*. Writers in France, England, and Vienna were clearly less inclined to isolate a theme such as "virtuosity" or "public concerts" and make it the object of an entire philosophical discussion, especially in the first half of the century. London's *Musical World*, for instance, under the editorship of J. W. Davison, took a serious, hard-line stance toward musical taste and vigorously promoted the classics. Yet in the 1840s it published no essays addressed in general to the subject of virtuosity. Why Germany? It is not that journalists outside Germany did not care about the issue, but they embedded their

Essays on Virtuosity

The numbers given in parentheses in the pages that follow
are pages from whichever essay in this list is being referenced.

Triest, Wilhelm. "Ueber reisende Virtuosen: Abhandlung" (On traveling virtuosos: Essay). *Allgemeine musikalische Zeitung* 4, nos. 46–48 (11, 18, and 25 August 1802). Essay.

Fink, G. W. "Ueber den Dilettantismus der Teutschen in der Musik" (On the dilettantism of Germans in music). *Allgemeine musikalische Zeitung* 35, no. 1 (1 January 1833), cols. 7–13; and "Bravourstücke für verschiedene Instrumente" (Bravura pieces for various instruments), vol. 35, no. 33 (14 August 1833).

Krüger, Dr. Eduard. "Ueber Virtuosenunfug" (On virtuoso nonsense). *Neue Zeitschrift für Musik* 13, nos. 17–22 (26 and 29 August; 2, 5, 9 and 12 September 1840). Fictional exchange of letters between Music Director and Dilettante.

Krüger, Dr. Eduard. "Das Virtuosenkonzert: Gespräch" (The virtuoso concert: conversation). *Neue Zeitschrift für Musik* 14, nos. 40–43 (17, 21, 24 and 28 May 1841). Socratic-style conversation between Virtuoso, Music Director, and a Dilettante.

Kahlert, August. "Das Concertwesen der Gegenwart" (Concert life today). *Neue Zeitschrift für Musik* 16, nos. 25–28 (25 and 29 March, 1 and 5 April 1842). Essay discussing concert life in general.

Gollmick, Carl. "Das heutige Virtuosenwesen" (Virtuosity today). *Neue Zeitschrift für Musik* 17, no. 45 (2 December 1842).

Hirschbach, Heinrich. "Componist und Virtuos" (Composer and virtuoso). *Neue Zeitschrift für Musik* 18, no. 30 (13 April 1843).

[Unsigned.] "Virtuosen-Unfug" (Virtuoso nonsense). *Signale für die musikalische Welt* 5, no. 29 (July 1843).

Granzin, Ludwig. "Das heutige Virtuosenthum in seiner Wirkung auf den Dilettantismus: Gesprächsweise Gedanken" (Virtuosity today and its effect on dilettantism: conversational thoughts). *Neue musikalische Zeitung für Berlin* 1, nos. 21–22 (26 May and 2 June 1847).

commentary within concert reviews or articles framed by other, more concrete topics. A journal like Leipzig's *Neue Zeitschrift für Musik*, in contrast, bore a distinctly philosophical profile. Of all the periodicals of the time, it was least directly tied to the worlds of publishing and public concerts,

and could thus afford to take a distance from quotidian, journalistic matters.[17] Its editor, Robert Schumann, expressed his contempt for virtuosity
only in reviews of sheet music, leaving the more philosophical issues to
friends in his intellectual circle, the self-styled "Davidsbund" or League
of David.[18] Another reason these essays emerged in central and northern
Germany is that virtuosity posed particular problems for the musical life
of its predominantly medium-sized towns (Dahlhaus, many have regret-
ted, characterized the musical culture of Leipzig and similar cities as
"provincial").[19] After discussing this, I will further show how the German
context shaped one of the recurring themes of polemics against virtuosity:
the intrusion of ego or personality into musical performance.

Because of their uncommon length and interest, the essays by Eduard
Krüger, August Kahlert (both associated with Schumann's critical circle)
and Wilhelm Triest will get special emphasis in my discussion. I include
Triest's 1802 essay "On Traveling Virtuosos" because, though far earlier than
the other essays, its content in many respects set the terms of the debate.
(The most obvious reason critics did not take up Triest's lengthy and thorough discussion immediately after he published it is that it coincided with
the Napoleonic wars, which decimated freelance concert life in the German
states for at least a decade.)[20] Triest's pioneering essay organized and articulated a series of resentments against instrumental virtuosos that, as Erich
Reimer has shown, had already been brewing among German musicians
in the later eighteenth century. Specifically, Capellmeisters and court musicians had been mounting a critique of the virtuoso concerto as a genre,
defending their professional territory against freelance performers who
were springing up everywhere but possessed few traditional credentials, particularly in the area of music theory.[21] In protecting their pride, the
court-based professionals developed a new term, the "true virtuoso" (*wahre
Virtuos*), to signify a musician with a broad range of learning, opposing it to
the merely excellent instrumentalist who might cobble together a simple
Italianate concerto (implicitly, a "pseudo-virtuoso").[22] In his essay, Triest
employed the terms "wahre Virtuos" and "ächte Virtuos" (755–56), showing that he belonged to this milieu. Forty years later, the concertgoing
public, the number of traveling virtuosos, and the venues for musical debate
had expanded phenomenally. Yet as I will show, the basic structure of
Triest's essay as a professional defense and ethical critique remained.

One aspect of the opposition to virtuosos stemmed from the character of the musical life in Germany's towns. Cities like Paris, London, and Vienna teemed with performers, making virtuosos a pervasive element of the cultural landscape. But a major performer appearing in Braunschweig or Halle could appear as an intruder, upsetting the placid order of a town and upending its local heroes. In his early essay (1802), Triest drew extensive attention to the contrast between large cosmopolitan capitals and the German towns. "We Germans," he wrote, "have no principal gathering place, no central point (foyer) of science and arts that serves the culture of the land as the heart serves the body" (745n.). Musically as well as politically, Germany existed as a collection of relatively small, independent units. In spite of this fragmentation, a sense of national unity was being forged through networks of communication, especially journals such as the *Allgemeine musikalische Zeitung*, and the transregional choral festivals that featured collective singing of folk or folkish songs, which grew rapidly in the decades after 1815.[23] In the four decades following Triest's essay, the geopolitical landscape had not changed dramatically. As late as 1871, over two thirds of all Germans officially classified as "urban" dwellers were in small or medium-size towns.[24]

The decentralized character of German musical life meant a different balance of power between professionals and amateurs. In a cosmopolitan capital such as London, the high concentration of professional musicians made for a unilateral structure of musical authority. Triest wrote that "large capital cities . . . tend to dominate in a dictatorial fashion the entire area around them in matters of musical taste," and contrasted this situation with that of Germany (744–45). In midsize German cities, such "vertical" hierarchy could exist in only a limited sense, giving professionals a stronger position among themselves, but a weaker position vis-à-vis the population. Each city had a coterie of professional musicians that commanded respect, but could not dominate the scene or direct public taste in the same sense. A highly learned musician, such as Gottfried Weber in Darmstadt, might be recognized as an authority, but his influence over the city's total musical activity appears narrow when the depth of amateur music-making is taken into account. Amateurism, in this context, had an independence, dignity, and visibility unavailable in the major capitals. In polemics against virtuosity, it was the virtuoso's ambiguous status between professional and amateur that made him a critical, in the sense of crisis-provoking, figure. Reflections on virtuosity thus turned frequently to amateur musical culture or "dilettantism," the latter not yet a derogatory term.

German professional musicians embodied their highest professional virtues in the figure of the Capellmeister, who was distinguished by the breadth of his musical knowledge, above all in the hallowed rules of counterpoint. In traveling virtuosos, these professionals saw that executive skill on an instrument was becoming divorced from wider musical and philosophical learning, and sought to defend the dignity of the Capellmeister's training. When Triest proposed solutions to the problem, for instance, he insisted that the performer "must have a thorough knowledge of the theory of music and of composition in particular; furthermore, a clear view of aesthetics and psychology . . . in a word, a more refined, if not learned, inner education than is usual among our virtuosos" (760).[25] Though much had changed by the 1840s, the Capellmeister and the values he represented were still in force. Thus Carl Gollmick, in his 1842 attack "Virtuosity Today," urgently pleaded with the modern virtuoso: "Give us just once, if you are a pianist, a free fantasy with an elegant and securely developed fugue theme, as our simple forebears did" (185). Without demonstrated musical learning, the virtuoso appeared to be nothing more than a glorified dilettante, yet he enjoyed the prestige and financial rewards on par with, if not excelling, those of the local Capellmeister.

The Capellmeister's relevance to polemics against virtuosity is most evident in two essays by Eduard Krüger: "On Virtuoso Nonsense" (1840), which is cast as a fictive conversation between a Music Director and a Dilettante, and in "The Virtuoso Concert" (1841), a trialogue among Music Director, Virtuoso, and Dilettante. The dialogue format, presenting an exchange of conflicting positions, gives Krüger's essays a refreshingly undogmatic tone (probably modeled after Schumann's pioneering trialogues among Raro, Florestan, and Eusebius). But both gently position the Music Director (a synonym for Capellmeister) as the Socrates figure: his views will eventually convince the others, and they manifestly represent Krüger's own opinions in displaced form. Krüger's Music Director is cast as a conservative, almost exclusively concerned with the pure, "straight" performance of oratorios and cantatas by Bach and Handel, but also showing that he recognized Beethoven's works as comparably serious. He vigorously confronts both the Dilettante and the Virtuoso on questions of musical learning. In a testy, impatient moment he asks the (violin) Virtuoso: "Have you, beyond your own instrument, composed anything? Have you expressly devoted yourself to composing, or studied?" ("Virtuosenkonzert," 160) The Music Director also finds time to regret the Virtuoso's uprootedness. As the Virtuoso's words make clear, a battle for authority and public approval was at stake: "We children of the devil, as we are often called publicly and secretly, ruin the mind of the public by pulling them away from their interest in sublime oratorios and enticing them into the world of sin" (159).

At the opposite end of the spectrum from Capellmeisters stood the dilettantes—amateurs who passionately pursued, played, and patronized music, but who were not musicians by profession and had not necessarily studied theory. The term *dilettante* is difficult to pin down. Their numbers included singers as well as instrumentalists, and the best among them made appearances on public concerts. Essays on virtuosity, however, fairly consistently use it to designate any nonprofessional musician, and this is how I will use it here. In a cosmopolitan context, dilettantes rarely entered into general comments on virtuosity, but in the German towns they could not be ignored. As late as 1852, a critic in Berlin could write that "in present times the *dominance* of dilettantism, and the advantages and disadvantages that the dilettantish pursuit of the arts exerts on art, is not seldom a topic of discussion."[26] He was writing about a city that, like many places in Germany, had a prominent *Liedertafel* but no permanent symphony orchestra—that is, a flourishing amateur musical life with greater visibility than the institutions representing "symphonic" values. This was no isolated observation. Kahlert, writing in 1842, felt that the dilettantes were stronger than they had ever been. Whereas the dilettante "in former times accepted the criticism of the Capellmeister when he counted wrong," today's amateur "makes claims to so-called general education [*Bildung*]" and thus oversteps his boundaries: "The dilettant has now transferred out of the practical domain into that of the tastemaker [*Kunstrichter*]" (98). And the taste such dilettantes promote, the critic Heinrich Hirshbach lamented, is the taste for virtuosity: "That a single significant, intelligent piece of music says more, and is more useful for art, than a hundred virtuosos combined, is still not understood by the dilettantes" (120). We are accustomed to thinking of Germany's musical culture as serious-minded, but the critics I am concerned with here worried that Germany's amateurs were not serious enough, adoring virtuoso or pseudo-virtuoso music to an alarming degree.

In the battles over virtuosity, the dilettantes had their greatest advocate in Gottfried Fink, editor of the influential Leipzig *Allgemeine musikalische Zeitung*. Fink's views merit fuller exposition because they provoked Robert Schumann to mount an aggressive front against virtuosity, a position he disseminated in the *Neue Zeitschrift für Musik* but had already formulated in the early 1830s.[27] Fink believed that Germany's thriving dilettantism was an achievement to be proud of. In Germany, he argued in a nominally folkish vein, music was not meted out to the people by dukes and aristocrats from above, but emerged from a native, inborn genius for and love of music, and he supported his point by citing pockets of "spontaneous" musical activity in Saxony, in the villages of Thuringia, and among the kaisers.[28] As the head of a journal with direct links to the publishing firm Breitkopf & Härtel, he had a vested interest in promoting virtuoso music. Yet his defenses of dilettantism and of virtuoso pieces, in two leading articles from the year 1833 (see table), articulate a coherent philosophy that can hardly be written off as mercenary. He concedes that "we live in the age of bravura," but he refuses to see this as a bad sign.[29] He accepts the hierarchically subordinate position of virtuoso pieces within the field of music, but does not thereby judge them inessential. If music is a tree, he writes using a metaphor that gets overworked, virtuoso pieces form only the "fruit" and the "fluttering leaves," rather than the "roots" and the "trunk," though the tree would hardly seem beautiful without the fruit and the leaves. Virtuoso pieces are in Fink's view important sources of novelty and regeneration—they keep music sounding fresh and alive, and through this they serve a higher purpose: "And so bravura and virtuoso pieces too are required and necessary for the growth and development of art in all souls" ("Bravourstücke," 535). Fink's point that virtuoso pieces serve as agents of artistic nourishment leads him to his crowning argument, that his serious-minded opponents (like Schumann) are not interested in artistic progress or in a thriving future for art: "It is only a paralyzing thought to view art forever as something finished, never as something becoming" (535). He advocates, furthermore, a relativism of taste: "There is enough room on this round earth for all kinds of wood and fruit, and the tongue of every person tastes for himself what he prefers" (533), and is able to affirm the ethical importance of fleeting, transient pleasures: "Change is life's best partner in everything that is called pleasure" (539).

Fink's position is appealingly democratic, tolerant, and sensible, linking the publication of music to the higher purposes of, and dissemination of, art. Together with his appropriation of the Hegelian idea of "becoming," it is no wonder that Schumann, who considered himself the progressive and the dilettantes regressive, felt compelled to found his own journal independent of any publishing concern, where he could promulgate his anti-virtuoso stance.[30] Opposition to virtuoso music is one of the cornerstones of the *Neue Zeitschrift*, announced in the journal's prospectus of 1834 and followed through in innumerable reviews.[31] Against Fink, Schumann comes off as an unregenerate elitist, representing the prerogatives of a professional composer against the inclinations of the consuming public. His main strategy, in the early issues of the *Neue Zeitschrift*, is to treat virtuosity purely at the level of compositional aesthetics—as revealed in published sheet music—rather than in terms of performance and reception. He does not discuss the whole phenomenon of live events and the performer's charisma, nor comment on whether a piece might give its dilettante consumer pleasure (as Fink does). That Schumann opposes virtuosity to symphonic values becomes clear in his review of Herz's Second Piano Concerto, where he tells performers, "When their hearers cry out at the fine intervals and trills 'Superb!' they should answer, 'Even this has its utility for us Beethovenians.'"[32] Virtuosity, for Schumann, must contribute to that animation of mind that will render music a "poetic" art, and most bravura music fails by merely tickling the senses. In constructing music as an object of contemplative, solitary listening, Schumann speaks for the minority party of fellow professionals (the Davidsbund) against the legions of amateurs and virtuosos (the Philistines) who seem to think of music as an activity—something done. The sole explicitly social strain in his critiques of published virtuoso pieces lies in repeatedly linking them to "fashion," implicitly opposed to inner experience and cultivation.

The Fink-Schumann face-off was, then, a confrontation between the musical public and the professional class, and Fink brought the issue of social status right into the open: "Those who can't quite laugh it off, they get angry, most of them musicians by profession. They are wrong" ("Dilettantismus," 9). By associating musical amateurs with democratic values, Fink claims the high moral ground against his elitist adversaries: "Mutual agreement between people, and respectful recognition and friendliness of one class toward the others, carries in general far greater advantages than the arrogant dominance of this or that class would admit" ("Dilettantismus," 11). In a passage apparently aimed directly at Schumann's party, he even introduces the politically charged rhetoric of "free choice": "Preferences must be free. . . . The Bachians and all 'ians' must not immediately declare insane every person who does not share their preferences with the same enthusiasm" ("Dilettantismus," 12). That Fink's perspective left a permanent mark on the debates over virtuosity is evinced by Krüger's 1841 dialogue, where the Dilettante (echoing Fink) begs for a less righteous attitude from the Music Director: "Take the world with a lighter heart. . . Don't always play the reformer. . . . In the end we can't be sure whether you, or the learned ones in general, or any other select party has captured the true taste" ("Virtuosenkonzert," 169).

Performing the Self

Away with all personality! So long as you do not overcome the dark despot, your individual I, you will not enter the ivory portals of the realm of truth.— All virtuosity in the usual sense is personality. (Krüger, "Virtuosenkonzert," 172)

The middle classes of the nineteenth century were obsessed with reflections on the self. In Peter Gay's sweeping view, their innovation was to model the self as an "inner" space, defining this inner terrain through their engagement with Romantic novelists and poets, through letter writing, diary-keeping, autobiography, and biography—all of them quintessentially nineteenth century genres of writing. And yet, Gay writes, "what makes the Victorians' self-scrutiny important . . . is not that they invented introspection or were the first to brood about it but that they made it available, almost inescapable, to a wide public."[33] To cultivate inwardness, in other words, was not simply to withdraw from all engagement with the world, for the bourgeoisie found numerous ways of externalizing that inwardness, of making it public information. Thus the boundary between public and private, and especially the need to keep a common ground between them, produced some of the deepest anxieties and conflicts experienced by the nineteenth century middle classes. The fight against virtuosity necessarily engaged with these tensions. It was constantly marking and policing a boundary between a privileged inner self and a devalued "performativity" construed as external and lacking in substance. One reason the battle was strongest in central-northern Germany may be that its middle classes were cultivating this interiorized model of selfhood (often associated with the psychology of Protestantism) and integrating it into their musical pursuits. Critics advocated the inner self against the outer world not only for performers but also for the audiences: suspicion that middle-class audiences only went to concerts to show themselves, to see and be seen, was rampant, and it was far stronger for audiences at virtuoso concerts than at symphony concerts.[34] To show how the self and its ethical integrity entered into overview discussions of virtuosity, I will first address the issue of the performer's character and then the complex network of relationships between performer, work, and public.

To someone living in a midsize German city, accustomed to stability and familiarity, the figure of the virtuoso posed considerable problems. In large cities, Triest wrote, a virtuoso's personal character is not much of an issue, since he has a busy social life and is rarely seen up close, "but in midsize and smaller cities, whose visual field is narrower, and where people are used to bringing their powers of judgment upon even the least significant persons and things, the foreigner in particular will not escape a close scrutiny of his inner character" (770–71). Such close observation would not be a problem if the traveling lifestyle did not expose the artist to the risks of moral collapse. Triest, thinly disguising an attack on the notoriously dissipated violinist Lolli (1725–1802), lists common "immoral characteristics" such as a "lack of modesty, strange moodiness, and an addiction to sensual indulgences such as gambling, women, and drink" (772–73). All of this would not be particularly relevant if music were not "an art that proclaims expression and the stirring of feelings as its principal goal, and so exactly ties the represented with the representer (the virtuoso)" (773). Music, in other words, is an art whose ethical purpose ("the furthering of humanity," as he puts it) can only be served by virtuous performers. Critic Ludwig Granzin, writing in 1847, extended this opinion to the general musical education of women and children, which requires "beyond the talent for art and its proper cultivation also an intellectual and moral foundation" (177).

Carl Gollmick elaborated this position most fully in his anti-virtuoso polemic "Virtuosity Today" (1842), but with intensified moralistic fervor.[35] Gollmick classifies virtuosos into three groups: the "unavoidable" (itself subdivided into three groups, the "school crowd," the "child prodigies," and the "virtuosi ambulanti"), the "solid," and the "untouchable." His second and idealized category, the solid, describes unambiguously the stable, small-town German musician. This performer has "remained true to his faith. Unconcerned with the external world and criticism, this modest artist lives his inner god, and his virtuosity has developed with his life as the movements of a healthy body with the movements of a healthy soul" (184).[36] It is not a coincidence that the sketch of this second class is shorter and more abstract than the others. Gollmick's "solid" virtuoso is something of a straw man, a model against which he can profile his real target: the "homeless *virtuosi ambulanti*."[37] The itinerant virtuoso is hopelessly divorced from his roots. He travels through many lands, ruins himself in "modish taste," returns "to his home a stranger," and betrays "in foreign lands" the maiden to whom he had promised himself. In this Faustian sell-out to international fashion, the healthy relationship between artistic purpose and personal character falls apart: "Despite external fine manners, impressive medals, despite the salon style, etc., he looks very weak on the inside, and it helps nothing, when our virtuoso is a German, that he props the foreign traveler above his genealogy" (183). Whereas the solid virtuoso is warm and brotherly, and "his favorite reward is the handshake of a social equal" (184), the untouchable cosmopolitan has lost contact with this basic human grain: "His social distancing from me is comparable only to his overwhelming aesthetic greatness" (185). Gollmick, in sum, was disgusted with the virtuoso bigwigs who sweep into town, seduce the public, and leave with huge quantities of money. And he was not alone. Krüger's Music Director voices the same opinion, becoming bitterly nostalgic about former times, when he and the Virtuoso played Beethoven quartets together: "To me you were Prometheus and Pandora, when you had not yet left the country to train your fingers, the source of immense fame and boundless journalistic praise" ("Virtuosenkonzert," 160).

The xenophobic strain in these comments is not aimed at asserting German musical superiority. The problem is an internal one: German musicians are so susceptible to the lures of the virtuoso path that they lose their inner honesty, rectitude, and conscience—the ethical qualities essential to a good musician—to a highly externalized, public sense of identity, marked as foreign. Such mapping of national identity onto personal character becomes unusually explicit in a review, from the same critical milieu, of French pianist Mortier la Fontaine:

> Even with his thorough musical education he still knew how to show the light, graceful, tasteful bearing that make the French so amicable in society. He struck me as a French *philosophe*, who delivers the world-shaking dogmas not with a serious, troubled face, not with a ponderous, almost mystical secretiveness, but with that pleasant smile, with that piquant lightness, with that *bonhomie* unique to our neighbors on the other side of the Rhine.[38]

Such oppositions between the Frenchman's polish and grace and the German's ponderous intellectuality may reveal a subtext of Schumann's choice of Henri Herz and Friedrich Kalkbrenner as targets of his more biting criticisms. Herz and Kalkbrenner were among the many German-born pianists whose virtuosity eventually landed them in Paris and enabled them to acquire aristocratic manners, money, and glory.[39] Although he never said it explicitly, Schumann may have perceived in Herz's "superficial" music a loss of German depth or character like that identified by Krüger, Gollmick, and other colleagues.[40] More important, it was sheet music by composers like them that most appealed to Germany's extensive dilettantism, and Schumann sought to make his critiques a bulwark against that trend.

Critics attended not only to the virtuoso as an autonomous individual, but also in relationship to the society he belonged to and to the audiences he played for. Many worried that the enthusiasm for virtuosos was unhealthy or misdirected, and as they attempted to explain why, they kept returning to the notion of a balance between individual and society. Sociologist Richard Sennett, in his book *The Fall of Public Man*, offered a comparably pessimistic interpretation of the relationship between public virtuosos and the conditions of modern selfhood.[41] Before the hegemony of "inwardness," Sennett argued somewhat schematically, the self was formed in the optimistic public spirit of the Enlightenment. A model for this self was the "actor." People could adopt a role or assume an identity in public situations with a positive sense of purpose. They were under no illusion that this role or identity was "natural," but they did not think of it as "false" or as a betrayal of an "inner" truth. To act in public and to act in private were clearly different, but not contradictory or competing. The great change, in Sennett's view, came with the urbanizing momentum of the early decades of the nineteenth century. Writing specifically about France, he argues that the dense, fleeting appearances of urban life produced in people a suspicion of outer appearances, a distrust of manifest character, and a fear of involuntarily revealing the self in a corrupted public space. Virtuosos became cult figures in the 1830s and '40s precisely by solving this problem of bringing the self into the public. The virtuoso showed how to "feel in public," and audiences marveled at his facility and boldness in doing so. Moreover, the virtuoso's behavior gave audiences license to react with strong emotion in the concert hall, thus moving them to bridge the normally unbridgeable private-public gap. Sennett implies that audiences of this period bore a certain *ressentiment*—a subliminal wish that the needs of an inward or autonomously conceived self could be fully met by, and realized in, the public world—and that the virtuoso was something of a fantasy of this ideal realized.[42]

A parallel impulse to what Sennett describes is found in the writings of Romantic philosophers around 1800, who, operating in the wake of the Enlightenment, sought to reintegrate the self with transcendental forces or an absolute whole. As Gerald Izenberg has formulated it: "In Romantic imagery and concept . . . the idea of infinite individuality is always linked with the notion of an all-inclusive totality other and greater than the self, in a relationship not of reciprocity but of dependency."[43] A brief detour into Hegel's notion of the self, which at least anticipates the Romantic trend, is necessary here because his ideas are echoed in the essays on virtuosity. Hegel's self only achieves its true realization when an individual subject, in all its concrete particularity, becomes aware of itself as part of a larger, more absolute whole or object. One of Hegel's favorite illustrations was none other than the figure of Christ: the genius of Christianity was that it represented a "Self that is at the same time *this* individual, and also the *universal* Self."[44] The self becomes more realized as it achieves a sort of double-vision that embraces the subjective and objective as separate and even contradictory, yet is able simultaneously to reconcile them conceptually into a larger unity. A political exemplification of this subject-object relationship emerges in the *Philosophy of Right*. Hegel faults both the Greek and the Roman republics for failing to create a political system in which all individuals might recognize themselves reflected at a higher level—people under this system thus lacked the objective complement to their subjective individuality. The modern state, in contrast, "has prodigious strength and depth because it allows the principle of subjectivity to progress to its culmination in the extreme of self-subsistent, personal particularity, and yet at the same time brings it back to the substantive [*substantielle,* as in objective] unity and so maintains this unity in the principle of subjectivity itself."[45]

Mary Hunter has recently shown how these heady ideas affected Hegel's discussion of musical performance, as well as pedagogical music treatises, in the early nineteenth century. Hegel's performer must submit to the objectivity of the work being played, but his submission takes an active form—a spiritual exertion necessary to bring the work to sounding life, and hence part of its full realization: "The Romantic sense of the 'genius of performance' involves the performer's psycho-spiritual capacity to transform himself into an other. But not just any other: this capacity creates a miraculous merging of his own self with that of the composer to represent a new subjectivity."[46] Hunter lays out the broader philosophical context for this union of the self with the other or the beyond, particularly compellingly in the case of Novalis, and shows that this Romantic trend left traces in musical pedagogy. Musical performance may, in her view, have been a privileged site where people could observe or experience the unity of subject and object: "Interpretative performance at this time was in many quarters considered to be a public display of precisely that most humanly and philosophically central phenomenon."[47]

The essays under discussion here tend to read the virtuoso phenomenon in the opposite way: as a singular failure of the subjective and objective to arrive at their desired complementarity. The issues were addressed most directly in the polemics by Kahlert and Krüger. Both writers, like so many in the central and northern German milieu, were steeped in Hegel's ideas, which were being disseminated in universities all over Germany, and they imported the philosopher's ideas of the self, or perhaps only the watered-down version thereof, into their considerations of virtuosity.[48] Of the two, Kahlert is somewhat less thoroughly Hegelian, but he does draw a distinction between modalities of the self. In a comparison of musical performance with stage acting, he remarks on the virtuoso's tendency to draw attention away from the work, so that "his beloved I [*sein liebes Ich*] becomes the main point of the whole task" (105). Shortly thereafter, however, Kahlert takes some comfort in the fact that "the nobler dispositions will not lose their higher self [*höheres Selbst*] in virtuosity" (106).

Krüger's dialogue between Music Director and Virtuoso employs a much more explicitly Hegelian vocabulary.[49] The virtuoso defends his tendency to bring personality into his public concert tours, claiming he has only a very short career and needs all the help he can get. The Music Director replies: "It is not this little personality that I am attacking . . . that is harmless and not worthy of further consideration . . . No! I mean also the core of personality in the deeper sense, the substantive subjectivity [*substantielle Subjektivität*]. Understood in this way, personal arts, as represented by virtuosos and actors, are an essential manifestation [*wesentliche Phänomenon*] thereof, without which they cannot achieve full life. It is the confusion of these two hierarchically separate perspectives that bring about the disgusting exaggeration of the personal-vain" ("Virtuosenkonzert," 164). In other words, there are two ways the self can be brought into musical performance: one merges the self with the work and transforms both; the second keeps the self outside of substantiality by failing to form a compelling bond with the work. Ethically, Krüger's Music Director demands that the performer get outside himself, not to serve slavishly the idealized work (in the manner of *Werktreue*), but to effect the full realization of his own subjectivity. In this line of thought, the musical work stands in for the Hegelian absolute or objective, with which the performer's self must be brought into relation.

This philosophical background is necessary for understanding Krüger's principal polemical point. His Music Director explains to the Dilettante exactly what sort of music was associated with the untransformed subjectivity of the performer, "his dear, silly I." It is music of "lyric" character, as opposed to "epic" or "dramatic" music, and this map of styles leads to his vehement repetitions of his argument: "I am impugning the value of subjectivity, of the incidental and personality, in the public context [*Öffentlichkeit*]. . . The aristocracy of the epic and the dramatic above the lyrical, i.e., for the concert hall—that is what I am claiming" (172). In both passages the Music Director invalidates the lyrical not on its own terms, but only in relation to public space. The only music appropriate to public spaces, by implication, are genres such as the oratorio and symphony, which bypass the lyrical and stage the collective effort of numerous individuals. Instrumental virtuosos not only appear alone in public space, but they play their own pieces and thus fail to establish an objective pole in which the performer's individuality might be reflected and elevated.

Toward the end of the article Krüger broadens this argument still further. Virtuoso concerts in general, as an institution, isolate musicians from one another in competition and keep them from working together. They are thus inimical to the general interest of art and society, and reform should proceed from state-organized music education: "That would be a worthy task for conservatories, academies, and national associations: to drive the nail out of the head of virtuosos, instead of praising a capable number of self-educated monads [*Monaden*] as they usually do. To educate the inner sense for art, morally decent aesthetics, that would be the true foundation of art education" (173). In suggesting a political solution to the problem of virtuosos, Krüger's argument brings us full circle to Triest's pioneering essay of 1802. When Triest finished diagnosing the problems, his proposed solution (an amazingly precocious one) was to bring instrumentalists under the protection of a state agency:

> Everywhere where an artist can count on good support, one would establish a sort of art-jury, consisting of the most artistically experienced and other understanding men, sanctioned by the high powers, and whose noblest duties would be of two kinds: partly to make sure that no artist submits to the public, partly that the good artists (the true virtuoso), according to his skill, should receive a steady salary without having to make his living with letters of recommendation and charlatanry. (756)

The forays into politics, philosophy, and ethics surveyed here show that the battle against virtuosity addressed issues far beyond aesthetics alone. In the extended essays by Schumann's Davidsbund circle and others, it touched on fundamental, and sometimes unresolvable, issues about what made societies and individuals healthy and cohesive. Very little of this social subtext can be glimpsed in the platitudes about superficiality or sensuality that were built into most critics' vocabulary by the second half of the nineteenth century. Obviously, the bulk of the attacks on the virtuoso phenomenon in the period 1810–40 were not driven by Hegelian philosophical baggage or by a look at its overall social and cultural implications. But charges of egotism and vanity formed one of the cornerstones of the battle against virtuosity even in its microcosmic appearances, as passing comments in concert reviews, and egotism could only seem objectionable if public music were conceived *a priori* as a means for transcending the self—as a medium for the transmission of socially shared sentiments and aspirations.

Liszt and the Critique of Virtuosity

Culturally grounded interpretations of the virtuoso Liszt tend to see him as the epitome of his age, embodying its Romantic idealism, its taste for spectacle and self-promotion, and its modernity-driven fascination with mechanical speed and power.[50] Even Liszt's contemporaries, such as Joseph d'Ortigue and Heinrich Heine, saw in Liszt an intensified reflection of the contemporary world (see their articles in parts II and III of this volume). It is no surprise, then, to find that some critics hostile to virtuosity made Liszt the embodiment of everything they detested in it. He was accused of greed for setting high ticket prices. His playing was faulted as harsh, mechanical, and overly technical. Audiences were berated for letting themselves get carried away by his nerve-shaking intensity and losing sight of true aesthetic values. And he was frequently accused of mangling Beethoven with his tempo changes and embellishments that put his personality above all else.[51]

Yet what is most remarkable in the reception of Liszt is how often he was viewed as a shining exception to the usual problems of a culture obsessed with virtuosity. Perhaps the most dramatic example is Berlin's famously severe and widely read music critic Ludwig Rellstab. In 1839, Rellstab delivered in his journal *Iris im Gebiete der Tonkunst* a prophecy concerning modern virtuosity: "There will come a time, and perhaps soon, when people will have become so saturated by this genre (virtuosity) that they will greet it with true revulsion, and its return will seem forever impossible."[52] By his own admission, Rellstab expected Liszt to confirm this prediction, but when he finally heard Liszt play in 1842, he reversed his opinion.[53] Rellstab was joined by several other critics in asserting that Liszt transcended the usual ills of the virtuoso throng. "Too many pianists," wrote a grumpy Viennese critic in 1846, "try to make themselves into virtuosos. How many pianists can attain any real artistry? Very few indeed, the first of whom is Liszt."[54]

What was it about Liszt's performing style and concerts that protected him from the darts of anti-virtuosity critics? How did he escape attacks by those who worried about materialism, sensuality, and decadent or dilettante taste? Above all, how did he, with his overwhelming personal magnetism and individuality, parry the charge of egotism? To answer these questions we need to attend to those aspects of Liszt's playing and concerts that were *not* typical of their time. It can be easy to forget that, for all his popularity, most listeners in the 1830s and '40s only had a chance to hear Liszt play two or three times. In the year-to-year concert seasons, audiences were hearing and lionizing virtuoso pianists whose style differed greatly from that of Liszt (in contrast to the later nineteenth century, when Liszt's pianism had become the international standard). There is a real sense in which pianists like Alexander Dreyshock and Theodor Döhler, not Liszt, epitomized their age, making them the targets of anti-virtuoso polemics.[55] Liszt was not simply "better" or more "advanced," but different in his approach—to the piano, to repertory choice, and to the framing of the concert event.[56] By all these means he drew attention away from his isolated self and linked it to an aesthetic object (the work) or a social object (the public). This is how he managed to defy the anti-virtuosity position of the Davidsbund, with its concern for the balance of individual and society.

Liszt framed his concerts in ways that drew audience attention toward the event's social, political, cultural, or humanitarian purpose. This had been his goal ever since he defined the musician as a quasi-religious figure with a power to influence all of society in his 1835 essay "On the Situation of Artists," and it is this that turned Rellstab's opinion around. In the Prussian capital, Rellstab explained, Liszt supported the students, donated enormous sums to numerous charities, honored the reigning king, indulged the connoisseurs with Bach, Scarlatti, and Handel, and pleased the public by taking requests and responding to encores—all of it directly related to his pianism. National and patriotic themes, reflected in a fair amount of Liszt's concert repertory, also removed his concerts from a sense of egotism or personal indulgence. By far the most consistent and thoroughgoing framework for linking his virtuosity to public interest was to give humanitarian charity concerts in large numbers and with a certain ostentation. By channeling his unique talent to larger socially useful ends, he was putting his subjective individuality in service of the objective social body. There were episodes, such as his first visit to Leipzig, where his ticket prices—often double the normal rate—provoked scandal.[57] But for the most part, Liszt's audiences were persuaded he was not giving so many concerts from a profit motive.

In this, Liszt escaped one of the most common concerns of critics who polemicized generally against virtuosity: the perception that modernity was characterized by a crass materialism, and that virtuosos epitomized it.[58] H. Hirschbach, another Davidsbündler, claimed straight out that "the apparently so overwhelming productive power in execution lies . . . in the tone of modern society: it wants to be entertained" (119). As with other arguments against virtuosity, this one dwelled on ethics to the near exclusion of aesthetics. Writers paid most attention to the accumulating wealth of concert artists, their high prices, their sacrificing of the "ideal" art to the interests of Mammon. Paganini and Liszt, lacking ties to permanent professional institutions, were obvious and open targets, but the whole class of touring virtuosos was under siege. A Hamburg critic, whose words were found worthy of reproduction by the Leipzig journal *Signale*, claimed the malaise was specific to the 1830 generation of musicians:

> In earlier times, too, one traveled as a virtuoso, but not with this extremely immoral greed that reduces art to a corrupt prostitute, not with this concertizing in every little tiny city. The feeling was purer back then; one only aspired to ask the world for its opinion, then went back home, gave piano lessons, and studied. This is the way Moscheles, Hummel, Kalkbrenner, Romberg, and Rode traveled. But giving lessons now seems honorless; the great virtuoso has it more splendid, nobler, more comfortable, more elegant, when he becomes a wealthy musician-merchant. ["Virtuosen-Unfug," 217]

The implicit idealization of a geographically stable, socially useful, not especially worldly virtuoso, who abstains from material temptations, resonates with the perspective of the Davidsbund. There is not a word here about music as a sounding art, or about how this career fails the ideal.[59] Liszt contradicted this ideal model in most ways, and yet charges of materialism were rare.

The aesthetic or sounding equivalent to such materialism was the reputedly "mechanical" sound of the *stile brillante*—the vocabulary of figurative patterns exploited in the concert music of Hummel, Weber, Moscheles, and other pianists of the pre-Liszt generation. What was "mechanical" in the minds of its detractors was the repetitive, rhythmically four-square shape of these figures, unrelieved by songful lyricism or sustained harmonies, as well as the sheer percussiveness of the piano (Schumann called it "empty tinsel"). Liszt's general break from *brillante* figuration may have contributed significantly to his freedom from the pervasive mechanist critique of piano virtuosity. All of his rivals—pianists like Sigismond Thalberg, Theodor Döhler, or Alexander Dreyschock—remained rooted in the *stile brillante*, even as they were taking advantage of the resources of the modern instrument. Even Chopin made extensive use of its characteristic four-note patterns, though rendering them less mechanical by syncopating them against their (sub)metrical backgrounds and blending them with the pedal (Examples 1a and 1b). Liszt's bravura thrives far less on patterns of this sort, and when he does employ them, notably in his filagree cadenzas, he blurs them together as an indistinct cloud of sound entirely foreign to the "noteyness" of the *stile brillante* (Example 2). Liszt also harbored an alternative sound ideal to that of earlier pianists. The *stile brillante*

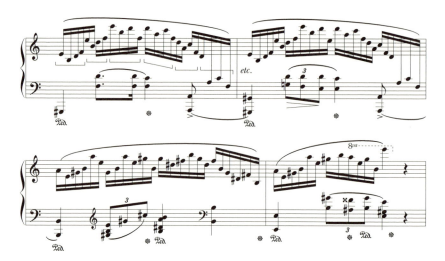

Example 1a. Chopin, Etude, op. 25, no. 11.

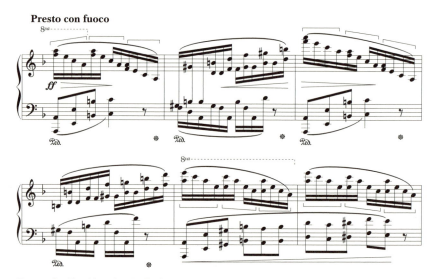

Example 1b. Chopin, Ballade, op. 38.

accepts the percussive attack of the piano—the materiality of its sound—
and indeed capitalizes on that sound for effects that delight the listener's
ear. Chopin's pianism, while considerably more plastic and sweeping,
never forces the instrument's sonorous boundaries. Liszt's concert music, by
contrast, often rejects the piano's limitations. It strives for orchestral effects

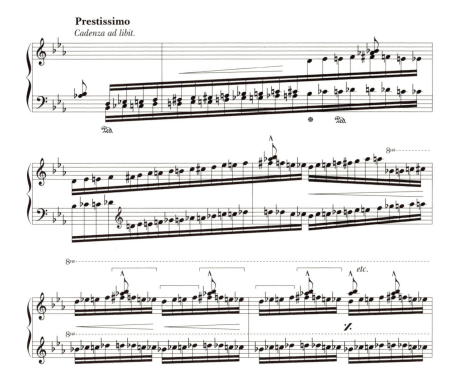

Example 2. Liszt's *Sonnambula* fantasy.

even at the expense of sonorous beauty—for example, a large chord repeated six or eight times fortissimo in imitation of a climactic tutti—and thereby rejects his instrument's bounded materiality. In striving for such "impossible" sounds, Liszt's pianism pulls away from the material and reaches toward its antipode: the ideal.

Another common critique of virtuosity that Liszt evaded to a surprising degree was the charge of excessive egotism—surprising because of the supreme self-confidence and individualism he always projected. As noted earlier, philosophically minded watchdogs faulted virtuosity for its glorification of the "kleines Ich," the individual self with no representation in the social or aesthetic object, and they isolated the "lyrical" (versus the "epic" or "dramatic") as the musical trace of such unredeemed subjectivity.[60] While Liszt did not think according to such categories, he clearly felt that music of decisively lyrical character was not well suited to the public concert as he imagined it. As much as he admired Schumann's novel piano works, for example, he did not feel he could pull them off in concert and almost immediately ceased performing the excerpts from *Carnaval* that he had attempted to promote.[61] Nor did he perform during his tours his own character pieces from the *Années de pèlerinage*, though they had been recently composed and he was uncommonly proud of them. A further telling example is his frequent omission of Chopin's contribution to the *Hexaméron*, the only variation with a dreamy tone, in concert. He also seems to have avoided pieces that, on account of their brevity, might be reminiscent of salon repertory. In Vienna he once substituted the *Lucia* fantasy for a pair of etudes announced on the program, explaining most implausibly to the audience that the etudes were "too exhausting."[62] Soon thereafter, he reintroduced the Chopin etude but transitioned from it into a fantasy on a Hungarian tune, as though it might not have a sufficient effect on its own.[63] In a similar manner, he typically segued directly from his transcription of Schubert's "Ave Maria" into another piece, such as a transcription of Schubert's "Ständchen" or the "Erlkönig."[64]

Liszt did not retreat from sustained lyricism altogether. His performing repertory included the first movement of Beethoven's "Moonlight" Sonata (sometimes with, sometimes without the other movements), a few of Chopin's mazurkas, and more consistently, a pairing of his transcriptions of Schubert's "Ave Maria" and "Ständchen." These pieces, uniquely formed islands of quiet, lyric expression on his concert programs— sustained melodic expressions without dramatic, heroic, or epic framing that might relate them to a larger aesthetic idea. One thing they all have in common, of course, is that they were written by composers that one did not hear often on virtuoso concerts. The Chopin and Schubert excerpts, in particular, were rightly understood as propaganda on behalf of these composers. Even in these moments of lyricism, then, Liszt was presenting himself as the servant of cultural diffusion, and the listener's attention was drawn as much toward the composer represented as it was toward Liszt's own world of feeling or egoistic center. In such circumstances, it was hardly possible to perceive Liszt as indulging in the kind of introverted lyricism that critics of virtuosity disliked so much. In the case of *Ave Maria*, furthermore, Liszt exploited the upper registers of the keyboard to conjure up halos of light and divinity around the melody (Example 3), in a sense channeling his virtuosity toward an incandescent realization of the mother's holy image, and prompting comments such as: "Magical were the bell tones and the chorale-like, lightly accompanied, evenly exhaled, sigh-like prayers."[65] There was thus no risk that the *Ave Maria* transcription, lyrical as it is, might appear as the projection of Liszt's "little I."

The great warhorses of Liszt's concert repertory kept lyrical effusions strictly at bay, in favor of the dramatic and epic emphasis that Krüger had

Example 3. Liszt transcription of Schubert's "Ave Maria."

admitted to public music. Many of his most frequently programmed pieces—the *Ungarischer Sturmmarsch*, the *Réminiscences de Robert le diable*, Weber's *Invitation to the Dance*, the *Erlkönig* transcription, the *Puritani Polonaise* (after Bellini), the *Tarantella*, and the *Grand Galop chromatique*— thrive on propulsive dance rhythms and heroic march rhythms, with no admixture of lyrical melody or anything that can be construed as inward-turning. In the opera fantasies, of course, complete lyrical melodies do appear. But when Liszt played "Là ci darem la mano" in the *Don Giovanni* fantasy, to take an example, there was little chance that audiences would identify the song with Liszt's own subjective presence: the aria belonged to Zerlina and Don Giovanni, or perhaps to Mozart, but not to Liszt. Indeed, a recurring response to Liszt's playing of this duet was that he seemed to merge with the characters of Zerlina and Don Giovanni.[66] More important, Liszt completed this fusion of his performing self with dramatic object in the non-melodic parts of his opera fantasies as well. In contrast to his virtuoso peers, who tend to present arias in relatively "pure" or "objective" form (Thalberg was legendary for this), Liszt presents them within larger music-dramatic processes—anticipations, sudden contrasts, intrusions, and climaxes—that help preserve a sense of dramatic tension, when not the actual drama being recalled. In variation 2 of the *Don Juan* fantasy, for instance, Liszt treats the theme to a variation on scherzo and *chasse* topics, estabishing a playful, coquettish mood that can easily be seen as linked to the dramatic substance of the gallant seduction scene, even though Mozart only hints at such musical means (Example 4). Here Liszt

Example 4. Liszt, *Réminiscences de Don Juan,* variation 2.

varies not just the melodic and harmonic structure, but the dramatic substance of the famous duet, in effect fusing his own subjective invention directly to Mozart's dramatic object.

Liszt's frequent performances of pieces understood as "classical" was yet another means by which he freed himself from the usual criticism of egotism. It was not so much that Liszt subordinated himself to the solemn text of the classical masters. This submissive approach, what Dahlhaus called the model of "interpretation," risked tipping the balance of subject (performer) and object (work) too much in favor of the object.[67] More than one critic appreciated Liszt precisely for his blend of restraint and soulfulness. In reference to Liszt's playing of Hummel's popular Septet, critic Heinrich Adami wrote: "Effects were developed that the composer himself certainly did not think of. . . . And yet with all the brilliance of conception, the musical fidelity [*Treue*] was not at all missing; and so it should be in music as in acting: *The performer would be at once master and servant of the poet.*"[68] Here interpretive fidelity is not tied to the letter but primarily to the spirit of the original creator. The same idea was articulated later, employing the philosophical language of subjective and objective: "Liszt is still the *most complete subjectivity* that exists in today's artistic world—no matter what composition of a new or old author he plays, it is not *this* figure that you encounter, but Liszt. You might perhaps maintain that the objective element of a composition must attain its coloration through the noble subjectivity of the performing artist, thus making it an individual interpretation [*Auffassung*]—granted. Yet Liszt has expanded the idea of interpretation; for him it means to give himself *to the foreign work*, in his complete brilliance, although only Liszt can do this."[69] Liszt alone, that is, seems to be able to mobilize his subjectivity in service to the work, rather than leaving subject and object perceptible as separate musical phenomena, as a variation on some kind of objective work. He thus embodied the model of the performer who, as Mary Hunter has shown, was being advanced by philosophers and pedagogues in the early nineteenth century: a performer who, through performative genius, gives to the work a life it does not have on its own.[70]

A suprising echo of this position is found in the concert reviews of Carl Gollmick. The curmudgeonly author of "Virtuosity Today," Gollmick seemed to aim his third model of the modern virtuoso—the "untouchable" cosmopolitan who only circulates in high aristocratic milieus—directly at Liszt.[71] Yet the hard-nosed voice of "Virtuosity Today" is absent from his earlier reviews of Liszt's concerts in Frankfurt and Mainz (1840), even if they do include some points of reproach. Gollmick finds Liszt's own pieces weak and formless, but unlike other critics who showed an aversion to such "Romanticism," he praises Liszt's classical interpretations overwhelmingly:

"His aesthetic substance lies in the representation of foreign creative pow-ers; indeed, his genius occasionally rises above them." In performances of Weber's *Konzertstück*, Hummel's B Minor Concerto, and Beethoven's Choral Fantasy, Gollmick heard "genuinely spirited interpretation and represen-tation of classical works, in which there lies a far greater service than to always give his own echo, which unfortunately is the case with so many 'dozens of concertizers.' . . . In this Liszt is at once poet and performer, and he can only be challenged by someone who understands how to enrich and elevate the beauties of foreign compositions, without at the same time employing certain effects."[72] Clearly, the work here has not just an objec-tive status but also a subjective one that the performer, and only the great performer, can bring out by entering into the spirit of the creator and blend-ing his own genius with it. It is this, not mere submission to the text of a classical score, that sets Liszt apart from the virtuoso mob. And yet, as the remainder of the review makes clear, Gollmick can find only a "sick" Romanticism elsewhere in Liszt's own concert pieces. In such pieces Liszt descends into the throng of virtuosos who "only give their own echo," a phrase strongly reminiscent of Krüger's Music Director, when he refers to the "little personality" or the "dear, silly I."

Strong partisans of symphonic values will want to view the gradual suppression or subsumption of virtuosity as a matter of pure aesthetic expe-rience—a "natural" process of refining taste toward what is truly good and beautiful (as Hanslick did). Here I have argued that symphonic values, on the contrary, were imposed upon a public that was initially gravitat-ing toward music of virtuoso character, both in 1802 (when Triest wrote) and in the 1840s. The battle issued from specific social locations: it voiced the interests of a class of professionals (composers, theorists, music direc-tors, and critics) struggling to maintain the dignity and prestige of their profession in the face of the striking democratization of musical life that marked the 1820s and '30s—a motivation shared by the London Philhar-monic, A. B. Marx, and the various essayists discussed. The debates also had a special relevance to the German cities, due not only to the struc-ture of their musical life but also to the strength of "interiority" as a model for experience and selfhood. How, then, did the critique of virtuosity seep into the consciousness of the general public and achieve the international hegemony it had by 1869, when Hanslick celebrated the supersession of the virtuoso era and of dilettantism? Why, to ask it another way, was Gottfried Fink the last influential critic to advocate the social virtues of pleasant, amateur music, losing ground to the stricter, more serious, and exclusive values of Schumann and his Davidsbund?

Understanding how a broad public eventually accepted and internalized symphonic values requires that we revise the common view of the nineteenth-century bourgeoisie as a complacent, self-assured class, cultivating the symphony in a sort of narcissistic affirmation of its superiority and universality.[73] Historian Peter Gay, in the five long volumes of *The Bourgeois Experience*, strives to replace this stiff image (a stereotype that formed in the context of modernism) with an image of a class in perpetual dynamic conflict, struggling to reconcile its contradictions and inconsistencies. The nineteenth-century bourgeoisie was receptive to, sometimes even desperate for, authoritative-sounding voices directing them toward the "good" or the "right" choices in music as in other aspects of life—all the more since music's recent democratization overwhelmed them with products and choices.[74] The dialogic format of the essays by Krüger, Kahlert, and Granzin may itself register that the music-loving public felt pulled in different, sometimes irreconcilable directions. Thus a hard-nosed critic such as Ludwig Rellstab could be enormously popular, even as he criticized his readers' supposedly superficial tastes and challenged them to transcend them, in effect dividing them against themselves.

An equally important question is whether the social, ethical, and political ideas addressed in the German essays on virtuosity survived, at some subliminal level, in the clichés that were habitually and uncritically attached to virtuosity by 1870. Recurrent adjectives such as *cheap, superficial, dishonest,* and *flashy,* no matter how mechanically repeated, certainly register some degree of ethical criticism for a middle-class perspective and gather considerable critical strength from the ethical subtext. What is more remarkable, however, is how these adjectives (like Schumann's fleeting mentions of "fashion") take on the appearance of disinterested, purely aesthetic responses or comments. They have been transformed from products of social contestation into the "natural" appearance of virtuosity—in other words, ideology. The critical essays from the 1830s and '40s discussed here, because written in a formative period in the bourgeoisie's relationship to music, deny such transparency and bring the social and ethical contexts up front.

It would be overstating the case to say that the battle against instrumental virtuosity was over in 1870. As late as 1904, Parisian musical life was rocked by the *guerre des concertos,* in which a coterie of symphony-centered zealots were calling for the total exclusion of concertos from orchestral concerts.[75] Like the Philharmonic Society of London's similar gesture ninety years earlier, this was an unsuccessful attack: a need for the concerto, for the pleasures of virtuoso performance, reasserted itself, reflecting an ambivalence characteristic of the music-loving classes. Symphonic values did not expunge virtuosity; they transformed it from a separate musical value into a hierarchically subordinate position on a single scale of musical value. Likewise, the growing power of Hanslick's highly competent musical "artists" did not erase the "dilettantes," but established the latter as a poor relation, thus giving "dilettantism" the pejorative sense it still has today.

NOTES

1. Eduard Hanslick, *Geschichte des Concertwesens in Wien*, 2 vols. (Vienna: 1869–70, repr. New York: 1979), vol. 1, p. 370.

2. Ibid., p. 371.

3. Ibid., p. 368.

4. Anon., "Virtuosen-Unfug," *Signale für die musikalische Welt* 4, no. 29 (July 1843): 220.

5. Discussions of the critique of instrumental virtuosity are rare and tend to appear in the context of articles on other subjects. Erich Reimer most directly addresses the topic for the period around 1800 in two articles: "Die Polemik gegen das Virtuosenkonzert im 18. Jahrhundert: Zur Vorgeschichte einer Gattung der Trivialmusik," *Archiv für Musikwissenschaft* 30, no. 4 (1973): 235–44; and "Der Begriff des wahren Virtuosen in der Musikästhetik des späten 18. und frühen 19. Jahrhunderts," *Basler Jahrbuch für historische Musikpraxis* 20 (1996): 61–72. Susan Bernstein gives a subtle account of the rhetorical strategies that oppose virtuosity to "depth" or "meaning" in the first three chapters of *Virtuosity of the Nineteenth Century: Performing Music and Language in Heine, Liszt, and Baudelaire* (Stanford, Calif.: 1998). For an excellent discussion of Liszt's struggle with the negative valuation of virtuosity, see Robert Wangermée, "Conscience et inconscience du virtuose romantique: A propos des années parisiennes de Franz Liszt," in *Music in Paris in the 1830s*, ed. P. Bloom (Stuyvesant, N.Y.: 1987), pp. 553–73. See also Albrecht Riethmüller, "Die Verdächtigung des Virtuosen," in *Virtuosen: Über die Eleganz der Meisterschaft—Vorlesungen zur Kulturgeschichte* (Vienna: 2001), pp. 100–24.

6. The string quartet was already accepted as a smaller cousin to the symphony in the early nineteenth century, due in part to the broad admiration for Haydn's quartets and in part to the devotion of violinists such as Ignaz Schuppanzigh, Carl Möser, and Pierre Baillot to the genre.

7. Cyril Ehrlich, *First Philharmonic: A History of the Royal Philharmonic Society* (Oxford, Eng.: 1995), p. 4. Emphasis added.

8. On London concert programs preceding the foundation of the Philharmonic Society, see Simon McVeigh, *Concert Life in London from Mozart to Haydn* (Cambridge, Eng.: 1993), pp. 101–18, and the extensive data presented in Laura Alyson McLamore, "Symphonic Conventions in London's Concert Rooms, circa 1755–1790," Ph.D. diss., University of California, Los Angeles, 1991.

9. The aesthetic writings of Crotch are explicated in Howard Irving, *Ancients and Moderns: William Crotch and the Development of Classical Music* (Aldershot, Eng.: 1999). What is especially interesting about Crotch's aesthetic ideas is that they legitimated instrumental music without any evident influence from German idealism. He was essentially working within eighteenth-century categories such as the pleasant and the sublime. Irving writes:

"Crotch's full acceptance in 1818 of a mixed style that could both entertain and edify, a style in which sublime musical effects are extended legitimately to the 'lesser' musical genres of symphony and opera, and in which these sublime effects can be identified in music by comparatively recent and even living composers, marks a point at which, for the first time, a conception reasonably close to classical music began to be promoted widely among the British concert audience" (p. 86).

10. Quoted in Ehrlich, *First Philharmonic*, p. 12.

11. Quoted in ibid., p. 6.

12 See John Spitzer, "Metaphors of the Orchestra—The Orchestra as Metaphor," *Musical Quarterly* 80, no. 2 (1996): 238–45.

13. Quoted in Ehrlich, *First Philharmonic*, p. 5.

14. *The Spectator*, 13 January 1831. Quoted in Ehrlich, *First Philharmonic*, p. 16.

15. To name only a few of the more influential journals that emerged in this period: *La Revue musicale* (Paris, 1828), *Neue Zeitschrift für Musik* (Leipzig, 1834), *Cäcilia* (Mainz, 1824), *Berliner allgemeine musikalische Zeitung* (Berlin, 1824), *Iris im Gebiete der Tonkunst* (Berlin, 1830), *Allgemeine musikalische Zeitung* (Vienna, 1829).

16. Arno Forschert, "Adolf Bernhard Marx und seine *Berliner allgemeine musikalische Zeitung*," in *Studien zur Musikgeschichte Berlins im frühen 19. Jahrhundert*, ed. Carl Dahlhaus (Regensburg: 1980), pp. 394–95.

17. Leon Plantinga, *Schumann as Critic* (New Haven, Conn.: 1967), pp. 34ff.

18. On Schumann's relative disregard for philosophy, see ibid., pp. 111–14.

19. Carl Dahlhaus, *Nineteenth-Century Music*, trans. J. Bradford Robinson (Berkeley and Los Angeles: 1989), p. 145.

20. For a thorough illustration of how the wars affected concert life in Berlin and how the city rebuilt its concert life, see Christoph-Hellmuth Mahling's copiously documented article, "Zum 'Musikbetrieb' Berlins und seinen Institutionen in der ersten Hälfte des 19. Jahrhunderts," in *Studien zur Musikgeschichte Berlins im frühen 19. Jahrhundert*, pp. 27–284.

21. Reimer, "Die Polemik gegen das Virtuosenkonzert im 18. Jahrhundert": 235–44.

22. Reimer, "Der Begriff des wahren Virtuosen": 61–72.

23. Dieter Düding, *Organisierter gesellschaftlicher Nationalismus in Deutschland (1808–1847): Bedeutung und Funktion der Turner- und Sängervereine für die deutsche Nationalbewegung* (Munich: 1984).

24. David Blackbourn, *History of Germany, 1780–1918: The Long Nineteenth Century* (Oxford, Eng.: 1997), p. 152.

25. Triest's view that the virtuoso must have a broad education, not only in music but in other sciences, is closely related to earlier understandings of the term *virtuoso*. The Renaisssance gentleman could display his virtue (*virtù*) through a variety of pursuits including music, scholarship, and especially warfare. A common meaning of "virtuoso" in the seventeenth century was a person of generally wide learning. Around 1700 the term was applied to musicians with theoretical and practical knowledge, and in the course of the 1700s it was increasingly applied to executive skill on an instrument. For an etymological history of the term, see Susan Bernstein, *Virtuosity of the Nineteenth Century*, pp. 11–12, and the first chapter in Marc Pincherle, *Le Monde des virtuoses* (Paris: 1961).

26. Otto Lange, "Künstler und Dilettant," *Neue Berliner Musikzeitung* 6, no. 32 (11 August 1852): 249. Emphasis added.

27. The background and substance of the Fink-Schumann controversy is presented in Plantinga, *Schumann as Critic*, pp. 32–39. For parallel critiques of virtuosity around 1830 in the French and English presses, see Jim Samson, *Virtuosity and the Musical Work: The Transcendental Studies of Liszt* (Cambridge, Eng.: 2003), p. 73.

28. Triest had linked this native inclination toward music-making with the problem of modern virtuosity: the Germans' "attachment to thoroughness and endurance in studying

and practicing" (col. 737) was admirable, but had the side effect of producing "our preference for the mechanical in music, the brilliance of our instrumental music and the quantity of our traveling virtuosos" (col. 738).

29. G. W. Fink, "Bravourstücke für verschiedene Instrumente mit Orchesterbegleitung," *Allgemeine musikalische Zeitung* 5, no. 33 (13 August 1833): 533.

30. The first reference to the journal that would eventually be founded is in a diary entry of 8 March 1833. See John Daverio, *Robert Schumann: Herald of a "New Poetic Age"* (Oxford, Eng.: 1997), p. 111.

31. For a more complete discussion of Schumann's positions on piano music, see Plantinga, *Schumann as Critic*, pp. 16–23, 196–218.

32. Robert Schumann, *Music and Musicians: Essays and Criticisms*, ed. and trans. F. R. Ritter, 8th ed., 2 vols. (London: n.d.), vol. 2, p. 89.

33. Peter Gay, *The Naked Heart* (London and New York: 1995), p. 6. This book is volume 4 of Gay's five-volume series *The Bourgeois Experience: Victoria to Freud*.

34. A characteristic complaint of this kind comes from the article "Virtuoso Nonsense": "So long as one has not seen these heros [virtuosos], like one has not read the novel that is momentarily *en vogue*, merely to have seen him or read it, a person is far behind in culture, and must catch up in order to pass as educated" (p. 218).

35. See also Gollmick's essay "Die Epidemie des Klavierspielens" in *Feldzüge und Streifereien im Gebiete der Tonkunst* (Darmstadt: 1846).

36. It is difficult to guess what musician might have exemplified this ideal, but pianist Adolph Henselt might have fit the bill. August Kahlert had written of him in 1839: "He saw in his mind an ideal, which he took it upon himself to pursue . . . he closed himself completely in his room and lived alone as a resident in his ideal tone pictures, with which he, like a magician, battled in order to control them . . . he does not play for the public and ask what the public would like most to hear." *Cäcilia* 20 (1839), 62–65.

37. This category is Gollmick's subdivision "c" of the "unavoidable" virtuosos, but it is nearly identical to the "untouchable" category, which is elaborated at great length. The main difference between them seems to be their nationality: the *virtuosi ambulanti* are Germans who have left and returned, whereas the "untouchable" virtuosos seem to be foreigners.

38. "Bei aller gründlichen musikalischen Bildung hat er sich doch die leichte, graziöse, geschmackvolle Tounure, die den Franzosen so liebenswürdig in der Gesellschaft macht, zu bewahren gewusst. Er erscheint mir wie ein französischer Philosoph, der die weltbewegenden Dogmen nicht mit ernstem Stirnrunzeln, nicht mit einer gedankenschweren und fast mystischen Geheimthuerei, sondern mit jenem gefälligen Lächeln, mit jener pikanten Leichtigkeit, mit jener Bonhommie, wie sie den überrheinischen Nachbaren eigen ist, vorträgt." *Berliner Figaro*, 26 March 1844.

39. Most of the leading pianists in Paris in the 1820s and early '30s were of German origin, including Herz, Friedrich Kalkbrenner, Stephen Heller, and J. P. Pixis. Even Liszt, who in his younger years was considered "German" by many observers in Paris, would qualify here.

40. In an article on Rossini, Schumann wrote of Herz: "Herz, the stenographer, who possesses no heart [Herz] save in his fingers, makes four hundred talers with a set of variations, while Marschner scarcely got more for the entire opera of *Hans Heiling*" (Schumann, *On Music and Musicians*, p. 235; original source: *Robert Schumanns Gesammelte Schriften über Musik und Musiker*, 5th ed. [Leipzig: 1914], vol. 2, p. 162). For another instance, see his disappointed reaction to a variation set of C. Krebs: "Herz and Lafont have varied the same theme. Let him go to them and learn French manners, coquettish ways, if he wishes to please with those" ("Variations for the Pianoforte," in Schumann, *Music and Musicians*, ed. Ritter, vol. 2, p. 429).

41. Richard Sennett, *The Fall of Public Man* (New York: 1974). See esp. chap. 8, "Personality in Public," which includes a discussion of Paganini and Liszt.

42. See Sennett's section "Charisma and *Ressentiment*," in ibid., pp. 277–81.

43. Gerald N. Izenberg, *Impossible Individuality: Romanticism, Revolution, and the Origins of Modern Selfhood, 1787–1802* (Princeton, N.J.: 1992), p. 8. The classic exposition of this element of Romanticism as manifest in English poetry is M. H. Abrams, *The Mirror and the Lamp: Romantic Theory and the Critical Tradition* (New York: 1953). See also his *Natural Supernaturalism: Tradition and Revolution in Romantic Literature* (New York: 1973).

44. Jerrold Siegel, *The Idea of the Self: Thought and Experience in Western Europe Since the Seventeenth Century* (Cambridge, Eng.: 1995), p. 403. My summary of Hegel's approach to the self is based on Siegel, pp. 397–426.

45. Ibid., p. 414.

46. Mary Hunter, "The Idea of the Performer in Early Romantic Aesthetics," *Journal of the American Musicological Society* 58, no. 2 (Summer 2005): 370.

47. Ibid., p. 383.

48. On the Hegelian influence in the writers of the *Neue Zeitschrift* circle, see Kariol Musiol, "Das Mozart-Bild des Davidsbündlers August Kahlert: Ein Beitrag zur Äesthetik der Spätromantik," in *Mozart-Jahrbuch 1983*, ed. R. Angermüller and D. Berke (Kassel: 1983), pp. 239–46; and in the same volume, "Der Einfluss der Philosophie Hegels auf das Mozart-Bild in der ersten Hälfte des 19. Jahrhunderts," pp. 257–61. Schumann, though decidedly less philosophical than these writers, would have encountered Hegelian ideas as a student of law in Heidelberg (1829–30). Hegel had lectured there from 1816–19, and theologian Karl Daub kept the Hegelian legacy alive there until his death in 1836. It should be noted here that although Hegel's writings were deeply influential in this period, their elusiveness led to much debate and to at least two starkly opposed camps of interpretation.

49. Krüger's familiarity with Hegel's ideas even leaves a direct trace in this article. The Dilettante says "Nun, wenn das nicht auf ein Hegel'sches Sophisma hinaus läuft, so weiss ich nicht, wo mir der Verstand geblieben" ("Virtuosenkonzert," p. 171).

50. This is the general approach of Richard Leppert and Stephen Zank, "The Concert and the Virtuoso," in *Piano Roles: Three Hundred Years of Life with the Piano* (New Haven: 1999), pp. 236–81; of James Deaville in "Liszt's Virtuosity and his Audience: Gender, Class, and Power in the Concert Hall of the Early 19th Century," *Hamburger Jahrbuch für Musikwissenschaft* 15 (1998): 281–300; and of Paul Metzner in *Crescendo of the Virtuoso: Spectacle, Skill and Self-Promotion in Paris During the Age of Revolution* (Berkeley: 1998).

51. English critic Morris Barnett, for example, reviewing Liszt's performance of Beethoven's "Emperor" Concerto, wrote: "The many liberties he took with the text were evidence of no reverential feeling for the composer. The entire concerto seemed rather a glorification of self, than the heart-feeling of the loving disciple." *Morning Post* (London), 18 August 1845.

52. *Iris im Gebiete der Tonkunst* 10, no. 41 (20 December 1839): 202.

53. Rellstab's *volte face* aroused the consternation of critic C. W. Spieker: "Men who were once calm and alert, with a pure taste and deep knowledge of music, like L. Rellstab, are moved as if in a magic circle by the power of the string-tamer, and sink in stupefied ravishment to the feet of the god from the champagne-surge of the pearly streams of golden tones." *Frankfurter patriotisches Wochenblatt*, 25 January 1843.

54. B. Thenmann, "Spiegelbilder aus Wien," (Wiener) *Theaterzeitung*, 18 July 1846, p. 682. I wish to thank William Weber for this reference.

55. Christopher Gibbs's essay in this volume shows, for example, how rich the world of piano concerts was in Vienna when Liszt played there in 1838.

56. Because my only purpose is to measure Liszt against some of the consensual views of the anti-virtuosity position, I leave aside the issue of how his virtuosity, and virtuosity more generally, positively embodied or epitomized the values of his historical era, a subject treated in several recent studies: Jim Samson, *Virtuosity and the Musical Work*, pp. 66–83; James Deaville, "Liszt's Virtuosity and its Audience"; Lawrence Kramer, "Franz Liszt and the Virtuoso Public Sphere: Sight and Sound in the Rise of Mass Entertainment," chap. 4 in *Musical Meaning: Toward a Critical History* (Berkeley and Los Angeles: 2002); Paul Metzner, *Crescendo of the Virtuoso*; Leppert and Zank, "The Concert and the Virtuoso."

57. Dana Gooley, *The Virtuoso Liszt* (Cambridge, Eng.: 2004), pp. 157–59.

58. For a trenchant reading of Liszt and contemporary anxieties over modernity, see Leppert and Zank, "The Concert and the Virtuoso."

59. Triest's earlier diagnosis of the same problem—the overexploitation of small towns to make money (found in column 740)—throws this critic's nostalgia into relief. If there were "purer" times, they were certainly not in the days when Hummel and Rode hit their stride.

60. Useful overviews of Liszt's concert programs are found in Michael Saffle, *Liszt in Germany, 1840–1845* (Stuyvesant, N.Y.: 1994), pp. 185–94 and app., and in Geraldine Keeling, "Liszt's Appearances in Parisan Concerts, 1824–1844," *Liszt Society Journal* 11 (1986): 22–34, and 12 (1987): 8–22.

61. "The public did not care for them, and the majority of pianists did not understand them. In Leipzig, even, where I played the Carneval at my second concert in the Gewandhaus, I did not succeed in obtaining my usual applause. . . . The frequent ill-success of my performances of Schumann's compositions, both in private circles and in public, discouraged me from including and keeping them in the programmes of my concerts which followed so rapidly on one another." Letter to J. W. von Wasielewski, 9 January 1857, published in *Letters of Franz Liszt*, ed. La Mara, trans. C. Bache, 2 vols. (New York: 1894), vol. 1, p. 310.

62. Dezsö Legány, *Franz Liszt: Unbekannte Presse und Briefe aus Wien 1822–1886* (Vienna-Cologne-Graz, 1984), p. 63. This report concerns Liszt's 1839 visit to Vienna. The pair of etudes was probably the same pair he had played in Vienna in 1838, one by Chopin and the other by Moscheles. It is possible that he planned to play two of the Paganini etudes, which he brought to Vienna in 1840.

63. Ibid., p. 80.

64. There are numerous variations on this as well. According to C. W. Spieker's review in *Frankfurter patriotisches Wochenblatt*, 25 January 1843, Liszt leapt directly from *Ave Maria* into *Erlkönig*.

65. C. W. Spieker, review in *Frankfurter patriotisches Wochenblatt*, 25 January 1843. Acccording to the music critic of Berlin's *Spenersche Zeitung* (7 January 1842, probably A. Schmidt), the *Ave Maria* "portrayed the sounds of the evening bells."

66. For a selection of responses registering this effect, see Gooley, *The Virtuoso Liszt*, pp. 27–29.

67. Dahlhaus opposes two models of performance, "virtuosity" and "interpretation," in *Nineteenth-Century Music*, pp. 134–41.

68. Legány, *Franz Liszt,* pp. 28–29. Emphasis original.

69. Dr. K., *Allgemeine Wiener Musik-Zeitung*, 26 March 1846. Quoted in Legány, *Franz Liszt*, p. 98. Emphasis original.

70. Hunter, "The Idea of the Performer," pp. 370–73.

71. One small piece of evidence shows with little ambiguity that Gollmick's third class of virtuosos, the "untouchable," was modeled directly on Liszt. In Gollmick's elaboration of the third class, he writes: "Do you see how his face bears not the expression of light-hearted pleasantness, but how his serious, finely chiseled features, his entire bearing

resembles that of a diplomat?" ("Virtuosity Today," p. 184). Eleven months later, after encountering Liszt at a private soiree, Gollmick writes: "My previous impression that Liszt was only a calculating diplomat soon disappeared." *Frankfurter Konversationsblatt*, 4 and 5 November 1843.

72. *Frankfurter Konversationsblatt*, 16 and 17 August 1840.

73. An example of this view, rooted in the Marxist intellectual tradition, can be offered from Hans Heinrich Eggebrecht: "[An aesthetic position that] presents music as an autonomous, internally coherent, concept-less world in itself, reflects the particular artistic need of bourgeois consciousness, that he seeks in the fictive, especially music, the emancipation that the real world denies him." Eggebrecht, *Musikalisches Denken* (Wilhelmshaven: 1977), p. 116.

74. Thus Kahlert wrote: "The unbelievable spread of dilettantism in our times [is evident in] the increasing production of piano instruments, the ease of traffic between large and small cities, the musical lending libraries, the journals, the spread of concerts and opera. Everyone hears so much, and so many different kinds of things, that his musical temperament *[Gemüth]* has no time to settle" (pp. 97–98).

75. See Pincherle, *Le Monde des virtuoses*, p. 21.

Prophet and Populace in Liszt's "Beethoven" Cantatas

RYAN MINOR

In a century when particularist national identities increasingly dominated music's public spheres, Franz Liszt moved with ease between nations and social movements: the Christian Socialism of the Saint-Simonians in France, a flourishing Hungarian nationalism, the "New German" avant-garde of Weimar and Bayreuth. Simply put, the generic breadth of Liszt's music and the wide range of his friendships, posts, and tours across the continent encapsulate an ideal of European cosmopolitanism unmatched by his musical peers. But Liszt's fluency in navigating the rough waters of nineteenth-century nationalism also brings to mind his virtuosity more generally. And for the most part, we have come to view Liszt's continental peregrinations and his support of multiple national projects solely through the lens of his career as a traveling virtuoso and pedagogue, or as a reflection of his outsized and seemingly adaptable persona. So conceived, nations and national publics figure primarily as easy referents of theatrical gesture (such as Liszt's "Hungarian" costume, donned after the 1838 floods) or as anonymous, hapless participants in a nascent mass culture nurtured by the "virtuoso public sphere."[1] In the schemata of Liszt's conquering virtuosity, Europe's peoples function all too easily as willing dupes in a cynical attempt to extract disposable identities—as well as cash—from audiences and the public spheres they have come to represent.[2]

Yet Liszt's engagement with Europe's national publics extended well beyond costumes and cadenzas. Although the question of opportunism may never entirely cease to haunt his cosmopolitan enthusiasms—cynical intent is impossible to disprove—recent considerations of Liszt's virtuosity have begun to complicate this charge by emphasizing the careful negotiations between Liszt and his many audiences.[3] Moreover, the myriad national projects to which Liszt contributed shared a number of lateral connections. Both

Liszt's cosmopolitanism as well as the nations it served were underwritten by a constellation of ideals—populism, collective sovereignty, and the increasingly interchangeable liturgies of church, nation, and art—whose convergence marks the cultural and political landscape of Europe in the nineteenth century. And in this sense, it was neither particularly difficult nor inconsistent for Liszt to have supported, and even adopted, multiple nationalities across the continent; there is perhaps no better evidence to support Carl Dahlhaus's supposition that nineteenth-century nationalist composition "was seen as a means, not a hindrance, to universality."[4]

Nowhere is this clearer than in the case of Liszt's choral music, where the promotion of a noble communal subject frequently underlies a variety of works spanning nations, genres, and political persuasions. To be sure, the corporate body at the heart of the choral music remains an abstraction; it is an "imagined community," a heady rhetorical construct borne more of high-minded idealism than any sustained engagement with the "real" peoples the works claim to envoice.[5] And as Paul Merrick has shown, much of Liszt's choral music stems from many of the same political, aesthetic, and religious convictions that informed those piano and symphonic works better known to us today; it would thus be a mistake to portray the choral compositions simply as good-natured community service written in penance for an otherwise high-flying solo career.[6] But a consideration of Liszt's choral music suggests that his commitment to the many social, political, and religious movements of the nineteenth century is a good deal more complicated than the sheer opportunism imputed to his virtuoso persona. Many of Liszt's choral works evince a kind of communal magnanimity—that is, a figurative attempt to employ "the people" as guiding muse and participants rather than audience alone—that has not always figured prominently in the reception of his virtuosity. Crucially, however, these choral compositions also betray an ambivalence as to the limits of that magnanimity.

This essay explores some of these complexities by focusing on Liszt's "Beethoven" cantatas of 1845 and 1870—two works that place front and center how a communal voice might be simultaneously national and universal, how the figure of the collective is to be reconciled with that of the singular artist, and how the burden of genres and musics past may be balanced with the onus of musical progress. In other words, the cantatas render in choral form several tensions marking Liszt's controversial career and nineteenth-century musical culture more generally. And although both compositions are largely forgotten today, they figured prominently in Liszt's compositional career. The 1845 cantata was his first work for mixed chorus and orchestra, and its performance at the unveiling of Bonn's Beethoven statue cemented Liszt's place among a cosmopolitan public of

Beethoven admirers. By contrast, the 1870 cantata was one of Liszt's final compositions for chorus and orchestra. It was written for Weimar's centenary celebration of Beethoven's birth, as well as for that year's meeting of the Allgemeine Deutsche Musikverein—a joint provenance that, as we will see, marks not only the nationalization but also the political manipulation of Beethoven's memory in service of a "New German" teleology of musical history. Negotiating these questions of nationality, progress, and the politics of memory is the chorus lying at the heart of both cantatas. Its varied treatment in the two works illuminates both the promise and the limitations of collective sovereignty in Liszt's aesthetics and indeed the larger musical world.

Contexts: Artist, God, *Volk*

Liszt traced his lifelong interest in choral music back to an 1825 visit to London, in which he was impressed by the massed children's choirs and St. Paul's Cathedral.[7] But although a noble seriousness underlies most of Liszt's compositions for chorus, it was only in the latter half of the century that he regularly began to write explicitly religious music. Many of his first choral compositions, much under the influence of Lamennais and the Saint-Simonians, were political in nature.[8] In addition to his advocacy of the German nationalist movement in "Das deutsche Vaterland" and the "Rheinweinlied" of the early 1840s, Liszt's choral works from the end of the decade illustrate a continued concern for political causes across Europe.[9] Chief among these later compositions is a triumvirate of *Männerchor* works from the late 1840s—*Le Forgeron, Hungaria 1848*, and an *Arbeiterchor*—stemming from Liszt's support of the workers' and Hungarian nationalist movements.[10] But Liszt's work, along with that of most European artists and thinkers, became less overtly political in the years following the failed 1848 revolutions. The 1850s witnessed sustained efforts at both large- and small-scale religious compositions, as well as secular occasional works stemming from his time in Weimar, such as choruses for the 1850 Herder festival.

His first large-scale religious work was the *Missa Solennis* of 1855, composed for the consecration of the cathedral in Gran. After several years' time concentrating mainly on the symphonic poems, Liszt announced his desire to "solve the oratorio problem"; the first of these compositions, finished in 1862, is *Die Legende von der heiligen Elisabeth*.[11] The work is built on chant melodies bearing a connection to Elisabeth (such as the hymn "In festo, sanctae Elisabeth"), Hungarian folk song and rhythms, and Liszt's telltale "cross" motive of a minor third enclosed within a perfect fourth.

Given its penchant for harmonic and dramatic effect, the oratorio comes as close as any of Liszt's works to his premise that the "religious music of the future" must unite the theater and the church.[12] (The *Christus* oratorio of 1866–72 comes close, however, as does the *Missa Solennis*—so much so that Hanslick complained that Liszt had "brought the Venusburg into the church.")[13] In fact, the *Elisabeth* oratorio was staged during Liszt's lifetime—albeit without his blessing—and its operatic performance became something of a cause célèbre among Wagnerian circles, Hans von Bülow having designated it a "spiritual drama."[14] But following *Christus* and the second "Beethoven" cantata, Liszt tended to eschew these works' lengthy forms and large performing forces. The intimate sacred compositions of his last decade, such as *Via Crucis* of 1878–79, have an intensity of both religious fervor—Liszt called it an "inner necessity of a Catholic heart"—and harmonic daring.[15] Hence *Ossa Arida* from 1879, for unison men's voices and organ with two players, has become a perennial favorite among biographers and analysts alike due to the radical conglomeration of thirds with which it begins.

As this short sketch of Liszt's choral works suggests, there is a general movement from the more explicitly political and secular works in the earlier stages of his compositional career toward the religious, and musically more ambitious, works of his middle and later years. Of course, such a scheme remains just that; the line between secular and sacred is often ambiguous at best, "high art" music in general grew increasingly complex in its formal and harmonic vocabularies throughout the century, and the changing political scene following both the 1848 revolutions and the Franco-Prussian War inevitably influenced the social contexts of choral music more generally. Yet these broader developments should not be seen as external elements that a consideration of Liszt's choral music must factor out; rather, they are the very preconditions of these works. As the political, religious, and musical landscapes shifted in the nineteenth century, so too did Liszt's contributions to the choral movement.

Liszt's choral music must also be understood within the institutional context of the choral societies, for it is here, in the cultural and political world of associational life, that choral music most explicitly participated in the public sphere of European nationality. In Germany in particular, liberalism, democracy, and nationalism all found fertile ground in these primarily bourgeois institutions seeking to exercise cultural and political autonomy.[16] Moreover, it was in the network of associations that the push for German unification found some of its most vociferous support among bourgeois liberals.[17] As the institutional locus for political movements claiming to represent "the people" rather than the church or particularist states, associations such as choral societies sought legitimization in what has become the highly overdetermined category of *das Volk*.[18] In line with the edifying promises accorded choral singing as well as associational life more generally, bourgeois intellectuals utilized the notion of the *Volk* as both the subject and object of their ennobling enterprise: that is, they argued that their associations were already constituted by the *Volk* and simultaneously functioned as disciplinary role models for an inchoate, ever-emerging *Volk*.[19] At once a rhetorically beneficial subject position and a distant object in need of ennobling pedagogy, the category of *das Volk* provided useful cover for a bourgeoisie whose high-minded claims to homespun indigeneity also kept at arm's length the more radical populism its liberal ideals spawned, but rarely embraced (universal suffrage, for instance, was not part of the liberal platform).[20]

Liszt's own choral aesthetics reflect this ambivalence. Indeed, the changing fortune of an imagined *Volk*—the extent to which the choral collective is accorded the figurative status as autonomous generating subject or dependent impoverished object in the exchange of religious, musical, or national sentiments—constitutes a central axis along which Liszt's choral music can be organized. His written formulation of the matter comes in the essay "On the Situation of Artists" (1835), in the section on "religious music of the future." Here, as John Williamson has pointed out, the influences of both Lamennais and the Saint-Simonians join forces to promote a model of religious song modeled after the songs of the people (such as the "Marseillaise").[21] Such music will be "patriotic, moral, political, and religious in nature . . . written for the people, taught to the people, and sung by the people." Yet this music is not from the people. In a clever modification of the dictum *vox populi vox dei*, Liszt retains both God and *Volk*, but the latter now serves as muse rather than author: "Come, O hour of deliverance, when poets and musicians, forgetting the 'public,' will only know one motto, 'The people and God.'"[22] The "religious music of the future" will ultimately stem from the genius, the artist-priest. The extent of this mediation, the tipping point between an avant-garde prophet's supervisory role and the collective's push for sovereign subjecthood, is a central animating tension in Liszt's contributions to the choral movement. And as the "Beethoven" cantatas make clear, this tension is amplified by both the musical conflict pitting the chorus's generic past against the progressive thrust of Liszt's *Zukunftsmusik*, as well as the societal implications of investing the chorus with its most idealistic utopian visions.

Although both cantatas quote extensively from the slow movement of Beethoven's "Archduke" Trio, op. 97, the Weimar work is not an updated version of the Bonn one, as Alan Walker has claimed.[23] The cantatas could hardly be more different: between them lie twenty-five years of Liszt's development as a composer, Beethoven's posthumous memorialization, and, most significant, the hardening boundaries between a communal voice issuing from below—understood as the collective recipients of Beethoven's legacy—and an increasingly authorial voice legislating from above. Indeed, it would not be a stretch to claim that the two works are differentiated by the revolutionary promise of the *Vormärz* and the straightened politics of Bismarck's new Germany, an era less immediately receptive to an earlier ideal of collective agency.[24] Who would claim Beethoven's legacy, how the music of the future would accommodate that of the past, and the respective roles that the artist-genius and the chorus-of-*Volk* would play in this musicosocial transformation are guiding themes of the two cantatas.

Bonn, 1845: Music and Presence

From the start, Liszt's multifaceted involvement with the Beethoven monument—as financial donor, composer, conductor, and resident virtuoso—attracted no small amount of publicity. He not only paid for the festival's hastily built concert hall (figure 1); he also featured prominently in two of the three concerts that made up the celebrations (figure 2). One newspaper quipped that it was a "Beethoven festival in honor of Liszt," and this view of both the 1845 festival and Liszt's cantata for it has remained intact by less sympathetic critics to this day.[25] The cantata has recently been portrayed by Alexander Rehding, for instance, as a kind of self-promoting monumentalism. But while the work's monumental aspirations are undeniable, it is less clear that the cantata represents Liszt as the sole recipient of those aspirations. Rehding's contention that the cantata served only to promote Liszt, to "consolidate his reputation as the chosen heir" and "instrumentaliz[e] Beethoven to further his own immortality," downplays the text of Liszt's cantata, which explicitly promotes the collective as Beethoven's immortal heir. And his reading of the cantata is also complicated by the other occasional works written for the festival, all of which emphasize a similar communal subject as guardians and recipients of Beethoven's timeless music.[26] Put quite simply, the "self" in Liszt's "self-promotion" is not Liszt alone, but Liszt among—and for—many.

As Liszt saw it, the cantata's text (written by the Jena poet and professor Bernhard Wolff) "is a sort of Magnificat of human genius conquered by God in the eternal revelation through time and space—a text which might apply equally well to Goethe or Raphael or Columbus as to Beethoven."[27] With Beethoven as such absent from most of the cantata, the role of

Figure 1. The "Artists' Concert" where the Bonn cantata was performed.

protagonist is taken on by the chorus of the *Völker* (see excerpts from the text, below). In Wolff's text, the *Völker* are caught in the currents of time, destined to perish because they never achieve permanence in the "book of world history." A prince may represent the people in a historical sense, but the *Volk* searches for someone among its ranks that can tell of its suffering, its aspirations, and its humanity to later generations. It is the genius, sent from the *Volk* but crowned by God, who lends those on earth "the reflection of brightest eternity." Beethoven is celebrated as such a genius, and the cantata ends with repeated *Heil*s to the composer.

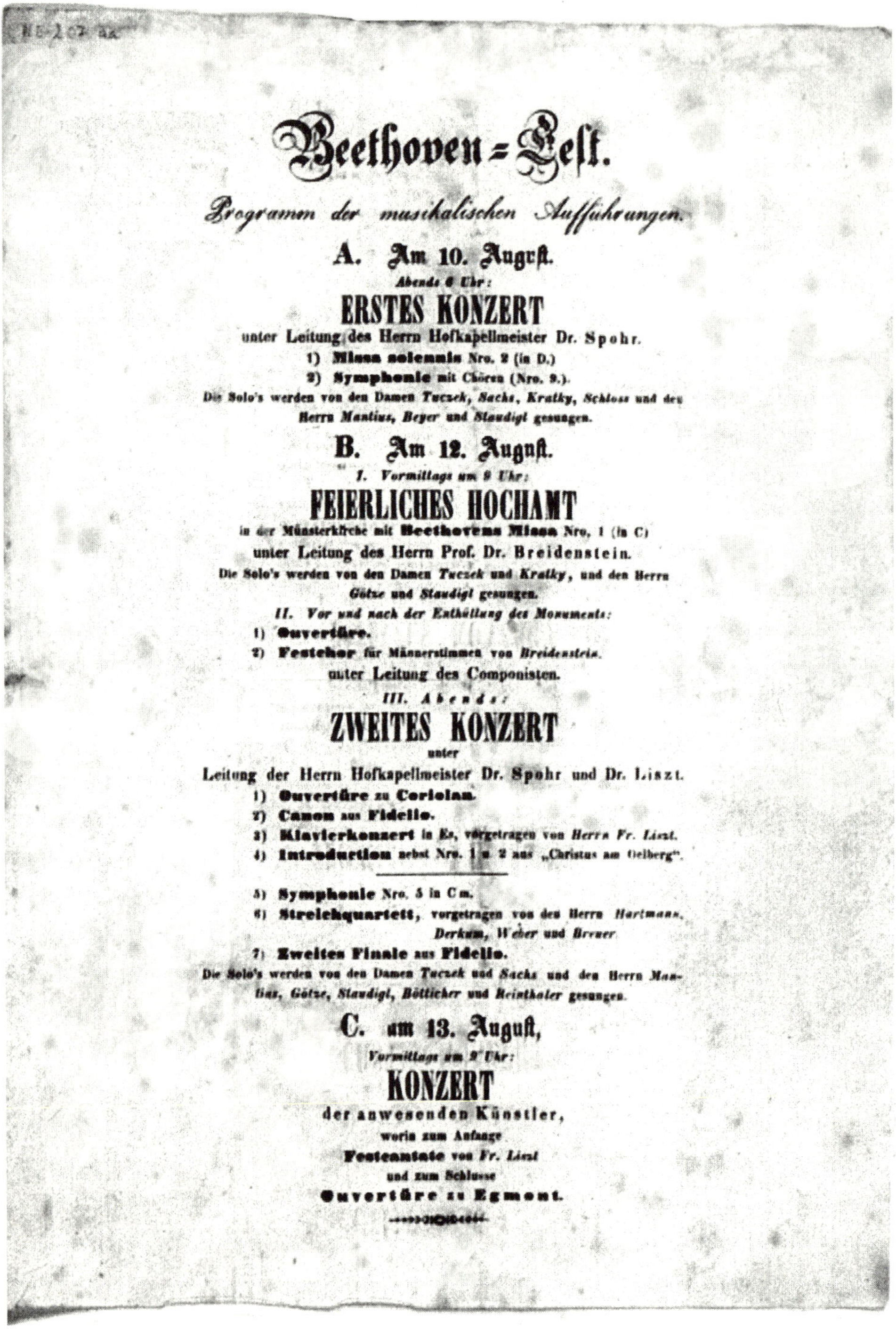

Beethoven-Fest.

Programm der musikalischen Aufführungen.

A. Am 10. August.

Abends 6 Uhr:

ERSTES KONZERT

unter Leitung des Herrn Hofkapellmeister Dr. Spohr.

1) **Missa solemnis** Nro. 2 (in D.)
2) **Symphonie** mit Chören (Nro. 9.)

Die Solo's werden von den Damen *Tuczek, Sachs, Kratky, Schloss* und den Herrn *Mantius, Beyer* und *Staudigl* gesungen.

B. Am 12. August.

I. Vormittags um 9 Uhr:

FEIERLICHES HOCHAMT

in der Münsterkirche mit **Beethovens Missa** Nro. 1 (in C)

unter Leitung des Herrn Prof. Dr. Breidenstein.

Die Solo's werden von den Damen *Tuczek* und *Kratky*, und den Herrn *Götze* und *Staudigl* gesungen.

II. Vor und nach der Enthüllung des Monuments:

1) **Ouvertüre.**
2) **Festchor** für Männerstimmen von *Breidenstein.*

unter Leitung des Componisten.

III. Abends:

ZWEITES KONZERT

unter

Leitung der Herrn Hofkapellmeister Dr. Spohr und Dr. Liszt.

1) **Ouvertüre zu Coriolan.**
2) **Canon aus Fidelio.**
3) **Klavierkonzert** in Es, vorgetragen von Herrn Fr. Liszt.
4) **Introduction** nebst Nro. 1 u. 2 aus „Christus am Oelberg".

5) **Symphonie** Nro. 5 in Cm.
6) **Streichquartett**, vorgetragen von den Herrn *Hartmann, Derkum, Weber* und *Breuer.*
7) **Zweites Finale aus Fidelio.**

Die Solo's werden von den Damen *Tuczek* und *Sachs* und den Herrn *Mantius, Götze, Staudigl, Bötticher* und *Reinthaler* gesungen.

C. am 13. August,

Vormittags um 9 Uhr:

KONZERT

der anwesenden Künstler,

worin zum Anfange

Festcantate von *Fr. Liszt*

und zum Schlusse

Ouvertüre zu Egmont.

Figure 2. Program for the Bonn musical festivities.

Excerpts from the Bonn Cantata's Text

I

Kommt und bringet euer Bestes,
kommt, ihr Hohen und ihr Niedern
mit den reichsten, schönsten Liedern.
Heut ist wahrhaft ein Tag des Festes

Come and give of your best,
come, high-born and lowly,
with the richest, most beautiful
  songs,
today is truly a day of festivity.

Es ist der Weihetag der Genius!

It is the day consecrated to genius.

II

Gleich den Wogen des Meeres
rauschen die Völker alle
vorüber im Zeitenstrom.

Like sea waves,
all peoples rush by
in the river of time.

Heute kommt, was morgen fleucht,
heute wirkt, was morgen stirbt,
für den Untergang erzeugt,
nimmer Dauer sich erwirbt.

What comes today is gone
  tomorrow,
what is effective today dies
  tomorrow,
doomed to its decline,
never gaining permanence.

III

Die Völker, die vorüberzogen,
versanken in die Nacht der Nächte:
nur ihrer Herrscher Namen geben Kunde
von ihrem Tun dem späteren Geschlechte.

The peoples who passed by
sank into the night of nights:
only the names of their rulers tell
later generations of their deeds.

In dem Buch der Weltgeschichte . . .
tritt der Fürst ein für sein Land.

In the book of world history…
the ruler speaks for his country.

Aber soll der Menschheit Streben
Auch entfluten mit dem Leben?
Wird denn Nichts den fernsten Jahren
Was sie wirkt aufbewahren?

But should humanity's ambitions
also recede with its life?
Will nothing of what it achieved
be retained for posterity?

Arme Menschheit, schweres Los!
Wer wird von dir entsendet
an der Tage Schluss?
Der Genius!
In seinem Wirken ewig wahr und groß.

Poor humanity, heavy fate!
Who from you will be sent
at the end of time?
The genius!
Forever true and great in his effect.

IV

Er . . . der Menschheit eint mit Gott . . .	He . . . who joins humanity with
ist's, der das Schicksal versöhnet.	God . . .
	is the one who placates fate.
Heilig! heilig! heilig!	Holy! holy! holy!
Des Genius Walten auf Erden,	The genius's sway over earth
er umhüllt das himmlische Werden,	envelopes heaven,
der Unsterblichkeit sicherstes Pfand.	the surest pledge of immortality.
Solch' ein Fest hat uns verbunden!	Such a festival has united us!
Und es soll in fernsten Tagen	And until the end of time
noch sein Bild der Nachwelt sagen,	his image will tell posterity
wie die Mitwelt ihn verehrt.	that his contemporaries honored
	him.
Heil! Heil! Beethoven Heil!	Hail! Hail! Beethoven, hail!

As Rehding points out, Wolff's text seems surprisingly anti-royalist, given both the financial support by several royal houses and their physical presence at the festival. Especially in the *Vormärz*, an appeal to the *Volk* or *Völker* was not without political meaning, particularly in conjunction with a text that stressed a rupture between the *Volk* and its political representation.[28] Yet the anti-royalist bent to Wolff's text is also offset in several ways. For one, the *Volk* is never explicitly the Germanic *Volk*, and repeated references to *Völker* generalize the sentiments beyond any particular nation. Not unlike the *Völker* populating Beethoven's *Der glorreiche Augenblick* of 1814, this is an essentially anonymous grouping of peoples that any of Europe's nations could have formed. (Although Rehding notes that the liberal German national flag can be made out in illustrations of the Bonn festival.[29]) Notably, the chorus switches to second-person in those sections of the cantata that narrate the plight of the *Völker*—a change in poetic voice that distances the Bonn festivity and its performers from the freighted text. At the same time, however, the chorus claims at the cantata's close that "this celebration has united us," and this self-referentiality serves to reconnect the choral participants to the liberal narrative that forms the core of the cantata's text.

Wolff's use of a communal protagonist may seem odd in a text ostensibly about Beethoven, but it was by no means unusual; virtually all of the text's sentiments were expressed on other occasions during the Bonn festivities. Indeed, an examination of the other festival texts reveals a consistent attempt, varying only in intensity, to articulate a collective subject as the beneficiary of Beethoven's music, his perceived timelessness, and the Bonn festivity itself. Four works serve as useful points of comparison: a *Festchor* by H. K. Breidenstein, also written for the statue's unveiling, with a text by Wilhelm Smets; two "festival greetings" for the arrival of Beethoven's statue in Bonn on 23 July, written by E. M. Kneisel, secretary of the Bonn committee; and "Beethoven," a festival poem written for the unveiling by Wolfgang Müller, a Rhenish doctor and future member of the 1848 Frankfurt parliament.[30] (A drawing of the statue at the heart of the festivities is shown in figure 3.)

Just as Wolff employs imagery of redemption and the genius's heavenly provenance (Beethoven is "crowned by God," revealing his "immortality"), Müller's poem refers to Beethoven as the savior who accomplished what others could not: "They [those who lived before Beethoven] were only like voices in the desert; / you are the savior who found the shore."[31] Smets's ode also uses religious imagery—"From heaven the beams of consecration / fall upon the sons of earth"—and Kneisel's second *Festgruß* claims that Bonn had been "chosen" as Beethoven's dwelling.[32] This biblical rhetoric accrues a more specific meaning in conjunction with the nationalist and sometimes martial language of the poems. Müller refers to the Ninth Symphony as a "song battle" *(Liederschlacht)*, the sounds of which announce an approaching chorus of the *Völker*.[33] Smets invokes the "all-conquering power of the human voice" and the "powerful fatherland," and Kneisel, by far the most subdued, emphasizes Bonn's connections with "all of Germany in association [*im Verein*]."[34] Wolff's text, on the other hand, avoids any national references.

If, as Kneisel's poem claims, the monument signals Beethoven's communal reentry, it also signals a temporal one as well, and it is in this removal of the temporal boundaries between the dead composer and the festival participants that the Bonn texts offer perhaps their most radical proposal: namely, that a Beethovenian timelessness could be conferred upon the Bonn celebrants. In Wolff's text this claim is made at the end, when the chorus announces that the monument was erected by Beethoven's contemporaries (*Mitwelt*): "In distant days / his image will tell posterity [*Nachwelt*] / how contemporaries honored him." Turning the Bonn participants into Beethoven's "contemporaries" not only erases the time between the ceremonies and the composer's death eighteen years earlier, it also gives the celebrants a timelessness of their own. Without a past, and defined only by the future—via the monument they leave for posterity—the Bonn

Figure 3. Beethoven statue in Bonn, by Ernst Hähnel.

"contemporaries" who built the statue themselves gain an immortality and a twofold place in the "book of world history": both as the *Volk* from which Beethoven came and whom he represents, and as those who honored him.

A similar claim is made in the other festival texts. For Smets, the festival participants are an anticipatory generation from every time and place ("Vorgeschlecht von jeder Zone, jeder Zeit") that will honor Beethoven. Beethoven enables the *Volk*'s posterity as much as its statue guarantees his: as the object of praise of "every *Volk*" he ensures a continuity in time and space for those who honor him, and in building the statue, Smets's "Vorgeschlecht" sees its own immortality as well as Beethoven's certified. It is worth noting in this context that Smets's poem consistently addresses Beethoven in the present tense, a circumstance fitting a composer and a *Volk* without a past. Smets's is a Beethovenian *Volk* that has escaped time and space: it is a *Volk* of the future.[35] For Müller, Smets, and indeed Wolff, Beethoven represents nothing less than the very promise of posterity, a future in and enabled by music. Those who recognize in Beethoven and his music the galvanizing force of communal expression can find the means of both creating and prolonging heaven on earth. But it is important to recognize that this music, not unlike the festival in its honor, is not simply an object of veneration. It is also one of generation. And it is in this sense that we turn to the cantata Liszt wrote to Wolff's text, for it is in the literal performance of Beethoven's music (the "Archduke" variations) that the work's communal subjects claim to be united—both with themselves and, it seems, with Beethoven himself, who is now claimed as a contemporary.

In Liszt's cantata the extended quotation of Beethoven's music comes at the end of the work. As Berlioz was the first to point out, it serves as an apotheosis.[36] The moment is carefully prepared; it not only concludes the central narration of the cantata—the emergence of the genius—but is itself enclosed by self-referential markers beginning and ending the cantata: an announcement at the beginning of the work that "today is a festival day" and the claim at the work's close that the festival has united its participants. Thus the "festival" to which the chorus refers, that which unites its participants, is not simply the Bonn festival in general but the middle narrative of the cantata, and most specifically the performance of Beethoven's music at that section's close. Not only does the inclusion of the "Archduke" material illustrate the communal effect of performing Beethoven's music, but Liszt's treatment of it, which both quotes the music and fuses it with his own, also serves to erase the temporal boundaries between Beethoven and the Bonn celebrants.

Yet before Beethoven arrives to escort his celebrants into heroic timelessness, Liszt makes sure to provide his forlorn *Volk* due pathos. Example 1

Example 1. Liszt, *Bonner Beethoven-Kantate,* no. 3, mm. 1–25.

Example 1 continued

Example 1 continued

shows the beginning of the cantata's third section, the depiction of the *Völker* that lack representation and a temporal anchor in the "currents of time." This andante—"sad," according to Liszt's tempo marking—begins with a wandering cello line that suggests B minor, the local tonic, yet avoids a stable cadence. Its metric grouping is even more unstable, as the fermatas and accents avoid strong beats and create a continued sense of metric displacement. At measure 8 the "wandering," evocative of the *Völker* without their genius, is followed by a rather maudlin accompanimental figure consisting of a descending tetrachord—the "emblem of lament"—in the lower strings and a repeated theme above it. This ostinato-like theme spans four beats, in contrast to the notated triple meter of the tetrachord below it; similarly, its dissonant passing tones against the bass add a further note of pathos.[37] The chorus's hesitant declamation in mm. 12–17 follows suit. If we are not entirely transported to a Baroque lament, Liszt's music nonetheless conveys certain stylistic traits that confer a similar sense of seriousness and nobility upon the collective subject depicted in the text.[38]

Following the B-minor lament it is announced that the prince will stand up for his country (Example 2). With a switch to B major, a dash of rhythmic brio—quick, marcatissimo triplets—and a broad new melody whose dip into flat six at measure 40 references the harmonic flavor of the whole cantata, the music appears to announce the *Völker*'s savior. A high-lying D-major tenor solo on this material starting at measure 49 seems to confirm this impression; just as the chorus sang of the *Völker*'s plight, so too would a gallant tenor sing of its redeemer. Although this setting appears almost too laudatory for the text's ultimate message, such heroic music marking the prince's advocacy for his people may have been a conciliatory gesture in light of the work's more radical sentiments. Still, Liszt does offer one discordant note. At measure 48, when the text first refers to the "Fürst" and his purely political representation of the people, the harmony suddenly shifts from B major to G minor, as if to register that the heroic figure promoted in the preceding music and text is not its ultimate hero. The prince's G-minor chord, a quick shudder that leads to the tenor's D-major, signals

Example 2. *Bonner Beethoven-Kantate*, no. 3, mm. 37–50.

Example 2 continued

Example 2 continued

dystopia rather than utopia, the minor flat-six as opposed to the major flat-six in which the genius will eventually appear. Indeed, this B-major section is immediately followed by an operatic soprano recitative emphasizing the shortcomings of the prince. The genius is announced finally at measure 129 with a return to E major and the fanfare that began the cantata; it is preceded, notably, by flat-six C major. The final section of the cantata ensues, starting with the "Archduke" quotation in C major.

It seems that Liszt had a particular fondness for the "Archduke" Trio. The work figured prominently in his Parisian concerts in the later 1830s, and he performed it throughout Germany in the years leading up to the Bonn festival.[39] Yet the fact that he would choose the slow movement for his artist-prince, and that he would give this quotation the tempo marking *Andante religioso*, corresponds to a number of tropes in both Beethoven reception in general and the Bonn festivities in particular. For one, by the time of Liszt's cantata an interpretive tradition was in place which viewed the Beethovenian slow movement generally in religious terms. Berlioz referred to the Adagio of the Fourth Symphony as the song of the Archangel Michael, and Friedrich Schmidt, an advisor to the Saxon court, contributed a poem to the 1846 *Beethoven-Album* in which the slow movement of the Ninth Symphony takes place on the "other side of the clouds."[40] Carl Czerny, moreover, specifically claimed that the third movement of the "Archduke" Trio has a "holy-religious" character.[41] The same Friedrich Schmidt also added words to the "Archduke" variations for the Bonn celebrations, although it is not clear whether he did so after learning of Liszt's cantata; Schmidt's setting, entitled "Hymne von Goethe und Ludwig van Beethoven," used the text "wer darf ihn nennen" from *Faust*.[42]

Schmidt's title reflects the hymnlike character of the opening measures: its simple, stepwise melody, calm homophony, and measured phrase divisions (Example 3). Yet beyond these opening measures, there is little stylistic reference to religious music per se, especially given the avowedly secular genre of theme and variations. The religious nature of the movement seems to stem more from a prevailing sense of godly presence than one of human prayer. T. W. Adorno's mid-twentieth-century description of the "Archduke" movement captures some of this sense: he heard an effect of "expressing tranquility through motion," which he likened to the "personification and hypostatization of the 'immanence' or 'presence' of God."[43] In the "Archduke" variations this tranquility was a result of renouncing the "symphonic mastery of time"; the gesture "is that of setting time free, as if with an exhalation of breath, and as if it were impossible to linger on the paradoxical peak of the symphonic. Time claims its right. . . ."[44] Time does indeed "claim its right" in the movement, and on several levels.

Example 3. Beethoven, "Archduke" Trio, op. 97, beginning of third movement.

Example 3 continued

Obviously, the nature of theme and variations itself involves the sort of repetition and return that would generally deny the sense of constant development demanded by the "symphonic mastery of time." The "Archduke" variations in particular always adhere closely to the theme, which remains audible and for the most part unchanged throughout. Moreover, the theme itself is structured around a return of sorts: the second phrase, starting at measure 17, leads back to the material of the opening measures at mm. 19–20, thus momentarily drawing this material into an almost cyclical relationship to itself. In general, the music's expansive temporal and spatial unity accords with Liszt's statement, quoted earlier, that the text celebrates "human Genius conquered by God in the eternal revelation through time and space."

For the most part, Liszt's quotation (Example 4) is straightforward. He puts the music in C major rather than the original D major. His boldest

Example 4. *Bonner Beethoven-Kantate,* no. 4.

step, at least for present-day listeners, is the addition of Wolff's text to Beethoven's instrumental melody. But no contemporary seems to have voiced any objections to it; adding texts to Beethoven's instrumental music was simply a common practice.[45] What did draw response from critics was Liszt's orchestration, which garnered almost unanimous praise.[46] His practice of "developing instrumentation" throughout the quotation is clear from the start.[47] The theme is first played by horns, bassoons, and trumpets; at the repetition of the first phrase, the lower horns and trumpets drop out and winds and the tenor solo enter; and at measure 13 in the trio, the tenor sings not the melody but an arpeggio line implied, but never written out as such, in Beethoven's original.

The rest of the variations continue much in this manner, with changing orchestration as well as varied voicing for the chorus and soloists, who often alternate the theme, an accompanimental line taken from Beethoven, or a descant lightly varying or implied in the original. Liszt simplifies some of the inner voices, evens out some of the syncopation, and skips entirely the second and third variations, perhaps because their filigree passagework could not so easily have been rendered by the large chorus. The transposition from D major to C major is important: it places the material in connection with the harmonic palette of the rest of the cantata, where C major as flat six was so frequent. Flat six itself may have had an idyllic connotation in the nineteenth century: Thomas Keith Nelson has proposed that it functions as the "Arcadian Pastoral," an "oasis apart from the ongoing drama."[48] Although the variations were perched on the mediant rather than flat six in Beethoven's trio (that is, D major in a B-flat-major work), in Liszt's cantata the variations, set on flat six, seem a world away from the E-major fanfare. Yet at measure 131 (Example 5), Liszt makes the flat-six relation dramatically clear. Shortly before the end of what would be the fifth and last variation in the original, Liszt breaks off the quotation on the dominant, and after a fermata and a low tremolo on A♯ and B, the opening fanfare of the cantata sounds in measure 134, with the bottom Bs raised to C♯s as yet another flat-six coloring. The chorus sings "Heil Beethoven!" on unison Es, and soon the entire chorus and orchestra enter on the "Archduke" material, this time in a "variation" in the tonic E major starting at measure 143 composed entirely by Liszt himself. With the tremolos, *fff* marking, repeated *Heil*s, and exclusion of all melodic material except the core of the "Archduke" theme, this moment would seem to mark Beethoven's apotheosis.

This is also the very moment where we might locate another apotheosis as well, for here the massed performance forces come together as they have not before, and it is directly after this last "quotation" of the "Archduke"

Example 5. *Bonner Beethoven-Kantate,* no. 4, mm. 128–50.

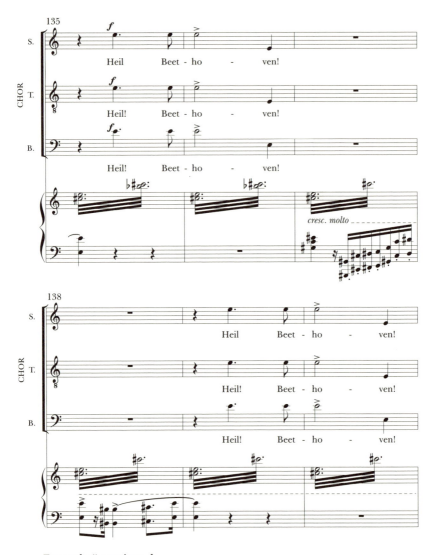

Example 5 continued

Example 5 continued

Example 5 continued

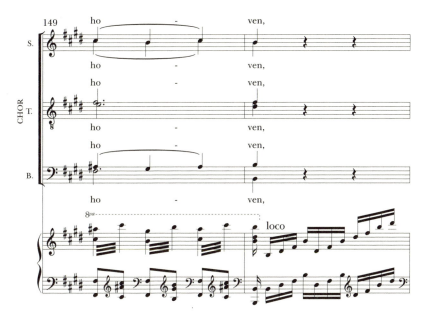

Example 5 continued

music that the fanfare enters once again, and the chorus claims that the festival has united them: unified through Beethoven's music, the Bonn collective seems to have its own apotheosis. To be sure, Liszt's cantata all but names Beethoven a god. But could Beethoven, the "heaven-sent" genius-prince and godly presence in Liszt's "Archduke" variations, also cohabit that music along with the festival participants, as the Bonn texts claim? Put another way: can the flat-six idyll accommodate only a deity?

Perhaps—but perhaps not. The difficulty lies in both Beethoven's and Liszt's compositions. Adorno saw in the "Archduke" variations and those of Beethoven's op. 111 a leave-taking. This reading of the latter work, itself immortalized in Thomas Mann's *Doktor Faustus*, has received considerable attention from scholars concerned with Adorno's diagnosis of Beethoven's late style.[49] But Adorno's comments addressed both variation movements, and they seem particularly relevant to Liszt's quotation of the earlier one:

> [T]he true power of illusion in Beethoven's music—of the "dream in stars eternal"—is that it can invoke what has not been as something past and nonexistent. Utopia is heard only as what has already been.

The music's inherent sense of form changes what has preceded the leave-taking in such a way that it takes on a greatness, a presence in the past which, within music, it could never achieve in the present.[50]

Adorno located the leave-taking at the end of the movements. The choice is logical, since the last set of variations marks a noticeable change in both the variation procedure and Beethoven's harmonic vocabulary (Example 6). The variation is much more developmental than the others: it moves to F major before its dominant cadence at mm. 147–48, and the repeat of the first phrase modulates to E major by measure 155, signaling harmonic fluctuations that do not resolve until measure 174. Phrases are broken up and repeated at mm. 152–54 and mm. 157–62, which furthers the sense of "symphonic" development. This "developing variation" (literally and figuratively) signals the reemerging "symphonic mastery of time," in Adorno's words. The end of the variation seems to regain some of its timeless expansiveness, but it flows immediately into the next movement: once again at the "peak of the symphonic," the music endows the "presence in the past," the variations suspended in time, with a utopian greatness as the open cadence leads into the final movement.

It is precisely this moment, when the illusion of godly presence and "stars eternal" dissipates in Beethoven's variations, that Liszt intervenes (see measure 131 in Example 5) by pulling the "Archduke" music into the E-major tonic and providing his own variation of Beethoven's theme. Where Beethoven takes his leave, Liszt brings him back, and where Beethoven reenters time, Liszt denies it altogether. Liszt absorbs the open-ended, "leave-taking" variation into the festival music, and at the "new" variation starting at m. 143 it is no longer the case that Liszt's music is looking back on Beethoven's, or that Beethoven's is sounding in posterity. The two are contemporaneous. And their contemporaneity is reflected in the text: it is here that the singers claim to inhabit Beethoven's *Mitwelt*. Of course, taken alone the "Archduke" variations quite literally demand music in, if not of, the future—a *Nachwelt*—since they end on an open cadence, a B-flat seventh chord.[51] In 1870 Liszt was to solve this problem by placing the quotation at the beginning of the cantata, as an extended slow introduction. But in 1845 Liszt not only composed music to follow Beethoven's (the restatement of the fanfare and prince themes), music that seems to absorb Beethoven's own; he also recomposed Beethoven after the latter had taken his leave. In writing an additional "variation," and doing so in the tonic, Liszt and the collective he envoices did more than claim contemporaneity, a mutual presence in music. They made Beethoven's music their own.

Example 6. Beethoven, op. 97, third movement, fifth variation.

Example 6 continued

Weimar, 1870: Absence and Telos

Such claims had a different resonance in Weimar twenty-five years later. The intervening years had brought with them a panoply of composers and schools; there was, as Ferdinand Hiller proudly (if ambivalently) noted, "too much music."[52] For most contemporaries Beethoven was firmly a cultural memory: the likes of F. G. Wegeler, Ferdinand Ries, and Anton Schindler, all of whom knew Beethoven personally and had attended the Bonn festival, had no equivalents at the Weimar celebrations save for Liszt himself. The disappearance of a living memory of Beethoven gave way to the need for an heir apparent, and naming Beethoven's successor lay at the heart of the New German debates that had engulfed the German musical establishment for over a decade (and would continue to do so).[53] Brahms, of course, was made the standard-bearer on one side, although at this point he had yet to write a symphony; Berlioz had been dubbed the "French Beethoven."[54] The *Weihekuss* (kiss of consecration) Liszt purportedly received from Beethoven in 1823 had set in motion a series of popular images that sought to claim his Beethovenian pedigree not only for German nationalist narratives but for pan-European ones as well; Danhauser's well-known *Liszt at the Piano*, picturing Beethoven's bust and, among others, Rossini and Hugo, was initially titled *Eine Weihemoment Liszts*.[55] Perhaps most famously, Richard Wagner's commemorative "Beethoven" essay of 1870 places Beethoven in a nationalist telos ending with Wagner himself.

Such a telos had its institutional home in the Allgemeine Deutsche Musikverein (hereafter ADMV), which was founded by Franz Brendel explicitly to promote the New German cause.[56] Although the association seems never to have had a particularly large membership, its concerts of new music organized for the annual meetings received substantial attention in the press, and the association was seen as a vigorous proponent of property rights for its composers.[57] Liszt was named honorary president in 1873, and served as its public representative. Unlike the Bonn festivities, there was presumably little dispute whether Liszt would be a suitable composer for the association's festival cantata. Along with Liszt's contribution, there were works by Beethoven and compositions from ADMV members, such as a piano quintet by Joachim Raff, a Lacrymosa by Felix Draeseke, and Saint-Saëns' *Les Noces de Prométhée*. Beethoven was represented by the *Missa Solennis* and several other late works (opp. 106, 131, and 135).[58] Liszt's cantata, which was both a "new" work and quotes Beethoven's music, served as a link between the two honored parties of the Weimar festival: it aims to praise Beethoven as well as the music of the future.[59]

Liszt's Weimar cantata shares with its Bonn forebear a distinct lack of national sentiment, although musical references to Bach and Wagner provide a strongly Germanic accent.[60] The Weimar work also follows the Bonn one in ending on a self-referential note, with the claim "the highest that life preserves of spiritual power, to him it was given today, to him it was imposed. Hail Beethoven, Hail!" The 1870 cantata, likewise scored for chorus, orchestra, and soloists, similarly employs an extended quotation of the "Archduke" variations, although this time as an opening movement. But here—and most notably here—the similarities end. Beethoven and his music now seem to be memories: both in the literal sense, since almost a half-century had passed since his death and its quotation of the "Archduke" material recalls not only Beethoven's original but also the 1845 work, and in the sense that Beethoven and his music were no longer claimed as a living presence. Now the object of a purely cultural memory—there are no claims for its everyday currency—Beethoven's music seems to sound only at a distance. Example 7 shows the beginning of the cantata and its mysterious introduction by the strings and horns. Heard in retrospect, the introduction first outlines the mediant, followed by the submediant, before arriving at Beethoven's original D-major tonic for the subsequent "Archduke" material. But as it sounds, without harmonic context, the chord progression is not without mystery. It seems to be taking us to a faraway place: the introductory chords function as a quotation mark.[61] Whereas the fanfare opening and closing of the 1845 cantata will eventually signal a fusion with Beethoven's music, its living presence, the opening measures of the 1870 work signal that music's distance.

Unlike the Bonn cantata, the Weimar one gives the "Archduke" variations in full, in their original D-major tonic, and they even end on the original's open cadence on the B-flat seventh chord—a momentary foray into a more chromatic space that has led one commentator to claim mistakenly that Liszt wrote the ending himself.[62] In Axel Schröter's words, the 1870 quotation is a "pure translation" of the trio's variations for full orchestra; he even retains the violin and cello lines note for note.[63] The variations have no text. The hymn topos of the opening measures in the original variations (to which the title of Schmidt's 1845 setting alluded) is emphasized in Liszt's orchestration for wind choir and horns, such that the tone of communal worship in Beethoven's original now seems to be honoring Beethoven himself. Liszt's orchestration is an act of faithful homage: it suggests Beethoven's full canonization, but with it the crystallization of his music into inviolable citation.

The "Archduke" material, which Liszt published separately, is labeled as an introduction.[64] The cantata that follows is not a small-scale work, as

Example 7. Liszt, *Beethoven-Cantate*, no. 1, opening.

Liszt himself acknowledged.[65] The text was written by Adolph Stern, a member of the ADMV board of directors, and upon Liszt's request the poet and historian Ferdinand Gregorovius made several changes.[66] The text is quite lengthy, and although Liszt offers a mostly syllabic setting with little textual repetition, the work is arguably too long.[67] Even more so than he had in *Christus* or *Die Legende von der heiligen Elisabeth*, both recently completed, Liszt frequently assigns large chunks of text to unaccompanied recitative for the soloists as a means of getting through it all. But unlike the earlier oratorios there are no individual numbers—real or implied—nor any substantive musical repetition to break the narrative into readily intelligible parts after the end of the instrumental introduction; the only recurring motivic material is a short deformation of the "Archduke" theme that is occasionally employed to refer to the coming prophet. For the most part, the cantata consists of long patches of unaccompanied recitative, homophonic choral declamation, and orchestral quotations from Beethoven's instrumental music. Recognizing the work's potential shortcomings, Liszt wrote to Baron August, "Supposing that it's a flop, at least it will be a painfully deserved one."[68]

At the heart of the problem lies the text, which is shown on the next two pages in a highly shortened, though substantively unaltered, version. Despite its length, the text offers little more than a standard narrative of emergence: darkness penetrated by the light of a star; the coming of the prophet; and an encomium to the genius figure (Beethoven is only named at the end).[69] It is a standard story, and indeed one familiar from Beethoven's own "Trauerkantate" for Joseph II and its famous soprano solo with chorus—later incorporated into *Fidelio*—on the text "Da stiegen die Menschen ans Licht." But in Beethoven's work the "emergence" is countered by Joseph II's death, and the subsequent return of the opening lament makes the otherwise standard narrative much more poignant. In Liszt's cantata, the only substantial embellishment to this narrative is a description of sounds and sights that the cantata's choral subjects do not understand. They are awoken by an unknown sound ("Do you hear the melody, not bells, not song?") and they are perplexed by stars above the Rhine. Unable to interpret the phenomena, they call for the wise old man for an explanation; he foresees the coming of a "melodic prophet," sent from God, who will transform human suffering into symphonies. The cantata closes with a paean to music as Beethoven's star rises again to the heavens.

If the cantata is nominally set in 1770, insofar as it narrates Beethoven's arrival on earth, its references belong solely to 1870. This is evident most notably in the cantata's narration of the circumstances before Beethoven arrives. In place of the total darkness and despair found in the Bonn cantata, the Weimar narrative simply describes a winter night full of heavenly light. Although Stern employs strongly religious language to portray Beethoven as a savior figure—he is the heaven-sent prophet who will sound the "great last judgment"—Beethoven seems to enter a world considerably less needy of salvation; all that the community portrayed in the cantata seems to lack is an explanation of Beethoven's appearance. This change in focus marks a systemic tension in the cantata, which tries to posit Beethoven as a singular prophet and simultaneously allow for other prophetic voices, namely those articulating the New German credo. If the Weimar cantata solved the problem of writing music to follow the "Archduke" variations by placing them at the beginning of the work, it created a possibly bigger problem of narrating Beethoven's arrival *after* his

Sternenschimmernde,	Stars glittering,
eisesflimmernde	an icy glimmering
Winternacht voll himmlischen	winter's night full of heavenly
Scheins . . .	glow . . .
rauschen die Wellen,	the waves rush,
glänzen silbern die Fluthen	silvery gleams the flow of the
des Rhein's.	Rhine.
Kam nicht ein Tönen,	Was that not a note
das uns vom Schlummer . . .	that woke us from our slumber?
erweckte?	
Viel Töne schwirren leise,	Many sounds whir softly,
bald froh, bald seltsam trübe.	now merry, now clouded strangely
Ja, eintausend Sterngebilde	Yes, a thousand stars
erglänzen ob dem Rhein.	sparkle over the Rhine.
Hört ihr die Weise?	Do you hear the melody?
Nicht Glockenschall, nicht Sang.	Not bells, not song.
Sehet empor, und der Himmel	Look above, heaven gleams
schimmert und blaut,	bluely,
wie wir's nimmer und nimmer	as we've never ever seen it before.
geschaut.	
Seltsamer Schauer hält uns umfasst.	A peculiar shiver holds us tight.
Ruft unsern weisen würdigsten	Call our wise and most worthy
Greis.	sage.
Er wird uns deuten den	He will explain to us the
Wunderschein.	wondrous glow.
Vater, Berather!	Father, adviser!
Kannst du uns deuten das Wunder	Can you explain to us the night's
der Nacht?	wonder?

Es lebt die alte Sage	There is the old legend
von Zeiten fromm und fern,	from distant, pious times
von einem Feiertage	of a festival day
ihn kündiget ein Stern.	announced by a star.
Wenn tief die Himmel klingen	When heaven deeply rings
in Sphärenmelodien,	in melodies of the spheres,
dann kommt am Himmels Bogen	then on heaven's arch
ein Cherub ernst und mild,	comes a cherub solemn and gentle
durch Winternacht gezogen	drawn through the winter's night,
in einen Stern gehüllt.	enveloped in stars.
Es wird der Seele Sehnen	The soul's longing
nach jenen Harmonien	for those harmonies
aus seinem Busen tönen,	will sound out of its bosom;
in Schmerzens Melodien	in pain's melodies
des Menschen tiefste Klage,	symphonies will speak
den Zweifel seiner Brust,	man's deepest laments,
in Symphonien sagen	the doubts of his breast,
und seine reinste Lust.	and his purest delight.
Zu des Aethers verschwiegenen	To the secluded bliss of the
Wonnen,	ethers,
zum Geheimniss der ewigen Sonnen,	to the mystery of the eternal suns,
reichet den Schlüssel nur einzig	only music provides the key.
der Klang.	
Die Völker all dem lauschen	All peoples listen to him,
so still wie im Gebet,	still as in prayer,
sein Ton kann nicht verrauschen,	his music cannot die away
so lang die Welt besteht.	as long as the world exists.
Der Stern ist aufgegangen in dieser	The star has ascended in this
Winternacht,	winter's night,
gesegnet welchem leuchtet die	blessed is he for whom the golden
goldne Strahlenpracht.	ray of splendor lights the way.
Heil Beethoven, Heil!	Hail Beethoven, hail!

music had sounded. Given the thoroughly contemporary music that narrates this emergence—signified above all by a bold quotation of the *Tristan* chord in measure 213, as the chorus describes the "peculiar shiver" they feel hearing such new music—the cantata must constantly negotiate the demands of praising both the historical Beethoven and a rather more abstract Beethoven identifiable as a contemporary, a *Zukunftsmusiker*.

Although Stern's text is itself caught between narrating a prophetic redemption and undermining the need for that redemption, this tension is magnified in Liszt's musical setting. Indeed, it lies at the heart of the Weimar festival itself, which sought both to honor Beethoven and to celebrate contemporary music. Put simply, if Beethoven's music—represented by the quotations—functions as a redemptive or transformative force in the cantata's musical narrative, it thus minimizes the music that precedes it. Liszt's music of the future would be superseded by Beethoven's music of the past. And to some extent, this is precisely what happens. There is, for instance, a general move from the more chromatic *Zukunftsmusik* preceding Beethoven's arrival to a more diatonic harmonic vocabulary organized in part around quotations of several Beethoven works at the moment of his arrival: the opening notes of both the *Eroica* symphony and the *Fidelio* overture, and the first theme of the 1805 "Leonore" Overture. The work ends on a triumphant, "Beethovenian" note, with repeated tonic chords and the *Eroica* motif dominating in the orchestra. The pure diatonicism of this quotation (it lacks the famous C♯) seems to have transformed the chromaticism that preceded it, marking Beethoven's heralded emergence and the omnipotence of his music.

On the other hand, this diatonicism is thematic, not structural. The cantata occupies a thoroughly chromatic space: it is formed around E major, A-flat major, and C major. In its pervasive chromatic modulations and lack of extended tonic-dominant tension, Liszt's cantata is New German music to the core. A slightly more extended example of the cantata's progressive harmonic practice is given in Example 8. The setting of "Zu des Aethers verschwiegenen Wonnen" at mm. 693–702 is built on cascading arpeggios and the beginning of the chorale melody, but it focuses attention onto the harmonic sequence E-flat major—B minor—D major—B-flat minor—C major. The text claims that only music itself offers the key to "secluded bliss," and Liszt's music rather neatly illustrates this seclusion in its traversal of two pairs of hexatonic poles.[70] E-flat major and B minor, for instance, share no common tones, and in functional harmonic language the chords can be related only with difficulty; B minor is the enharmonic minor six of E-flat major's parallel minor. As opposite hexatonic poles they suggest the ultimate in harmonic distance, and it is precisely this sense of distance the text claims music can bridge, moving not only between one but two pairs of poles before ending the sequence. It is hard to imagine a stronger or more telling contrast to the 1845 cantata, and not simply because of the different harmonic language. In the Weimar work, the "music of the future" sounds at a distance—a "secluded bliss" in the ether. In the Bonn work, by contrast, the music of the future is the music of the here and now—of the *Mitwelt*—whose bliss is anything but secluded.

But it seems that seclusion, no matter how blissful, comes at a cost: the collective does not understand such music. Hence the "Archduke" theme reappears, in modified form, as an intriguing yet inscrutable promotion for a

Example 8. *Beethoven-Cantate,* no. 2, mm. 690–702.

Example 8 continued

kind of music the chorus cannot yet call its own. Indeed, it is the treatment of the "Archduke" theme in the cantata proper—its "deformations" or mis-quotations by the incomprehending chorus—that provides the narrative pretense for the chorus to ask an old, wise man to explain the sounds. At measure 165 (Example 9), immediately preceding the text "Do you hear the melody," an elementary version of the "Archduke" theme is heard in the orchestra; ascending in half-steps to its ultimate destination, E major, it lingers on D major in mm. 175–84. Clearly referring to the D-major variations that opened the cantata, this version of the theme is an undeniable invocation of music already heard, of remembered music. Yet the text, which refers to the "bright star" marking Beethoven's heavenly emergence, insists upon its newness and the nascency of the "Archduke" material.[71]

What is this music? It has yet to crystallize into a clear musical thought—the community claims "never ever" to have seen such a vision, and cannot yet comprehend it or its accompanying music—yet it obviously alludes to the variations already heard. The deformation of the "Archduke" material is symptomatic of the cantata's uneasy promotion of Beethoven as both the ghostly trace of the musical past and as an emerging avatar of the musical future. Of course, this ambivalence was systemic to the Weimar festivities as a whole, and Liszt's cantata compensates for it with an increasing reliance on short, atomized quotations of Beethoven's music. The music of remembrance and presence is supplemented by that of music-historical knowledge. Naturally, the cantata undeniably claims Beethoven as its true prophet. But in relying on the old man to explain Beethoven's music, music that is "not yet" understandable, the cantata supplements its musical prophet (Beethoven) with a hermeneutic one (the New German exegete). He is called upon by the chorus to explain the sounds they do not understand—"only he alone," they claim, can make sense of it all—and in doing so his function signals the abandonment of a communal, participatory role of the chorus in Liszt's cantata: this is the music of the future as spectacle, not collective act. The cantata replaces as the recipients and bearers of musical understanding the community of listeners singing its text with the community of listeners attending the ADMV meeting. Indeed, the old man's narration of the genius's emergence is matched by a marked increase in the number of musical citations—those of Beethoven's music, as well as the chorale melody "Wie schön leuchtet der Morgenstern," references any member of the ADMV would presumably have recognized immediately.

After Beethoven's "arrival" and the chorus's promise to honor its genius, the "Archduke" material returns once again on the text "The star is risen." Like the new variation in the Bonn work, this one, at least at its start, is relatively faithful to the original. Although Liszt puts it in duple meter, it

Example 9. *Beethoven-Cantate*, no. 2, mm. 164–71.

is completely homophonic and maintains Beethoven's melodic shape. Musically, this moment may seem like a long-awaited arrival. Yet, crucially, the text stresses something else: a leave-taking. It announces that Beethoven's star has now risen; he is no longer with the celebrants in the cantata. In contrast to the Bonn work, the Weimar cantata emphasizes not Beethoven's presence but his absence at the climax of its narrative. Certainly he is not absent from the cultural, referential memory to which the cantata appeals; his is a spiritual presence, one the text promises will never die (*verrauschen*). But there is no claim to an everyday presence among the celebrants. He must be summoned, as he was in the mysterious chord progression introducing the variations, and his music will require exegesis to be comprehensible.

Like the Bonn work, the text ends on a self-referential note, and the C-major "Archduke" music is pulled into E major for the close of the work. To a degree, Liszt ends the Weimar cantata as he did the Bonn one, with the chorus singing a newly composed variation of Beethoven's music and *Heil*s in his honor in the final measures. But there is an important difference: whereas the 1845 cantata sought to deny Beethoven's leave-taking, by claiming his enduring presence in the communal performance of his music, the 1870 cantata *starts* with his leave-taking (the final, developmental variation with the open-ended cadence) and subsequently narrates his arrival, only to announce that leave-taking yet again at the end. The cantata repeatedly reenacts his departure. It folds together the historical Beethoven, whose star has once again risen to the heights from which it came, and the referential Beethoven, the citations of whom now operate no differently than the chorale melody likewise announcing a star.

Thus, to continue the metaphor, two stars shine at the end of the Weimar cantata, one for each of its prophets: the canonized Beethoven of music-historical reference; and the group of composers gathered in Weimar who understand those references, and in whose name Liszt's often ambivalent cantata seeks to claim Beethoven as one of their own. (The Bonn cantata, by contrast, had no use for stars: Beethoven was very much still "on earth," embodied in those performing his music.) In this cantata musical meaning is no longer completely immanent to the work; it is reserved for those who possess the requisite cultural memory to recognize and process the quotations. The chorus in the cantata does not possess this cultural memory, and must ask the wise man for an explanation. To be sure, many associations in nineteenth-century Germany such as the ADMV saw the education of the public as part of their mission, and in this sense there is nothing necessarily exclusionary about the cantata's delineation between those who understand the music and those who do not.[72] But the very fact that this discrepancy is central to the narrative of the cantata illustrates the distance between the Bonn and Weimar works.

Liszt's Bonn cantata promised a new temporality, one in which past, present, and future coincided, and the collected *Volk* joined Beethoven in an eternal *Mitwelt* of communal and musical presence. We might follow Walter Benjamin in approaching such a promise as that of messianic time: "Only a redeemed mankind receives the fullness of the past—which is to say, only for a redeemed mankind has its past become citable in all its moments."[73] Benjamin had a messiah other than Ludwig van Beethoven in mind, of course, but given the messianic properties attached to Beethoven in the 1845 work, such a characterization is not far off. In Wolff's text, the *Volk* bereft of its genius was destined to perish in "the books of world history," and it is Beethoven who comes to provide mankind with its revolutionary temporality, a past that has been recovered for an eternal present. This messianic temporality is driven home by the coexistence of Liszt's own festival music with the citation of Beethoven's "Archduke" material. In the 1870 cantata, by contrast, citing Beethoven has little to do with the "fullness of the past," but rather its crystallization, the legitimization of an aesthetics of the future cut off from both the past and the community at large. Whereas Beethoven's music seemed to provide the emancipatory means toward a communal future *within* music in 1845, by 1870 his music came to embody a future *of* music. What in Bonn had functioned as the gift of musical participation had become in Weimar the onus of musical progress, whereby the ossification of Beethoven as object of a new musical telos mirrors as well the ossification of the chorus, its role reduced to somewhat dimwitted spectators to whom both music and telos must be explained. In place of the Vormärz effusions of the Bonn work, the Weimar cantata substitutes the straightened realities of a political and cultural landscape that was significantly less likely to seek inspiration or even legitimization in "the people." Perhaps Liszt had heeded the call of Peter Cornelius (another New German publicist) for composers to acknowledge that "the times of naïve creation, of sweet dreams of music, are past, that they have acquired reflection and self-criticism . . . that their composing and striving has thus to be 'post-March,' not 'pre-March' [i.e. Vormärz]."[74]

But although the Beethoven cantatas clearly participated primarily in a German public sphere, and in both festivities Liszt's fellow participants attempted to honor Beethoven specifically as a German composer, it is important to point out that in both compositions neither the collective nor the figure of the artist-prophet is assigned a clear nationality. The works are indicative of Liszt's nationalist principles more broadly, in which a Herderian conception of national culture rooted in the *Volk* joined forces with a liberal belief in collective agency and autonomy. It is a cosmopolitan aesthetic found throughout Liszt's choral compositions. The *Elisabeth* oratorio, for instance, was finished in Rome, is dedicated to Ludwig II of Bavaria, tells the story of a Hungarian, and takes place at the Wartburg near Weimar. The 1874 choral ballad *Die Glocken des Strassburger Münsters* shares a similar background: with a text by Longfellow, a setting in Alsace, a musical forebear in Palestrina, and a premiere in Hungary that served as a fund-raiser for Bayreuth, the ballad illustrates how strongly a national and cultural eclecticism informed Liszt's choral music well after the particularizing moment of German unification.

Of course, this kind of cosmopolitanism is not unrelated to a broader eclecticism supporting Liszt's music more generally. The fundamental interdependence of secular and sacred aesthetics throughout Liszt's oeuvre is one obvious example; so, too, is a wide confessional embrace witnessed, for instance, by the inclusion of the Bachian chorale "O Haupt voll Blut und Wunden" in the otherwise Catholic *Via Crucis*. Yet if the transportable "Volksgeist" ethos underlying much of the choral music is one of many wide-reaching tendencies that come together in Liszt's music, it is a crucial one all the same. After all, the imagined voice of a noble collective is hardly limited to the choral music alone. Liszt's call in 1835 for a religious music speaking as both God and *Volk* relates not only to the choral works of the 1840s that followed it, but the first version of the *Harmonies poétiques et religieuses* (1834) that preceded it. Although the piano work does not employ musical textures that immediately bring to mind a communal voice (such as the instrumental hymns in *Ce qu'on entend sur la montagne*, the instrumental "Hirtenspiel" in *Christus*, or indeed subsequent versions of the *Harmonies*), its opening quotation of Lamartine explicitly suggests the work's generation in a collective subject: "We pray with your words, we weep with your tears, we plead with your song."[75]

Such a mixture of singular and plural, of the individual and the communal, brings us back to the opening question posed by this essay—the extent to which we might see in Liszt's advocacy of "the people" a mitigating force that discussions of his virtuoso personality and his multinational enthusiasms have tended to overlook. Works such as the 1834 *Harmonies* point the way toward a conception of the virtuosic solo works that is itself oriented around a communal aesthetic. Dana Gooley's discussion of charity as a guiding force in Liszt's concertizing is another fruitful approach.[76] Obviously, the goal is not to whitewash Liszt's career, to turn someone whose concerts seemed to exclude the "middle bourgeoisie" almost purposefully (and who, after all, tried to marry a woman with over 30,000 serfs) into an unimpeachably virtuous folk hero.[77] But Liszt's music and his career also illustrate a conviction that nations, the people who constitute them, and the cultures that define them shared an intrinsic value. Clearly the Weimar "Beethoven" cantata illustrates some of the limits to such idealism, as does the ambivalence of the "On the Situation of Artists" essay at the beginning of his compositional career. Yet to point out that prophet and populace do not maintain a steady equilibrium in Liszt's choral works is to suggest no more—and no less—than that this imbalance reflects the contradictory forces of the nineteenth century more generally.

NOTES

1. The term is Lawrence Kramer's, although I hasten to add that his account does not necessarily promote this simplistic approach toward Liszt's audiences. "Franz Liszt and the Virtuoso Public Sphere: Sight and Sound in the Rise of Mass Entertainment," in *Musical Meaning: Toward a Critical History* (Berkeley: 2002), pp. 68–99.

2. Erika Quinn, for instance, writes: "Throughout the rest of his life [i.e. after the 1838 floods], Liszt used nationalist sentiments to serve his own personal purposes when possible." "Composing a German Identity: Franz Liszt and the *Kulturnation*, 1848–1886," Ph.D. diss., University of California, Davis, 2001, p. 58. For a comparative approach, see Gerhard J. Winkler, ed., *Liszt und die Nationalitäten: Bericht über das internationale musikwissenschaftliche Symposium Eisenstadt, 10–12 März 1994* (Eisenstadt: 1996).

3. See, for instance, Dana Gooley, *The Virtuoso Liszt* (Cambridge, Eng.: 2004).

4. Carl Dahlhaus, *Nineteenth-Century Music*, trans. J. Bradford Robinson (Berkeley: 1989), p. 37.

5. The term was coined by Benedict Anderson, *Imagined Communities: Reflections on the Origin and Spread of Nationalism* (New York: 1991).

6. Paul Merrick, *Revolution and Religion in the Music of Franz Liszt* (New York: 1987).

7. The visit is reported in Alan Walker, *Franz Liszt: The Virtuoso Years 1811–1847* (Ithaca, N.Y.: 1987, rev. ed.), p. 113.

8. The canonical account of the Saint-Simonians' musical aesthetics, as well as Liszt's interest in the movement, is found in Ralph P. Locke, *Music, Musicians, and the Saint-Simonians* (Chicago: 1986).

9. Dana Gooley has recently emphasized Liszt's contributions to the German nationalist movement following the 1840 "Rheinkrise"; see "Liszt and the German Nation, 1840–1843," in *The Virtuoso Liszt*, pp. 156–200.

10. On these three works see Merrick, "1848: Revolutions and a Mass," in *Revolution and Religion*, pp. 26–35.

11. *Letters of Franz Liszt*, trans. Constance Bache (London: 1894), vol. 2, p. 33.

12. This formulation comes from Liszt's "De la situation des artistes," in *Sämtliche Schriften*, vol. 1: *Frühe Schriften*, ed. Rainer Kleinertz (Wiesbaden: 2000), pp. 56–59, here 59.

13. Michael Saffle notes that Liszt himself quoted Hanslick's critique; see his "Sacred Choral Works," in *The Liszt Companion*, ed. Ben Arnold (Westport, Conn: 2002), pp. 335–63, here 362 n. 13.

14. An impressively single-minded promotion of the oratorio's Wagnerian credentials comes from Hans von Wolzogen, "Liszts 'heilige Elisabeth' auf der Bühne," *Aus Richard*

Wagners Geisteswelt: Neue Wagneriana und Verwandtes (Berlin: 1908), pp. 275–88. For an interesting account of *Elisabeth*'s staged performances in Vienna, see Cornelia Szabó-Knotik, "Changing Aspects of the Sacred and Secular: Liszt's *Legend of St. Elisabeth* in the Repertory of the K.K. Hof-Operntheater in Vienna," in *Nineteenth-Century Music: Selected Proceedings of the Tenth International Conference,* ed. Jim Samson and Bennett Zon (Burlington, Vt.: 2002), pp. 169–78.

15. La Mara, ed., *Franz Liszts Briefe,* (Leipzig: 1893–1905), vol. 8, p. 415.

16. On democracy and associational life, see most recently Stefan-Ludwig Hoffmann, "Democracy and Associations in the Long Nineteenth Century: Toward a Transnational Perspective," trans. David F. Epstein, *Journal of Modern History* 75 (2003): 269–99. See also Klaus Tenfelde, "Die Entfaltung des Vereinswesens während der industriellen Revolution in Deutschland (1850–1873)," in *Vereinswesen und bürgerliche Gesellschaft in Deutschland,* ed. Otto Dahn (Munich: 1984), pp. 55–114; and Dieter Düding, *Organisierter gesellschaftlicher Nationalismus in Deutschland (1808–1847): Bedeutung und Funktion der Turner- und Sängervereine für die deutsche Nationalbewegung* (Munich: 1984). For an interesting comparative case, see Robert Putnam's *Bowling Alone: The Collapse and Revival of American Community* (New York: 2000), much discussed recently in the American media.

17. Much has been written on associations in nineteenth-century Germany; most influential has been Thomas Nipperdey, "Verein als soziale Struktur in Deutschland im späten 18. und 19. Jahrhundert: Eine Fallstudie zur Modernisierung I," in *Gesellschaft, Kultur, Theorie: Gesammelte Aufsätze zur neueren Geschichte* (Göttingen: 1976), pp. 174–205. See also Dahn; Christiane Eisenberg, "Working-Class and Middle-Class Associations: An Anglo-German Comparison, 1820–1870," in *Bourgeois Society in Nineteenth-Century Europe,* ed. Jürgen Kocka and Allen Mitchell (Providence, R.I.: 1993), pp. 151–78; and Ralf Roth, "Von Wilhelm Meister zu Hans Castrorp: Der Bildungsgedanke und das bürgerliche Assoziationswesen im 18. und 19. Jahrhundert," in *Bürgerkultur im 19. Jahrhundert: Bildung, Kunst und Lebenswelt,* ed. Dieter Hein and Andreas Schulz (Munich: 1996), pp. 121–39.

18. See, for instance, Wolfgang Tilgner, "Volk, Nation und Vaterland im protestantischen Denken zwischen Kaiserreich und Nationalsozialismus (ca. 1870–1933)," in *Volk-Nation-Vaterland,* ed. Horst Zilleßen (Gütersloh: 1970), pp. 146–49.

19. See Bernhard Giesen, *Intellectuals and the German Nation: Collective Identity in an Axial Age,* trans. Nicholas Levis and Amos Weisz (New York: 1998). On the role of the *Volk* in Enlightenment thinking, see *Das Volk als Objekt obrigkeitlichen Handelns,* ed. Rudolf Vierhaus (Tübingen: 1992).

20. On this imbalance, see Wolfgang Kaschuba, "Deutsche Bürgerlichkeit nach 1800: Kultur als symbolische Praxis," in *Bürgertum im 19 Jahrhundert: Deutschland im Europäischen Vergleich,* ed. Jürgen Kocka with Ute Frevert (Munich: 1988), pp. 9–44.

21. John Williamson, "Progress, Modernity and the Concept of an Avant-Garde," in *The Cambridge History of Nineteenth-Century Music* (New York: 2001), pp. 287–317, here 295.

22. Liszt, "De la situation des artistes," p. 59.

23. Alan Walker, *Franz Liszt: The Final Years 1861–1886* (New York: 1996), p. 209 n. 36.

24. On the change in German choral aesthetics following unification in 1871, see chapter 3 of my "National Memory, Public Music: Commemoration and Consecration in Nineteenth-Century German Choral Music," Ph.D. diss., University of Chicago, 2005.

25. There are several first-person accounts of the festival: H. K. Breidenstein, *Festgabe zu der am 12ten August 1845 stattfindenden Inauguration des Beethoven Monuments* (Bonn: 1845; repr. Bonn, 1983) as well as his *Zur Jahresfeier der Inauguration des Beethoven-Monuments: Eine actenmässige Darstellung dieses Ereignisses, der Wahrheit zur Ehre und den Festgenossen zur Erinnerung* (Bonn: 1846; repr. Bonn, 1983); Hector Berlioz, "The Musical Celebration at Bonn," in *Evenings at the Orchestra,* ed. and trans. Jacques Barzun (Chicago: 1999), pp. 326–44;

and Henry F. Chorley, "Beethoven's Music at Bonn," in *Modern German Music*, vol. 2, ed. Hans Lenneberg (New York: 1973), pp. 276–90. Of the many secondary accounts, see in particular: Hans-Josef Irmen, "Franz Liszt in Bonn oder Wie die erste Beethovenhalle entstand," in *Studien zur Bonner Musikgeschichte des 18. und 19. Jahrhunderts*, ed. Marianne Bröcker and Günther Massenkeil (Cologne: 1978), pp. 49–65; Lina Ramann, *Franz Liszt als Künstler und Mensch*, vol. 2, part 1 (Leipzig: 1887) pp. 249–65; Walker, *Franz Liszt: The Virtuoso Years*, pp. 417–26; Ingrid Bodsch, ed., *Monument für Beethoven: Zur Geschichte des Beethoven-Denkmals (1845) und der frühen Beethoven-Rezeption in Bonn* (Bonn: 1995); and Esteban Buch, *Beethoven's Ninth: A Political History*, trans. Richard Miller (Chicago: 2003), pp. 133–55.

26. Alexander Rehding, "Liszt's Musical Monuments," *19th-Century Music* 26, no. 1 (2002): 52–72, here 67.

27. Letter from 28 April 1845, in *Letters of Franz Liszt*, vol. 1, p. 96.

28. On the political content of Wolff's text, see Andreas Eichhorn, *Beethovens Neunte Symphonie: Die Geschichte ihrer Aufführung und Rezeption* (New York: 1993), p. 301. On the Vormärz period, see in particular Christopher Clark, "Germany 1815–1848: Restoration or Pre-March?" in *Nineteenth-Century Germany: Politics, Culture and Society, 1780–1918*, ed. John Breuilly (New York: 2001), pp. 40–65 and David Blackbourn, "The Age of Revolutions, 1789–1848," in *The Long Nineteenth Century: A History of Germany, 1780–1918* (New York: 1998), pp. 45–174.

29. Rehding, "Liszt's Musical Monuments," p. 64.

30. See the following individual notes for citations of these texts. In general, an excellent sense of contemporary Beethoven reception—poems, addresses, reminiscences—can be gleaned from a Festschrift published just after the festival: Gustav Schilling, ed., *Beethoven-Album: Ein Gedenkbuch dankbarer Liebe und Verehrung für den grossen Todten, gestiftet und beschrieben von einem Verein von Künstlern und Kunstfreunden aus Frankreich, England, Italien, Deutschland, Holland, Schweden, Ungarn und Russland* (Stuttgart: 1846). For an interesting comparison with obvious correlates to Liszt's second, 1870 cantata, see the (confusingly titled) *Erstes Poetisches Beethoven-Album: Zur Erinnerung an den grossen Tondichter und an dessen Säcularfeier, begangen den 17 Dezember 1870*, ed., Hermann Joseph Landau (Prague: 1872). A more in-depth consideration of both festivals, the two cantatas, and their social contexts can be found in chapter 2 of my "National Memory, Public Music."

31. Müller, "Sie waren nur wie Stimmen in der Wüste; / Du bist der Heiland, der das Ufer fand," in Landau, *Erstes Poetisches Beethoven-Album*, p. 255.

32. Smets, "Vom Himmelssaal der Weihe Strahl / herab auf Erdensöhne fällt," in Breidenstein, *Festgabe*, p. 31.

33. On the importance of the Ninth Symphony for Vormärz liberalism, see Eichhorn, *Beethovens Neunte Symphonie*, pp. 298–317.

34. "Es tönt durch's All ein mächt'ger Klang, / dass ist der Wesen Wettgesang: / vom Sternenreigen hehr und gross, / zum Westgesäusel tief im Moos, / vom Donnerhall und Wasserfall, / vom Rauschen durch den Eichenwald, / zum süssen Lied der Nachtigall, / das wehmuthvoll im Hain erschallt, / vom Meereswogen Sturmgeroll / zur all bezwingenden Gewalt der Menschenstimme, rein und voll." In Breidenstein, *Festgabe*, p. 31.

35. In Müller's case the claims of posterity take on more explicitly religious connotations. Through Beethoven, Müller promises, "The world is God and God the world," and a "golden new time" is promised those who follow the "banner-bearer of future noble times:" "Soon we will hover with you in the ether / like holy spirits between worlds of stars."

36. In Berlioz's words, "This hymn [the "Archduke" theme] . . . finally bursts forth with the majesty of an apotheosis." Berlioz, "The Magical Celebration at Bonn," in *Evenings at the Orchestra*, p. 340. On Beethoven's apotheosis in nineteenth-century reception, see Arnold Schmitz, "Die Beethoven-Apotheose als Beispiel eines Säkularisierungsvorgangs," in *Festschrift*

P. Wagner zum 60. Geburtstag, ed. K. Weinmann (Leipzig: 1926), pp. 181–89, and his *Das romantische Beethovenbild: Darstellung und Kritik* (Berlin: 1927; repr. Darmstadt, 1978); see also Günther Massenkeil, "Die Bonner Beethoven-Kantate (1845) von Franz Liszt," in *Die Sprache der Musik: Festschrift Klaus Wolfgang Niemöller zum 60. Geburtstag am 21. Juli 1989*, ed. Jobst Peter Fricke (Regensburg: 1989), pp. 381–400, and, more recently, Scott Burnham, *Beethoven Hero* (Princeton, N.J.: 1995).

37. On this lament topos, see Ellen Rosand, "The Descending Tetrachord: An Emblem of Lament," *Musical Quarterly* 55 (1979): pp. 346–59.

38. The chromatic chordal progression that follows, illustrated by the move toward F-minor in mm. 18–25 before the B-major modulation at measure 32, shows Liszt's use of the most "advanced" harmonic means to portray the plight of the *Völker* caught in the "night of nights."

39. See Axel Schröter, "*Der Name Beethoven ist heilig in der Kunst.*" *Studien zu Liszts Beethoven-Rezeption, Teil 1: Text* (Linzig: 1999), pp. 217 n. 102, 225. See also Michael Saffle, *Liszt in Germany 1840–1845: A Study in Sources, Documents, and the History of Reception* (Stuyvesant, N.Y.: 1994).

40. On Berlioz's comment, see Alessandra Comini, *The Changing Image of Beethoven: A Study in Mythmaking* (New York: 1987), p. 250. Schmidt's poem, which provides an impressionistic text for each of the four movements, is given in Schilling, *Beethoven-Album,* p. 9.

41. See Schröter, *Der Name Beethoven,* p. 217.

42. Friedrich Schmidt, "Hymne von Goethe und Ludwig van Beethoven zusammengefügt und zur Bekränzung des Bonner Denkmales bei dessen feierlicher Enthüllung am 11 Aug. 1845, dargebracht von Friedrich Schmidt, Ritter, Großherzogl. Sächs. Geh. Regierungsrath" (Weimar: 1845). The exact circumstances of Schmidt's setting remain somewhat of a mystery; see, however, Friederike Grigat's catalogue entry for the work in Bodsch, *Monument für Beethoven,* p. 278.

43. Theodor W. Adorno, *Beethoven: The Philosophy of Music*, ed. Rolf Tiedemann, trans. Edmund Jephcott (Stanford, Calif.: 1998), p. 88. Adorno saw in this "tranquility through motion" "the female element, the *Shekinah.*" His understanding of *Shekinah*, a Jewish mystical concept of God's hidden presence, seems to have come from his friend Gershom Scholem; see Scholem, *Von der Mystischen Gestalt der Gottheit: Studien zu Grundbegriffen der Kabbala* (Zurich: 1962), p. 136, and Adorno, *Beethoven,* pp. 226–27 n. 191.

44. Adorno, *Beethoven,* p. 90.

45. Franz Wegeler began publishing texts to Beethoven works in 1797, with the composer's approval, and Friedrich Silcher published three volumes of such texts, including his addition of a text from H. Stieglitz's "Bilder des Orients" to the "slow" movement from the Seventh Symphony to create a men's chorus entitled "Persischer Nachtgesang." Even in 1892, when one might assume such an act would be blasphemous, Hans von Bülow famously set words to the variation theme of the *Eroica* in honor of Bismarck's seventy-seventh birthday. See Helmut Loos, "Zur Texterung Beethovenscher Instrumentalwerke: Ein Kapitel der Beethoven-Deutung," in *Beethoven und die Nachwelt,* ed. Helmut Loos (Bonn: 1986), pp. 117–37. Silcher's "Persischer Nachtgesang" is reproduced in Schilling, *Beethoven-Album,* p. 4.

46. August Schmidt wrote, for instance, "Mehrere Stellen würden dem geübtesten Kapellmeister in der Instrumentirung große Ehre machen," in *Wiener allgemeine Musik-Zeitung* 101 (23 August 1845): p. 403. Breidenstein, who felt that Liszt's inexperience in writing for chorus was evident in the uncomfortably high soprano part, praised the instrumentation as "truly magnificent." Breidenstein, *Zur Jahresfeier,* p. 21. In the context of this praise it is worth repeating that the cantata was Liszt's first composition for orchestra.

47. The term "developing instrumentation" is mine, and refers simply to Liszt's practice in this work—already noted by Axel Schröter—of maintaining one instrument from a previous grouping in the subsequent one. See Schröter, *Der Name Beethoven*, pp. 219–22.

48. Thomas Keith Nelson, "The Fantasy of Absolute Music," Ph.D. Diss., University of Minnesota, 1998, vol. 2, pp. 379–80.

49. See Elvira Seiwert, *Beethoven-Szenarien: Thomas Manns "Doktor Faustus" und Adornos Beethoven-Projekt* (Stuttgart: 1995); and, most recently, Berthold Hoeckner, "Echo's Eyes," in *Programming the Absolute: Nineteenth-Century German Music and the Hermeneutics of the Moment* (Princeton, N.J.: 2002), pp. 224–65.

50. Adorno, *Beethoven*, p. 175.

51. B♭ is, of course, flat six in Beethoven's D major. But I am not sure that this particular flat six has any bearing on Liszt's own use of the sonority (C in E major) in his cantata. Beethoven's is a seventh chord, whose kinetic nature does not lend itself to the suspension of time, and the entire variation movement was on the mediant of the trio's global tonic—and thus the B♭ at the end of the variations is not perched away from the tonic but returning to it.

52. Ferdinand Hiller, "Zu viel Musik," in *Aus dem Tonleben unserer Zeit* (Leipzig: 1871), pp. 1–16.

53. On the New German debates, see Robert Determann, *Begriff und Ästhetik der "Neudeutschen Schule": Ein Beitrag zur Musikgeschichte des 19. Jahrhunderts* (Baden Baden: 1989); and Imogen Fellinger, "Brahms und die Neudeutsche Schule," in *Brahms und seine Zeit*, ed. Constantin Floros et al. (Hamburg: 1983), pp. 159–70.

54. Constantin Floros, "Brahms—der zweite Beethoven?" in *Brahms und seine Zeit*, pp. 235–58.

55. Comini, *Changing Image of Beethoven*, p. 207.

56. The ADMV remains underresearched; most of its documents are located in the Goethe- und Schiller-Archiv in Weimar, awaiting inspection. Arthur Seidl's history of the association only covers the first fifty years, and is devoted mainly to its organizational structure. See his *Festschrift zum fünfzigjährigen Bestehen des Allgemeinen Deutschen Musikvereins: Im Auftrage des Vorstandes verfaßt von Arthur Seidl* (Berlin: 1911). See also Dietrich Kämper, "'Anbahnung einer Verständigung': Das Tonkünstlerfest 1887 des Allgemeinen Deutschen Musikvereins in Köln," in *Musicae Scientiae Collectanea: Festschrift Karl Gustav Fellerer zum 70. Geburtstag am 7. Juli 1972; Überreicht von Kollegen, Schulern und Freunden*, ed. Heinrich Hüschen (Cologne: 1973), pp. 250–62.

57. On the "success" of the ADMV, see James Deaville, "The Organized Muse? Organization Theory and 'Mediated' Music," *Canadian University Music Review* 18, no. 1 (1997): 38–51; and Quinn, "Composing a German Identity," pp. 200–233.

58. *Tonkünstler-Versammlung zu Weimar, zugleich als Vorfeier zu Ludwig van Beethoven's 100-jährigen Geburtsfeste veranstaltet vom Allgemeinen Deutschen Musikverein: Fest-Programm für die Tage vom 25.–29. Mai 1870*, Staatsbibliothek zu Berlin, Stiftung Preußischer Kulturbesitz, DB617.

59. In this regard Liszt's work was not entirely alone; a "Beethoven-Ouvertüre" by Eduard Lassen made up of themes from *Fidelio* and the *Egmont* overture was also performed.

60. Cosmopolitanism and its universal ideals are, of course, not entirely foreign to strains of German nationalist thought. Bernd Sponheuer gives an excellent historical outline of some ways German musical nationalism was formed around ideals of universality in "Reconstructing Ideal Types of the 'German' in Music," in *Music & German National Identity*, ed. Celia Applegate and Pamela Potter (Chicago: 2002), pp. 36–58. See also Quinn and Daniel Beller-McKenna, "How Deutsch a Requiem? Absolute Music, Universality, and the Reception of Brahms's *Ein deutsches Requiem*, op. 45," *19th-Century Music* 22 (1998): 3–19.

61. The music sounds, in Carolyn Abbate's words, as a tombeau: "The living composer plays his imperfect recording of a dead master's sounds; at the same time a past master brings a present composer back from stasis or death. There is a double exposure, a sound that is gone—concealed or lost—and yet is audible through a present sound. Tombeaux repeat sounds from the past without repeating them phonographically as a facsimile." Carolyn Abbate, "Outside the Tomb," in *In Search of Opera* (Princeton, N.J.: 2001), pp. 185–246, here 190.

62. Kristin Wendland, "Secular Choral Works," in *The Liszt Companion*, pp. 365–401, here 394.

63. Schröter notes, however, that Liszt maintains the principle from 1845 of according each variation its own instrumentation. Schröter, *Der Name Beethoven*, pp. 222–23.

64. The orchestral introduction was published as an "overture": *Zur Säkularfeier Beethovens: Overture* (Leipzig: 1870). For its subsequent performances, see Ramann, *Franz Liszt als Künstler*, vol. 2, part 1, p. 417. The cantata in its entirety was performed in Pest in December of 1870; to my knowledge this was the last German-language performance of the work. The program for the Pest concert can be found at the Stiftung Weimarer Klassik, Goethe- und Schiller- Archiv, Weimar, GSA 59/242. Liszt arranged an Italian translation by G. M. Angelini for a possible performance in Italy; see his letter to Sgambati from 25 November 1880 in *119 Római Liszt-Dokumentum*, ed. Eösze László (Budapest: 1980), p. 107. The letter, though written in French, has only been published in Hungarian, and I am grateful to Eliza Johnson-Ablovotsky for translating it for me.

65. Letter to Princess Carolyne, 6 May 1869, in *Franz Liszt: Selected Letters*, ed. and trans. Adrian Williams (Oxford, Eng.: 1998), p. 704.

66. Schröter, *Der Name Beethoven*, p. 362.

67. More than a thousand measures follow the introduction. There is no recording of the work, but I estimate it runs about an hour and a half. At issue is not the length per se but whether the work can support it. And as I suggest, the text's flimsy narrative makes this rather difficult.

68. Letter to Baron August, 8 March 1870, in Williams, *Franz Liszt: Selected Letters*, pp. 712–13.

69. Princess Carolyne seems to have thought more of the text than Liszt did; in a letter to Adeleide von Schorn of February 1870 she called the verses "dignes de Schiller—les plus beaux que je connaisse sur la musique." *Zwei Menschenalter: Erinnerungen und Briefe*, ed. Adelheid von Schorn (Berlin: 1901), p. 173.

70. On hexatonic poles, see Richard Cohn, "Maximally Smooth Cycles, Hexatonic Systems, and the Analysis of Late-Romantic Music," *Music Analysis* 15, no. 1 (1996): 9–40. Here, using Cohn's designations, the first pair (E-flat major and B minor) occupies the western pole, the second pair (D major and B-flat minor) the southern pole, and C major the northern pole.

71. Several measures later, at mm. 206–11, a short orchestral interlude follows, which is built on the same material as the "Archduke" reference starting at measure 164. The first five notes are identical to those of the "Archduke" theme, and the second measure corresponds to the original in the same way. But a 7–4 meter clearly obscures the rhythmic contour of Beethoven's theme (although it also enhances its sense of temporal expansiveness and timelessness), a three-note line linking the first two measures descends rather than ascends, as it does in the original, and Liszt replaces the supertonic harmony in the second measure with the subdominant.

72. See Quinn, "The General German Music Association and Its Liberal Mission," and Roth, "Von Wilhelm Meister zu Hans Castorp."

73. Walter Benjamin, "Theses on the Philosophy of History," in *Illuminations*, ed. Hannah Arendt, trans. Harry Zohn (New York: 1977), pp. 253–64, here 254.

74. Peter Cornelius, *Literarische Werke III: Aufsätze über Musik und Kunst*, ed. Edgar Istel (Leipzig: 1904), p. 100, cited in Williamson, p. 300.

75. For some preliminary thoughts and context on this issue, see Klaus Wolfgang Niemöller, "Zur religiösen Tonsprache im Instrumentalschaffen von Franz Liszt," in *Religiöse Musik in nicht-liturgischen Werken von Beethoven bis Reger*, ed. Walter Wior et al. (Regensburg: 1978), pp. 119–42.

76. See Gooley, *The Virtuoso Liszt*, pp. 167–71.

77. Ibid., p. 69. On the living conditions of Princess Carolyne's serfs, see Alan Walker, *Franz Liszt: The Weimar Years, 1848–1861* (Ithica, N.Y.: 1989), p. 30.

"Just Two Words. Enormous Success"
Liszt's 1838 Vienna Concerts

CHRISTOPHER H. GIBBS

For the cosmopolitan and peripatetic Franz Liszt five European cities most shaped, supported, and sustained his life and career: Vienna, Paris, Weimar, Budapest, and Rome—indeed, the last twenty-seven years of his "vie trifurquée" Liszt more or less evenly divided among the final three.[1] Paris was where, in his early teens, he adopted a new language and first came to international attention. The remaining city, Vienna, holds a special position. It lies less than sixty miles from his birthplace in Raiding, a small town in what was then the German-speaking part of Hungary. As a boy of nine Liszt and his father moved to Vienna. They lived there continuously for only eighteen months (1821–23), during which time Liszt studied with Czerny and Salieri, met Beethoven, published his first work, and gave prominent public concerts.[2] After moving to Paris in September 1823, he did not return for fifteen years, until his pathbreaking concerts of 1838 at the age of twenty-six; he came back on tour the next year, and the next, as well as in 1846, and later visited Vienna numerous times, even on occasion performing.[3] In the mid-1840s there was talk of him succeeding Donizetti as Kapellmeister, a move that would have made Imperial Vienna rather than the backwater Weimar his base of activity.[4]

The present documentary essay focuses on the crucial seven-week visit in the spring of 1838, which changed the course of Liszt's life. Because of his earlier educational experiences there, Vienna had already proved a potent force, although in biographical tellings its role remains somewhat obscured by the relative paucity of documentation, and is in any case overshadowed by more sensational accounts of his subsequent training, young adulthood, and first legendary romances in France. The trip to Vienna in 1838 marked a turning point. Comparing his life to a classical five-act drama, Liszt later remarked that the second act (1830–38) concluded with the "return performances in Vienna, the success of which determined my path as a virtuoso."[5] (The third act of concert tours would last nearly ten years and take him across Europe and beyond.) Not only did Vienna deeply affect Liszt, but so too did he leave a mark on the musical life of this most musical of cities. As one critic put it at the time: "The good Viennese are quite changed" (Die guten Wiener sind wie ausgewechselt).[6] Lending the sojourn further personal significance are the biographical issues that emerged from Liszt's stay there, issues concerning his artistic, professional, and domestic situation, such as his legendary generosity, nationalist fervor, career aspirations, and the state of his deteriorating relationship with Marie d'Agoult, his companion for the past five years and the mother of his children.

Liszt's time in Vienna, from 10 April to 26 May, is well documented in private and public sources, the latter with lengthy articles in the local and foreign press, which were followed by his own published account. This took the form of an open letter to the French violinist Lambert Massart that appeared in the 2 September issue of the *Revue et Gazette musicale de Paris*, and soon thereafter was translated for German, Austrian, and Hungarian periodicals.[7] The importance of the trip in initiating the path Liszt pursued for the next decade has encouraged biographers to relate the events in far more detail than for other cities, and yet considerable confusion, misinformation, and an absence of local context make it difficult to assess meaningfully its significance. This essay aims to provide some sense of the cultural and musical climate in Vienna, to suggest ways in which Liszt's reencounter affected both him and the city, and to clarify what was customary and what was novel about his activities.[8] I shall look at the evidence from the "horizon of expectations" of the time, paying scant attention to what we know of Liszt's subsequent life and career.[9] Difficult as it may be to "bracket" such knowledge, there are advantages in trying to appreciate what would have been considered typical and atypical in the spring of 1838, how Liszt was viewed at this relatively early stage in his career, when he was much more the virtuoso than the composer, and before many, although certainly not all, of the legends surrounding him had taken hold. I will also speculate about what Liszt hoped to accomplish in Vienna and about the importance of this episode in his exceedingly careful and self-aware career development. I will consider in particular the artistic importance of his reconnection with the city of Beethoven and Schubert after years immersed in the musical life of France and Italy.

The documentary evidence for this investigation comes not only from Liszt's own published account and letters, from the memoirs, letters, and diaries of others, from articles and reviews in the press, but also from those sources that allow us to reconstruct the nature of musical and concert life in Vienna.[10] By beginning with some background information concerning the general musical scene in the 1830s, I hope to set up an informed context in which to consider what Liszt programmed, when and where he played, with and for whom, what prices he charged, and how he and others, not just the critics, viewed the results.[11] His "enormous success" in Vienna offers the chance for a case study in the creation of a musical celebrity, a figure who would later become a central figure in musical Romanticism (*FLC* 315/86).[12]

Liszt arrived in Vienna at a particularly notable moment, with more than one critic remarking that 1837–38 was an unusually exciting season. A commentator in the *Humorist* exclaimed: "Concerts! Great Concerts! Everyone announces a great concert, but then gives a small one! No one announces a small concert that in fact turns out to be great. 1838 is a concert year! But a good one! Its planet is called: Liszt! When this planet leaves our orbit then I will lay down and not let the notes out and not attend any other concerts."[13] That season two other musical stars besides Liszt shone in the Viennese firmament: Clara Wieck and Sigismond Thalberg. Their presence provides an unusual opportunity to assess the situation of the piano virtuoso and composer. First, however, it would be wise to take a look at concert life in Vienna before the arrival of this notable trio.

Virtuosity in Vienna before Liszt

Nicolò Paganini's Viennese debut, which like Liszt's would initiate years of touring, occurred exactly one decade earlier: the spring of 1828, a year after Beethoven's death and eight months before Schubert's. (Schubert attended at least one of Paganini's concerts and is said to have commented that he "heard an angel singing.")[14] The violinist gave fourteen concerts over the course of four months (29 March to 24 July).[15] His performances challenged critics to come up with sufficient superlatives. The poet, critic, and editor Ignaz Castelli wrote, "Never has an artist caused such a terrific sensation within our walls as this god of the violin. Never has the public so gladly carried its shekels to a concert, and never in my memory has the fame of a virtuoso so spread to the lowest classes of the population."[16]

With the deaths of Beethoven and Schubert, as well as of some leading performers closely associated with them, most notably the celebrated violinist Ignaz Schuppanzigh, an era in Vienna ended, closing what Raphael Georg Kiesewetter, in one of the first music history surveys, called "The Epoch of Beethoven and Rossini (1800–1832)," and what Eduard

Hanslick, some thirty-five years later, would dub the "Epoch of Beethoven and Schubert, 1800–1830" in his classic history of Vienna's musical life. Now began, in Hanslick's estimation, "The Era of the Virtuoso: Thalberg and Liszt, 1830–1848."[17] Yet many aspects of Vienna's concert scene continued as they had for decades, with a season that began around late October and ended in May. (Paganini's summer appearances were unusual and initially unplanned—he kept on extending his stay and adding concerts.) Much of it was still guided by the same institutions Beethoven and Schubert had known. Each season the Gesellschaft der Musikfreunde, founded in 1812, presented Society Concerts (Gesellschafts-Concerte) devoted to orchestral music, as well as Evening Musical Entertainments (Musikalische Abendunterhaltungen) offering chamber and vocal music. The Concerts Spirituels also featured orchestral and choral works, but at what was generally regarded as a lower level of execution. Charity concerts were common, especially around Easter, typically given either by established organizations or in response to a specific circumstance, such as to honor a noted figure or in response to some natural disaster.

Beyond the institutional and charitable offerings, composers and performers presented their own concerts (an "Akademie," as it was usually called), which they organized themselves and from which they reaped the financial rewards (or not). The frequency of such events escalated considerably in the 1830s, with an increasing number of virtuoso performers coming from abroad. Prodigies—or young performers of sometimes questionable ability who claimed to be worthy of attention—regularly gave concerts. Concerts almost always included an orchestra, usually one associated with a theater (such as Theater an der Wien and Theater in der Josephstadt) and conducted by figures like Leopold Jansa, Georg Hellmesberger, and Karl Holz.

The format tended to be fairly uniform: an overture to start (most frequently one by Beethoven or Mozart), followed by a work for the featured performer, in either a concerto or a solo piece. Vocal music often came next, or a "declamation," delivered by an actor from the Imperial Court Theater. Concerts usually ended with the featured performer, sometimes playing an original composition or improvising. The participating instrumentalists were mostly members of one of the city's orchestras, for either the Court or one of the suburban theaters; some were also professors at the Conservatory, yet another institution that regularly presented concerts. In addition, there was the stable of actors from the Court Theater who gave the declamations.[18] Despite rivalries and factions, these dominant musicians and actors performed together; visiting artists, including Wieck and Liszt, had to obtain their services.[19] Charity concerts brought performers together, sometimes in rather unusual combinations. At one such occasion, on 13 March 1831, sixteen pianists, two seated at each of eight instruments, performed the overtures to Rossini's *Semiramide* and Beethoven's *Egmont* as arranged by Czerny. The playbill lists a veritable who's who of Viennese pianists at the time: Czerny, Franz Chotek, Theodor Döhler, Joseph Fischhof, Georg Lickl, Albin Pfaller, Wenzel Plachy, Thalberg, and "eight other excellent artists and friends of art."

Musicians also gave benefit concerts (as distinct from charity concerts) in the less altruistic cause of supplementing their personal incomes. The case of Leopold Jansa—a local violinist, conductor, composer, and professor at the Conservatory—is typical. His concert on 23 April 1835 at the hall of the Gesellschaft der Musikfreunde, the Musikverein, followed the expected format: after the *Egmont* Overture, came his own Concerto for Violin in E Major, and then Heinrich Proch's "Der Blinde Fischer," a new song with Waldhorn obbligato performed by Ludwig Tietze, Eduard Lewy, and the composer. This was followed by Thalberg playing one of his caprices "for the first time publicly," and the concert ended with Jansa, Proch, Karl Holz, and Joseph Lincke performing his Concerto for Two Violins, Viola, and Cello. Three years later, Jansa gave an Akademie that opened with Beethoven's *Coriolan* Overture, followed by his own Violin Concerto in B Minor, a declamation, Hummel's Piano Trio in E (with Aegid Borzaga and Fanny Sallamon), a duet from Pietro Generali's opera *La donna soldato*, and concluding with an impromptu for violin by Jansa. Such concerts show the expected heterogeneous combination of music and recitation, the participation of local colleagues, and the limited use of an orchestra to open the event and to accompany soloists.[20]

The magnitude of Liszt's series in 1838 becomes clearer when profiled against concerts by other virtuosos. Most relevant are the many pianists, both local and visiting, who performed in the 1830s, occasionally in a series of two or three concerts grouped together within a fairly short period. Among the leading foreign pianists to appear were Ludwig Schunke, Adolph Henselt, and Johann Nepomuk Hummel, all noted composers as well.[21] Pianists residing in Vienna included Carl Maria von Bocklet, whose students (among them Alois Tausig and Caroline Herrschmann) also gave concerts, and the young Louis Lacombe, a student of Czerny's. Bocklet (1801–81), who had premiered much of the chamber music of Beethoven and Schubert at Schuppanzigh's concerts, offered programs that were unusually spare and serious; four in 1835 are representative:[22]

10 April
    Overture
    Hummel, Piano Concerto in B Minor
    Aria from Mozart's *Titus*
    Improvisation

20 April
    Overture
    Hummel, Piano Concerto in A Minor
    Vocal work
    Improvisation

29 November
    Moscheles, Piano Concerto in E flat Major
    Weber, *Konzertstück*
    Improvisation

20 December
    Hummel, Piano Concerto in A flat Major
    Moscheles, *Concert fantastique* (manuscript)
    Improvisation

A large number of women pianists, following Leopoldine Blahetka in the 1820s, were regular presences in Vienna, among them Herrschmann, Nina Onitsch, and Nina Delack.[23] Fanny Sallamon appeared most often in the 1830s. Her concert at the Musikverein on 2 February 1832 began with the standard Beethoven overture but also, unusually, featured a Beethoven sonata, specifically the "Appassionata," of which Wieck's performance six years later would cause a stir:

    Beethoven, *Egmont* Overture
    Hummel, Piano Concerto in A-flat Major
    Lachner, "Fragen," song with cello obbligato, sung by Ludwig
        Tietze, with Joseph Merk and the composer accompanying
    Jansa, New Adagio and Rondo for Violin and Orchestra
    Beethoven, "Grosse Sonate" in F Minor

"For these comparisons will never end": Thalberg, Wieck, and Liszt

The rise of the instrumental virtuoso in the 1830s promoted a comparative musical culture. Performers were judged not only on their own merits but also in relation to others, with the foundational model being Paganini. Liszt aspired to be the "Paganini of the Piano," and it did not take long before exactly that label was repeatedly applied to him. The comparative contest was promoted in the press, which helped to create a culture of performing celebrities. A certain governing logic made comparisons far from odious, but rather inevitable.

By the time Wieck and Liszt appeared during the 1837–38 season, six celebrated musicians had won the official imprimatur of the special title k. k. Kammervirtuoso (Imperial and Royal Chamber Virtuoso): Paganini and Thalberg, cellist Joseph Merk, violinist Joseph Mayseder, and singers Giuditta Pasta and Jenny Lutzer.[24] The designation carried not only prestige—those honored tended to display the title proudly—but also privileges because they were considered "subjects of the Austrian Empire in all countries and always under the protection of the Austrian envoys."[25] Both Wieck and Liszt hoped they would be granted the title during their stays.

The principal comparative contest in Vienna was among pianists, even if the name of Paganini was invoked as a cultural and musical touchstone. Thalberg, at twenty-six just three months younger than Liszt, had already become the local standard-bearer. Although he was born in Geneva, Thalberg had been familiar to Viennese audiences for more than a decade and enjoyed especially close ties to the city as a member of a powerful aristocratic family, the Dietrichsteins.[26] He and Liszt had already had their run-in in print, the salon, and concert hall; Vienna renewed the contest. As Liszt wrote to Marie d'Agoult immediately after his second appearance: "The Thalbergites (for these comparisons will never end), who prided themselves on their impartiality to begin with, are beginning to be seriously vexed" (*FLC* 318/87).

Clara Wieck's presence expanded the field and provided the press with more to write about. Before she had played a single note in public, Adolph Bäuerle, the influential editor of Vienna's *Allgemeine Theaterzeitung*, wrote that this "famous artist, who has just triumphed in Prague, has arrived here and will give concerts in the middle of this month. We are making the public aware of the modest young artist who ranks alongside Liszt and Chopin in Germany. Vienna shall decide if she can hold her own next to Thalberg."[27]

Such comparisons were not only made in the press and among the musical cognoscenti, but also were very much on the minds of the artists themselves. As Clara Wieck's father, Friedrich, a noted piano pedagogue, was preparing her for her first concert, he wrote in her journal: "Although Thalberg's name is on every tongue here, they know very well that he plays coldly and is also not a masterful composer—he is also reproached because he plays only his own works" (7 December). The *Neue Zeitschrift für Musik* reported that the concert caused a "sensation that no artist has aroused since Paganini and Thalberg."[28] Clara called it "my triumph" in her diary and noted, "The audience generally affirmed that I have a higher standing than Thalberg. Father says, 'Why compare? Cannot two artists exist side by side?'" Yet Friedrich must have been pleased that the comparisons were being made to Clara's advantage, for following her third concert he boasted of her "complete victory over Thalberg" (14 December and 7 January). Clara's strategy extended to performing music by the competition on her next concert: "I played pieces by Liszt and Thalberg to silence those who thought I couldn't play Thalberg. There were 13 curtain calls, and not even Thalberg experienced that."[29]

Liszt was even more attuned to this competition among pianists. Indeed, aspects of it had already been partially played out the year before in his "duel" with Thalberg at a charity event in Paris. The result had been a draw, with the hostess, the formidable Italian Princess Cristina Belgiojoso allegedly declaring, "There is only one Thalberg in Paris, but there is only one Liszt in the world."[30] Rainer Kleinertz has argued that Thalberg was an "idée fixe" for Liszt during these years, and indeed his correspondence is filled with obsessive references to his rival.[31] In this context, a private letter Liszt wrote to Massart just after leaving Vienna is almost comical: "Thalberg, whom I don't like to quote and towards whom I only keep the most religious silence, said some nice enough words to me that capture well the situation in Vienna: 'In comparison with you I have never had more than a *succès d'estime* . . .' That is perfectly true, but I pray you not repeat it, as I want to avoid, as much as is possible, all comparisons. I more or less have that ambition."[32] We shall later examine some of the critical comparisons made in Vienna about the reception of Thalberg, Wieck, and Liszt, including a well-known article in the *Neue Zeitschrift für Musik* that ranked the virtues of each of them in order.[33]

When he returned to Vienna in 1838 Thalberg was well known to local audiences. He had appeared there as early as 1827, at age fifteen, playing frequently in private circles and public concerts.[34] He toured Germany in 1829, England the next year, and was establishing himself in Paris by the mid-1830s, all the while frequently returning to Vienna and participating

Figure 1. Playbill of Sigismond Thalberg's "Farewell Concert" on 1 December 1838.

in concerts given by the various musical societies and institutions, as well as in charity concerts, including one in 1830 to help victims of a serious flood that year. In addition, Thalberg's compositions, unlike Liszt's, were widely performed in Vienna by other pianists.[35] Because of his family, he enjoyed broad aristocratic connections and Court support. His three concerts at the Musikverein in November and December 1836, which Hanslick would later credit with initiating a new era, give a representative idea of his repertory. (The complete programs are given in table 4 at the end of this essay.)[36] Thalberg also planned three concerts late in 1838, but the first two were canceled.[37] (See figure 1.) As Friedrich Wieck commented, Thalberg, like Paganini before him, generally played his own music, which constituted a crucial difference from the programming of Clara Wieck and Liszt, who mixed their own works with those of others. Thalberg's concerts in late 1836 were well received, with a review in the Leipzig *Allgemeine musikalische Zeitung* stating that Thalberg, "the feted hero of the day, gave three concerts at high prices before audiences as large as they are elite. He played everything, without orchestral accompaniment, on a heavenly English piano that had been given to him in Paris by Erard."[38]

Exactly one year later the Wiecks arrived in Vienna, following concerts in Prague. Clara's public appearances between December 1837 and April 1838 were unprecedented in quantity for a pianist and could just as rightly be said to have been epoch making—indeed, that is exactly what Friedrich declared after her second concert, on 21 December: "Clara has founded a new era in piano playing in Vienna with this concert."[39] The eighteen-year-old pianist spent nearly five months in Vienna with her father; her extensive and unusual activities thus directly preceded Liszt's arrival and she stayed on expressly to meet and hear him. Recounting the full and fascinating story of her time in Vienna is beyond the scope of this essay; much of it is related in Friedrich's letters to his wife back in Leipzig, as well as in the diary Clara kept at the time (in which her father also often wrote).[40] She also made relevant comments in clandestine letters written to Robert Schumann, to whom she was already secretly engaged.

The Vienna concerts marked Wieck's first great career success, proving extraordinarily popular as well as lucrative. She was showered with gifts, including manuscripts by Beethoven and Schubert, and with honors, from a torte named after her to dedications of poems and music. Before Wieck, visiting performers tended to give just two or three concerts. (Paganini's fourteen in 1828 were unprecedented, all the more unusual in that most of them took place "off season.") Her visit thus began in the expected way: two concerts were announced (14 and 21 December); after the third on

7 January, she gave another on 21 January, which was billed as the "fourth and last" (see figure 2), but then "by request" she added two more (11 and 18 February).[41] (Table 5 at the end of the essay gives the complete programs of her solo concerts.)

Some aspects of her concerts were typical, such as the use of an orchestra (the one for the Josefstadt Theater under Heinrich Proch), the participation of local virtuosos and actors, and the mixture of genres and composers. From the beginning it is clear that she and her father planned her repertory carefully and waited for success with audiences before going on to program especially challenging pieces. The general seriousness of her concerts was remarked upon, including "early music"—Bach's Prelude and Fugue in C-sharp Major in particular caused quite a stir.[42] Her performance of Beethoven's "Appassionata" Sonata aroused special admiration, but also some controversy over her interpretation.[43] The celebrated writer Franz Grillparzer was inspired to write his well-known poem "Clara Wieck und Beethoven (f-moll Sonate)," which was widely reprinted at the time (Liszt included it in his open letter to Massart) and set to music by Johann Vesque von Püttlingen:[44]

A wizard, weary of the world and life, locked his magic spells in a diamond casket, whose key the threw into the sea, and then he died.

Common, little men exhausted themselves in vain attempts; no instrument could open the strong lock, and the incantations slept with their master.

A shepherd's child, playing on the shore, sees these hectic and useless efforts. Dreamy and unthinking as all girls are, she plunges her snowy fingers into the waves, touches the strange object, seizes it, and pulls it from the sea. Oh! What a surprise! She holds the magic key!

She hurries joyfully; her heart beating, full of eager anticipation; the casket gleams for her with marvelous brilliance; the lock gives way.

The genies rise into the air, then bow respectfully before their gracious and virginal mistress, who leads them with her white hand and has them do her bidding as she plays.[45]

Wieck's six concerts were, however, only part of her participation in Vienna's musical life, which extended to various charity events and Court appearances, not to mention the many occasions on which she played at

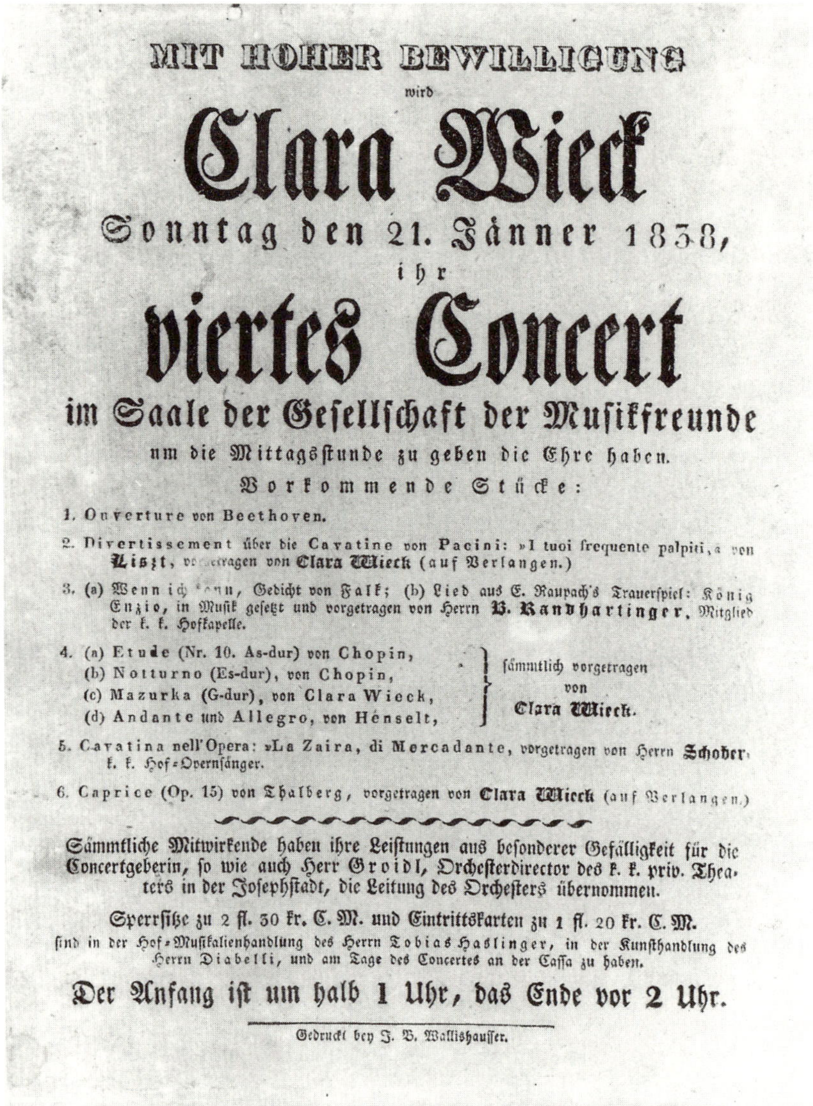

Figure 2. Playbill of Clara Wieck's concert on 21 January 1838.

the private homes of aristocrats and musicians. The list of her public and semipublic appearances alone is daunting (see table 1). I know of no other pianist before Liszt who gave so many individual concerts in such a concentrated period; the *Neue Zeitschrift für Musik* commented that no performer had done so since Paganini.[46]

Table 1. Clara Wieck's Appearances in Vienna 1837–38

14 December	Concert no. 1
21 December	Concert no. 2
26 December	Plays at Court for the Empress
28 December	Plays at the concert of Franz Glöggl
4 January	Plays at the Esterházy Palace
7 January	Concert no. 3
21 January	Concert no. 4
11 February	Concert no. 5 "By request"
18 February	Concert no. 6 "Last"
25 February	Plays at the concert of violinist Johann Mayer
26 February	First concert at Hoftheater
7 March	Plays at Court for Archduchess Sophie
9 March	Second concert at Hoftheater
14 March	Third concert at Hoftheater
18 March	Charity concert at k. k. Universitäts-Saale
25 March	Charity concert at k. k. Redoutensaale
5 April	Charity cconcert at Burgtheater
9 April	Concert for Baroness Erdmann and Countess Forgata

Liszt's Arrival in Vienna

Liszt's youthful Vienna appearances in the early 1820s had long since faded from memory when he returned in 1838. His recent concert repertory in France, Italy, and elsewhere was, not surprisingly, similar in some respects to what he would present in Vienna, although he had never before given so many concerts in such a concentrated time. In contrast to Thalberg, Liszt's own compositions played less of a role in his concerts. He continued to juxtapose virtuoso works with more serious and unfamiliar fare, including piano sonatas and chamber music.[47] Liszt also became increasingly engaged with the music of Beethoven and Schubert. In Paris he had performed Beethoven sonatas and chamber music, and accompanied singers, especially the celebrated tenor Adolphe Nourrit, in Schubert songs. In the year or so before coming to Vienna Liszt had put much of his energies into transcribing Beethoven symphonies and Schubert songs. This, too, may have been a reason for his desire to reengage with the city of these two masters. Beethoven had been dead just eleven years, Schubert less than ten. They were still in the living memory of the Viennese.

Part of the allure of Vienna, no doubt, was the chance to connect and reconnect with close associates of both Beethoven and Schubert, ranging from Czerny and the publisher Tobias Haslinger to less familiar figures like Johann Baptist Jenger, Ludwig Tietze, and Benedict Randhartinger (a fellow classmate from the time when they studied with Salieri), all three of whom joined him in concert. Liszt left a particularly moving account of hearing Baron Carl von Schönstein, an amateur singer Schubert had highly praised and to whom he dedicated *Die schöne Müllerin*, sing some Lieder privately one evening.[48] Vienna was a musical mecca for musicians of a certain sensibility who wanted to continue to participate in the substantive musical tradition of Haydn and Mozart, Beethoven and Schubert. Clara Wieck thought that once she and Schumann married they might move there, and their correspondence shows plans evolving. Schumann, who had not yet visited the city (he would go later in the year), was keen on the idea: "Don't you know that one of my oldest and fondest wishes is to live a number of years in the city where Beethoven and Schubert lived?"[49] At some point Liszt evidently made a comment about doing the same thing, for Clara informed Robert, "I am really afraid that Liszt might move to Vienna, which he wanted very much to do."[50]

Liszt had been planning his return to Vienna for some time, well before the floods in his native Hungary, which he claimed (and posterity has generally believed), prompted his swift departure from Venice and Marie d'Agoult in April 1838. According to his later published account, it was only in early April that he learned of the devastating flood of the Danube the previous month:

I had become accustomed to considering France my homeland, forgetting completely that it was really another country for me. . . . How could I not believe that I was the child of a land where I had loved and suffered so much! How could I possibly have thought that another land had witnessed my birth, that the blood coursing through my veins was the blood of another race of men, that my own people were elsewhere. . . ? [After reading of the flood] I was badly shaken by it. I felt an unaccustomed sense of compassion, a vivid and irresistible need to comfort the many victims. . . . Oh, my wild and distant homeland! Oh, my unknown friends! Oh, my vast family! Your cry of suffering has summoned me to you! . . . I left for Vienna on the 7th of April and planned to give two concerts there: the first for my countrymen, and the second to pay for my traveling expenses.[50]

Here, as in his letters, in contemporaneous press accounts, and in a police report from the time, it is absolutely clear that Liszt presented only one concert to aid the flood victims.[52] Yet many biographies of the composer state that he gave eight such charity concerts, raising a huge amount of money for the cause. Although recent scholars have usually gotten the facts right, Liszt's most influential modern biographer, Alan Walker, has consistently perpetuated errors concerning what he calls Liszt's "eight charity concerts," and seems determined to press the point that Liszt's sole motivation for the trip was nationalistic: "Hungary, and Hungary alone, was the reason Liszt found himself in Vienna."[53]

Not only was there just one charity concert, but there is also good reason to question whether Liszt's trip was really prompted by the flood, by "Hungary, and Hungary alone." He had hoped to conquer Vienna and intended to concertize there without any charitable impetus. Plans were announced in the German press late in 1837.[54] Friedrich Wieck mentioned it in a letter to his wife in November, and Clara passed it on in a Christmas Eve letter to Robert (Liszt is "not yet here but is daily expected").[55] Throughout his life Liszt was a long-range planner, and Vienna was an attractive place—probably the most attractive—to start a new stage of his career, which he had been ruminating about for some time already.[56] Dana Gooley has argued that the charity concert for the flood victims was a "pretext" for going to Vienna and that Liszt's principal motive was more likely the desire to show up Thalberg on his own turf and perhaps to make money and to get away from d'Agoult.[57] It is, of course, impossible to determine his motivations, which no doubt were many and complex, but they were surely not as simple and altruistic as often presented.

By mid-March the seriousness of the Danube flood, which marked a defining moment in Hungary's history, was widely publicized. Given the extent of the devastation, it is hardly surprising that there were many events to help the cause, most of them before Liszt's—indeed, his concert was one of the very last. As early as 19 March the forever calculating Frederick Wieck commented that it was time to leave Vienna: "We must go—Clara can only lose from this point on. If she remains here she must play six more times for other causes—[the English singer Clara] Novello would like to replace us here. The terrible misfortune in Pest makes it difficult to give concerts just for one's personal gain." By this point Clara had given her six individual concerts. As she wanted to meet Liszt, she left Vienna briefly to perform two concerts in Pressburg and upon returning, Friedrich noted: "The abundance of concerts is frightful" (3 April). Clara wrote to Robert: "Concerts for the people in Pest are endless, and they are always packed."[58] Table 2 lists some of the concerts for the flood victims leading up to the one by Liszt.[59]

Table 2. Selected Charity Concerts for Flood Victims of Pest and Ofen in 1838

29 March	Concert at the Conservatory (including Beethoven's *Eroica* Symphony)
1 April	Arcadius Klein in k. k. Redoutensaale (featuring Clara Novello, Richard and Carl Lewy, Baron Carl von Schönstein, Moritz Saphir, and others)
1 April	Concert at k. k. grossen Universitäts-Saale ("Eine grosse musikalische-declamatorische Akademie," with Georg Hellmesberger conducting)
3 April	Concerts Spirituels (featuring Clara Novello, Julie Rettich, Fanny Sallamon, and Ignaz Ritter von Seyfried conducting Beethoven's Fifth Symphony)
5 April	Charity concert (featuring Clara Wieck)
5 April	Joseph Geiger, piano (featuring Joseph Staudigl, Aegid Borzaga, Benedict Randhartinger, Jenny Lutzer, and conducted by Hellmesberger)
7 April	Moritz Saphir's Akademie
11 April	August Anders, fourteen-year-old pianist
15 April	"Musikalische Akademie" for Pest and Ofen
16 April	Adolph Pfeiffer, twelve-year-old flutist from Pest (also featuring Jenny Lutzer)
18 April	Franz Liszt's charity concert

In short, the Vienna Liszt arrived at in April 1838 was inundated, one might say, by charity concerts, which were in any case typical at that time of the season and were greatly expanded that year because of the flood. The fact that Liszt gave one (and only one) to help the crisis was not unusual, although that it was his first concert is noteworthy. It was a keen strategic move, but in certain respects he had no other viable option.[60] He knew what he was doing—in a letter to d'Agoult five days before the concert he told her: "When you receive these lines I shall already be a consecrated man in Vienna [un homme sauvé à Vienne]" (*FLC* 313/84).

Liszt left Venice on 7 April and reached Vienna at midnight on Tuesday the tenth. "My arrival is reported in all the newspapers, and if I am not laboring under delusions as big as Mallefille's fists, I shall create an immense effect. My first concert, for the flood victims, will probably be next Wednesday. In the next forty-eight hours I shall have heard Clara Wieck (who has stayed expressly for me) and also have seen some of the important people again, Metternich, Dietrichstein, et al." (*FLC* 311/83). In a letter from the next day, 13 April, he recounts that the event would indeed take place on Wednesday the eighteenth and that it had already been announced.

Liszt initially planned to stay about two weeks, and the various prolongations of the trip created real tensions with d'Agoult.[61] Like Paganini and Wieck before him, he kept on adding dates, with Haslinger arranging his appearances and managing most of his affairs during the trip. (Concerts, even by established organizations, were not planned or announced much in advance; the idea of a season schedule was invented considerably later.) Liszt soon encountered some of the city's cultural power brokers, including the Hungarian Count Thaddeus Amadé, a former patron of his who, Liszt gleefully reported, "does not like Thalberg and is already ablaze with joy when hearing me" (*FLC* 312/83). He met Count Moritz Dietrichstein, long a prominent force in the musical life of Vienna (and the person to whom Schubert dedicated his "Erlkönig," op. 1), who is commonly identified as Thalberg's father from an affair with Baroness von Wetzlar (with whom, incidentally, Liszt and d'Agoult had just spent time in Venice).[62]

Before appearing in public Liszt played privately for various prominent musicians, including his former teacher Czerny, Mayseder, Merk, Fischhof (who taught piano at the Conservatory), and the Wiecks, who were staying at the same hotel (Zur Stadt Frankfurt). According to many accounts, Liszt held court there. Years later the pianist Heinrich Ehrlich, a student of Thalberg's and in his teens at the time, recalled that Liszt's sitting room was "like an army camp in which all sorts and conditions mingled indiscriminately. . . . He was equally kind to all, but kindest and most bewitching to any young artist in whom he had discovered talent. Was it any wonder that wherever he went he was followed by a swarm of admirers, that he was adored, idolized?"[63] Liszt clearly enjoyed a very rich social life. As he put it to d'Agoult: "I have made no friend here, but still have many courtiers. My room is never empty. I am the man à la mode" (*FLC* 321/89).

Some of the most vivid and informative accounts about Liszt's activities while in Vienna come from the Wiecks. Later in her life Clara, now Clara Schumann, had become exceedingly negative about Liszt and detested his music. (In 1851, for example, she admitted that he still played like the "devil," but stated that his compositions were "just too terrible.")[64] Yet their initial Viennese encounter in 1838 was one of considerable mutual admiration. Liszt had wanted to meet the eighteen-year-old for some time already, and was tremendously impressed by her both personally and musically.[65] "She is a very simple person, very well brought up, ... entirely preoccupied with her art, but nobly and without childishness. She was flabbergasted when she heard me. Her compositions are truly very remarkable, especially for a woman. They have a hundred times more invention and real feeling than all the past and present fantasies of Thalberg" (*FLC* 313/85). Liszt soon dedicated his *Études d'exécution transcendante d'après Paganini* to her, and although she did not dedicate a work to him, Robert Schumann did so with his Fantasy in C, op. 17, some months later.

Liszt spent a good amount of time with the Wiecks during the early part of his stay in Vienna; he reported some of their encounters in letters, as did the Wiecks, and mention even appeared in the press. These reports are helpful in that they give an idea of how frequently Liszt performed in private during his time in Vienna. No doubt there were many soirées and occasions about which we know little or nothing. At Fischhof's, on Wednesday 11 April, the day of his arrival, Liszt played some of his own etudes, as well as etudes by Chopin, preludes and fugues by Mendelssohn originally written for organ, and Schumann's *Fantasiestück* at sight. The next day he again played some of his etudes, the *Reminiscences of I puritani*, and the scherzo from Czerny's Sonata in A-flat, op. 7.[66] The Wiecks' first reactions are found in Clara's diary where Friedrich wrote: "We heard Liszt today at [piano-maker] Conrad Graf's who was sweating as his piano did not survive the great duel—Liszt remained the victor. He cannot be compared with any other player—he is unique. He arouses fear and astonishment and is a very kind and friendly artist. His appearance at the piano is indescribable—he is original." To which Clara added: "He immerses himself in the piano. ... (The Viennese say: he goes under and Clara rises thereby)—[Liszt's] passion knows no bounds; not infrequently he injures the beauty in that he tears the melody apart and uses the pedal too much, which must make his compositions less comprehensible to the laymen if not to the connoisseurs. He has a great intellect; one can say of him 'His art is his life.'"

Clara introduced Liszt to some of Schumann's new compositions and reported on his enthusiastic response, especially to *Carnaval*.[67] On 18 April she played it for him, together with his own fantasy on Pacini's "I tuoi frequenti palpiti": "He acted as if he were playing along and moved his whole body convulsively." Liszt was flattered that she had not only programmed this work at her 21 January concert, but also performed it at soirées and before the empress, "which is an entirely new honor for me" (*FLC* 313/85). On 19 April at Haslinger's, Liszt performed Beethoven's "Archduke" Trio in B-flat, op. 97, together with Mayseder and Merk, and a four-hand version of his *Grand Galop chromatique* with Clara.[68] Friedrich reported:

> He plays Clara's *Soirées* at sight and how he plays them! If he could rein in his power and his fire—who could match his playing? Thalberg has written the same. And where are the pianos that can produce even half of what he can and wants to do . . . ?

> Liszt does not have a nice tone (fingers too thin) and there is little melody in his compositions—yet still full of feeling. In many ways he is the opposite of Henselt—he does not like to play his own compositions.

> It is *strange* that the ages of the four new players: Liszt, Thalberg, Henselt, and Clara—do not even add up to 100. Liszt's musical powers of comprehension surpass all bounds of imagination."[69]

Liszt's initial encounters with the Wiecks and with prominent Viennese musicians, many of whom had had personal ties to Beethoven and Schubert, convinced him that he was on the right course. He informed d'Agoult that "there was an enthusiasm of which you can have no idea. Without a doubt I am going to have an *overwhelming success* on Wednesday morning [with the concert for Pest.]" "Best of all," he reported, he would not have to stay longer than the agreed-upon time, and a second and third concert were already planned that should earn some money (*FLC* 313/84). The first concert, for the flood victims, occurred at 12:30 P.M. on Wednesday 18 April. (See figure 3.) Liszt reported rapid-fire to d'Agoult later that afternoon: "The post is leaving. Just two words. Enormous success. Cheering. Recalled fifteen to eighteen times. Packed hall. Universal amazement. Th[alberg] hardly exists at present in the memory of the Viennese. I am truly moved. Never have I had such a success, or one that can be compared with it" (*FLC* 315/86). He used the same phrase about Thalberg being forgotten in a letter to his mother a week later.[70] It took but this single experience for Liszt to begin saying that he would like to stay in Vienna awhile: "My thoughts are confused," he confesses in the same letter to d'Agoult.

On 23 April, just after his second appearance (an evening concert), Liszt opens his letter to d'Agoult: "Forgive me for talking to you once again of my Viennese successes. You know that I am by no means inclined to exaggerate the effect I produce, but here there is a furor, a mania of which

Figure 3. Playbill of Franz Liszt's charity concert for the flood victims of Pest and Ofen on 18 April 1838.

you can form no idea. Seats for today's concert were already sold out by the day before yesterday, and doubtless tomorrow nothing will be left for the third." He discloses what profits these concerts will bring in, "all expenses paid," and states that there is no reason not to give more: "I could easily give another half dozen concerts, but want to restrict myself to another two, which will make four in three weeks." He is pleased that with this money he can live with d'Agoult "in tranquility this summer" and decides not go to Hungary: "What's the point? You are my homeland, my heaven, and my sole repose" (*FLC* 318–20/87–89).

Liszt's View of Vienna

The rest of this essay will examine Liszt's remaining weeks in Vienna. I shall begin with an overview of his activities drawn from his writings, as well as from those of some with whom he came in contact, and then move on to a more detailed look at his public concerts and their reception. The most immediate information about Liszt's activities upon his arrival is found in his letters. Those he wrote to d'Agoult (her contemporaneous letters to him for the most part do not survive) typically offer a mixture of giddy excitement and nonchalance, proud reportage and depressed complaints. It is as if, after the initial effusions, Liszt realized he had better check himself and switch to a world-weary tone; he states that he had not "yet made a single interesting acquaintance" (*FLC* 316/87), proclaims that his "life is prodigiously monotonous" (*FLC* 327/92), and makes extravagant claims of being miserable without her. His enthusiasm is far more convincing, however, than his professed boredom, especially when placed alongside comments he made to others in which no reservations were expressed. In a letter to Adolphe Nourrit sent soon after leaving Vienna, he praises the city, "where I spent one [*sic*] of the best months of my life, spoilt, adulated and, better than that, *seriously understood* and accepted by an outstandingly intelligent public."[71] A private letter that he wrote to Massart at the same time summarizes his activities and accomplishment: "I will not bore you any more with my success in Vienna. In short, seven concerts for my own benefit, the least successful of which, that is to say the first, netted 3500 francs. Three charity concerts, one for the benefit of the flood victims, one for the institute for the blind and the Sisters of Mercy, and another; a concert at Court, for the Empress and Archduchess Sophie (notwithstanding all the small intrigues and cabals at Court). A personal and artistic effect unheard of in Vienna, a popularity always increasing, and the sympathetic esteem and enthusiasm of the crowd, such was the result of my five-week stay in Vienna."[72]

Although the surviving correspondence is one-sided, we can surmise that Liszt was under considerable pressure to return to Venice. He constantly needed to reassure d'Agoult that he would be with her soon, and noted that although he was not having much fun, he would at least make money: "That's the best of it" (*FLC* 316/87). Money, in fact, is a recurring theme in his correspondence from Vienna (and not just with d'Agoult), the central issue being how much he could make for himself, not how much he might give to charity; indeed, he writes very little about the flood victims or about Hungary. There is no doubt that in Vienna, as throughout his long career, Franz Liszt was an exceedingly generous man and artist, probably unparalleled among musicians of his century, but that generosity need not be exaggerated, as is commonly done regarding this episode in his life. Nor should we underestimate his keen interest at the time in personal gain, especially as he had a mother, mistress, and two children to support. Liszt, who came from humble origins, realized in Vienna that he could make a considerable amount of money—something that was commented upon in the press.[73] The most relevant and repeated story from the trip that casts Liszt as unconcerned with mundane pecuniary matters, however, concerns the remark he allegedly made to Princess Metternich, with whom he did not get along, after she asked him how business had been at his concerts in Italy. Liszt famously responded: "I make music, not business."[74] The anecdote immediately made the rounds in Vienna—Clara recounted it in her journal on 6 May—and Liszt would tell it himself for years to come. And yet on one of the occasions when he had to inform d'Agoult that he would be extending his trip, Liszt explains: "I am making absolutely splendid business" (Je fais de très brillantes affaires) (*FLC* 321/89).[75]

Liszt's letters to d'Agoult from mid-April (their number drastically declined in May, or at least do not survive) waver on the issue of whether, when, and how she should come to Vienna herself, or whether they should perhaps meet halfway in Klagenfurt. At one point he sent her money for the trip.[76] She then became ill in early May and apparently began complaining about her state of health.[77] In any case, a trip to Imperial Vienna was probably not really viable given the illicit nature of her relationship with Liszt, or was simply not something she wanted to endure. Liszt repeatedly professes his great unhappiness and asks himself in the letters why he ever came to Vienna in the first place.[78]

Fame and fortune may have initially been high priorities for Liszt, but after arriving in Vienna he seems to have become increasingly excited by the musical values and regional sentiments he encountered there.[79] Any shift in priorities has been partially obscured by the account he wrote and published months after the trip; the views he expressed therein are rather different from what he stated while in Vienna. This shift is also obscured by well-known comments written many years later in Marie d'Agoult's memoirs, where she states, "Franz had abandoned me for such small motives! It was not to do a great work, not out of devotion, not out of patriotism, but for salon success, for newspaper glory, for invitations from princesses."[80] According to her account, she was for the first time keenly aware of the difference in their social status and felt the trip had changed him. She says she was devastated by his admission that he had been unfaithful to her: "The way in which he spoke about his stay in Vienna brought me down from the clouds. They had found armorial bearings for him—a republican, living with a *grande dame*! He wanted me to be heroic. The women had thrown themselves at his head; he was no longer embarrassed over his lapses, he justified them like a philosopher. He spoke of necessities. . . . He was elegantly dressed; his talk was about nothing but princes; he was secretly pleased with his exploits as Don Juan. One day I said something that hurt him: I called him a *Don Juan parvenu.*"[81]

No doubt these colorful comments were critical in convincing later commentators of the significance of the Vienna trip for Liszt's personal life. Biographers of as different stripes as Ernst Newman and Alan Walker agree on the fundamental significance of his unaccompanied trip. Newman finds that "the decisive moment in their story was Liszt's departure for Vienna in 1838; though their union was to last, at least in outward form, for another six years, it was already virtually over in inner fact, though neither of them seems to have been fully conscious of this at the time."[82] Walker believes that "the roots" of the couple's estrangement "can be traced back to Liszt's departure for Vienna in 1838."[83]

The scholar, like a child watching parents divorce, runs the risk of getting caught in the middle and taking sides in what became a nasty, albeit fascinating, breakup. The passage just quoted from d'Agoult's memoirs may not be accurate, and much of what she says is unbelievable and not supported by documents from the time. Her memoirs are supplemented by some fictional writings to which, as Walker has rightly observed, they often bear a close similarity.[84] While her later writings have proven to be eminently quotable, they should not carry the same weight that befits what she actually wrote in 1838, her diary and letters, which relate nothing about problems with Liszt. In correspondence with Ferdinand Hiller, Louis de Ronchaud, and Adolphe Pictet that spring and summer, she mentions him only to pass along his gossip from Vienna and to take some pride in his success there.[85] None of Liszt's surviving letters from Vienna discuss flirtations, romantic conquests, or other women (except for Clara

Wieck, a safe subject). In short, d'Agoult's memoirs and fiction, too often treated as if they were authentic documents from 1838 in uncritical biographies, must be approached with considerable skepticism. At that time her relationship with Liszt was still relatively young. She had recently given birth to their second child, Cosima, and soon after his return would become pregnant again. The bond was not yet doomed, nor had Liszt abandoned Marie.

Liszt's letters from Vienna focus on his triumphs and money, interspersed with considerations on whether d'Agoult should come and declarations of his love. They are far less rich in detail than the Wiecks' candid observations about local musical and social life. In his later published account he remarked:

> Not a year passes that the Viennese are not visited by two or three renowned artists. I saw Thalberg again there, but he had unfortunately decided not to perform publicly. Kalkbrenner had been announced, but we learned to our great regret that when he arrived in Munich he decided to return to France. I was still in time, however, to meet an interesting young pianist, Mademoiselle Clara Wieck, who had secured a very fine and legitimate success for herself this past winter. Her talent charmed me; she possesses genuine superiority, a true and profound sense of feeling, and she is always high-minded.[86]

There are a large number of references to Thalberg, whom he calls the "Ostrogoth," sprinkled throughout the correspondence. The "big news" at the end of April was of his rival's coming to Vienna and their dining together at Dietrichstein's on 28 April. "I am very glad about the arrival of the Ostrogoth, for I can now be accommodating with no great effort" (*FLC* 321/89). He informed his mother that Thalberg "has bought a beautiful horse and often rides in the Prater. Yet he positively refuses to play in private or in public."[87] But from Clara Wieck's diary we learn that Thalberg had played already. When the Wiecks returned to Vienna from a brief trip to Graz at the end of April, they discovered Thalberg's arrival: "The competition in Vienna continues," Friedrich wrote on 6 May. Liszt performed at a charity concert that day, and Thalberg played his *Moses* fantasy, as well as some etudes at Baron Eduard Tomascheck's.[88] Wieck noted that he apologized for "being out of practice and said he believed that most of the time he plays very well. Today he was embarrassed," to which Clara added: "Thalberg behaves in a very likable manner and continually requested us not to judge him by today's performance."

The presence of the three virtuosos was recognized in various ways, such as their becoming honorary members of the Gesellschaft der Musikfreunde.[89] The prominent artist Joseph Kriehuber created lithographs of Thalberg and Liszt, and Staub of Wieck, which were sold to the public.[90] (See figures 4a, 4b, and 4c.) Liszt informed Marie: "Fifty copies of my portrait have been sold in a single day."[91]

What Liszt most wanted, however, was to be named k. k. Kammervirtuoso. Thalberg had received the honor in 1834 and proudly used the title at home and abroad; it appeared on playbills and on the title pages of some of his compositions. Indeed Liszt made some snide remarks about this in his testy review of Thalberg's compositions in January 1837, where he implied the honor derived from personal connections rather than from artistic merit.[92]

Clara Wieck was given the title k. k. Kammervirtuosin in mid-March, the seventh musician to be so honored; she, too, attached the title to programs and publications. As her diary and correspondence make clear, this all had long been in the planning; various negotiations were necessary because she was young, foreign, and Lutheran.[93] Friedrich noted on 15 March: "The Kaiser's patent was presented. I have never paid 7 fl. for a seal and 1 new Austrian ducat with such joy" and he then gave the citation:

> To the Piano Virtuoso Clara Wieck, By the Grace of God, In consideration of her outstanding artistic skill and as a public gesture of the highest satisfaction with her artistic accomplishments, His Majesty the Kaiser, has decided with the highest cabinet approval on the 13th of this month to bestow the title of k. k. Kammervirtuosin on her, a decision which this present degree confirms with satisfaction.

Despite Liszt's disparaging comments about Thalberg, it is clear that he too lobbied for the Imperial title, which now numbered Paganini, Thalberg, and Wieck among the select. At first he apparently thought that Count Amadé could help, but Liszt did not enjoy the imperial support that his competition did, especially Thalberg, and his suit was unsuccessful. This rejection was indicative of what appears to have been rather widespread opposition to Liszt from some in the Court.[94] Soon after his arrival he presented himself, but Princess Metternich, "as a matter of etiquette, did not receive me the first time" (*FLC* 313/84). The diplomat Philipp von Neumann recorded in his diary Liszt's successful visit soon thereafter: "He astonished us by the self-sufficiency of his manners. He is a product of 'la jeune France' beyond anything one can imagine."[95] Performing at Court proved harder to arrange and dates kept on getting postponed. It was a frustration

Figure 4a. Lithograph by Staub of Clara Wieck (1838).

Figure 4b. Lithograph by Kriehuber of Sigismond Thalberg (1838).

Figure 4c. Lithograph by Kriehuber of Franz Liszt (1838).

Liszt conveyed to d'Agoult: "I am adulated, cajoled, and feted by every-one, with the exception of half a dozen individuals, rather influential ones for that matter, who are fuming and fretting about my successes. Princess M[etternich] is behaving better toward me than she did in the early days. Thalberg is more to the liking of these people. But they don't know what to do about it, because of the great mass of people who have come out unanimously in my favor, thereby consigning the Ostrogoth to the sec-ond rank. A Viennese bon mot: 'L… is das Mandl, Th… das Weibl'" (Liszt is the man, Thalberg the woman) (*FLC* 327/92).

In fact, there was active suspicion about Liszt's politics and morals. Informing d'Agoult that his Court appearance was postponed, he remarked: "By the strangest chance, you played a part in my lack of favor, the Empress's devoutness being taken advantage of for the benefit of some childish animosities or other" (*FLC* 321/89). It was hurtful information that Liszt might better have kept to himself, but it shows there were consequences due to the nature of his personal life. A secret report dated 25 April from Count Josef Sedlnitzky, the powerful chief of police, presents the conclu-sions of an investigation into Liszt's background, especially concerning rumors about his alliances with the likes of George Sand and Abbé Lamennais. Sedlnitzky also mentions the elopement with Marie and con-cludes: "He appears to me indeed as a vain and superficial young man, who affects the eccentric manners of the young French of today, but who is good-natured and, apart from his value as an artist, of no real significance."[96]

Although things improved, with members of the Imperial family attend-ing many of his concerts (as duly noted in the press), Liszt played at Court only once. A few days before he wrote Marie: "After all the intrigues, all the cabals which I have told you about, it is a veritable small triumph for me. I don't need to explain this subject to you. You know me" (*FLC* 329). The event was on the evening of 17 May, in "the apartments of her Majesty."[97] The next day he wrote to his mother: "Despite all the petty cabals and Court intrigues, I played for the Empress yesterday. The suc-cess was complete and my friends extremely pleased."[98] He goes on to tell her that he expects to be appointed k. k. Kammervirtuoso, the honor he mocked, yet desired, and in the end did not obtain.

Liszt's Concerts: In Vienna's View

Summarizing Liszt's trip soon after he left, the Leipzig *Allgemeine musikalische Zeitung* reported:

> Liszt, after giving a charity concert on behalf of the unfortunate inhabitants of the two neighboring cities, Pest and Ofen, performed six more concerts and one soirée musicale. Each of these netted him on average between 1,600 to 1,800 silver Gulden. He also played twice for the Imperial Court in the private residence and just as many times for charitable causes. He even played to help out a female singer who was passing through. And he performed in the salons of the foremost families of this Imperial city, in the homes of various artists, in the showrooms of the finest instrument makers, as well as at his own lodgings. It is not in the character of this childlike, amiable young man to refuse any request, or behave in a self-important or precious manner. The subtly uttered wish of a true friend of art is all that is required, and he is ready at the piano. He will fantasize at the keyboard for an hour just for one overjoyed listener, without thinking of stopping.[99]

This account indicates the enormous scope of Liszt's private and public appearances, and except for mistakenly saying that he played at Court twice rather than once, it helps explain some of the general confusion in the Liszt literature concerning how many public concerts he gave. Because his first appearance was the charity concert, it did not count, so to speak, at least in Liszt's own enumeration and in the way subsequent concerts were listed on the playbills. This created inconsistencies at the time, in the press, and even in Liszt's own letters. For example, Liszt wrote to d'Agoult on 8 May: "This morning [was] my fourth concert (which is actually my sixth, although those for the people of Pest and [the 6 May charity concert] in the Redoute don't count)" (*FLC* 326/91). His final appearance (25 May) was billed as a "Soirée musicale," and that meant it figured differently as well.[100] As reported, Liszt appeared as the featured artist on two further charity concerts; that of 6 May is the one he mentioned to d'Agoult, which benefited the poor, blind, and elderly, and the other, on 24 May, was for the Sisters of Mercy.[101] (See figure 5.) Liszt included these charity concerts in his numbering, which therefore brought the total to ten concerts, still not including an appearance he made at a concert given by the soprano Angelica Lacy in the Augartensaale on 15 May or his playing at Court on 17 May.[102] Table 3 below lists Liszt's public appearances as

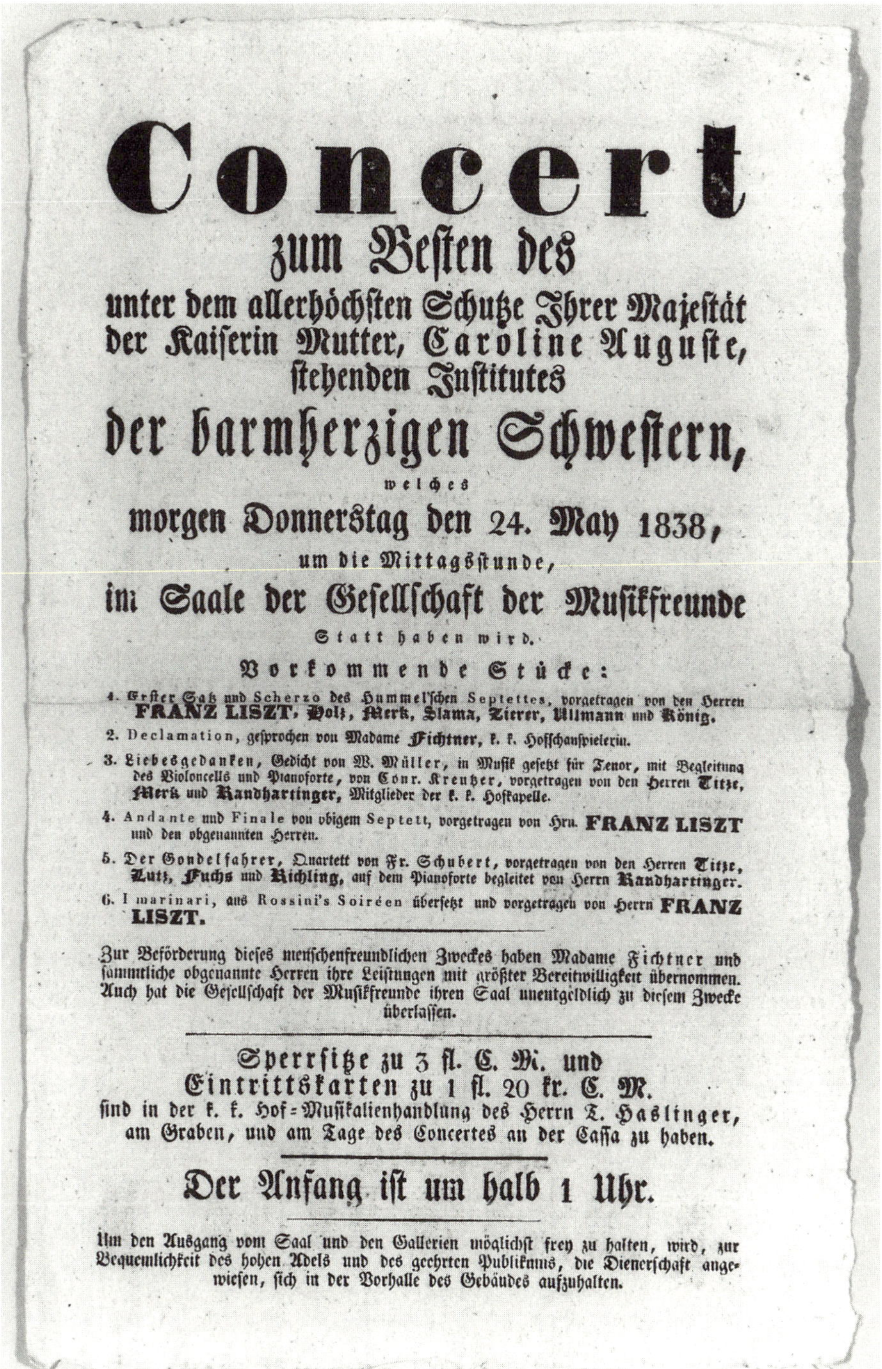

Concert

zum Besten des

unter dem allerhöchsten Schutze Ihrer Majestät
der Kaiserin Mutter, Caroline Auguste,
stehenden Institutes

der barmherzigen Schwestern,

welches
morgen Donnerstag den 24. May 1838,
um die Mittagsstunde,
im Saale der Gesellschaft der Musikfreunde
Statt haben wird.

Vorkommende Stücke:

1. Erster Satz und Scherzo des Hummel'schen Septettes, vorgetragen von den Herren **FRANZ LISZT**, Holz, Merk, Slama, Zierer, Ullmann und König.
2. Declamation, gesprochen von Madame Fichtner, k. k. Hofschauspielerin.
3. Liebesgedanken, Gedicht von W. Müller, in Musik gesetzt für Tenor, mit Begleitung des Violoncells und Pianoforte, von Conr. Kreutzer, vorgetragen von den Herren Titze, Merk und Randhartinger, Mitglieder der k. k. Hofkapelle.
4. Andante und Finale von obigem Septett, vorgetragen von Hrn. **FRANZ LISZT** und den obgenannten Herren.
5. Der Gondelfahrer, Quartett von Fr. Schubert, vorgetragen von den Herren Titze, Lutz, Fuchs und Richling, auf dem Pianoforte begleitet von Herrn Randhartinger.
6. I marinari, aus Rossini's Soiréen übersetzt und vorgetragen von Herrn **FRANZ LISZT.**

Zur Beförderung dieses menschenfreundlichen Zweckes haben Madame Fichtner und sämmtliche obgenannte Herren ihre Leistungen mit größter Bereitwilligkeit übernommen. Auch hat die Gesellschaft der Musikfreunde ihren Saal unentgeldlich zu diesem Zwecke überlassen.

Sperrsitze zu 3 fl. C. M. und
Eintrittskarten zu 1 fl. 20 kr. C. M.
sind in der k. k. Hof-Musikalienhandlung des Herrn T. Haslinger, am Graben, und am Tage des Concertes an der Cassa zu haben.

Der Anfang ist um halb 1 Uhr.

Um den Ausgang vom Saal und den Gallerien möglichst frey zu halten, wird, zur Bequemlichkeit des hohen Adels und des geehrten Publikums, die Dienerschaft angewiesen, sich in der Vorhalle des Gebäudes aufzuhalten.

Figure 5. Playbill of the charity concert for the Sisters of Mercy on 24 May 1838.

announced in the playbills and table 6 at the end of the essay gives the complete programs for his principal concerts.[103]

Table 3. Liszt's Appearances in Vienna 1838

18 April	Charity concert for the Hungarian Flood Victims
23 April	First concert
29 April	Second concert
2 May	Third concert
6 May	Charity concert for Versorgungs- und Beschäftigungs-Anstalt für arme erwachsene Blinde
8 May	Fourth concert
14 May	Fifth concert
15 May	Plays at a concert given by soprano Angelica Lacy
17 May	Plays at Court
18 May	Sixth concert
24 May	Charity concert for the Institut der barmherzigen Schwestern
25 May	Soirée musicale

Liszt's "enormous success," the concert for the flood victims on 18 April in the Musikverein, was different in certain respects from his following appearances. It being the first, it naturally received the most attention in the press. It was the only one of his principal concerts that used an orchestra. Karl Holz, Beethoven's close associate in his final years, led the orchestra in Cherubini's *Les Deux Journées* overture, followed by Liszt performing Weber's *Konzertstück* for piano and orchestra. Although this would become one of Liszt's warhorses, the *Allgemeine musikalische Zeitung* noted that the work was out of favor at the time, and it was only the brilliance of his performance that helped make a strong case. According to their account: "The thunderous applause knew no bounds; and such a tribute of recognition must have affected the virtuoso deeply, accustomed though he was to homage, for hot tears rolled down his cheeks."[104]

Thalberg had offered use of his Erard piano to Liszt for this concert, on which occasion he played two Graf pianos as well.[105] Friedrich Wieck observed: "*Konzertstück* by Weber on Thalberg's English grand—*Puritaner Fantasie* on the Conrad Graf—*Teufelswalzer* and *Étude* (twice) on a second Graf—all three destroyed but everything full of genius—tremendous applause—the artist informal and kind—everything new and unbelievable—only Liszt."[106] As at most of his concerts, there was a "declamation," in this instance a poem by the satirist Moritz Saphir (editor of the *Humorist*) delivered by Julie Rettich, and a Lied, Beethoven's "Adelaide," sung by Benedict Gross. He ended with his *Valse di bravura* and his Grand Etude in G Minor, which had to be repeated, and he was recalled twelve times.[107]

"'Reserved seats already sold out!' This, as all music lovers know, are the most important words on a concert announcement and themselves a powerful verdict on the event itself." So the *Humorist* began its review of his next concert, which took place on Monday, 23 April, at 7 P.M. in the presence of the emperor's mother, her daughter the Archduchess Sophie, and a large assemblage of "musical and literary celebrities."[108] The following five concerts, like the first, were held at 12:30; afternoon concerts were more common than evening ones in Vienna, in part for reasons of lighting and heating. This was not a preplanned series—concerts kept getting added on as Liszt extended his stay. Press reports indicate that they were sold out in advance—with one critic stating that there had never been such a demand for tickets in the history of the Musikverein.[109] The ticket prices, 3 florins c. w. for reserved seats and 1.20 for the remainder, were the same as what Wieck and most others charged at the time.[110] Over his career Liszt was sometimes accused of overcharging, but that was not the case in Vienna. Because the orchestra was not used and he could sell many more seats, however, the profits were higher.

The exceptionally enthusiastic reception of the initial concerts set the tone for intensive comment in the press, as well as in more personal accounts. Throughout his Vienna stay, the critical response was almost unanimously enthusiastic; there were generally no pro- and anti-Liszt factions or debates over what he did well or poorly, which one sometimes encounters during his career. Much of the reception is fairly interchangeable with what had been expressed, or would be, in other cities before and after. Two years later, after concerts in Dresden, Robert Schumann remarked in a glowing review of a Liszt concert: "All of this has been described a hundred times already, and the Viennese, especially, have tried to catch the eagle in every way: with pitchforks, poems, by pursuit, and with snares. But he must be heard—and also seen; for if Liszt played behind the scenes, a great deal of the poetry of his playing would be lost."[111]

In addition to the abundance of criticism issuing from Vienna, its level was also high. Friedrich Wieck remarked on 7 December that "criticism of music here is refined and correct—and judgment made with great intelligence. They are very much interested in true music here and the taste is far better than the reputation." Liszt seems to have been similarly impressed. While overvaluing comments from writers often bought into the hype, trafficking in gossip and fanning the flames of competition, the detailed reviews of figures like Heinrich Adami of the *Allgemeine Theaterzeitung*, who went to all of the concerts, provide valuable documentation of the events. Indeed, press accounts are particularly useful for their reportage—we learn what was new and unusual about Liszt in comparison with other performers. From a large amount of public and private commentary, I will concentrate on briefly distilling five issues that often arise: 1) the nature and quality of Liszt's playing; 2) his repertory; 3) comparisons with other virtuosos; 4) his stage presence and manners; and 5) the phenomenon of Liszt as a celebrity. Most of these factors are interrelated in some way.

Quality. Critics struggled to find the "right words" needed to praise Liszt's playing.[112] Liszt was particularly pleased with two long articles about him, the first by Saphir in the *Humorist* and the other by Ignaz Kuranda in the *Telegraph*, and requested separately from d'Agoult and his mother that they arrange to have them translated into French and reprinted.[113] Both articles are written in extravagantly poetic language; there are not many details about the events themselves, just effusions about the performer. The *Allgemeine musikalische Zeitung*, which reprinted part of Saphir's piece (thereby making it quite widely known), called it a better "portrait" of Liszt than Kriehuber's lithograph. Part of the lengthy article states:

> Liszt knows no rule, no form, no law; he creates them all himself! He remains an inexplicable phenomenon, a compound of such heterogeneous, strangely mixed materials, that an analysis would inevitably destroy what leads to the highest charm, the individual enchantment: namely, inscrutable secret of this chemical mixture of coquetry and childlike simplicity, of whimsy and divine nobleness.
>
> After the concert, he stands there like a conqueror on the field of ballet, like a hero in the lists; vanquished pianos lie about him, broken strings flutter as trophies and flags of truce, frightened instruments flee in terror into distant corners, the listeners look at each other in mute astonishment as after a storm from a clear sky, as after thunder and lightening mingled with a shower of blossoms and buds and dazzling rainbows; and he the Prometheus, who creates a form from every note.[114]

Reading less flowery commentaries one is struck by two common observations that resonate with criticism elsewhere: the orchestral nature of Liszt's playing and his commanding physical presence. Many conclude that you had to *see* him to get the full impact and be able to understand the reaction he evoked in his audiences. Most listeners had never experienced anything like it. In contrast to Thalberg's reserved presence at the keyboard, Liszt's movements were sometimes considered excessive.

Critics had long remarked on the sheer power of Liszt's playing, on its orchestral ambitions, and reported that he "defeated" pianos, breaking strings right and left. The Vienna concerts were no different, especially the first concert with its three pianos and broken strings. Pietro Mechetti wrote in the *Wiener Zeitschrift für Kunst* that "many passages in his works suggest that one of his immediate objectives seems to be to turn the piano as much as possible into an orchestra."[115] Upon hearing Liszt's transcription of Rossini's overture to *William Tell*, Saphir commented on how brilliantly he was able to convey all the orchestral sounds on the piano.[116] Adami praised Liszt's "wonderful symphonic handling of the piano."[117]

Repertory. The fact that after the Pest charity concert Liszt dispensed with the orchestra for the rest of his concerts changed the nature of the events.[118] He appeared in most parts of the program and was onstage far more than was usual. We have seen that Thalberg principally played his own compositions and that in comparison Wieck offered a much wider variety of serious and popular works. Liszt praised the "enlightened eclecticism" of Viennese audiences and satisfied this with the range of the pieces he offered, including chamber music (the Hummel Septet, a piece he performed frequently and would later arrange for piano solo), vocal music, transcriptions, and sonatas; a wide variety of both elevated fare (Beethoven sonatas) and popular (opera fantasies, etudes, and gallops). In total he performed some fifty pieces by eighteen composers, many of them public premieres, all apparently from memory, and only repeating a work from an earlier program as an encore or by request. One such request was for a relatively new addition to his repertory, *Hexaméron*, a set of "Bravour-Variationen" on a march from Bellini's *I puritani*. Liszt wrote the introduction, a variation, some transitions, and finale of this piece, with the other variations contributed by leading pianists of the day: Thalberg, Pixis, Herz, Czerny, and Chopin.[119] (See figure 6.) Liszt improvised just once in the public concerts. Rather than encore Weber's *Invitation to the Waltz* as the audience wanted on 18 May, he launched into an improvisation based on the piece. According to a report in the *Telegraph*, an audience member was so taken as to give out a loud cry of enthusiasm, distracting Liszt, who cut his playing short. "The short improvisation had nonetheless given us a deep insight into the inner life of the artist."[120]

Figure 6. Playbill of Franz Liszt's concert on 14 May 1838.

Comparisons. I have already commented that not only critics but also the performers themselves were constantly making comparisons between and among the leading pianists of the day, principally Liszt, Thalberg, and Wieck, as well as Henselt, Bocklet, Chopin, Kalkbrenner, and others. One of the best-known comparisons was written by Joseph Fischhof for the *Neue*

Zeitschrift für Musik in mid-April, therefore before any of Liszt's public concerts, but after he heard him play privately. He ranks Liszt, Wieck, Thalberg, and Henselt according to a long array of qualities, including purity of playing (T, W, H, L); improvisation (L, W); feeling and warmth (L, H, W, T); versatility (W, L, T, H); beauty of touch (T, H, W, L), and so forth—even "Egoismus" (L, H) and "no grimacing while playing" (T, W) are considered. He concludes that Liszt is the representative of the French Romantic school, Thalberg of the voluptuous Italian, and Wieck and Henselt of the sentimental German.[121]

Thalberg, as the hometown favorite, was the pianist typically invoked by the critics. Many reviews of Liszt's concerts mention him, usually to Liszt's advantage—Liszt is a genius, Thalberg a talent. An interesting diary by a nineteen-year-old Viennese woman, Therese Walter, an amateur musician whose family hosted musical soirées Liszt attended, gives some idea of how pervasive a topic of conversation this comparison was among concertgoers. Reacting to a poem by Josef Zedlitz that cast Liszt as Byron and Thalberg as Goethe, she remarks that the comparison is apt to a point, especially for Liszt, but that the talented Thalberg is not in the same league as Goethe. The drama between the two pianists, she believes, would make an excellent subject for a play.[122]

As we have seen, Wieck had recently enjoyed a phenomenal success in Vienna, but Liszt overshadowed her. Adami was the most candid:

> I do not want to diminish the accomplishments of this excellent artist, but inadvertently one is reminded that much, or rather all, in art and in life depends on that one lucky moment, and that frequently chance and circumstance determine the degree of one's reputation. What if that young artist had arrived here after Liszt? What would the outcome of her appearance have been then? This question is easily and without much afterthought answered by those who have heard both perform. In posing it, I sincerely do not want to disavow the acclaim that Clara Wieck has received, or to judge the enthusiasm for her exaggerated, or even laughable. Rather, my intention is to draw attention to the fact that much of a virtuoso's fortune and reputation depend on the choice of the right moment. Clara Wieck has presented us with superb artistry. Should we begrudge her the laurel wreaths that a public devoted to the beautiful laid at her feet as a sign of grateful remembrance; just because another came along whose genius surpasses hers? Those who think along such lines will just as quickly retract the enthusiasm with which they greeted Liszt as false or inauthentic when another star appears on the artistic

horizon. Let us not resent what anyone achieves by talent or genius. The domain of art is inexhaustible. The creative force of the genius is invincible. And even if we consider something today as unsurpassable, we will never be certain that something even more superior may not appear tomorrow![123]

Clara seems to have felt similarly. Although she did not perform in Vienna following Liszt's arrival, she did concertize in Graz soon after hearing him and before returning to Leipzig. She confided in a letter to Schumann: "Once again I survived playing at the theater. The applause was as usual, but my playing seemed so bland and so—I don't know how to put it— that I almost lost interest in continuing my tour. Ever since I heard and saw Liszt's bravura, I feel like a beginner."[124] Her father wrote to her mother after Liszt's first appearance: "It was the most remarkable concert of our lives, and it will not be without lasting influence on Clara. The old schoolmaster will take care that she does not follow his many tricks and eccentricities."[125]

Manners. It was not just the way Liszt played, what he played, and how he looked that fascinated audiences—his style and manners were also completely new to them, especially the way he would regularly engage in conversation with the audience, in French generally, and foster such an informal atmosphere. As Dana Gooley has rightly observed, the press generally said little about any Hungarian connection for Liszt, but tended to identify him as French.[126] Adami reports that "Liszt appears each time well before the start of the concert and mingles with the public, speaking and conversing with everyone, leading the ladies to their seats, creating space and order, is here, then there, and generally makes himself the host of the hall. All this is completely new for Vienna, one must see it for oneself."[127] Clara noted in her diary on 6 May that while Liszt "is playing in his concerts, he speaks with the ladies sitting around him, always stays with the orchestra, drinks black coffee, and behaves as if he were at home. That pleases everyone now, and he creates a furor. Lenau calls him 'the greatest musical magician.' His behavior is totally French and artless." The Leipzig *Allgemeine musikalische Zeitung* observed:

> Every corner of the hall was packed to the rafters, even the pit which had been cleared and turned into regular seating. It was so full that there was hardly room enough for the artist and his instrument. There he sits then, in the midst of an exclusive circle of ladies, a jewel in the crown, conversing first with the one on his right, then with the

one on his left, all with a mix of innocence and the ingratiating charm learned in the world of the Parisian salons. And it is in this mix that his indescribable and unprecedented appeal lies. Even members of the highest aristocracy feel at ease here. We are no longer dealing with a public concert but rather a gathering of guests invited to experience the greatest aesthetic appreciation, an assembly where everyone knows everyone, where the joy of participation sparkles in every eye, and where all are united by the same cause; this shared engagement even succeeds in lessening the differences between classes. But when the master touches the keys once more, the roaring sea calms down. Dead silence returns, as if decreed by powerful Neptune himself.

As we see in this report and many others, the audience itself was notable; the press related for each concert the presence of the highest nobility and of the "artistic nobility of our musical city."[128]

Liszt as phenomenon. For a variety of musical and extramusical reasons, therefore, a Liszt appearance was no longer just a concert; he was a "musical Faust," a "magician" who mesmerized audiences.[129] One after another, critics remarked that nothing like this had ever happened in Vienna, with the possible exception of Paganini a decade earlier. As Clara wrote to Schumann, Liszt "has caused a stir as Vienna has never known. He is truly an artist whom one must see and hear for oneself."[130] Therese Walter's diary provides a glimpse of a young woman who was clearly entranced by the virtuoso, fascinated by the gossip about his life, his relationships with Marie d'Agoult and other women, thrilled when she is given Kriehuber's lithograph, and overwhelmed by his musicianship. Such a private account reflected what readers found almost daily in the press, where the social mixed with the artistic, the man with the art, the celebrity with the artist. The *Allgemeine musikalische Zeitung* assessed the situation in this way:

The arrival of this phenomenon among pianists was so unexpected, and his stay of such short duration, that the longing to hear and admire him is quite pardonable. And so, invitation upon invitation from the highest nobility and most distinguished families press and cross each other daily, nay hourly; and the modest, unassuming artist, doubly amiable by his obliging courtesy, which can refuse no one anything, is quite out of breath; at times, indeed, he would need to divide himself in two.[131]

The Vienna *Anzeiger* provided a summary of Liszt's trip soon after he left:

> People intrigue to get tickets, and on a hot summer's day sit in the hall for a full hour before the start of the concert. The orchestra is removed so that the elite of the ladies of fashionable society may have seats near the virtuoso. Liszt remains the same, but new merits are daily discovered in him. People exchange anecdotes about his life, wait for him in the street, try to catch a word or two from him, order his portrait, buy his handwriting—in short, he becomes the vogue. Any pretext is used to make his acquaintance; he is regularly besieged with dinners, suppers, and parties. The honor of inviting him and receiving him graciously is coveted by even the great and mighty. And this is where his Parisian upbringing stood him in excellent stead. With amiable ease of manner, cheerful, chatty, and courteous, he moved in the world to which he had long been accustomed.[132]

To be sure, Liszt had experienced adoring audiences and enthralled critics before, and it would be some six years before Heinrich Heine coined the term "Lisztomania," but according to his own accounts he had never encountered anything like what happened to him in Vienna in the spring of 1838. That this enthusiasm and adulation merged with what he perceived as higher musical values and understanding made the experience all the more welcome—and seductive.

Liszt and the Viennese Tradition

The Viennese public tremendously impressed Liszt, as one can see in his letter to Adolphe Nourrit quoted earlier and as he repeated in his published account:

> Playing for such an intelligent and friendly audience, I was never given pause by the fear that I would not be understood, and without appearing foolhardy, I was able to play the most serious works of Beethoven, Weber, Hummel, Moscheles, and Chopin; portions of Berlioz's *Symphonie fantastique*; fugues by Scarlatti and Handel; and finally, those dear etudes, those beloved children of mine that had seemed so monstrous to the inhabitants of La Scala.
>
> This I must say: ever since I have been playing the piano and in all my frequent contacts with the music lovers of all nations, I have never encountered an audience as sympathetic as the one in Vienna;

it is enthusiastic without being dazzled, difficult to please without being unjust, and its enlightened eclecticism allows for all types of music, for nothing is excluded through prejudice.[133]

One composer Liszt does not mention here is Schubert, whose music he performed more than any other during the visit, both accompanying Lieder and offering the new Lied transcriptions. A further crucial exposure was to Schubert's *Divertissement à la hongroise* (D818), which led to his *Mélodies hongroises (d'après Schubert)* and eventually to a wide range of "Hungarian" music. (It is somewhat ironic that the principal musical significance of the trip with respect to his homeland—since he never actually made it to Hungary as he had hoped—came by way of Schubert.)

Viennese critics hailed Liszt as an inspired interpreter of Beethoven.[134] He performed two of Beethoven's piano sonatas (A-flat Major and C-sharp Minor) and "Adelaide" on his concerts, as well as the "Archduke" Trio at one of Haslinger's soirées. Unlike Liszt's early personal encounter with Beethoven (even though there is considerable uncertainty about its extent), there is no indication that he had met Schubert while studying in Vienna, nor is anything known about his exposure to his music at that time. After settling in Paris, he began to encounter it, even though Schubert was rarely played in France at the time.[135] He started to perform Schubert Lieder and then to transcribe them.[136] With the return to Vienna this engagement with Schubert's music increased dramatically. Although Liszt's promotion of Beethoven's music was significant, especially as it affected the view of his late works, Beethoven's name needed little help. The consequences of Liszt's activities for Schubert reception, on the other hand, were profound, as the composer was still relatively little known outside of Vienna. Liszt first performed two of his Schubert transcriptions on his second appearance (23 April). The premiere of what was in essence a new subgenre evoked general comment about the viability and advisability of the idea.[137] The critic in the *Humorist* praised the "indescribable magic" of his transcription, *Ständchen*, and said of the reworkings: "They were neither variations nor potpourris. These were the simple, heartfelt songs of the divine departed one, from the motives of which the great composer cast thoughtful, simple, and yet so artistic flowers at the tear-stained grave of the great beloved song poet."[138] Adami initially reacted to the "original" pieces thus: "They are not so much brilliant concert pieces, as one usually encounters today, but rather musical impromptus, in which the song chosen constitutes the foil."[139]

After Liszt accompanied Tietze in "Erlkönig" at the next concert, Adami stated that he doubted the accompaniment had ever been played so effectively and commended the singer for his successful performance, given the potential to be overshadowed by Liszt.[140] A critic for the *Wiener Telegraph* agreed: "What poetry did Liszt not bring to Schubert's "Erlkönig"! Has one ever heard the song performed this way? At this speed, with this coloring, with this magic cloak of romanticism?"[141] But it was Liszt's transcription *Erlkönig* that would become one of his most popular repertory pieces and a staple encore throughout his career.[142] It was apparently first performed publicly as an encore at the 18 May concert. Adami wrote that it would be difficult to say which composition he played best, since everything was performed so brilliantly. Yet if the question be pressed, *Erlkönig* "would be the greatest and most extraordinary of all his performances. I do not believe that 'Erlkönig' has ever been sung as masterfully and made as deep and powerful an impression on its audience as at this concert where the voice and the accompaniment merged as a direct whole from an inspired artistic soul. Where, moreover, could one find a singer who in the performance of this song would be capable of matching the accompaniment of a Liszt."[143] The success of the Schubert transcriptions soon led to their publication. In May Haslinger released four songs under the title *Hommage aux Dames de Vienne*, and Anton Diabelli followed with *12 Lieder*.[144] (See figure 7.)

Adieu Vienna

Vienna gave Liszt the opportunity to reengage intimately with a gloried musical tradition. The *Humorist* bid him farewell noting that such remarkable triumphs had been enjoyed by few others in "the city that claims Mozart, Haydn, and Beethoven among her own."[145] His final concert, a "Soirée musicale" on 25 May, was held at the Musikverein at the unusual time of 10:30 in the evening before a sold-out audience. (See figure 8.) Adami states that: "Never was there, nor will there ever be again, such a concert. It almost seemed as though this time he wished to exhibit the most dazzling riches of his art, to make the parting doubly hard for us."[146]

Liszt began with his transcription of the *Wilhelm Tell* Overture, presented his *Rondeau fantastique: Yo que soy el contrabandista*, accompanied Johann Vesque von Püttlingen in two of the singer/composer's own songs, and performed Berlioz for the first time in Vienna—the second and fourth movements from *Symphonie fantastique*. The evening concluded with three Schubert transcriptions—*Sei mir gegrüsst*, *Erlkönig*, and *Die Post*—followed by the *Valse di bravura* as an encore.[147] According to Adami: "I will only say that the public was in a state of excitement even before the first piece and that with the performances of *Erlkönig* and *Bravourwalzer* the enthusiasm

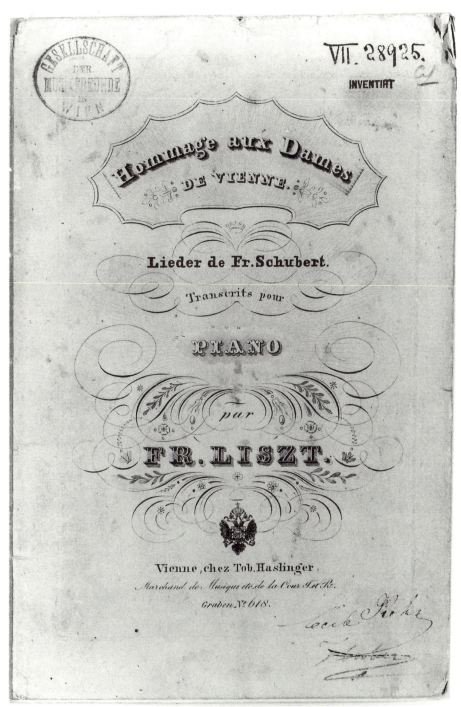

VII. 28925.

INVENTIRT

Hommage aux Dames

DE VIENNE.

Lieder de Fr. Schubert.

Transcrits pour

PIANO

par

FR. LISZT.

Vienne, chez Tob. Haslinger,

Marchand de Musique etc. de la Cour I. et R.

Graben No 618.

Figure 7. Cover of "Hommage aux Dames de Vienne," Liszt's transcriptions of four Schubert songs (1838).

Figure 8. Playbill of Franz Liszt's "Soirée musicale" on 25 May 1838.

mounted to a level such as I have never experienced at a concert."[148] Liszt set off for Italy the next day: "Before he quitted Vienna, a parting dinner was given at which the composer sat up till morning, toasting, etc. Liszt, then wrapped in his cloak, threw himself into his carriage, but was surprised at the end of the first stage by a party of friends, who had hastened before him for the gratification of 'more last words.' Such was his success in Vienna."[149]

Some three weeks earlier, on 8 May, Liszt had written to d'Agoult words she no doubt wanted to hear: "I am mortally sad. At every moment I ask myself why I came here, what I have to do here, of what use to me are these plaudits of the multitude and the meaningless noise of puerile celebrity. Yes, Marie, I am mortally sad." A week later he sounded the same woeful chord: "And I, too, my poor angel, am mortally sad . . . what made me decide to come here at all?" (*FLC* 326, 330/91, 93).

Like Liszt himself, perhaps, we shall never know exactly why he came to Vienna—was it primarily out of a patriotic desire to help the Hungarian flood victims, was it for career advancement, to expand his musical horizons and inaugurate a new act in his life, to gain distance from d'Agoult, or for some complex mixture of these factors and others? Whatever his intentions, once he came and triumphed, the initial reasons mattered less anyway. Both he and Vienna experienced a new kind of musical celebrity, one that juxtaposed, and sometimes combined, virtuosic display and substantive compositions. Upon his return to Italy, Marie thought him changed, much more worldly and affected. For his part, after fifteen years of living, creating, and performing in the French and Italian musical and social spheres, Liszt had reconnected with the region of his birth and with the music that meant the most to him. At the age of twenty-six he was searching for direction in his life and career. Vienna allowed him to envision new vistas. As he soon wrote in his account of the episode:

Always surrounded by a group of good friends who catered to my every wish, always beset by the sound of the music I made, always on the eve or the morrow of giving a concert, I spent my time in Vienna in a manner that was far too extraordinary to give me the right to add anything else about it, except to say that I came away with the fondest memories of my stay there and the regret that it had been so short.[150]

Table 4. Thalberg's Three Concerts, 1836

20 November 1836   Sunday, 12:30, Musikverein

      1   Cherubini, *Anacreon* Overture

      2   Thalberg, New Fantasy

      3   Persiani, Aria from *Ines di Castro*, sung by Sophie Löwe

      4   Franchomme, Variations for cello, performed by Aegid Borzaga

      5   Declamation

      6   Thalberg, Third Caprice

8 December 1836   Thursday, 12:30, Musikverein

      1   Beethoven, *Egmont* Overture

      2   Meyerbeer/Thalberg, Fantasy on motives from *Les Huguenots*

      3   Gluck, Aria from *Iphigenia aus Tauris*, sung by Ludwig Tietze

      4   Jansa, Capriccio for Violin, performed by Leopold Jansa

      5   Declamation by Mr. Löwe

      6   Thalberg, New Fantasy on "God Save the King" and "Rule Britannia"

16 December 1836   Friday, 12:30, Musikverein

      1   Cherubini, *Faniska* Overture

      2   Thalberg, Caprice

      3   Bellini, Aria from *I puritani*, sung by Mr. Schober

      4   Ghys, *Thème varié*, performed by Mr. Ghys

      5   Declamation by Mad. Fichtner

      6   Thalberg, Fantasy on "God Save the King" and "Rule Britannia" (by request)

Table 5. Wieck's Six Concerts, 1837–38

14 December 1837   Thursday, 12:30, Musikverein

1   Proch, Overture

2   Pixis, Concert-Rondo

3   Donizetti, Aria from *Anna Bolena*, sung by Mr. Hirsch

4a   Henselt, Etude, "Wenn ich ein Vöglein wär', flög ich zu dir"

4b   Chopin, Nocturne (F-sharp, op. 15, no. 2)

4c   Arpeggio-Etude, op. 10, no. 11

4d   Henselt, Andante and Allegro

5   Beriot, Violin Concerto (first movement), played by Henry Blagrove

6   Wieck, Concert-Variations on the cavatina from Bellini's *Pirata*, op. 8

21 December 1837   Thursday, 12:30, Musikverein

1   Kreutzer, Overture

2   Wieck, Concertino for Piano and Orchestra, op. 7

3   Randhartinger, "Elfengesang," sung by the composer

4a   Bach, Prelude and Fugue in C-sharp Major [encored]

4b   Chopin, Mazurka in F-sharp Minor

4c   Chopin, Etude in G-flat Major

5   Declamation by Mr. Marr of Maltiz's "Der graue Gast"

6   Orchestral Entr'acte

7   Henselt, Variations on a theme from Donizetti's *Liebestrank*, op. 1 [finale encored]

7 January 1838   Sunday, 12:30, Musikverein

1   Mozart, *Magic Flute* Overture, performed by the three Eichhorn brothers with their father

2   Beethoven, Sonata in F Minor, op. 57, "Appassionata"

3 Weiss, "Verlornes Minneglück," poem by Janitschka Jr., for tenor with horn and piano accompaniment, performed by Franz Mum, Eduard König, and the composer

4a Chopin, Nocturne in B Major

4b Wieck, *Hexentanz*, Impromptu, op. 5, no. 1

4c Henselt, Lied ohne Worte (A-flat Major)

4d Henselt, Etude with the motto: "Wenn ich ein Vöglein wär', flög ich zu dir"

5 Lafont, Potpourri for two violins, performed by the Eichhorn brothers

6 Wieck, Concert-Variations on the cavatina from Bellini's *Pirata*, op. 8

21 January 1838   Sunday, 12:30; Musikverein

1 Beethoven, Overture

2 Pacini/Liszt, Divertissement on the cavatina of "I tuoi frequenti palpiti" (by request)

3a Poem by Falk

3b Randhartinger, Lied from the tragedy *König Enzio*, performed by the composer

4a Chopin, Etude in A-flat Major

4b Chopin, Nocturne in E-flat Major

4c Wieck, Mazurka in G Major, op. 6, no. 5

4d Henselt, Andante and Allegro

5 Mercadante, Cavatina from *Zaira*, sung by Mr. Schober

6 Thalberg, Caprice, op. 15 (by request)

11 February 1838   Sunday, 12:30, Musikverein

1 Proch, New Overture

2 Mendelssohn, *Capriccio brillant*, with orchestra, op. 22

3 Schubert, "Die zürnende Diana," sung by Mr. Schmidbauer

4a Sechter, Fugue for Clara Wieck's Album

4b Wieck, Mazurka, op. 6, no. 5 [encored]

4c Henselt, Allegro with the motto: "Orage, tu ne saurais m'abattre" [encored]

5 Müller, "Das Erkennen," sung by Mr. Schmidbauer

6 Chopin, Variations on "Là ci darem la mano," op. 2

18 February 1838 Sunday, 12:30, Musikverein

1 Mozart, Overture

2 Wieck, Concertino for piano and orchestra (by request)

3 Lachner, "Bewusstseyn," poem by Rellstab, for tenor with horn and piano accompaniment; performed by Gottfried and Eduard König

4 Beethoven, Piano Trio in B-flat Major, op. 97, performed by Professors Böhm and Merk

5 Overture

6a Henselt, New Etude in E-flat Minor, op. 2, no. 8

6b Henselt, Andante with the motto "Exaucé mes voeux," op. 2, no. 3

6c Bach, Prelude and Fugue in C-sharp Major (by request)

Table 6. Liszt's Eight Concerts, 1838

18 April 1838   Wednesday, 12:30, Musikverein

1 Cherubini, *Die Tage der Gefahr* Overture

2 Weber, *Konzertstück*

3 Declamation by Julie Rettich of Moritz Saphir's "Des Kindes zuversicht"

4 Bellini/Liszt, *Reminiscences des Puritains*

5 Beethoven, "Adelaide," sung by Benedict Gross

6 *Valse di bravura* and Grande Étude in G Minor [encored]

23 April 1838   Monday, 7 P.M., Musikverein

1 Hummel, Septet for piano, flute, oboe, horn, viola, cello, and bass, performed by Messrs. Zierer, Ullmann, König, Holz, Merk, Slama, and Liszt

2 Declamation by Marie Denker

3 Lachner, "Das Waldvöglein," performed by Jenny Lutzer, Richard Lewy, Jr., horn, and Karl Levy, piano

4a Schubert/Liszt, *Ständchen*

4b Schubert/Liszt, *Lob der Thränen*

5 Pacini, Cavatina, "I tuoi frequenti palpiti," sung by Jenny Lutzer

6 Pacini/Liszt, Fantasy on the cavatina "I tuoi frequenti palpiti"

29 April 1838   Sunday, 12:30, Musikverein

1 Czerny, Piano Sonata in A-flat, Andante and Scherzo

2 Schubert, "Liebesbotschaft," sung by Ludwig Tietze

3 Declamation by Marie Denker of Moritz Saphir's "Rococo Gedicht"

4a Moscheles, Two Etudes

4b Chopin, Two Etudes

5 Schubert, "Erlkönig," sung by Ludwig Tietze

6 Rossini/Liszt, "La serenata" and "L'orgia," Fantasy on motives from Rossini's *Soirées musicales* [last section encored]

2 May 1838		Wednesday, 12:30, Musikverein
	1	Beethoven, Sonata in A-flat
	2	Schubert, "Das Ständchen," sung by Benedict Gross
	3	Meyerbeer/Liszt, *Reminiscences des Huguenots*
	4	Schubert, "Der Hirt auf dem Felsen," sung by Benedict Gross, with clarinet played by Professor Josef Friedlowsky
	5	Liszt, Etude in A-flat *Grand Galop chromatique* [encored]

8 May 1838		Tuesday, 12:30, Musikverein
	1	Meyerbeer/Liszt, *Réminiscences de la Juive*
	2	Schubert, "Widerspruch," for four male voices, sung by Messrs. Tietze, Lutz, Fuchs, and Richling with Emanuel Mikschik, piano
	3	Chopin, New Etudes Moscheles, New Etudes
	4	Schubert, "Der Wanderer," sung by a "dilettante"
	5	Schubert, "Der Gondelfahrer," for four male voices, sung by Messrs. Tietze, Lutz, Fuchs, and Richling with Emanuel Mikschik piano
	6	HEXAMÉRON, Bravour-Variationen (*) on the march from Bellini's *I puritani*, composed by Chopin, Czerny, Herz, Liszt, Pixis, and Thalberg (*) Introduction by Liszt, Variation One by Thalberg; Variation Two by Liszt; Variation Three by Pixis; Variation Four by Herz; Variation Five by Czerny; Variation Six, Andante, by Chopin; Finale by Liszt [the Czerny variation may have been omitted on this occasion]

14 May 1838	Monday, 12:30, Musikverein

1 Beethoven, Sonata in C-sharp Minor

2 Schubert, "Das Fischermädchen," "Der Kreuzzug," "Die Forelle," performed by Benedict Randhartinger, ["Die Forelle" encored]

3 Kessler, Etude (Andante in A-flat)
Handel, Fugue in E Minor
Kessler, Octave-Etude
Scarlatti, "Cat's Fugue" in G Minor

4 Randhartinger, "Elfengesang," "Mannestrotz," sung by the composer

5 HEXAMÉRON, Bravour-Variationen (*) on the march from Bellini's *I puritani*, composed by Chopin, Czerny, Herz, Liszt, Pixis, and Thalberg (by request)

(*) Introduction by Liszt, Variation One by Thalberg; Variation Two by Liszt; Variation Three by Pixis; Variation Four by Herz; Variation Five by Czerny; Variation Six, Andante by Chopin; Finale by Liszt

18 May 1838	Friday, 12:30, Musikverein

1 Liszt, Romantic fantasy (on two Swiss melodies)

2 Beethoven, "Neue Liebe, neues Leben," sung by Mr. Lutz, accompanied by Johann Baptist Jenger

3 Weber, *Invitation à la valse*

[Liszt then added an improvisation on Weber]

4 Schubert, "Auf dem Strome," "Die Post," sung by Mr. Lutz

5 Rossini/Liszt, "Li marinari" and "La tarantella," from Rossini's *Soirées musicales*

[Encore: Schubert/Liszt, *Erlkönig*]

25 May 1838		Friday, 10 P.M., Musikverein
	1	Rossini/Liszt, *Wilhelm Tell* overture
	2	Vesque, "Ständchen" (poem by Uhland), sung by Ludwig Tietze
	3	Liszt, *Rondeau fantastique: Yo que soy el contrabandista*
	4	Vesque, "Ermunterung" (poem by Egon Ebert), for voice and horn with piano accompaniment, performed by Ludwig Tietze, Professor Lewy, and Liszt
	5	Berlioz/Liszt, fragments from *Symphonie fantastique*, a) Scène du bal, b) Marche de supplice
	6	Schubert/Liszt

1 *Sey mir gegrüsst*
2 *Erlkönig*
3 *Die Post*
[Encore: Liszt, *Grande Valse di bravura*]

NOTES

I am grateful to Nancy B. Reich for sharing with me sections of her translation of the diaries of Clara Wieck. I appreciate the help I received from Otto Biba and his associates at the archives of the Gesellschaft der Musikfreunde in Vienna. My thanks to Anja Hechong Boenicke and Irene Zedlacher for checking German translations and to Judit Gera for assistance with Hungarian sources. Funding for part of the archival research in Vienna was provided by grants from the American Council of Learned Societies, the Austrian Cultural Institute, and Bard College. I also wish to acknowledge the helpful suggestions offered by Christopher Hatch and Dana Gooley on earlier drafts of this essay.

1. A useful table of where Liszt spent his last years is given in Derek Watson, *Liszt* (New York: 1989), pp. 134–35. One might add another site of major importance: Bayreuth. Although Liszt did not spend much time there, it is where he died and is buried.

2. Liszt's first published work was the "Diabelli" variation he contributed to a collection the publisher Anton Diabelli assembled in 1824 and which included works by fifty composers (among them Schubert, Czerny, Hummel, Moscheles, and Weber). Another set on the same insipid tune, by Beethoven, op. 120, was released separately; see Otto Erich Deutsch, *Schubert: A Documentary Biography*, trans. Eric Blom (London: 1946), p. 348. For information about Liszt's various concert activities, see Emmerich Karl Horvath, *Franz Liszt: Kindheit* (Eisenstadt: 1978), vol. 1, p. 75; and Iwo Zaluski and Pamela Zaluski, *The Young Liszt* (London: 1997), pp. 32–48.

3. Liszt made sure that most of his major later works, from tone poems to the grand oratorio *St. Elisabeth*, were performed in Vienna; during the last two decades of his life he visited nearly every year and stayed with his "cousin" Eduard in an apartment in the Schottenhof; see Eduard Ritter von Liszt, *Franz Liszt: Abstammung, Familie, Begebenheiten* (Vienna: 1937).

4. See letter to Marie d'Agoult of 14 April 1846, Adrian Williams, *Franz Liszt: Selected Letters* (Oxford, Eng.: 1998), p. 235; Alan Walker, *Franz Liszt: The Weimar Years, 1848–1861* (New York: 1989), p. 110.

5. Peter Raabe, *Liszts Leben* (Tutzing: 1968), p. 12.

6. *Allgemeiner Musikalischer Anzeiger,* 21 June 1838, pp. 97–100, in Dezsö Legány, *Franz Liszt: Unbekannte Presse und Briefe aus Wien, 1822–1886* (Budapest: 1984), p. 33 (hereafter *Presse und Briefe*); translated in Adrian Williams, *Portrait of Liszt by Himself and His Contemporaries* (Oxford, Eng.: 1990), p. 107.

7. Translations of "Lettre d'un bachelier ès-musique; A M. Lambert Massart" appeared in the *Neue Zeitschrift für Musik* 9, no. 32 (19 October 1839): 128); *Anzeiger* 11, no. 5 (31 January 1839): 33; *Allgemeine Theaterzeitung* 32, no. 40 (25 February 1839): 198; and *Társalkodó* 24, (23 March 1839): 94; see *Franz Liszt: Sämtliche Schriften*, ed. Detlef Altenburg, vol. 1, ed. Rainer Kleinertz, assisted by Serge Gut (Wiesbaden: 2000), pp. 178–205; English translation in *An Artist's Journey: Lettres d'un bachelier ès-musique, 1835–1841*, ed. and trans. Charles Suttoni (Chicago and London: 1989), pp. 100–44. The often discussed issue of which of the early published writings Liszt wrote solely himself or with the assistance of Marie d'Agoult seems fairly clear in this case; for one thing she was not with him in Vienna and would have hardly endorsed some of what Liszt wrote in the essay. In a letter to his mother

later that summer he asks her to tell Massart that "I have written him an open letter in the *Gazette musicale*, and that he will receive it shortly" (Williams, *Selected Letters*, p. 95).

8. The best narrative account is Emmerich Karl Horvath, *Franz Liszt: Italien* (Eisenstadt: 1986), vol. 3, pp. 77–125. Invaluable is Legány's *Presse und Briefe*. Meticulously annotated and filled with essential materials, it should be noted that the selection of journals presented for the 1838 concerts is limited and entries are sometimes abridged. See also Robert Stockhammer, "Die Wiener Konzerte Franz Liszts," *Österreichische Musikzeitschrift* 16 (1961): 437–42. See also Alan Walker's problematic account in *Franz Liszt: The Virtuoso Years, 1811–1847* (New York: 1983), pp. 253–82.

9. Specifically, a project that takes into account what Hans Robert Jauss calls "the horizon of expectations" needs to know which compositions were available to Liszt's contemporaries and which they considered significant—the works, in short, that established his fame at a specific historical moment. The concept of the "horizon of expectations" *(Erwartungshorizont)* is set forth for reception theory by Jauss in the essay "Literary History as a Challenge to Literary Theory," in *Toward an Aesthetic of Reception*, trans. Timothy Bahti (Minneapolis: 1982), pp. 3–45.

10. This essay is part of a larger project examining aspects of concert life in Vienna during the 1820s and '30s. I gathered much of the information that follows from Viennese archives, including the program collections of the Gesellschaft der Musikfreunde, the Österreichische Nationalbibliothek, and the Stadt- und Landesbibliothek. These are invaluable resources as many concerts were barely mentioned, if at all, in the Viennese press, let alone the easier-to-access Leipzig *Allgemeine musikalische Zeitung* and *Neue Zeitschrift für Musik*; hereafter cited as *AmZ* and *NZfM*.

11. Vienna's musical life has received surprisingly little study since Eduard Hanslick's important *Geschichte des Concertwesens in Wien*, 2 vols. (Vienna: 1869); see Alice M. Hanson, *Musical Life in Biedermeier Vienna* (Cambridge, Eng.: 1985); and Richard von Perger, *Geschichte der k .k. Gesellschaft der Musikfreunde in Wien. I Abteilung: 1812–1870* (Vienna: 1912).

12. Liszt's letters to Marie d'Agoult are cited with the sigla *FLC*; the first number refers to the French edition and the second to Adrian Williams's translation in *Selected Letters*. When only one number appears it refers to the French edition because the letter does not appear in Williams's collection and therefore is given in my own translation. See Serge Gut and Jacqueline Bellas, eds., *Correspondance Franz Liszt, Marie d'Agoult* (Paris: 2001).

13. Saphir Moritz, *Humorist* 2, no. 17 (18 May 1838): 315; see also the comment by J. B. Sorger in *Der Sammler* that Liszt was "indisputably the most important phenomenon" among an "astonishing crowd of musical celebrities," cited in Horvath, *Liszt: Italien*, p. 80.

14. Paganini's first performance was just three days after Schubert's own triumphant concert on 26 March, the first anniversary of Beethoven's death. This proved to be Schubert's only public concert devoted entirely to his own music; flush with its good receipts, he took his friend Eduard von Bauernfeld to the violinist's concert; see Otto Erich Deutsch, *Schubert: Memoirs by His Friends*, trans. Rosamond Ley and John Nowell (London: 1958), pp. 67, 186, 228.

15. A handwritten index of the programs of Paganini's fourteen concerts is in the archives Gesellschaft der Musikfreunde, as well as some of the actual programs.

16. G. I. C. de Courcy, *Paganini: The Genoese*, 2 vols. (Norman, Okla: 1957), vol. 1, p. 65.

17. *Geschichte der europäisch-abendländischen oder unserer heutigen Musik* (Leipzig: 1834); see Herfrid Kier, *Raphael Georg Kiesewetter (1773–1850): Wegbereiter des musikalischen Historismus* (Regensburg: 1968), pp. 91–95; *Geschichte des Concertwesens in Wien* (Vienna: 1869), pp. 139ff.; see also Carl Dahlhaus's commentary on the shift in the naming of eras in *Nineteenth-Century Music*, trans. J. Bradford Robinson (Berkeley: 1989), pp. 8–15.

18. Among the most active and prominent performers in the 1830s were violinists Joseph Mayseder, Leopold Jansa, Joseph Böhm, Heinrich Proch, Karl Holz; cellists Aegid Borzaga, Joseph Merk, Joseph Lincke; hornists Eduard Constantin Lewy, Eduard König; clarinetist Anton Friedlowsky; and flutist Aloys Khayll. Singers who appeared most frequently at concerts included Ludwig Tietze (or Titze), Joseph Staudigl, Benedict Gross, Benedict Randhartinger, and Jenny Lutzer. The most active actors taking part in concert life in 1838 were Julie Rettich, Sophie Schröder, Mathhilde Wildauer, Johann Daniel Löwe, and the venerable Heinrich Anschütz, who had delivered poet Franz Grillparzer's famous funeral oration for Beethoven in 1827.

19. Clara Wieck noted in her diary the "intimidating coldness of local musicians" (3 December) and Friedrich complained that "the cabals are frightful"; he initially had particular problems working with Holz and Jansa (14 February). The diaries of Clara Wieck, which are forthcoming from Olms Verlag in German and English editions co-edited by Gerd Nauhaus and Nancy B. Reich, are cited here by the date of entry.

20. The concert was on 4 March 1838, see review in *NZfM* 8, no. 35 (1 May): 139. Wieck was originally supposed to play on this concert (see diary entry for 4 March).

21. Schunke gave a program on 12 May 1833 at the Musikverein that featured 1) Beethoven, *Prometheus* Overture; 2) Schunke Concerto (Allegro, Adagio, Rondo); 3) Aria by Mercadante; 4) Solo for harp; 5) Declamation by Sophie Schröder; 6) Fantasy. Examples of two Hummel concerts from 1834 are (15 May): 1) Overture to Mozart's *The Marriage of Figaro*; 2) New concerto (manuscript); 3) Cavatina from Mercadante's *La Donna Caritea*; 4) Hummel, *Oberons Zauberhorn*, op. 116, for piano and orchestra; 5) Mozart aria; 6) Improvisation by Hummel; and (22 May) 1) Beethoven's *Prometheus*; 2) Hummel, Concerto in A-flat, op. 113; 3) Aria from Mozart's *The Marriage of Figaro*; 4) Hummel, *Le Retour de Londres* (manuscript); 5) Declamation; 6) Free fantasy by Hummel. Henselt performed Beethoven's C Minor Piano Concerto at the *Concerts Spirituels* on 10 March 1836.

22. Bocklet gave three concerts later in 1838, after Wieck and Liszt: (9 December) Overture; Bach, Three Preludes and Fugues; Beethoven's E-flat Piano Concerto; Free fantasy; (26 December) Beethoven's *Coriolan* Overture, Moscheles's *Concert fantastique*, Weber's *Konzertstück*, Free fantasy; (30 December) Weber's *Euryanthe* Overture arranged for piano, Beethoven's Piano Trio in B-flat Major with Leopold Jansa and Aegid Borzaga, Simon Sechter's "Die Verlobung," Free fantasy.

23. See Hanslick's discussion of women pianists in *Geschichte*, pp. 326–27.

24. *NZfM* 8, no. 25 (27 March): 100.

25. Friedrich Wieck listed some of the benefits in Clara's diary on 8 March: "They are listed annually in the court calendar of the Kaiser, 2) they are considered citizens of Vienna, 3) they receive letters of recommendation from the Staatskanzelei [Chancellory] wherever they go and whenever they want it, 4) they are considered subjects of the Austrian Empire in all countries and are always under the protection of the Austrian envoys, and 5) they may go to Vienna whenever they will, etc." Liszt states in a letter to d'Agoult that the honor carries a stipend of 2,000–3,000 francs a year (*FLC* 317).

26. In most of the scholarly literature Count Moritz von Dietrichstein is considered Thalberg's father, although there is some dispute whether Thalberg was his natural or adopted son. Yet Liszt states quite clearly in a letter that he met "the two Dietrichsteins" and that it was Moritz's older brother, Prince Franz Joseph von Dietrichstein who was the "father of Th[alberg]." He says the prince "is an old man with white hair and an affectionate and princely manner; he has been extremely charming and attentive to me. . . . His brother, Count Moritz D., seemed a man of polish" (*FLC* 313/84). The most recent research, by Dudley Newton, suggests that Thalberg was the son of Joseph Thalberg, who was himself the son of Prince Franz Joseph. See "Sigismund Thalberg," in *Liszt Society Journal* 16 (1991): 38-60.

27. *Theaterzeitung*, no. 244 (December 6, 1837): 996.

28. *NZfM* 7, no. 51 (26 December 1837): 204

29. Eva Weissweiler, *The Complete Correspondence of Clara and Robert Schumann*, 3 vols. (New York: 1994), vol. 1, p. 80.

30. Williams, *Portrait*, p. 91. As Williams points out, there are many variants of the verdict. D'Agoult's is the most famous: "Thalberg is the first pianist in the world, Liszt the only one!"; see Dana Gooley, *The Virtuoso Liszt* (Cambridge, Eng.: 2004), pp. 18–77, and Walker, *The Virtuoso Years*, pp. 232–43.

31. "Subjektivität und Öffentlichkeit: Liszts Rivalität mit Thalberg und ihre Folgen," in *Der junge Liszt: Referate des 4. Europäischen Liszt-Symposions: Wien 1991*, ed. Gottfried Scholz (Munich: 1993), p. 58.

32. Letter of 3 June 1838, quoted in *Liszt: Sämtliche Schriften*, p. 616.

33. The comparisons eventually became part of history. Hanslick—who was not even a teenager at the time, although later commentators sometimes make it seem as if he were describing events he experienced himself—dated Thalberg's concerts in late 1836 as the beginning of a new era and called him the "true father of a new school of piano": "In the realm of virtuosity this period, 1830–48, is the most important. Its highest brilliance, fame, fortune, and decline lie within. One might date the reign of sovereign virtuosity between 1836, Thalberg's first epoch-making season, and Liszt's final concert year in 1846." He commented on Wieck's first appearances: "A half-open rose with all the allure of the bud and the full fragrance of a blooming Centifolie! No wonder child, and yet still a child and already a wonder. It was a further new side of virtuosity: after Thalberg's salon appearances as a veritable musical Pelham, now appears in Clara Wieck as a maidenly innocence and poetry." Of Liszt's concerts that year, Hanslick drew particular attention to their large number, the absence of an orchestra, to his varied, demanding, and often high-minded repertory, and finally to the general phenomenon he created, when "ladies lost their hearts and critics their heads." Hanslick, *Geschichte*, vol. 1, pp. 331, 325 (Thalberg), 332 (Wieck), and 335 (Liszt).

34. He played Hummel's B Minor Concerto and later Kalkbrenner's D Minor Concerto and Beethoven piano concertos. A facsimile of the program for a concert benefiting flood victims is given in *Franz Schubert Dokumente 1817–1830*, ed. Till Gerrit Waidelich, vol. 1 (Tutzing: 1993), pp. 574; cf. 323, 336.

35. It is interesting to note that most of those performing Thalberg's music were either women (Sallamon, Onitsch, Herrschmann, Delack, and Wieck) or prodigies (Louis Lacombe, Louis Engel, Heinrich Ehrlich, the last of whom studied with Thalberg).

36. In addition to the three concerts for which programs are given in table 4, Thalberg played a private evening concert (Privat Abend-Unterhaltung) on 21 December at which he performed: 1) Beethoven, *Prometheus* Overture; 2) Thalberg, Fantasy; 3) Beethoven, "Neue Liebe, neues Leben" (sung by Ludwig Tietze); 4) Ott, Rondino for Waldhorn (performed by Eduard König); 5) Hackel, *Vor der Schlacht*; 6) Solo for pedal harp (played by Therese Brunner; 7) Beriot and Benedict, Variations for Violin and Piano (performed by Thalberg and Henri Vieuxtemps); 8) Hackel, "Gebeth," men's chorus to a poem by Friederike Susan, with harp and physharmonika (performed by Therese Brunner and Georg Lickl); review in *AmZ* 39, no. 7 (15 February 1837): 115

37. Three programs are given in George Kehler, *The Piano in Concert* (Metuchen, N.Y./London: 1982), vol. 1, pp. 759–62, but the first two were not given. An announcement was printed stating: "Wegen plötzlich eingetretener Unpäßlichkeit können die beiden für den 18. und 22. November d. J. angekündigten Concerte des S. Thalberg nicht Statt finden"; see review in *AmZ* 41, no. 9 (27 February 1839): 167. The "farewell concert" did take place on 1 December: 1) Thalberg, Variations on Motives from Beethoven's Symphonies; 2) Schubert, "Ständchen," accompanied by Joseph Fischhof; 3) Thalberg,

Two Etudes; 4) Beriot, Variations for Violin by Beriot, performed by Johann Mayer; 5) Aria; 6) Thalberg, *Moses* Fantasy, by request. The k. k. Kammervirtuoso also participated in a charity concert on 27 November 1838 (Concert zum Besten der Armen von der Gesellschaft der adeligen Frauen zur Beförderung des Guten und Nützlichen) at the Musikverein: 1) *Moses* Fantasy; 2) Lied for soprano and waldhorn; 3) Declamation; 4) Randhartinger, "Sehnsucht" with waldhorn; 5) Schubert, "Gondelfahrer" (accompanied by J. B. Jenger); 6) Thalberg, Variations on romance and chorus from Rossini's *La donna del Lago*. Both concerts were also reviewed in the *Humorist* 2, no. 191 (17 November 1838): 764; no. 202 (3 December 1838): 808.

38. Review in *AmZ* 39, no. 7 (15 February 1837): 115.

39. *Friedrich Wieck Briefe aus den Jahren 1830–1838*, ed. Käthe Walch-Schumann (Cologne: 1968), pp. 82, 87.

40. For a discussion of her time in Vienna see Nancy B. Reich, *Clara Schumann: The Artist and the Woman* rev. ed. (Ithaca, N.Y.: 2001), pp. 78–83; and Janina Klassen, "Souvenir de Vienne: Künstliche Präsentation und musikalische Erinnerung," in *Ich fahre in mein liebes Wien: Clara Schumann—Takten, Bilder, Projektionen*, ed. Elena Ostleitner and Ursula Simek (Vienna: 1996), pp. 61–72. See also *NZfM* 7, no. 51 (26 December 1837): 204.

41. Three were originally planned it seems; see Clara Wieck diary entry for 7 December.

42. For information on Wieck's repertory during this phase in her career, see Pamela Susskind Pettler, "Clara Schumann's Recitals, 1832–50," *19th-Century Music* 4, no. 1 (1980): 70–76.

43. Moritz Saphir, in the *Humorist*, and the critic for the *Telegraph* wrote against her; see Wieck diary entries for 19, 23, and 27 January.

44. The poem was widely printed—first in the *Wiener Zeitschrift für Kunst* (9 January), then in *NZfM* 8, no. 8 (26 January 1838): 30; and later Liszt included it in his Vienna article, thus getting it further published in other French, German, and Hungarian periodicals. It was also reprinted in Hanslick (*Geschichte*, p. 334) and in many biographies of Clara Wieck. Püttlingen's setting uses motives from Beethoven's sonata and was published by Diabelli (reviewed in *NZfM* 8, no. 24 [23 March 1838]: 94). Püttlingen, with whom Liszt would perform in May, also composed under the name J. Hoven.

45. Translation by Charles Suttoni in Liszt, *An Artist's Journey*, p. 143.

46. *NZfM* 8, no. 22 (16 March 1838): 86–87.

47. See Geraldine Keeling, "Concert Announcements, Programs and Reviews as Evidence for First or Early Performances by Liszt of His Keyboard Works to 1847," *Studia Musicologica Academiae Scientiarum Hungaricae* 34 (1992): 397–404.; and Keeling, "Liszt's Appearances in Parisian Concerts, 1824–44," *Liszt Society Journal* 11 (1986): 22–34, and 12 (1987): 8–22.

48. Deutsch, *Schubert: Memoirs*, pp. 100, 211, 332; Liszt, *An Artist's Journey*, p. 144; and *FLC* 330/93. Clara Wieck also commented on this remarkable amateur; see diary entry for 4 December.

49. Weissweiler, *The Complete Correspondence*, vol. 1, p. 119.

50. Ibid., p. 166.

51. Liszt, *An Artist's Journey*, pp. 138–40. Much more dramatic is the version Marie d'Agoult related years later in her *Memoirs*. Often the two accounts are conflated in biographies to provide a compelling narrative but one that may not be accurate; see Comtesse D'Agoult, *Memoires, 1833–1854*, ed. Daniel Ollivier (Paris: 1927), p. 141.

52. The report is given in Julius Kapp, *Franz Liszt* (Berlin: 1909), p. 62; many letters make clear that only the first concert was for Pest—the most explicit is to Massart on 3 June in which Liszt states he gave three charity concerts and "seven for my own benefit"; quoted in Serge Gut, *Franz Liszt* (Paris: 1989), p. 52.

53. Walker, *The Virtuoso Years*, p. 254. Walker states that Liszt "hurried to Vienna, arriving there in mid-April, and at once arranged to give a series of charity concerts for the victims. . . . Between April 18 and May 25 Liszt gave eight concerts which raised the colossal sum of 24,000 gulden, the largest single donation the Hungarians received from a private source." He repeats the claim in the recent *Reflections on Liszt* (Ithaca, N.Y.: 2005), p. 27, and gives an even more inaccurate account in the *New Grove Dictionary of Music and Musicians* where he states Liszt "gave ten recitals for the victims of the floods; six had been planned but four more were added by popular demand" ("Liszt, Franz," *Grove Music Online* ed. L. Macy [Accessed 20 February 2006], http://www.grovemusic.com). Klára Hamburger also asserts that Liszt's eight concerts were for the flood victims (*Franz Liszt*, trans. Gyula Gulyás [Budapest: 1980], p. 42).

54. *Der Adler* reported in early January, long before the spring floods, that Liszt would "soon visit Vienna in order to perform in public"; see Gooley, *The Virtuoso Liszt*, p. 235.

55. Friedrich Wieck's letter is given in Wolfgang Seibold, *Robert und Clara Schumann in ihren Beziehungen zu Franz Liszt: Im Spiegel ihrer Korrespondenz und Schriften* (Frankfurt am Main: 2005), p. 60; for Clara's letter to Robert see Weissweiler, *The Complete Correspondence*, vol. 1, p. 60.

56. See, for example, Liszt's letter of 18 December 1837 to Abbé Lamennais: "Will my life be forever tainted with this idle uselessness that weighs upon me? Will the hour of devotion and manly action never come?" and so forth (*Letters of Franz Liszt*, ed. La Mara, trans. Constance Bache, 2 vols. [London: 1894; repr. New York: 1968], vol. 2, p. 21) and to Massart: "As I have told you often before, for me everything is *future*. But it's not necessary that this future be put off forever. *In two or three years, my cause will be definitely lost or won*, at least as far as piano is concerned" (quoted in Gooley, *The Virtuoso Liszt*, p. 56).

57. Gooley, *The Virtuoso Liszt*, pp. 123, 236–37, cf. p. 56.

58. April 3–4, Weissweiler, *The Complete Correspondence*, vol. 1, p. 134 (translation amended). The *NZfM* reported, "Concerts to help Pest are being given in countless numbers, and the number of participants is large." *NZfM* 8, no. 32 (20 April 1838): 127); many are discussed in *NZfM* 8, no. 44 (1 June 1838): 175.

59. I am aware of only two concerts following Liszt's concert—a "Grosses musikalisches Frühlingsfest" on 2 May under the direction of Michael Leitermayer, and one on 21 April, reported in the *Humorist* 2, no. 67 (27 April): 267.

60. Dana Gooley discusses Liszt's strategic use of charity—his "glow of goodness"— in *The Virtuoso Liszt*, pp. 201–62.

61. Liszt told Cristina Belgiojoso on 13 April that he planned to stay in Vienna for about two weeks (Williams, *Selected Letters*, 86); see also his letter to the publisher Breitkopf & Härtel (La Mara, *Letters of Franz Liszt*, vol. 1, p. 23). Charles Suttoni also quotes an unpublished letter to Count Amadé in which Liszt states "my stay in Vienna has to be extremely short (because of engagements I have undertaken in Italy in May)." Liszt, *An Artist's Journey*, p. 139.

62. *Mémoires, Souvenirs et Journaux de la Comtesse d'Agoult (Daniel Stern)*, ed. Charles F. Dupechez, 2 vols. (Paris: 1990), vol. 2, p. 170. Concerning Thalberg's father see n. 26 above.

63. Williams, *Portrait*, p. 106.

64. Berthold Litzmann, *Clara Schumann, ein Künstlerleben, nach Tagebüchern und Briefen*, 3 vols. (Leipzig: 1902–10), vol. 2, p. 263 and vol. 1, p. 418.

65. Liszt's letter to the publisher Hofmeister about Clara Wieck in Seibold, *Robert und Clara Schumann*, p. 61. Robert Schumann learned of this letter (Hofmeister had sent it to him) and told Clara about it (5 January 1838); Weissweiler, *The Complete Correspondence*, vol. 1, p. 73.

66. *NZfM* 8, no. 34 (27 April 1838): 135.

67. Liszt wrote to Robert Schumann from Vienna on 5 May stating that "speaking frankly and freely, it is absolutely only Chopin's compositions and yours that have a powerful interest for me." La Mara, *Letters of Liszt*, vol. 1, p. 24; also quoted in Williams, *Portrait*, pp. 90–91.

68. *AmZ* 40, no. 20 (16 May 1838): 323; see Clara Wieck diary entry for 19 April 1838. Hofmeister had recently published the four-hand version of Liszt's *Grand Galop chromatique*.

69. Friedrich Wieck made similar comments in a letter to his wife: "The powers of musical perception of this Liszt truly verge on unbelievable. If he had been given the right training and could rein in his power no one could play after him." Williams, *Portrait*, p. 102.

70. The letter to his mother is in Klára Hamburger, *Franz Liszt: Briefwechsel mit seiner Mutter* (Eisenstadt: 2000), pp. 129–30. The claim is echoed after his next concert on 23 April, when he invokes the ur-virtuoso: "In living memory no one has had such as success in Vienna, not even Paganini" (*FLC* 318/87), and again the next week: "With no exaggeration, never since Paganini has anyone made such an impression" (*FLC* 321/89).

71. Williams, *Selected Letters*, p. 94.

72. Letter of 3 June 1838; quoted in Gut, *Liszt*, p. 52.

73. An article in the Leipzig *Allgemeine musikalische Zeitung* commented on Liszt's newly found ability to make money and on his generosity: "It was in Vienna that Liszt, according to his own account, made the important discovery that his art could bring financial rewards as well as fame and honor. In France he had performed largely for his own personal pleasure and that of society. Yet, the abundant revenue served him only as a means for worthy acts hidden from view. Quietly he did many good deeds; he generously supported those in need, presented his friends with precious souvenirs, and hosted splendid feasts which were attended by princes, counts, excellencies, state officials, musicians, writers, painters, and art dealers, all united by the bonds of conviviality and joy. They in turn gave sumptuous dinners at Dommayer's tasteful establishment in Hitzing. Streams of champagne flowed freely, and Saphir gave full reign to his poetic fancy and improvised toasts to all present" (*AmZ* 40, no. 35 [29 August 1838]: 583).

74. Williams, *Portrait*, p. 106

75. There are countless variants of this famous story; my favorite is in James Huneker, *Franz Liszt* (New York: 1911), p. 244, which has Prince Metternich apologize later for his wife's remark: "I trust you will pardon my wife for a slip of the tongue the other day; you know what women are!"

76. See *FLC* 326/92; Liszt sent d'Agoult 200 florins to make the trip (*FLC* 323).

77. Marie d'Agoult's journal breaks off on 25 April until June, although she does make comments about her health in letters to others.

78. *FLC* 326/91. It is a phrase he uses elsewhere, perhaps echoing what d'Agoult tells him about her state.

79. That Liszt told d'Agoult that patriotism drew him to Vienna is evident in her letter to Ferdinand Hiller from 20 April; in Marie de Flavigny, comtesse D'Agoult, *Correspondance générale: 1837–octobre 1839*, ed. Charles F. Dupechez (Paris: 2004), vol. 2, p. 179.

80. D'Agoult, *Memoires*, p. 147. The translation is from Newman, *The Man Liszt: A Study of the Tragi-Comedy of a Soul Divided Against Itself* (New York: 1970), pp. 77–78; Walker uses this translation, without crediting its source, but misleadingly changes the tense so that it seems like a genuine diary entry: "Franz has left me," and so forth (*The Virtuoso Years*, pp. 261–62).

81. Newmann, *The Man Liszt*, p. 78 (translation amended).

82. Ibid., p. 85.

83. Walker, *The Virtuoso Years*, p. 260.

84. Ibid., pp. 259–63.

85. See comtesse D'Agoult, *Correspondance générale*, pp. 179, 185, 196.

86. Liszt, *An Artist's Journey*, p. 142.

87. Based on an accurate numbering of Liszt's concerts, this letter can now be dated with certainty to 18 May not 14 May; see Hamburger, *Liszt: Briefwechsel mit seiner Mutter*, p. 133.

88. This was probably Baron Eduard Tomascheck, the nephew of the noted Czech composer Václav Jan Tomáček. In Robert Schumann's diary he refers to a "Tomascheck aus Wien," see *Robert Schumann: Tagebücher, 1836–1854*, ed. Gerd Nauhaus, vol. 2 (Leipzig: 1987), p. 244.

89. Liszt's letter from Venice of thanks (1 June), Legány, *Presse und Briefe*, p. 117; La Mara, *Letters of Franz Liszt*, vol. 1, p. 26.

90. The Wieck lithograph was distributed by Diabelli; see *NZfM* 32 (20 April 1838): 127. Clara's diary shows she sat for Staub on 1 March.

91. *FLC* 321/89. For Liszt see *NZfM* 38 (11 May 1838): 151; for Clara see *NZfM* 32 (20 April 1838): 127. Kriehuber did other lithographs of Liszt in 1838 and in following years; see Ernst Burger, *Franz Liszt: A Chronicle of His Life in Pictures and Documents*, trans. Stewart Spencer (Princeton, N.J.: 1989), pp. 105, 109.

92. The article originally appeared in the *Revue et Gazette musicale de Paris* 4, no. 2 (8 January 1837): 17–20; see *Sämtliche Schriften*, vol. 1, pp. 350–56. See also letter to d'Agoult on 13 February 1837 where Liszt tells her that Chopin believes "un Dietrichstein" paid Fétis to write favorably about Thalberg. At another time he wrote to her that Rudolph Apponyi, an Austrian ambassador in Paris, was assisting Thalberg and working against him; see *FLC* 265. The comment is similar to one he made to Chopin that Thalberg was "an aristocrat who is even more a failed artist," Liszt, *An Artist's Journey*, p. 25.

93. Weissweiler, *The Complete Correspondence*, vol. 1, p. 83; see also Wieck's diary for 8 March in which Friedrich discusses the obstacles that have been overcome.

94. See Wieck's comment in a letter to his wife that "many are against him [Liszt]" at Court and that he did not enjoy the success there that Clara had (*Wieck Briefe*, p. 93).

95. Williams, *Portrait*, p. 102.

96. Kapp, *Liszt*, p. 62; Gooley, *The Virtuoso Liszt*, p. 126.

97. According to Legány, Liszt performed together with three singers from the Italian opera company (Poggi, dall'Occa, and Brambilla). He played a Fantasy on Themes of Rossini, a Tarantella and Polonaise on Motives from Bellini's *I puritani*, his transcription of Schubert's "Ständchen," and his own *Valse di bravura* (Legány, *Presse und Briefe*, p. 51).

98. Hamburger, *Liszt: Briefwechsel mit seiner Mutter*, p. 133.

99. *AmZ* 40, no. 35 (29 August), p. 581; see also *Wiener Zeitschrift für Kunst* (5 June 1838), p. 534; cited in Legány, *Presse und Briefe*, p. 50.

100. This enumeration is consistent with the playbills, which announced that his first appearance was for a concert "Zum Besten der in Pesth und Ofen durch Ueberschwemmung Verunglückten," the second was not numbered, and then the third as his "Second Concert" and so forth until the final "Soirée."

101. The programs were: (6 May): 1) Beethoven, Overture; 2) Reading of Schiller's "Die Ideale" by Ludwig Löwe; 3) Cavatina and Chorus from Mercadante's *Donna Caritea*, sung by Madame [Sophie] Schoberlechner dall'Occa; 4) Weber, *Konzertstück*; 5) Duet from Mercadante's *Emma d'Antiochia*, sung by Madame Schoberlechner dall'Occa und A. Poggi; 6) Weber's chorus "Lützow's Jagd"; and (24 May): 1) Hummel, Septet, first movement and Scherzo; 2) Declamation; 3) Kreutzer, "Liebesgedanken," for tenor, cello, and piano performed by Tietze, Merk, and Randhartinger; 4) Hummel, Septet, Andante, and Finale; 5) Schubert, "Der Gondelfahrer," performed by Titze, Lutz, Fuchs, Richling, accompanied by Randhartinger; 6) Rossini/Liszt "I marinari" from *Soirée*, and as an encore the duet "Suoni la tromba" from Bellini's *I puritani*.

102. Liszt only performed his reworking of Schubert's "Ständchen" and his *Valse di bravura* on this program; reviewed in *Humorist* 2, no. 79 (18 May), p. 315; a copy of the playbill is in the archives of the Gesellschaft der Musikfreunde in Vienna.

103. The information for table 6 is drawn from the playbills and checked against reviews and personal accounts; programs or performers were sometimes changed, pieces were repeated and encores added, and Liszt did not accompany singers in all cases, although that is nowhere indicated in the playbills. Facsimiles of the programs for 18 April and 6 May are in Burger, *Chronicle*, p. 104.

104. *AmZ*; on the popularity of Weber's *Konzertstück* in Liszt's career, see Gooley, *The Virtuoso Liszt*, pp. 78–116.

105. Thalberg had requested that his father make it available to Liszt for the charity concert, although Liszt was not sure at first whether he should accept the offer (*FLC* 309).

106. Adami noted in a number of his reviews that Liszt played on a Graf piano: "It should be mentioned that Liszt in all of his concerts played on one and the same piano, an excellent Graf instrument." Legány, *Presse und Briefe*, p. 49.

107. Ibid., p. 26.

108. *Humorist* 2, no. 67 (27 April 1838): 267.

109. Legány, *Presse und Briefe*, p. 27; see also the comment in the *AmZ*: "Haslinger's office was besieged daily by throngs of subscribers. Peopled demanded, bargained, and schemed to obtain a ticket." *AmZ* 40, no. 35 (29 August 1838): 581.

110. c. m. denotes *Conventionsmünze* (assimilated coinage) as distinct from w.w., meaning *Wiener Währung* (Viennese currency), which was valued at less than half.

111. Williams, *Portrait*, p. 123.

112. Legány, *Presse und Briefe*, p. 24.

113. A translation of Saphir's article in the *Humorist* (2, no. 64 [21 April 1838]: 253–54) later appeared in J. Duverger [Marie d'Agoult], *Notice biographique sur Franz Liszt* (Paris: 1843); a section also appeared excerpted in *AmZ* 40, no. 20 (16 May 1838): 324–25, which therefore made it much better known, and Lina Ramann quoted it at length in her biography, *Franz Liszt als Künstler und Mensch* (Leipzig: 1880–94). The Kuranda article which he asked his mother to have translated into French by Ernest Legouvé or Berlioz and published in a Parisian journal was "Franz Liszt," *Der Wiener Telegraph: Conversationsblatt für Kunst, Literatur, geselliges Leben, Theater, Tagesbegebenheiten und Industrie* 3, no. 51 (27 April 1838): 209.

114. *AmZ* 40, no. 20 (13 May 1838): 324–25; *Humorist* 2, no. 64 (21 April 1838): 254. Translation adapted from Piero Weiss and Richard Taruskin, *Music in the Western World: A History in Documents* (New York: 1984), p. 365.

115. Williams, *Portrait*, p. 104 (translation amended).

116. *Humorist* 2, no. 85 (28 May 1838): 340.

117. Legány, *Presse und Briefe*, p. 39.

118. He did play with orchestra at the charity concert on 6 May, performing Weber's *Konzertstück* again.

119. Liszt first played *Hexaméron* in Vienna to end his 8 May concert and repeated it by request to end his next one. Liszt had first played it on 18 February in Milan; see *NZfM* 8, no. 27 (3 April 1838): 108.

120. *Telegraph* (30 May 1838); see also Legány, *Presse und Briefe*, pp. 46–47.

121. *NZfM* 8, no. 34 (27 April): 136; reprinted in *The Musical World* (17 May 1838).

122. Teréz Walter, *Liszt Ferenc Árvízi Hangversenyei Bécsben 1838/9*, trans. and ed. Béla Csuka (Budapest: 1941), pp. 53, 55.

123. *Allgemeine Theaterzeitung* (25 April 1838): 366; although most of the review is given in Legány, this passage is omitted (*Presse und Briefe*, p. 28).

124. Weissweiler, *The Complete Correspondence*, vol. 1, p. 164.

125. See Wieck, *Briefe*, pp. 93–94; Williams, *Portrait*, p. 103 (translation amended).

126. Gooley, *The Virtuoso Liszt*, p. 125.

127. Legány, *Presse und Briefe*, p. 41.

128. Ibid., p. 31.

129. Ibid., pp. 38, 41.

130. Weissweiler, *The Complete Correspondence*, vol. 1, p. 163.

131. *AZfM* 40, no. 20 (13 May 1838): 323.

132. Williams, *Portrait*, p. 107; see also Legány, *Presse und Briefe*, p. 33.

133. Liszt, *An Artist's Journey*, pp. 141–42.

134. See the excellent study by Axel Schröter *"Der Name Beethoven ist heilig in der Kunst":* *Studien zu Liszts Beethoven Rezeption*, 2 vols. (Sinzig: 1999), vol. 1, pp. 142–46. For reviews of Liszt's Beethoven interpretations see Legány, *Presse und Briefe*, pp. 35, 53; and Horvath, *Liszt: Italien*, p. 84.

135. Liszt probably would have made some passing comment later in life about meeting Schubert that would have been recorded somewhere. All that remains is anecdotal—he allegedly told August Göllerich that they never met (Walker, *The Virtuoso Years*, p. 73 and Williams, *Portrait*, p. 6). Chrétien Urhan, who exerted tremendous influence over Liszt (as well as over Chopin and Berlioz), was the first important figure in Schubert's French reception, performing Schubert's music as a violist and also making reworkings. About Schubert's French reception, see J. G. Prod'homme, "Schubert's Works in France," *Musical Quarterly* 14 (1928): 495–514; Willi Kahl, "Schuberts Lieder in Frankreich bis 1840," *Die Musik* 21 (1928): 22–31; and Xavier Hascher, "Schubert's Reception in France: A Chronology (1828–1928)" in *Cambridge Companion to Schubert*, ed. Christopher H. Gibbs (Cambridge, Eng.: 1997), pp. 263–69.

136. There are two common mistakes about Liszt's first reworking of Schubert's music, *Die Rose*. That the reworking dates from 1833, not 1834 or 1835, is clear from a letter to Valérie Boissier, mother of one of Liszt's pupils, on 31 May 1833 that thanks her for her approval of this reworking (see Robert Bory, "Lettres inédites de Liszt," *Schweizer Jahrbuch für Musikwissenschaft* 3 [1928]: 11–13). Second, the song is set to Schlegel's poem "Die Rose," not Goethe's "Heidenröslein," with which it is often confused.

137. The musical range of Liszt's Schubert Lied reworkings is large, not only with respect to the musical material used, but also the nature of the musical transformations. One class, which Liszt sometimes called "partition de piano" when arranging other composers, denotes a high degree of fidelity. Alan Walker calls this type "transcription," which is "strict, literal, objective." Liszt's reworkings of Beethoven symphonies and the *Symphonie fantastique* are examples of this kind. The other category—often called "paraphrase" or "fantasia"—is described by Humphrey Searle as "original works based on material from elsewhere" and by Walker as a "free variation of the original." The paraphrase relies on the idea of "metamorphosis"; usually Liszt takes one melodic idea and submits it to increasingly elaborate ornamentation and technical virtuosity. Publisher's catalogues, work lists, and scholarly literature, editions, reviews, manuscripts, and other sources give little consistent indication of the variety of Liszt's reworkings. On the basis of the two broad categories, it is commonly felt that he made only transcriptions of Schubert songs, although Walker states that "one or two of them do stray over the border and behave albeit fleetingly, like paraphrases." Yet more than one or two display considerable departure from the original, and many others occupy a middle ground between transcription and paraphrase. Most of Liszt's reworkings of Schubert Lieder retain the original tonality (*Ständchen* and the two versions of *Ungeduld* are transposed), but not all adhere to the original structure. See Searle, *The Music of Liszt* (London: 1966); Walker "Liszt and the Schubert Song Transcriptions," *Musical Quarterly* 67 (1981): 50–63; and Gibbs, "The Presence of *Erlkönig*: Reception and Reworkings of a Schubert Lied," Ph.D. diss., Columbia University, 1992,

pp. 212–50. The classification of Liszt's Lied reworkings is well discussed by Diether Presser in "Studien zu den Opern- und Liedbearbeitungen Franz Liszts," diss., Cologne, 1953, pp. 133ff.

138. *Humorist* 2, no. 67 (27 April 1838): 267.

139. Legány, *Presse und Briefe*, p. 29.

140. Ibid., p. 32.

141. Otto Brusatti, *Schubert im Wiener Vormärz* (Graz: 1978), p. 93.

142. See Gibbs, "The Presence of *Erlkönig*," pp. 244–45.

143. Legány, *Presse und Briefe*, pp. 46–47.

144. The song transcriptions Haslinger released were *Ständchen*, *Die Post*, *Lob der Tränen*, and *Die Rose*; and Diabelli released in 1838: *Sey mir gegrüsst, Auf dem Wasser zu singen, Du bist die Ruh, Erlkönig, Meeresstille, Die junge Nonne, Frühlingsglaube, Gretchen am Spinnrade, Ständchen* ("Horch, horch"), *Rastlose Liebe, Der Wanderer, Ave Maria*. The covers of some of these are given in Burger, *Chronicle*, 106.

145. *Humorist* 2, no. 85 (28 May 1838): 340.

146. Williams, *Portrait*, p. 105; Legány, *Presse und Briefe*, p. 45. In a letter Liszt stated that Haslinger planned three soirées (*FLX* 328/29).

147. The playbill announced Schubert's "Die Allmacht"—a song Liszt would arrange decades later for orchestra, tenor, and male chorus—sung by Joseph Staudigl, but no review or other document indicates it was performed.

148. Legány, *Presse und Briefe*, p. 45.

149. *The Musical World* 10, no. 138 (1 November 1838): 134–35; see *AmZ* 40, no. 35 (29 August 1838): 583.

150. Liszt, *An Artist's Journey*, p. 144; this is just one more instance of words that d'Agoult would hardly want to hear, let alone ghostwrite.

Liszt, Wagner, and Unfolding Form:
Orpheus and the Genesis of *Tristan und Isolde*

RAINER KLEINERTZ

Liszt's possible influence on Wagner is usually discussed primarily with regard to harmony.[1] The step from the triadic harmony of the *Ring* to the chromaticism of *Tristan und Isolde*, in particular, is often linked to Liszt's symphonic compositions of the Weimar period. In a well-known letter of October 1859 to Hans von Bülow, Wagner himself admitted that since his acquaintance with Liszt's compositions he had become "quite a different fellow as a harmonist."[2] Further influence by Liszt on Wagner involving structural aspects of musical form has seemed less plausible, in part due to the different genres to which the two composers devoted themselves. Whereas Liszt, in his symphonic compositions of the early Weimar period (around 1850), experimented with features of sonata form,[3] Wagner, in *Opera and Drama* (1852), presented a theory of "poetic-musical periods," which he would use as the formal basis of his music dramas.[4] Considering, however, that Wagner interrupted the composition of the *Ring* in 1857, shortly after having heard two of Liszt's symphonic poems for the first time, the question arises whether these works perhaps exerted a greater influence on Wagner than generally admitted.

Immediately after Breitkopf & Härtel published the first six symphonic poems in 1856, Liszt sent the scores to Wagner, putting Wagner in possession of *Tasso, Les Préludes, Prometheus, Orpheus, Mazeppa,* and *Festklänge.* A personal encounter some months later seems to have deepened Wagner's comprehension of these works. During Liszt's visit to Wagner in Zurich (and St. Gall) from 13 October to 27 November 1856, he played his own compositions on the piano—including the recently composed *Faust* and *Dante* symphonies. And at the festivities for Liszt's birthday on 22 October, some of his symphonic poems were played on two grand pianos.[5] But it was a concert at St. Gall, Switzerland, on 23 November 1856, where Liszt conducted his *Les Préludes* and *Orpheus*, that awoke Wagner's profound admiration for these works, especially *Orpheus*. Only six days after the concert, Wagner told von Bülow that Liszt's new compositions had won his wholehearted support:

> I acknowledge without any contradiction the eminent value of his creations. In St. Gall—where they organized a sort of festival for us—he let me listen to his *Orpheus* and the *Préludes*, the first of which I consider a totally unique masterwork of the highest perfection. Also the *Préludes*, whose main motif I would like to be somewhat more original, are beautiful, free and noble.[6]

The next day, in a letter to Otto Wesendonck in Paris, Wagner expressed the same admiration for *Orpheus*:

> To speak only of pleasant things, I will share with you the favorable outcome of the concert. Liszt's *Orpheus* has profoundly won me over: this is one of the most beautiful, most perfect, indeed most incomparable tone poems: the work was a great pleasure for me! The public considered the "Préludes" as more commendable, they had to be repeated.—Liszt was quite delighted by my unfeigned appreciation of his works and expressed his joy in a very touching way.[7]

His opinion had not changed when he recounted the event in the third part of *My Life*, printed privately in 1875:

> To my delight Liszt rehearsed the orchestra in two of his compositions, *Orpheus* and *Les Préludes*, to a point of masterly perfection; despite the extreme limitations of the instrumental resources available, their execution left nothing to be desired in point of beauty or panache. I was especially taken with the restrained orchestral piece *Orpheus*, to which I have always accorded a special place of honor among Liszt's compositions; the public on the other hand preferred *Les Préludes*, of which the main parts had to be encored.[8]

Especially in the context of Wagner's slightly critical position toward the more effective *Préludes*, there can be no doubt that his admiration for *Orpheus* was sincere and that the reasons lay in specific features of this symphonic poem. Friedrich Schnapp, an editor of the book *Lisztiana*, remembers that on a lost sheet with questions on his symphonic poems, Liszt had annotated to *Orpheus*: "R. Wagner found there a wavering between bliss and woe *[Wonne und Weh]*, which moved him profoundly."[9] Whereas this might refer in a more general sense to the character or the "content" of the piece, Wagner clearly emphasized form in his famous open letter on Liszt's symphonic poems of 15 February 1857:

> Supposing one has been irresistibly driven to see the worth of this phenomenon [Liszt's symphonic poems], the uncommon richness of inventive power which at once confronts us in these great tone-works brought before us as by a stroke of the magician's wand, then one might at first be bewildered again by their *form*. . . . Onward, then—to "Form"!—Ah! dear child! were there no Form, there would certainly be no artworks, but quite certainly no art judges either; and this is so obvious to these latter that the anguish of their soul cries out for Form, whereas the easygoing artist—though neither could he, as just said, exist without Form in the long run—troubles his head mighty little about it when at work. . . . After hearing one of Liszt's new orchestral works, I was involuntarily struck with admiration at its happy designation as a "symphonic poem." And indeed the invention of this term has more to say for itself than one might think; for it could only have arisen with the invention of the new art-form itself. . . . I further ask: if Music's manifestation is so governed in advance by Form, as I have already proved to you, whether it is not nobler and less trammeling for her to take this Form from an imagined Orpheus or Prometheus motive, than from an imagined march or dance motif?[10]

For Wagner, Liszt's symphonic poems replaced the traditional sonata form with a new conception of form. And whereas the traditional, "classical" form was in Wagner's view based on the march or dance, i.e. on rhythmic movement and consequently on periodic phrasing, Liszt's new form owed its specific structure to a poetic motive such as the myths of Orpheus or Prometheus. As an example of the "classical" model, Wagner offers Beethoven's third *Leonore* overture:

> But he who has eyes, may see precisely by this overture how detrimental to the master the maintenance of the traditional form was bound to be. For who, at all capable of understanding such a work, will not agree with me when I assert that the repetition of the first part, after the middle section, is a weakness which distorts the idea of the work almost past all understanding; . . . the evil could only have been avoided by entirely giving up that repetition; an abandonment, however, which would have done away with the overture-form—i.e.,

the original, merely suggestive (*nur motivierte*), symphonic dance-form—
and have constituted the departure point for creating a new form.[11]

Liszt's symphonic poems suggested to Wagner not only individual realizations of programmatic ideas, but also fundamentally an alternative idea
of form for symphonic composition. In this context it is notable that
Wagner's open letter refers especially to *Orpheus*, as he pointed out in a
letter to Liszt from 8 February 1857: "Tell the dear Child [Marie von
Sayn-Wittgenstein, Princess Carolyne's daughter] that she will soon receive
a letter from me, as she requested, but not about 'Indian poetry' (droll
idea!) but about that of which my heart is full, and which I can call by no
other name, than 'Orpheus.' But I must wait until I am in the right
mood."[12] Considering that less than a month after the St. Gall concert, on
19 December 1856, Wagner wrote down the first dated sketches for *Tristan
und Isolde* ("for the time being music without words"), it is worth looking
closer at the symphonic poem *Orpheus*, and then examining its possible
consequences for Wagner's theory and practice.[13]

Probably the most significant impression Liszt's *Orpheus* made on Wagner
was that it was unusually uniform. There is no clear exposition of themes,
there are no contrasting motives, and above all, there are neither transitional nor development sections.[14] The whole piece seems to move slowly
but surely and regularly along a chain of small units, sometimes identical,
sometimes varied or slightly altered. The aim of this constant phrase movement is a single fortissimo climax, followed by a short epilogue. Easily
distinguishable form units are a short harp prelude with a characteristic
motif in the horns and two different chords in the harps (mm. 1–15), a
violin solo (mm. 84ff.) with a corresponding violoncello solo (mm. 114ff.),
a return of the beginning (mm. 15–26) in fortissimo (mm. 144–55), a large
crescendo leading toward the climax (mm. 180–94ff.), and finally a short epilogue recalling the melody of the violin solo and ending in a series of
chords (mm. 206–25). Harmonically, Liszt indicates a tripartite plan: in measure 72 the key changes from C to E, and in measure 128 returns to C. There
is, however, no thematic plan corresponding to these key changes.[15] Unlike
Les Préludes, there is no resemblance to sonata form and there is no example of Liszt's well-known method of thematic transformation.[16] The
question then remains: what aroused Wagner's admiration?
   A closer look reveals a surprising structural disposition: a great number of small elements are literally repeated (a–a) or more or less varied
(a–a'). This formal principle of parallel units is already present in the
opening chords, where a syncopated horn motif is accompanied by a

chord, first on E♭, then on A₇. The same procedure is continued in the following measures, showing already a tendency to extend this parallelism to a larger scale: the a–a' of mm. 15–26 form together a larger-scale A, which is repeated in the same key, but with different orchestration, in mm. 26–37 (A'). In the following section (mm. 38–71) Liszt shortens the units to two or three measures, adding at the same time a third and fourth unit (mm. 47–54), which unfold the starting impulse of the first elements to shape a short melody, leading back toward the repetition of the whole (mm. 55–71). For a more didactic overview we may describe mm. 38–54 as a (38–40), a (41–43), b (subdivided into two units, 44–46 and 47–54). In many cases it is difficult to decide if a new melodic unit should be denoted as a more or less identical repetition "a," as a variant of the former unit "a'," or as a contrasting element "b." Since the b component of an a–a–b "set" always contrasts with the pair of a's, through its expansiveness and its closing or transitional character, it is here always denoted as "b," even when it starts with the same motivic idea as one of the a's. Measures 38–54 form altogether an A which is literally repeated—with the exception of a variant in mm. 66–71—in mm. 55–71. The lento in mm. 72–84 introduces a contrast with its English horn melody (developed from the horn syncopations in mm. 1–37), but is itself organized in the same manner, with the units related as a–a'–b. So the eleven small units of the whole section (mm. 38–84), which leads toward the entry of the violin solo in bar 84, form a large scale A(38–54)–A'(55–72)–B(72–84).

This formal disposition inevitably calls to mind what Alfred Lorenz called "bar-form," and particularly his notion of "potenzierte Barform."[17] This "exponentiated bar-form," as the concept might be translated, consists of two parallel *Stollen* (A–A) and a succeeding *Abgesang* (B), which can be divided into an a–a–b on a smaller scale, and so on.[18] Even if the principle might seem similar to that in Liszt's *Orpheus*, it must be emphasized that the concept "bar-form" and the related idea of a lyrical form as used by Wagner in *Die Meistersinger von Nürnberg*, as well as Lorenz's particular construction of an architectonic form in Wagner's dramas, are all contrary to the formal principle I am identifying in *Orpheus*.[19] Liszt's intention is not to create "closed" formal sections, but to develop or "unfold" small elements into greater units. The same formal idea, which because of its open, dynamic character might be called "unfolding form," is continued on a still larger scale in the central section of the piece, from measure 84 to 179 (see Example 1). The small a–a–b construction of mm. 84–92 is the beginning of a large-scale A–A'–B (84–114). But then this A–A'–B as a whole forms again a large α to which is joined an α' (114–44) and a β part (144–79).[20] The following Lento espressivo (180–94), can be

Example 1. Liszt, *Orpheus*, mm. 84–179.

Example 1 continued

regarded as a continuation of this β section as well as an intensifying bridge towards the fortissimo climax of the symphonic poem as a whole.

To avoid any misunderstanding: this is not an attempt to adapt Lorenz's system to Liszt's symphonic poem, but to explain how Liszt proceeds in creating larger units out of small melodic elements. The fundamental difference is that *Orpheus* has no "architectonic" form, that the whole cannot be explained as "bar-form" or "arch form" or anything else. Liszt's form is dynamic, a constant process of "making music," but unlike purely "rhapsodic" music, the quasi-improvised elements unfold into ever larger units. So even the parts designated here as b or B are neither clearly contrasting nor closing, but have a dialectic function: on the one hand they continue the impulse given by the repeated a section, and on the other hand they form a bridge toward the beginning of a new a–a–b section. An especially clear instance of this is the first B section (mm. 72–84), which takes melodic elements such as the syncopated horn motif from the very beginning (mm. 1–2), and the neighbor-note figure of the A parts (measure 38ff.), and assembles them into a lyric melody, while creating at the same time an introduction to the central section that begins with the violin solo at measure 84.

The intensification section in measures 180–94, as well as the climactic section in measures 194–206, evade a description as a–a–b. The intensification starts with a two-measure sequence that leads toward an augmentation of the dotted quarter-note with the following eighth-notes into a dotted half with quarters. This augmentation leads toward a varied repetition of the two-measure sequence (mm. 186–89), now crescendo, followed by a fragmented sequence in measures 190–94. The last measure is already the beginning of the climactic section which presents first (mm. 194–98) the theme from measures 15ff., followed by eight measures of relieving tension. The epilogue (mm. 206–14), again, can easily be described as a–a–b: it starts with a reminiscence of the violin solo (from measure 84), which is repeated and subsequently augmented to half-notes "perdendo" (mm. 210–14), before the piece fades away in a series of nine "mysterious" chords.

The overall form is illustrated in chart 1, which is to be read from left to right. Each column stands for one of the small units (a, a', etc.). The height depends on the number of measures.[21] The different shades refer uniquely to the function as a, a', or b within a larger section. Chart 2 displays the tonal structure of the entire piece. It can be seen that many a–a or a–a' units, but not all, have the same tonality and that the b sections normally change toward another key. Of special interest is the fact that the large scale sections (A–A'–B) correspond even in harmonic aspects. Thus mm. 15–26 (A) and 26–37 (A') are harmonically identical, as are the following mm. 38–54 (A) and 55–71 (A'). The B parts of mm. 72–84 and 102–14 are also completely identical not only in their melodic and formal shape, but also in their harmonies, forming a sort of yoke over the different A–A' parts in mm. 38–71 and 84–102.

On the whole, there is a clear predominance of the tonic C and the dominant G, followed by B-flat, the relative of G minor. The central section (mm. 84–194) stands more or less for a development, which in a literal sense does not take place. It starts in C-sharp minor followed by F minor/F (the mediant of D-flat minor [=C-sharp]), E, G-sharp minor/G-sharp, C minor/C, E-flat, C, and, finally, after a long dominant section (mm. 155–94) leads back to the tonic C. Harmonic development, however, seems not to be the form-building principle. Apparently the succession of harmonies is not motivated by their own "logical" development, but is a mere consequence of shifts from a to b sections.

The tonal organization unveils perhaps the most important achievement of Liszt's unfolding form: in *Orpheus*, symphonic music unfolds without need of motivic-thematic work and without harmonic development. The differentiation between "thematic" and "transitional" sections becomes as

Chart 1. *Orpheus* Overall Form

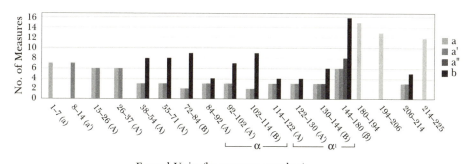

Formal Units (by measure number)

Chart 2. *Orpheus* Harmonic Plan

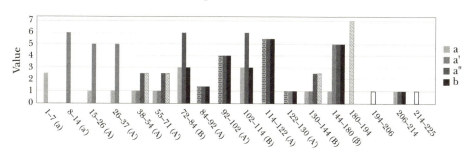

Formal Units (by measure number)

Note: The value 1 is the tonic C, the other harmonies are posted above (e.g., E♭ as 2.5). Major keys are blank, minor keys dotted. Stripes indicate modulating parts.

superfluous as that between harmonically stable and modulating sections. Different keys can easily be juxtaposed, such as, for instance, in the first fourteen measures E-flat and A⁷, without need of an immediate functional relation towards a tonic. (They are linked, however, by the chromatic descent of their fundamental notes B♭ and A which lead toward the G in measure 15.)

When he published *Orpheus*, Liszt added a short preface explaining the fundamental idea. It should be emphasized that this preface is not a "program" in the proper sense, and that the piece is not in its course determined by programmatic events. The whole stands for the mythological musician who by his singing evokes his lost Eurydice, interpreted as the

"Ideal," which he will never be able to capture and which evaporates as he reaches for it:

> Today, as in the past and forever more, Orpheus, which is to say Art, must spread its melodious waves and vibrant chords, like a sweet and seductive light, over contrary elements that tear and bleed in the soul of each individual, as well as in the innards of society in general. Orpheus mourns Eurydice—Eurydice, that emblem of the ideal engulfed by evil and sorrow, whom he is able to wrest from the monsters of Erebus, to free from the depths of the Cimerian darkness, but whom he, alas, can not preserve on this earth. . . . If we were to formulate our idea completely, we would have wished to render the serenely civilizing character of the melodies that radiate from every work of art—their suave energy, their august empire, their sonorities, so nobly soothing to the soul, their undulation sweet as the breezes of Elysium, their gradual rise like the vapors of incense, their diaphanous and airy-blue Ether enveloping the world and the whole universe as if in the atmosphere, or in a transparent cloak of ineffable and mysterious Harmony.[22]

The subject of Liszt's symphonic poem is the act of harmonious singing itself. Out of the prelude-like harmonies, motives and short themes take shape and are gathered in units of constantly greater scale. The single tone g (later altered to g♯), presented by the horns at the very beginning, evokes harmonies and small melodic patterns that will be combined in different ways during the whole piece. A first "highlight" is the elegiac melody in the English horn (mm. 72ff.), continued by the oboe. Then the insisting, pleading chant of the solo violin (mm. 84ff.), which leads to the repetition of the elegiac melody as its *Abgesang*. Both melodies are to a certain extent "developments" of the patterns presented in the first fifty-five measures (see tables 1 and 2.) That the piece as a whole did not become "'shapeless'" is due to a singular form of structural organization: the smallest units of mm. 2–4 are bound together in greater units of mm. 8–16, which, at least in the central part of the piece (mm. 84ff.), are gathered into units of far greater scale (mm. 31–36). The result, however, is no "architectonic form," but a constant process, which leads toward the climax and finally fades away. The "secret of form" in Liszt's *Orpheus*—to borrow a phrase Lorenz applied to his work on Wagner—is not "closed forms" or a concrete "form model," but rather a constant unfolding of small, "open" elements into greater units.

Table 1. *Orpheus:* Themes and Motives

Introduction (motif a), mm. 1–4

Theme Ia, mm. 15–22

Theme Ib, mm. 38–44

Theme II, mm. 72–79

Theme III, mm. 84–92

Table 2. *Orpheus:* Order of Themes and Motives

	Introduction (Motif a)	Theme Ia	Ib	II	III	II	III	Ib	Ia	Ia'	II	Ia	III	Epilogue
Measure	1	15	38	72	84	102	114	130	144	155	180	194	206	214

Wagner Reconsiders Instrumental Music

In his *Orpheus*, Liszt resolved a problem that had worried Wagner since his first compositional sketches for the *Ring*: how to avoid the periodic structure of music (which Wagner himself had still used in *Lohengrin*) without becoming "formless," in a sort of constant accompanied recitative, and without maintaining the difference between "closed" aria sections and dramatic development in recitative sections. Wagner's own theoretical solution was the concept of the "poetic-musical period" (*dichterisch-musikalische Periode*) as presented in *Opera and Drama*. The "verse melody" should remain in the same key for as long as the sentiment of the text remains unchanged. But when this sentiment changes (as from "bliss" to "woe"), the music should modulate to a foreign key and return to the first key only when the former sentiment returns.[23] This organization of music would assure its independence from "absolute music," which according to Wagner was generically based on the "Tanzmelodie," i.e., music of periodic structure with reprise.[24]

Wagner's concept of the "poetic-musical period" was closely connected with two axioms of his theory of composition in *Opera and Drama*: on the one hand, he remained trapped in a sort of periodic organization, which is perceptible not only in his theory, but also in his early sketches for *Siegfried's Tod*.[25] On the other hand, the "poetic-musical period" resulted from Wagner's famous verdict on "'absolute music,'" which included all forms of instrumental music. Since such forms could not be based on poetic verse and its dramatic sentiments, they were unable to express dramatic ideas and had to remain in the "architectonic" form of "absolute music." For Wagner, all forms of instrumental music were originally based on dance, and through the aria these forms had even conquered opera:

> The Disconnected was so peculiarly the character of operatic music. Only the separate tone-piece had a Form coherent in itself; and this was derived from absolute-musical good pleasure, maintained by custom, and imposed upon the poet as an iron yoke. The connecting principle, within these forms, consisted in a ready-made theme making place for a second, a middle-theme, and repeating itself according to the dictates of musical caprice. In the larger work of absolute instrumental-music—the Symphony—alternation, repetition, augmentation, and diminution of the themes made out the movement of its separate section, which strove to vindicate itself before the Feeling by establishing the utmost possible Unity of Form, through the coordination (*Zusammenhang*) and recurrence of its themes. The vindication

of their recurrence, however, rested on a merely imagined, but never realized assumption; and nothing but the Poetic Aim can really bring about this vindication, because it downright demands the latter as a necessary condition for its being understood.[26]

Wagner points out that all forms of instrumental and dramatic music were based principally on the contrast and recurrence of themes, and on what we may call "motivic-thematic work." As the formal organization of these pieces was a consequence of the musical material and not of the poetic motivation, all these forms had to be rejected.

Not even from program music—either overtures or program symphonies—did Wagner expect a solution.[27] In both he saw the danger of the lack of inner correlation between the program, which the listener had to know in advance, and the more or less arbitrary form:

> The ground of this apprehension consists herein: unqualified or fantastic musicians, denied that higher consecration, have set before us tone-works departing to such an extent from the customary Symphonic (dance-) form, of which they simply had not gained the mastery, that the composer's aim stayed absolutely unintelligible if his bizarre dance-forms were not followed step by step with an explanatory program. Hereby we felt that Music had been openly degraded, though solely because on the one hand an unworthy idea had been given her to express, on the other, this idea itself had not come to clear expression; which mostly arose from all its scanty stock of intelligibility having been derived from the traditional, but arbitrarily mangled dance-form, and bungled in the application.[28]

Surprisingly, only a few weeks after becoming closely acquainted with Liszt's symphonic poems, Wagner expressed a profoundly different opinion of independent instrumental music and even revoked one of his most important "dogmas": his verdict on instrumental music and especially on program music:

> After hearing one of Liszt's new orchestral works, I was involuntarily struck with admiration at its happy designation as a "symphonic poem." And indeed the invention of this term has more to say for itself than one might think; for it could only have arisen with the invention of the new art-form itself. . . . What, now, would that new form be?— Of necessity a form dictated by the subject of portrayal and its logical development. And what would be this subject?— A

poetic motif. So!— prepare to be shocked— "Programme-music." . . .
I pardon everybody who has hitherto doubted the benefit of a new
art-form for instrumental music, for I must own to having so fully
shared that doubt as to join with those who saw in our program-music
a most unedifying spectacle.[29]

In Liszt's symphonic poems Wagner encountered a new approach
where logical development (the "form") originated in a "poetic motif" rather
than in the traditional sonata form. Thus the traditional form-building
elements—the alternation of themes, their development, and their recurrence—had become superfluous. For Wagner, Liszt's symphonic poems
were no longer significant deviations from the traditional form, motivated
in an "extra-musical" program, but new forms in themselves, as the individual realizations of a poetic motive:

Now we have recognized the march- and dance-form as the irremov-
able foundation of pure Instrumental-music, and we have seen this
form lay down the rules of construction for even the most complex
tone-works of every kind so rigorously, that any departure from
them, such as the non-repetition of the first period, was considered
a transgression into formlessness and had therefore to be avoided
by the daring Beethoven himself—to his otherwise great detriment.
On this point, then, we are at one, and admit that in this human
world it was necessary to afford divine Music a point of attachment,
nay—as we have seen—a "conditioning moment," before ever she
could come to an appearance. I ask now, whether March or Dance,
with all the mental pictures of those acts, can supply a worthier
motive of Form than, for instance, a mental image (*Vorstellung*) of the
main and characteristic features in the deeds and sufferings of an
Orpheus, a Prometheus, and so forth? I further ask: if Music's manifestation is so governed in advance by form, as I have already proved
to you, whether it is not nobler and less trammeling for her to take
this form from an imagined Orpheus or Prometheus motive, than
from an imagined march or dance motive?— Surely no one will
have an instant's doubt about it, but rather allege the difficulty of
obtaining an intelligible musical form from these higher, more individual images (*Vorstellungen*), since it has hitherto appeared impossible
to group them for the ordinary understanding (I don't know whether
I am expressing myself correctly) without employing those lower, more
general motives of form.[30]

The mention of "Orpheus" as well as the concert in St. Gall within the same text (his open letter on Liszt's symphonic poems) leave no doubt that it was specifically this symphonic poem that provoked these reflections, thus altering one of the fundamentals of Wagner's theory. Nor can there be any doubt that this experience must have affected Wagner's own compositional practice.

Toward *Tristan*

Considering not only the letter on Liszt's symphonic poems, but also that Wagner wrote down some of the earliest sketches for *Tristan und Isolde* on 19 December 1856, within a month of the St. Gall concert, and that these sketches—in contradiction to his former theory on music and drama— were described by him as "yet music without words" (vorläufig Musik ohne Worte), it is worth taking a closer look at the genesis of the opera.[31] Among the earliest sketches for *Tristan* we find the melodic idea that appears in the second act after Brangäne's words "Bald entweicht die Nacht!" In the sketch (Example 2) it is associated with different words ("Sink hernieder, Nacht der Liebe"). These words, slightly varied, exist in the final version as well, but there they are attached to a different melody.[32] The fact that the motif is attached to different words is not as surprising as the conventional periodical structure of the whole. A two-bar "antecedent" leads toward the highest note d″, from which point the "consequent" returns with a cadence to the final note g′. Thus the varied sequence of the head motif B–G–C♯ to D–B–F♯ in bar 3 is integrated into a four-bar period, recalling more the music of *Tannhäuser* and *Lohengrin* than the phrasing achieved in *Die Walküre* and *Siegfried*. The following line ("Hell dann leuchtet")

Example 2. Wagner, sketch for *Tristan und Isolde*, Act 2.

shows a varied version of the "antecedent." Apparently, Wagner intended a more or less strophic form. This sketch is not dated, but it can be presumed that it was written down shortly before or after the first dated sketches from 19 December 1856.[33]

The sketches from 19 December 1856, then, show Wagner's attempt to overcome this conventional form and move toward a broader melodic unfolding. The four measures of the former sketch are retained (now without any text), but then repeated in varied form, followed by several melodic variations that should enable some broader development.[34] Wagner brought these sketches together some days later in the so-called "Notenbriefchen" for Mathilde Wesendonck (Example 3).[35] Here the first four measures are repeated, intensified by raising the highest note from d" to e" (mm. 5–8), while the following ten measures start almost identically, but then continue freely as a series of sequences and variations that lead back toward the tonic G. The overall form of mm. 1–18 can easily be described as A–A'–B, which is underlined by the parallel beginnings of the smaller units (mm. 1, 3, 5, 7, etc.). The fact that the initial sketch, as well as this slightly later attempt at "forming," do not mention any particular text line from *Tristan*, underlines what Wagner told Marie von Sayn-Wittgenstein in a letter from this time concerning his *Tristan* sketches: "All this is still only music" ("Das ist Alles nur erst noch Musik").[36]

We can see from another sketch for the second act (Example 4) that this was not pure coincidence.[37] The total of thirty-one measures can be divided into an opening section (eventually) A(1–4)–A(5–8) and a continuing section mappable as B (9–12, 13–31). Robert Bailey comments: "Here, Wagner's intention from the very beginning seems to have been to make a complete musical complex. He began with the melody from beginning to end in ink and only later added the block-chordal harmonization in three parts in pencil. As a pure melodic conception then, Wagner was more concerned with the expansion of his generating idea than with the development of various elements implicit in it."[38]

In both cases, it is important not whether or how Wagner followed a "model" presented by Liszt, but that Wagner was concerned with problems of musical form without any guiding text or action. That the solution he found was more or less similar to Liszt's principle of "unfolding form" emphasizes the importance of his encounter with *Orpheus*. This is not contradicted by the fact that Wagner did not preserve the sketched form in the final version of *Tristan und Isolde*, but changed it significantly, since in the printed score both motives are developed in a very similar way, adapted to the requirements of the drama.[39] The "love theme" is first presented during eleven measures (starting with Isolde's "Wie sie es

Example 3. Wagner, sketch sent to Mathilde Wesendonck.

Example 4. Wagner, sketch for *Tristan und Isolde*, Act 2.

wendet") that are clearly organized as 2+2+7. The first two measures are almost literally repeated (a–a). The last seven (b) start with a sequence of the first measure, which is continued by a sequence of half measures and ended by a rhythmically and melodically augmented unit in two measures. These eleven measures are varied by the next seventeen measures in a different key over the pedal f (from "[nun laß mich gehorsam] *zeigen*"), organized as 3+3+11 measures. The following eight measures have a transitional character, leading toward a slightly varied repetition of the first eight measures (from Isolde's "[die mir das Herze brennen] *macht*"), now in B major. Even though we refrain from interpreting the whole as A–A'–B or A–A'–B–A", it is evident that the large-scale form is a continuation of the building principle of the motif itself. Here, as well as in Liszt's *Orpheus*, the traditional development techniques are no longer consequences—"development"—of the thematic material, but are rather its constructive principle.[40] When Dahlhaus states that in *Tristan*, as well as in Liszt's symphonic poems, sequences are no longer a principle of development, but of exposition, he grasps only part of the truth:[41] Liszt, and subsequently Wagner, made use of a formal principle that brought to an end the difference between exposition and development.[42]

The most striking example is the Introduction to Act 3.[43] Here, where Wagner did not need to take into account a text or an immediate dramatic action and where he could make use of musical material from the Prelude to Act 1, Wagner is the closest to Liszt's formal principle in *Orpheus*. This principle is already revealed in the first ten measures: the "longing motif" from the very beginning of the work, now in a diatonic variant in F minor, is first presented in two parallel units (a–a) followed by a larger unit (b), which starts the same way but then takes a different shape that leads toward an open ended pianissimo on the dominant C major. Here, these ten measures might have been repeated, but Wagner interposes a five-bar reminiscence from Act 1 (c), starting in measure 26 in the parallel A-flat major, then sequentially continued via G-flat minor and E-flat minor back to the dominant C major.[44] Only then is the whole (a–a–b–c) repeated. The two sections (1–15 and 16–30) are thus clearly related one to another as A and A'. The remaining twenty-four measures (B) present the motif from the beginning in a more dissonant, intensified version, divided again in a–a–b (2+2+4) and a–a–b (2+2+6), but now without the reminiscence section. After the curtain is raised the whole introduction is finished by seven descending measures (b), ending in the tonic F minor, by which point the sad melody of the English horn has already started.[45]

This process of unfolding is perceptible over large spans of *Tristan*. One quite obvious example is the "Sterbegesang" of the great love scene in

Act 2 ("So starben wir, um ungetrennt," mm. 1377ff.).[46] The four-tone motif Eb–Ab–Ab–G is repeated in a series of ascending sequences forming an a–a'–a" (4+4+8) and brought to a close with a new melodic line b ("ganz uns selbst gegeben"). These twenty-four measures are repeated in the same key with additional viola figuration and the text divided between Tristan and Isolde. Both "strophes" (A–A') then culminate in the great melodic gesture of revolving eighth-notes in the continuation of Brangäne's chant ("Habet Acht!").

In *Tristan* as well as in *Orpheus*, to summarize, the form-building principle is not the "architectonic" or "arithmetical" relation of the whole to its parts, but the unfolding process of a small melodic unit in a series of repetitions and sequences that are gathered into greater units on a larger scale. Such unfolding occurs without a drive toward cadential closure, and without a need to open out into a transitional or developmental process. These are the criteria that further distinguish unfolding form from periodic forms, which can also take something of an a–a–b shape (especially 2+2+4).[47]

The aim of the present study is clearly not to explain *Tristan und Isolde* according to a single principle, still less to claim that Wagner learned any "system" from Liszt and then simply made use of it. Considering, however, the harmonic audacity of the *Tristan* score and the tendency toward sequences, which according to Carl Dahlhaus form the structural counterpart of the chromaticism, it should not come as a surprise to find formal structures that recall the unfolding form of *Orpheus*.[48] But it is equally evident that there is a great methodological danger in finding and forcing into a system that which one seeks to find, thus repeating the fundamental error of Alfred Lorenz's study on Wagner's "secret of form." This is why only a few examples from Wagner's *Tristan und Isolde* are analyzed here, examples that are not necessarily representative of the whole. They show only the existence of formal principles similar to those in Liszt's *Orpheus*. In the context of a three-act musical drama and within a different compositional practice, Wagner could not merely "transfer" this principle to his *Tristan* score. However, the documents, writings, and music examples cited here should leave no doubt that the personal relationship between Liszt and Wagner during Liszt's Weimar period (1847–61) included an important cross-fertilization that was not limited to details of harmony or orchestration, but extended to phrasing and form as well.

NOTES

1. See, for instance, the article by Alexander Rehding, "Liszt und die Suche nach dem 'TrisZtan'-Akkord," in *Acta Musicologica* 72 (2000): 169–88.

2. Letter from Paris, 7 October 1859: "There are many things that we admit among ourselves, e.g., that since I became familiar with Liszt's compositions I've become a wholly different creature, as harmonist, from what I was before" (So giebt es Vieles, was wir unter uns gern zugestehen, z. B. dass ich seit meiner Bekanntschaft mit Liszts Compositionen ein ganz anderer Kerl als Harmoniker geworden bin, als ich vordem war). Richard Wagner, *Sämtliche Briefe*, ed. Gertrud Strobel et al., 14 vols., 2nd ed., (Leipzig: 1967), vol. 11, p. 282. See Richard Wagner, *Prelude and Transfiguration from "Tristan and Isolde,"* ed. Robert Bailey (New York and London: 1985), p. 21.

3. See Rainer Kleinertz, "La Relation entre forme et programme dans l'oeuvre symphonique de Liszt," *Ostinato rigore* 18 (2002): 85–98.

4. Wagner, *Oper und Drama*, ed. Klaus Kropfinger (Stuttgart: 1984), pp. 305ff. Alfred Lorenz based large parts of his analysis of Wagner's *Ring* on these pages from *Oper und Drama*: *Das Geheimnis der Form bei Richard Wagner*, 4 vols. (Berlin: 1924–33), vol. 1, pp. 18ff.

5. See Richard Wagner, *My Life*, ed. Mary Whittall, trans. Andrew Gray (Cambridge, Eng.: 1983), pp. 537, 540.

6. Wagner to Hans von Bülow, 29 November 1856, *Sämtliche Briefe*, vol. 8, p. 204.

7. Wagner to Otto Wesendonck, 30 November 1856, *Sämtliche Briefe*, vol. 8, pp. 211–12.

8. Wagner, *My Life*, p. 542.

9. Lina Ramann, *Lisztiana: Erinnerungen an Franz Liszt in Tagebuchblättern, Briefen und Dokumenten aus den Jahren 1873–1886/87*, ed. Arthur Seidl, rev. Friedrich Schnapp (Mainz: 1983), p. 9.

10. Richard Wagner, *Prose Works*, trans. William Ashton Ellis, 8 vols. (London: 1892–1899), vol. 3, pp. 242–43, 247. The letter was first published on 10 April 1857 in the *Neue Zeitschrift für Musik* 46, no. 15: 157–63. The text of this published version is identical with that of the collected edition of Wagner's writings *Gesammelte Schriften und Dichtungen*, 10 vols., 2nd ed., (Leipzig: 1887/1888), vol. 5, pp. 182–98, whereas the manuscript (Nationalarchiv der Richard-Wagner-Stiftung Bayreuth; published in *Sämtliche Briefe*, vol. 8, pp. 265–81) differs considerably.

11. Wagner, *Prose Works*, vol. 3, pp. 245–46; *Sämtliche Briefe*, vol. 8, pp. 273–74.

12. *Correspondence of Wagner and Liszt*, trans. Francis Hueffer, 2 vols. (London: 1888), vol. 2, p. 183; letter dated 27 January 1857. The letter mentioned here is the open letter on Liszt's symphonic poems.

13. "Vorläufig Musik ohne Worte." Wagner to Marie von Sayn-Wittgenstein in the same letter in which he sent these sketches, 19 December 1856. *Sämtliche Briefe*, vol. 8, p . 230.

14. Liszt himself ironically observed, in a letter to Alexander Ritter (4 December 1856), that his symphonic poem *Orpheus* was bound to be dismissed with contempt because "it has no proper *working-out* section." Liszt, *Briefe*, ed. La Mara, 8 vols. (Leipzig: 1893–1905), vol. 1, p. 273. Analytical approaches to this enigmatic piece have been made by Arnfried Edler, *Studien zur Auffassung antiker Musikmythen im 19. Jahrhundert* (Kassel: 1970), pp. 127–69; Sigfried Schibli, "Franz Liszt: 'Orpheus,'" *Neue Zeitschrift für Musik* 147, nos. 7/8 (July–August 1986): 54–56; Serge Gut, *Franz Liszt* (Paris: 1989), pp. 360–61; Thomas Spencer Grey, "Richard Wagner and the Aesthetics of Musical Form in the Mid-19th Century (1840–1860)," Ph.D. diss., University of California, Berkeley, 1988, pp. 371–75.

15. It is difficult to see in these key changes the basis of an overall A–B–A' form, given that the two A-parts do not match up, and that the B-part is not sufficiently contrasting. The latter starts with the English horn/oboe solo (see table 1, theme II) which is not entirely new but rather a consolidation of the short motives and themes presented hitherto.

It has more closing (Abgesang) than initiating character and is repeated later on in mm. 102ff. and (modified) in mm. 180ff.

16. Grey, *Richard Wagner and the Aesthetics of Musical Form*, p. 371. Richard Kaplan interprets the form according to sonata principles: "*Orpheus* has the 'sonata without development' form common in slow movements; the only development takes place in what Rosen calls the 'secondary development section' following the first theme area in the recapitulation." "Sonata Form in the Orchestral Works of Liszt: The Revolutionary Reconsidered," *19th-Century Music* 8 (1984): 150. My fundamental objection to this argument is that *Orpheus* lacks not only a development section, but also thematic contrast, a reprise in the proper sense, and a harmonic contrast that would be resolved in the reprise. From a slow movement in "sonata without development" form one would expect at least a clear bipartite plan, something like A–B–A'–B' with a return to the tonic in A'. Kaplan is certainly right to stress the importance of sonata form in Liszt's symphonic poems, and I don't wish to discard in principle any influence of sonata form in *Orpheus*. But it seems not to be the leading form-building principle. In a brief analysis, Keith Johns understands *Orpheus* as "a ternary structure that incorporates aspects of variation form" in accordance with the key changes in mm. 72 and 128. See his book *The Symphonic Poems of Franz Liszt*, ed. Michael Saffle (Stuyvesant, N.Y.: 1997), p. 60. Wolfram Steinbeck states categorically: "Die Anlage des Werkes ist einzigartig unter den Symphonischen Dichtungen. Weder steht auch nur schemenhaft die Sonatensatzform im Hintergrund wie bei den meisten anderen Symphonischen Dichtungen, noch finden sich Ansätze zur Mehrsätzigkeit in der Einsätzigkeit, wie zumindest bei der Hälfte der Werke. Auch folgt es keiner anderen herkömmlichen Form." Steinbeck, "Musik über Musik: Vom romantischen Sprachproblem der Instrumentalmusik zu Liszts Symphonischer Dichtung *Orpheus*," *Schweizer Jahrbuch für Musikwissenschaft* 15 (1995): 176.

17. Lorenz, *Das Geheimnis der Form bei Richard Wagner*, pp. 176ff.

18. In German *potenzieren* means especially "to raise to the power of (2, etc.)." Translated here as "exponentiated," Lorenz explains it in the first volume of *Das Geheimnis der Form bei Richard Wagner:* "In view of the preceding, the essence of the exponentiated *Bar* is not difficult to understand. The *Stollen* consist themselves of *Bars*; the *Abgesang* too can contain a *Bar* or *Bars*. This art-form is the peak of organic-dramatic beauty. For it is clear how naturally the exponentiations must develop, when an *Abgesang*, made after two *Stollen*, itself becomes an initiation, is itself repeated entirely (like a large *Stollen*), and thus becomes in the truest sense of the word an exponentiated intensification of the first elements, resulting in a large *Abgesang*. This procedure can . . . repeat itself still three or four times, so that a third and fourth level of exponentiation originates. Every intensification whips up a new one through its stollen-like repetition—an organism of unbelievable beauty comes to life!" (p. 176). For a discussion of these terms, see Stephen McClatchie, *Analyzing Wagner's Operas: Alfred Lorenz and German Nationalist Ideology* (Rochester, N.Y.: 1998). Bar-form is discussed at p. 129ff., and "potenzierte" form at p. 135ff.

19. See Curt Mey, *Der Meistergesang in Geschichte und Kunst: Ausführliche Erklärung der Tabulaturen, Schulregeln, Sitten und Gebräuche der Meistersinger sowie deren Anwendung in R. Wagners "Die Meistersinger von Nürnberg"* (Leipzig: 1892).

20. The beginning of this α' part is clearly recognizable by the entrance of the violoncello solo corresponding to the violin solo in mm. 84ff. So even the large-scale relation α–α' is not only constructed but can be perceived during audition.

21. If a phrase ends in the same measure in which a new unit begins, this measure is counted twice so that the addition of the number of measures of the smaller units is usually greater than the total number of measures of the section.

22. In the original French: "Aujourd'hui comme jadis et toujours, Orphée, c'est-à-dire l'Art, doit épandre ses flots mélodieux, ses accords vibrants comme une douce et irrésistible lumière, sur les elements contraires qui se déchirent et saignent en l'âme de

chaque individu, comme aux entrailles de toute société. Orphée pleure Eurydice, Eurydice, cet emblême de l'Idéal englouti par le mal et la douleur, qu'il lui est permis d'arracher aux monstres de l'Erèbe, de faire sortir du fond des ténèbres cimmériennes, mais qu'il ne saurait, hélas! conserver sur cette terre. . . . S'il nous avait été donné de formuler notre pensée complètement, nous eussions désiré rendre le caractère sereinement civilisateur des chants qui rayonnent de toute œuvre d'art; leur suave énergie, leur auguste empire, leur sonorité noblement voluptueuse à l'âme, leur ondulation douce comme des brises de l'Élysée, leur élèvement graduel comme des vapeurs d'encens, leur Éther diaphane et azuré enveloppant le monde et l'univers entier comme dans une atmosphère, comme dans un transparent vêtement d'ineffable et mystérieuse Harmonie."

23. See *Oper und Drama*, ed. K. Kropfinger, pp. 305–306; Thomas S. Grey, "A Wagnerian Glossary," in *The Wagner Compendium*, ed. Barry Millington (London: 1992), pp. 238–39. On the history and the problem of this term, see Werner Breig, "Wagners Begriff der 'dichterisch-musikalischen Periode,' in *Schlagen Sie die Kraft der Reflexion nicht zu gering an": Beiträge zu Richard Wagners Denken, Werk und Wirken*, ed. Klaus Döge et al. (Mainz: 2002), pp. 158–72.

24. See "Das Kunstwerk der Zukunft," in *Gesammelte Schriften und Dichtungen*, vol. 3, pp. 90ff.

25. Robert Bailey, "Wagner's Musical Sketches for *Siegfried's Tod*," in *Studies in Music History: Essays for Oliver Strunk*, ed. Powers, Strunk, and Strunk (Princeton, N.J.: 1968), pp. 459–94.

26. *Oper und Drama*, p. 362, part 3, chap. 6. English translation in Wagner, *Prose Works*, vol. 2, pp. 347–48.

27. In Part 3 of *Opera and Drama*, Wagner mentions the modern opera overture: "Every man of common sense must know that these tone-pieces—provided there was aught to understand in them at all—should have been performed *after* the drama, instead of *before* it, if they were meant to be understood. Vanity has betrayed the musician—even in the most favorable cases—into wanting to fulfill the Foreboding in the very overture itself, and that, with an absolute-musical certainty about the whole plot of the drama." Wagner, *Prose Works*, vol. 2, p. 340n. His critique of program symphonies was aimed mainly at Berlioz (*Oper und Drama*, p. 78). Wagner exemplified his Berlioz critique repeatedly with the adagio of the *Roméo et Juliette* symphony. *Sämtliche Briefe*, vol. 8, pp. 276–77.

28. "On Liszt's Symphonic Poems," in Wagner, *Prose Works*, vol. 3, pp. 247–48. For the original version, see Wagner's letter to Marie von Sayn-Wittgenstein from 17 November 1857, *Sämtliche Briefe*, vol. 8, pp. 275–76.

29. Wagner, *Prose Works*, vol. 3, pp. 243, 246, 248–49.

30. Ibid., p. 243.

31. This remark clearly does not say that there were no sketches for the text of *Tristan* at all, as discussed in John Deathridge, Martin Geck, and Egon Voss, *Wagner-Werk-Verzeichnis* (hereafter WWV): *Verzeichnis der musikalischen Werke Richard Wagners und ihrer Quellen* (Mainz: 1986), p. 443, but that the sketched melodic line, which was to be sung, was still wordless music.

32. Nationalarchiv der Richard-Wagner-Stiftung, Bayreuth, B II a 5, p. 21 (WWV 90, Musik, If).

33. This would suppose that the verses set to music here existed before or soon after 19 December 1856. They are considerably changed in the final version of the poem. Egon Voss supposes that the sketches with text are slightly later than those without text from 19 December 1856. Considering, however, the simple strophic character of the sketch in example 2, it might well be earlier than the more "formed" sketches without text from 19 December 1856 and in the "Notenbriefchen" for Mathilde Wesendonck (see Example 3). In any case, this is not crucial in our context. The important point is that all

these sketches, with their demonstrated interest in melodic forming, seem to have been written down after the St. Gall concert. See Egon Voss, "Die 'schwarze und die weiße Flagge': Zur Entstehung von Wagners "Tristan," *Archiv für Musikwissenschaft* 54 (1997): 210–27.

34. These sketches are published by Robert Bailey in "The Genesis of *Tristan und Isolde* and a Study of Wagner's Sketches and Drafts for the First Act," Ph.D. diss., Princeton University, 1969, p. 33, and "The Method of Composition," in *The Wagner Companion*, ed. Peter Burbridge and Richard Sutton (London and Boston: 1979), pp. 309–13.

35. Nationalarchiv der Richard-Wagner-Stiftung, Bayreuth, A II a 5, fol. XIV (WWV 90, Musik, Ie), on the first page, titled "sleepless" (*Schlaflos*). This sheet is possibly identical with the sheet of music that Wagner sent to Otto Wesendonck on 22 December 1856 and where he comments: "Ich kann mich nicht mehr für den Siegfried stimmen, und mein musikalisches Empfinden schweift schon weit darüber hinaus, da wo meine Stimmung hin passt, in das Reich der Schwermuth." *Sämtliche Briefe*, vol. 8, p. 231.

36. Bailey, "Genesis," p. 39.

37. The transcription follows Bailey, omitting corrections and variants.

38. Bailey, "Genesis," pp. 39–40.

39. See Wagner, *Sämtliche Werke*, ed. Isolde Vetter and Egon Voss (Mainz: 1990–1993), vol. 8, p. 46ff. (act 2, sc. 1, m. 419ff.).

40. Lorenz was partly conscious of this difference when he defended Wagner's "sequences" against Guido Adler: "Adler . . . goes to the battlefield against 'sequences' in Wagner. He overlooked that in many ways it is a matter not of sequence, but of formal construction." Lorenz, *Das Geheimnis der Form*, p. 191n.

41. Carl Dahlhaus, *Zwischen Romantik und Moderne* (Munich: 1974), p. 45.

42. See Dieter Torkewitz, "Modell, Wiederholung—Sequenz: Über Liszts Technik der Intensivierung, mit einer Anmerkung zu Wagner," in *Franz Liszt und Richard Wagner, Referate des 3. Europäischen Liszt-Symposions Eisenstadt 1983*, ed. Serge Gut (Munich and Salzburg: 1986), pp. 177–88.

43. This instrumental piece is to a large extent identical with the music of the fifth Wesendonck-Lied "Im Treibhaus" (WWV 91A). The Lied was finished 1 May 1858, the complete draft of the third act of *Tristan und Isolde* including the Introduction is dated 9 April 1859. Facsimile and transcription in Ulrich Bartels, *Analytisch-entstehungsgeschichtliche Studien zu Wagners "Tristan und Isolde" anhand der Kompositionsskizze des zweiten und dritten Aktes* (Cologne: 1995). For my argument this is of little importance, since both dates are clearly after Wagner's encounter with Liszt's *Orpheus*. The genesis illustrates, however, that the Introduction is not directly linked to dramatic action.

44. A variant of the "love renunciation motif," first presented in the Prelude, mm. 29ff.

45. The form of this introduction has been analyzed the same way by Lorenz, who calls it in his terminology an "exponentiated bar-form": "The prelude will so easily be recognized, by anyone who has compared the previous discussion with the score, as an exponentiated bar with double-themed *Stollen*, that I can leave as established this plan without further explanation. The clear manner of construction and regular proportions spring to the eye." Lorenz, *Das Geheimnis der Form*, p. 132.

46. See ibid., pp. 118–19. Lorenz's dogmatism makes it impossible for him to perceive mm. 1377–435 as a unit in which the continuation of Brangäne's chant ("Habet Acht! Schon weicht dem Tag die Nacht!") arches over and concludes the two "strophes" of the "Sterbegesang" ("So starben wir, um ungetrennt"). He divides both into two different periods (XVI and XVII).

47. Several theorists call this "Satzprinzip." A famous example is the beginning of Beethoven's Piano Sonata in F Minor, op. 2, no. 1.

48. See Carl Dahlhaus, *Wagners Konzeption des musikalischen Dramas*, 2nd ed. (Munich, 1990), p. 140. In fact, the relation is a dialectical one: the chromaticism is simultaneously a consequence of the sequences that originate in a new form idea.

Publishing Paraphrases and

Creating Collectors:

Friedrich Hofmeister, Franz Liszt, and the

Technology of Popularity

JAMES DEAVILLE

The most neglected aspect in our study of the life of the musical artwork is the publisher. We may know detailed information about the genesis of a piece, yet we are unable to answer basic questions about how that work was disseminated in print: Who was the publisher? What was his relationship with the composer? How many copies of a given piece were published, how often, over how many years? What were the financial arrangements for individual publications? These questions remain largely unanswered even for such studied composers as Bach, Beethoven, and Wagner. According to sociologist Pierre Bourdieu, the neglect resides in "the ideology of creation, which makes the author the first and last source of the value of his work."[1] This ideology has made us unwilling to assign credit to the business of culture.

Liszt's oeuvre has suffered from this same bias: no comprehensive study of the role of his music publishers has been undertaken.[2] This essay will help fill the lacuna by closely studying and analyzing for the first time the activities of one publisher, Friedrich Hofmeister in Leipzig, on Liszt's behalf. The basis for these considerations is the discovery of complete print-run statistics for Liszt works published by Hofmeister, as well as a series of unpublished letters between Liszt and the firm, and the balance sheet for the *Réminiscences de Lucia di Lammermoor* (LW A22).[3] These important business records have only now come to light because the Hofmeister archive remained in tight private possession until 1952, and after the expropriation of the company by the GDR, the records were relegated to the relatively inaccessible state archive in Leipzig.[4] The print-run figures are valuable for their contribution to our knowledge about individual Liszt works, but they gain in importance because of the comparisons they permit with other Hofmeister publications of the period, especially those by composers like Schumann and Chopin. Hofmeister's firm was only one member in a complicated international web of music publishers that made the same works of Liszt available to the purchasing public across national boundaries, yet broader comparisons are not possible since the business records of those other companies no longer exist or are inaccessible.[5] Still, study of the statistics and the other documents, in comparison with materials from the Schlesinger archive maintained by Musikverlag Zimmermann in Frankfurt am Main, and the C. F. Peters archive at the state archive in Leipzig, gives a clearer picture of early Liszt publishing practices and provide new insights into German music publishing in the first half of the nineteenth century. Above all, these new sources allow us to explore the nexus between composer, publisher, and public. Hofmeister was inventing nothing less than a technology of popularity: he created collectors among the public by publishing the works that Liszt so successfully performed for them.

Let us first take a brief look at the publisher.[6] Friedrich Hofmeister, born in 1782, opened his music shop in Leipzig on 19 March 1807. Within a year, he started publishing music, largely songs and piano music by composers like Henri Cramer and Friedrich Wieck. In the following years, the publisher on the one hand risked investing in works by Beethoven, Carl Maria von Weber, and Heinrich Marschner, and on the other maintained a catalogue of popular and pedagogical music that would sell large numbers of copies. (Table 1, following this essay, presents the print-run statistics for various works by Beethoven.) During the same period, the guitar method of J. T. Lehmann, to take an example of a more popular publication, appeared in printings of 1,000 copies each. Hofmeister's choice of composers eventually covered the full range, from relatively unknown, young, "serious" figures like Chopin and Schumann through celebrated popular ones like Joseph Labitzky (1802–81) and Norbert Burgmüller (1810–36). After 1847, Hofmeister gradually yielded control to his sons Adolph Moritz (1802–70) and Wilhelm (1824–77). As of 1852, composers had to deal solely with the two sons, who continued their father's policies and commitments, and new catalogue items were largely popular in nature. The firm had various owners in the twentieth century, was expropriated by the GDR, opened a branch in Frankfurt, and still exists in Leipzig today.

There is no documentation for Liszt's earliest contact with Hofmeister, which must predate his publication of *Die Rose* (LW A17, composed 1833),

Harmonies poétiques et religieuses (A18, 1833–34) and *Apparitions* (A19, 1834) in November of 1835. It remains unclear how or why Liszt settled on Hofmeister as his primary German publisher, which Hofmeister would remain for the next five years; it stands to reason, however, that Liszt would be associated with a leading German music publisher, who at the time seems to have enjoyed good ties with Liszt's Parisian friend, music publisher Maurice Schlesinger. The following list presents the works of Liszt that Hofmeister published, identified here by the title given in the publisher's handwritten Druckverzeichnisse.

Liszt Compositions Published by Hofmeister

Plate	Title, etc.	Date of first printing
2069	*La Rosa*	17 November 1835
2070	*Harmonies poétiques*	17 November 1835
2071	*Apparitions,* liv. 1	17 November 1835
2139	*Réminiscences,* op. 9	14 October 1836
2173	*Grande Valse,* op. 6	14 January 1837
2185	*Divertimento,* op. 5, no. 1	17 February 1837
2209	*Fantaisie,* op. 5, no. 2	28 April 1837
2241	*Apparitions,* liv. 2	21 December 1837
2242	*Rondeau fantastique,* op. 5, no. 3	8 September 1837
2269	*Fantaisie des Huguenots,* op. 11	23 February 1838
2276	*Grand Galop,* op. 12	9 March 1838
2277	*La même à 4 mains* [The same for four hands]	9 March 1838
2340	*12 Etudes,* liv. 1, liv. 2	9 February 1839
2441	*Fantaisie,* op. 13, *Lucia*	10 March 1840
3562, 3563	"Hussitenlied"	1 September 1865
4579	*Nicolai Ouvertüre*	15 October 1852
6882	*Zelle*	30 December 1871
6978	*Grand Galop leicht*	31 July 1873

Liszt by and large remained faithful to Hofmeister in the second half of the 1830s. In a letter from 5 April 1838, he acknowledged Hofmeister's activity on his behalf: "Up to the present I have had none but the most pleasant business relations with Herr Hofmeister, who has the kindness to publish the greater part of my works in Germany."[7] However, an incident in 1839 soured the relationship: according to a Liszt letter from 1855, Hofmeister pirated the 1826 French edition of the twelve etudes, a version that Liszt himself had previously renounced.[8] In the following year Hofmeister published the *Réminiscences de Lucia* (LW A22) and in 1852 the organ version of Nicolai's *Kirchliche Fest-ouvertüre* (LW E2).[9] However, Liszt would turn to other German publishers during the 1840s and afterward.[10]

In his later business dealings, Liszt sent the publishing firm a letter in 1869 that criticized the company's continuing interest in his virtuoso-era works.[11] This unpublished letter answers the firm's request for renewed German publication rights for three works: the *Grand Galop chromatique* (LW A43), which Liszt calls "aged"; the *Réminiscences de Lucia* (LW A22), which he calls "worn out"; and the *Hugenotten Fantasie* (*Grande fantaisie sur des thèmes de l'opéra Les Huguenots*) (LW A35), which he dismisses as "a thankless piece with very little success."[12] While Liszt gave permission for the first two pieces, he could not do the same for the third because of "the differences that occurred years ago between your house and that of Schlesinger in Berlin, which resulted in legal proceedings."[13] Although the disagreement originally concerned the question of which publisher had the rights over the *Huguenots* fantasy, Heinrich Schlesinger actually took Hofmeister to court in 1843 over a defamatory statement that the latter had published in 1842 in the *Allgemeines Buchhändler-Börsenblatt*, and Liszt, at Hofmeister's insistence, was forced to give a deposition in court against Schlesinger, who was a friend.[14] The court case may well have been another factor behind his leaving Hofmeister.

The dispute itself is of interest as an example of the close relationship between publishing and performance. Heinrich Schlesinger in Berlin asserted that his brother Maurice in Paris, who had purchased "toute la propriété" for the *Huguenots* Fantasy from Liszt, had ceded him the German publication rights for the work in 1837. In the words of Heinrich Schlesinger: "Since the compositions of Mr. Liszt had only a small number of sales in Germany at the time, and this fantasy—because of its colossal technical difficulties—promised even fewer sales, we had a few copies printed for us in Paris. . . . When we saw Mr. Hofmeister's edition, we demanded in writing on 9 January 1838 that he suppress his [edition] as an illegal one. Since the item appeared to us to be of so little commercial value, we did not pursue taking him to court. . . . [However,] Mr. Liszt's presence in Berlin [in the winter and spring of 1841–42] and the roaring applause that the Fantasy on Motives from the *Huguenots* received caused us—with approval of the composer—to proceed with the engraving of the plates and a new cover."[15] In other words, publishing the piece by Liszt became important to Schlesinger by virtue of the composer's and music's acquired popularity.

In sorting out the composer-publisher relationship between Liszt and Hofmeister, it is clear that Liszt's personal ties to Hofmeister were limited. Outside the five years between 1835 and 1840, during which Hofmeister published Liszt's new works, there is virtually no correspondence between them, and references in other letters are quite few. One reason is to be found in Liszt's desire, after retiring from his virtuoso career in 1847, to distance himself from his virtuosic works, which he associated with the Hofmeister years. The problems in this relationship may also be attributable to Hofmeister's personality, which was difficult, as reflected in his dealings with other composers like Marschner and Schumann: he was cold and calculating, cheap, and even dishonest, traits that were not a good basis for a long-term relationship or friendship with Liszt.[16] Hofmeister's sons do not seem to have shared his difficult personality, but as Liszt's letter from 1869 implies, the father's retirement did not remove his problems over the company's actions in the past.[17]

Regardless of the firm's relationship with its composers, the new documents from the Hofmeister archive reveal how extensively the company published during the nineteenth and early twentieth centuries, its period of greatest activity. The print indexes (Druckverzeichnisse) record dates of publication and print runs for over 10,000 pieces of printed music between 1808 and 1930. At least nineteen of those plate numbers are for works by Liszt. The indices also preserve some balance sheets for individual pieces, but only one for a work by Liszt, *Réminiscences de Lucia di Lammermoor* of 1840 (LW A22).[18] In total, Hofmeister printed almost 50,000 copies of pieces by Liszt between 1835 and 1930. While the new statistics help us identify some unknown first editions, my interest here is what these figures reveal to us about Hofmeister's contributions to the popularity of individual works by Liszt, compared among themselves and with the works of other composers. But I should note that my findings are only valid for Germany, due to international laws at the time that limited individual publisher's activities to their own countries. A complicated network of international agents meant that a given work by Liszt could hypothetically appear in five approved European editions at once or in close proximity (Austria, France, Germany, Great Britain, Italy).[19] More often, three "national" editions of Liszt's works were published simultaneously through international agreements, such as the *Réminiscences de Lucia*, which appeared in 1840 in an authorized edition under the imprints of Latte in Paris, Hofmeister in Leipzig, and Ricordi in Milan. With regard to Liszt's piano music, the configuration of international publishers was not always the same, and thus for Paris of the late 1830s and early 1840s, music publishers Brandus, Latte, Schlesinger (Paris), and Troupenas all appear in his definitive works list, in varying conjunction with Hofmeister, Schott, Schlesinger (Berlin), Schuberth, and Breitkopf & Härtel in Germany, and Diabelli, Spina, Haslinger, and Mechetti in Austria.[20] While compositions like the first version of the transcriptions of Beethoven Symphony nos. 5 and 6 (LW A37b) and of the Symphony no. 7 (LW A37b) enjoyed exclusive publishing arrangements with Breitkopf & Härtel and Haslinger respectively, it was to the composer's advantage to have his music disseminated as widely as possible. It is no coincidence that the music Liszt featured on tours between 1838 and 1847 was most significantly represented in multiple international editions, a point to which we shall return.

The three publications of 1835, all printed on 17 November, do not suggest the work of a popular or even promising composer, neither by print runs nor by the company's modest advertisement in the Leipzig *Allgemeine musikalische Zeitung*.[21] First printings of 100 copies were standard for a relatively unknown composer, which Liszt was in Germany in 1835. The diminishing publication activity for all three pieces (table 2) bespeak the unsuitability of these early works as repertory for the concerts of Liszt's virtuoso tours, beginning in 1838.[22] This is especially evident in the case of the *Apparitions* (LW A19), which appeared in only 100 copies between 1839 and 1855, quite a contrast with the 500-plus annual print runs for the popular virtuosic pieces. In establishing the relative value of "esoteric" early works like the *Apparitions* and *Harmonies poétiques et religieuses* (LW A18), we may well marvel over their harmonic and formal audacities, yet it is just those experimental qualities that set them apart from Hofmeister's cash cows like the etudes of Adolph Henselt or dance music for piano by Charles Mayer.[23] Such evidence supports the contention that marketability (thus popularity), and not aesthetic considerations drove the diffusion of the music by publishers, and thus Hofmeister can be justified for printing so few copies of these seminal early piano works. While aesthetic factors might well have contributed to the public's preference for certain pieces, the publisher's judgment of the music had business as its primary concern, as we shall see. These editions also indirectly provide the first proof of a link between Liszt's extraordinary virtuosic performances and sales of his music, since he did not perform the works on the road and they did not sell well. This may beg the question of whether the lack of popular success for these three pieces motivated Liszt not to perform them, or whether his failure to program them obviated any appreciation from the public that could buy the sheet music. But the fact remains that Liszt did not play the works in public and the music did not sell.

Ultimately, the difficulty of a piece by Liszt—the issue of playability— did not hinder its sales, since the Hofmeister figures reveal that people bought sheet music they could not possibly play because they had seen and heard Liszt perform it, whereby the notes on the page served as a souvenir of that "transcendental" experience. At the same time, a piece of music was not assured of popularity just because it was a difficult, flashy operatic fantasy. The *Réminiscences de la Juive* (LW A20) is a good case in point: Hofmeister's German edition never made it beyond 800 copies during the nineteenth century (table 3). Before the tours (1838–47) this edition had already experienced a precipitous decline in numbers, from 250 copies in the first year 1836–37, to 100 in the second year, to 50 in the next four years. Liszt himself did not program the work in Germany, both a cause and effect of its lack of popularity.

Before addressing the question of why the *Réminiscences de la Juive* did not work well in print or in concert, we must consider the general realm of operatic paraphrases, fantasies, etc.—compositions that should have proven more accessible to the general public and thus more "popular" than newly composed works like the *Apparitions* (LW A19) or the *Harmonies poétiques et religieuses* (LW A18), or even a Schubert arrangement like *Die Rose* (LW A17). As Charles Suttoni observes, "It was the public's familiarity with these [opera] melodies that drew them both to the opera house and the concert hall"—and, I would add, to the music store.[24] Timeliness was an important goal for the production of paraphrases, since they had to appear either while the work was still onstage or while its melodies remained in the public's memory. Indeed, Liszt completed his fantasies normally at least within one year of the opera's premiere. While those reminiscences and fantasies Liszt published with Hofmeister represented widely performed operatic scenes and arias, commentators like Suttoni and Leslie Howard place them within an early phase, as compared with the post-1840 reminiscences on *Robert le diable*, *Norma*, and *Don Juan*.[25] They suggest that the early transcriptions tend to be overly long and their virtuosic effects obscure the originating melodies, which would have weakened the attraction for the public. (It should be noted, however, that the assessment of a progression in Liszt's style during the period in question is not uncontested and merits a fuller study.) Perhaps because performance records indicate that Halévy's *La Juive* was much performed and greatly appreciated in Germany as *Die Jüdin*, Liszt's reminiscences may well have missed their audience despite a certain virtuosic appeal.[26] Thus it is not until measure 131 that a complete theme from the opera appears, and much of the work is freely conceived as a showpiece, with Halévy's "delicately exotic" Boléro—the terms are Suttoni's—getting lost in the fray. Still, the opera was popular and Liszt was beginning to enjoy fame, so the novelty of the work ensured a limited initial sales interest.

Encouraged by the preliminary success of the *Réminiscences de La Juive* (LW A20), and by the overall balance sheet of Liszt sales (750 copies in the first fourteen months of Liszt publication), Hofmeister took the important step of increasing the initial print run for the next Liszt piece, the *Grande Valse di bravura* (LW A32a), to 150, a number that would become standard for Liszt works (table 4). Since the first Hofmeister publications in 1835, Liszt had begun concertizing extensively to great acclaim, especially from the spring of 1838 on, and thus the publisher had every reason to believe he was backing a "winner." However, it is not coincidental that Liszt programmed the waltz moderately in Germany, that the publication sold only moderately in that market, and that once he ceased playing it in Germany, in 1842, it stopped selling. Neither his correspondence nor the music itself inform us why Liszt did not widely perform the piece, which Howard calls "flamboyant and witty."[27] The same scenario essentially holds true for the *Grande fantaisie sur des motifs de Niobe (Divertissement sur la cavatine de Pacini "I tuoi frequenti palpiti")* (LW A24), with 150 as the initial print run (figure 1). It also sold 250 copies within its first year beginning in February 1837, before the tours in Germany (table 5). After 1838, Hofmeister printed only 50 copies of the *Grande fantaisie* per year (1840, 1841, 1842, and 1845). Pacini's popular cavatina was the best-known number from his 1826 opera, which survived into the 1830s and later in a variety of variation and fantasy elaborations by such composers as Franz Hünten, Heinrich Panofka, and Joseph Dessauer.[28]

Beginning in early 1838, Hofmeister and Liszt entered the world of mass publishing with three major virtuoso piano works that would be popular during the German tours and would sell in great numbers during the nineteenth century, thus increasing the publisher's reputation and earning substantial profits. The fantasy on *Les Huguenots* (first version, LW A35), the reminiscences of *Lucia* (LW A22), and the *Grand Galop chromatique* (LW A43)—coincidentally, the major pieces on Liszt's first public concert in Germany, in Dresden on 16 March 1840—sold over 37,000 copies in Hofmeister's German editions before 1930. At the same time, the *Huguenots* fantasy (figure 2) did not significantly depart from the publication pattern of the *Niobe* fantasy, although it ultimately sold more copies (1,725 in all; see table 6). Hofmeister printed 300 copies in 1838 (initial print run of 150), followed by 50 or 100 copies per year through 1843, then 50 in 1846 and in 1848, and no further printings until 1854. Liszt's later assessment of the work's internal problems helps to explain the unusual discrepancy between his own active promotion of it in Germany and its modest sales in that market during the tours.[29] The inordinate length of the first version of the *Huguenots* fantasy—over twenty minutes—probably also

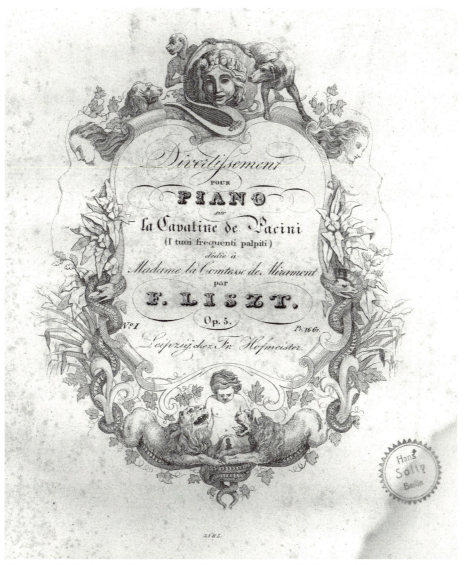

Figure 1. Hofmeister edition, *Grande fantaisie sur des motifs de Niobe / Divertissement sur la cavatine de Pacini ("I tuoi frequenti palpiti")*.

Reminiscences

DES

HUGUENOTS

GRANDE FANTAISIE

dramatique

pour le Pianoforte

composée et dediée

à Madame la Comtesse M. D'A.

PAR

F. LISZT.

Op.11. — ✦ — *Pr. 1 Thlr. 8 Gr.*

Propriété des Editeurs.

Leipzig, chez Fred Hofmeister.

PARIS,   **MILANO,**
chez M. Schlesinger.   chez J. Ricordi.

Enregistré aux Archives de l'Union.

2269.

Composed and published 1836

Figure 2. Hofmeister edition, *Réminiscences des Huguenots*.

influenced subsequent performance and sales. Of course, once Schlesinger in Berlin published a significantly shortened, revised version in 1842, demand for the first version would have diminished. Largely based on the love duet between Valentine and Raoul at the end of Act 4, with other thematic material surrounding it, Liszt's fantasy (original version) presents a different, more coherent, and organic concept of the work than other paraphrases, including the *Huguenots* fantasy by Sigismond Thalberg, which in traditional potpourri fashion presents three high points from the opera, each elaborated in succession.[30] If Liszt's work receives higher praise today on the basis of aesthetic considerations, the Thalberg composition may have found more eager listeners in its day. The German concert-going public not only was accustomed to hearing the type of paraphrase promulgated by Thalberg, but would also have found the potpourri style more readily accessible.[31] While Liszt's paraphrases from the 1840s—created specifically for performance on tour—continued this level of sophistication, tending to focus on a single character, they were swept up in the "Lisztomania" of the times, with audiences eager to hear his latest creations on their favorite operas.

The publication life of the *Réminiscences de Lucia di Lammermoor* (LW A22) anticipates and reflects this direction. Hofmeister first released it in early 1840, when Liszt was already embarking upon his German tours, and thus Hofmeister must have felt justified issuing it in the unusually high initial print run of 300 copies, followed two weeks later by another 200 (table 7). While print runs and frequencies of publication lag behind those for the *Grand Galop chromatique* (discussed below), the figures for *Lucia* nevertheless reveal a sensation. We are fortunate that for the *Lucia* fantasy, the Hofmeister records preserve a balance sheet for the first four years of publication (figure 3). For the first time, we can observe a publisher's expenses and income for a major virtuosic piece by Liszt. Figure 4 presents the details. For our purposes, it is less important to know the taler's absolute value than the relative issues of cost and profit (although it should be noted that the music for the *Niobe* fantasy, for example, cost 1 taler). Hofmeister made twice as much money on the first four years of the *Lucia* fantasy than he spent on it. He did this because he sold copies for twice what it cost him to produce them, and his other expenditures were minimal.[32] Liszt's honorarium, for example, was 40 talers—Hofmeister needed to sell less than 80 copies of Liszt's piece at 14 groschen each to cover Liszt's honorarium, and within the first three months he had already sold 500.[33] In all, the firm printed nearly 15,000 copies of the piece, a remarkable number by nineteenth-century standards. Obviously, publishing Liszt was a profitable business, but more important, we again observe how publisher and public lived in

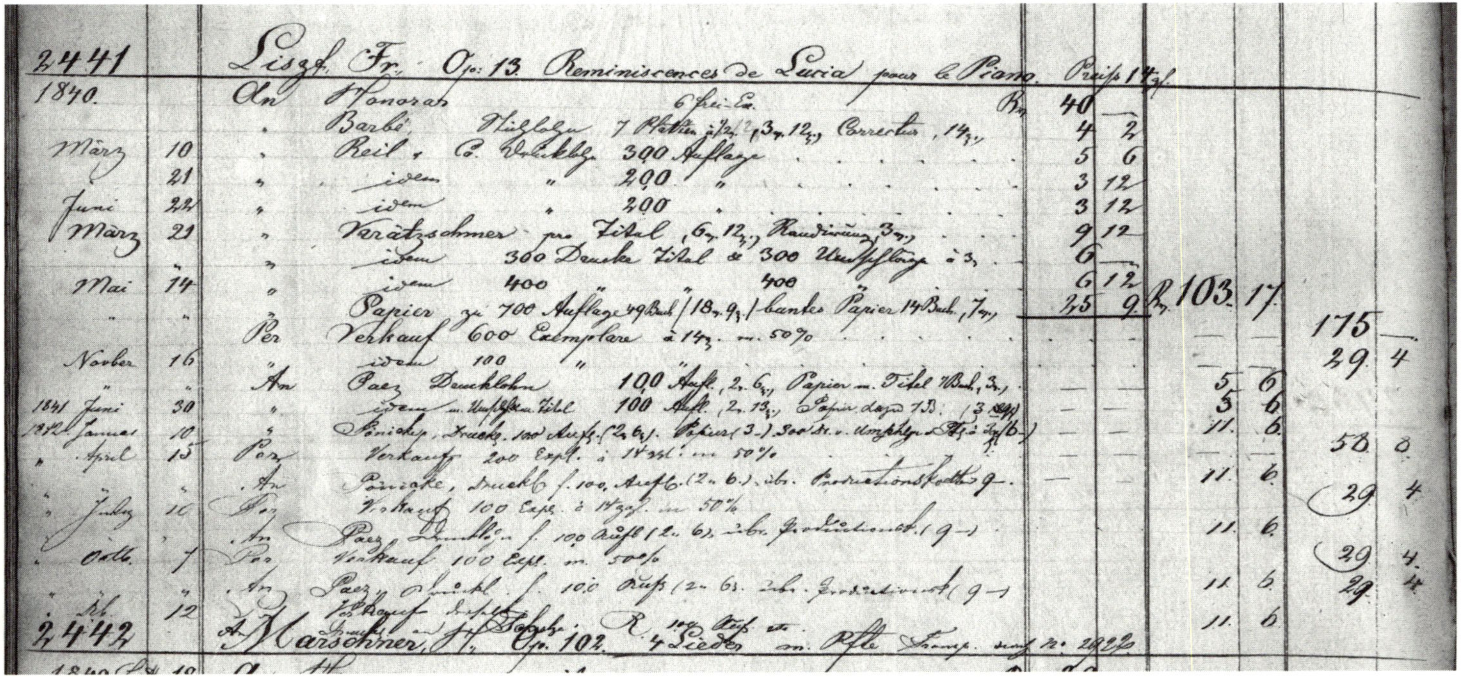

Figure 3. Hofmeister balance sheet detail for *Réminiscences de Lucia di Lammermoor*, 1840–43.

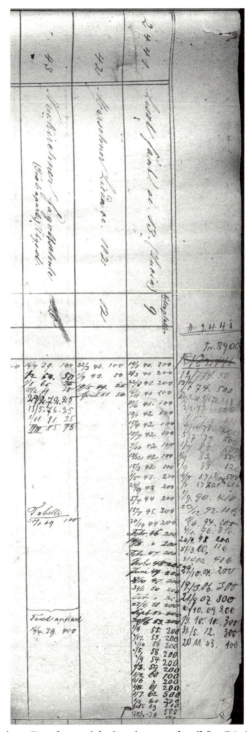

Figure 4. Hofmeister Druckverzeichnis print-run detail for *Réminiscences de Lucia di Lammermoor,* 1840–43.

a symbiotic relationship: Hofmeister both responded to and created the Lisztomania of the day through the popularizing technology of publishing.

The most successful of the Hofmeister publications of Liszt was the *Grand Galop chromatique* (LW A43), which became Liszt's signature piece in Germany and sold over 20,000 copies total in Hofmeister's two- and four-hand editions. After an initial print run of 150 copies on 9 March 1838 (table 8), two more printings of 100 each within the first year, and a modest run of 200 during 1839, sales of the German edition took off once Liszt began the tours. Here the correlation between performance and publishing is clear: 950 copies the first tour year; 600 in 1841; 1,400 in 1842; and 1,100 in 1843, with the number trailing off to 300 in 1844, the year in which he performed in Germany only through March. This amounts to 3,550 copies within six years, more than Hofmeister printed for the entire oeuvre of Chopin. During the course of the century, a normal decay of sales occurred, but for an ephemeral piece, *Grand Galop* proved unusually resilient, enjoying a reprint of 600 copies every two to three years. Not only is the frequency of printings during the early 1840s remarkable (every one to three months), but the size of print runs is also unusual for a Hofmeister publication of piano music: 100 copies, then 200 copies, and starting with 1843, 300 copies at a time. Such large numbers were a risk for the publisher, and the cautious Hofmeister expanded the print runs only when he could ensure sustaining high sales levels.

As a piece of salon dance music, the galop brings us more squarely into the realm of the domestic than either the free compositions or the works based on other compositions. Unlike those pieces, the galop was also functional music, which gave the sheet music a certain usefulness for the socially climbing middle class of the time.[34] If we were to remark that the sheet music to Liszt's *Grand Galop chromatique* could have attained popularity because it was functional music of lesser difficulty than the composer's other tour music, it must be noted that the issue of technical demands is relative. While the question of the technical capabilities of musicians of the day—amateur and professional—has yet to receive scholarly attention, this music is of a difficulty not to be compared with that for galops by other Hofmeister composers like Panofka or Burgmüller, especially when played at Liszt's tempo: "The tempo of the dance was so fast that one could hardly follow it with the ear, and even less with the eye, for whoever looked at the fingers of the concert-giver got lost in their rapidity."[35] Liszt customarily played the *Grand Galop chromatique* at the end of a virtuoso concert, as a "rouser," suggesting that purchasers were bringing Liszt's transcendence—and possibly a remembrance of his performance—into their residences when they bought this "functional" music. While it has been popular in Liszt scholarship to dismiss crowd-pleasing works like the *Grand Galop*, the new Hofmeister statistics give concrete evidence of how Liszt became a household word—or household item—through such popular music. As Charles Rosen notes, "Only a view of Liszt that places [pieces like] the Second Hungarian Rhapsody in the center of his work will do him justice."[36]

The Hofmeister statistics for Liszt's virtuosic works take on greater significance when used for comparison. While the same data for other Liszt publishers is at best incomplete, we know that Breitkopf & Härtel intended to publish a group of six symphonic poems in an initial print run of 150 copies. The firm explained to the composer in May of 1856 that the number represents "the minimum required to disseminate the work to any extent among the public and at the same time to place at your disposal adequate copies."[37] Of course, the general public would not be the primary consumers of the scores, which are a far cry from the piano sheet music from the late 1830s and the '40s.[38] Later in the century, Liszt's piano music continued its earlier high flight, as evidenced by print-run statistics from C. F. Peters.[39] The *Rigoletto: Paraphrase de concert* (LW A187) of circa 1855 appeared in Peters's German edition of March 1891 in an initial printing of 1,000 copies, with another 2,500 copies printed over the next three years. The *Miserere du Trovatore* (LW A199) was issued in January 1893 with 1,000 copies and with 500 more in both 1895 and 1897.

The Hofmeister figures also allow us to compare his promotion of Liszt with that for other composers, with revealing results. We might expect that composers like Schumann or Chopin were important market items for Hofmeister, but then we would be assuming that aesthetic considerations—or worse yet, our own construction of the canon—drove the dissemination of music. Actually, the most successful composers for Hofmeister were concert virtuosi like Liszt, Henselt, and Mayer, while Schumann and Chopin did not do well for the publisher, at least not initially.

Let us take a look at Schumann's Intermezzo, op. 4, and Toccata, op. 7, two of the most important Schumann pieces in the Hofmeister catalogue, albeit relatively minor works within the composer's oeuvre. The works clearly did not meet the publisher's expectations at first, for after an initial printing of 100 copies each in, respectively, 1833 and 1834 (tables 9 and 10), they did not again reach that same print-run level for another thirty years. In fact, during Schumann's lifetime, Hofmeister printed only 175 and 300 copies of these pieces, quite a striking contrast with his publication of Liszt. Interestingly, both of the Schumann works significantly increased in sales during the 1860s, which corresponds with the increased touring activity of Clara on behalf of her deceased husband—again, proof of the link between performance and publication. These increases after a substantial amount of time defy the trend, seen with Liszt and other composers, of a consistent decline in sales. In the case of Schumann and Chopin, the eventual canonization of the composer led to heightened interest in these and other works, while more popular music, including Liszt's *Grand Galop*, lost their appeal over time. Chopin's Impromptu, op. 51 (table 11) increased in sales only well after the first printing and after the composer's death, perhaps in connection with Liszt's promotion of Chopin through his book, which found wide distribution in Germany.

When comparing Liszt's publication status with that of other composers, it becomes apparent that the same nexus of performance and publication is in operation. Two unpublished letters from Heinrich Schlesinger reflect how important that relationship was for publishers. In a letter to his brother Maurice in Paris dating from 1844, Heinrich remarked that he "would take [Theodor] Döhler's *Gr. Fantaisie de Concert sur la Favorita de Donizetti p. Piano* for an honorarium of 800 Fr., if Döhler performs it in concerts."[40] He makes the point even more forcefully when writing about Jacques Rosenhain's fantasy on Halévy's *La Reine de Chypre* for piano: "I will take [it] for 300 Fl. only if Rosenhain plays it in concerts, otherwise not."[41] In the case of these composers, however, the publisher was able to dictate his terms, which would not have been the case with Liszt in the early 1840s. In a letter from 1838, Liszt himself recognized the value of performances for the publication of his *Hexaméron*: "In any case [it] will not really be published until I perform it in Paris. For some years this will be the inevitable misfortune of all the pieces I write."[42]

Looking ahead into the later nineteenth century, the composer's renown or canonic status would overtake live performance as a driver of popularity in the publication of piano music. As the phenomenon of virtuosity lost its most outstanding proponent in 1847, as the critique of the practice mounted, and as the spirit of the age shifted from optimism to pessimism, the need for the entertaining, popular performance of the virtuoso fell away. Certainly neither Brahms nor Grieg, to mention two pianist-composers after 1850, needed or used the vehicle of public performance to sell their sheet music, which did quite well according to the records of C. F. Peters. And an established figure like Mendelssohn dominated the market in initial and subsequent printings by virtue of his canonic stature.[43]

So, did Hofmeister miss the boat by using the popularizing technology of the press to promote Liszt's *Grand Galop* over his *Harmonies poétiques*, Schumann's Intermezzo, or Chopin's Impromptu? We must say no, for if a publisher made it his task to discover genius, he would not have been in business for long. In fact, Hofmeister could only afford to publish Schumann, Chopin, Alkan (and even the more esoteric works of Liszt) on the backs of Liszt, Lehmann, Henselt, and Mayer. Publishing and audience demand went hand-in-hand—we may not be able to say that Hofmeister made Liszt, but he certainly helped make the sensation around Liszt. Yet we must also give Hofmeister credit for taking a risk with such patently unpopular works as the *Harmonies poétiques* and *Apparitions*.

Of the many questions that remain, one is of particular interest: Why were "Lisztomaniacs" purchasing in great numbers pieces that were beyond their technical capabilities? The prevailing assumption has been that piano music of the ninetheenth century was bought to be performed. However, in light of the tremendous sales figures for Liszt's virtuoso music in connection with such a momentous historical occurrence as his virtuoso tours throughout Europe and the resulting Lisztomania, we are invited to rethink the reasons behind those purchases. As Walter Benjamin helps us theorize, this was an issue of collecting and empowerment.[44] In a seminal article from 1986, Beverly Gordon argues that the physical presence of the souvenir "brings back into ordinary experience something of the quality of an extraordinary experience."[45] If certain possessions can also be considered to be functions of an "extended self," thus creating meaning in life for subjects, then we could posit that owning one of Liszt's latest virtuoso hits was the result of desires both to possess an artifact inscribed with his transcendent power and to participate vicariously in the Lisztomania of the times.[46]

As shown through the correlation between performance and publishing, the individual would purchase Liszt pieces that he or she had heard in concert or that were prominently featured in the Liszt craze ("You just have to get this. . ."). The publisher satisfied the urges of the emerging bourgeoisie to gather artifacts for the purpose of memory, empowerment, and self-transcendence at a difficult time, when the bourgeoisie was seeking identity and stability in the midst of social and economic turmoil. He was ultimately creating collectors of cultural goods, who could find at least temporary liberation in published music. Sheet music was only part of this material culture—publishers were quick to toss off large numbers of lithographs and biographical pamphlets during and after Liszt's visits.[47] Here we see how, by catering to popular taste, the publisher was meeting important human needs of his times.

Print Runs for Hofmeister's Publications

The tables below are derived from Hofmeister's three printed volumes of print indexes (Druckverzeichnisse). In addition to the month/year and raw figure for each print run we have also provided a graphic interpretation of each work's printing history. Below the graph we have listed, variously, the catalogue number, title and composer, instrumentation, work or opus number, number of plates, designer of the cover page, and other printing information as presented in the original entries of the Druckverzeichnisse.

Source: Sächsisches Staatsarchiv Leipzig, Musikverlag Friedrich Hofmeister, Druckverzeichnisse, 43–45

Table 1. Beethoven Publications from Hofmeister

a. Three Trios, op. 9

MONTH AND YEAR	PRINT RUN
September 1809	100
October 1820	100
May 1824	50
October 1828	25
February 1832	25
July 1834	50
March 1843	50
January 1855	50
TOTAL	450

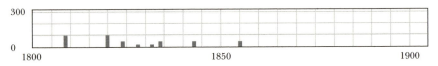

#110 Beethoven, 3 Trios, Op. 9 No. 1 (Zum 2 mal gemacht)
22 Platten. Titel Zinn No. XVII No. 1

b. Excerpts from *Fidelio*

MONTH AND YEAR	PRINT RUN
October 1819	300
July 1829	50
May 1832	50
July 1835	50
October 1837	50
March 1841	50
June 1845	50
August 1860	50
TOTAL	650

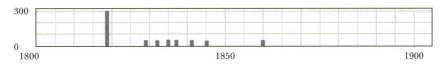

#637 Beethoven. Aus Fidelio f. Pfte. 2ᵉ Aufl.
6 Platten

c. Ballet Music for Four Hands

MONTH AND YEAR	PRINT RUN
1822	300

#847 Beethoven. Musique de Ballet à 4 mains.
Stein

d. *Coriolanus* Overture

MONTH AND YEAR	PRINT RUN
April 1824	200
February 1856	50
February 1860	50
April 1865	50
TOTAL	350

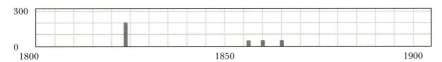

#1005 Beethoven. Ouvertüre Coriolan 4 ms.
14 Platten

e. *Egmont* Overture

MONTH AND YEAR	PRINT RUN
October 1824	200
November 1828	50
October 1830	100
September 1836	50
December 1836	50
November 1838	50
December 1841	50
November 1845	50
April 1851	50
October 1854	50
October 1859	50
TOTAL	750

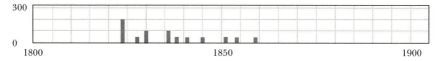

#1022 Beethoven. Ouv. Egmont f. Pfte.
8 Platten

f. *Prometheus* Overture

MONTH AND YEAR	PRINT RUN
October 1824	200
January 1843	50
January 1858	50
TOTAL	300

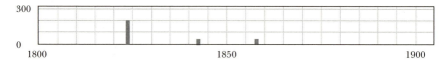

#1041 Beethoven Ouv. Prometheus f. Pfte.
6 Platten

Table 2. Liszt Publications from 1835

a. *Die Rose*

MONTH AND YEAR	PRINT RUN
November 1835	100
February 1836	50
August 1836	50
September 1837	100
June 1839	50
August 1840	50
November 1842	50
June 1846	50
July 1872	25
February 1881	25
June 1891	75
TOTAL	625

#2069 Liszt, La Rose f. Pfte.
5 Platten Stein Krätsch.

b. *Harmonies poétiques et religieuses*

MONTH AND YEAR	PRINT RUN
November 1835	100
February 1836	50
August 1836	50
August 1837	50
May 1838	50
June 1839	50
August 1840	100
June 1842	50
April 1844	50
January 1849	50
November 1866	25
May 1874	25
April 1883	75
December 1908	125
TOTAL	850

#2070 Liszt, Harmonies poetiques p. Pfte
8 Platten Titel/Kupfer No. 51

---

c. *Apparitions*

MONTH AND YEAR	PRINT RUN
November 1835	100
February 1836	50
August 1836	50
March 1838	50
May 1838	50
October 1839	50
June 1842	50
September 1855	25
May 1871	50
June 1871	25
March 1885	75
April 1904	100
TOTAL	675

#2071 Liszt, Apparitions p. do. Liv. 1
10 Platten Titel/Stein Krätsch.

Table 3. Liszt, *Réminiscenses de la Juive*

MONTH AND YEAR	PRINT RUN	MONTH AND YEAR	PRINT RUN	MONTH AND YEAR	PRINT RUN
October 1836	100	October 1838	50	March 1844	50
December 1836	50	September 1839	50	July 1846	50
February 1837	50	April 1840	50	June 1852	50
August 1837	50	March 1841	50	February 1867	50
June 1838	50	September 1842	50	June 1873	50
				TOTAL	800

#2139 Liszt, Reminiscences p. Pfte. Op 9.
24 Platten Titel/Stein Krätschm.

Table 4. Liszt, *Grande Valse di bravura*

MONTH AND YEAR	PRINT RUN	MONTH AND YEAR	PRINT RUN	MONTH AND YEAR	PRINT RUN
January 1837	150	September 1842	50	June 1879	25
June 1837	100	October 1845	50	March 1882	75
June 1838	100	September 1850	50	January 1889	75
June 1838	50	November 1866	25	December 1895	75
May 1840	50	June 1869	25	August 1905	100
September 1840	50	July 1873	25	TOTAL	1,150
July 1841	50	January 1876	25		

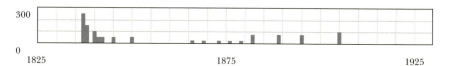

#2173 Liszt, Grande Valse p. Pfte. Oe. 6
12 Platten Titel/Stein Krätzschm.

Table 5. Liszt, *Grande fantaisie sur des motifs de Niobe / Divertissement sur la cavatine de Pacini ("I tuoi frequenti palpiti")*

MONTH AND YEAR	PRINT RUN	MONTH AND YEAR	PRINT RUN	MONTH AND YEAR	PRINT RUN
February 1837	150	October 1838	50	November 1845	50
July 1837	50	March 1840	50	May 1859	25
December 1837	50	May 1841	50	April 1872	25
June 1838	50	July 1842	50	October 1886	75
				TOTAL	675

#2185 Liszt, Divert. f. Pfte. oe. 5. No. 1
18 Platten Kupfer No. 83 und 8

Table 6. Liszt, *Fantaisie des Huguenots*

MONTH AND YEAR	PRINT RUN	MONTH AND YEAR	PRINT RUN	MONTH AND YEAR	PRINT RUN
March 1838	150	August 1843	50	December 1874	50
June 1838	50	February 1846	50	December 1876	25
June 1838	50	February 1848	50	February 1878	75
October 1838	50	February 1854	50	May 1881	75
September 1839	50	February 1859	50	May 1884	75
April 1840	50	November 1862	50	November 1887	75
November 1840	50	October 1865	50	November 1891	75
April 1841	50	March 1867	50	July 1900	75
February 1842	50	September 1869	50	January 1912	125
September 1842	50	October 1873	25	TOTAL	1,725

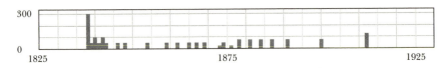

#2269 Liszt, Fant des Huguenots op. 11
29 Platten Titel/Stein Pönicke

Table 7. Liszt, *Réminiscences de Lucia di Lammermoor*

MONTH AND YEAR	PRINT RUN	MONTH AND YEAR	PRINT RUN	MONTH AND YEAR	PRINT RUN
March 1840	300	January 1850	200	February 1877	500
March 1840	200	December 1850	200	December 1878	200
June 1840	200	June 1851	200	May 1879	116
November 1840	100	September 1852	200	July 1879	600
June 1841	100	June 1853	200	July 1882	500
January 1842	100	April 1854	200	September 1883	500
April 1842	100	April 1855	200	November 1887	616
July 1842	100	December 1855	200	November 1887	500
October 1842	100	October 1856	200	September 1890	410
December 1842	200	May 1858	200	December 1892	116
March 1843	100	March 1859	200	June 1894	200
May 1843	200	February 1860	100	January 1896	316
September 1843	200	June 1860	200	September 1898	200
April 1844	200	August 1861	200	March 1900	116
October 1844[?]	200	July 1862	500	April 1900	416
July 1845	200	February 1865	500	October 1904	200
February 1846	200	May 1869	500	March 1906	300
August 1846	200	April 1870	500	August 1907	300
February 1847	200	? [cut off]		October 1909	200
October 1847	200	July 1874	50	October 1910	300
December 1848	200	July 1874	500	May 1912	300
June 1849	200	June 1876	161	November 1923	100
				TOTAL	14,956

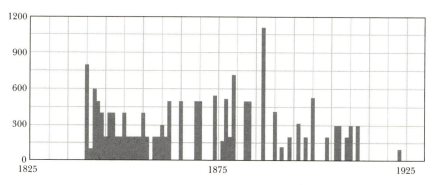

#2441 Liszt Fant. Oe 13 (Lucia)
9 Platten

Table 8. Liszt, *Grand Galop chromatique*

MONTH AND YEAR	PRINT RUN	MONTH AND YEAR	PRINT RUN	MONTH AND YEAR	PRINT RUN
May 1838	150	October 1843	300	July 1874	50[0]
May 1838	100	May 1844	300	February 1875	500
September 1838	100	January 1845	200	March 1878	500
April 1839	100	November 1845	200	September 1879	116
November 1839	100	July 1846	200	January 1880	616
January 1840	100	August 1847	100	January 1882	500
March 1840	50	March 1848	200	December 1882	116
April 1840	200	May 1849	200	September 1883	512
July 1840	100	June 1850	200	February 1886	616
July 1840	100	November 1851	200	May 1888	116
September 1840	200	May 1855	100	March 1889	616
November 1840	200	July 1856	100	November 1891	619
March 1841	200	January 1857	100	April 1896	200
July 1841	200	July 1857	100	June 1896	116
November 1841	200	May 1858	100	January 1900	300
January 1842	200	September 1858	100	January 1902	200
February 1842	200	July 1859	100	February 1903	200
April 1842	200	March 1860	200	June 1904	200
April 1842	200	April 1861	200	November 1904	200
September 1842	200	June 1862	500	August 1906	300
June 1842	200	July 1865	500	July 1908	300
March 1843	200	February 1868	300	September 1912	300
April 1843	300	May 1869	500	February 1921	500
June 1843	300	June 1871	500	November 1930	300
				TOTAL	17,743

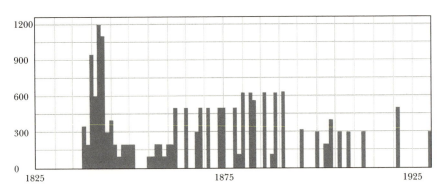

#2276 Liszt, Grand Galop pour Piano Oe 12
9 Platten Titel/Kupfer No 159

Grand Galop chromatique
Edition for Four Hands

MONTH AND YEAR	PRINT RUN	MONTH AND YEAR	PRINT RUN	MONTH AND YEAR	PRINT RUN
March 1838	150	February 1856	50	March 1885	75
July 1838	50	June 1858	50	October 1886	100
April 1839	50	September 1863	50	January 1889	100
January 1840	50	March 1867	50	June 1891	75
January 1840	50	August 1869	50	May 1893	75
September 1840	50	November 1871	50	November 1894	75
June 1841	50	September 1873	25	February 1896	100
April 1842	50	December 1874	50	February 1899	100
January 1843	50	December 1875	25	August 1902	100
June 1843	50	June 1876	50	March 1905	100
April 1844	50	April 1877	100	September 1906	200
November 1845	50	May 1879	100	April 1909	125
February 1849	25	May 1881	100	April 1916	90
April 1851	50	September 1883	100	TOTAL	2,940

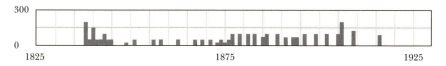

#2277 Le même à 4 mains

Table 9. Schumann, Intermezzo, op. 4

MONTH AND YEAR	PRINT RUN	MONTH AND YEAR	PRINT RUN	MONTH AND YEAR	PRINT RUN
October 1833	100	May 1863 I	50	March 1871	100
December 1839	25	March 1864 II	50	November 1872	100
February 1846	50	May 1864 I	50	December 1872	100
April 1848	50	June 1865 I	50	April 1873	200
August 1850	50	June 1865 II	50	May 1875	300
February 1856	50	January 1866 I	100	October 1875 II	200
March 1858 I	50	January 1866 II	100	September 1877 I	200
July 1859	50	April 1867 II	50	September 1877 II	200
November 1859 I	50	June 1867 I	100	July 1878 I	1000
June 1860 II	50	December 1868 II	100	July 1878 II	1000
August 1860 I	50	February 1869 I	100	January 1883 II	75
June 1861 II	50	March 1869 II	100	January 1883 I	75
July 1861 I	50	May 1869 I	100	June 1885 II	200
January 1863 II	50	September 1870	100	October 85 I	100
				TOTAL	5,675

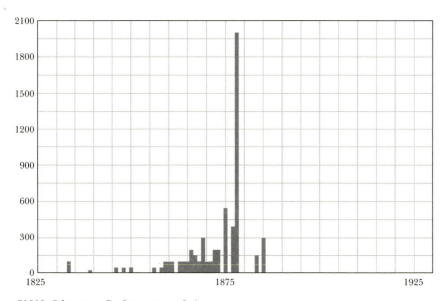

#1903 Schumann, R. Intermezzo 3–4
21 Platten
in 2 Lieferungen

Table 10. Schumann, Toccata, op. 7

MONTH AND YEAR	PRINT RUN	MONTH AND YEAR	PRINT RUN	MONTH AND YEAR	PRINT RUN
June 1834	100	July 1865	50	July 1876	100
November 1835	50	January 1866	100	September 1877	200
December 1846	50	April 1867	50	July 1878	1000
October 1851	50	October 1867	100	October 1879	75
March 1853	50	November 1868	100	September 1880	75
January 1858	50	February 1869	150	January 1882	75
July 1859	50	January 1870	200	April 1883	75
April 1860	50	January 1871	150	January 1884	300
May 1861	50	January 1872	100	April 1884	100
October 1862	50	February 1872	50	March 1885	75
November 1863	50	June 1872	200	July 1885	200
June 1864	50	November 1875	200	April 1886	75
				TOTAL	4,450

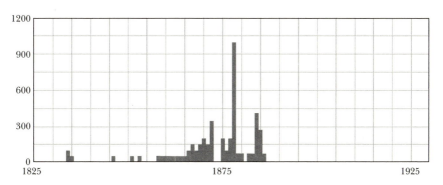

#1969 Schumann, Toccata oe. 7
9 Platten

Table 11. Chopin, Impromptu, op. 51

MONTH AND YEAR	PRINT RUN
March 1843	50
April 1844	100
October 1850	50
March 1852	50
June 1853	50
April 1854	50
July 1855	50
January 1856	100
August 1857	50
May 1858	50
September 1858	50
TOTAL	650

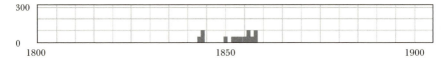

#2900 Chopin Impromptu Op 51
2/m 9 Platten

NOTES

Various colleagues and institutions have significantly contributed to this essay. First and foremost I must thank the Sächsisches Staatsarchiv Leipzig and their employees, who not only made the Hofmeister materials accessible, but also enabled and approved reproduction of the sources. Herr Norbert Molkenburg of C. F. Peters Verlag kindly allowed me to work with items from the Peters archive maintained within the Sächsisches Staatsarchiv Leipzig. I am grateful to the Social Sciences and Humanities Council of Canada for providing funding for my research in Leipzig. Jim Samson, Jeff Kallberg, Sanna Pederson, and Michael Saffle have all contributed valuable insights into the topic. Finally, I thank Christopher Gibbs and Dana Gooley for their careful editing of and helpful comments on drafts of this essay.

1. Pierre Bourdieu, "The Field of Cultural Production, or: The Economic World Reversed," in *The Field of Cultural Production*, ed. Randal Johnson (New York: 1993), p. 76.

2. One of the reasons for this lacuna is the complexity of Liszt's publishing history, in terms of his substantial oeuvre, the large number of publishers he used, and his practice of extensively revising and reissuing works. The best overview of his publishing activities is furnished in Albi Rosenthal's "Franz Liszt and His Publishers," *Liszt Saeculum* 38 (1986): 3–40.

3. The Liszt numbers (LW) are taken from the works list prepared by Rena Charnin Mueller and Mária Eckhardt for the *New Grove Dictionary of Music and Musicians*, 2nd ed., vol. 14 (London: 2001), pp. 786–872. According to this system, piano works are prefaced by the designation *A*.

4. While the state archive system of the GDR maintained quite restrictive access policies, the complete holdings of the Sächsisches Staatsarchiv Leipzig have been open to the general public since 1989.

5. Within Germany, there exists no trace of an archive for Schuberth, while only the *Briefkopierbücher* and first editions survive in a closed archive for Liszt's Berlin publisher Schlesinger. B. Schott's Söhne in Mainz and Breitkopf & Härtel were two important German publishers of Liszt's music, yet their archives—which by and large survived the Second World War—are largely inaccessible to scholars today because these holdings remain in the hands of the companies. Ricordi in Milan, responsible for Liszt publishing in Italy, does not possess the needed print-run statistics (although they do preserve valuable Liszt autographs). And documents from Liszt's primary Austrian publisher, Haslinger, seem to have disappeared altogether (they may be in private possession, as a collection).

6. Biographical information about Friedrich Hofmeister and historical details about his company appear most fully in the publication *Tradition und Gegenwart: Festschrift zum 150jährigen Bestehen des Musikverlages Friedrich Hofmeister* (Leipzig: 1957).

7. "Ich habe bis zu dieser Stunde nur die trefflichsten Beziehungen zu Herrn Hofmeister gehabt, der die Güte hat, den größten Teil meiner Werke in Deutschland zu veröffentlichen." Letter from Liszt to Breitkopf & Härtel, 5 April 1838; repr. in Oskar von Hase, *Breitkopf & Härtel: Gedenkschrift*, 4th ed., vol. 2 (Leipzig: 1919), p. 146.

8. "Hofmeister's printing of the twelve etudes . . . is simply a reprint of the volume of etudes that was published in France when I was in my thirteenth year. I have long disavowed this edition and . . . replaced it by the second [edition]. . . . As a result, I regard the [Breitkopf &] Härtel edition of the twelve etudes as the *only legal one*." "Die Hofmeister'sche Auflage der 12 Etuden . . . ist einfach ein Nachdruck des Heftes Etuden, welches, als ich in meinem

13ten Jahr war, in Frankreich veröffentlicht wurde. Ich habe diese Ausgabe längst desavouirt und durch die zweite . . . ersetzt. . . . Folglich erkenne ich blos die Härtel'sche Ausgabe der 12 Etuden als die *einzig rechtmässige.*" Letter from Liszt to Alfred Dörffel, 17 January 1855, in *Briefe*, ed. La Mara, vol. 1 (Leipzig: 1893), p. 189.

9. The Sächsisches Staatsarchiv Leipzig preserves Liszt's unpublished contract with Hofmeister for this piece, under the call number Musikverlag Friedrich Hofmeister, 5/1.

10. Liszt had also been publishing with Schott in Mainz since the mid-1830s and continued with them into the 1840s, while after 1840 he had Breitkopf & Härtel in Leipzig, Schuberth in Hamburg and Leipzig, Schlesinger in Berlin, and Cranz in Leipzig as his major German publishers, with Kistner in Leipzig joining them after 1848.

11. Unpublished letter from Liszt to Hofmeister (Jr.), from Rome, 16 September 1869; Sächsisches Staatsarchiv Leipzig, Musikverlag Friedrich Hofmeister, 5/2.

12. "Der greisen '*Galop chromatique*'. . . , der abgenützten 'Reminiscences de *Lucia*'. . . der *Hugenotten Fantasie,*— ein undankbares Stück, von sehr geringen [*sic*] Erfolg."

13. "Die vor vielen Jahren stattgefundenen Differenzen zwischen ihrem [*sic*] Verlag und den [*sic*] Schlesinger'schen in Berlin, worauf gerichtliche Verhandlungen erfolgten."

14. Friedrich Hofmeister, "Die Schlesinger'sche Musikalienhandlung in Berlin," *Allgemeines Buchhändler-Börsenblatt* 9, no. 50 (12 December 1842): 393–94.

15. "Da damals die Compositionen des Herrn Liszt nur geringen Absatz in Deutschland hatten, diese Fantaisie ihrer colossalen Schwierigkeiten wegen, noch weniger Absatz versprach, so liessen wir in Paris eine Anzahl Exemplare für uns drucken. . . . Als uns Herrn Hofmeister's Ausgabe zu Gesicht kam, fordertern wir ihn schriftlich den 9. Januar 1838 auf, dieselbe als eine widerrechtliche zu unterdrücken; und da der Gegenstand uns in Bezug auf commerziellen Vortheil zu unbedeutend schien, so unterliessen wir die Ausstellung eines Processes. . . . Herrn Liszts Anwesenheit in Berlin und der rauschende Beifall, den die Fantasie über Motive aus den Hugenotten sich erwarb, veranlassten uns mit Genehmigung des Componisten den Stich der Notenplatten und eines neuen Umschlagtitels zu veranlassen." Paste-in of corrected version of article from the *Allgemeines Buchhändler-Börsenblatt* of May 1842, from Berlin, 26 May 1842; Frankfurt am Main, Archiv des Musikverlags Zimmermann, Briefkopierbuch.

16. *Tradition und Gegenwart*, pp. 23–25.

17. Ibid., pp. 19–20.

18. The balance sheets bound in Sächsisches Staatsarchiv Leipzig, Musikverlag Friedrich Hofmeister, Druckverzeichnisse, 43, contain details about all expenditures and income for a given work, including on the one side the composer's honorarium, engraving costs, and printing costs, on the other sales revenues. Unfortunately, the balance sheets only exist for works published between 1840 and 1845, which excludes Liszt's earlier publications with Hofmeister.

19. Axel Beer discusses these networks in his authoritative study *Musik zwischen Komponist, Verlag und Publikum: Die Rahmenbedingungen des Musikschaffens in Deutschland im ersten Drittel des 19. Jahrhunderts* (Tutzing: 2000), p. 66.

20. Ricordi in Milan was the only Italian publisher for Liszt's piano compositions before 1848, whereas for the small number of those works that appeared in Britain (less than ten), Liszt had at least five publishers: Boosey, Wessel, Mori & Lavenu, Cocks, and Cramer, Addison & Beale.

21. Fr. Hofmeister, "Anzeigen," *Intelligenz-Blatt zur Allgemeinen musikalischen Zeitung*, no. 11 (November 1835), p. 1.

22. Information about the repertory of Liszt's German tours, the focus of this study, appears in Michael Saffle's valuable documentation *Liszt in Germany 1840–1845: A Study in Sources, Documents, and the History of Reception* (Stuyvesant, N.Y.: 1994).

23. Alan Walker, *Franz Liszt: The Virtuoso Years, 1811–1847*, rev. ed. (Ithaca, N.Y.: 1987), pp. 157–58, 312–13.

24. Charles Suttoni, "Operatic Paraphrases," in *The Liszt Companion*, ed. Ben Arnold (Westport, Conn.: 2002), p. 179.

25. Ibid., pp. 180–82; Leslie Howard, notes to *Liszt at the Opera I* (Hyperion Records, CDA66371/2, 1990) and *Liszt at the Opera V* (Hyperion Records, CDA67231/2, 1998).

26. In a letter to Marie d'Agoult, 22 May 1836, Liszt noted the effect of the *Réminiscences* in concert. *Franz Liszt: Selected Letters*, ed. and trans. Adrian Williams (Oxford, Eng.: 1998), p. 64.

27. Leslie Howard, notes to *Rarities, Curiosities, Album Leaves and Fragments* (Hyperion Records, CDA67414/7, 1999).

28. Regarding the migrations of Pacini's aria, see Hilary Poriss's valuable study, "Making Their Way Through the World: Italian One-Hit Wonders," *19th-Century Music* 24, no. 3 (2001): 197–224.

29. See the aforementioned letter of Liszt to the publisher from 1869.

30. Gerhard Winkler, "'Ein' feste Burg ist unser Gott': Meyerbeers Hugenotten in den Paraphrasen Thalbergs und Liszts," in *Der junge Liszt: Referate des 4. Europäischen Liszt-Symposions, Wien 1991*, in *Liszt Studien 4*, ed. Gottfried Scholz (Munich: 1993), pp. 100–34.

31. Regarding the different audiences for Liszt and Thalberg in a French context, see Dana Gooley's fascinating study, "Liszt, Thalberg and the Parisian Publics" in his *The Virtuoso Liszt* (Cambridge, Eng.: 2004), pp. 18–77.

32. The mechanism for the sale of the music within Germany is not that different from the situation today: customers identified music for purchase from advertisements, etc., they would request it from their local music store, and as stock of specific items dwindled, stores sent orders to publishers, which they filled.

33. The term "honorarium" is taken directly from the Hofmeister documentation and does not imply anything more than a one-time payment to a composer. If a composer requested "free copies" (*Freiexemplare*) of the work, those costs would be deducted from the honorarium. At the time (late-1830s and 1840s), Liszt and his fellow composers did not receive royalties. As Liszt's contract of 1852 with Hofmeister for the organ version of Nicolai's *Kirchliche Fest-ouvertüre* reveals, he was not only ceding publication rights to the publisher, but was also selling ownership of the piece. Sächsisches Staatsarchiv Leipzig, Musikverlag Friedrich Hofmeister, 5/1. In comparison with Liszt's honorarium of 40 talers, Hofmeister in 1840 gave Heinrich Panofka 26 talers for his *Elegy*, op. 17, and his Fantasy, op. 18, and gave J. P. Pixis 17 talers for the four-handed arrangement of his Third Duo.

34. See William Weber's *Music and the Middle Class* (New York: 1975), which despite its age remains unsurpassed in its assessment of the relationship between social class and music in nineteenth-century Europe.

35. Liszt concert review by F. Raabe in the *Königliche preussische Staats-, Kriegs- und Friedenszeitung*, 12 March 1842, cited in Gooley, *The Virtuoso Liszt*, p. 206.

36. Charles Rosen, "The New Sound of Liszt," review of Alan Walker's *Franz Liszt: The Virtuoso Years, 1811–1847*, *New York Review of Books* 31, no. 6 (April 12, 1984): 20.

37. "Das Minimum, welches erforderlich war, um die Werke im Publikum einigermaßen zu verbreiten und zugleich Ihnen hinreichende Exemplare zur Verfügung zu stellen." Letter from Breitkopf & Härtel to Liszt, Leipzig, 9 May 1856; cited in Oskar von Hase, *Breitkopf & Härtel*, vol. 2, p. 167.

38. The question of the public response to Liszt's symphonic poems is raised by Keith Johns in "The Performance and Reception of Liszt's Symphonic Poems in Europe and North America, 1849–1861," in *The Symphonic Poems of Franz Liszt*, ed. Michael Saffle (Stuyvesant, N.Y.: 1997), pp. 83–138. Johns, however, problematically, assumes that the opinions expressed by critics in newspapers and journals are the same as those of concert audiences.

39. Figures from the *Auflagenbuch*, 1874– , Sächsisches Staatsarchiv Leipzig, Musikverlag C. F. Peters, 5222.

40. "Döhler's gr. Fantaisie de Concert sur la Favorita de Donizetti p. Piano nehme ich für das Honorar von 800 Fr. an, wenn Döhler dieselbe in Concerten vorträgt." Letter from Heinrich to Maurice Schlesinger, Berlin, 28 April 1844; Frankfurt am Main, Archiv des Musikverlags Zimmermann, Briefkopierbuch.

41. "[Ich] nehme Rosenhayn's Fant. s. l. Reine de Chypre p. Piano nur dann für 300 Fl. wenn sie Rosenhayn in Concert spielt, sonst nicht." Letter from Heinrich to Maurice Schlesinger, Berlin, 9 May 1842; Frankfurt am Main, Archiv des Musikverlags Zimmermann, Briefkopierbuch, 395.

42. The undated letter was published by Jacques Vier in *Franz Liszt: L'Artiste, le clerc* (Paris: 1950), pp. 48–49, and translated by Dana Gooley in *The Virtuoso Liszt*, p. 56.

43. When Peters issued Theodor Kullak's edition of the *Lieder ohne Worte* in 1877, the initial printing was 3,000 copies, followed by 8,000 in 1878, 5,000 yearly from 1879 to 1881, 6,000 in 1882, and culminating in 10,000 copies in 1883 and 1884. Interestingly, these figures parallel those for the more costly "Pracht-Ausgabe."

44. Walter Benjamin, "Unpacking My Library: A Talk About Book Collecting," in *Illuminations*, ed. Hannah Arendt (New York: 1955), pp. 59–67.

45. Beverly Gordon, "The Souvenir: Messenger of the Extraordinary," *Journal of Popular Culture* 20 (1986): 135.

46. Russell Belk, "Possessions and the Extended Self," *Journal of Consumer Research* 15 (1988): 160.

47. In an unpublished letter to F. E. C. Leuckert in Breslau, from Berlin, 25 January 1843, Schlesinger offers to send the publisher his most recent Liszt works as well as portraits of the virtuoso, in advance of concert appearances in Breslau. Frankfurt am Main, Archiv des Musikverlags Zimmermann, Briefkopierbuch, 448–449.

PART II

BIOGRAPHICAL
DOCUMENTS

Liszt on the Artist in Society

INTRODUCED AND TRANSLATED BY RALPH P. LOCKE

In 1835, Liszt wrote and published a long, remarkable essay to which he gave the title *De la situation des artistes, et de leur condition dans la société* (On the Situation of Artists, and on Their Condition in Society).[1] The twenty-three-year old poured into it his excitement about the books, ideas, and musical works that were engaging him at the time, as well as his ambivalence about how Paris was treating the latest piano star: Liszt himself, who was at that point, in his own words, only an "embryonic" composer. *On the Situation of Artists* also prefigured many of Liszt's projects, career choices, and obsessions during the ensuing half-century until his death in Bayreuth at age seventy-four.

The essay was published in six installments in the *Gazette musicale de Paris* between May and October 1835. A substantial addendum appeared in November 1835 in response to a long critique from a German-born journalist writing under the pseudonym Germanus Lepic.[2] In the addendum Liszt restated his main objections to the musical life of the day: that performers and composers had too readily accepted a subordinate place in modern European society, were narrowly educated, and were debasing their talents by offering formulaic entertainment to wealthy aristocrats in salons and to average citizens in public dance halls. The article by Lepic had accused Liszt of ingratitude and of borrowing the misery of others: "You have been adulated, spoiled by the world," the critic sniped, safe in his pseudonymity, "so you have no cause to complain!" Liszt rightly rejected this criticism as "totally *ad hominem*" and a distraction from the real issues at hand. He explained that when wealthy people hired him to play in their homes, he found himself treated as "nothing but a rather pleasant 'means of amusement.'" "The most beautiful works of Beethoven, Mozart, and Schubert," if he risked playing them, met with "inept silence," whereas "miserable bagatelles" occasioned "noisy transports [of delight]."[3]

Neither this spirited November addendum nor any of the six main *Situation* installments has thus far been translated into English. My translation of the sixth installment (the last of the series) is given below. It attempts to flow idiomatically in clear, present-day English, yet also capture some of the passion, playfulness, and occasional oddity of Liszt's 1830s-era French. I have added brief explanations of distinctive wordings and literary allusions in the notes, based in part on the commentary provided by Rainer Kleinertz and Serge Gut in the superb critical edition of Liszt's complete early writings.[4]

The first four installments of the *Situation* essay explore the different ways in which artists and their art—in the broad sense—have been treated by Western societies through the ages. Liszt argues that music and other arts are capable of exercising worthy social functions. He cites the Greek bard Tyrtaeus (whose odes persuaded the Spartans to join in battle against the Messenians), the chanted choruses in Attic tragedies, and the music of Catholic worship and various non-Western ritual traditions across the centuries. He then contrasts the decay of musical and artistic life in current-day France, calling as witnesses a wide range of literary and philosophical figures, from the brilliant Victor Hugo to the musically sophisticated Joseph d'Ortigue, and from the Abbé Félicité-Robert de Lamennais (whose antimonarchist book *Paroles d'un croyant* [Words of a Believer, 1834]—was condemned by the pope) to the Saint-Simonians (whose leaders were jailed by the French government in 1833 after the movement had launched a relentless train of bold social and political demands, including that divorce be legalized).

Though these first four installments emphasize the degraded state of musical life and the desperation of many musicians' lives, they also hint at some hopeful alternatives. In the lengthy fifth installment, Liszt expands these glimpses into a full-blown set of concrete proposals: improvements he would like to see at the Conservatoire and other music schools, but also in such areas as chamber music, light and serious opera, orchestral concerts, recitals by solo instrumentalists and singers, music journalism, and "religious music," a term given a new spin.

This last category leads Liszt to insert a startling statement he had written the year before (though not published at the time) when he was still digesting the ideas of the Saint-Simonians—which he had experienced with fascination in 1832—and blending them with those of Lamennais. Indeed, he may have written the statement under the direct guidance of Lamennais, at whose country house in La Chênaie he made retreat for a month during September–October 1834. Liszt here announces that traditional religion has lost its moorings—"the altar creaks and totters"—and calls for a new kind of music that will combine religious and "humanitarian" (i.e., ethically inspiring) messages with the expressive means and impressive resources of modern symphonic and operatic art. He urges in particular that a contest be established for "national, moral, political, and religious tunes, canticles, songs, and hymns that will be taught in the schools." Of all the proposals in the *Situation* series, this one, had it been enacted, would have done the most to push the art of music far from the state of unchallenging and socially innocuous entertainment in which Liszt claims to find it. He notes, pointedly, that such frankly social and political uses of music were not unprecedented—even, or perhaps especially, in France: "The *Marseillaise*, which, more than all the legendary tales of the Hindus, Chinese, and Greeks, has *proven* to us the power of music—the *Marseillaise* and the wonderful songs of the Revolution were the awesome and glorious forerunners [of these humanitarian hymns that the government should commission]."[5]

The abundance of literary allusions in the first four installments and parts of the fifth, as well as the generally rhapsodic style, suggests that Liszt may have been relying on his current mistress (and the eventual mother of his three children), Marie d'Agoult, to help him put his thoughts into prose. We know from surviving letters that, between 1837 and the late 1840s, he would sometimes let Marie edit articles in his name and, on at least one occasion, write one in its entirety. (The same occurred in reverse: in 1843 he would rework in detail, and apparently at Marie's request, an article of hers on a topic far from music but of great interest to him: neo-Hegelian philosophy and its ramifications in the writings of revolutionary-democratic poet Georg Herwegh.)[6] Even so, all of Liszt's articles from his years with Marie d'Agoult seem to have been based on his views and on specific arguments and musical points that he had explained to her or even written out for her to incorporate. We also know that he later permitted his second longtime mistress, Princess Carolyne von Sayn-Wittgenstein, to perform a similar role for him, the results of which included not just articles (on Berlioz, on Wagner), but also several books (on Chopin and on the music of the Hungarian gypsies). Was Liszt already relying on Marie d'Agoult in the articles of 1835–36? This possibility (or, in some eyes, accusation) was briefly raised during his lifetime, then went into abeyance for decades, only to become the object of heated debate among prominent Liszt scholars in the mid- and late twentieth century, continuing into the twenty-first.[7]

Recently, the editors of the critical edition of Liszt's writings have taken the firm position that the Comtesse d'Agoult had little or no role in any of Liszt's articles before 1837, and that the *Situation* series is entirely Liszt's in both "conception" and "formulation."[8] Other Liszt scholars, though, suspect that the truth about the *Situation* series is closer to what Charles Suttoni proposed in an appendix to his superb translation of Liszt's immediately subsequent series of sixteen articles, entitled *Lettres d'un bachelier ès-musique:* that the words may sometimes be Marie d'Agoult's, but "the basic, underlying substance . . . behind them reflects all the ideas about the nobility and social function of art, the humanistic Romanticism that [Liszt] had absorbed from the Saint-Simonians, Lamennais, and others, independent of the countess. . . . The 'author,' the person responsible for these articles[,] is Liszt."[9]

If collaboration lay behind the *Situation* essay, its traces are particularly evident in the first four installments. In contrast, the fifth and sixth installments can be attributed more directly to Liszt, apparently down to the smallest details. For one thing, these last two sections suddenly become very concrete in their recommendations about musical life; literary allusions and high-flown style are greatly curtailed, though by no means absent. More important, the manuscript of the installment translated here (the sixth and, by intention, last) survives: it is entirely in Liszt's distinctive handwriting and preserves his own crossings-out, improved wordings, and remarks to the typesetter about matters of layout and typography, including which words to set in italics and which in small capitals.

The sixth installment consists largely of a summary of the wide-ranging proposals laid out in the fifth. The manuscript, at first glance, suggests that Liszt was writing at furious speed, in a flood of intense, typically Romantic excitement about the issues that he was addressing.[10] But, upon closer examination, one notes that the corrections were not made later (i.e., squeezed in above words that Liszt had crossed out when rereading the whole text). Rather, Liszt penned the new words on the same line as the rest, immediately to the right of what he had just written and then crossed out. This suggests that even as he was gathering his thoughts and setting them down, he was taking care to find the most appropriate way of formulating them.

Whatever the "compositional process" here, the structure of the sixth installment and its particular rhetorical strategies suggest a mind under fine rational control, a mind that was shaped by having heard and read—during childhood, adolescence, and early manhood—the Bible, church sermons, political polemics, and philosophically tinged poems and novels. We note many balanced phrases, sometimes echoing, directly or indirectly, the famed *parallelismus membrorum* of the biblical books of Psalms and Proverbs. Equally striking are the many chains of words or phrases (usually consisting of three elements) that form a verbal crescendo. Often the final, climactic element in the chain invokes realms of the spirit, as when Liszt writes that artists do truly suffer but that this is "because of their isolation, their self-centeredness, and their lack of faith." More generally, the vocabulary abounds in religious metaphors and also in equally inspiring secular ones (such as visions of brothers or soldiers struggling, in solidarity, against a common enemy or marching "arm in arm" toward a virtuous social goal or military triumph). Liszt writes, for example, about how, having reached a point of "disgust" with what he saw around him, he underwent a *noviciat*, a word that normally means the humbling process of entering a religious order, but here indicates his decision to plunge himself into a study of the gratifying and generally appreciated roles that music had played in the religiously unified societies of earlier millennia. Similarly, he writes that true artists will henceforth take on—joyfully, it seems—a social role that God has "imposed."

Other elements of prose style—syntax, verb tenses—likewise can suggest a vision, nearly apocalyptic, of art and humanity moving toward a brighter, better future. Liszt announces the creation of a grand social movement of musicians who will insist that the French government set in motion eight major musical projects:

1. A competition every five years for works in the major musical genres
2. Music education in the schools, and "religious" (moral and civic-spirited) songs composed for the children to sing
3. Reform of church music
4. State-sponsored festivals of symphonic music
5. Active encouragement of opera, recitals, and chamber music
6. A new and different music school, with branches in the provinces
7. Courses in music history and aesthetics at that school, or those schools
8. Inexpensive editions of the greatest musical works of the past and present, and scholarly studies and dissertations that explore and explain them

Liszt launches this "program" of eight points in the present tense, as if the movement already existed and as if he were empowered to speak on its behalf: "We ask and demand. . . ." Artfully, he avoids the solicitous-sounding conditional (e.g., "we would like," "there should be").[11]

Scholars rightly point out that various of the proposals and *cris de coeur* in these early articles were to echo in Liszt's writings, compositions, professional activities, and private life through the subsequent decades. Liszt's dissatisfaction with the career of a performing virtuoso, already apparent here, would culminate in his abandoning public performance in the late 1840s, much as the religion-tinged rhetoric found here seems to anticipate his taking Minor Orders in the Catholic Church in 1865. His call for a grand quinquennial competition for musical works in large forms (point 1) would take a somewhat different form in his efforts at organizing a musical commemoration of Beethoven in Bonn in 1845. Liszt himself later composed numerous sacred works, as he envisaged here (point 3), making imaginative use of the most up-to-date stylistic resources, such as harmony that is highly chromatic, sometimes bordering on the atonal (e.g., *Via crucis* and *Ossa arida*). To his distress, these works were largely ignored by the Catholic hierarchy.

In his middle years, Liszt would transfer from France to Germany and Central Europe his call for a "société universelle" (all-encompassing organization) of musicians who wish to "raise and ennoble the condition of artists." He built up a substantial symphonic and operatic establishment in Weimar and attempted to create a Goethe Foundation in that city.[12] He trained hundreds of pianists at no cost in his later decades. He also spurred the founding of the Allgemeine Deutsche Musikverein (Pan-German Musical Union, likewise in Weimar, 1861) and—in several phases, beginning in 1840—of the Budapest Conservatory.

In addition, certain aspects of his eight-point program would be carried out by others, for better or worse. The monks of Solesmes, in the late nineteenth century, restored (as urged in point 3) a more dignified and historically grounded version of Gregorian chant. Chamber music concerts (point 5) increased enormously in the course of the late nineteenth and early twentieth centuries. And inexpensive yet reliable editions of music (point 8), about which he wrote a separate article in January 1836, indeed became a prominent and admirable feature of musical life during the century ahead.[13] On a broader level, governments arose in the twentieth century that harnessed music and the other arts to influence the attitudes and behaviors of their respective citizens. But the cultural machinations of the Nazis, Soviet-era Eastern Europe, and Maoist China would have been condemned by Liszt and other progressive artists and intellectuals of his day as a perverse parody of his 1834 call for a new, state-sponsored religio-political musical repertory (briefly restated in the sixth installment, under point 2).[14]

Still, many of the chagrined observations in the *Situation* articles sound distressingly familiar to us as we ponder the *vie musicale* that surrounds us, wherever we live. Perhaps it is time to take inspiration from the passionate but always well-grounded analysis and solutions offered by this impatient, brilliant, and socially committed twenty-three-year-old artist and visionary.

• • •

FRANZ LISZT

On the Situation of Artists and Their Condition in Society

(Final Installment)

Gazette musicale de Paris
11 October 1835

Let us summarize what has been said thus far.

From the point of view where we have placed ourselves (and it is super-fluous to add that we have not chosen it on a whim but only out of the need to raise ourselves to a point from which we can have the most complete view of the facts) we have noted that everywhere are:

Sufferings, humiliation, bitterness, misery, loneliness, and persecution FOR THE ARTIST;

Barriers, exploitation, financial cuts, inadequate or harmful institutions, *manacles* and *gags* FOR THE ART.[15]

And everywhere, from musicians of all types—performers, teachers, or composers—we have heard laments, expressions of hopelessness,[16] words of discontent and of anger, prayers for change or reform, yearnings for a greater and more satisfying future; yearnings that are sometimes confused and contradictory, but that give evidence that a new yeast is fermenting.

Whether more or less openly, more or less deeply, ALL ARE SUFFERING.

Whether it be in their contact with the public or with high society; whether it be at the hands of the theater and opera house directors, the reviewers and columnists, the employees in the Ministry of Fine Arts, the owners of sheet music stores, and so on—whether it be, in short, through their civic, political, or religious connections, or their mutual relationships: connections that carry no official approval—relationships that fall short of a true bond—

It makes no difference. *All are suffering*, and the sense of suffering that many of them have is, much of the time . . . not legitimate, not right. But at other times they feel it because of actual injustices that *result from* their isolation, their self-centeredness, and their lack of faith.[17]

Schiller said somewhere: "Every time art has lost its way, it has been the artists who were at fault."[18] Might we not add: Every time artists—rather than uniting, either to resist oppressive conditions and harsh demands, or to walk arm in arm toward the goal that has been divinely assigned to them—break ranks, repress their awareness of their own dignity, and submit, one by one, day by day, to the consequences of silently accepting their *inferior position*, the fault is certainly theirs to a great extent.

But let us not start in on matters that will be discussed elsewhere.

Once again, we repeat, the situation of artists, their condition in society, what they have been, what they are, what they will necessarily be, in city, church, theater, and concert hall—all these complex questions that we have taken it as our task to broach are at once highly important and extremely delicate; they are indissolubly tied to the toughest problems. Just sketching them in a selective and imperfect way has required us to undergo a quite laborious apprenticeship and numerous reflections.

After having sated ourselves to the point of disgust with the study of facts and details of the present day,* we climbed up, step by step, through all the previous historical levels in order to refresh ourselves at the eternally fruitful and life-giving spring of traditions.[19] As we contemplated the magnificent destinies that the mind of antiquity assigned to music, and as we evoked the illustrious legislators and philosophers who instructed their peoples to the tune of the lyre, we asked ourselves, "What can have caused modern music's disgrace, its social abdication?[20] And how did those who were first, consent to make themselves the last?"[21]

Then, the more attentively we examined, in their origins and their results, the ways that art—that *eternal phenomenon*[22]—gradually developed and diversely evolved, and as we penetrated deeper into the intimate relations between music and poetry, religion, the human heart, and man as an entire whole in body and soul, at the same time music's mysteries and real worth revealed themselves to us.

And, from that point on, our faith began to revive.

Now, sure of the convictions that we have acquired, we cry unceasingly that a great work, a grand religious and social MISSION stands *imposed* upon artists.

So, in order that no one objects that we use these words haphazardly, in a vague or indeterminate sense; and in order, furthermore, to convey, in an effective manner, the general sympathies that, day by day, only grow and are made more alive through the unbroken parallel motion of the progress of art with the moral and intellectual progress of artists; and, fi-

---

*And, in this regard, we believe we have omitted nothing of any importance. If need be, we could quote a host of proper names and facts that correspond to them, but the reader will easily understand why we abstain from doing so.

nally, in order to assist in bringing about, as best we can, that future which everyone senses and desires, we call ALL MUSICIANS, all those who have a broad and deep feeling for art, to form a common, brotherly, religious bond among themselves and to *establish a universal society*, having the aims:

1. To promote, encourage, and activate the upward movement, extension, and unconstrained development of music.

2. To raise and ennoble the condition of artists, providing remedies for the abuses and injustices that they suffer, and determining what measures are necessary to maintain their dignity.

In the name of all musicians, in the name of art and social progress, we ask and demand:

First, the founding of a competition for religious, dramatic, and symphonic music, to occur every five years. The best compositions in those three genres will be performed in solemn fashion over the course of a month at the Louvre, and then acquired and published at governmental expense. In other words: the founding of a new MUSEUM.

Second, the introduction of musical instruction into primary schools; its propagation in other schools—and, for this purpose, the *creation* of a new religious music.*

Third, the reorganization of the musical activities in all the churches of Paris and the provinces, and the reform of plainchant singing there.

Fourth, large gatherings of Philharmonic Societies, on the model of the great musical festivities in England and Germany.

Fifth, an opera house, concerts, and chamber music concerts, all organized according to the plan that we indicated in the preceding article about the Conservatoire.

Sixth, a PROGRESSIVE SCHOOL of music, established separate from the Conservatoire by eminent artists; a school whose branches will extend into the main provincial cities.

---

* I said earlier what this music will be like.[23]

Seventh, a professorship in the history and philosophy of music.[24]

Eighth, the inexpensive publication of a Collection of the most remarkable works of all early and modern composers, from the rebirth of
music up to our days. This publication, embracing in its entirety the
development of the art, starting with folk song and arriving gradually,
and in historical order, at the choral symphony of Beethoven, might
take the title of MUSICAL PANTHEON.[25] The biographies, dissertations, commentaries, and explanatory notes that will of necessity
accompany it will form a veritable ENCYCLOPEDIA of music.

*

Such is the program that we have presented in summary fashion (reserv-
ing the right to come back to it in greater detail) to all those who are
interested in art in France.

We believe we know all too well the present situation of things to give
credence to any supposed "practical impossibilities" that some persons
might perhaps by chance raise in objection.

NOTES

1. For a critical edition of the text of Liszt's wordings and allusions in the *Situation*
articles and the addendum on *"subalternité,"* see Franz Liszt, *Sämtliche Schriften,* ed. Detlef
Altenburg, vol. 1, ed. Rainer Kleinertz, incorporating research of Serge Gut (Wiesbaden:
2000), pp. 1–75. The German translations on facing pages (by Liszt acolyte Lina Ramann,
now revised by Kleinertz) sometimes give further insight into likely interpretations of
Liszt's usually clear but occasionally elliptical prose. The two earlier editions are largely
reliable, although much less fully annotated: Fr[anz] Liszt, *Pages romantiques,* ed. Jean
Chantavoine (Paris: 1912), pp. 1–83; and Franz Liszt, *Artiste et société: Édition des textes en
français,* ed. Rémy Stricker (Paris: 1995), pp. 13–56, 393–56. Chantavoine's volume, reports
Stricker (p. 8), omits parts of certain texts. The volume consists of the *Situation* articles, as
well as most but not all of the immediately subsequent series of essays, *Lettres d'un bachelier
ès-musique.*

2. Lepic was evidently Pierre Alexandre (Adolphe) Specht, still known today (among
certain specialists, at least) for having translated important articles by Heine into French;
see Liszt, *Sämtliche Schriften,* vol.1, pp. 565–66; and Thomi Hupfer, *Franz Liszt als junger Mann:
Eine Leserei* (Bern: 2001), pp. 13n, 15n, 118, 137n, 141, 354–55. *Specht* and *(le) pic* are, respectively, the German and French words for a woodpecker or nuthatch.

3. Liszt, *Sämtliche Schriften,* vol. 1, p. 70. Liszt's word, which I translate as a "means of
amusement" is the somewhat unusual, though not unprecedented, *amusoir,* printed in italics, as if Liszt is quoting someone or drawing attention to the oddity of the word. *Amusoir*
might also be translated more pointedly as "an inanimate device that provides amusement"
(by analogy to other *-oir* nouns: *tiroir, encensoir, peignoir*).

4. Kleinertz and Gut's critical commentary is admirably thorough and helpfully cross-referenced (Liszt, *Sämtliche Schriften*, vol. 1, pp. 547–67). My translation incorporates a few details from an excerpt translated (smoothly but somewhat freely) by Alan Walker in his *Franz Liszt: The Virtuoso Years, 1811–1847*, rev. ed. (Ithaca, N.Y.: 1987), pp. 159–60. Like the editors of the *Sämtliche Schriften* (see their comment, vol. 1, p. 504), and of the original publication in the *Gazette musicale*, I do not always follow Liszt's manuscript in its (inconsistent) use of uppercase for certain words and phrases.

5. Quotations from *Sämtliche Schriften*, vol. 1, pp. 56–58. For the quotation, I have adapted the wording in Franz Liszt, *An Artist's Journey: Lettres d'un bachelier ès-musique, 1835–1841*, trans. and annotated by Charles Suttoni (Chicago: 1989), pp. 236–37, after consulting two other worthy translations: *Music in the Western World: A History in Documents*, selected and annotated by Piero Weiss and Richard Taruskin (New York: 1984), pp. 366–67; and Paul Merrick, *Revolution and Religion in the Music of Liszt* (Cambridge, Eng.: 1987), pp. 19–20. On the Saint-Simonians' distinctively propagandistic use of music and its echoes in this 1834 *appel* by Liszt, see Ralph P. Locke, *Music, Musicians, and the Saint-Simonians* (Chicago: 1986), esp. pp. 15–36, 45–67, and 101–106. I explore Liszt's reactions to the movement and its aesthetic views in more detail in "Liszt's Saint-Simonian Adventure," *19th-Century Music* 4 (1980–81): 209–27 and corrigenda in 5 (1981–82): 281.

6. Editors' commentary, in Liszt, *Sämtliche Schriften*, vol. 1, pp. 495–96.

7. See, most strikingly, Émile Haraszti, "Franz Liszt—Author Despite Himself: The History of a Mystification," *Musical Quarterly* 33 (1947): 490–516; Liszt, *Artist's Journey*, pp. 238–45 (Appendix E: "Liszt as Author"); editors' commentary, in Liszt, *Sämtliche Schriften*, vol. 1, pp. 484–503 ("Zur Autorschaft"); and Alan Walker, "Liszt as Writer," in *Reflections on Liszt* (Ithaca: 2005), xvi–xvii, 217–38 ("Liszt the Writer"), and 241–44.

8. Editors' commentary, in Liszt, *Sämtliche Schriften*, vol. 1, p. 497.

9. Liszt, *Artist's Journey*, pp. 244–45. The gap in time between the *Situation* addendum and the first of the *Lettres d'un bachelier ès-musique* is only three weeks if one counts Liszt's open letter to George Sand as the first of the *Lettres* (though it does not yet bear the *Lettres* series title).

10. Two of the pages (the first and next to last) are reproduced in Liszt, *Sämtliche Schriften*, vol. 1, pp. 505–506.

11. Chantavoine too readily terms the neologisms in Liszt's early articles "superflus et barbares" (unnecessary and crude)—Liszt, *Pages romantiques*, p. 38n. The particular case that he identifies, *embryonique*, is unfair. After all, the dictionary of the Académie française would not recognize an adjectival form for the noun *embryon* until the 1930s (6th ed.), when it settled on *embryonnaire*. What was an imaginative young writer to do in 1835? (The German equivalent, at least nowadays, is *embryonal*.)

12. See the plan sketched out in Liszt's essay "De la Fondation-Goethe à Weimar," in *Sämtliche Schriften*, vol. 3, ed. Britta Schilling-Wang (Wiesbaden: 1997), vol. 3, pp. 22–151.

13. Franz Liszt, "Des publications à bon marché," *Sämtliche Schriften*, vol. 1, pp. 326–31.

14. On 1830s-era calls for what I term "art as a means of social control" and on later echoes (or, to some extent, perversions) of them, see Locke, *Music and the Saint-Simonians*, pp. 17–18, 226–34.

15. *Manacles and gags* is an evocation of "manacles on our hands and gags in our mouths," a line from the first page of Hugo's famous preface to his collection of poems, *Les Orientales* (1829).

16. *palinodies* (hopelessness): literally "recantations" or "retractions."

17. Liszt's entire sentence (including a rhetorical ellipsis) reads: "*Tous souffrent*, et beaucoup d'entre eux sentent qu'ils souffrent . . . illégitement, iniquement, d'ordinaire; mais souvent aussi par suite de torts réels, *à cause* de leur isolement, de leur égoïsme et de leur manque de foi."

18. The quotation is from Schiller's essay "On the Use of the Chorus in Tragedy," which served as preface to his 1803 play (with choruses), *The Bride of Messina*. In 1851 Schumann would compose an overture to that play.

19. *la source . . . des traditions*: Liszt's plural, though awkward in English, is surely intended to suggest the multiple cultural contexts that he pondered (China, etc.).

20. The word *déchéance* can also mean "decadence," "dethronement."

21. Here Liszt plays on the words of Jesus: "The last shall be first" (Matthew 19:30 and 20:16; Mark 10:31; and Luke 13:30).

22. The phrase *chose éternelle*, italicized by Liszt, is presumably a quotation.

23. Liszt said this in an appendix to a previous installment, no. 5, of this series.

24. *"Une chaire d'histoire et de la philosophie de la musique"* presumably would be established at the new Paris music school that Liszt envisioned, as stated in the fifth installment of the *Situation* series (Liszt, *Sämtliche Schriften*, vol. 1, p. 38, lines 30–31). The word *chaire* is a resonant one, referring originally to an ecclesiastical "pulpit" and consequently applied to professorships in philosophy and other fields at the University of Paris (the Sorbonne). Alan Walker joins this call for an academic *chaire* in music (the seventh point in Liszt's program) to the preceding one, thereby reducing the total number of points from eight to seven. (He renames Liszt's "first" through "eighth" in a lettered list, *a* through *g*, and later refers to Liszt's "seven-point plan," in *Franz Liszt: The Virtuoso Years*, pp. 159–60.) Walker's wording also implies, perhaps inadvertently, that there will be a chair of music history and aesthetics in each of several provincial cities: "a school whose branches shall extend to all the provincial towns having a chair in the history and philosophy of music" (p. 160). Inserting an "and" before "having" brings Walker's sentence back into line with Liszt's apparent meaning.

25. Perhaps a *double entendre*. The marble-sheathed Pantheon of ancient Rome was a spacious temple dedicated to all the gods (and later transformed into a Christian church). The Panthéon in Paris had almost the opposite history: originally built as a church, completed in 1780, it was transformed during the French Revolution into a location for commemorating important French writers, leaders, and so on, as indicated in the inscription that it still carries today: "Aux grands hommes, la patrie reconnaissante" (From a grateful fatherland, to the [memory of its] great men).

The First Biography: Joseph d'Ortigue on Franz Liszt at Age Twenty-Three

INTRODUCED AND EDITED BY BENJAMIN WALTON
TRANSLATED BY VINCENT GIROUD

In conclusion to a somewhat ungenerous review of François-Joseph Fétis's 1830 music primer, *La Musique mise à la portée de tout le monde*, Joseph d'Ortigue (1802–66) admitted that his criticisms of the book were perhaps harsh and overly detailed (they certainly were), but justified himself with a statement of intent:

> It is time to go beyond the petty and narrow criticism from another age and . . . to bring into music, as into all other orders of ideas, the foundations of a wider criticism, that alone can raise this art to the rank that it ought to occupy in the ensemble of human experiences, by showing the essential connections that it has with them and its participation in the work of civilization as a whole.[1]

The value of such a mini-manifesto as a defense of the review itself is debatable, aggrandizing what was merely another installment in the war between the two critics that rumbled on through the early 1830s. But it works very well as a summary of d'Ortigue's approach to critical writing in general, which always sought to reconnect music with contemporary social developments as a step toward recovering its ancient power. This ambition is already evident in d'Ortigue's first major work, the anti-Rossini pamphlet *De la guerre des dilettanti* (1829), in which Rossini's perceived technical failings are diagnosed as symptoms of moral decadence, and resurfaces frequently in his writings of the following years across a wide variety of journals in a way that marks the critical shift from the Rossinian 1820s to the Germanic Romanticism of the following decade.[2] Where d'Ortigue's cousin (and fellow Provençal) Castil-Blaze—his elder by eighteen years—

had conquered the Parisian musical world of the Restoration with a combination of practical musical versatility and technically expert criticism, d'Ortigue embodied the more aesthetically uncompromising beliefs of the subsequent generation.[3]

He had arrived in Paris shortly before the July Revolution of 1830 as an earnest proselytizer for a type of music criticism that played down musical detail in favor of an insistence on music's importance within the wider world. Nowhere was this exploration of the connections of music and society more strongly articulated than in the opening of his exceptionally long Liszt biography, published in the *Gazette musicale de Paris* on 14 June 1835.[4] The *Gazette*, launched by the publisher Maurice Schlesinger the previous year and including both d'Ortigue and Liszt among its named editors, offered the perfect forum for a new, E. T. A. Hoffmann–inspired approach to music criticism that was visible both in the biography and in Liszt's own essay series, "On the Situation of Artists and on Their Condition in Society," which began to appear the month before the biography, and would continue until the following October.[5] Indeed, d'Ortigue's account of Liszt's life, which formed some kind of "special issue" of the journal, acts in part to claim the twenty-three-year-old composer for the new Romantic aesthetic, connecting him explicitly to the lineage of Beethoven in opposition to Rossini, and emphasizing his post-Restoration attainment of artistic maturity. Liszt is memorably introduced as the most striking embodiment of all the cultural currents of his artistically overheated age: "Religious aspirations and arid doubts, enthusiasms and depressions, excesses of independence and the search for authority, his soul absorbs it all." To write about Liszt is therefore to write about the position of all artists, and beyond that all contemporary humans: Liszt is pure living, breathing, performing *Zeitgeist*. Or, more accurately perhaps, he is the personification of *mal du siècle*, as well as of all the utopian hopes, spiritual searching, and artistic hyperbole that recur artistically in so many forms throughout the decade—including d'Ortigue's own semi-autobiographical novel, *La Sainte-Baume* (1834), in which later critics have perceived a portrait of Liszt both in the pious, lovelorn hero of the tale and in the figure of the seducer turned monk, Frère Paul.[6] The Liszt of d'Ortigue's biography, too, is a true romantic protagonist, fashioned according to a variety of intellectual influences, which are combined to create a young Franz who shows musical genius in all necessary ways, personal and artistic, confirmed both by the opinions of musical connoisseurs and by the popular science of phrenology.

The collection of tales that make up Liszt's life history here—including the first mention of the encounter with Beethoven that would later be transformed into the famous *Weihekuss*—has been the main focus for later biographers, either to be woven into their own narratives or to be debunked.[7] And the article clearly has great documentary value, both as the first serious biography of the composer, and for the quotes from Adam Liszt's diaries, apparently lent to d'Ortigue by Liszt's mother and long since lost. Furthermore, by 1835 Liszt and d'Ortigue were good friends and intellectual confrères, not least in their shared admiration for the charismatic Abbé de Lamennais. D'Ortigue had been an ardent supporter of Lamennais since staying at his Breton retreat at La Chênaie in 1830, and it was through him that Liszt met the controversial *abbé* in 1834.[8] Whether their friendship makes the biography more or less reliable is open to question. D'Ortigue's earlier biographies of other musician friends (Berlioz and George Onslow) had both used material supplied directly by their subjects, thereby combining authenticity with the opportunity for creative self-fashioning.[9] It is not unreasonable to suppose that something similar happened here, whether from information provided by Liszt or by his mistress and sometime ghostwriter Marie d'Agoult. Yet the philosophical framing of the biography, which consists of a detailed (and at times obscure) exploration of Liszt's relationship to his age on either side of a more straightforward central exposition of the composer's life, is undoubtedly d'Ortigue's own, as witnessed by his reproduction at one point of a large chunk from an earlier review, and is as interesting in its creation of a particular view of Liszt as any of the specific anecdotes contained within.

Many of d'Ortigue's ideas, of course, are forged from the same potent amalgam of 1830s philosophies and fads that d'Ortigue sees imprinted on the mind and soul of Liszt. And part of the slightly perverse retrospective appeal of d'Ortigue at this time comes from the fervent passion he displays in expounding ideas—such as the superiority of the artist over common humanity, of Beethoven over Rossini, symphony over opera, spirituality over sensuality—which, however misdirected, still retained the freshness and force of novelty, and would later quickly harden into ideological platitudes. Moreover, d'Ortigue was just discovering the heady thrill of developing a prose style that would be judged, at least by like minds whose opinion mattered most, by the grotesque Hugolian coloring of its images, such as Liszt throwing himself "naked and palpitating into the chaos in which the entire age is fermenting, in which the bones of the eighteenth century are boiling, mixed haphazardly with elements of the past in full dissolution and the fertile but shapeless germs of the future."

Yet as the same quotation also indicates, d'Ortigue only served up such tasty images in the service of his historical models. Of particular importance here was the "palingenetic" development of music cited toward the end of the biography to introduce the section on the organ, which at first reading seems strangely out of place.[10] The turn to palingenesis (spiritual rebirth) drew on the work of Pierre-Simon Ballanche, whose *Essais de palingénésie sociale* (1827–29) had offered a creative interpretation of social development that mapped out the gradual attainment of universal freedom (as had existed before the Fall) through the workings of divine providence.[11] Ballanche's combination of social progress within a religious frame appealed to d'Ortigue, and in 1833 he produced a "palingénésie musicale," outlining a progression from the style of Palestrina, through the dramatic style dominant from Monteverdi to Rossini, and climaxing in the all-inclusive symphonic style of Beethoven.[12] Clearly not a model that thrived on historical nuance (or indeed accuracy), this could be transferred easily enough into the Liszt biography, with the organ representing the lost grandeur and unity of sacred music, followed by the separation of music from its true religious function, leading on the one hand to the development of the piano and to the orchestra on the other. Now a new synthesis was in sight: Rossini and his followers (ever the negative pole of d'Ortigue's dialectics) had introduced pianistic figuration into their orchestral writing, while Beethoven and his confrères (Weber, Schubert, Hummel, Moscheles) had translated orchestral effects for the piano. Here d'Ortigue saw the seeds of Ballanchian redemption, unifying music and humanity again "in the regenerated soil of Christianity." And Liszt, by this model, was the one who had developed the orchestral capacities of the piano to the greatest extent and therefore, by implication, the one who would bring about the return to music's lost spiritual potential.

But is Liszt the real savior here? D'Ortigue expresses doubts about the capacity of the piano to match Liszt's exacting requirements, and any final rhetorical leap toward Liszt as virtuoso organist remains ultimately undescribed. Caught within his historical frameworks, between the conflicting demands of music as hermetic or socially transformative (as dictated by Lamennais), as poetic or absolute, the gaps in d'Ortigue's argument reveal some of the same tensions that d'Ortigue so vividly perceives in Liszt himself. D'Ortigue describes Liszt's playing ecstatically, but takes him to task for rhythmic freedom and charlatanism; meanwhile, the course of Liszt's life as depicted by d'Ortigue is defined temporally by the alternation of extreme spirituality and equally extreme sensualism, and temperamentally by the two separate personalities he describes within the composer's single body. The image of Liszt's sinister alter ego at war with his devout self is both dramatic and (unintentionally) comical in its stark opposition of the dangers fostered by reading Byron and Voltaire rather than Pascal and Lamennais. Yet the innate instability of the dialectic between spirit and senses, faith and irony that causes d'Ortigue both to praise and condemn the thrillingly sensual aspect of Liszt's playing, also illuminates the instability of d'Ortigue's wider claims for Liszt as the agent of any kind of socio-religious musical transformation. This becomes clear at the very end of the biography, when d'Ortigue, having adroitly sidestepped the promised technical description of the composer's works to develop his theories of palingenesis, then directly juxtaposes the *Fantaisie* on themes from Berlioz's *Lélio* (1834) with the circumstances of its composition at Lamennais's house at La Chênaie. "One can easily imagine that the deepest and most intimate sympathies of [Liszt's] soul must go naturally out toward this extraordinary man," d'Ortigue writes of Lamennais, before briefly describing the piece.

The implication, then, is that Lamennais inspired the work. But, as with the discussion of the organ, it is a point that d'Ortigue does not quite make. Why? Because to do so too explicitly would be to reveal its impossibility, as impossible as Heine's quip from the following year about Liszt performing a fantasy on Ballanche's *Palingénésie*, "whose ideas he translated into music, something very useful for those who find it impossible to read the works of this famous writer in the original."[13] The effectiveness of the joke relied on the fact that in the synesthesic atmosphere of the time such a performance was at once completely ridiculous and almost plausible; a reading compounded by Liszt's comment to Heine that afterward people kept requesting to hear his fugue on Ballanche's work.[14] Ultimately, d'Ortigue wanted more from Liszt than could be demonstrated in his handful of compositions and by his devastating yet troubling performances (too rhythmically wayward, too close to mannerism), and despite the critic's devotion to revealing the creative mind of the artist through external circumstances, these circumstances could only ever shed a partial light on Liszt as musician; just as (to resurrect another dualism) Liszt the musician could not (yet) live up to the expectations created by Liszt as embodiment of his age.[15] Preoccupied as we still are by the attractive yet elusive links between music and society, one of the appealing aspects of d'Ortigue's enthusiastic intentions and inevitable failure perhaps then lies in the way that it mimics our own experience.

By the time of Liszt's return to Paris from Switzerland in 1836, d'Ortigue praised his transformed technique and compositional skills, but noted that the mystical, religious tone of his earlier works had given way to an ironic, skeptical, negative, Rossinian style: the style of the Lisztian Other. D'Ortigue hoped that the composer could recover his equilibrium, and in later years, while the critic's own ideas on religious music became more uncompromising (increasingly focused on plainchant), the two men remained close—helped, no doubt, by Liszt's own definitive turn toward the spiritual. In the 1860s, not long before d'Ortigue's death, there were even references in Liszt's letters to a "travail liturgique" that they planned together.[16] Its nature is unclear, but no doubt it was a long way from the first thrill of the Byronic Liszt at the piano in 1835, "inebriating, fascinating, and terrifying," in the words of d'Ortigue, revealing a sublimity constituted and sustained in part by the critic's own celebratory prose; a sublimity that might reflect the multifaceted character of the age, or point toward spiritual regeneration, but that would always ultimately outstrip even the most ambitious of d'Ortigue's interpretative strategies, leaving him nothing but recourse to the deeply Romantic (and always revocable) trope of linguistic inadequacy: "One has to see him; one has to hear him, and fall silent."

JOSEPH D'ORTIGUE

Frantz Liszt

Gazette musicale de Paris
14 June 1835

The great work of the human mind today consists in its effort to pull itself away in every intellectual sphere from all ties to convention, to replace the arbitrary prescriptions and shackles of pure form with the free action of nature; and in its tendency to move back toward the fundamental and immutable laws governing beings. People who mistake the arduous and ephemeral play of human activities for the essential order, and call any agitation a disorder, are troubled when facing the process and effort we are describing, and see in it only violent symptoms of endless upheaval. Yet for anyone who does not misunderstand the principle and direction of its movement, it is clear that our age is searching at once for order within freedom, for freedom within order, and for tranquility within the two; which is to say that it ardently desires the reestablishment of the complete and natural course of the primary laws on which mankind's stability and development are based.

It has perhaps not been sufficiently noted that this general need is particularly felt among artists. And as we attempt here to describe the way it shows itself in this class of society, we believe we are placing art on the noblest ground: we are considering it in its relationship with man's most elevated and powerful instincts; we are placing it, in short, on a par with the fundamentals of civilization.

It was on such bases that we made a previous attempt to appraise the work of a young composer who, through the ups and downs of his career, is sustained by an indomitable confidence and a virile sense of independence.[17] It is from that same perspective that we now propose to examine the talent of an even younger artist, one who occupies an extremely elevated rank among our pianists: nobody denies his talent, to be sure, yet leaving matters of technique aside, this talent is far from being unqualifyingly embraced; the only reason for this, in our opinion, is that he is judged too much from the perspective of the individual, without taking into account his intimate affinity with the body of prevailing ideas and his relationship to the true direction of art.

The comparative method by which a man confronts his times, however, could not possibly offer more interesting aspects or truer parallels than in the case of the artist now being considered. We do not believe that any contemporary has drawn more broadly from the common reservoir of his time or reflected its diverse characteristics as fully as he has. Subjected at a very young age to the crucible of society, so impressionable, and, as it were, so responsive to it, he reflects the most vivid and faithful imprint of the various social types that have reproduced themselves in him. Religious aspirations and arid doubts, enthusiasms and depressions, excess of independence and search for authority—his soul absorbs it all, experiences it all every day; and it is not clear when its power reveals itself at its most astonishing, whether that it absorbs all those emanations inwardly or that it uses them up and pours them out in his artistic inspiration in the form of ardent, passionate emotions.

Clearly this essay is simultaneously the history of the gradual development of the faculties of an individual and a survey of the current situation of art, each being part of the same whole. The artist whose name heads these pages is, properly speaking, as much their subject as their text. We study plants in their own soil, whence they draw their nutrients. In our conception, the artist occupies the foreground of a painting whose background is the general aspect of the period. We see in him one of the most outstanding expressions of contemporary artistic thought. Finally, this kind of biographical sketch cannot be complete and must, above all, be discrete lest it prove harmful, even through praise, to certain social relationships.[18] Far from being suspected of having been written for the sole and vain purpose of entertainment and amusement, this study, we believe, should be seen as a thorough picture of what can be achieved in an extraordinary mind, both spontaneously and through its successive actions, by the highest degree of artistic feeling, when joined with various powerful influences.

Frantz Liszt was born in the Hungarian village of Raiding on 22 October 1814 [Recte: 1811], the year of the comet. We mention this detail because the young virtuoso's parents saw a premonition of sorts in the coincidence between the appearance of the phenomenon and the birth of their child. Adam Liszt, Frantz's father, was not a professional musician; he was employed in the administration of the estates of Prince Esterhazy, the son of old Prince Anton Esterhazy, who had sheltered the young Haydn and appointed him his Kapellmeister. By securing for himself the greatest genius of his day and guaranteeing him an easy and pleasant existence, this prince is owed the gratitude of all artists, since it is thanks to the comfort Haydn enjoyed in his position that musical Europe gained the multitude of masterpieces that will live as long as art itself. In the first years of the eighteenth century the chapel of the house of Esterhazy was organized with the greatest care, while the corpus of religious music to which Mozart, Cherubini, and several other famous composers had contributed was one of the finest in Europe.

Adam Liszt was a frequent card-game partner of Haydn, and was on close terms with him. Haydn, whose character was always calm and whose imagination was seldom fired up, was kept mercilessly busy at work. The card game was nearly the only pastime the great man enjoyed.

No first-rate pianist, Adam Liszt[19] was nevertheless a notably talented performer. A consummate musician, he could play almost any instrument. Had his family been richer and had fourteen or fifteen siblings not demanded the greatest share of the sacrifices required to develop a brilliant career which would have given him opportunities for advancement, he could have become a distinguished artist. Such opportunities came up several times, but he was never able to take them. This is the most poignant of all the disappointments of human life, when material considerations force man's noblest part, his intelligence, to renounce the free and full exercise of his faculties, condemning him to the sad contemplation of his inactivity, while remaining intimately aware of his diminished power. It is truly a kind of death, the most appalling of all, when the soul keeps outliving itself, driven by the single idea, ever-present and ever-accusatory, of its own annihilation!

With Adam Liszt's career illusions having vanished, his dreams of glory dissipated, a deep-seated sadness and melancholy filled his life: he devoted himself to his administrative career with intelligence and probity, yet his distaste for it caught up with him and he ended up regarding it with horror. The unique dispositions he had already noticed in his son, however, aroused in his mind the idea of the possibility of a felicitous compensation; a consoling hope was born. In a sense, he transferred onto Frantz the development he had dreamed of for himself. He often said to him: "My son, you are predestined! You will be that ideal artist whose image had fascinated my youth in vain. What I only glimpsed in me shall inevitably be accomplished in you. My abortive genius will be reborn in you. In you I want to be rejuvenated and continued."

It was in roughly the same terms that the mother of one of our most illustrious virtuosos, then still a child, predicted to him his future glory: "Nicolo," she told him one day as she took him on her knees, "you will be a great musician. A radiantly beautiful angel appeared to me last night; he bade me choose a wish to be realized: I begged him to make you the first among violinists, and the angel promised it to me." This child, once grown up, was known as Paganini.[20]

A few circumstances relating to Frantz's childhood need to be disclosed. Beyond their own intrinsic interest, these details are also precious insofar as they can cast light on the artist's orientation as he grew older; moreover, as free and spontaneous expressions in which the soul's leanings already reveal themselves, these details can explain certain facts that might otherwise be mistaken for studied oddities and affectations of character. Adam Liszt kept a daily record of his son's life. All that concerned his health, studies, pastimes, pious exercises, conversations, travels, and successes was consigned therein with the minute, scrupulous exactitude of a loving father. This memoir is in the possession of Madame Liszt, to whose kindness we are indebted for communicating it to us. We will follow it from time to time in our retelling of this initial period that ends with Adam's death:

> Following the inoculation of the vaccine began a period of illness, during which the child alternately experienced nervous pains and intermittent fevers that several times threatened him with the loss of his life. Once, when he was 2 or 3, we thought he had died. We ordered a coffin for him. This alarming state of affairs lasted until the age of 6! . . .
>
> From his childhood, Frantz showed religious leanings through a natural inclination of his soul, and a keen artistic sense already blended with feelings of piety that possessed all the sincerity of his age.
>
> At the age of 6, he heard me play on the piano a concerto in C sharp minor by Ries. Bending over the keyboard, Frantz was listening intently. That same evening, on his way back from the garden where he had gone for a walk, he sang the theme of the concerto. We asked him to do it again. He did not know what he was singing. That was the first intimation of his genius. He asked insistently that we start him on the piano. After three months of lessons, fever overtook him again and necessitated an interruption. His taste for study did not prevent him from liking to play with children of his age; yet he was more inclined to live alone with himself.

Later, M. de Chateaubriand's *René* wrung tears from him for six months; he read and reread it ceaselessly; that book contributed more and more to developing his love of solitude.[21] He had applied to himself this saying of René's: "A secret instinct is tormenting me." He wrote these words in all his notebooks.

His work was uneven, yet diligent until the age of nine. At that time he gave his first public performance, in Oedenburg; he played Ries's concerto in E flat and improvised. Fever had overtaken him once more before he sat at the piano and the performance increased it. For a long time Frantz had felt an extreme desire to appear in public, and he showed great assurance and daring there.

Prince Esterhazy, to whom he was introduced by his father, encouraged him and gave him a few hundred francs. That was not much for the heir to Haydn's Maecenas. In Pressburg, however, where his father took him soon afterward, he enjoyed the protection of several noblemen, notably Count Thadeus Amadeus and Count Zanary. These noblemen gave him, during a six-year period, a pension of 1,200 to 1,500 francs.

A year after leaving Pressburg, Adam Liszt decided to give up his position and sell everything he owned in order to settle in Vienna with his wife and son. The sale of his furniture brought him the sum of 600 francs. This decision was made against the advice of his wife and his friends, who all agreed that he was mad.

Upon his arrival in this city, Frantz was immediately put into the hands of Czerny, who made him start with Clementi sonatas. Humiliated to find himself treated like a schoolboy, Frantz took a dislike to his master, but once Czerny had given him works by Beethoven and Hummel, Frantz felt a real sympathy for him, and he gave full recognition to his tact and personality.

Old Salieri also displayed much warm affection for the little virtuoso. It was under this able master that Frantz studied the different clefs and took instruction in religious music.

When he visited music publishers, he never found the pieces he was shown difficult enough. Once, the publisher set before him a concerto in B minor by Hummel; leafing through the score, the boy said it was nothing and he would play it well at first sight. These words were heard by leading Viennese pianists who, astonished by the child's boast, took him at his word and took him up to the salon where the piano was kept. The boy sight-read the concerto with equal amounts of skill and assurance. From that occasion, he ventured to sight-read several times in public.

Frantz had been in Vienna for eighteen months when he gave a major concert that was attended by Beethoven.[22] Far from intimidating the child, the presence of the illustrious composer exalted his imagination. Beethoven encouraged him, albeit with the reserved tone he invariably took in the last years of his life; this should be ascribed either to his personal sorrows or to the black melancholy into which his infirmities plunged him.

In 1823 Adam Liszt, worried by his son's seemingly indeterminate progress, took him to Paris. His trip through Germany was a triumph. The father's main ambition was for Frantz to enter the Conservatoire to study counterpoint and composition. The two foreigners went to M. Cherubini with letters of recommendation from Prince von Metternich. They were received with a harsh response: *No foreigner can enter the Conservatoire.* M. le Directeur forgot he was himself Italian. The father begged, insisted, supplicated; the result he obtained was that M. Cherubini grudgingly agreed to hear his son; he received many compliments and the firm assurance that Frantz was refused entry.[23] The unhappy father gave himself up to discouragement and despair. At that point they were summoned to the Palais-Royal for the New Year's festivities. The child prodigy electrified the entire audience. The Duke of Orleans fell under his spell and bade him ask for anything he wanted. The *pulcinella* over there, the child answered, pointing to a handsome mannequin hanging in front of the tapestry.

An entire year went by, during which the young Listz was like a doll for all the ladies in Paris. He was in demand everywhere, flattered, caressed, spoiled, each of his droll or impertinent remarks, pleasantries, or caprices repeated, reported, publicized; all were found adorable.[24] By the age of twelve, he had inspired passions, provoked rivalries, aroused hatreds; all heads were turned, he was doted upon. One evening at the Théâtre-Italien, as every box vied for his company, he felt himself smothered in an ardent embrace; he struggled to pull himself away and see who was embracing him: it was Talma.[25] We believe that such adulation had an influence on his talent and frame of mind. Yet its immediate effect was to make him forget the chaste and naive thoughts of his youth and look back with pity on his innocent exercises and pious ecstasies. Not regarding himself a child anymore, he almost blushed at the memory of his childhood; ahead of his age through his capacities and talent, he wanted to be ahead as well in adopting a curt and decisive manner and a disdainful, affected cynicism. His father felt the need to subject him to a regimen of obstinate work. He forced him, after his meals, to play twelve Bach fugues. Transposing them into different keys was mere child's play for Frantz.

In May 1824 his father took him to England; he performed at George IV's court with immense success. There are two anecdotes concerning his London stay. Invited to a soiree, Liszt arrived quite late, almost at the end. Among the virtuosos who had been heard was a rather mediocre pianist; he had performed a solo, failing to produce any impression among the audience. Liszt was asked to sit at the piano and unwittingly played the piece already performed by the virtuoso; he electrified the entire audience. It did not occur to anyone that the piece could be the same as the one already heard. Certain comparisons were whispered that were far from favorable to the earlier pianist. Friends of the latter, on the other hand, tried to excuse him, putting the blame on the excessive coldness or severity of the piece he had chosen. Things had reached this point when Mme Pasta, who was present, took it upon herself to look at the score left on the piano and discovered that the two pieces were identical.

There was at the time in London a distinguished phrenologist-doctor, Mr. Deville.[26] Out of curiosity, some people introduced Liszt to him as a lazy boy, devoid of natural talents, a boy whose family did not know what to do with him. The phrenologist carefully examined the child's skull, passed his fingers over a few bumps, and confessed that the subject did not seem to him as ill-favored as was thought. However, he advised Frantz not to devote himself to the study of dead languages. Suddenly, as he was pressing both his index fingers on the corners of the forehead, he exclaimed with enthusiasm: Why, this is a born musician! Let them make an artist of him and you will see what he will become. —Well, he was told, this child is none other than the young Liszt, whom you have already heard about. —Mr. Deville tenderly embraced the virtuoso, and was delighted to have found such justification for the truth of his system.

Liszt returned to Paris in September and resumed the same style of life as in the previous year. He made a second trip to England in April 1825. He went to St. Paul's Cathedral, where he heard the choir of seven to eight thousand children from the charity schools singing anthems and psalms in unison; he retained from this one of those rare and strong impressions that we should take care not to repeat in order to preserve the memory.

At the end of 1825, the jury audition and rehearsals took place for his opera *Don Sanche ou Le Château d'amour*, with a libretto by Messrs. Théaulon and de R.[27] The opera had four performances at the Académie royale de Musique; after the premiere, Adolphe Nourrit brought the author onstage to receive the applause of the parterre.

This theatrical debut did much for Liszt's reputation. His father deemed the moment favorable for organizing a major tour in the provinces. In early 1826, they left for Bordeaux, where Frantz gave several highly successful public performances; at one of these concerts Rode played with him. On another occasion, attending a meeting of Bordelais music lovers, Liszt played a sonata of his composition that he introduced as being by Beethoven. Whether the gentlemen could not refrain from a certain exaltation upon hearing the very name of Beethoven or were genuinely deceived by the magic of the performance—or else felt they had to find beautiful anything they thought to be by the greatest artist of Germany and Europe—the prank was successful; the sonata was found sublime. With further successes, he toured through Toulouse, Montpellier, Nîmes, Marseilles, Lyons.

His health, meanwhile, had become stronger in the course of the trip. While his gaiety occasionally bordered on insolence, he retained a pious disposition. In Lyons, where he stayed for a while, the conscience of his destiny grew more strongly in him and manifested itself more distinctly in his thoughts. Having returned to Paris in that same year, he studied counterpoint under M. Reicha. His father, who had put so much effort into bringing him before the public, began to feel dismayed to see him become a child prodigy. He therefore encouraged his son's solitary leanings and, whenever he had money, was happy to see him closeting himself away for six months of work. In this quiet life Frantz's religious propensities took a new turn. He saw the serene days of his childhood return. Such piety sounds all the more remarkable since it was neither sustained nor fed by his father's example. Yet his burning, contemplative soul, while indulging in ecstasies worthy of Saint Teresa, was full of admiration for suicide, without perhaps being aware of the contradiction. This proves how powerful some ideas of the age were on his mind while he gravitated toward God with a natural movement. Love of mankind was gradually taking shape within him, beginning with charity. He loved the poor; whenever he had money, he gave it to them; when he had none, he gave at times his handkerchief, at other times his rings and jewels. One day, as our young artist was walking across the boulevard, he was approached by a little street-sweeper who asked him for a sou: Liszt could only find a five-franc coin on him. —Take this, he said, and go and get some change. —The little Savoyard went, and without thinking asked the pianist to take his broom. The latter, upon seeing himself alone, holding a broom in the middle of the boulevard, was at first tempted to feel humiliated. —But after all, he said to himself, this broom is the livelihood of a man like me; this instrument, no matter how dirty, is no more vile in God's eyes than my rosewood piano. —And he placed himself proudly in an erect position, holding the broom to the ground with his fully extended arm, facing the stares of the crowd on both sides of the boulevard and the rich people going by in their splendid carriages with a self-assured air as he waited for the little beggar to return.

During the period in question, the *Pères du désert* were his only reading.[28] He went to confession often. He felt a call to the priesthood. He came to dislike music and devoted himself to it only to obey his father's inflexible will. The fear of missing his calling, on the one hand, or, on the other, of betraying his father's hopes, gave him unbearable anguish and aroused endless scruples in his mind; his soul was constantly bubbling over like a vase that overflows not because it is too full, but because a hidden fire continuously stirs the water inside.

Perhaps one could say about the feeling for art what has been said regarding the feeling of love, that it is close to religious devotion. It can scarcely be doubted, in the circumstances we are discussing, that our musician was driven to religion by art, as he was later drawn back to it by love. It was in such a mystical frame of mind that he visited Geneva, Lausanne, and Berne in 1827. He read pious books exclusively. On his return, he kept pestering his father with requests for permission to go to confession. Adam Liszt feared that he would throw himself wholly into excess of this kind and did not always grant it; not to cause pain to a much loved father, Frantz did not insist. His piety was nonetheless intelligent and admitted a certain freedom of ideas and opinions. It was not, like that of many religious people, rigid, narrow-minded, dulled by routine, and stupid; it was sincere as well, more understanding, and altogether catholic in perspective. The litanies were his favorite prayer. The endlessly repeated phrase, *Take pity on us! Take pity on us!* seemed sublime to him. He saw in those four words the cry of all pain, the repentance of all sin, as well as a kind of lugubrious refrain for all categories of the evils and crimes of mankind. For him that exclamation summarized both man's infinite misery and God's infinite mercy, and he said that if he could have prayed in moments of oblivion, he would have recited the litanies.

In the spring of the same year, he made his third trip to England, which was a triumph. He had a success at the Drury-Lane Theatre and was called back for encores.

On his return to Paris, his health worsened perceptibly. In order to restore it, his father took him to take the waters in Boulogne. This trip, however, had a tragic outcome for both of them. No sooner had Adam Liszt arrived in the city than he was attacked by an inflammation that within three weeks led him to the tomb.

Only our musician could explain the profound impression made on such a tender heart and such an exalted imagination by the death—so unexpected a month before—of a father who had counted his own life for nothing in order to live entirely through his son. Until then the idea of death had not struck young Frantz. This idea, somewhat speculative and general to the point of vagueness, had not yet awakened in him the possibility of a realization that might affect him personally. "Then I shall die some day? What! *I* die! *I*, who speak, who feel; can *I* die? I have some difficulty in believing it: for, after all, that others should die is perfectly natural: one sees that every day: we see them pass by, and get accustomed to it; but to die one's self! to die bodily! that is rather too much." Those words, by an author who often hides the profundity of his thoughts behind a facade of levity and insouciance, convey precisely enough the state of indifference in which Liszt had always found himself concerning this terrible concept of death.[29] It lay far beyond the sphere of his practical existence, and never having glimpsed it save in his remotest thoughts, he had neither sounded it out nor explored it as he did all matters of which he had direct experience. Suddenly death appeared to his feeble eyes in all its overwhelming force as a mystery: unhappy for the impious, glorious for the Christian, of nothingness for the skeptic, consecrated for the artist, sorrowful for the spouse and the son. He bent, he collapsed under the powerful embrace of this unknown, strange thing that he had heard called Death. Death was to him the first revelation of life.

This event that had struck what he held dearest in the world put a brutal stop to the development of his ideas, and suspended for a time the exercise of his activity. His soul, crushed by such a violent jolt, sunk into the abandonment of all duties and reshaped itself around an obsession with isolation and abandonment. Silent grumblings, reproaches, remorse, scruples, perhaps superstitious terrors, the actual cause of which he could not sort out, rose from the depths of his consciousness and, like lugubrious phantoms, swirled over the ever-present image of his dead father. A recourse to religious consolations was not in his mind; had it been, he would not have found in himself enough impulse or energy to invoke them; had they been offered to him, one can believe that they would have glided over his soul like worthless dew on a marble statue. The indifference and coldness of his father's dying moments had pushed his religious feelings into the remotest and darkest recesses of his heart. He no longer felt in himself either love or tears.

A father's death is the root of the past torn out; the death of a child is a form of the future being extinguished. An orphaned son is a frail sapling violently separated by a cruel knife from the maternal stock. It tires, languishes, and dies, unless its sap can instantly feed itself on beneficent soil. Like a wilted stem bending gradually toward the ground, young Liszt was imperceptibly expiring, bending toward the earth that carried within it the remains of his father, when his eyes moved away from the past, where a tomb was all he could still see, to look at the future. Then, his life appeared to him divided into two parts: on the one side, he saw that his career of obedience had spent itself; on the other side, he glimpsed a career of freedom to be fulfilled. Proudly raising his lowered head, still enveloped in the shadows of death, he resolved to walk straight toward the light that shone in the distance.

Thus ended with his father's life a submissive period during which he had obtained great successes as a performer. His manner of playing was full of impetuosity. Through the torrents of a slightly nebulous passion, one could see shining occasional flashes of genius; also visible were a few of those divine sparks which he now produces so profusely that they seem like golden stars shot endlessly from a vast conflagration. Subjected, however, whether to the demands of his masters or to the whims of audiences, or to the authority of his father, his imagination could only furtively devote itself to its fancies; he was found wanting both for excessive vagaries and for excessive timidity; he was not himself yet; he was only a premonition.

So, looking back at his past, he resolved to examine himself severely, with a view to pulling himself away from those various influences and sorting out the elements of his piano playing that had been forced on him by authority, or adopted by him as concessions, to the detriment of what was individual in him. In short, he resolved to trim from his acquired habits those that might have disturbed the exercise of his natural habits. This was not accomplished unhesitatingly or without trial and error. Like a pendulum whose motion is interrupted by an obstacle, he wavered for some time before finding his balance, but his powerful will overcame all difficulties. Thus, before throwing himself into the stormy course of freedom, he reimmersed himself in a broad, calm, and reasoned doctrinal orderliness. He looked for ways of subjecting his faculties to a law of equilibrium and harmony, and he attempted to conquer the sort of powerful peace which, as Saint Augustine put it both accurately and profoundly, is the tranquility of order. He decided that a brief period of organization should precede the indefinite period of freedom. An eaglet about to soar in flight, he preened his feathers, shook the dust of the eyrie off his wings while testing their strength, before spreading them in the limitless domain of space.

He thus conceived the training of the artist within himself in combination with the training of the social being, since the artist is the social being's highest and fullest expression. Taking up his position in the world under this twofold persona, he set off toward his destiny with firm and noble self-confidence.

Having returned from Boulogne to Paris, Liszt supported himself by giving lessons. His wide-ranging literary interests began at that moment; until then he had felt this curiosity only intermittently. At this point intervened a development important both in itself and for the nature of its consequences on the life of our musician, namely his first and major initiation into life through feelings of love and the resultant suffering and atonement.[30] We do not consider it our task to narrate this period of crisis; we will be content to offer the following observation as a kind of moral from the event we are passing over in silence: the aristocracy admires talent; it seeks, encourages, applauds, and rewards it. Yet, even as it rewards it, it does so by considering it a thing to be paid for with money. Never will a nobleman give his daughter to an artist; he will tell you that there has never been a lowering of rank in his family or, if once there were, he does not wish to repeat such a scandal. All the knowledge, genius, and renown of the artist cannot, in the nobleman's eyes, hold its own against the title of gentleman, as common, banal, and at times devalued as it may be. So that the most inept, stupidest, wretchedest nobleman still enjoys a social glamor far superior to that of the artist. Such people have been told that they were noble *in a literal sense,* that a purer blood than that of other men ran through their veins, and they believed it.

Suffering turns into purification only insofar as the mind adheres to it by a free act of the will and the heart opens itself freely to the promptings of grace, clad in mystery. Only then does the most absolute sacrifice bring a powerful consolation and a wonderful virtue that amply make up for the violent effort it cost. Then God offers himself to the human being as compensation. Like Silvio Pellico, Liszt lost himself in God.[31] All earthly beauties vanished from his thought before the idea of God that was so intimately present to him. With the whole vigor of his soul and his entire youthful energy, he plunged, lost himself, drowned himself in that divine spring, expanding through the contemplation and endless absorption of all that is incorruptible, immeasurable, infinite within the uncreated essence. Every day he renewed his inner sacrifice. He struck up a friendship with M. Urhan and drew new strength from their conversations.[32] With this friend he was able to free himself from the painful necessity of hiding a part of himself; in his relations with M. Urhan it was not simply the artist but the man as well, the Christian who revealed himself openly. To say that this mode of living was quiet, saintly, regenerated, is also to say that it was happy. In this religious fever, he remembered one day that he was a musician, because music was not then part of him. He made plans to compose religious music, as the music so designated nowadays did not seem to him in all reason to adopt the form of human thought; he was struck by the idea that he would create sacred music. Meanwhile, in his solitary improvisations he depicted the joys and ecstasies of Communion; he also depicted the world as he glimpsed it in his lofty detachment from earthly things.

When the soul gets a taste of the supernatural life with such plenitude and superabundance, it is usually at the expense of the life of the body. Liszt fell ill; his vital faculties soon wore themselves out in the prodigious activity of his intelligence and sensitivity. A decline that lasted six months, the progress of which was terrifying, persuaded some that he was dying. Several obituaries appeared in newspapers about him, the man for whom a coffin had been built when he was two years old.[33]

While the artist revived, he nevertheless firmly resolved to live as if dead to the world. He could not get used to society again; human noise was unbearable to him, producing a horrible dissonance with the vibrations of his soul. Yet this resolution did not hold. It often happens that after an illness, when the body is born again in health and life returns through every pore, the feeling of existence provokes the imagination to a certain eccentric disposition and imparts to it such a strength and such an impulse that it takes flight far beyond the boundaries it had at first forbidden itself to cross. Once those limits have been overstepped, it knows no restraining powers. Then, exalted by this vital exuberance, by this boiling blood that roars through its veins and brings a kind of drunkenness to the brain, it no longer grasps except through a confused, troubled medium what were previously the clearest notions and the most distinct perceptions; it desires ardently to blend into life outside and eventually throws itself into physical pleasures as onto an object of prey. We do not believe one should attribute to such a cause the short period of loss of faith that succeeded the period of heavenly bliss and mystical contemplation that appeared to have ended the earthly career of our artist. We tend rather to think that his sudden insouciance toward everything—religion, his future, genuine feelings of love, fame even—in short, a total indifference came to him on a wind that found its way bearing the ideas of the age, though he may have been unaware of this influence. Thus, in the middle of his fervor, a sneer of self-contempt arose in his soul. As the Holy Scriptures, ancient philosophy, and modern moral philosophers all agree to put it: man is of two pieces. Liszt himself experienced this, to his grief. Alongside his own and true self he saw a second self arising, like a sinister genie, usurping the first; a mysterious, evil power which mastered and dominated him. Thus, when he reproached himself with a sardonic giggle for having believed in God, whenever he derided religion, love, freedom, and art, it was not *he* who laughed and spoke in that way: it was the other. In reading Pascal and the *Essai sur l'indifférence*, it had been *he*; but during this period when he read Volney, Rousseau, Dupuis, Voltaire, Byron; when he reasoned too proudly, when he mocked and hated, when his head became coldly exalted by suicide and nothingness, it was not *he*, it was the other.[34] This dogmatic, nihilistic cynicism was not his, it did silent violence to his soul; it was an anomaly, as Liszt himself came to realize; an anomaly that can be explained like other anomalies, human life being what it is, as de Maistre has said. As we have said, this condition did not last long; impiety was not natural to him. Still, the rumor of this change spread quickly to the outside world. The news that *Liszt was no longer religious* caused a sensation among a crowd of pretty women. He was credited at once with twenty affairs; he was not having a single one. Around that time a woman to whom he felt attracted by a purely artistic sympathy introduced him to Italian music. His inclinations at the time were highly conducive to this initiation into an altogether sensuous music. He himself summarized the situation of his soul at the time in a few compositions, notably in his *Fantaisie sur la Fiancée*, the only one he then published; it is a piece of expressive mockery, of Byronic verve, its forms coquettish, brilliant almost to a fault, much in the manner of M. Herz.[35]

The doctrines that nourished Liszt as long as the aforementioned condition lasted soon produced in him the disgust they ought naturally to inspire. No longer being sustained in the cultivation of his art by the faith that produces courage and enthusiasm, a profound boredom set in. Boredom gave rise to the need for work, and thus the need to know and to become active. A kind of self-challenge restored all his energy. *I must become Paganini*, he said suddenly; since then this idea has never left him. He felt the need to undertake broad musical, literary, and philosophical studies before presenting himself to the outside world. He resumed his intimate contemplative life, and while superficially retaining his artistic relations and social life, he knew how to give them up, then as now, in favor of the inner religious feeling. Always preoccupied with thoughts of his future, living ten and fifteen years ahead, he viewed as secondary the successes that drive the ambitions of so many other virtuosos. He went on frequent retreats. During these he dreamed of Paganini and Mme Malibran. At the same time, he looked back on his past so as to think more clearly about his future. He wondered whether he should ground his existence in marriage. No, he said to himself. Should he travel abroad, increase his fame, make a fortune? No again, always no. One idea pursued him, tormented him, obsessed him: the need to find truth in his art. With each retreat the worldly never failed to say: *It is caused by an unhappy love affair!* In this the natural wisdom of the worldly was mistaken; no passion was involved, save the passion for art. However, one must concede that this passion can at times be truly unhappy, that is, when it finds itself in touch with the laughter and cold irony of society.

Liszt emerged from his solitude to undertake a second trip to Switzerland. Having arrived in a house in the country near Geneva, he spent the entire evening playing the piano. A woman said to him: *So you have come here to melt Mont Blanc!* The six months of his Swiss stay were perhaps the fullest of his life. Back in Paris, he went frequently to the Porte-Saint-Martin Theatre, where *Marion de Lorme* and *Antony* were being performed.[36] He connected a memory of his stay near Mont Blanc to a character from one of these two plays. In his desire to learn everything, or at least to know everything, he struck up a friendship with one of the heads of the Saint-Simonian movement, M. Barrault; the new doctrine had appealed to him through certain ideas of progress and betterment that the leaders of this school had been able to disseminate with talent and enthusiasm, and it contributed to furthering the range of his studies.

The successive, highly diverse phases of our musician's life after the death of his father, as just reported here, took place within the years 1828 and 1829. Then came 1830. Liszt witnessed the three-day revolution; he saw the people, indignant at the violation of their rights, rise *en masse;* he witnessed their enthusiasm for the fight, their moderation during the fight, and the dignity with which they became restful again after the fight. This fierce struggle between power and freedom, the fall of power, the quiet triumph of freedom, must have produced in his soul a shock of the sort whose memory remains forever vibrant. He conceived at the time a revolutionary symphony. A few months later, in 1831, a concert took place at the hall of the Saint-Simonians on rue Taitbout. Mme Malibran had just sung an aria which Liszt accompanied on the piano. As they walked back to her box, she took the arm of her accompanist. At each row the singer was stopped on her way with congratulations from every side. As she was responding right and left, Liszt saw General Lafayette standing before him. Leaving Mme Malibran on the spot, he leapt forward to embrace the old general, who with his customary goodness welcomed this spontaneous testimony of sympathy and admiration.[37]

We have followed Frantz Liszt from his birth to the period when his experience, his well-established reputation, his social position, as well as his precocious talent have put him in the rank of the most consummate artists. Since that time, he has pursued his unrelenting work and the course of his dazzling successes. Also since that time, he seems to have entered a different period, whether in extending his talent in a new direction or refining it, which we do not believe we can examine at this time. His art is the expression of his life; all the vicissitudes of the latter are reproduced in the qualities and defects of the former. A sudden, intuitive genius rather than a positive, rational, analytical mind, he resonates, he vibrates under each shock and countershock from external things. In a feat of prodigious sympathy, his soul has associated and identified with everything great and generous in contemporary society. Yet, in his burning curiosity to know everything, learn everything, and become involved in everything, he has often found in the fine-looking fruit from which he hoped to draw refreshing juice, nothing but arid dust. He has thrown his soul, naked and palpitating, into the chaos in which the entire age is fermenting, boiling the bones of the eighteenth century, mixed haphazardly with elements of the past in full dissolution, and the fertile but shapeless germs of the future. Jolted among so many diverse principles, his soul has retained their various emanations. With nothing but the torch of reason in hand, his soul tore at the entrails of society, but where it sought a clear spring it found only muddy waters, and where it sought a rock on which to rest, it saw nothing but a mystery, an abyss in which its flickering light was extinguished. Hence his extended disenchantments, anguish, and doubts, the endlessly reborn spiritual labors in which hope succumbed without support until a ray of truth, an expectation, a religious breeze restored provisionally the quiet and peace of his soul. Hence also his propensity to mix sorrow with all his pleasures and despair with all his sorrows. And then, casting his eyes around, the artist saw celebrities, major intellectual figures, poets, journalists, philosophers; he took their works, devoured them, reading with an acute sensibility, laying bare the heart of the writer. With this insatiable, nervous curiosity he read dictionaries with the same application as a poet, studying Boiste and Lamartine for four uninterrupted hours at his fireside with the same investigative spirit and the same interpretive effort.[38] Then, once he had penetrated the thought of the writer, he would call on him, asking him to explain his thoughts face to face. In this way Liszt has struck up friendships with MM. de Lamartine, de La Mennais, Hugo, de Vigny, Sainte-Beuve, Ballanche, de Sénancour, Mme Dudevant, etc. etc.; he has assimilated their feelings and ideas, and every day he draws from their inspiration all he can transfer into his art.[39] These relationships have made him discover in himself innumerable points of contact with other destinies. In the same spirit he studies the distinctive qualities of his young musical friends: Chopin, Hiller, Mendelssohn, Dessauer, Urhan, V. Alkan, and Berlioz, who was for him an apparition.[40]

Just as our musician sees in all the arts, and particularly in music, a reverberation and a reflection of general ideas in the same way that he sees God in the universe, so should he be seen when performing on the piano. His performance is his speech and his soul. It is the most poetic and most synthetic summary of all his impressions, of everything that has a hold on him. The impressions he would evidently find it most difficult to render in words or express with neat and precise ideas are reproduced at the piano to the full extent of their vagueness, with a truthful energy, an instinctive force, a power of feeling, and a magical charm that could never be equaled. In this instance his art is passive, it is an instrument, an echo; it expresses and translates. At other times it is active; it is he who speaks; his art the organ used to broadcast his ideas. This is why a Liszt performance is no mechanical or material exercise, but above all a composition, a genuine artistic creation.

His performance is a waterfall, an avalanche that tumbles downward, a torrent of harmony that reproduces in its immeasurable swiftness the thousand reflections and nuances of the rainbow; it is a diaphanous, vaporous form suspended in midair by the sounds of an aeolian harmony; its shimmering clothing made up of flowers, stars, pearls, and diamonds; then come accents of despair articulated in the midst of suffocation; it is a delirious joy; it is a prophetic voice speaking a great lamentation; it is a virile, proud speech that commands, subjugates, terrifies; it is a sigh being poured forth, the last groan of a dying man. One has seen him, in Weber's *Konzertstück* for piano and orchestra, grab hold of a tutti from the orchestra on his instrument and drown in his thunder the hundred voices of the orchestra and the thousand bravos that burst then from the hall. One has recently seen him, at the Hôtel de Ville, unleashing so much emotion in a duet performed with his young pupil, Mlle Vial that gradually losing warmth and expression and succumbing to fatigue, he collapsed, senseless, at the foot of his piano.[41] How is it that, from our own experience, seeing Liszt sit down at his piano to play the simplest thing—a *caprice*, a waltz, an *étude* by Cramer, Chopin, or Moscheles—we suddenly feel our breast choked by a sob? Yet it is above all in performing Beethoven that the pianist becomes a giant. Beethoven—whose music some narrow or hateful minds still persist in seeing as mere change, as if change could occur without introducing into art a new fundamental principle, as if change could be anything other than the embodiment, the external manifestation of a new type, of an inner development—Beethoven is for Liszt a God before whom he bends his head; he considers him a sort of redeemer whose coming has already been marked in the musical world by the liberation of poetic thought and the abolition of the reign of conventional rules. Oh! One has to see him give voice to one of those songs, these poems called sonatas, that once vulgar designation! One has to see him, with his windblown hair, hurling his fingers from one end of the keyboard to the other to land on a note that explodes with a clamorous or silvery sound, like a bell struck by a bullet; his fingers seem to grow longer, like springs being released, as if at times freeing themselves from his hands. One has to see him raise his sublime eyes to the sky to search for inspiration, then, gloomily, fix them on the ground; or see his radiant and inspired features, like those of a martyr, radiating in the joy of his tortures; or see that terrible look he occasionally darts at the listener, inebriating, fascinating, and terrifying him; and that other, dulled look which, deprived of light, fades away; one has to see his nostrils dilated to let out the air that escapes from his breast in tumultuous waves, like those of a horse flying across the plain. Oh! One has to see him, one has to hear him, and fall silent, for here we feel too much how admiration weakens our expression.

Liszt's musical performance, however, is far from having the privilege of being faultless, like the ever so correctly icy and elegantly monotonous performances of some of his fellow virtuosos. He has real defects, the causes of which we will seek, and which we will indicate with impartiality. First, it seems to us that, while on the one hand the talent of our musician has benefited much in regard to the grandeur of his inspirations

from having studied the laws of universal development, the dominant characteristics of the age, and the broadest social relations, on the other hand
certain relationships limited to the sphere of intimate life, certain petty
preoccupations, certain personal requests, all-powerful in a salon, but
utterly powerless elsewhere, may have had seductive influences on a talent too magnificent for some to let it develop by itself. In short, in saying
that his dealings with the most remarkable men of our time have been
more beneficial to him than the company of the most fashionable women,
we believe we make our idea clear enough, and avoid being accused of
intending to apply to the man what, in our mind, only concerns the artist.

Secondly, whether Liszt at times exaggerates his feelings or distorts the
expression of the feelings that animate the composer, it is nonetheless true
that he has been accused of not being totally immune to a certain charlatanism in his mannerisms and playing. While admitting that this is a fine
defect, since it is born from a great warmth of the soul and a disposition
to add spice to an often cold composition through powerful performance, it is fair to say that at times Liszt justifies the saying that the sublime
is neighbor to the ridiculous, though many are the worldly who most
often see the ridiculous in what is sublime.

Finally, Liszt's playing errs on the side of rhythmic freedom. Generally,
he considers the piece he plays a theme for the fancies of his imagination.
He often produces an admirable thing out of a mediocre piece, and only
he can do that. We know that several compositions would have no effect
if a certain latitude as regards tempo and rhythm were not left to the performer. Yet it can also occur that the character of a piece depends solely
on rhythmic unity and, should this character be removed from it, even
the most brilliant performance is no compensation. For instance, we cannot approve of the manner in which our virtuoso renders M. Berlioz's
Marche au supplice, which he has so artfully translated for the piano, and
various other pieces, such as the scherzo of Beethoven's C-sharp Minor
Sonata. Not that he does not possess rhythmic sense; but he abandons himself too much to his impetuosity, which at times makes the task of the
orchestra that accompanies him very difficult.

Liszt's ideas and opinions may have been almost invariably vague and
unstable because of the immense need for development he has always felt;
his life may in a way have embodied nothing but a passionate, ongoing
eclecticism; nevertheless, he has constantly directed his efforts toward
one goal: to work with a view to disengage his art more and more from
the formal bonds by which it is still constrained, as attested to by the current state of Italian music, to harmonize it with what is most intimate in
ideas, affections, and human feelings and to elevate it to the level of a social

and religious mission. That at least is the idea; we will presently see what he imagines with regard to the form. He too has felt that art could become a civilizing element, a tent of peace open to all exhausted or disenchanted minds that might come to gather there; and that music—the most sympathetic of all the arts, and the only one whose power excites the unanimous emotions of masses of individuals by gaining more strength from their numbers—could be considered a neutral ground where, owing to the vague and indeterminate character of its expression, men came to unite with that much less distrust since the impressions made by this art are undefined. Music, in this sense, is the only *socializing* art.

As a composer, Liszt has so far produced little. His main works are his *Fantaisie sur la Fiancée*, the one on Paganini's *campanella*, a duet for two pianos on themes by M. Mendelssohn, a symphonic fantasy for piano and orchestra on two themes by M. Berlioz, and the piano arrangement of the latter's *Symphonie fantastique*.[42] Even though these works cannot be regarded as original,* since in keeping with the method followed by most composer-pianists they are either translations or written on preexistent themes, they nevertheless imply inspiration as much as merit. As the system adopted by the composer is already set out in them, we will devote our final pages to its examination. But in order to do so, we will indulge in a digression that will first enable us to shed light briefly on the question that remains to be treated, while also giving us the opportunity to expose the palingenesic and fundamental point of view, the only genuine one as we see it, from which the history of music is to be considered.[43]

It would be tempting to believe, as one surveys the history of modern music, that Christianity, which is both the source and principle of all that is true and beautiful in every genre, has expressed itself musically in an instrument that it has charged with a specific role and a special mission. It has done so by endowing this instrument with a certain royal, sovereign character and by including it within its essential eternity. The instrument in question is the organ. The idea we are putting forward may not be as paradoxical as it appears at first sight. For one thing, the organ is not an individual invention; it does not belong to a particular figure; like Gothic architecture, it is a social, collective, anonymous invention, the product of a whole civilization, the expression of a common feeling, and the realization of a universal thought. And if we reflect on this name *organ, organum*, we will find there a proof, a highly philosophical one in our view, of the

---

*M. Liszt has just published some *Harmonies poétiques et religieuses* for the piano. [Editor's note: this work first appeared in the *Gazette musicale* the previous week, on 7 June.]

origin we are attributing to it: it is the *organ* of that very thought and of Christian art.

This particular destination, this mission assigned to the organ, appears both in its structure and in the role it has fulfilled in musical history. We can only mention the first of these two points. To demonstrate the second, it is enough to establish on the testimony of historians that the organ created first, harmony; second, rhythm and measure; and third, that the orchestra and most modern instruments are descended from it. Thus the whole of musical art developed in the Middle Ages from the organ, which itself came out of Christianity, just as civilization comes from Christianity, manifested and perpetuated in a visible form by the Church.

The organ is thus the pivot on which all the developments of modern music turn. Its whole mission can be viewed from two perspectives: first, from the angle of *immutability*, in that it represents what is fixed and invariable in art; second, from the angle of *variety*, insofar as harmony, the orchestra, and instrumentation derive from it; these two perspectives can be compared to Gerbert's distinction between the two kinds of music, plain and measured.

As we consider it from the second of the above angles, however—as the generator of instruments and the orchestra—we see two further perspectives.[44] The organ is one and manifold; manifold because it contains all of the various instruments whose union forms the orchestra within it; and one because those same instruments it embraces in the unity of its structure are controlled by the same hand and, by being fused within a single harmony, contribute to the overall effect. So long as Catholicism was, in a way, the regulator of human thought, the organ alone ruled in the musical realm. The orchestra did not exist or, to state it better, existed only partially and fragmentarily. But once art, following a new impulse, was secularized and deserted the temple, the organ lost its empire and fell silent in the abandoned temple. The organ, however, has still enjoyed an indirect, remote sovereignty, by reproducing itself in the outside world in two ways corresponding to the two characteristics we noted when we considered it the generator of instruments. From the angle of harmonic unity, it has reproduced itself in the form of the piano; from the angle of the multiplicity of instruments, it has reproduced itself in the form of the orchestra. Through one, it has entered salons and concerts; through the other, it has taken over the theaters.

Thus is established the sovereignty of the organ, and whenever it is still called today *king of the instruments*,* it is clear that this expression is used with a real—though vague—feeling for this truth.

---

*Several of our readers no doubt are aware of this saying by Liszt: *The organ is the pope of the instruments.*

Leaving aside the question of knowing how the orchestra and the piano have progressed to the point at which we see them today, we will note two tendencies in their latest developments. While some composers—Rossini and his school—have brought numerous figurations and accompanimental formulas into the orchestra that had been provided for them by the mechanism of the piano, and which they had found, so to speak, ready-made under their fingers, elsewhere a new school has been formed which tries to appropriate for the piano certain combinations and effects that belong to instrumentation. The shining stars of this second school are Beethoven, Weber, Schubert, Moscheles, and Hummel. Thus, while the former have tried to bring the piano into the orchestra, the latter transfer the orchestra to the piano. Consequently, the orchestra and the piano, both proceeding from the organ like two branches from the same tree, are now arguably tending to come closer and meet, perhaps with a view someday to reattaching themselves to the common root and drawing a new sap from the regenerated soil of Christianity.

This is how we view the crux of the current problem of instrumental music; one should attach the various compositions of our young musician to the second system that we have tried to outline. We could not possibly analyze each of his pieces separately, but obviously in all of them Liszt has aimed to apply orchestration to the piano, that is to say, to make the piano *instrumental* and in dialogue with itself. He intends to continue and to complete the revolution started by his masters. Indeed, this is a grand, fertile idea, one that can tempt a young and strong imagination, since a revolution completed is as fine a thing as a revolution begun. It certainly will not be denied that the virtuoso is endowed with everything necessary to achieve great progress on the piano. We only fear lest his talent, which knows no difficulties, mislead him regarding the inherent defects of his instrument and over certain resources that are not so much those of the piano as his very own.

We must single out his *Fantaisie symphonique sur le chant du Pêcheur et le choeur des Brigands* by Mr. Berlioz, the latest and most important work by Liszt. He composed it last autumn when staying at La Chênaie with the Abbé de La Mennais. It can be easily understood that the deepest and most intimate sympathies of his soul should draw him naturally toward this extraordinary man. Liszt found in him more than a friend, and today he prides himself on being his disciple. The composition in question displays the most unexpected and delightful effects in the transformations of its two principal themes. He was able to derive from the two subjects incidental phrases full of originality, which are thrown into relief by a passionate and colorful orchestration. The bold new harmonic combinations reveal a very thorough knowledge, and the piece as a whole proves that, whenever he wishes, this most astonishing of pianists will be able to hold a high rank among the most able orchestrators.

We have reported the life of Liszt in every detail; we have followed him from step to step in all the phases of his existence, until that moment when the artist reached his maturity. By making the musician better known, we are also convinced that we have made the man better appreciated. Among the many diverse influences that have acted on that soul, which is both expansive and introverted, and open to all influences of his age, a triple anxiety, a triple need, has never ceased to make itself felt: the need to believe, the need to know and the need to act. And these three things—faith, which raises us toward God; science, which makes us know man; action, which is merely the positive, outer manifestation of our love for our fellow men—form a complete man; and it is only by covering this immense range that man comes closer and closer to the full extent of his necessary earthly development.

—Joseph d'Ortigue

NOTES

1. "La Musique mise à la portée de tout le monde, par M. Fétis," *Le Correspondant*, 27 August 1830; reprinted in Joseph d'Ortigue, *Écrits sur la musique: 1827–1846*, ed. Sylvia L'Écuyer (Paris: 2003), pp. 225–30. The timing of the article, just a month after the July Revolution, places it at a particularly ripe time for imagining new directions in critical writing.

2. The full title of the pamphlet is: *De la guerre des dilettanti, ou de la revolution opérée par M. Rossini dans l'opéra françois; et des rapports qui existent entre la musique, la littérature et les arts* (Paris, 1829). The extensive collection of d'Ortigue's journalism from 1829 to 1847 edited by Sylvia L'Écuyer offers an enormously useful overview of d'Ortigue's thought; together with an extensive biographical introduction, it is much the best source of information on the critic available (and to which I am greatly indebted here). D'Ortigue's own collection of articles, published in 1833 as *Le Balcon de l'Opéra*, has also been recently reissued by Minkoff (Geneva: 2002).

3. D'Ortigue's mother was cousin to Castil-Blaze's father; there is little evidence that the two were in contact once both were in Paris. D'Ortigue would eventually inherit his relative's coveted position as music critic of the *Journal des débats*, but not until decades later.

4. The article was republished the following year in German as "Adam Liszts Tagebuch": in *Neue Zeitschrift für Musik* 4 (1836): 13–16, 19–21, 23–4, 27–30, 31–3, 39–40. In November 1839, Liszt wrote to Marie d'Agoult: "I plan to get him to redo my biography: which will now form a complete volume and immediately be translated into German and probably into English." Adrian Williams, ed., *Franz Liszt: Selected Letters* (Oxford, Eng.: 1998), p. 118. The extended length of the original article might suggest that this could have been the initial intention as well, but in many ways it worked best within the *Gazette*, where it appeared a week after the publication there of Liszt's early single-movement composition *Harmonies poétiques et religieuses*, and in the middle of the composer's set of articles on the position of artists in society.

5. "De la Situation des artistes et de leur condition dans la société," *Gazette musicale de Paris* 3, 10, and 17 May; 26 July; 30 August; 11 October 1835; reprinted in Franz Liszt, *Pages romantiques*, ed. Jean Chantavoine (Paris: 1912; repr. 1985). Ralph P. Locke annotates the sixth installment on pp. 291–302 of this volume. On the history and philosophy of the *Gazette*, see Katharine Ellis, *Music Criticism in Nineteenth-Century France: "La Revue et Gazette musicale de Paris," 1834–80* (Cambridge, Eng.: 1995), esp. 48–55.

6. Émile Haraszti, *Franz Liszt* (Paris: 1969), p. 219, seems to have been the first modern critic to link Liszt with Anatole de Rhumilhey, the protagonist of d'Ortigue's novel, and the idea is explored by L'Écuyer in d'Ortigue, *Écrits*, pp. 84–85, where passages from the novel and the *Gazette* biography are placed side by side to demonstrate their similarity. L'Écuyer also proposes the monk Frère Paul as another possible model for the composer (p. 85).

7. On the genealogy of the *Weihekuss* tale, see Allan Keiler, "Liszt and Beethoven: The Creation of a Personal Myth," *19th-Century Music* 12 (1988): 116–31; and Alan Walker, "Beethoven's *Weihekuss* Revisited," in *Reflections on Liszt* (Ithaca, N.Y.: 2005), pp. 1–10. It is notable, however, that d'Ortigue makes no mention of the kiss itself, despite its origin being located here by several recent writers on the composer.

8. On d'Ortigue's relationship with Lamennais see L'Écuyer's biographical introduction in d'Ortigue, *Écrits*, esp. pp. 46–51. The literature on Liszt and Lamennais is more extensive; see in particular Alexander Main, "Liszt's *Lyon*: Music and the Social Conscience," *19th-Century Music* 4 (1981): 228–43; Paul Merrick, *Revolution and Religion in the Music of Liszt* (Cambridge, Eng.: 1987); and Arthur McCalla, "Liszt Bricoleur: Poetics and Providentialism in Early July Monarchy France," *History of European Ideas* 24 (1998): 71–92.

9. "Galerie biographique des artistes français et étrangers: V. Hector Berlioz," *Revue de Paris*, 23 December 1832; *Le Balcon de l'Opéra*, pp. 295–324; and in d'Ortigue, *Écrits*, pp. 277–90, where Berlioz's contributions are indicated in bold type. Like the Liszt biography, it was the first serious biography of the composer; a manuscript copy survives that shows the information from Berlioz that d'Ortigue wove directly into the article. D'Ortigue's biography of Onslow, on the other hand, took the form of an anecdote about a visit to the composer's country house, in which d'Ortigue quotes Onslow's own description of his biography directly ("Biographie musicale: George Onslow," *Revue de Paris*, 17 November 1833; in d'Ortigue, *Écrits*, pp. 352–61). In a letter to d'Ortigue, Onslow expressed displeasure that the critic had not disguised Onslow's contributions, since it gave the impression that the article had been commissioned by the composer (see *Écrits*, p. 352).

10. D'Ortigue's interest in the history of the organ recurs in numerous writings in the early 1830s, and in a letter of April 1832 to Renduel, the publisher of *Le Balcon de l'Opéra* and *La Sainte-Baume* (and of many of the most important romantic texts from the 1830s), d'Ortigue mentioned plans for a "historical and philosophical work" titled *De l'Orgue* and suggested to him by Victor Hugo; the work never appeared. See Adolphe Jullien, *Le Romantisme et l'éditeur Renduel* (Paris: 1897), p. 169.

11. On Ballanche, see Arthur McCalla, *A Romantic Historiosophy: The Philosophy of History of Pierre-Simon Ballanche* (Leiden: 1998), and "Liszt Bricoleur," which explores the differences between Ballanche's conception of historical progress and Lamennais's more activist model.

12. "Palingénésie musicale," *La France catholique* (November 1833): 25–7, 33–7; repr. in *L'Artiste* (8 and 15 December 1833): 221–24, 235–40. Perhaps d'Ortigue planned to expand the thoughts in these articles, or else perhaps Liszt had not seen them, since in the second of his own articles for the *Gazette musicale* ("De la situation des artistes," 10 May 1835), he mentions that "a musical palingenesis by [d'Ortigue] has been announced several times; we strongly hope that this important publication will not be delayed."

13. Heine, "Nuits florentines," *Revue et gazette musicale de Paris* (May 1836); quoted in McCalla, "Liszt Bricoleur," p. 86.

14. Liszt, *Lettres d'un bachelier ès musique* 7: "À M. Heine," *Revue et gazette musicale*, 8 July 1838; quoted in McCalla, "Liszt Bricoleur," p. 86.

15. L'Écuyer links d'Ortigue's biographical, anecdotal approach to that of his contemporary friend Charles Augustin Sainte-Beuve; see *Écrits*, pp. 106–10.

16. Letter from Liszt to Carolyne von Sayn-Wittgenstein, 12 May 1861, quoted in d'Ortigue, *Écrits*, 177.

17. A reference to d'Ortigue's biography of his close friend Hector Berlioz. See note 9 above for further information about the article.

18. A reference perhaps to Marie d'Agoult, unmentioned here only weeks after Liszt had left Paris to join her in Switzerland.

19. Here d'Ortigue resumes a habit of misspelling the name *Liszt* as *Listz,* as he had in fact already done in the title of this biographical study. Although we have retained the endearing addition of a *t* in *Frantz,* we have corrected his (inconsistent) misspellings of Liszt's last name, as well as two instances of *Mendelssohn* spelled as *Mendelshon.*

20. The appearance of Paganini, and the implied connection between him and Liszt, echoes the violinist's presence in the Berlioz biography, in which he is quoted giving approval to Berlioz's music at the famous 1832 concert.

21. *René*, by the vicomte de Chateaubriand, originally formed part of the author's immensely influential *Génie du christianisme* (1802)—the foundational text of Romantic Christianity—but was rereleased as a separate novel the same year.

22. This is the first claim of Beethoven's (doubtful) attendance at the concert, but the description is also notable for lacking any mention of the famous *Weihekuss*, by later accounts supposedly bestowed by Beethoven on Liszt at the same event. See note 7 above.

23. This story, for many years another staple of Liszt biography, also occurs for the first time here; two months later, Liszt's own account of the occasion would appear in the *Gazette musicale* (30 August 1835) in the fifth part of "De la situation des artistes."

24. The premature obituary of Liszt that had appeared in *Le Corsaire* in October 1828 also mentions the doting female attention from this time.

25. François-Joseph Talma (1763–1826), the greatest French actor of both the Empire and the Restoration.

26. James De Ville (1777–1846), the best-known English phrenologist in the 1820s and 1830s. Other famous heads that he felt included those of William Blake, George Eliot, and the Duke of Wellington.

27. *Don Sanche* was premiered at the Opéra on 17 October 1825; the second librettist was de Rancé.

28. A collection of fourth-century early monastic texts known in English as the *Apophthegms of the Fathers*.

29. Translator's note: This quotation comes from chapter 37 of Xavier de Maistre's *A Nocturnal Expedition Round My Room*; we are citing the translation by Edmund Goldsmid (Edinburgh: privately printed, 1886), p. 65.

30. A reference to Liszt's thwarted relationship with the seventeen-year-old Caroline de Saint-Cricq, daughter of King Charles X's minister of finance.

31. Pellico (1789–1854), the Italian playwright who had been imprisoned throughout the 1820s for his opposition to the Austrian government in Italy, in 1834 had published a book of pious maxims, *Dei doveri degli uomini*, which appeared in French translation the same year.

32. Chrétien Urhan, the devout violinist, violist, and eccentric composer, is now best remembered as the first soloist in Berlioz's *Harold en Italie*, and for turning his back to the stage in the orchestra at the Opéra in order to avoid the earthly temptations on show. His participation in many of the Beethoven chamber music performances in Paris in the early 1830s with the Baillot Quartet were regularly praised by d'Ortigue, who also published two longer appreciative sketches of him: "Album [...] Chrétien Urhan," *Revue de Paris* 4, March 1832, pp. 61–64, a review of Urhan's two quintets, reprinted in *Le Balcon de l'Opéra*, pp. 324–32, and *Écrits*, pp. 259–62; "Revue musicale," *La Quotidienne*, 4 December 1833, a review of Urhan's concert at the church of Saint-Vincent-de-Paul for St Cecilia's day, in *Écrits*, pp. 366–70.

33. Only one obituary, in *Le Corsaire*, appears to have been published; the decline in Liszt's health at this point, triggered by the death of his father, was almost certainly more closely bound to his break with Caroline de Saint-Cricq than is made clear here.

34. The *Essai sur l'indifférence en matière de religion*, by Liszt and d'Ortigue's revered guru Lamennais appeared in 1817; all the writers appreciated by Liszt's "other" were famous for their irreligious views.

35. The *Grande fantaisie sur la tyrolienne de l'opéra "La Fiancée" de Auber* was published in 1829 by Troupenas as Liszt's op. 1.

36. D'Ortigue's chronology here seems to be slightly confused: Dumas's *Antony* and Hugo's *Marion de Lorme* both date from 1831; the authors took advantage of the brief disappearance of censorship in the wake of the 1830 revolution to stage shocking subjects.

37. General Lafayette, a hero already from the revolution of 1789, had played his part in the brief reprise in 1830 when his appearance on the balcony of the Hôtel de Ville in Paris, tricolor in hand, had served to legitimize the new reign of Louis-Philippe.

38. Pierre-Claude-Victoire Boiste (1765–1824) produced his most famous work, the *Dictionnaire universel de la langue française* in 1800; later editions were edited by Charles Nodier.

39. Madame Dudevant was the real name of George Sand.

40. Josef Dessauer (1798–1876), a Bohemian composer best known for his Lieder, had been in Paris in 1831–32.

41. The concert in question took place on 9 April 1835.

42. The *Grande fantaisie sur la tyrolienne de l'opéra La Fiancée de Auber* was published by Troupenas as Liszt's op. 1 in 1829, and the *Grande fantaisie di bravura sur La clochette de Paganini* by Schlesinger as op. 2 in 1834; Schlesinger also published the arrangement of the *Symphonie fantastique* in the same year (reviewed by d'Ortigue in *Le Temps,* 13 January 1835). The other two works mentioned here remained unpublished in Liszt's lifetime; the duet for two pianos—the *Grosses Konzertstück über Mendelssohns Lieder ohne Worte,* S. 257—does not seem to have been performed complete (following Liszt's collapse at the concert in 1835) until 1984. Meanwhile, the symphonic fantasy (on two themes from Berlioz's *Lélio*) for piano and orchestra, S. 120, is the same piece that d'Ortigue mentions later as composed while Liszt was staying at the country house of the Abbé de Lamennais; the work was reviewed by d'Ortigue in *La Quotidienne* on 24 December 1836; reprinted in *Écrits sur la musique*, pp. 514–17.

43. On d'Ortigue's use of Ballanche's idea of palingenesis, see my introduction.

44. Much of the following four paragraphs appeared first (with slight changes) in the *Le Temps* review of Liszt's *Symphonie fantastique* arrangement from 13 January 1835.

Ludwig Rellstab's
Biographical Sketch of Liszt

INTRODUCED AND TRANSLATED BY ALLAN KEILER

The brief biographical sketch of Liszt by Ludwig Rellstab, which comes at the end of a modest volume in which he gathered together his essays on Liszt's Berlin performances during the early months of 1842, originally published in the *Vossische Zeitung*, is one of a small group of biographies of Liszt that appeared during his virtuoso years. These some half-dozen publications, in both French and German, began with Joseph d'Ortigue's biography published in the *Gazette musicale de Paris*, in June 1835. Only in 1843 did a second biography in French appear, by one J. Duverger, which, as we shall see, has interesting connections to Rellstab's. In between these two works there appeared, in addition to several biographical notices in standard musical lexicons, biographies in German by Johann Wilhelm Christern and Gustav Schilling, as well as Rellstab's. All coincided with Liszt's tours of Germany in the early 1840s.

It is easy to dismiss these contemporary reports as inaccurate and misleading. More often than not they are consigned to the dustbin of history as unworthy relics, to be superseded by the cold and objective truth of modern scholarship.[1] More recently the tide has changed. Scholars have begun to recognize how significantly these accounts mirror the social and cultural fabric through which Liszt's public persona, in all its complexity and contradiction, was fashioning itself during his most active years as a virtuoso.[2] What lends these early works particular relevance, however, is that Liszt was often on friendly terms with their authors, involving himself in one way or another with their biographical projects.

In the summer of 1834, Liszt was becoming more self-aware and focused about his artistic goals, attempting to create a self-image that would reflect his ideas about art and society. He spent nearly a month in the fall at La Chênaie with Abbé Félicité-Robert de Lamennais, to whom he had been introduced by d'Ortigue, and whose views on the relationship of religion and the arts were appealing. Only weeks before the appearance of d'Ortigue's biography, Liszt, using Marie d'Agoult as his collaborator, had presented himself to the French public as an author, with the first part of his *De la situation des artistes et de leur condition dans la société*.[3] Perhaps it was Marie herself who suggested the idea of a biography at so opportune a time; both would have found d'Ortigue a more than acceptable biographical agent.

After the events in Pest in January 1840 surrounding the presentation of the sword of honor to Liszt, and the ensuing furor in the Parisian press, Liszt attempted to encourage large-scale accounts of his concert activities and to exercise greater influence over projected biographies.[4] Indeed, establishing an acceptable biographical image in the press would become an important part of his strategies of self-management. By April he had already approached his friend Franz von Schober, an eyewitness to the events in Pest, urging him to publish an account of them that he knew would be sympathetic. Realizing that he had gone too far, he wrote to Schober on January 3 explaining, "I am afraid I was very indiscreet in asking you to be so good as to undertake this work. . . . But I will not speak of it anymore."[5] But speak of it he did, at the end of August: "A propos of Hungarian! I shall always value highly the work on my sojourn in Pest."[6] Schober eventually agreed to Liszt's proposal, in the form of a collection of articles on the Hungarian concerts he had written for the German press in 1842, which were published the following year as *Briefe über F. Liszts Aufenthalt in Ungarn*.

Liszt was more than pleased with Schober's chronicle of his Hungarian sojourn, but felt that unless at least some version of it could be adapted for the French press, it remained only a partial solution to the kind of damage control he was seeking. In the meantime, a second opportunity for a new, German biography arose in the person of Johann Christern, a prolific but uninspired Hamburg music teacher and composer, though, as a writer on musical subjects, not much more than a hardworking dilettante.[7] Christern was enthusiastic enough about Liszt's playing, which he had heard in Hamburg in the autumn of 1840 and again in the fall of 1841, and enterprising enough to want to capitalize on the excitement generated by most prolonged series of concerts Liszt had given so far in Germany, nine in all, and to prepare a biography for Liszt's German audiences. It is hard to say how much contact or discussion Liszt had with Christern. There is little evidence of the "authentic reports" promised on the title page. Profit was certainly a factor, at least for the publisher, Schuberth, for a list of Liszt's compositions is added as an appendix, with a reminder attached that two of the works listed were published by Schuberth and the whole list available from the publisher. In this connection, the rather bold statement in the first paragraph of the foreword, that Liszt was as great a composer as he was a virtuoso, makes some degree of sense.[8]

Christern's biography appeared, it has been estimated, sometime during the last two months of 1841, and it is doubtful whether Liszt had the time or inclination to occupy himself with it much beyond those months.[9] With his sights fixed squarely on Berlin, his thoughts would have turned to Ludwig Rellstab, the most widely read and influential music critic in the Prussian capital, whose well-known dislike of virtuosos would have made him a likely adversary Liszt could not afford to overlook. Although Rellstab is most often remembered today for having invented the title of "Moonlight" for Beethoven's Piano Sonata in C-sharp Minor, op. 27, no. 2, and, with more justification, for having provided the texts for the first seven songs of Schubert's *Schwanengesang*, he was astonishingly prolific as music critic, novelist, poet, and librettist. Indeed, there are no fewer than twenty-four volumes in the complete edition of his works. Although he studied piano with Ludwig Berger and theory with Bernhard Klein, both devoted to Beethoven and his legacy, Rellstab began his career as an artillery officer before turning to writing. In 1826 he became principal critic for the *Vossische Zeitung*, a post he held for more than two decades. Stylistically his critical writing is subjective, often impressionistic, and, under the influence of Jean Paul, the German Romantic poet whom he adored, it can be dense, bitingly ironic, and at times obscure. Although cosmopolitan in outlook, he is generally considered conservative in his musical and aesthetic sympathies. His dislike of Italian opera and the Rossini craze is well-known. In addition to Mozart, Haydn, and the early and middle works of Beethoven, he admired Cherubini, Weber, and Mendelssohn. Of the newer Romanticism he was wary and often critical.

Liszt's letter to Marie d'Agoult on 6 January, the day following his third appearance in Berlin in only five days, conveys how much thought he had given not only to Rellstab's reviews but to a meeting with Rellstab himself: "Here are some newspapers. I prefer to send you Rellstab's articles because Rellstab *ought* to be an adversary of mine. He is the *critic* par excellence in Berlin. I refused to call on him first—after my first concert he came to see me, and although of different minds on a number of points we can get on, as you will see from the lines that he has written about me."[10]

What, then, did Liszt find in Rellstab's reception that so pleased him? Certainly Rellstab's comparison of his virtuosity with Thalberg's, in his first review, must have brought him immense satisfaction: "Liszt encompasses all of Thalberg's abilities within his own. If Liszt doesn't offer what Thalberg offers, he could certainly do so. And while Liszt could accomplish any task that Thalberg can, the reverse is not true."[11] As for Liszt's playing on its own terms, Rellstab emphasized a number of traits that would continue to appear like leitmotives in subsequent reviews. For one thing, Rellstab argued, one must speak in poetic, not simply technical terms of Liszt's playing. Furthermore, Liszt's virtuosity is not limited to technical mastery alone but is inexorably bound up with his personality and intellect. Where he cannot follow Liszt, however, is his "pronounced lingering over individual traits" at the expense of the whole, as he writes in connection with Liszt's performance of the "Moonlight" Sonata.[12]

August Kahlert, in the *Neue Zeitschrift für Musik*, not to mention Mendelssohn, Schumann, and Wagner, all drew attention to the willful self-absorption that was so prominent a force in Liszt's playing.[13] But whereas Mendelssohn reacts with biting sarcasm to Liszt's utter disregard of the text of Beethoven's Violin Sonata in C Minor, op. 30, no. 2, and Schumann expresses moral outrage at Liszt's "obstinate independence" in a performance of the "Emperor" Concerto, Rellstab remains evenhanded and detached, even generous in the degree to which he allows Liszt his point of view.[14] He has many critical things to say, for example, about Liszt's performance of the "Moonlight" Sonata, one that is "not so much Beethoven's Sonata as what Liszt finds deepest within his own self about it, how it has stimulated and shaken him up."[15] He goes on to remark, in an unusual show of critical generosity, that nevertheless, "as I have said, Liszt continues to enjoy this right; after all is said and done he could follow no other law. Here criticism is not going to say what ought to be, but only what is."[16]

Why was Rellstab so willing to grant so much more leeway to Liszt than to others? In this regard the comparison that Rellstab drew with Paganini is instructive, as is the fact that he included a translation of most of the obituary Liszt wrote upon the violinist's death in 1840.[17] Paganini's lapses of taste, his errors of judgment, he says, are "inborn," the result of a "natural instinct," enclosing him in an "intellectual prison" brought about by his very nature. Liszt's lapses are merely "inculcated," "learned," the result of his youth and inexperience, the excesses he developed during his formative years in Paris. How much this view of Liszt is dictated by his admiration for what he saw as Liszt's intellectual brilliance, his generosity of spirit, his openness and curiosity, and how much by Liszt's tactical success in appealing to German nationalistic sentiments is hard to say. Both probably played a role. Of the warm friendship that surely developed between Rellstab and Liszt during those early months of 1842, one should not discount the more personal side, that of the understanding and trust that comes from a gradual recognition of shared experience and ideals. To judge from the biographical sketch alone, it is likely that Rellstab and Liszt spent some time together, going over published biographical material as well as whatever was on Liszt's mind with respect to Rellstab's projected biography.[18] No doubt common experiences emerged during their discussions that would have brought them together in personal ways. Rellstab's father, like Liszt's, wanted a career in music but was forced to abandon the possibility (his father's illness made it necessary for him to enter the family business). Partly to compensate, again like Adam Liszt, he hoped to realize his thwarted ambition through his son, driving him quite mercilessly in his musical studies.[19]

Rellstab's small volume appeared in March 1842 with the title *Franz Liszt. Beurtheilungen-Berichte-Lebensskizze*. It contains a half-dozen or so individual reviews of concerts, and among the articles that make up the *Berichte*, more general ones; the concluding "Liszt in Berlin" and "Liszt, ein Ereignis des öffentlichen Lebens," the longest and most detailed examinations of Liszt's artistic personality, are the ones to which Rellstab refers in the first paragraph of the biographical sketch translated below.[20] Although we do not know all of the circumstances that led to the volume's creation, we do know that it was at the request of an "unnamed, but easily recognized hand," as he tells us rather mysteriously in the preface, that Rellstab gathered these writings together. As for the biographical essay, there is some reason to believe that it was Liszt himself who suggested the idea to Rellstab, for it would give Liszt an opportunity to correct what he saw as errors and lapses of judgment on the part of his biographers, a concern that appears quite often in letters to Marie throughout 1842.[21] As the reader will see, Liszt contributed valuable information and points of view to Rellstab, although he was, as usual, selective about what he chose to include and ignore.

The publication of Rellstab's book did not end Liszt's involvement with biographical projects. He was still keen for a French-language biography, one that would satisfy the French intellectual elite, all the more so in early 1842 with the appearance of biographies by Christern and Rellstab that were making much of his German nationalistic stance. As early as February, he had asked Marie "to take charge as soon and as much as possible with my biography."[22] By November they had formed a plan to incorporate material from both Franz von Schober's collection of articles on German concerts and Rellstab's biographical sketch, under Marie's supervision, into a French-language biography of Liszt.[23] It appeared the following April, compiled and written by Marie—Liszt seems to have done little more than edit and reduce the length of the manuscript she submitted—under the first of her *noms de plume*, J. Duverger.[24]

Rellstab's book was treated harshly when it first appeared. Recognizing the value of the biographical sketch, one writer, with barely suppressed sarcasm, expressed surprise that Rellstab, usually a "calm and level-headed man," could show himself hardly less enthusiastic about Liszt than the "huge number of residents of the Prussian royal city."[25] But Rellstab, it seems, never wavered in his admiration of Liszt the virtuoso.[26] Indeed, he does not hesitate some four years later, in his homage to his teacher Ludwig Berger, whose teachings he revered above all others, to express sadness that Berger could not have known Liszt: "He [Berger] would have embraced him, in spite of his lapses of taste and abstruse singularities, with lively appreciation and greeted him with the greatest joy as king of the realm in which he himself was so mighty and noble a ruler."[27]

Life Sketch

From *Franz Liszt: Beurtheilungen–Berichte–Lebensskizze*
Berlin, J. Petsch, 1842

As we have already mentioned in the preface, we are obliged in this biographical essay by the limitations of space to reduce a more than lavish portrait to no more than a brief outline, even though Liszt's dazzlingly flamboyant life, deeply turbulent both on the surface and in its depths, a life endlessly puzzling psychologically, calls for the fullest possible treatment. Such a portrait, however, would have to be based on an extended period of work and a long and intellectually close relationship with the artist. A part of the relevant discussion, to which more of his personal circumstances and intellectual periods of development would give rise, is, by the way, obviated by the preceding attempt to present and explain in a general way the artist's views about life and art.

Liszt was born on 22 October 1811, in the Hungarian village of Raiding, in the district of Oedenburg. His father, Adam Liszt, was employed as a bookkeeping official by Prince Esterházy. With his intelligence and good sense he held fast to a higher aim, however, that far exceeded the circumstances of his life. Gifted with uncommon musical abilities—he played the cello very well and, of course, the violin, and later acquired a creditable proficiency at the piano—the principal happiness of his life was to be in close contact with the great musical talents brought together in the orchestra of Prince Esterházy at Eisenstadt. Adam Liszt lived in close contact with Joseph Haydn, and Hummel, who frequented Eisenstadt over a long period, also numbered among his musical friends; even Cherubini came there a few times. Since Adam Liszt took part in quartet performances and other chamber works, his talent, although that of a dilettante, must have been first-rate in view of the fact that he was able to hold his own in the presence of such professionals. The musical abilities of his son are at least in part a handsome legacy that nature all the more generously bestowed on him in the richest abundance.

Franz Liszt was the only child of his parents, their entire hope and their entire happiness. This was especially true for his father, who brooded endlessly over his own failed career, and thus thought all the more about directing his son toward what he himself had been deprived of. Franz was expected to become something significant, something that would stand out above the ordinary, although, to be sure, something as yet undecided. In light of the respect enjoyed by the clerical state, especially in the Catholic denomination, the sensitive temperament of the boy may have led his father to the thought that his son had aspirations toward the church. He asked him once, "Do you want to become a priest, Franz?" "No, I don't want to become a priest." "Then such a man as this one?" the father went on, indicating the portrait of Gluck and other famous musicians that hung in the room. "Yes, I would like to become such a man." How right it seems that the boy's wish was guided by an inner desire, a wish that he himself had hardly grasped!

The following event gives a decisive indication of his musical talent. One day Adam played the Concerto in C-sharp Minor of Ries; Franz, leaning on the instrument, listened with fierce attentiveness. In the evening, during a walk in the garden, he sang the melody of the theme. This ability to remember a by-no-means simple series of musical tones in one so young, in one whose memory was still untrained, was a sign of the most significant talent. It was at this point that his father gave in to his son's urgent pleas and began instruction with him on the piano. Franz was then six years old, so his musical instruction did not begin at an excessively early age, certainly to his good fortune.

In several biographical sketches it is reported that during this time and in the years following a tendency toward religious fervor already exhibited itself in the boy. Liszt indicates that these reports are thoroughly erroneous, especially the reference in the *Universal-Lexikon der Tonkunst* that he had at the time already read Chateaubriand's *René* and been profoundly moved by it, that he had sought solitude and had spent half a year in a deeply melancholic mood. There is no doubting these circumstances, but they occurred some ten years later, when he had already been living in Paris for a while. Tenderness and gentleness were, to be sure, in spite of the boy's liveliness, predominant in his character, but not so much as to lead him in any way, at that time, to spiritual eccentricities.

His musical progress under the guidance of his father was remarkable. After three years of instruction, his playing was so exceptional that he was able to appear in public. A concert in Oedenburg was arranged, in which he performed the Concerto in E-flat Major of Ries and a free fantasy, amid the enthusiastic applause of an astonished audience. That he was stricken with the "old fever," as it is referred to in some biographies, immediately before he began to play, is something the artist is unable to recall. Although he became ill several times with attacks of fever in this period of his boyhood, it seems to us that people have attributed too much importance to what is no more than a chance occurrence.[28]

There is no truth to the account, repeated everywhere, that Prince Esterházy presented the young virtuoso with a gift of 50 ducats. Because of his relationship with Adam Liszt, the Prince may have been the individual most likely to support Franz's talent, a talent blossoming, so to speak, under his very authority, but he disregarded rather than supported it. It was rather the Hungarian Counts Amadé and Zapary who, with the most worthy and genuine appreciation of the boy's rare talent, offered him, after a brilliantly successful concert in Pressburg, a yearly stipend of 600 florins C.M. for a period of six years.[29] It was this stipend that enabled the father to resign his position and, freed from other obligations, to pursue his plans for his son's artistic education. Of course, neither of these noble-minded men could have known what rich fruit this seed would eventually bear; indeed, they have without question earned the thanks of the entire world of music.

It was in Vienna, in 1821, with this help, that the boy's talent was able to develop further. Although already overwhelmed with his teaching duties, Carl Czerny, with truly noble unselfishness, was prepared to take charge of the boy's training at the keyboard, while Salieri took charge of his studies in composition. Thinking it probable that, as far as fundamental problems of technique were concerned, there was still much catching up for his brilliant student, Czerny gave him at first Clementi sonatas and, it is true, the easier ones. This injured the young virtuoso's pride, however, because he was certainly able to play them at sight without hesitation. As for Czerny, he was not happy with details of execution, with touch, fingering, and so on, and held the talented boy, who wanted so urgently to press on ahead, to these indispensable fundamentals with absolute strictness. Because of this, ill feeling arose in the boy at first, and he devised various sly tricks in order to escape from what appeared to him as tyrannical and humiliating schooling. He thus wrote down bad fingerings for himself and then complained to his father about his teacher, who was demanding something so incorrect from him. But before long the schism was healed when more difficult tasks were put before the ambitious boy, and both affection and trust were restored.

Meanwhile, Liszt was hard at work composing. Although Salieri did not put him through a rigorous study of counterpoint, a direction in music in which he himself was not entirely at ease, he nonetheless lavished real affection on him, keeping him working diligently on genuine exercises in composition. He had him write small sacred pieces—Liszt still remembers a *Tantum ergo*, for example, that he composed under the supervision of his teacher—and also worked with him on score reading, how to accompany, and so on. After a year and a half of the most diligent study, during which the young virtuoso frequently aroused the astonishment of musical connoisseurs—he once played, among other things, at sight and without once faltering, the Concerto in B Minor of Hummel, one of the most demanding works for the piano—the moment apparently arrived when he was ready to be heard successfully in Vienna. Indeed, the fame of this remarkably endowed boy had already spread throughout the entire imperial city, even as far as the solitary Beethoven, to whom he was introduced by Professor Schindler, his well-known biographer. According to Schindler's own account, Beethoven is supposed not to have been exactly friendly during this visit, whereas Liszt really does not recall having encountered anything unfriendly on the part of the great master, whose innermost nature was invariably full of love. Beethoven even attended the young virtuoso's concert, arranged soon after, something extremely rare given his total seclusion and his melancholy disposition, and gave him the most decisive, though in its way the most formal sign of praise.[30]

The audience erupted nevertheless with the greatest enthusiasm, overwhelming the astonishingly talented boy with the most generous tribute of applause. As a result, Adam Liszt thought it appropriate to arrange a second concert soon after. These two concerts took place in Town Hall and in the small Redoutensaal. Liszt played the Concertos in A Minor and B Minor of Hummel as well as several other pieces, and a free fantasy, which he was especially fond of doing in those years, constructing them in the most felicitous ways.[31]

The success of these two concerts provided Adam Liszt with the means to continue his son's education under even more favorable circumstances, by transplanting it to a more important setting. Paris was the goal toward which Adam Liszt, as circumspect as he was zealously ambitious, was aspiring. In spite of many a spectacular decline, Paris was still the training ground for the most thorough musical education, indeed the most stimulating and varied scene when it came to the arts. In 1823, he journeyed to Paris by way of Munich and Stuttgart, where Liszt performed publicly to the greatest applause, yet where, having grown into the most astonishingly complete and unique artist that we now recognize him to be, he has not been heard since his early years of training.

To provide his son with the Conservatory's outstanding musical training was the father's chief purpose in departing for Paris. Cherubini, however, who stood at the head of this institution, denied him admission on grounds that he was foreign. We will not go into the matter of whether this admittedly existing rule could bear no exception. We refuse to believe it, inasmuch as Cherubini himself was not native-born. Cherubini's bitter isolation and dismissive nature may well be at least partly responsible. This initial setback, however, was in no way damaging to his success. Liszt became quickly well-known through his talent, and after having played to the greatest acclaim before the Duke of Orleans, the present King of France, became everyone's object of admiration, and the highest social circles fought for the privilege of paying homage to the astonishing child. Gold, fame, adulation poured down on him with equal immoderation not simply because he was a musical prodigy, but also on account of his other intellectual gifts, which aroused the greatest interest. Even if the triumph was genuinely earned, the extravagance of the reception plainly presented dangerous pitfalls for the boy's intellectual development. Nevertheless, the serious opposition of a strong, thoroughly noble and unselfish will, from a father who kept only the highest artistic goals in view, a father blessed by nature to his very core with a good heart, were the best defenses against these dangers. His son happily put behind him the critical transition from childhood to youth.

With respect to music, Liszt had made continuous and painstaking progress in the intervening years. He studied counterpoint with Reicha for more than a year, proceeding as far as its most complex procedures, a direction that he nevertheless openly admits to subsequently abandoning as something less appealing to his nature, and therefore more or less losing the confidence he had once acquired in it. His father had him do exercises conscientiously. He thus had to play among other things a number of Bach fugues every afternoon, a practice to which we owe perhaps the truly marvelous mastery with which he still performs to this day this most difficult of tasks. Often he had to transpose these to other keys, something which, as stated in the *Lexikon der Tonkunst*, was "child's play" for him.*

Liszt made several trips from Paris, in particular two to England, which brought him, in addition to the acclaim that was as frequent there as in France, a broadening of his artistic views in many directions. A tour of the provinces, to Bordeaux, Toulouse, Montpellier, Rheims, Marseilles, and Lyon took place during this period. A certain playful tendency, as in his early studies with Czerny, even now showed itself occasionally. In Bordeaux, for example, he played a sonata of his own before a famous

---

* When, in looking through biographies with Liszt, I came to this place, he exclaimed in quite a lively manner: "Child's play? Not at all. It was very difficult for me and I hesitated and often went wrong. I can do it, of course, but it is even now a difficult task for me." He wanted to give it a try on the spot, but in so doing he really got tangled up. It seems to us no inconsiderable feature of the artist's natural candor that he is ready to disclaim exaggerated rumors about himself and to give to the biographer a more modest version.

violin virtuoso and passed it off as one of Beethoven's, managing thereby to arouse utter admiration. What has passed from French biographies into German, concerning a difficulty that is supposed to have happened to him there—which is why he would not speak about his stay there—is pure fiction, or appears to rest entirely upon errors.[32]

During this period Liszt was also diligently composing, not only for his instrument. In addition, he made a name for himself with a small-scale opera, *Don Sanche, ou Le Château d'amour* on a text that the prolific Theaulon had provided him. He speaks highly and with gratitude of Paer for his friendly help and advice in this youthful undertaking, which was received with encouraging applause, running through four or five performances at the theater of the Académie royale.

Around this time, Liszt suffered an inner crisis. Adrift in youthful turmoil, not satisfied with musical success alone, without a safe outlet for, or the means to appease or resolve the urgent feelings driving him, he sought them—an error that often occurs—not deep within himself, but in external things redeemed only by their high-mindedness. He thus lapsed into fervid religiosity. Understandably, his sensible father opposed this tendency, which the son, as a consequence, concealed as carefully as possible within his inner life. Only in the evening, when he went to bed, did he give full play to the urgings of his heart, stole out of bed, and poured out his young soul for hours in the most fervent prayers. Anyone who is able to comprehend psychic struggles will be able to recognize in such lapses the noble and profound character of the soul that has submitted to them. He sought consolation in the sustained reading of works which, nevertheless, strengthened his mawkish inclinations. *Les Pères du désert* was now his favorite book, indeed nearly the only one with which he occupied himself.[33] Music was close to repugnant to him; he pursued it only in order to satisfy his father. The tours of the French provinces already referred to, and later on a trip to Switzerland, followed by a third trip to England, appear to have been the means by which his father attempted to struggle against his son's inclinations, which were gradually taking root in him. The last tour was a continuous series of triumphs of his brilliant virtuosity, which he achieved particularly at the Drury Lane Theater. Nonetheless, not only these psychic conflicts, but the acute nervous stimulation inseparable from music had upset his physical health. In order to restore it, his father went to Boulogne with him. Only here, where his son regained his health, did his father meet his death, on Saint Augustus Day, 1827.[34]

Liszt felt this painful blow with all the fervor of a youthful heart, for in spite of his father's strictness, he had nevertheless respected and loved that part of him that never deviated from the most noble principles, that

held fast to an ambition directed toward higher ideals. In his youthful innocence, he felt the need then and there to urge his mother, who was still
living in Hungary, to settle in Paris, where she has since made her home
and where she lives with her son on the closest terms. And yet in the natural order of things, one tends to feel the freedom and independence that
accompany one's growing maturity as something beneficial. And so it was
with Liszt. Unreservedly self-motivated intellectually, he entered upon a
new phase of his life.

The immediate steps along this path were not without the most bitter
struggles. He had won the love of a brilliant young girl, who possessed
both position and wealth.[35] Even in France those prejudices, or shall we
say those superficial, base views about life, appeared not to have been completely uprooted by the storms of revolutions, which strive to exert their
material might over the highest intellectual nobility. The girl's father was
opposed to the union. Liszt gave in with a pride more noble than the pride
of birth. But the pain he suffered acted with destructive force on his passionately fervent heart. He was forced to undergo a harsh psychological
struggle that suddenly took him away once again from the most varied
artistic activity that had taken possession of him with the most passionate
force—he was practicing, composing, teaching—and led him to those
mystically gloomy regions that had once before enveloped him. This second critical period, gradually gaining strength, was much more violent
than the first. He buried himself in reclusive reflection and study, threw
aside his art, stripping it of all worldly connection, shut himself up with
his books, avoided all human contact. He saw his mother for months on
end only at mealtime, facing her at the table completely silent.

Prayer was the only consolation his heart would allow. At the same
time, an inquiring impulse drove him to seek out truth, to struggle free
of these circumstances. He read an immense amount and also attempted
to gain, through his reading of philosophical texts, clarity about the doubts
that tormented him. Beside the usual old favorites he read during difficult times, he chose works that formed a contrast with them—Voltaire,
Rousseau, Schelling. And in point of fact it was finally his intellectual
strength that brought him back on the right path. Perhaps his physical
crisis also hastened the crisis his soul was undergoing. Having allowed his
dreams, his notions, and his hopes to lead him astray for so long, he not
only returned to the firm foundation of truth, to the sunny kingdom of
art and of life, but took hold of it with his whole being. But what is
expressed in this connection in several biographies about him, that he threw
himself into a frenzy and whirlpool of worldly pleasures, is an interpretation of his altered direction both untrue and unworthy, an interpretation

he simply yet decisively rejects. His intellectual powers healed and sustained him now continuously. He felt the need to look inward for his aspirations. As an adult, both physically and mentally, he now felt he was no longer in the condition in which he first entered public life as a child. He felt it as his obligation, imposed on him by virtue of the brilliant, truly miraculous successes of his youth, to live up to his artistic promise through his achievements. "More mature and stronger, I didn't want to content myself with less than was the case when I was a child." "I had been," he joked, "the *petit prodige*. Now I felt a calling, an obligation to myself to become the *grand prodige!*"

All his efforts were directed toward this one aim. He practiced, if now with more abandon, yet with tremendous persistence. He composed a great deal, trying out all manner of fashions depending on his intellectual mood of the moment. He supported himself by giving lessons, for which he had the most extraordinary talent and much more aptitude than one would assume from his artistic temperament.[36] Altogether his scientific knowledge of the piano is one that has been acquired with the greatest sense of purpose, and in this connection he has taken notice of everything of importance that has taken place in the world of music.

In his mood of exceptional vitality and passionate inclination, every intellectual happening must have seized him with the most singular impact. One such example is the July Revolution, which fell within this period of his life and filled him with the most passionate enthusiasm. By the same token, he had created other hopes for himself from its consequences, and in this connection allied himself completely with the youth of France. He even abandoned the artistic intentions he had conceived in the first enthusiasm for this historical event. He wanted to write a *Sinfonie révolutionnaire* whose themes he had put together from a Hussite song, a Protestant chorale, and "the Marseillaise." On the whole what he wanted to express in it was more the idea of a Reformation that reconciles, and thus to make the historical moment symbolically comprehensible in religious terms. The political turn that the events took led him away, however, from his purpose.

Saint-Simonism, in full bloom at the time, also took hold of him with gripping force. But it was more its fundamental ideas than the later degenerate forms that attracted him. Its governing idea, which paid due course to both heart and mind, is to construct human society solely on a peaceable (or *friedseligen*, as Liszt has expressed it) foundation and to acknowledge only three essential distinctions—a kind of intellectual or spiritual Trinity—in the activity devoted to the preservation of the whole—the scientific, the artistic, and the industrial—and, to the contrary, to abolish all external barriers and differences. Such was the foundation of the system that won his warm sympathy. Later, when its principles came to be violated, when strange, untenable forms developed from a falsely understood application of these principles, he lost no time in detaching himself from them.

This period of his life lasted until 1833. Because of a personal event, the following year was of decisive significance for the artist. He entered, although under conflicting circumstances, an affair of the heart. The details are not meant for the general public.[37] As a consequence of this relationship it happened that he left Paris for a rather long time, going first to Switzerland, then Italy. This period was exceptionally productive for him artistically, with a series of independent compositions that he has not yet published, nor even yet arranged and written down as a unit. He has nevertheless gathered part of them together in a large work of several volumes, to which, as already mentioned, he has given the title *Années de pèlerinage*. It is above all from what he sends out into the world of this collection that his importance as a composer will be judged. The two samples that he offered in his concert (cf. p. 22)[38] promise something extraordinarily beautiful.

As far as events are concerned, the artist's life from this period on has become almost entirely a public one. The exceptional stage he has reached as an artist affords him everywhere the same successes he has achieved before our eyes. Paris, Italy, England, but above all Hungary, his homeland, and our German homeland have all witnessed them enthusiastically. The most brilliant, indeed truly uplifting successes have been those in Hungary. To the enthusiasm that the artist aroused was added the Hungarians' pride in their famous countryman and their gratitude for the huge charitable donations he made as a result of the concerts he presented in the imperial city of Vienna, to which he had hastened from Italy after the unprecedented disaster of the Danube floods. In the context of this union of three powerful elements of enthusiasm and respect, he was named an honorary citizen of two Hungarian cities and, in the Theater in Pest, with the acclamation of the crowd, a sword of honor was presented to him by the greatest nobility of the land with the entreaty that by accepting it he would agree to preserve above all his Hungarian nationality. For the sword, in Hungary, is the national symbol of the rights of free male citizens (*freien Männerrechts*).*

In a similarly brilliant, genuinely royal manner Liszt was acclaimed in the Rhineland, where he won for himself a second home, a kind of citizenship of the heart and mind, through his concerts for the Beethoven

---

* Soon to appear are letters which a friend of Liszt's is bringing out about his Hungarian sojourn that will give us a more detailed description of these events.[39]

monument and the completion of the Cologne cathedral and by a leisurely tour of the towns along the Rhine, including a visit to the island of Nonnenwörth. On 22 August 1841 he enjoyed an unusual and brilliant triumph there, when the Choral Society of Cologne, fetching him from the island in a magnificent steamboat adorned with flags of every description and discharging mortar fire, afforded him a journey filled with song and pleasure such as never before have sparkled on the waves of the Rhine.

What happened here in our home city—the way the enthusiasm for his extraordinary appearance turned out to be something truly popular— we have already described in our reports about those events, at least as far as the facts are concerned, in the most cursory way.

What remains for us to accomplish is to take another look at the unique character of his artistic and intellectual career and to see how it has turned out. Inasmuch as we have already attempted to describe and explain it abundantly, we want now to confine ourselves more to matters of fact. We think it would be interesting in that connection to go back to a childhood anecdote that the artist himself has confirmed to us and given a more detailed account.

The phrenology of Franz Gall has found its many opponents, yet it has been confirmed on occasion in remarkable ways. Liszt himself, when he was fifteen, was presented the occasion for a Gallean examination. He was taken to London, to the famous phrenologist Deville, to whom he was introduced as a boy who would not amount to anything, who showed no ability at all. The scholar was asked if he might detect, by examining his skull, any tendency that might promise some hope for his development. Deville touched the boy's head and said, then and there, strongly affected, "Have you given him a chance with music? That would certainly be my advice." One can easily imagine the happy impression this judgment made on everyone present.

Perhaps Deville, with more investigations, might have been able to make further claims of the greatest importance, for though Liszt's other intellectual gifts have not turned decisively into achievements, they belong nonetheless, in themselves and in degree, to the most extraordinary. They have led him along the wondrous path on which we have accompanied him. But will the brilliance of this rarest of individuals leave behind a permanent impact as well? Is there bound up with the brilliant light a deeper fire, an inner, enduring, fertile warmth? Let us for the present leave this question unresolved and consider where he stands now.

Liszt stands on the summit of virtuosity. He has intellectualized its mechanical life to a degree as no one before him. The appearance of Paganini, which affected him to an indescribable degree, had a significant impact on him in this regard. In a dignified and deeply considered article in the *Revue musicale,* "Paganini à propos de sa mort," an article of decisive importance for shedding light on Liszt's intellectual and artistic efforts, he has spoken out with absolute clarity on his views about this artist and the manner in which one can become the heir to his fame. We quote the following passage from it.*

> I do not hesitate to say: a figure like Paganini can never appear again . . . but there are other ways in which it is possible to achieve a comparable renown and a higher authority.
>
> To regard art not as a certain means to achieve selfish advantage or a sterile fame, but as a congenial force, one that brings people together and unites them; to elevate one's life to that high rank whose ideal is talent; to make artists aware of what they can and must be; to prevail over public opinion through the superior force of a noble way of life—this is the task to which an artist must be devoted who feels strong enough to lay claim to a share of the inheritance of Paganini.
>
> Although difficult, the task is not absolutely impossible. Today, the path to success remains broad for all those who strive for prestige. Everyone who dedicates his art to a principle or a conviction may consider himself assured of a sympathetic reception. Everyone anticipates a new organization of the political conditions of society. Without overstating the significance of the artist in the transformation of society, without proclaiming in grandiose expressions, as one has so often done, his mission and his apostolate, we believe that his position is allotted him by the design of Providence, and that he too is called upon, for his part, to collaborate in the creation of a stable and ethical universe.
>
> From this moment on, may the future artist, with his whole heart, renounce every egotistical and vain role, of which, we believe, Paganini was a last and famous example. May he set his purpose not in himself but beyond himself; may virtuosity be for him a means, not an ultimate goal; may he call to mind that *nobility obliges,* as an old proverb expresses it, just as we are able to say today with as much, nay more, justification, *genius obliges.*

We may well take this as a statement of the solemn promise according to which Liszt has set out upon his career. Who would be able to claim

---

* From the translation that appeared in no. 25 of the *Magazin für die Lit. des Auslandes* (1842).[40]

for him a more worthy conception of it, inasmuch as it is associated with decency in both thought and action?

Whether it is, after all, the noblest career, insofar as art is concerned, to which he can lay claim, or whether there was for him a calling to a higher path and the strength to achieve it is another question. As we have already stated many times, it seems to us that the enormous process of maturing with regard to Liszt's inner life has not yet been brought to a close, for the nature of such an intellect does not mature as tranquilly or quickly as do those of a lesser order. He still struggles on the stormy sea of passion; he is a torrent bursting forth that is still searching for its proper channel. The things that he values and loves the most are more revealing to us than what he personally gives us, which is capable of the most varied interpretations.

We do not want to mention here those eternal geniuses placed at the very summit of art by universal acknowledgment, although it is always a significant sign that Liszt appears to assign Beethoven the highest place among them. Let us rather turn to those with whom he has lived, struggled, and developed. As far as keyboard virtuosity is concerned, he reveres Chopin, respects Moscheles, gives all the others their due, although he has a profound aversion against mechanical perfection without intellectual acuteness. How he especially loves Schubert as a composer we have seen. As for the French, Berlioz is the one for whom he feels the closest kinship. The lighter, newer French music of Auber, Adam, Halévy has little effect on him. He feels that comic opera has closed its account with Boieldieu. It is understandable, then, when the artist says that his mind is drawn irresistibly toward or away from paintings, scholarly literature (especially religious-philosophical literature), or poetry in similar ways. He is conversant with French *belles-lettres* in an unusually comprehensive way. The more recent works of Romanticism, especially Victor Hugo, have inspired him profoundly. He knows German literature less well, only a few things of Lessing, Goethe's *Faust*, and some recent works, which have attracted attention in our circle, too. Rather than instructing him in what is true and authentic in German learning, however, they give him false notions about us. He feels the strongest kinship with Lord Byron. He is the poet, as Liszt himself admits, whom he has embraced, to whom he has abandoned himself completely. The choice is decisive as far as his intellectual development is concerned. It more than anything else shows the hope to be justified, if we may thus express it, that the very same intellectual development still has to await a new phase, perhaps a final affirming and ennobling transformation. Were any remote or unfamiliar intellectual and poetic force suited to negotiate the passage from these passionate conditions into those of higher enlightenment and discretion, it would be, in our opinion, that of Jean Paul, whose ethical authority and titanic powers of fantasy were able to awaken, in ways that we cannot admire enough, the highest faith and the truest and noblest convictions.

Still, in the most unadulterated and surest way, powerfully maturing forces become reconciled of their own accord.

In the noble and worthy tasks that the artist has set himself, may he add these last, the noblest and most worthy. In their perfect and harmonious fusion, all moral and artistic elements collapse into one point, which lies, to be sure, in the unconquered realm of the ideal! It is not our right but his alone to decide how closely he makes contact with the full extent of his being and his powers. No one has the power fully to achieve, but each has the power to strive; few, however, have the decisive courage. Still, the eagle flies toward the sun!

NOTES

1. I have not attempted to correct every factual error in Rellstab's biography, which I think would be both tedious and unnecessary. At least some of the errors belong to the long uncritically anecdotal history of Liszt biography—for example, the legend that Adam Liszt was on friendly terms with Joseph Haydn—and these will eventually be eliminated as Liszt biography achieves a more critical attitude toward such anecdotal material.

2. See, for example, Dana Gooley, *The Virtuoso Liszt* (Cambridge, Eng.: 2004), whose use of contemporary documents, including the early biographies of Liszt, has considerably enriched our understanding of the virtuoso Liszt within the social and political context of the 1840s.

3. Liszt's *De la situation* appeared in six installments, 3 May, 10 May, 17 May, 26 July, 30 August, 11 October, in the second volume (1835) of the *Gazette musicale*; the sixth installment is included in the present collection, see pp. 291–302.

4. Liszt's reception of this nationalist Hungarian sabre precipitated a public relations crisis both in the Danube region and beyond, as explored in depth in Dana Gooley's *The Virtuoso Liszt*, pp. 129–55.

5. La Mara, ed., *Letters of Franz Liszt*, trans. Constance Bache, 2 vols. (London: 1894), vol. 1, p. 42.

6. Ibid., p. 47.

7. See Carl Engel, "Views and Reviews," *Musical Quarterly* 22 (1936): 354–61, for a short biography of Christern and a partial list of corrections and comments Liszt made in a copy of Christern's biography, acquired by the Library of Congress in 1924.

8. The more lasting interest shown in Christern's biography comes from the handwritten corrections that Liszt made in the published text, presumably for a second edition, one that never materialized. The corrections are interesting as far as they go, but each one has to be evaluated on its own terms. Alan Walker, for example, goes too far when he reads these corrections as evidence of the "remarkable objectivity with which [Liszt] viewed himself as a biographical topic" in *Franz Liszt: The Virtuoso Years 1811–1847* (New York: 1983), p. 4. For all the valuable factual corrections Liszt makes, he perpetuates errors, some unknowingly, to be sure. As for his attempts to "remove exaggeration," Liszt is selective, removing some and leaving others, particularly those overwritten tributes to his strong German nationalist sentiments, which clearly could only have pleased him.

9. See Engel, "Views and Reviews," p. 357.

10. Serge Gut and Jacqueline Bellas, eds., *Correspondance Franz Liszt, Marie d'Agoult* (Paris: 2001), p. 871.

11. Ludwig Rellstab, *Franz Liszt: Beurtheilungen-Berichte-Lebensskizze* (Berlin: 1842), p. 2.

12. Ibid., p. 7.

13. August Kahlert's "Das Concertwesen der Gegenwart" appeared in *Neue Zeitschrift fur Musik* 16 (1842). Kahlert (1807–64) wrote prolifically on the philosophy and aesthetics of music and its history, forming a close friendship with Schumann as well as with poets and philosophers of the period. He was a regular contributor to the *NZfM* as well as other German periodicals. See also Axel Schröter, *"Der Name Beethoven ist heilig in der Kunst": Studien zu Liszts Beethoven-Rezeption*, vol. 1 (Sinzig: 1999), p. 167ff.

14. See Schröter, *"Der Name Beethoven,"* p. 168.

15. Rellstab, *Franz Liszt*, p. 7.

16. Ibid.

17. Ibid., p. 52.

18. Apparently on comfortable enough terms with Liszt, Rellstab was willing to accede, for example, to the request of students to intercede with Liszt about reducing ticket prices for them. See Rellstab (1842), pp. 28–29.

19. On Rellstab's early years, see Jürgen Rehm, *Zur Musikrezeption im vormärzlichen Berlin: Die Präsentation bürgerlichen Selbstverständnisses und biedermeierlicher Kunstanschauung in den Musikkritiken Ludwig Rellstabs* (Hildesheim: 1983), p. 50ff.

20. The whole of Rellstab's book was reprinted in *Liszt Saeculum*, in seven installments between 1978 and 1984.

21. In the preface, Rellstab merely says that "complying with a different wish" he has added a biographical sketch to his collection of articles. He goes on to explain that his sketch is merely a preparation for a much larger work—this too is hinted at in the opening paragraph of the biography—and that the value of his work so far comes, in part, from the personal communications with Liszt. It would be surprising, then, if the "different wish" was not that of Liszt himself.

22. The letter to Marie, written 15 February, goes on to say: "I am being asked for it from all sides. It is a terribly important thing to me." Gut, *Correspondance*, p. 885. Once again, on 11 April, Liszt brings up the matter of a biography with Marie: "I won't press you for a biography, but you cannot imagine how annoyed I am with this pile of biographical notices that are swarming all over German papers. You will do me an important service in putting all of this in order" (p. 901). At this point, as he tells Marie, he intends to have the intended biography signed by Belloni, who was Liszt's secretary at the time.

23. By this time, both the Schober and Rellstab accounts had appeared, both in March. Liszt was pleased enough to consider using them in some way as part of the intended biography in French. This is what he explained to Marie, in a letter of 29 November 1842. By that point he realized that merely to translate both as part of a projected biography would make too long a work so that, as he tells Marie, "it will be necessary for you to make the necessary abbreviations." Gut, *Correspondance*, p. 941. For her part, Marie had already suggested Pascallet as a possible publisher. Once again, the following day (November 30), Liszt wrote to Marie about the intended biography. Liszt had already written to Rellstab to supply documents and had already gone over a manuscript that is far too long: "you must be so good as to give another two weeks of your attention to this annoying task" (p. 953). Unfortunately, what to do about Schober and Rellstab had not been settled: "One will have to see," Liszt tells Marie, "in what proportion one will have to intermingle Schober and Rellstab with the Pascallet Biography."

24. The Duverger biography written and assembled by Marie d'Agoult is a compilation of sorts. Marie follows the narrative order of Rellstab's sketch for the most part, expanding and elaborating when she saw fit. As for Schober, a translation of one of the articles in his book is incorporated as one of the appendices, along with Liszt's essay on Paganini. In addition, she had before her original documents, one of them perhaps the childhood diary of Liszt, which has been published as *Franz Liszt Tagebuch 1827*, ed. Detlef Altenburg and Rainer Kleinertz (Vienna, 1986).

25. C.F.B., *Allgemeine musikalische Zeitung*, 11 May 1842; see also Rehm, *Zur Musikrezeption im vormärzlichen Berlin*, pp. 103ff.

26. Gooley (*The Virtuoso Liszt*, pp. 181ff., for example) has argued that Rellstab came to dislike Liszt's Beethoven interpretations more and more, which I think is overstated. I do not see much evidence that Rellstab changed his views significantly about Liszt's approach to Beethoven during the course of a mere two months, when Liszt was performing in Berlin. His reviews and articles show that he reacted to individual performances of Beethoven as he heard them. Some he disliked—for example, Liszt's performance of the "Moonlight" Sonata (pp. 6–7); others he thought extraordinary—for example, the "Appassionata" (pp. 21–22), except for the rushed tempo of the last section of the last movement, or the Third Piano Concerto (p. 27), about which he had no reservations whatsoever. Mostly his dislikes centered around exaggerations of tempo.

One can learn a great deal about Rellstab's ideas about Beethoven interpretation from a passage in his *Ludwig Berger, ein Denkmal* (Berlin: 1846), pp. 75ff. As he relates therein, he spent an evening in the company of Ferdinand Ries, Bernhard Klein, and Ludwig Berger, who began to discuss how Beethoven's sonatas should be performed. Each of the three then demonstrated his views to Rellstab, choosing the first movement of the "Pathétique" Sonata. Rellstab found Berger's performance the most inspired, the closest to what was demanded by the music. In discussing Berger's performance, he emphasized the grand rhetorical sweep and the varied poetic imagery called to mind by the performance, characteristics which he found again and again in Liszt's performances of Beethoven. Indeed, his whole description of Berger's interpretation would be more than appropriate for what he found worthy of praise in Liszt's playing of Beethoven, except, of course, when Liszt, for whatever reason, chose to emphasize contrasts too drastically, or tampered in some way with the overall unity of shape or form.

27. Rellstab, *Ludwig Berger*, p. 81.

28. The concert in Oedenburg took place in October 1820, at the Old Casino. Liszt appeared as a guest in a concert by the blind flautist Baron von Braun. That Liszt, who had turned nine just four days earlier, was attacked by fever before the concert is one of a number of childhood events or anecdotes initiated by d'Ortigue, who wrote, "La fièvre l'avait repris avant de se mettre au piano et cette exécution l'augmenta." (He was overtaken by fever again before sitting down to the piano and his playing increased it) (see p. 312 in this volume). Although Liszt apparently suffered bouts of fever as a child, there is no evidence that he suffered such an attack before his appearance in Oedenburg. The anecdote retains its effectiveness because it dramatizes the success that Liszt is supposed to have achieved at one of his very first appearances as a child. So biographers continue to include it. Ramann goes further than most in dramatizing the obstacles that Liszt had to overcome, and the anxiety Adam Liszt suffered from the whole affair; see *Franz Liszt. Artist and Man 1811–1840*, tran. E. Cowdery (London: 1882), pp. 39–40. Walker adds to Liszt's success still more by mistranslating d'Ortigue: not "his playing increased it" but incorrectly, "yet he was strengthened by the playing" (*Virtuoso Years*, p. 68).

It is interesting that Liszt has no recollection of illness, but he could very well have forgotten. More to the point is Rellstab's description; he argues, with characteristic good sense, that too much has been made of such incidents. More relevant still is the issue of biographical method that this anecdote raises. We are not dealing with a single anecdote of childhood fever. Many others occur. What is fascinating is how virtually all are described as occurring concurrently with some act of creative expression—along with the first discovery of talent, for example, accompanying Liszt's first lessons, at public performances, and so on. This linking of fever, metaphorically connected to fire, in the context of the rise and expression of talent, that is, of the origins of creativity, has a long history as a biographical motif, to use an expression of Ernst Kris and Otto Kurz (see their *Legend, Myth, and Magic in the Image of the Artist: A Historical Experiment* [New Haven: 1979], esp. pp. 86ff.). The purpose of such a motif is to provide some form of explanation, however fanciful, even magical, for the mystery of talent and creativity: talent arises by a harnessing of power and an expenditure of energy after a long internal struggle. In the case of Liszt, as in most cases when biographical motives are fashioned, there is some truth to the realistic basis on which these anecdotes are constructed—Liszt suffered from fevers as a child. As far as the concert in Oedenburg that Rellstab refers to is concerned, however, nothing concrete is known; the invention is necessitated by the desperation to explain the unknown.

29. *Conventionsmünze*, or assimilated coinage, the silver florins reintroduced in 1818, with a ratio of 1:2.5 to the older currency, or Viennese currency.

30. The famous concert at which Beethoven is said to have been present is not, as Rellstab mentions in the following paragraph, the concert in Town Hall, but rather the

second concert, in the small Redoutensaal (13 April 1823). Rellstab's account differs in interesting ways from previous ones. His is the first to separate the concert from a visit to Beethoven's house the week before, and the first to mention, although indirectly, the so-called *Weihekuss* (kiss of consecration). Rellstab discussed these events, as the reader will see from his account, with Liszt himself, and this alone invites discussion. What intrigued Rellstab is the account of the events he read in Anton Schindler's *Beethoven in Paris* (Münster: 1842). Schindler had written that Liszt and his father were received in an unfriendly manner by Beethoven during their visit to the composer's house. Rellstab could not have known that the two entries in Beethoven's Conversation Books that mentioned such a reception were added by Schindler after Beethoven's death. Nevertheless, the fact of an unfriendly reception seems to have circulated to some extent, because d'Ortigue mentions just such a reception (although he places it at the concert and not in Beethoven's house) in his biography. One should not make too much of Liszt's response to Rellstab—that he remembers no show of unfriendliness on the part of Beethoven—because one cannot verify that an unfriendly reception ever took place, although the Conversation Books make clear that Liszt and his father, along with Schindler, visited Beethoven a week before the concert.

It was no doubt Schindler's idea that Beethoven attend the concert of the young prodigy and provide him with a theme on which to improvise. The whole venture was foolhardy and Schindler, who was particularly close to the composer during the course of 1823, knew it better than most. Beethoven's deafness had kept him away from public concerts, he disliked prodigies, and, at the moment, was full of anxious concern over the publication and performance of his *Missa Solemnis*. To ask the composer under such circumstances to provide a theme for a prodigy with whom he was barely acquainted was an impertinence that would have offended anyone close to the composer. Schindler knew all this, yet his inflated view of his relationship with Beethoven, and the need to shore up his sense of importance by impressing people with what he alone could accomplish because he had Beethoven's ear led him into rash situations from which he could extricate himself only with great difficulty. Given these circumstances, it is not unlikely that Adam Liszt and his son were not received in the friendliest manner, but that is all one can say.

Adam Liszt believed, unfortunately, that Schindler could accomplish the impossible. Indeed, he surely had Beethoven's presence in mind when he indicated in the program for the concert that audiences could expect a "free fantasy on the pianoforte by the concert-giver, on a written-out theme most humbly requested from Someone in the audience." See Emmerich Karl Horvath, *Franz Liszt*, vol. 1, *Kindheit* (Eisenstadt: 1978), p. 80, where the program is given in its entirety.

In spite of the symbolic importance that Liszt biographers would begin to attribute to the concert of 13 April 1823, contemporary events suggest that the whole affair was little more than a fool's errand on the part of Adam Liszt and Schindler. For one thing, Beethoven did not attend, a fact clear enough in the Conversation Books. In the following weeks, along with the usual playful mockery of Schindler, Beethoven is treated to a report of the concert by his nephew Karl, whose knowledge is clearly secondhand, and Johann, his brother, who seems to have attended the concert. Franz's playing was also a disappointment, for although the reviewers praise his skill and fluency, he appears not to have mustered sufficient strength for the technical demands required of both a concerto by Hummel, and a grand set of variations by Moscheles. Ironically, the greatest disappointment of the afternoon was Franz's improvisation. Performers were always courting disaster with promised improvisations because they were at the mercy of whatever challenge they accepted from the audience. Could it be that Adam Liszt's grandiose promise rankled teachers and their students in Vienna, encouraging prospective rivals to prepare difficult or inappropriate themes for Franz, who was, after all, a relative newcomer. This actually seems to be what happened. One of those in the audience who had prepared a theme was Johann Pixis, a well-known composer and teacher in Vienna who had prepared a theme from a Haydn quartet. As it turned out, one of Pixis's students, who had positioned himself unbeknownst to his teacher close to Franz, handed him a rondo theme that because of its excessive length—it was twenty-four measures long—was utterly inappropriate as a theme on which to improvise. No wonder that reviewers faulted him in his improvisation. The actual details of the concert can be found in a little-known review in *Der Sammler* (29 April 1823), which Michael Saffle has brought to our attention, in "Liszt Research Since 1936: A Bibliographic Survey," *Acta musicologica* 58 (1986): 231–81; the text of the review is given on p. 279. See also my "Liszt and Beethoven: The Creation of a Personal Myth," *19th-Century Music* 12, no. 2 (Fall 1988): 116–31, where a case is made, on the basis of the Conversation Books, that it is utterly unlikely that a second visit on the part of Liszt and his father to Beethoven's house took place sometime after the concert, and therefore utterly unlikely that the scene of the *Weihekuss* took place there, either.

Such disappointment and embarrassment, in this case for Franz and his father, is often the natural breeding ground for denial and idealization. Exactly when the two began to reconstruct the events in such a way as to psychically transform them into what they had so deeply wished to happen is difficult to say. It may have begun as a conscious exaggeration, indeed, falsification on the part of Adam Liszt, as part of an attempt to impress people with his son's successes. As Bernard Gavoty has related, Adam Liszt told Cherubini, when he and his son spoke to the director of the Paris Conservatory about the possibility of his son's entrance, that "Beethoven heard him and kissed him in front of the entire hall," presumably part of a conversation with Cherubini that is described in an unpublished letter of Liszt to his friend Janka Wohl (see Gavoty, *Liszt: Le virtuose 1811–1848* [Paris: 1980], p. 66ff.). Whatever one thinks of the veracity of such evidence, it is possible that something along these lines happened spontaneously, becoming the starting point for psychic elaboration.

One of the most interesting and too little unexplored aspects of Beethoven worship in the nineteenth century is what we might call the pilgrimage literature, those accounts, both imagined and real, in which common motives are elaborated in a Proppian-like process, motives that generally circle around the expression of a holy pilgrimage, generally involving a first encounter with Beethoven, during which great emotional turmoil is experienced by the visitor as Beethoven is gradually humanized so as to arouse the deepest pathos. The climax of most versions is the sought-after sign of recognition and approval, often a paternal blessing of some sort. Czerny has left one such account ("Erinnerungen aus meinen Leben," English trans., *Musical Quarterly* 42 [1956]: 306ff.); so has Rellstab himself, in the second volume of his *Aus meinem Leben* (Berlin: 1861), pp. 224ff. The most famous fictional account is Wagner's *A Pilgrimage to Beethoven*, written in 1840, in which a young artist, the author-narrator, is first turned away by the housekeeper but finally admitted. These pilgrimage stories circulated much as in oral history, with details shared, omitted, and altered, the whole process creating a kind of fetishistic attachment to the person and memory of Beethoven. Liszt's elaboration, with its roots in actual fact, becomes ultimately a fantasy of artistic genealogy that acquired the deepest significance in Liszt's psychic life.

31. The two concerts described by Rellstab took place 1 December 1822, where Liszt played the A Minor Concerto, and 13 April 1823, where he played the B Minor Concerto. Liszt made several other public appearances, as well as appearances in private homes, in Vienna during the years 1822–23. Among recent biographers, only Emmerich Karl Horvath has given a full account of these appearances; see *Franz Liszt: Kindheit*, p. 75ff.

32. The difficulty of which Rellstab speaks remains unclear. One assumes that he is referring to the biography of d'Ortigue and the *Universal-Lexicon der Tonkunst*. In this we learn that in Liszt's tour of the French provinces in 1826, Bordeaux is where he passed

off one of his own sonatas as one by Beethoven, but there is no biographical mention of any difficulty Liszt might have suffered in that city. Of other cities Liszt visited during the tour, it is Lyons where he is said to have experienced a new awareness and sense of determination about his career and as a result returned to Paris in order to study counterpoint with Reicha. If the implication of cause and effect has any merit, then it may be that Liszt came to the realization in Lyons that he still required further training in order to fulfill his destiny. By the time of Ramann and later biographers—Ramann is vague about place—but during Liszt's tour of the provinces he began to suffer from the mental crisis that affected him during the year or two before his father's death (1827), a time when he presumably turned away from music to the priesthood, a complete about-face as far as Liszt's mental state is concerned. From these facts alone, it is clear that the whole psychological character of Liszt's adolescent years has still to be dealt with properly. See d'Ortigue's "Biographical Study of Franz Liszt" in this volume; Gustav Schilling, *Encyclopädie der gesammten musikalischen Wissenschaften, oder Universal-Lexikon der Tonkunst* (Stuttgart: 1837), vol. 4, p. 416; Ramann, *Franz Liszt: Artist and Man*, p. 122ff.

33. It is hard to tell whether *Les Pères du désert* is the title of a particular text or, more likely, refers to a popular genre of texts containing the lives of the desert fathers and a digest of their writings. One such possibility would be *Principales Vies des pères des déserts d'Orient . . . : avec un précis de leur doctrine spirituelle et de leur discipline monastique*, published in Avignon in 1825.

34. One cannot blame Liszt's biographers for assuming that Liszt passed through a period of adolescent struggle and rebellion. That he was a prodigy, guided by a father who was relentlessly dedicated to his son's career, at least partly out of a need to compensate for his own failed career as a musician, would suggest to anyone with common sense that Liszt's adolescent years were psychologically difficult for him. Rellstab's analysis of Liszt's adolescent years is far more temperate and cautious, and therefore more believable, than those of contemporary biographers. He holds to the tradition, initiated by d'Ortigue, that Liszt would lapse or withdraw into some form of melancholy and morbid religiosity when in the throws of psychic struggle, although he rejects, with Liszt's help, the idea that this behavior was already present when Liszt was six or seven years old. There is certainly evidence for such behavior, on the other hand, in the years before and after the death of Liszt's father.

Rellstab may be off the track, however, when he argues that Adam Liszt opposed these morbid religious tendencies in his son. If it is true that Liszt grew dissatisfied and restless when it came to music, especially with the demands and expectations his father placed on him, it is more likely that it was Adam Liszt who would seek to gain his son's compliance and find some way to oppose his growing willfulness by encouraging him, perhaps even demanding that he dedicate himself through religious devotion to the virtues of paternal obedience and respect. This is at least one way to view the contents of Liszt's recently published childhood diary (*Franz Liszt Tagebuch 1827*). Liszt kept this small diary for a brief period during his sixteenth year, from 1 April (incidentally, only a few days after Beethoven's death) through 21 July, a month before the death of Adam Liszt. It is made up entirely of popular pietistic religious texts, those that Adam Liszt would no doubt have known and perhaps used during his studies in the Franciscan order in Malacka. A frequently cited text in the diary, *L'Imitation de Jésus-Christ*, would have been required reading for Adam at Malacka. Nearly all the entries entered into the diary by the sixteen-year-old Franz, each dutifully introduced with the sign of the cross and the sequence of numbers from one to seven, portray a severe and demanding God requiring hard work and obedience. It is not hard to see Adam Liszt as the driving force behind the diary.

35. The young girl was Liszt's biographically enshrined first love, Caroline de Saint-Cricq, the seventeen-year-old daughter of Count Pierre de Saint-Cricq, who was minister

of commerce under Charles X. Liszt may have come to know the family as a member of the parish of the Church of Saint-Vincent-de-Paul, where he was confirmed in 1829, as there were Saint-Cricqs in the parish. The period of their relationship extends from around the latter part of 1827 into the fall of 1828. See Henri Doisy, *Les Débuts d'une grande paroisse: Saint-Vincent-de-Paul Montholor* (Roven: 1942), pp. 286ff.

36. Rellstab shows himself here, as he often does in his biography, to be psychologically perceptive about Liszt. Most biographers are content to describe and enumerate Liszt's many activities that center around pedagogy, which, it should be emphasized, include not only his teaching but his interest in original sources and autographs, critical editions, and so on. But Rellstab seems to sense that teaching fulfilled significant needs for Liszt, needs that are already present in his adolescent years. Perhaps Liszt's interest began in simple emulation of Czerny, who was more competent and benevolent than his father in the role of teacher. This is the impression one gets from a letter he wrote to a Parisian lady, in 1824, in which he suggests how she might go about improving a score she had given him. (The letter is published in Mária Eckhardt, "Liszt in his Formative Years—Unpublished Letters 1824–1827," *New Hungarian Quarterly* 27, no. 103 [1986]: 93–107). Ultimately, the explanation for Liszt's lifelong dedication to teaching, perhaps even dependence on it, goes well beyond the generosity of spirit that Eckhardt and other writers propose. Indeed, it touches on complicated ego issues of self-worth and status that have yet to be examined.

37. Rellstab refers here, with tact and discretion, to Liszt's relationship with Marie d'Agoult. The two met late in 1832 or early 1833. Near the end of May 1835, both left Paris, separately, meeting in Basel to begin a union that lasted more than a decade. By the time of Rellstab's biography, they had had three children together. In October of 1839, their relationship had begun to slowly disintegrate, running its course with considerable anguish and recrimination until April 1844, when the two parted.

38. Rellstab is referring here to his article "Zusammenfassung der folgenden Concerte," one of the essays published together with his sketch of Liszt's life. The samples he refers to, *Au lac de Wallenstadt* and *Au bord d'une source,* were performed at the concert of 2 February 1842.

39. Rellstab refers here to Franz von Schober's *Briefe über F. Liszt's Aufenthalt in Ungarn* (Berlin, 1843).

40. Liszt's article on Paganini, "Sur la mort de Paganini," was published in the *Revue et Gazette musicale,* 23 August 1840, and included as an appendix to J. Duverger, *Notice biographique sur Franz Liszt* (Paris, 2nd ed., May 1843).

From the Biographer's Workshop:
Lina Ramann's Questionnaires to Liszt

INTRODUCED AND ANNOTATED
BY RENA CHARNIN MUELLER
TRANSLATED BY SUSAN HOHL

By 1874, Franz Liszt was sixty-three years old and well into his fabled "vie trifurquée," the trisected year he spent in the cities of Rome, Weimar, and Budapest on a schedule he was to maintain until his death. Since 1869 he had devoted much of his time giving master classes to a select group of musicians, many of whom eventually became the next generation of virtuosi and teachers, not only at the keyboard but also as conductors. Within the year Liszt was also to become one of the founders of the Royal Academy of Music in Pest and would serve as its first president, all the while continuing his unstinting efforts to aid the robust musical associations in Germany—in particular, the Allgemeine Deutsche Musikverein, for which he had served as honorary president since 1859. His touring years as a performer seemed but a dim memory. Since 1847, he had not given a piano recital for a fee, although he had appeared onstage, reinventing the role of the orchestral conductor. He was the salaried Hof-Kapellmeister of the Weimar court from 1848 to 1858; after 1859, conducting by invitation constituted a major portion of his livelihood, in addition to the modest revenues received from publishers for the sale of his music. His money was invested with Rothschild's in Paris; his fiscal affairs were managed by his companion, the Polish princess Carolyne Sayn-Wittgenstein, and anything that arose of a legal nature was handed over to his so-called cousin Eduard Liszt, one of the Royal Imperial public prosecutors in Vienna.[1]

In 1874 Liszt was still the stuff of legend and the subject of numerous articles in music periodicals. Although he had ceased for the most part writing for these journals himself, his name as well as those of his closest disciples were prominent in articles, especially those dealing with the movement in

Germany known as the New German School (Neu-Deutsche Schule), the group of contemporary composers centered in Weimar around Liszt, but also including Wagner (and Berlioz, simply by association).[2]

In 1876 his Weimar-years companion, Princess Carolyne, was ensconced permanently in Rome, hard at work on her monumental review of Catholic dogma, *Causes intérieures de la faiblesse extérieure de l'Église en 1870*.[3] Since the eleventh-hour cancellation of their intended marriage in 1861, Carolyne and Liszt had maintained separate living establishments in Rome and the princess had devoted herself to her gigantic critique of church doctrine, which one might view as retribution—after all, it was the pope who had "thwarted" her nuptials to Liszt.[4] By the time of her death in 1887, twenty-four volumes of this work had been published, two of which were contentious enough to be put on the *Index librorum prohibitorum*. Not surprisingly, Liszt thought it best to distance himself well from Carolyne's magnum opus. He had taken Minor Orders in 1865, and although he had not gone further in pursuit of an ecclesiastical career, he maintained a strict and carefully regimented routine of religious observation, invariably wearing his Roman collar. Although his appearance sometimes engendered a puzzled and slightly pejorative response from those who knew him well, the countenance of l'Abbé Liszt was not at all at odds with the persona of the virtuoso who had once electrified audiences with his keyboard wizardry.[5]

And so, by the mid-1870s, we have an incongruous portrait of man and musician: the nineteenth-century musical superstar and the fervently religious Catholic. While Liszt himself seemed not to be bothered by this, Princess Carolyne thought he needed better public relations. She had been a formidable manager of Liszt's business from the very beginning of their relationship, to the point of organizing his musical household almost as soon as she arrived in Weimar from the Ukraine in March 1848. While her intentions were honorable, she was less than experienced in the organization of a musician's atelier, and her catalogue of Liszt's compositions cannot be trusted for precise dating.[6] In 1874, perceiving that there was no accurate catalogue of Liszt's works and no informed biographical statements available, the princess, as she had done before, took matters into her own hands: she encouraged Liszt in a major biographical effort with a Nuremberg music teacher named Lina Ramann (1833–1912).

Ramann was no stranger to things Lisztian and was already a widely traveled pedagogue. In the mid-1850s she had sailed to America and spent a year in and around Chicago, bringing music to rural communities without permanent musical establishments. Finding the semi-frontier conditions hard, and the weather even worse, she was forced by illness to return to Germany.[7] By 1858 she headed a music school for young women in

Glückstadt and had begun to publish widely. Her first contact with the composer came at the Leipzig Tonkünstler-Versammlung in 1859, where Brendel, already a Liszt disciple and the editor of the *Neue Zeitschrift für Musik*, introduced them.[8] The following year, she dedicated the second part of her *Technische Studien* to the composer, who responded graciously by letter. Ramann's personal contact with Liszt in the next decade was sporadic, but she continued to send him examples of her publications.[9]

Ramann was present at the first performance of *Christus* in Weimar in 1873, and shortly thereafter Liszt visited her in Nuremberg. From that point, Ramann showed herself intensely interested in promoting Liszt and his music through her journalistic and pedagogical writings.[10] More important, she seemed able to overcome Liszt's apparent lack of interest in a biographical project. In Nuremberg she first broached the subject of an analytical publication—specifically, her wish to write something about *Christus*. As she related in her diary, Liszt, somewhat taken aback that anyone would want to plunge into such a task, replied in uncharacteristically brusque fashion that he could not prevent her from doing so since the score was now published.[11]

Why was Liszt so cool to Ramann's project? The reason probably lay in the contemporaneous reception of his orchestral music. After sour reviews greeted the German premieres of a good number of the symphonic poems and other major orchestral works, Liszt actively discouraged their performance, except when hard-pressed. Leading the attack was the powerful Viennese critic Eduard Hanslick (1825–1904), who as early as 1857 castigated *Les Préludes*. Fast becoming the most influential music critic of his time, Hanslick had been an admirer of Liszt the pianist, but Liszt the orchestral composer, as one of the representatives of the New German School, was the target of some of his most vitriolic prose. In the second edition of his seminal work, *Vom Musikalisch-Schönen* ("On the Musically Beautiful," 1858),[12] Hanslick named Liszt specifically and attacked his conception of the new idiom, the Symphonic Poem (*Symphonische Dichtung*).[13] Liszt's public reaction to Hanslick's invective was silence. In the later 1850s and 1860s, counterarguments were mounted by Richard Wagner, largely from his exile in Switzerland.[14] Arguments came now as well from Liszt's principal disciples, among them Hans Schellendorf von Bronsart (1840–1913), Brendel, Peter Cornelius (1824–74), and Richard Pohl (1826–96).[15] Thus formed the great battle between Hanslick—championing what would come to be called "absolute" music, music removed from any notions of extramusical associations emanating from art or literature—and the advocates of the Weimar school, for whom the new concept of "program music," often inspired directly by paintings or poetry, was the key to the future. Following these polemics, Liszt's star as a composer seemed to be dimming: the critical view of his oeuvre in the musical press in Germany became a thorn in his side, and he judiciously advised his students to refrain from programming his newer music, both symphonic and keyboard, if they wanted to further their careers. Some of these warnings were heartbreakingly resigned: In an 1859 letter to Johann von Herbeck in Vienna, Liszt wrote, "My intimate friends know perfectly well that it is not by any means my desire to push myself into any concert programme whatever."[16] Later, his newer music, even that from 1865 on, both secular and sacred, was to confound all who surrounded him, Wagner included.[17]

It was at this point that the Ramann biographical project entered the equation. Beginning in 1874, in addition to letters, she sent him written questions on pieces of foolscap, to which he dutifully replied. The planned work initially did not seem lengthy, but Ramann became the first to find that Liszt studies invariably spiral wildly out of hand. The composer had little patience with what Ramann now saw as her "mission," although in 1875 he did agree to her proposal of an edition of his writings. He voiced his antipathetic feelings to the princess, who joined the venture like a galleon in full sail. What had started as Ramann's attempt to publish some small articles and critiques of Liszt's music grew into the princess's "official" biography, albeit authored by Ramann, a project that would occupy both women even after Liszt's death in 1886.[18] After a halting start, Liszt (in Weimar) and Ramann (in Nuremberg) visited each other several times, and in 1876, Ramann decamped to Rome for an extended stay with Princess Carolyne.

The work was far from easy. Along the way there were some heated exchanges between the two ladies, with Ramann asserting a high degree of independence and ultimately making it clear that she was not going to be Carolyne's ghost writer. In particular the princess sought to disparage Liszt's liaison with Countess Marie d'Agoult, the mother of his children, who had died in 1876. But despite the many obstacles put in her path by the recalcitrance of her subject, to say nothing of the omnipresence of the princess, difficult but well-meaning, the first volume of what would eventually be a three-part work appeared in 1880.

Only then did Liszt find fault with the harsh portrait of Marie d'Agoult, something the composer apparently had done nothing to prevent earlier. He was troubled by the details in the section describing their 1835 flight from Paris to Switzerland. From his markings in the dedication copy of Ramann's first volume in the Weimar archive, a volume conspicuous for the minimal number of annotations he made in it, it is clear that he perceived this episode as having been badly handled, and one suspects the influence of the princess here.[19] Liszt softened the portrait of Marie and corrected the more egregious errors in the text, and the entire chapter was then rewritten according to Liszt's prescription for an 1881 London edition in German of Ramann's first volume. Here Liszt refuted the widely reported charge that it was *he* who had seduced the countess, making clearer that it had been a mutually arrived-at decision. Testimony from Marie d'Agoult's brother and husband—that "Liszt is a man of honor"— found its way into that 1881 publication and became the climax of the chapter. An English translation was issued in 1882.[20]

The subject matter covered in Ramann's questionnaires and letters took the events of Liszt's life up through 1879, but Ramann's first volume had carried the story only through 1840.[21] Volume 2 was divided into two parts, published separately: the first part, which appeared in 1887, shortly after the composer's death, dealt with the so-called *Virtuoso Period* (*The Years 1839/40–1847*) and contained a chronological catalogue of his works from 1839 to 1847; part two, published in 1894, subtitled *Collecting and Work: Weimar and Rome* (*The Years 1848–1886*), continued the catalogue from 1848 to his death.[22]

In the mid-1890s Ramann, having completed her formal biographical project, assembled a further collection of unpublished documents with an eye toward issuing them as a separate book, but her attention was diverted by another project exploring Liszt as pedagogue. Collecting information from pupils and acquaintances of the composer, she put together a series of commentaries—glosses—on important keyboard works, eventually publishing them under the title *Liszt Pädagogium*.[23] Clearly, with this slender volume Ramann returned to the Liszt she felt closest to—the piano prophet and teacher. As for the envisioned compilation, which was to include letters exchanged between Liszt and Ramann, the questionnaires transcribed here, as well as a number of highly important letters from Princess Carolyne to her, Ramann never got beyond a title and preface. For the title of the collection she chose *Lisztiana*, borrowing Liszt's own sign-off in his letters to Marie d'Agoult ("Lis(z)tiana"), a sly move which she could never have slipped by the princess while she was alive. By the mid-1890s Ramann was infirm and unable to bring the material to completion, and in 1896 she gave all of her library to the recently established Liszt-Museum in Weimar. A collection of immense breadth and quality, both in printed and manuscript material, originally it had contained not only letters and documents but all of Liszt's musical sketch and draft books, which he carried with him in the years of his European tours (1839–47).[24]

In a "Nachschrift" dated December 1902, some ten years before her death, Ramann handed over the task of editing the collection to Arthur

Seidl (1863–1928). Seidl (no relation to the noted conductor Anton Seidl) was an eminent writer on music, a major Wagnerian, and between 1899 and 1903, the music critic of Munich's *Neueste Nachrichten*. Seidl also proved incapable of getting the book published within his lifetime,[25] however, and when he died in 1928 the manuscript lacked an index, necessary pictures, and facsimiles, and it was still in need of much editorial revision. Friedrich Schnapp, a brilliant scholar who would publish important work on Busoni, E. T. A. Hoffmann, Mozart, and Schumann, as well as Liszt, took over the project from Seidl.[26] However, the tumultuous politics of World War II and the Cold War intervened. Weimar was part of the Communist German Democratic Republic, funding was limited, and with Goethe and Schiller the most important proponents of the "heilige deutsche Kunst," the German Communists gleefully handed over all important Liszt scholarship activity to their sister Communist state, Hungary, until well into the 1980s.[27] Only in 1983, some ninety years after its inception, and in the year of the death of the work's third editor, did Schott Verlag finally publish *Lisztiana*.[28]

Although we only reproduce the questionnaires here, Ramann makes it clear in her biography that, in addition to using Liszt's responses in the questionnaires, she amplified her annotations retrospectively from correspondence with Liszt, Princess Carolyne, and others.[29] Nonetheless, we must view her reporting of verbatim conversations with Liszt with more than a fair amount of circumspection, since apart from the letters and questionnaires, no documents survive to record their interaction. The same situation holds true to some degree with the questionnaires—except here it is Liszt we must question. It would not be inaccurate to say that nearly every one of the fifteen extant questionnaires contains erroneous information imparted by the composer to Ramann with equanimity. How could this be the case?

As we have pointed out, at the beginning of this process Liszt was sixty-three years old, and he was being asked specific questions about works he had composed and events that had taken place as long as fifty years earlier. By and large, his responses were amazingly precise when one takes this span of time into consideration. Some of this unintentional misinformation, unchecked by Ramann, did get into print, and to correct it has been the work of succeeding generations of Liszt scholars. For his part, Liszt was bemused by the preoccupation of his would-be biographer with uncovering the specifics of how and where he worked. When Ramann asked what he thought was apparently an unimportant question, Liszt ironically responded, "Don't entangle yourself in too many details. My biography is far more to be imagined than taken down in dictation."[30] While some of the questionnaires were dated by Ramann, others were not; but for the most part, dates for the unmarked questionnaires were obtained from ancillary materials by Ramann's designated successor, Seidl.

At the beginning Ramann did not organize her questions chronologically: the first questionnaire (August 1874) asked the composer about his Etudes, op.1, moved directly to the question of the symphonic poems, and then returned to the earliest Lied compositions—that is, from the 1820s to the 1850s and then back to the 1840s. The third questionnaire from the same month, which has not survived, dealt with piano music, orchestral works, church music, organ works, and Lieder. This suggests that her aim was to question Liszt about his oeuvre by genre. Interspersed with questions about specific compositions are questions concerning individuals—Liszt's parents, Marie d'Agoult, and his children are all dealt with several times. Ramann repeated questions when she felt she didn't have enough specific information, and Liszt grew impatient in his responses to the repetitions. Sometimes, the questions were too painful for him to deal with on paper, such as the query about his son Daniel, who had died in 1859; he replied that they should talk about those events in person. Ramann also sent questionnaires to his publishers, inquiring about dates of publication. A few responded with separate letters or postcards.[31]

With the publication of *Lisztiana* in 1983 we finally received insight into the publication turmoil that surrounded the first full-scale biography of Liszt, a vibrant artist who was, arguably, the linchpin of the nineteenth century in nearly every facet of musical activity. While Liszt's motto, *génie oblige*, seemed to be his working aesthetic, we see that he was quite terse with Ramann, providing her only with the barest essentials about his compositions and his myriad musical activities. Despite this, Ramann, in the high nineteenth-century style, produced tomes that positively reeked of hero worship. From our perspective, it is easy to understand Ramann's effulgence as she produced something akin to what Princess Carolyne wanted all along. And though subsequent generations of historians and biographers have sought to tone down Ramann's portrait, Liszt stands as dazzling a figure to us today as he did to his contemporaries.

NOTES TO THE INTRODUCTION

1. Eduard (1817–79), the youngest son of Liszt's grandfather Georg's third marriage, was really Liszt's uncle, but because of their closeness in age, he called him his cousin.

2. The term had been launched by Franz Brendel in an 1859 speech in Leipzig marking the twenty-fifth anniversary of the *Neue Zeitschrift für Musik*, founded by Schumann but now seemingly a mouthpiece for the "Music of the Future," Wagner's *Zukunftsmusik*. It saw Liszt and his school as the standard-bearers of Germany's musical future, reconciling the pure German of Bach and Beethoven with the Franco-Italian influence on German music (Handel, Gluck, Mozart).

3. Published in Rome by J. Aureli, 1872 and years following.

4. There are several studies of this complicated event: Paul Merrick's "Liszt's Transfer from Weimar to Rome: A Thwarted Marriage," *Studia Musicologica Hungaricae* 21 (1979): 219–38; Donna Di Grazia, "Liszt, the Princess, and the Vatican: New Documents Concerning the Events of 1861," Master's thesis, University of California, Davis, 1986; and the same author's "Liszt and Carolyne Sayn-Wittgenstein: New Documents on the Wedding That Wasn't," *19th-Century Music* 12, no. 2 (Fall 1988): 148–62. Both Di Grazia works located and translated for the first time the primary source documents in Rome relating directly to the ecclesiastical problems encountered in 1861. Also Alan Walker, *Liszt, Carolyne and the Vatican: The Story of a Thwarted Marriage*, ed. Michael Saffle (Stuyvesant, N.Y.: 1991).

5. One of the most famous observations came in 1865 (albeit published many years later) from Ferdinand Gregorovius (pseud. Ferdinand Fuchsmund): "Yesterday I saw Liszt, befrocked as an *abbé*—he was getting out of a carriage; his black silk cassock fluttering ironically behind him—Mephistopheles disguised as an Abbé." *Römische Tagebücher von Ferdinand Gregorovius* (Stuttgart: 1892), p. 300.

6. Between 1850 and 1854, the princess put together a list of titles, presumably in chronological order, of Liszt's published and unpublished oeuvre. The manuscript is found today in Weimar (WRgs MS 141,1), but its accuracy has been found wanting. (The siglum WRgs used throughout this essay and translation is an abbreviated version of the RISM [Répertoire international des sources musicales] siglum assigned to the Goethe- und Schiller-Archiv in Weimar [D-WRgs]). For a description of the way in which the princess's catalogue was compiled, see Rena Charnin Mueller, "Liszt's *Tasso* Sketchbook: Studies in Sources and Revisions," Ph.D. diss., New York University, 1986, pp. 75–82; hereafter "Liszt's *Tasso* Sketchbook." Liszt's own *Thematic Catalogue*, compiled 1850–55 and published by Breitkopf & Härtel (1855), was, by its publication date, chronologically flawed as well. It appeared a year before all of the symphonic poems and many other major orchestral works were printed, thus giving a foreshortened view of the composer's output. It would not be revised until 1877, and a complete thematic catalogue for the composer has yet to be issued.

7. See Eva Rieger, "So schlecht wie ihr Ruf? Die Liszt-Biographin Lina Ramann," in *Neue Zeitschrift für Musik* 147, nos. 7–8 (July–August 1986): 16–20.

8. As a student in Leipzig, Ramann had been a pupil of Lysinka, Brendel's wife, herself a piano student of John Field; see Rieger, "Lina Ramann," p. 17.

9. Books she sent Liszt included her *Technische Studien* (Hamburg: 1860), *Aus der Gegenwart* (Nürnberg: 1868); *Bach u. Händel* (Leipzig: 1868); *Die Musik als Gegenstand des Unterrichts und der Erziehung* (Leipzig: 1868); *Allgemeine musikalische Erziehungs und Unterrichtslehre* (Leipzig: 1870).

10. James Deaville speaks of Ramann's commission for a Liszt biography from Julius Schuberth in 1874, which apparently gave way to Breitkopf & Härtel at some point in the late 1870s; see "Lina Ramann and La Mara: Zwei Frauen, ein Schicksal," in *Frauen in*

der Musikwissenschaft, Dokumentation des internationalen Workshops Wien 1998, ed. Markus Grassl and Cornelia Szabó-Knotik (Vienna: 1999), pp. 239–52.

11. Ramann, *Lisztiana*, ed. Friedrich Schnapp (Mainz: 1983), pp. 20–22; hereafter *Lisztiana*. See also Walker, *Franz Liszt: The Virtuoso Years, 1811–1847* (New York: 1983), pp. 6–11; hereafter *The Virtuoso Years*; and *Franz Liszt: The Final Years, 1861–1886* (New York: 1996), pp. 275–79; hereafter *The Final Years*.

12. First published in four installments in the *Blätter für Literatur und Kunst: Beilage der Oesterreichische-Kaiserlichen Wiener Zeitung* (25 July 1853, 1 August 1853, 15 August 1853, and 13 March 1854), the first edition in book form was issued by Rudolf Weigl in Leipzig later in 1854; by 1918 there had been a dozen editions. See *Eduard Hanslick: On the Musically Beautiful,* trans. and ed. Geoffrey Payzant (Indianapolis: 1986). Citing Hanslick's autobiographical *Aus meinem Leben* (Berlin: 1894), vol. 1, pp. 237–38, Payzant notes that the work had earlier "been refused by the two most important publishing houses in Vienna" (p. xii).

13. See Walker, *Franz Liszt: The Weimar Years, 1848–1861* (New York: 1989), pp. 360ff.; hereafter *The Weimar Years*. It is interesting that by 1858 Hanslick's sole exposure to the new idiom was *Les Préludes*.

14. Wagner was more outwardly antagonistic toward Hanslick, even in print (he later considered naming the Meistersinger pedant who eventually came to be called Beckmesser, "Hans Lick").

15. As the current editor of the *Neue Zeitschrift für Musik*, the journal established in 1834 by Robert Schumann, Brendel was primarily responsible for the eventual conflagration because of the lopsided amount of space he gave to what has been described as "the exaggerated philosophical and cultural pretensions of the writings by and about Wagner and Liszt beginning to proliferate around this time." Thomas Grey, "Eduard Hanslick," *New Grove Dictionary of Music and Musicians,* vol. 10 (London: 2000), pp. 827–33.

16. See La Mara, *Briefe*, vol. 1, pp. 332–34; translated in Constance Bache, *Letters of Franz Liszt,* 2 vols. (New York: 1894), vol. 1, pp. 399–402.

17. Some of Wagner's most vitriolic comments were made in front of Liszt and later preserved for posterity through the diaries of his wife, Cosima, who was Liszt's daughter. See Cosima Wagner, *Die Tagebücher*, ed. Martin Gregor-Dellin and Dietrich Mack, 2 vols. (München: 1976–77). The English translations are available in an edition by Geoffrey Skelton (New York: 1978–80).

18. The princess survived Liszt by only eight months, and died in Rome in March 1887.

19. WRgs MS 59/350. Corrections to vol. 1 by Princess Marie von Hohenlohe-Schillingsfürst, Carolyne's daughter, are found in WRsg MS 59/323; Ramann's own corrections are in WRgs MS 59/353.

20. The English translation by Miss M. E. Cowdery suffered from the translator's evident lack of musical expertise, although it did contain a new preface and many of Ramann's corrections, especially those suggested by Liszt in the chapter on Marie d'Agoult. Walker (*The Final Years,* p. 279) mentions a concurrent, aborted American translation undertaken by Sara Hershey Eddy of Chicago, described in a January 1884 letter from Mrs. Eddy to Carrie Lachmund (not to her husband, the Liszt pupil Carl Lachmund, as Walker states); this translation has never been found.

21. It is important to note that Ida Marie Lipsius, under the pseudonym La Mara, was also engaged in a biographical project on Liszt in the late 1870s. She later turned her full attention to the editing of Liszt's letters, and as James Deaville has pointed out, used similar questionnaires in her research for the letter volumes, apparently in a like-minded quest for veracity: see Deaville, "Lina Ramann," p. 245ff.

22. It also included an index of his writings, a listing of the contents of the six volumes Ramann herself had edited for Breitkopf & Härtel between 1880 and 1883, the project that delayed the completion of the final part of the biography. Liszt's writings are now being issued in a new series entitled *Sämtliche Schriften* by Breitkopf & Härtel under the general editorship of Detlef Altenburg (1989–).

23. *Liszt Pädagogium: Klavier-Kompositionen Franz Liszt's nebst noch unedierten Veränderungen, Zusätzen und Kadenzen nach des Meisters Lehrer Pädagogisch Glossirt* (Liszt pedagogy: Franz Liszt's piano compositions pedagogically interpreted according to his teachings from thus far unedited changes, additions, and cadenzas) (Leipzig: 1902). Ramann used information she had assembled from Liszt pupils and acquaintances (August Stradal, Berthold Kellermann, August Göllerich, Heinrich Porges, Ida Volckmann, and Auguste Rennebaum), printing fascinating information on performance practice for important works as varied as the B Minor Sonata, *Funérailles, Consolations*, three Hungarian Rhapsodies, and the *Robert le Diable* fantasy.

24. See Mueller, "Liszt's *Tasso* Sketchbook," for a complete description of all of the extant Weimar sketchbooks, which still retain their original numbering from the Ramann Bibliothek. The idea of a Franz-Liszt memorial foundation and museum was actually in the air before Liszt's death, initiated by the head of the Grand Ducal family in Weimar, Carl Alexander; see August Göllerich, *Franz Liszt* (Berlin: 1908), p. 194. After Liszt's death (31 July 1886) and that of Princess Carolyne (9 March 1887), the Liszt Museum was established, funded by a grant of 70,000 gulden from Marie Hohenlohe-Schillingsfürst, Carolyne's daughter. The foundation was inaugurated by the Allgemeine Deutsche Musikverein on 22 October 1887, which would have been the composer's seventy-sixth birthday.

25. From our vantage point, it is clear why Seidl was unable to complete the editorial work on *Lisztiana* in time for the 1911 centenary celebrations of Liszt's birth—it was an enormous task. To accomplish it he had to make himself into a Liszt scholar of Ramann's breadth—and it took him twenty-four years, something he recognized and apologized for in his 1912 memorial piece for Ramann ("*mea culpa, mea maxima culpa*"). Seidl devoted his principal efforts to the life and works of Richard Strauss, and his most important book, *Straussiana: Aufsätze zur Richard Strauss-Frage aus drei Jahrzehnten,* appeared in Regensburg in 1913. Clearly, Seidl's inspiration for the title of his *Straussiana* followed the fashion of Ramann's title for her compendium, *Lisztiana.*

26. When in 1926 Seidl felt at last that the Liszt book was ready for the public, he shepherded his manuscript through his press of choice, Gustav Bosse Verlag, where the materials reached the page-proof stage and then came to an abrupt halt. Seidl's health was also failing. According to the editorial preface by Friedrich Schnapp in the *Lisztiana* collection published many decades later, Seidl, shortly before his death in 1928, voiced to his wife, Dorothee, his wish that Schnapp would take over the final editorial work. (Schnapp, "Zur Textvorlage, zur Textrevision und zu den Bildbeigaben," *Lisztiana*, pp. 9–10.)

Schnapp tells of his painstaking revision of the already typeset text, the compilation of an index done together with Seidl's wife, and the preparation of the plates of the pictures and facsimiles ("[. . .] die Klischees der Bilder- und Faksimile-Beigaben herstellen lassen"). Then "disastrous circumstances" (*verhängnissvolle Zeiten*) overcame them, clearly an indirect reference to nascent Nazism, which threatened their very existence. Seidl and his wife may have been Jewish; Schnapp's religion is unknown, but it seems unlikely that he was Jewish, since he published during the war, in a markedly Nazi-oriented volume in honor of Peter Raabe. (Schnapp's "Verschollene Kompositionen Franz Liszt" came out in 1942 in *Von Deutscher Tonkunst: Festschrift zu Peter Raabes 70. Geburtstag*, ed. Alfred Morgenroth [Leipzig]. Raabe, the foremost Liszt scholar in Germany, succeeded Richard

Strauss as president of the Reichsmusikkammer in 1937). But the turmoil of the war had a devastating effect on Bosse Verlag.

Further biographical information on Schnapp is scant. He was a confidant of Wilhelm Furtwängler during the war when he (Schnapp) was acting as chief recording engineer for Nordwestdeutschen Rundfunk. Schnapp appears to have been one of those individuals who stayed well below the radar of high-flown Nazi publicity (unlike Peter Raabe, Liszt's principal biographer between the two world wars, who was in the thick of things), and when the East German state was established, he crossed over comfortably and was apparently not subject to any de-Nazification processes by his new employers. There is little evidence of his working in the West apart from publications issued by West German firms; he was a freelance musicologist without a permanent academic position and moved without restraint in the pursuit of his scholarly research, publishing jointly with such eminent scholars as László Somfai and Wolfgang Plath. He remains, and Pamela Potter agrees, that Schnapp was, indeed, a spectral character. See Pamela Potter, "Musicology Under Hitler: New Sources in Context," *Journal of the American Musicological Society* 49, no. 1 (Spring 1996): 70–113).

27. Schnapp's preface refers to a long period before interest in Liszt was renewed, an oblique reference to the post–World War II neglect of Liszt by the German Democratic Republic, where the Weimar archives were located. Originally, Ramann's *Nachlass* was split into three groups among the Weimar establishments: the musical manuscripts and her large collection of Liszt's printed music went to the Liszt-Museum; the manuscript materials for the biography went to the Goethe- und Schiller-Archiv; and the pictures were deposited in the Goethe-Haus on the Frauenplan, the headquarters of the Goethe Nationalmuseum. After World War II, most of the musical manuscripts in the small Liszt-Museum went to the Goethe- und Schiller-Archiv; the printed materials in the Liszt-Museum were shifted to the prints section of the National Forschungs- und Gedenkstätte der klassischen deutschen Literatur in Weimar and housed in both the Schloss-Bibliothek (formerly the Zentral-Bibliothek) and the Anna-Amalia-Bibliothek. In the 1990s, the prints were reunited in the Schloss-Bibliothek, and as a result escaped the devastating fire in September 2004 that destroyed many of the important collections housed in the Anna-Amalia-Bibliothek.

28. In "Verschollene Kompositionen Franz Liszts," Schnapp utilized much information from the still unpublished *Lisztiana* materials to document his work, without bothering to mention that it had been entrusted to him by Seidl.

29. Some of the original questionnaires have disappeared and survive only in the text of *Lisztiana*. Ramann also expanded on her queries by including a series of ten "Supplementary Letters" ("Ergänzende Briefe") dating from 1873, 1884, and 1886, some of which were printed for the first time in *Lisztiana* (pp. 427–35). These letters, all held in the Weimar "Ramann Bibliothek," contained interesting biographical material written in response to Ramann's inquiries from Cosima Wagner (I), Fritz Stade (II), Clara Schumann, along with Liszt's response to Clara (III), and the Grand Duke Carl Alexander (IV), the latter already printed in Adelheid von Schorn's memoir *Das nachklassische Weimar* (Weimar: 1912).

30. "Verwickeln Sie sich nicht in zu vielen Details: Meine Biographie ist weit mehr zu erfinden als nachzuschreiben," WRgs MS 59/351, 1, no. 15, dated 1878; reproduced in Ramann, *Lisztiana*, p. 407.

31. All extant items are in Weimar today in the Goethe- und Schiller-Archiv, WRgs MS 59/359, 4.

The Ramann-Liszt Questionnaires

In the following translation of the questionnaires, Ramann's original text is given in italics; Liszt's responses are in normal typeface. Footnotes at the bottom of the page represent commentary by the present author except where specifically noted. LW citations refer the reader to the List of Works by Mária Eckhardt and Rena Mueller printed in the *New Grove Dictionary of Music and Musicians*, 2nd ed. (London: 2001), vol. 14, pp. 785–872.

No. 1 / [August] 1874

What was your mother's first and last name?

Please write the answer here!
Anna Lager (born in Lower Austria); died in Paris in '66.

What was her father like? What did he do? Where did he live?

My father was a very capable and upstanding civil servant and worked as chief accountant for the princely house of Esterhazy. He also distinguished himself as a musician, playing several instruments, (piano, violin, cello, and guitar) and during the most celebrated period of the Esterhazy court orchestra, from the end of the last century through the beginning of this one, he became friends with Haydn and Hummel, and often performed with the ensemble as an amateur player.[1]

---

1. Ramann began with basic questions about Liszt's mother, Anna Lager (1788–1866) and father, Adam (1776–1827), but he misunderstood Ramann's second question: she asked "What was her father like" ("Wie deren Vater?"), meaning, what was his mother's father like, but Liszt went on to describe Adam in detail. It is in his answer about his father that we notice one of the most interesting aspects of the questionnaires: the terms Ramann used and with which we have become familiar as descriptions of the periods in Liszt's life were first used by Liszt himself in his responses—for instance, *Glanzzeit*, "most celebrated period," which Liszt used to refer to his father's tenure at the Esterhazy court during the period of Haydn and Mozart and not to his own years as a virtuoso.

When did you compose your Etudes op. 1 and where were they first published?

They were written in '27 in Marseille, and published soon afterward in Paris.[2]

When were they revised for the first and second times, respectively?

The 1st in '37, Italy, the 2nd in '49, Weimar.[3]

When did you first conceive the idea for your symphonic poems? In what sequence were they written?

Approximately the way they are listed in Härtel's edition. The first symphonic poem to be performed was Tasso, at Goethe's Memorial Celebration in August of '49, in Weimar.[4]

When did you devise the Dante—and when the Faust—symphonies?

During the Weimar period, in the mid-'50s.[5]

2. Liszt's answer about the date of composition of his first set of piano *Études*, op. 1 (LW A8), demonstrates just how difficult Ramann's move from interrogatory process to her final text was going to be. Liszt's recollection of the date of composition was off by a year. The works were indeed published in Paris, but by Dufaut & Dubois in 1826, and as op. 6 by Boisselot in Marseilles. (See "An Early Liszt Edition," *Liszt Society Journal* 14 [1989]: 9–10).

3. With Ramann's next question about the subsequent transformation of the *Études* into the *24 Grandes études pour le piano* (LW A39) and then the *Études d'exécution transcendante* (LW A172), Liszt replied with their dates and place of conception correctly, but only generally. An intermediate version of *Mazeppa* was published separately by Schlesinger in 1847 (LW A172/4). We know now that Haslinger in Vienna, the publisher of the first versions (LW A39) did not return the publishing rights to Liszt until January 1850. The composer began to revise the *Études* only later that year, completing the work in 1851 and handing them over to Breitkopf & Härtel, who published the set in 1852 (LW A172).

4. To Ramann's inquiry about the "first idea concerning the symphonic poems," Liszt's response is precise and accurate, but Ramann never picked up on his careful wording and discussed these revolutionary works strictly in the order of the 1856 publication. Ramann had asked about when the creative impulse had originated, and at first Liszt responded not about conception of the symphonic poem but their publication order. In fact, *Tasso* had begun life as a concert overture in June 1847, while he was on tour in Constantinople, in advance of a performance of the Goethe play planned for the 1849 Weimar Goethe Centenary Festival. Knowing that he would be obliged to perform a major new orchestral composition, Liszt had the piece ready for the 28 August 1849 premiere. Subsequently, in the early 1850s, he revised the work substantially, adding a large central section that effectively turned it into the first symphonic poem, and performed it in its new guise and with that appellation on 19 April 1854; see Mueller, "Liszt's Tasso Sketchbook," pp. 278–303. In hindsight, Liszt was stating clearly that *Tasso* (LW G2) had been the first work to use the term "symphonic poem" in print on a Weimar concert program: *Ce qu'on entend sur la montagne*, the first *printed* symphonic poem, was not the first to be conceived as such.

5. The information concerning the *Dante* (LW G14) and *Faust* (LW G12) symphonies again reflects Liszt's hazy recollection of the final stage of composition. In reality, Liszt's

Which are the first of your Lieder?	"Loreley," "Mignon" (the 2 books
And where did you compose them?	which were first published by
	Schlesinger in '42, and 10, 12 years
	later were included in the "Collected
	Songs" published by Kahnt).[6]

Do you still possess a copy of the essays	[No. They appeared in '35, and are
published in the Gazette musicale,	probably available in Leipzig, in a
"De la situation des artistes"?[7]	collection of the *Gazette musicale*.][8]
[And if yes, would you possibly entrust	
it to me for a short time?][8]	

ideas and sketches for *Dante* can be traced back to individual notations dating from 1839 and 1847, while ideas for *Faust* also originated in the 1830s and sketches survive that may date from 1847.

6. Ramann's query about the Lieder led Liszt to remember two of his most famous, but they weren't the earliest of his German settings. His first setting in the German language was Heine's text "Im Rhein, in schönen Strome" (LW N3, 1840). *Die Loreley* (LW N5) and *Mignon* ("Kennst du das Land?" LW N8) were written in 1841 and 1842, respectively. All three songs were published by Schlesinger in Berlin in 1843.

7. *De la situation des artistes et de leur condition dans la société* (On the Situation of Artists and Their Condition in Society) was issued in seven installments in the *Gazette musicale* (Paris) between 3 May and 15 November 1835.

8. Corrections to the original, inserted by the German editors.

No. 2/[August] 1874

A

Is it true, as Christern wrote of you in 1841, that as a nine year-old boy you immersed yourself "in the mystical philosophies of a certain Jacob Böhme" and focused your imagination on "apocalyptic visions"?[1]

I don't remember ever having read Jacob Böhme's writings.[2] My mystical tendencies were always restricted to biblical subjects (primarily the books of the New Testament), the biographies of several saints (especially Francis of Assisi) and the book *The Imitation of Christ*, which was written by either Gerson or Thomas A Kempis.[3]

B

Who owns your father's diaries, which are often referred to by Schilling in his book about you?[4] *If you have them, would you possibly permit me to take a look, and send them to me? I would return them very shortly!*

My mother kept a few volumes of these diaries. Since she passed away, I don't know where they've gone to.[5]

---

1. In October 1840, Johann Wilhelm Christern (1809–77) published an autobiographical sketch of Liszt in the Hamburg *Blätter für Musik und Literatur* titled "Franz Liszt, der Romantiker." Christern went on to publish his biographical sketch of Liszt as a pamphlet with Schuberth in 1841 (*Franz Liszt nach seinem Leben und Wirken aus authentischen Berichten dargestellt von Christern*). Liszt's personal copy of Christern's 1841 biography with his handwritten annotations was in Princess Marie Hohenlohe's collection and now resides in the Music Division of the Library of Congress.

2. Jacob Böhme (1575–1624) was an orthodox follower of Martin Luther's teachings, a mystic who lived most of his life in Görlitz, a Thuringian town not far from Weimar. His mystical writings found their way into the works of Tieck, Novalis, Ritter, Schlegel, and Schelling—he was a popular figure for the German Romantic writers. Clearly his Protestant theories on life did not interest Liszt.

3. To this day, *The Imitation of Christ* by Thomas à Kempis (1380–1471) stands, arguably, as the most influential devotional text after the Bible. It figured prominently in the works of such thinkers as Sir Thomas More, St. Ignatius Loyola, and John Wesley. During Liszt's lifetime, the authorship of the book was still a matter of some discussion, and Liszt shows that he is aware of the problem of attribution, mentioning one of the other claimants to the text, Jean de Charlier de Gerson (1363–1429), onetime Chancellor of Paris.

4. Gustav Schilling, *Franz Liszt: Sein Leben und Wirken aus nächster Beschauung* (Stuttgart: 1844).

5. Ramann's several attempts to locate Adam Liszt's diary were to no avail. Apparently, the only person outside the family to have handled the diary was Joseph d'Ortigue, who was given access to it by Liszt's mother for his "Étude biographique," published in the *Gazette musicale*, 14 June 1835. (See "The First Biography: Joseph d'Ortique on Franz Liszt at Age Twenty-three" in this volume.) Although the existence of the diary has been questioned (see Walker, *The Virtuoso Years*, p. 59n.), recent scholarship seems to accept the diary as real, but one of the many Liszt items still floating in the ether.

C

Do any of your childhood letters to your mother still exist?

Probably not—and in any case, they are entirely unimportant.[6]

D

How old were you when you learned to read and write?

7 years old—I taught myself how to write musical notation, and much preferred practicing music to practicing writing my letters; by the time I was 9 I had already scribbled quite a few notebooks full of musical notes.[7]

6. Klára Hamburger, *Franz Liszt: Briefwechsel mit seiner Mutter* (Franz Liszt: correspondence with his mother) (Eisenstadt: 2000), contains new translations and commentary.

7. Several of these items of juvenilia remain in Weimar in the GSA, mixed in with later materials in three large sketch portfolios, WRgs MSS 60/Z12 (the "Nagy" Pot-Pourri), Z18, and Z31.

No. 3/[August] 1874

[Piano Music, Orchestral Works, Church Music, Organ Works, Lieder][1]
[Lost]

1. German editors' bracketed note.

No. 4/[November] 1874

Do you perhaps still remember the
"Tantum ergo" that you wrote as a
"ten year-old" when you were study-
ing with Salieri? And—if so, would
you possibly copy it out for me?

Forgotten; but presumably the same
inspirational feeling appears again
in the Tantum ergo that was published four years ago by Kahnt in
the collection, *9 Sacred Songs.*[1]

Where is your opera "Don Sancho"?
And where can I obtain the story of
the text, or the text itself? I think it
would be interesting and desirable to
include an aria or some other excerpt
that was especially successful and
characteristic in your biography.
(Perhaps in facsimile?)

The score was stored for many
years in the library of the opera in
Paris, which was destroyed by fire.[2]

Your little song "Angiolin dal biondo crin" *interests me a great deal too.*
There is no sweeter lullaby in all the
world! Did you compose it for a spe-
cific child, because it seems so
artless?![3]

The setting was written for my
eldest daughter Blandine (Mme.
Ollivier—died 12 years ago—)[4]
in Italy, in the summer of '39, to
a poem by Marchese Boccella—
in Rome?

1. Liszt's first *Tantum ergo* (LW S1, 1822) was apparently *not* the same work that was
composed in 1869 and published by Pustet in Regensburg in 1871, with a second edition
published by Kahnt the very same year. The latter (LW J27) was written for 4-part women's
choir and organ and was originally issued as no. 4 of the *Neun Kirchenchorgesänge.*
2. *Don Sanche* (LW O1,1825) has been a subject of much discussion. Liszt wrote the
work with the assistance of his teacher of composition, Ferdinand Paër (1771–1839). Liszt
thought the score had been lost in a Paris fire, but parts of the manuscript survived, unbeknownst to the composer, rediscovered by Jean Chantavoine at the beginning of the
twentieth century and presently in the archives of the Bibliothèque Nationale. Performed
17 October 1825, the work was given four times and then withdrawn.
3. *Angiolin dal biondo crin* was the first song Liszt composed (LW N1). Conceived as a
lullaby for Blandine, it was published in 1843 by Schlesinger (Berlin), and then revised
for Schlesinger (Berlin) in 1856 and the 1860 Kahnt *Gesammelte Lieder.*
4. Blandine-Rachel Liszt was born 18 December 1835 in Geneva. She grew into a
handsome woman and in 1859 married Emile Ollivier (1825–1913), a rising politician,
and settled in France. She died 11 September 1862, two months after giving birth to their
only child, Daniel. Her death was a severe shock to Liszt, coming only three years after
the death of his youngest child, also Daniel (for whom the new baby had been named) in
Berlin on 13 December 1859.

You told me that "Die Loreley" and   Answer given in my letter.[5]
"Mignon" were the first Lieder you
composed. Yet I can't escape the thought
that Jeanne d'Arc au bûcher
(Dumas), "Il m'aimait tant" *(Mme*
de Girardin), and Poésie[s] lyriques
(Schlesinger, printed in 1843) to texts
by Victor Hugo belong to an earlier
period. Am I mistaken?

5. The 27 November 1874 letter to which Liszt referred Ramann for the answers to her questions about *Jeanne d'Arc* (LW N37), *Il m'aimait tant* (LW N4), and the *Poésies lyriques* (LW A42) covered a great deal of ground for the biographer. Ramann had asked where he found deliverance from spiritual pain, clearly annoying Liszt somewhat with this question; yet he found himself looking back over his oeuvre and picking out some of the works he remembered most fondly, and then referred her to one of the seminal analyses of his musical being, Felix Draeseke's pamphlet on the symphonic poems ("Liszts symphonische Dichtungen," *Anregung für Kunst und Wissenschaft,* vol. 2 [1857] and vol. 3 [1858]; see "Defending Liszt: Felix Draeseke on the Symphonic Poems" in this volume). In his first paragraph, Liszt says that he found his "palliatives" for any spiritual pain in the musical materials and general feeling in the "Tristis est anima mea" and the "Seeligkeiten" in *Christus* (LW I7), and similar materials in *Ce qu'on entend sur la montagne* (LW G1), based on Hugo's wondrous poem. He then refers Ramann to Draeseke's commentary on his works, where the writer has gotten to "the nucleus [*Kern*] of all my compositions." He goes on further to describe more musical "palliatives": the "Magnificat" ending the *Dante* symphony (LW G14), Psalm XIII ("Herr! wie lange willst du meiner so gar vergessen," LW I3), and the song "Ich möchte hingehen" (LW N31) to a text by Georg Herwegh (1817–75); see *Lisztiana,* pp. 41–42.

The remainder of the letter answers her questions, albeit inaccurately, about specific pieces with one especially interesting case: he remembers the "abandoned version of the Petrarch Sonnets" ("verworfene Version der Petrarca Sonette," LW N14) from the same "Conzert Getümmels" (concert turmoil). This highly interesting remark sheds great light on these works and ultimately on Ramann's modus operandi, which often sought to diminish the role of Liszt's former consort, Countess Marie d'Agoult, in the development of his compositional oeuvre. The Petrarch Sonnets found their way into the *Années de pèlerinage—Deuxième Année—Italie* (LW A55), published by Schott in 1858. However, the only sketches extant for these works appear in the *Lichnowsky* Sketchbook (WRgs MS 60/N8), and date from 1842 at the very earliest, see Mueller, "Liszt's *Tasso* Sketchbook," pp. 144–59. Liszt penned these untexted melodic lines only after his attention returned to Petrarch as a result of receiving a book of Hugo's poems from the countess, and while setting the text "Oh! Quand je dors" (LW N11), a verse he quoted in a letter written to Marie d'Agoult from Berlin 25 January 1842: "I would like also to send you a song of V[ictor] H[ugo]: 'Oh! In my dreams draw near my couch, As Laura appeared to Petrarch, etc [. . .]' Thanks for the volumes of Hugo. I will read them." Serge Gut and Jacqueline Bellas, *Correspondance de Liszt et de Madame d'Agoult, 1833–1840* (Paris: 2001), pp. 878–85. Clearly, Liszt didn't remember how he had come upon the Petrarch materials, and the countess's role in bringing them to Liszt's attention was not even a blip on the radar.

What kind of instruction did you receive in Vienna (1822) from Randhartinger?	None at all. Randhartinger was a fellow student of Salieri's—not my teacher.[6]
Did you have any other schooling at the time other than musical instruction?	No. My father gave lessons at that time in history, Latin, etc. to quite a few young noblemen, and no time to spend on me.[7]
What did you play at your 2nd concert in Vienna (1823) besides Hummel's B Minor Concerto and an "improvisational fantasy"?	Probably variations by Czerny, Moscheles, or Pixis, which were very much the fashion then.

6. Ramann pressed Liszt about his musical education in Vienna, which had been a subject of great controversy: speculation was rampant with his early biographers about lessons with Beethoven, Czerny, Randhartinger, and Salieri. Liszt responded only that Benedict Randhartinger (1803–93) had been a fellow pupil in Salieri's classes, not his teacher.

7. Liszt's somewhat rueful remark about his father's having little time to spend with him is the sole such critical remark concerning his parents of which this author is aware.

No. 5/[November] 1874

Did the performance of your "Don Sancho" receive any negative criticism from the press? And do you perhaps remember from which papers?

No. The 3 performances of the little 1-act opera were received with a certain approval—nothing more.[1]

Which newspaper was at all unfriendly in its attitude toward you at that time?

Prior to the '30s the newspapers bothered very seldom with music and musicians. The feuilletons which did concern themselves were organized later; specialty music newspapers first became reality in Paris through Fétis [. . .] as a result I had no real criticism until then—an omission which was abundantly made up for later.[2]

Is the date of the first performance of your opera perhaps still in your memory?

No—it was in '25, at the latest '26.[3]

Is there a cross or a stone marking your father's grave?

Unfortunately not. I'll tell you the reason for this personally.[4]

---

1. Walker (*The Virtuoso Years*, p. 115) says that the reviews were mixed, quoting the *Almanach des Spectacles* of 1826, which wrote "this work has to be judged with indulgence."

2. Liszt is recalling that before the *Revue musicale*, begun in 1827 by François-Joseph Fétis (1784–1871), few journals dealt exclusively with music and musicians. As a consequence he remained there without critical notices—a neglect that later was richly remedied—a sly comment on his travails with both the French and German press as he matured.

3. See note about *Don Sanche* (no. 2 in questionnaire no. 4 above).

4. As mentioned in my introduction, Liszt's reticence about this event mirrors his later inability to communicate with Ramann on paper concerning the death of his son, Daniel, in 1859.

| *What is the name of the cemetery where he is buried?* | I don't remember the name of the cemetery in Boulogne-sur-mer anymore.[5] My mother lies in the Montparnasse Cemetery in Paris.[6] Emile Ollivier (in whose home she passed away) made the funeral arrangements (in '66) and ordered the inscription on the gravestone, "Mulierem fortem quis inveniet?"[7] |

5. Walker tracked down the cemetery in which Adam Liszt was interred (Cimetière de l'Est, on the outskirts of Boulogne-sur-Mer) and reproduces the burial notice. Apparently Liszt was not present at his father's burial, and while the reasons for this could be many (that he was ill and too shaken to attend), clearly it was something else about which he could not write to Ramann. In the biography, Ramann waxed philosophical but gave few details, only some general remarks concerning Adam Liszt's final illness; see *The Virtuoso Years*, p. 125ff.

6. Anna Liszt died in Paris on 6 February 1866, in the home of her son-in-law, Emile Ollivier. The burial was scheduled for only two days later, and it did not give Liszt, who was in Rome, enough time to reach Paris.

7. German editors' note: The complete quotation runs "Qui inveniet feminam bonam, hauriet jucunditatem a domino" (Proverbs 18:22). [The King James Bible version of this text: "Whoso findeth a wife findeth a good thing, and obtaineth favor of the Lord."]

No. 6/[August] 1875

When was your eldest daughter Blandine born?	At Christmas, 1835, in Geneva.[1]
Did she remain in Switzerland for the duration of your Italian journey?	Yes, with her wet-nurse.[2]
Was Cosima born in the fall of 1837 or in the spring of 1838, in Como?	She was also born at Christmas, 1837, in Como.
Was the Countess with you in Milan?[3] In Venice?[4] Florence, Rome	Yes, of course: the Italian journey was arranged by the Countess.[5]

1. See biographical note about Blandine-Rachel Liszt (note 4 in questionnaire no. 4 above).

2. Walker says that Blandine was handed over to a local wet-nurse, Mlle. Churdet (*The Virtuoso Years*, p. 215). When Liszt and Marie d'Agoult left Geneva to continue their Swiss idyll, the infant was left behind in the care of a Pastor Demelleyer and his family; her parents would not see her again until January 1839, when she joined them in Milan. In the meantime, their second daughter, Francesca Gaetana Cosima, had been born in Como on 24 December 1837, and Marie was expecting their third child.

3. German editors' note: Liszt underscored "Milan" in red pencil and placed a question mark in margin.

4. German editors' note: Liszt struck through the question mark after "Venice" and added the other two cities.

5. The four years of travel in Switzerland and Italy were chronicled by Marie d'Agoult in *Mémoires de la comtesse d'Agoult*, ed. Daniel Ollivier (Paris: 1927). A modern, more complete edition by Charles Dupêchez, *Mémoires, Souvenirs et journaux de la Comtesse d'Agoult (Daniel Stern)*, came out in 1990. Liszt's own diary of the early period, now in the Bibliothèque Nationale in Paris, is discussed by Mária Eckhardt in "Diary of a Wayfarer: The Wanderings of Franz Liszt and Marie d'Agoult in Switzerland, June–July 1835," *Journal of the American Liszt Society* 11 (June 1982): 10–17. Since neither diary was available to Ramann, what she could consult were Liszt's articles published as *Lettres d'un bachelier ès musique*, which had appeared individually in the *Revue et Gazette musicale de Paris* and elsewhere between 1835 and 1841. These were travelogues, to some extent, but also serious statements about musical life in the cities he visited, mainly Geneva, Milan, Vienna, and Paris. Marie d'Agoult's contribution to the authorship of these works may have been substantial, but since the letters are so filled with musical detail, something she was not capable of, they must be read as primarily belonging to Liszt. Other contemporary accounts of their journey were written by their traveling companions, principal among them George Sand (*Lettre d'un voyageur* no. 10), and a Swiss major named Adolphe Pictet (*Une Course à Chamonix: conte fantastique* [Paris: 1838]). After Cosima's birth, the infant remained in Como with her wet-nurse, and Liszt and Marie d'Agoult continued on their travels. After Daniel's birth on 9 May 1839, the Feast of the Ascension, he also was left in the care of a wet-nurse. But in this case, neither parent saw Daniel until the autumn of 1841, at which point they found him severely malnourished.

Where did Cosima stay?	Like Blandine, with her wet-nurse.
When was Daniel born and where?	May, 1839, in Rome.
When did you bring your children together under your mother's care?	In October '39, I left the Countess in Florence; she returned to Paris alone; I devoted myself to concert tours, beginning in Vienna. The 3 children were brought to Paris, to my mother.[6]
Approximately how long did they stay with her?	From the end of autumn '39, until the summer '44, when I parted from the Countess for good. Blandine and Cosima then entered a distinguished private girls' school (in Paris), which was run by Mlle Laure Bernard (later governess to the children of the Duke of Nemours). I left the choice of the school up to the Countess d'A—— but refused to allow the children to live with her.

6. Neither Liszt nor Marie d'Agoult were cut out to be parents—at least, not for children under the age of consent. Liszt acknowledged his paternity for each child, but Marie d'Agoult used a false name on each birth certificate, which by French law limited her participation in their upbringing. Consequently, after their parting, when she would try to wrest control of their upbringing away from Liszt, she would fail (see Walker, *The Virtuoso Years*, p. 249). The composer was at the beginning of his virtuoso tours, never at home—indeed, he did not see his children for nine years between 1844 and 1853, although there were many letters exchanged. The countess was too busy running her salon and writing her novels and pamphlets to undertake any of the day-to-day management of the children's care—although it must be said that this was a common attitude for the gentry of the time. As a result, all three children were brought up principally by a succession of women somewhat removed from their parents. When, in November 1839, some six months after Daniel's birth, Marie d'Agoult returned to Paris to face the problem of how to manage her illegitimate children without further embarrassing her family, Liszt's mother stepped in to care for Blandine and Cosima in Paris, where they grew up with no contact whatsoever with their mother for eleven years. See Walker, *The Virtuoso Years*, p. 383.

What was the name of the Princess Wittgenstein's governess, into whose care you released your daughters?

Madame Patersi de Fossombroni, a very honorable older lady. My 2 daughters spent quite a few years in her care, beginning in the autumn of 1848; later they came to Berlin to stay with the mother of Hans v. Bülow.[7]

Were your daughters never under the care of their own mother?

The children often visited their mother, but never lived with her, because I did not consider this arrangement prudent.

In which establishment was your son brought up?

The notes about my dearly beloved son require further discussion which I will share with you personally.

When did you compose the children's hymn (Hymne de l'enfant à son réveil)?

Many years ago: last winter I modified quite a bit the edition which came out a short time ago in Pest.[8]

---

7. Liszt's response of "1848" to Ramann's query about when the girls were put under Mme. Patersi's care was off by two years. When the girls were old enough, they attended a Parisian boarding school, still under the supervision of Anna Liszt; but in 1850, when as precocious preadolescents Blandine and Cosima established surreptitious contact with their mother, Princess Carolyne entered the picture and prevailed upon the already angry Liszt to shift the care of all three children to an elderly family retainer brought out of retirement, Madame Patersi de Fossombroni, who had been Carolyne's own governess. In 1855, as it became clear that the aging Mme. Patersi could not go on for much longer, Liszt removed the children to Berlin in the care of the mother of Hans von Bülow, Franziska, something that caused both Anna Liszt and the children great pain. See Walker, *The Weimar Years*, pp. 27n., 236, 425ff.

8. One supposes that it was because of its title that Ramann, in the midst of this questionnaire dealing with Liszt's children, inquired about the composition of the *Hymne de l'enfant à son réveil* (LW A61/7, 1st version, pub. 1865; A158/6, 2nd version, pub. 1853). Liszt replied tersely about a work that began as a piano piece but had many incarnations between 1840 and 1853 and was finally published as the sixth number of the *Harmonies poétiques et religieuses* by Schott. His recollection of the edition published in Pest in the previous winter that he had recently modified is one for women's and mixed choral voices with varying accompaniments (LW J2).

What year did you lose your son?

He died on 3 December 1859, in Berlin, while staying with his sister Cosima, who lovingly and tirelessly cared for him. Together with Cosima, I accompanied the body of Daniel to the cemetery.[9]

To summarize briefly: The 3 children stayed with their very able wet-nurses in the areas around Geneva, Como, and Rome respectively, until the end of '39; then they came to Paris, to stay with my mother;[10] they never lived with the Countess; Blandine and Cosima were first raised in accordance with good taste in Madame Bernard's exclusive boarding school from '44 until the autumn of '48; always, I alone paid the not inconsiderable costs of their education;[11] Princess Wittgenstein helped me magnanimously during the years that my daughters were under the care of

9. Daniel Liszt began studying law at the University of Vienna in 1857. In the summer of 1859 he traveled to Berlin to spend his summer holiday with Cosima and Hans von Bülow. His sister found him to be undernourished and in poor physical condition, and despite her ministrations, his health worsened over the course of the autumn and he was unable to return to his studies. In hindsight, it seems clear he was suffering from some kind of severe lung disease, perhaps tuberculosis. As he grew sicker, Cosima agitatedly summoned Liszt, who arrived 11 December. Both he and Cosima were at Daniel's bedside when he died on the 13th (*not* the 3rd, as Liszt tells Ramann; Schnapp pointed out Liszt's mistake here in a footnote). His funeral took place on the 15th, and he was buried in the Catholic cemetery (see Walker, *The Weimar Years*, pp. 474–79). It must be said that this was not the first time Liszt was in error about an important death date: as early as August 1834, in a letter to Marie d'Agoult, Liszt cited 26 August as the anniversary of the loss of his father, not 28 August (see Gut/Bellas, *Correspondance*, p. 171).

10. Again, Liszt misspoke here: only Blandine and Cosima came to Paris in 1839; Daniel did not arrive until 1841.

11. Liszt shouldered the entire expense of the three children from the beginning, because the circumstances of Marie d'Agoult's departure from her husband and family had, in effect, severed her from her substantial financial resources. Liszt's concert tours were one way of ameliorating this monetary shortfall, which is one reason he undertook the English tours of 1840 and 1841. Marie d'Agoult was never as interested in Liszt's career as she should have been. To some extent, her attitude was very much that of the aristocracy

> Madame Patersi —(from '48 until '53 or '54); and likewise afterward, as both girls went to live with Frau von Bülow in Berlin.

of pre- (and post-) revolutionary France, where musicians stood alongside the servants, rarely breaking free of that societal constraint. Resentful of the time he spent on tour, and more than a little jealous of the gossip that put him in compromising positions with numerous women, she was furious at his unwillingness to take her anger seriously. In the spring of 1844, Marie was shaken by the press coverage of Liszt's rumored dalliance with a purportedly Spanish dancer named Lola Montez, which had begun in Dresden in February when she was seen in his company at a performance of Wagner's *Rienzi*. Lola then embarrassed Liszt by following him as he continued his tour in Germany and then came to Paris hard on his heels. This escapade led Marie d'Agoult to utter her famous demand that she did not object to being his mistress, but she did object to being *one* of his mistresses. Her revenge was taken shortly after she and Liszt parted in May 1844, when she wrote her novelization of their life, *Nélida*, under the *nom de plume* Daniel Stern. After their acrimonious parting, Liszt became even more adamant about keeping the children separated from the countess's new life in Paris as Daniel Stern, and this is the reason he was so angry when in 1850 he discovered that Blandine and Cosima had been to see their mother.

No. 7/[September] 1875

Franz Liszt.

Honorary Doctor[1] of the University of Königsberg,[2]
Member of the Royal Academy of Fine Arts in Berlin,[3]
President of the Hungarian Academy of Music in Budapest,[4]
Royal Hungarian Council,[5]
Chamberlain to the Grand Ducal Court of Saxony-Weimar,[6]
Honorary Citizen of the cities of Oedenburg, Pest, Weimar, and Jena,[7]
Knight of the Prussian Order "of merit,"[8]
Commander of the Orders: Franz Joseph, Legion of Honor, St.
  Gregory, Honor Guard, Oaken Crown, St. Michael, etc.[9]

1. Liszt was the recipient of many honors throughout his life, and although he graciously accepted them, the civil orders—as opposed to the ecclesiastical orders—seemed of little consequence. Several repetitions occur in this listing of honors and orders as Liszt composed it, without a written request from Ramann, who further confused matters by misdating it—see German editors' note below, which points out that Liszt's treasured distinction as honorary president of the Allgemeiner Deutscher Musikverein was omitted. The Allgemeiner Deutscher Musikverein grew out of a more informal Tonkünstler-Versammlung that took place in Leipzig, 1–4 June 1859. Liszt was appointed its first president, and he remained in this elevated office for twenty-five years. Richard Pohl's brochure *Die Tonkünstler-Versammlung zu Leipzig am 1 bis 4 Juni 1859: Mittheilungen und authentische Quellen* (Leipzig: 1859) described its concerts, personnel, and guiding philosophy. See also Walker, *The Weimar Years*, p. 511.

Information concerning each of the honors has been taken from Robert Bory, *La vie de Franz Liszt par l'image* (Geneva: 1936); Ernst Burger, *Franz Liszt: A Chronicle of His Life in Pictures and Documents*, trans. Stewart Spencer (Princeton, N.J.: 1989); Gut/Bellas *Correspondence;* Dezsö Legány, *Liszt and His Country, 1874–1886*, 2 vols. (Budapest: 1976), vol. 1, p. 8; and Walker, *The Virtuoso Years; The Weimar Years; The Final Years*. For three photographs of Liszt wearing his orders, see Ernst Burger, *Franz Liszt in der Photographie seiner Zeit: 260 Portraits, 1843–1886* (Munich: 2003), pp. 66–67.

2. Conferred 14 March 1842; letter to Marie d'Agoult from Tilsit dated 16 March. Facsimile of the diploma in Bory, *Liszt*, p. 105.

3. Conferred 14 February 1842; letter to Marie d'Agoult from Berlin, 15 February 1842.

4. The royal ordinance proclaiming Liszt's appointment was prepared in Vienna and dated 21 March 1875. It was printed in the Hungarian press a week later.

5. Conferred 13 June 1871; came with an annual pension of 4,000 forints.

6. Conferred 17 August 1861 by Grand Duke Carl Alexander, on the eve of Liszt's departure from Weimar.

7. The first conferred 18 February 1840. Liszt was named a magistrate of the county of Oedenburg, 3 August 1846. After World War I, the place name changed permanently

to Sopron when part of the province was ceded to the newly constituted Hungarian state. The Weimar honor, conferred 26 October 1860, is the most interesting, coming, as it did, on the eve of his departure for Rome; facsimile in Bory, *Liszt,* p. 161. The Freedom of the City of Jena was conferred October 1842.

8. Conferred March 1842.

9. Of these, the most interesting are the Commander of the Order of St. Gregory the Great, conferred by Pius IX, August 1859; and the Grand Commander's Cross of St. Michael, conferred 2 April 1866, Liszt's name day; investiture Paris, 2 May, immediately following.

No. 8/1875 [?][1]

Knight of the Order of Merit ('43)[2]
Commander of the Legion of Honor ('61)[3]
Commander of the Order of Franz Joseph ('74)[4]
Commander of the Weimar Order of the Falcon ('74) etc.[5]
Honorary Doctor of the University of Königsberg ('41 or '42)[6]
Chamberlain to the Grand Ducal Court of Saxony ('61)[7]
Honorary Citizen of Oedenberg, Weimar, Jena etc.[8]
Honorary Canon of Albano ('79)[9]
President of the Royal Hungarian Music Academy in Budapest.[10]

1. German editors' note: The above details, provided without accompanying questions from L. Ramann, in the master's own hand on two special, completely separate slips of paper (the second slip of paper was incorrectly annotated and ordered by L. Ramann; it originated at the earliest at the end of 1879, cf. the Canonical Honor of Albano) surprisingly omit the recently awarded honorary presidency of the Allgemeiner Deutscher Musikverein.

2. See note 8 in preceding questionnaire.

3. Liszt had expected to be named a Chevalier of the Legion of Honor in 1834. His nomination was postponed by Charles X as the result of a testy personal exchange he had with Liszt that year, as Liszt himself noted in his personal copy of Ramann I (WRgs MS 59/352/1). Conferral only came in April 1845. Liszt was nominated to be an officer in the Legion of Honor, 25 August 1860 (a copy of the certificate is reproduced in Walker), and less than a year later, he was named a commander by Napoleon III.

4. Conferred 11 January 1874. Earlier, on 7 June 1867, he had received the Commander's Cross of the Order of the Emperor Franz Joseph. On 30 October 1859, he had been elevated to the Austrian nobility and was technically entitled to use the prefix "von" before his name. Liszt never did this and allowed the title to pass to his cousin Eduard and the latter's heirs. Bory, *Liszt*, p. 161, reproduces the letter of conferral.

5. Invested by the Grand Duchess Marie Pavlovna on the occasion of his first Weimar concert 29 November 1841. Letter to Marie d'Agoult dated 7 December 1841. Clearly his parenthetical "74" is in error.

6. See note 2 in preceding questionnaire.

7. See note 6 in preceding questionnaire.

8. See note 7 in preceding questionnaire.

9. Installed 12 October 1879; the only promotion he accepted in the church hierarchy after he took Minor Orders (30 July 1865). Liszt never functioned as a canon as was required by the pontifical rubrics of the day. This honorary title is evidence that the entire fragmentary list could not have originated earlier than the end of 1879, since the title was conferred in October of that year.

10. See note 4 in preceding questionnaire.

No. 9/[November] 1875

When—in which year—was the composition "Pensée des Morts" written? Does it refer to a particular experience, or is it rather an expression of your feelings at that moment?

This fragment of the "Harmonies poétiques" was written (in Paris) in '34 (including the specific indication, "avec un profond sentiment d'ennui"—with a profound feeling of world-weariness. Note: ennui is used here in the sense described by Bossuet: "this inexorable world-weariness which is the basis of human life"—not as boredom in the ordinary sense, but rather as the suffering and sorrow common to all humanity.)[1] Now then: I took up the first 4 or 5 pages of the "harmonies poétiques" fragment in the year '50, in "Pensée des Morts," the closing of which develops out of the melodic shift (transformation?) from the preceding austere Gregorian chant, "de profundis clamavi ad Te, Domine!"[2] I forget how many numbers are to be found within the "Harmonies poétiques" in Kistner's edition (1850); I only remember that I played this humble work, which contains "Bénédiction de

---

1. In questionnaire no. 9, Ramann returned to matters of composition and dating, specifically, the "Pensée des Morts," which was to become part of the *Harmonies poétiques et religieuses*. Liszt's reponse was illuminating from a creative point of view; the dates as he recollected them, however, are wrong. All the works he mentions in the lengthy paragraph refer to compositions that span the period 1834–53. The "Fragment der Harmonies poétiques" (LW A18) was published simultaneously in Paris (Schlesinger) and Leipzig (Hofmeister) in 1835, and then reissued in the *Gazette musicale de Paris* (Supplement 23, 7 June 1835) from the Schlesinger plates. The anthology with the same title appeared in 1853 (Leipzig, Kistner, LW A158). The impression he gives is that between the publication in 1835 of the single piece and the collection of the set, beginning in 1847 with the pieces *Invocation* (LW A158/1) and *Bénédiction de Dieu dans la solitude* (LW A158/3), little activity took place that amounted to compositional work. In fact, quite the opposite was the case.

2. "From out of the depths I cry to you, oh God!" In a letter dated 30 October 1833, Liszt describes to Marie d'Agoult a "petite harmonie Lamartienne sans ton ni mesure" (a little Lamartinian harmony without tonality or meter); see Gut/Bellas, *Correspondance*, pp. 92–94, which places the *Harmonies poétiques et religieuses* (LW A18) a full year earlier than

Dieu dans la solitude," "Funérailles" and "Cantique d'Amour,"[3] for the Princess Carolyne Wittgenstein, and that I dedicated it to her.

"Funérailles" refers to the tragic events (1850) in Hungary.[4]

This kind of music is no longer of any use; it was my mistake that I did not prevent its publication. The prudent course of action is to restrict oneself to "playing music" and "musical playing." Unfortunately the critic has become far too frivolous, while art has become far too serious! Next year I will publish an orchestral work, entitled: "Les Morts" (after a prose-hymn by Lamennais). With this composition, as with "Pensée des Morts," there was no cause other than the remembrance of my dead parents, friends and children.[5]

previously known. The work in question had as its inspiration a poetic collection of the same name by Alphonse de Lamartine (1790–1869), an idol for Liszt from the time of their first introduction in Paris in the 1820s. At this time, Liszt was taken by the idea of incorporating Gregorian melodies into works for piano or piano and orchestra, which is clear from his response to Ramann citing "gregorianischen Intonation."

3. *Funérailles* (LW A158/7) was actually entitled "Funérailles, October 1849" when it was published in the *Harmonies poétiques et religieuses* set by Kistner in 1853, written in memory of the Hungarian martyrs executed 6 October 1849. (The *Cantique d'amour*, LW A158/10, was the tenth number in the set.)

4. In Liszt's explanation of the title for *Funérailles*, his recollection of the date is again faulty: the Hungarian uprising occurred in 1848–49. But his memory of the inspiration was crystal clear, and had it been published earlier—and more prominently—a major controversy concerning the extramusical associations of the piece might have been avoided. Numerous writers, beginning in the 1850s, have tried to connect the work with Liszt's reaction to Chopin's death, 17 October 1849, the only rationale being the rather mysterious date in the title and the repetitive rolling octaves that resemble those in Chopin's *Polonaise* in A-flat Major, op. 53. But Liszt's thoughts were with the unsuccessful Hungarian revolutionaries who were trying to depose their Austrian rulers (Sándor Petöfi, Lajos Kossuth, István Széchenyi, and Ferenc Déak), all of whom, along with László Teleky, József Eötvös, and the national poet Mihály Vörösmarty, would be further remembered by Liszt in his *Historische ungarische Bildnisse* (LW A335) in 1885.

5. Liszt wrote to Ramann about his plan for an orchestral work entitled *Les Morts* (LW G25/1) to be based on a "'Hymne in Prosa, von Lamennais,' which through the *Pensée des Morts* gave rise to thoughts of my dead parents, friends, and children." The work was conceived in 1860 as an orchestral piece in memory of Liszt's son, Daniel. It was dedicated to Cosima von Bülow.

No. 10/[November] 1875

When did Belloni begin to work as your secretary?

February '41—in Brussels, and he remained with me, ever loyal, honest and friendly, during my entire period of concertizing, which ended in the summer of '47 at a great military revue by Kaiser Nicolas, in Elisabethgrad (near Odessa); since that time I have not given any more concerts for my own profit.[1]

Is it true, as Schilling says, that you gave your first concert for solo piano in Rome?

Yes: in the Salon of Prince Dimitri Galitzin (Governor of Moscow) in Rome, Palazzo Poli. Count Michel Wielhorsky arranged the concert, and turned the profits over to me.[2]

---

1. Gaetano Belloni (1810–87) became Liszt's secretary and amanuensis at a point in the composer's life when he badly needed such assistance. Belloni made the traveling arrangements, bought the necessary supplies for their journeys, and functioned as a general factotum—with one important distinction: he was musically learned and began to put Liszt's musical household in order as well. By 1843, Belloni had assembled a kind of pressbook for Liszt, a folder entitled "Recensionen" (WRgs MS 59/261,1). It contained press clippings about Liszt's performances from December 1841 through April 1843. Belloni noted on the cover that he began collecting the notices in February 1843 in Breslau; most are unfortunately without mastheads, but they were identified on the basis of their contents by Rolf Dempe, an East German researcher working in Weimar in the 1960s. Belloni also urged Liszt to write down his concert repertoire; Liszt's original listing (WRgs MS 60/Z15a) was used subsequently in the preparation of the fair copies of what came to be called Liszt's *Programme Général*. Eventually, these sources served as the backbone of Liszt's Thematic Catalogue project, which resulted in the 1855 publication by Breitkopf & Härtel (revised in 1877); see Mueller, "Liszt's *Tasso* Sketchbook," 65ff.

2. Liszt's letter of 4 June 1839 to the Princess Cristina Belgiojoso declared, famously paraphrasing Louis XIV, "le Concert, c'est moi!" La Mara, *Franz Liszt's Briefe*, vol. 1. (Leipzig: 1893), pp. 24–26. It would not be until his first English tour in April–June 1840 that he advertised his performances as "pianoforte recitals," nomenclature suggested to him by the London publisher Frederick Beale. See Walker, *The Virtuoso Years*, pp. 355–56, citing Willert Beale, *The Light of Other Days* (London: 1890), vol. 1, pp. 16–17.

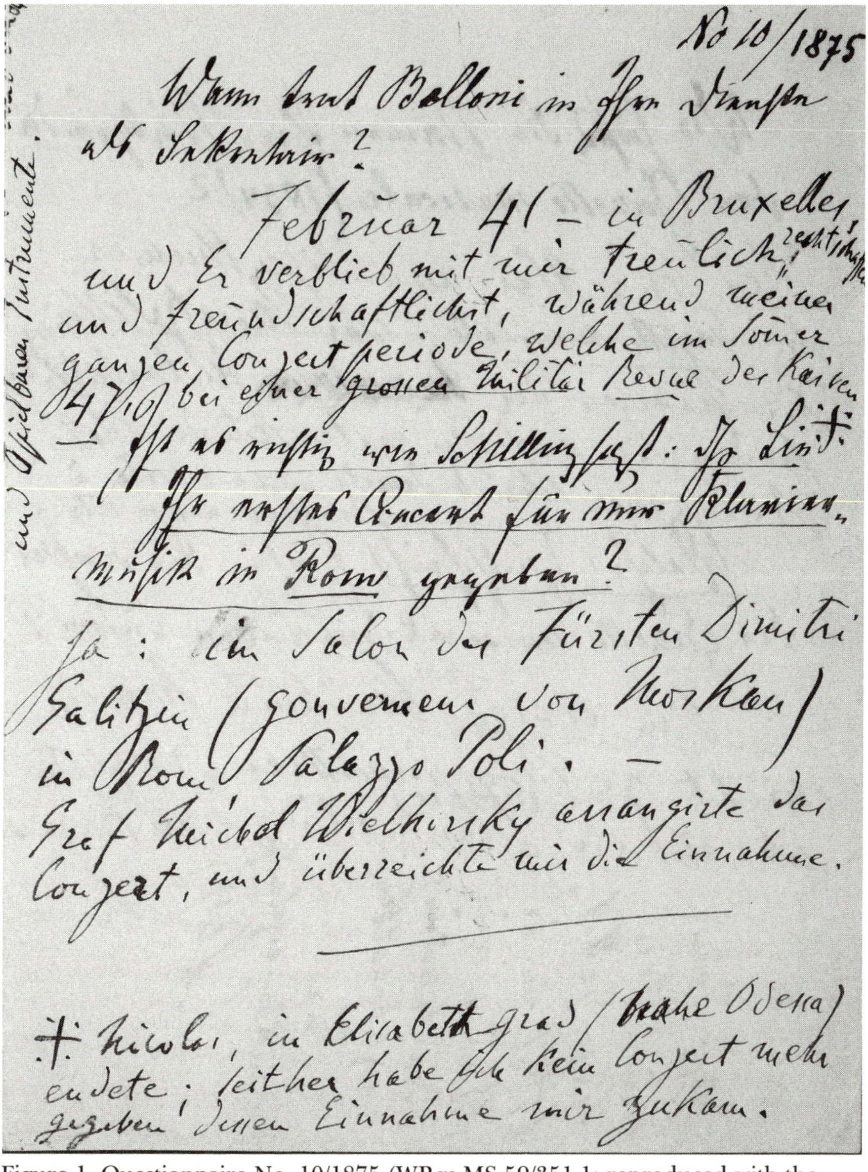

No 10/1875

Wann trat Belloni in Ihre Dienste als Sekretair?

Februar 41 – in Bruxelles, und Er verblieb mit mir treulich, rechtschaffen und freundschaftlich, während meiner ganzen Concertperiode, welche im Sommer 47 bei einer grossen Militär Revue der Kaiser

Ist es richtig wie Schilling sagt: Ihr Liszt: Ihr erstes Concert für nur Klaviermusik in Rom gegeben?

Ja: im Salon des Fürsten Dimitri Galitzin (gouverneur von Moskau) in Rom, Palazzo Poli. – Graf Michael Wielhorsky arrangirte das Concert, und überreichte mir die Einnahme.

Nicolai, in Elisabethgrad (nahe Odessa) endete; seither habe ich kein Concert mehr gegeben dessen Einnahme mir zukam.

Figure 1. Questionnaire No. 10/1875 (WRgs MS 59/351,1; reproduced with the kind permission of the Goethe- und Schiller-Archiv, Weimar). Ramann's questions, in German cursive script, left Liszt without enough room for his answers, and he was forced to add to his response in a footnote, marked with his customary dotted cross ⁜.

Figure 1 continued. The second, inner page of the folded questionnaire, containing the two questions about the *Gazette musicale*, as well as the *nota bene* carried over from the back of the questionnaire and written sideways, asking Ramann to leave more space for answers on the next questionnaire.

Haben Sie den Brief an das
Beethoven-Comité in Bonn (1839)
von San Rossore, oder von Florenz
aus geschrieben?

Wahrscheinlich von Pisa aus,
wovon man in einer Stunde nach
San Rossore fährt. In Florenz hatte ich
die Sache mit dem berühmten Bildhauer Bartolini,
besprochen.

Waren Sie auf der Insel Elba allein
oder begleitet?

Ich war nie auf der Insel Elba.

Und in San Rossore? allein?

Wie schon vertraulich gesagt war mein ganzer
Schweizer und italienischer
Aufenthalt, von 34 bis 39 nur ein
Duetto amoroso, molto agitato. Deshalb
befand ich mich stets in dem „wahrhaftigen égoïsme à deux."

Figure 1 continued. Third, inner page of questionnaire no. 10, with questions about the Beethoven Memorial, Elba, and San Rossore.

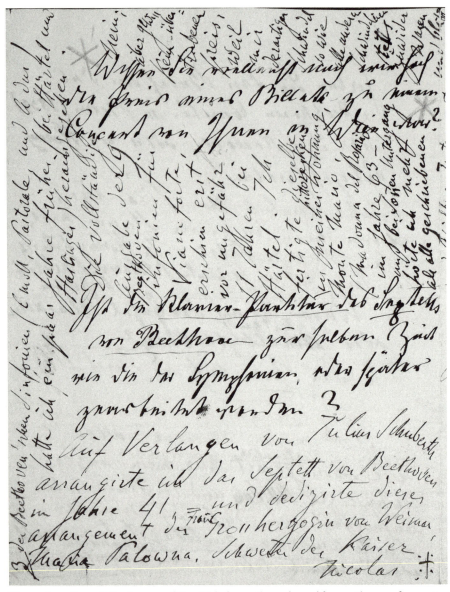

Figure 1 continued. Back page of the folded questionnaire, with questions and answers about the price of tickets and the Beethoven septet. As mentioned previously, Liszt was forced to squeeze his answers into the available space, writing in a manner called *gitterartig*—literally, a latticed style. The writer turned a sheet of paper 90 degrees and continued writing around, between, and through sentences already on the page in order to save space.

What were the names of your co-founding colleagues of the Gazette musicale *(1834)?*

The founder and owner of the *Gazette musicale* was Maurice Schlesinger; you will find the names of the other contributors on the first page of the paper. R. Wagner once wrote an article entitled, "A Visit to Beethoven," etc.[3]

Which newspapers did you help found and contribute to other than the Gazette musical?

So as not to compromise some very well-known names, I decline to answer this question.[4]

From where was the letter to the Beethoven Memorial Committee in Bonn (1839) written, from San Rossore, or from Florence?[5]

Probably from Pisa, which is an hour's travel from San Rossore. In Florence I discussed the matter with the famous sculptor, Bartolini.

3. Wagner's novella, "Eine Pilgerfahrt zu Beethoven" (1840) was his imaginary visit with an idol who "obligingly outlines the future Wagnerian music drama as the continuation of his own work: poetry and music to be united in a new synthesis; arias, duets and other divisions to be replaced by the continuous fabric of a drama." (Barry Millington, "Myths and Legends," in *The Wagner Compendium* [New York: 1992], p. 133.) First published in the *Revue et Gazette musicale de Paris* in four installments in 1840 as "Une visite à Beethoven: épisode de la vie d'un musicien allemande," it was later reprinted in the Dresden *Abend-Zeitung* (1841) as "Zwei Epochen aus dem Leben eines deutschen Musikers" with an additional subtitle, "Aus den Papieren eines wirklich verstorbenen Musikers," that showed Wagner's familiarity with E. T. A. Hoffmann's *Kater Murr* and his Meister Johannes Kreisler.

4. Liszt seems to be implying that he had something to do with the establishment of a well-known journal, and the one that most readily comes to mind is the *Neue Zeitschrift für Musik*, founded in 1834 by Robert Schumann. Schumann's lengthy review of the Berlioz *Symphonie fantastique* in the *Neue Zeitschrift für Musik*, done from Liszt's piano transcription that contained all of the instrumental cues, cemented both Berlioz's reputation as one of the most creative and important composers of the time and Liszt's position as a transcriber of miraculous powers. In 1836, Schumann published a German version of Joseph d'Ortigue's *Étude biographique* of Liszt, which he had reprinted from its 1835 *Gazette musicale* edition. And in 1837, Liszt published a long article on Schumann's piano music in the *Gazette musicale*, something that raised Schumann's stock as a composer: Schumann was still struggling for creative recognition and was deeply appreciative of Liszt's attention because at the time he was far better known in Germany as the editor of the *Neue Zeitschrift* than as a composer (Walker, *The Virtuoso Years*, pp. 346–47). Was Liszt suggesting that he had done much to propel the *Neue Zeitschrift* and its founder to the forefront of musical journalism at the time—efforts that went unrecognized (or unappreciated) by Schumann (and, later, Clara)? It remains a puzzle.

5. Ramann printed the entire letter of 3 October 1839 to the Beethoven Committee in Bonn in vol. 1 (pp. 549–50), giving Pisa as the place of origin. In his letter Liszt offered to pay the difference between the cost of the planned monument (50 to 60,000 francs) and the paltry amount raised thus far by subscription, on the condition that the statue

Were you alone when you went to Elba Island, or accompanied?[6]

I was never on Elba Island.

And in San Rossore? Alone?

As is already well-known, my entire stay in both Switzerland and Italy, from '34 until '39, was only a *duetto amoroso,* an amorous duet, molto agitato, this is why I found myself constantly involved in a maddening "égoisme à deux."[7]

Do you perhaps know how high the price of a ticket was to a concert of yours in Vienna?

No; however it was certainly not an exaggerated price, because that kind of swindle, like all swindling, was and remains repulsive to me.[8]

Was the piano transcription of the Beethoven septet made at the same time as those of the symphonies, or later?

I arranged the Beethoven septet at the request of Julius Schuberth in '41[9]—and dedicated this arrangement to the wife of the Grand Duke of Weimar, Maria Palowna,[10] sister of Czar Nicholas. I had published 3 of the Beethoven symphonies (the C minor, the Pastoral, and the A major) a few years earlier (by Härtel and Haslinger). The complete edition of the 9 Beethoven symphonies for pianoforte had first appeared approximately 11 years before, from Härtel. I finished this edition

was sculpted by the Italian Lorenzo Bartolini (1777–1850), whom he had come to know in Florence in 1838. Liszt's offer was accepted, and in 1840 he made good on it with a first installment of 10,000 francs. In the end, the monument was sculpted by a German, Ernst Julius Hähnel (1811–91). Both Liszt and Marie d'Agoult sat for Bartolini during this period. The Liszt sculpture is in Weimar in the Liszt-Museum; the bust of Marie d'Agoult, featured prominently in all Liszt iconographies, is lost; see Burger, *Chronicle,* pp. 102, 110.

6. German editors' note: L. Ramann's words *in company* are struck through by Liszt and the word *accompanied* written above them.

7. Literally, an "egotism for two."

8. The ticket prices for Liszt's 1838 Vienna concerts varied, depending on the venue. See the essay by Christopher Gibbs in this volume.

9. LW A69. The work was published in 1842, not the year before.

10. Correct spelling is Paulowna.

in my picturesque apartment, Monte Mario (Madonna del Rosario) in '63—and at sunset I heard more music than all written and playable instruments put together could produce.

NB. With the next questionnaire, please allow more room for answers.

Your
grateful and most devoted
F. Liszt

No. 11/Nov. 75 [answered December 1875]

How many "Hungarian Marches" did you compose, and in what order are they written? Which are orchestrated?

The Hungarian category is catalogued thus:

1. Rhapsodies (14 or 16?);[1] 6 of these are for orchestra,[2] and the same ones are also arranged for 4-handed pianoforte (published this spring by J. Schuberth).

2. Symphonic arrangement of the Rákóczy March: orchestral score,[3] followed by 2- and 4-hand versions for pianoforte— and also for 2 pianofortes, 4- and 8-handed arrangements (published by Schuberth)

1. Ramann's inquiry about "Hungarian Marches" led Liszt to try to simplify the confusing situation of his compositions based on Hungarian materials. He carefully separated the categories for her, listing the "14 or 16" Hungarian Rhapsodies first (LW A132), among the most famous of the composer's works, but not the earliest in the chronology. Liszt had, in effect, disavowed the earlier versions of the Rhapsodies, which had borne a variety of titles when they were first published, and did not include these early works in his first thematic catalogue in 1855. The term "Rhapsody" was a second thought and a later entry into the equation (LW A60b: *Magyar Rhapsodiák / Ungarische Rhapsodien / R[h]apsodies hongroises*; "Hungarian Rhapsodies," composed 1846–47, the revisions of A60a, published by Haslinger in 1847).

Liszt's "14 or 16?" refers to the last incarnation of the well-known series, also called *Ungarische Rhapsodien* (*Rhapsodies hongroises*, LW A132), actually fifteen works written between 1847 and 1853, one of which (the Rákóczi March) existed in two versions—thus a total of sixteen pieces, and issued by a variety of publishers in Berlin (H. Schlesinger), Leipzig (Senff, Kistner), Mainz (Schott), Paris (M. Schlesinger), and Vienna (Haslinger). This group was at least the third version of some of the pieces, some of which were published as early as 1840 with alternative titles but based on similar melodic materials. Four more rhapsodies would be written in the last four years of Liszt's life (LW A132/16–19).

2. Franz Doppler's (1821–83) initiative to transcribe six of the Hungarian Rhapsodies for orchestra found favor with Liszt, who revised and completed them for publication by Schuberth in 1874–75. To add to the already confused situation of the Rhapsodies themselves and their various guises, the six orchestral works did not retain their original numbering from the solo piano set. Their order in the orchestral versions with their equivalents for solo piano are Rhapsody 1 = no. 14; Rhapsody 2 = no. 12; Rhapsody 3 = no. 6; Rhapsody 4 = no. 2; Rhapsody 5 = no. 5; Rhapsody 6 = no. 9. The four-hand arrangements are LW B41.

3. LW G29, written between 1863 and 1871 (Schuberth, 1871); LW A60b/3 for piano solo; LW C33 for piano four-hands.; LW C25 for two pianos four-hand and eight-hand (Schuberth, 1871).

3. Hungarian Marches:
A) in D minor (dedicated to the King of Portugal) (NB. The 2 main themes are used in their entirety in the symphonic poem "Hungaria.")[4]
B) in E minor (Storm March) (It appears again soon in a much-improved second edition of the orchestral score and piano arrangements at Schlesinger, Berlin)[5]
C) Coronation March (orchestral score, 2- and 4-hand arrangement, from Schuberth)[6]
D) Quick March (published in Pressburg)[7]
NB. Actually, "Szószat and Hymnus" also belong to the Hungarian category (orchestral score and piano transcription).[8]

Were you specifically invited to lead the 1841–42 winter concerts of the Philharmonic Society before your trip from London to Russia? Or are the newspaper notices referring to this based only on rumors?

I wasn't invited to direct the Philharmonic Society, but rather to head (as music director) a German opera society that was hoping to do good business in London, but had gone bankrupt in Paris 6 weeks earlier—which is why I sent a few thousand Thaler to them

4. LW G24 (Fürstner, 1870–71); the original piano version, LW A65 (Cranz, 1840); the symphonic poem is LW G13 (Breitkopf & Härtel, 1857).

5. LW A112, first published as the *Seconde marche hongroise* by Schlesinger (Paris) in 1844, and then in a revised edition as the *Ungarische Sturmmarsch* by Schlesinger (Berlin) in 1876; LW G35 (Schuberth, 1876—this orchestral version is based on LW A112); LW B46, the piano four-hand version of LW A112 (Schuberth, 1876).

6. LW G33 (Schuberth, 1867); LW A248 (Schuberth, 1871); LW B32 (Schuberth, 1871).

7. LW A252 (Schindler, 1871).

8. LW G34, *Szózat und Hymnus: Zwei vaterländische Dichtungen von Vörösmarty und Kölcsey komponiert von Béni Egressy und F. Erkel*, for orchestra (Rózsavölgyi, 1873); LW A261, *Szózat und Ungarischer Hymnus*, for piano solo (Rózsavölgyi, 1873).

What was the name of the Prussian prince who gave you the manuscripts from Louis Ferdinand?[9] How many were there? Where are they? Was the Elegy (on themes by Prince L. F.) that Schlesinger published written at the time of your Berlin concerts of 1842?

there for their journey home—the result of a very elegant concert.

No Prussian prince sent me the manuscripts of Prince Louis Ferdinand, whose well-thought out, classically styled and melancholy quartet (F minor) I produced in my

then not-unpopular concerts in Berlin (January, February 42). At this opportunity I had the honor of mentioning other musical works by Prince Louis Ferdinand to the Princess of Prussia (now Empress of Germany). Her Majesty delighted me with the unusual, valuable gift of a volume of Prince Louis Ferdinand's works edited by the Mademoiselles Erard in Paris, within which Her Royal Majesty the Princess of Prussia graciously enclosed the autograph manuscript of the flute concerto by Frederick the Great (with the principal and accompaniment parts written in his own hand). Both gifts, in the same violet velvet jewel-cases within which they were presented to me in 1842 in Berlin, have been stored for the past 25 years in Weimar.[10]

9. Friedrich Christian Ludwig Ferdinand, Prince of Prussia (1772–1806), more widely known as Louis Ferdinand, died prematurely (and heroically) at the Battle of Saalfeld in 1806. A highly accomplished pianist, he studied with Ladislav Dussek (1760–1812), a strong musical influence on his compositional development (see Mueller, "Liszt's *Tasso* Sketchbook," pp. 204–6, 261–62). Prince Louis was also the dedicatee of Beethoven's Third Piano Concerto (op. 37, 1802). His String Quartet in F Minor, op. 6 (1806) was the basis for Liszt's *Elégie*, LW A94 (Berlin, Schlesinger, 1847; "Nouvelle édition," 1852).

10. The flute concerto is held in the Goethe- und Schiller-Archiv under the call number WRgs MS 60/Z36.

I renewed my thanks to the Princess of Prussia (at the beginning of the 1850s) with the dedication of the "Elegy on Themes by Prince Louis Ferdinand of Prussia." This little opus was published at the same time as the paraphrase "Lyre and Sword!" (by Schlesinger in Berlin).[11]

Is the following list of your waltzes complete? And is the list chronologically correct?
Valse di Bravura *(Geneva)*
" melancolique *(Vienna?)*
" a capriccio *(?)*
" infernale *or Rob.-Fantasy (?)*
Revision of the first three waltzes:
3 Caprices-Valses *(Weimar?)*
Soirées de Vienne *(?)*
Faust-Waltz (?)
Valse-Impromptu *(?)*[12]

The catalogue should simply state:
3 Valse-Caprices—
1. Valse de bravoure (2- and 4-handed)
2. Valse mélancolique
3. Valse sur des motives de "Lucia" et "Parisina" (Haslinger Publishing, Vienna)[13]
and: Valse Impromptu: (Schuberth)
NB. I wrote the theme of this Valse-impromptu in one of the many keepsake albums of the Czarina of Russia in '42, in Petersburg. Soon afterward (without my knowledge) it was published by Schuberth, under the title, "petite Valse."
Since I've hardly danced even half a waltz in my entire life, I also refrained from composing them.

11. *Leyer und Schwerdt nach Carl Maria von Weber und Körner*, LW A151, was a piano work based on a poem by Theodore Körner from a collection of the same name published posthumously in 1814; see Mueller, "Liszt's *Tasso* Sketchbook," pp. 204–6.

12. German editors' note: This entire list of composition titles is struck through back and forth; therefore his answer.

13. LW A88b, the collection of three waltzes written between 1836 and 1853 and issued with multiple titles. As Liszt revised these works from the 1830s, the publishers' penchant for descriptive titles clearly manifested itself, something the composer alludes to in his "NB" at the end of this question. Some of the reissued works were disavowed by Liszt in his thematic catalogue, and his explanation to Ramann demonstrates his wish to endorse certain versions that had not, in his mind, been superseded. No. 1 in B-flat major (second

In what year did your first face-to-face meeting with Richard Wagner take place?

Richard Wagner recounts it the best himself in one of his Parisian essays ('41 or '42):[15] later, in '44, I met him when he was court music director in Dresden, and there heard his "Rienzi";[16] and again a few years later, again in Dresden, where we suffered through a very agitated evening together—which was my fault—at the home of Robert Schumann. . .[17] If these memories seem appropriate to you for your work, I'll willingly tell you more personally. One should neither brag about such things, nor dismiss them.

version of *Le Bal de Berne, Grande Valse de bravoure*, LW A32a); No. 2 in E Major (second version of *Valse mélancholique*, LW A57); No. 3 in A Major (second version of *Valse de concert sur des motifs de Lucia et Parisina*, LW A88a); LW B1, piano four-hand version published as *Grande Valse di bravura* by Ricordi in 1837; LW A84c, the revised version of *Petite Valse favorite* (LW A84a), published as *Souvenir de Pétersbourg* (Schuberth, 1843).

15. "Face-to-face" presented a problem for Liszt in this reply. Wagner had reviewed Liszt's 25 April 1841 concert at the Salle Erard in Paris for the Dresden *Abendzeitung*, and this was printed 5 May 1841; see Walker, *The Virtuoso Years*, p. 365ff. At this famous concert, a fundraising event for the Beethoven Memorial and advertised as an all-Beethoven program, Liszt was to play the Fifth Piano Concerto (the "Emperor") with Berlioz conducting, but the raucous audience insisted that he first play his newly composed *Réminiscences de Robert le diable* (LW A78), which forced Berlioz and the orchestra simply to stand aside and listen. Wagner fulminated at what he saw as a breach of concert etiquette, especially with such a showy work, and vented at Liszt in his review. In *Mein Leben* (1869), he recounts an earlier meeting with Liszt engineered at a distance by Wagner's friend Ferdinand Laube, suggesting that Wagner visit Liszt when he arrived in Paris. The two meetings were apparently only separated by days. See Richard Wagner, *My Life*, trans. Andrew Gray, ed. Mary Whittall (New York: 1983), pp. 238–40.

16. Liszt saw *Rienzi* in Dresden in February 1844; see note 11, questionnaire no. 6 regarding Liszt and Lola Montez.

17. Liszt's acceptance of fault for an "agitated evening" with Schumann came very late. This event is often cited as the beginning of a rift between the Schumanns and Liszt that was to culminate, after Robert's death, in the unpleasantness of the Brahms-Joachim Manifesto of 1860 (see note 3, questionnaire 16). Ramann said little in her biography about the origins. The occasion was a dinner the Schumanns in Dresden hosted 9 June 1848 for Liszt (see Robert Schumann, *Tagebücher*, vol. 3, *Haushaltsbücher Teil 2, 1847–56*, ed. Gerd Nauhaus [Leipzig: 1982], p. 462). Arriving late, accompanied by Wagner, Liszt upset Clara's careful arrangements for pre-dinner music, which included her performance of Robert's Piano Quintet, op. 44, which Liszt later tactlessly described as "Leipzigerisch," a term that encompassed his antipathetic feelings toward the conservatory environment in general. Apparently, Liszt then slighted the recently deceased Mendelssohn, which made Schumann violently angry. The problem was twofold: on the one hand, it seemed

Was the composition (in manuscript) with which you honored the Liedertafel *in Munich (1843) published within your collection of 12 choruses for male voices in four parts (by Kahnt)? Which one is it?*	No—and it remains unused.[18]

What kind of symphonic work (overture?) did you perform in Copenhagen at the time of your concerts there (1841)?

None whatsoever—unless perhaps I might have composed a symphony (with countless movements) entitled "Newspaper Hoaxes."

I gratefully acknowledged the kind attentions of King Christian VIII of Denmark by dedicating to him my "Don Juan Fantasy," which was published a few years later.[19]

Where have you stored the manuscript of the flute concerto by Frederick the Great, which was presented to you by the Prince of Prussia?[20]

Beyond the three vocal quartets "Rheinweinlied," "Was ist des Deutschen Vaterland?" and "Studenten-Ratten-Lied," are there any others, and which ones, that were written on the Rhine?

3 choruses for male voices in four parts:
  a) "Rheinweinlied" (text by Herwegh)
  b) "Die Ratt' im Kellernest"
  c) "Reiter Lied" (text by Herwegh) (published by Schott)

that Liszt was insensitive to the fact that Mendelssohn, a close friend of Schumann's, had died suddenly in December 1847. But while Liszt's opinion of Mendelssohn had always been high, he felt that the Leipzig Conservatory, founded in 1843 by Mendelssohn and staffed by a faculty that was staunchly old school, was too conservative and not forward-looking enough for his taste. See Walker, *The Weimar Years*, p. 341ff., citing Berthold Litzmann (*Clara Schumann: Ein Künstlerleben* [Leipzig: 1902–08], vol. 2, pp. 121–22; and Schumann's letters edited by F. Gustav Jansen (*Robert Schumanns Briefe: Neue Folge* [Leipzig: 1904], p. 523).

18. Liszt dedicated the *Trinkspruch* for male chorus ("Giesst Wein in die Gläser, ihr Zecher!" LW M17) to the Stubenvoll Männerquartett in Munich. The work was not published until 1929 in the *Zeitschrift für Musik* (Leipzig).

19. *Réminiscences de Don Juan*, LW A80, Schlesinger, Berlin, 1843.

20. German editors' note: This question is struck through in Liszt's ink, since it had already been answered in response to the third question of this questionnaire. [See note 11 above.]

and also a few other "male choruses" which were published in a small collection (edited by Kahnt).[21] The male chorus "Was is des Deutschen Vaterland"[22] was performed a few times in Berlin in '42 and '43, and was published by Schlesinger in '43. Since then I haven't looked at this immature opus.

Did you live on the island of Nonnenwerth in the autumn of 1841, or in Cologne?

I traveled to Cologne often, but only for a few days at a time, to visit my friend Herr Lefevre, founder of the pianoforte manufacturer Eck & Company.[23] My summer residence in '42 and '43 was at Nonnenwerth (with the Countess d'Agoult, who enjoyed it there). The ceaseless visitors aggravated me very much during these summer months . . . and I would take care never again to attempt a quiet retreat in a place accessible to railroads and steamships.[24]

21. LW M2; LW M3; LW M4. The *Vierstimmige Männergesänge* were published by Schott in 1843.

22. LW M1.

23. Eck was also a major supplier of music paper to Liszt during his virtuoso tours. Eck & Lefevre published six of Liszt's songs in 1844. The famous third Liebestraum, "O Lieb, so lang du lieben kannst" (LW N18/3) was originally intended for this set but was lost in transit, and Liszt substituted *Morgens steh' ich auf und frage* with the publisher. The important conclusion derived from this is that the *Liebesträume* (LW A103, keyboard, and LW N18, songs), frequently the subject of much speculation as to which came first, the piano or vocal versions, began life as songs and were subsequently transcribed for the keyboard; see Mueller, "Liszt's *Tasso* Sketchbook," pp. 218–21.

24. Apparently Liszt felt besieged by the visitors from the numerous excursion boats that landed on the island to visit the nunnery, especially on liturgical feast days.

Did you donate a sum of 10,000 francs to the Beethoven-Memorial Committee (Bonn) only once, or several times? And how large was the total sum that you gave toward Beethoven's monument?

In my letter from Pisa in '38 or '39 to the Beethoven-Memorial Committee, I offered to underwrite the entire cost of the Beethoven Monument.[25] Later it was discovered that only ten thousand francs were needed, and I had paid this already in 1840. Even after the considerable preparations for the Beethoven Centennial in August of '45 there was no deficit (I took responsibility for that); in fact, there was a small surplus, even in spite of the establishment of the concert hall, which I initiated.[26]

In St. Petersburg (1842) was there any conflict between your views on the "duties and position of artists" and those of the people there?

In no way at all.

The favor which Czar Nicholas showed me in 1842[27] I completely lost during my second visit to St. Petersburg ('43), for the most part because of an exaggerated and in part false report from the chief of police in Warsaw at the time concerning my Polish sympathies, which it was my privilege not to deny. However, what some newspapers reported about my invented "deportation" from St. Petersburg is entirely false.

25. See note 5 in questionnaire no. 10.

26. Walker notes that Liszt told La Mara, "There was no loss, but a surplus of 1,700 Thaler" (*The Virtuoso Years*, p. 417n.).

27. Liszt's 1842 Moscow concerts were chronicled by T. Trofimova in "Liszt in Russia," published in *Sovetskaia Muzyka* 8 (March 1937): 55–60. Walker (*The Virtuoso Years*, p. 378, n. 39) gives the author's name as V. Khvostenko. Liszt's first visit was marred by the specter of his contretemps with the czar at one of the St. Petersburg recitals in 1842. Famously, the czar arrived late and then continued to talk while Liszt was playing. Liszt stopped in mid-phrase and sat at the keyboard with his head bowed as if in prayer, which finally caught the czar's attention. He asked why there was silence, to which Liszt haughtily replied, "Music herself should be silent when Nicholas speaks!"

No. 12/Dec. '75 [answered in April, 1876]

Can the Warsaw chief of police who so atrociously denounced you to Czar Nicholas be named? And if so, what was he called?

He should not be named—and he's called Abramovich. His ill-will was damaging to me once again later on.

What caused the Czar's disfavor? How long did it last? It can't have been very long, since you played for him in 1847 in Odessa?

The disfavor manifested itself in the lack of an invitation to the royal concerts, and in the absence of the Czar at my final concerts in St. Petersburg ('43)—I have never had the honor of speaking to Czar Nicholas since that time.[1]

I ended my career as a pianist in Elisabethgrad, not far from Odessa —(late in the summer of '47) where Czar Nicholas was holding a great military revue. I was invited there by one of the commanding generals, Osten Sacken, and played a few times in the theater.

Didn't you perform in St. Petersburg when you were in Russia in 1843? And was Moscow the only city where you concertized? Our German newspapers contained only very sparse coverage of your Russian tour.

Before I went to Moscow, and if I am not mistaken, also upon my return, I gave a few concerts in St. Petersburg, which were not unpopular. In 1843 I concertized in no other Russian cities but St. Petersburg and Moscow. At the

---

1. Despite this limited response to Ramann's question, her lengthy description of Liszt's 1843 visit in the biography (vol. 1, pp. 207ff.) contained many nuggets of what can only be described as gossip—verbatim conversations between Liszt and Adolphe Henselt (1814–89), the Imperial Court pianist, and a piquant story about Liszt arriving late for a concert because of a carriage ride with Princess Menschikov. Ramann went into great detail about Liszt's visit to a gypsy encampment in Moscow (vol. 2, pp. 211ff.), something that made a great impression on the composer and eventually found its way into a discussion of European gypsy music in his *Des Bohémiens et de leur musique en Hongrie* (Paris: 1859), pp. 177–79. But it is also notable for what is not there: real descriptions of Liszt's interactions with Russian composers, especially Glinka, Dargomischhsky, and Constantin Bulgakow, something that would only come later in the biographical matrix with the publication of the critical writings of Vladimir Stasov (1824–1906) and the critic Alexander Serov (1820–71).

beginning of June in the same year I returned to Nonnenwerth, to meet up with the Countess d'Agoult. My third and last tour to Russia was in '47, when I also played in Kiev in February, in Constantinople in May,[2] in Odessa at the end of June,[3] and finally in Elisabethgrad (my last concert for which I took receipts).

Is the "Prince of Prussia" who recalled you from Breslau to Berlin in February of 1843, our Kaiser?

Yes. I was recalled from Breslau to Berlin for the occasion of a royal concert at the palace of the Prince of Prussia, later Prince Regent, now King and Kaiser.[4]

A Berlin reporter indicated that on 11 January 1843, you played a "New Fantasy on Themes from Le Nozze di Figaro." Of your works on Mozartian themes, I know only the Don Juan Fantasy. Was this Figaro Fantasy written out, or was it improvised? If it was written out, where can it be found? Has it been published? By whom?

It remained only in sketches, and has been lost.[5]

2. Liszt's visit to Constantinople occurred slightly later than he remembered: he dated the beginning of his transcription of the Rossini Stabat Mater transcription in the *Tasso* sketchbook with the place name "Bujukdere," the artists' quarter in Constantinople where he was staying at the time, and wrote the date "5 Juin 47" at the end of the piece; see Mueller, "Liszt's *Tasso* Sketchbook," pp. 197–202.

3. Again, Liszt's recollection is off by a few weeks. On 17 July 1847, he wrote to his mother from quarantine in Galatz, just prior to his departure for Odessa (Hamburger, *Briefe an seine Mutter*, pp. 210–13). He remained in Odessa from the end of July through 17 September, accompanied by Princess Carolyne, giving six concerts there.

4. Wilhelm I, King of Prussia (1797–1888); Emperor of Germany 1871–88. He married Princess Augusta of Saxe-Weimar-Eisenach (1811–1890), the daughter of Grand Duke Carl Friedrich of Saxe-Weimar-Eisenach (1783–1853) and the Grand Duchess Marie Paulowna of Russia (1786–1859), the latter the sister of Czar Nicholas I of Russia. Carl Friedrich was technically Liszt's first patron, but it was at the initiative of his son and successor Carl Alexander (1818–1901) that Liszt first went to Weimar in 1842.

5. Liszt's *Fantasie über Motive aus Figaro und Don Juan* (LW A90), was found in the Liszt collection in the Goethe- und Schiller-Archiv in Weimar but not published until 1912 in

In Haslinger's music catalogues, 1840–48, I saw several times the listing, "Hungarian National Melodies" (Liszt). The Thematic Catalogue (1855, Breitkopf & Härtel) refers not to these national melodies, but only to the Melodie hongroise d'après Schubert. *How are they connected?*

A few volumes from my Hungarian works were first published in 1840 by Haslinger under the title, "Hungarian National Melodies": I later collected them in the edition of the Hungarian Rhapsodies.[6]

In what year did you compose "Geharnischte Lieder," which was published by Knop in Basel (and later by Kahnt)?

During a journey through Basel, (in the summer of '45) as thanks for the torchlight parade the Men's Choral Society there provided me.[7]

Is the Kahnt Edition a revision of the Knop Edition?

As with the Lieder, I used the opportunity provided by the Kahnt Edition to make a number of changes to the choruses for male voices in four parts.[8]

Did you compose the "Six Lieder" ("Du bist wie eine Blume," "Dichter, was Liebe sei, mir nicht verhehle," "Morgens steh ich auf und frage," "Die todte Nachtigall," "Mild wie ein Lufthauch," etc.) published by Eck & Co. in 1844 during the time you spent living near the Rhine?

Yes, at Nonnenwerth. The Eck partner, Herr Lefevre, was a friend of mine.[9]

---

the *Gesammelte Werke* in an edition "enhanced" by Feruccio Busoni. No other work exclusively devoted to *Figaro* is known to have existed.

　　6. See note 1 in questionnaire no. 11.

　　7. *Drei vierstimmige Männerchöre: Trost* I—*Vor der Schlacht* ("Es rufet Gott uns mahnend," LW M22); *Nicht gezagt* ("Nicht gezagt! Nicht geklagt!" LW M23); and *Trost* II ("Es rufet Gott," LW M24). The title "Geharnischte Lieder" occurs only in the piano transcription; see LW A207.

　　8. There is some disagreement about when these works were first issued in their solo piano versions: Jacob Milstein in *F. Liszt* (Moscow: 1971) claims that these works were first published by Kahnt in Leipzig in 1850 and 1852, and that the 1861 edition is another revision. The second versions of the choral settings were published by Kahnt in 1861.

　　9. See Liszt's response concerning Nonnenwerth in note 24 in questionnaire 11.

Were you the mediator for Berlioz and his brief musical stroll through Germany in 1843?

Berlioz came to Germany at that time of his own initiative. At the beginning of the 1850s I saw to it that the Weimar court invited Berlioz to conduct two court concerts. Berlioz accepted the invitation, and stayed for the performances of his "Cellini," which I conducted.[10] The first edition of "Cellini" (Braunschweig Litolf) appeared soon after, and is dedicated to Grand Duchess Maria Paulowna.[11]

Did you transcribe the overture to Berlioz's Francs-Juges *for piano following Berlioz's tour through Germany?*

Much earlier, at the same time as the "Symphonie fantastique" in 1833, in Paris.[12]

Were the lost scores for piano *of the Lear Overture and the Harold Symphony written in 1843, or do they fall into the Weimar period?*

During my Swiss travels, in '35—[13] In Weimar I transcribed only the "Cellini" excerpt, "Bénédiction et Serment" (published by

10. Berlioz traveled to Germany between December 1842 and June 1843, a trip that was initially hampered by his lack of knowledge of the language and chronicled by Wolfgang Griepenkerl in *Ritter Berlioz in Braunschweig* (Braunschweig: 1843). However, from a musical standpoint, it was extremely important. His second visit took place 14–21 November 1852. Liszt had hoped to have Berlioz present for the premiere of *Benvenuto Cellini* in Weimar in February 1852, during Liszt's first planned Berlioz "Festival," but difficulties with the preparations of the opera required a postponement until autumn. Arriving in November, the performances of a revised *Cellini* met with moderate success, but *Roméo et Juliette* and parts I and II of *La Damnation de Faust* were received warmly. Berlioz's conducting was praised as well.

11. A piano-vocal score appeared in 1856, but only the overture was printed in the *Werke* edition edited by Charles Malherbe and Felix Weingartner (Breitkopf & Härtel).

12. Liszt's solo piano version of the *Ouverture des Francs-Juges* (LW A31) was first published by Schott in 1845. Although no manuscript was thought to have survived, Jonathan Kregor of Harvard University has just discovered a discarded fragment of the work used as a collette on the manuscript of a Beethoven symphony transcription in Weimar.

13. On the basis of Liszt's response here, the *Ouverture du Roi Lear* (LW A30) was presumed lost by Ramann (vol. 1, p. 289), even though it had been listed in the 1855 Thematic Catalogue manuscript copy (WRgs MS 59/Z14) as published by Schott. However, Peter Raabe located the manuscript in Weimar in the course of preparing his catalogue for his 1931 biography and works list (*Franz Liszt: Leben und Schaffen*, vol. 2, p. 272), and in 1983, this author verified the existence of the manuscript for Peter Bloom and the *New Berlioz Edition*. The first edition of Liszt's transcription appeared in 1987 in the British Liszt Society Publications.

Litolf);[14] in Rome in '62 I transcribed the "Pilgrim March" from the Harold Symphony, "The Dance of the Sylphs" (from the Faust Symphony) and an improved version of the idée fixe and the "March to the Scaffold." One of Berlioz's associates, Rieter Biedermann, edited these 4 numbers.

Were the two songs "Faribolo pastour" and "Chanson du Béarn" that were published by Schotts Söhne in 1845 transcribed by you at that time, or do they belong to an earlier period? Which one?

"Chanson du Béarn" was written during my trip to Madrid, at the end of the summer of '44, in Pau (former residence of the Prince of Bearn, and birthplace of Henry IV); so also was "Faribolo pastour." These two little transcriptions are hardly known, and I have completely forgotten them.[15]

14. LW A178, published by Meyer in 1854. On Gottfried Meyer's death in 1849, his widow carried on the business successfully, and in 1851 she married the composer and pianist Henry Litolff (1818–91). Litolff had been a piano teacher of Hans von Bülow in the 1840s but never a pupil of Liszt's, although Liszt had heard him play and was extremely enthusiastic about his style. He is the dedicatee of Liszt's First Piano Concerto (LW H4, Haslinger, 1857). Liszt first transcribed the complete *Harold en Italie* for solo piano and viola (LW D5) in 1836–37 and writes about a performance of it to his mother in 1836, but no complete manuscript exists for this earliest version of the work and it was never published. "The Dance of the Sylphs" was first published in Liepzig and Paris in 1866; Schnapp notes that Liszt should have written "from the Dramatic Legend, 'La Damnation de Faust'" instead of "Faust Symphony." The cost of the first edition of the complete *Symphonie fantastique* transcription (LW A16a), printed in Paris by Schlesinger, was borne entirely by Liszt, and it was this edition that was used by Schumann for his famous review. Individual movements from the *Symphonie fantastique* were published separately (*Andante amoroso*, LW A16b; *Marche au Supplice*, LW A16c) and then issued nearly simultaneously by different publishers in Paris, Milan, Vienna, and Leipzig. Liszt revised the *Marche au supplice* in 1865 (Rieter-Biedermann), and the second edition of the entire symphony was completed in the years before 1876, when it was published by Leuckart.

15. LW A107 and LW A106, first published together by the Bureau Central in Paris in 1844 as *Faribolo Pastour: Chanson tirée du poème de Françonnetto de Jasmin et la chanson du Béarn transcrites pour piano*. Both works were dedicated to Countess Carolyne d'Artigaux, formerly Carolyne St. Cricq, a piano pupil of Liszt's from 1828 whom Walker describes as Liszt's "first love affair" (Walker, *The Virtuoso Years*, pp. 131, 408–09). In October 1844, Liszt met her unexpectedly in Pau, near the Spanish border, when he discovered that she had loaned the Erard piano for his concert.

Is the Spanish Rhapsody (?) an artistic expression of your Spanish tour in 1845? Who published it? (It is not in the Thematic Catalogue of 1855.)

Written as a reminiscence of my Spanish tour, in Rome (in about '63). When I left Weimar ('61), I asked Bülow to take over my publishing correspondence for me, and gave him a number of manuscripts which he placed according to his own judgment with different firms, for an appropriate royalty. I don't remember which publisher brought out the "Rhapsodie espagnole."[16] P. S. Gottschalg just told me that the "Spanish Rhapsody" (likewise the "Todtentanz," and the "Fantasy on Themes from 'The Ruins of Athens'") was published by Siegel in Leipzig.[17]

Is the Prince Eugen Wittgenstein, to whom you dedicated your Ballade (in D flat),[18] the spouse of the Princess W.?

Eugen Wittgenstein is the nephew of Princess Carolyne Wittgenstein, born Iwanowska. At that point he was posted with the Russian diplomatic service, as secretary to the embassy in The Hague. Eugen was an intelligent, very talented young man: he painted and composed extraordinary things: he became close friends with Berlioz in Paris, and often visited the Altenburg in Weimar (in the '50s). For a long time now he has lived in seclusion on his estate in Russia.

16. LW A114, published posthumously with a dedication to Lina Ramann (Licht & Meyer, 1887).
17. Alexander Wilhelm Gottschalg (1827–1908), another Liszt amanuensis from the 1850s, was an organist and secretary to Liszt in Weimar and Rome. He was incorrect about some information he imparted directly to Ramann. The catalogue numbers for "Todtentanz"and "The Ruins of Athens" are, respectively, LW H8 and LW H9; both were, indeed, published by Siegel, in 1865.
18. LW A117 (Kistner, 1849).

Would you like perhaps to give me the names of some of your Polish friends from the time of your Warsaw concerts?

In particular, Count Leon Lubincki. In Warsaw (February of '43) I met Madame Marie Kalergi (born Countess Nesselrode)[19] for the first time, whom you met 20 years later in Weimar and Kassel as Madame Moukhanoff. A remarkable and deeply kind woman. Her only daughter (from her first marriage), Countess Coudenhoven, lives in Vienna. Mme Moukhanoff was an intimate friend of my daughter Cosima.

And finally, I would like to ask the name of your Hungarian publisher.

A) Rózsavölgyi; the oldest and most respected firm in Pest, where in fact for many years there has been no Rózsavölgyi, just as at Breitkopf & Härtel there is no Breitkopf, and now at Schlesinger (in Berlin) and at Schott, there is neither a Schlesinger nor a Schott—a former quasi-student of mine, Herr Dunkl, functions as manager, and his brother-in-law Grinsweil serves as financial backer.[20]

B. My dear young friend Taborszky (of the firm Taborszky and Parsh, in Pest).[21]

---

19. Countess Marie Mouchanoff-Kalergis, born Countess Nesselrode (1822–1874) was a confidante of first Liszt and then of Cosima Liszt-Wagner.

20. The Pest firm of Rózsavölgyi, founded in 1850 by Gyula Rózsavölgyi (1822–61) and Norbert Grinzweil (1823–90). After Gyula Rózsavölgyi's death, Grinzweil went into partnership with János Nepomuk Dunkl.

21. Liszt had met János Mihály Táborszky in 1840 at a benefit concert he gave in Pest. Initially, Táborszky opened his firm in 1868 as a branch of Rózsavölgyi, but he soon became independent and joined with József Parsch to create Táborszky & Parsch. See Krummel and Sadie, *Music Printing and Publishing*, pp. 404, 442.

No. 13 [October 1876][1]

The instrumental arrangement (the score) of my "Elegie" (Moukhanoff)[2] was done[3] by me.

Your most grateful servant,
F. Liszt

Szegszard
October 27, '76.

In the famous Bach Prelude arranged by Gounod there is another, similar scoring.[4] In my opinion the combination of harmonium and harp can be used to advantage in many ways. I have often used it, for example in the "Hymn of the Christ-child at His Waking" and in the 2nd version of the Angel Chorus (from Goethe's Faust) etc.[5] The little version of the St. Cecilia Legend is also arranged for piano, harp, and harmonium;[6] and in the Stabat Mater of the Christus Oratorio the harmonium provides supporting accompaniment to the solo voice at several points.[7]

NB. The 4 arrangements of the Elegie Moukhanoff were completed by me.[8]

1. Format for this questionnaire follows the original. No question is cited.

2. LW D13a (piano, harp, hamonium), b (piano, cello), c (piano, violin), arranged from the original composition *Elegie I (Schlummerlied im Grabe)—En Mémoire de Marie Moukhanoff* (LW A266). The piano solo version, a piano 4-hand arrangement (LW B36), and D13a and b were published in 1875 by Kahnt; D13c followed in 1876 with the violin part said to have been arranged by Nándor Plotényi, a Hungarian student of Liszt's, something Liszt strongly disavows twice in this questionnaire.

3. German editors' note: L. Ramann's word *erfunden* (?), invented, has been erased and corrected in Germanic letters, to *getroffen,* made or done, by Liszt.

4. Liszt met Charles Gounod (1818–93) when he visited Paris in May–June 1861. Gounod's *Premier prélude de J. S. Bach* was originally arranged for strings and solo violin in 1853. The text of *Ave Maria* was added to the orchestral version in 1859.

5. Liszt's *Hymne de l'enfant à son réveil* ("O Père qu'adore mon père"), LW J2, exists in four versions composed in 1844, 1860–61, 1865, and 1874. Only the final version was ever published, by Táborszky & Parsch in 1875; see note 21 above, in questionnaire no. 12. LW L7, *Chor der Engel ("Rosen, ihr blendenden") aus Goethe's Faust II Theil,* was published in the *Goethe-Album* printed in celebration of the Goethe Centenary (Schuberth, 1849).

6. LW I1 (Kahnt, 1876).

7. LW I7 (Schuberth, 1872).

8. There are actually five arrangements: LW A266 (solo piano), B36 (piano 4-hand), and D13a, b, c; see note 4 immediately above. Liszt seems to be at pains to set aside any idea of a collaboration with Plotényi on this work.

No. 14 [December 1876]

Were your "Bravura Etudes after Paganini's Caprices" written in 1831? Or only after Paganini's death (1840)?

The "Fantasy" on the theme of the "little bells" by Paganini was published in Paris in '34 or '35(?)[1] at the same time as my "Piano Transcription of the Symphonie fantastique" of Berlioz,[2] and the fragment "avec un profond sentiment d'ennui!" from "Harmonies poétiques,"[3] before my trip to Switzerland. At that time I played the Fantasy (which is actually a set of variations) at a few concerts without success. After my first Viennese success, ('38) I took up the Paganini Etudes once again, and Haslinger (in Vienna) published (in '39) the first edition of my transcriptions of the Paganini Etudes.[4] Ten years later, in Weimar I simplified this first edition, (which was considered unplayable) and engaged Härtel to publish the second edition,[5] which has now

1. LW A14 (Paris, Schlesinger, 1834).

2. LW A16a, b, c; see note 1 in questionnaire no. 13.

3. LW A18, first published in the *Gazette musicale de Paris* in 1835; see note 1 to questionnaire 9. The remark "avec un profond sentiment d'ennui!" appears at the head of the work beneath the indications "Senza tempo" and "extrémement lent." The appearance of highly personalized indications such as this is directly related to the influence of Berlioz, whose new, startlingly individualized performance practice indications in the *Symphonie fantastique* were to rock the musical establishment as a result of Liszt's transcription of the work.

4. LW A52, *Études d'exécution transcendante d'après Paganini*, came out first with Schonenberger in Paris in 1840, not Haslinger. The dedication to Clara Schumann first appears in Haslinger's 1841 edition. Liszt at first announced his intention to transcribe all twenty-four of the Paganini Caprices, then reduced the number to twelve, but in the end, only six were written and published.

5. Liszt actually began revising in Lisbon on 2 February 1845, and the manuscript of this intermediate version, entitled *Variations de bravoure pour piano sur des thèmes de Paganini*, remained unpublished until 1989, when it was issued by Editio Musica Budapest in a version edited by Imre Mezö (LW A113). The edition best known today, *Grandes Études de Paganini* (LW A173; Breitkopf & Härtel, 1851), originally bore the title "Grandes Études

become rather popular thanks to Fräulein Mehlig[6] and other pianists, whose gracious fingers perform Number 6, "La Campanella," with brilliant success.

Am I right in assuming that Paganini's "Caprices" fundamentally contribute to the completely radical change in piano technique accomplished by you, which to a certain extent they have also determined? The latter to the extent that the work of transposing for piano the hair-raising figures, arpeggios, etc. showed you the way to a new technique.

That's for my biographer to say. When I face up to my stupidities, I can't be objective, and can only comfort myself with the thought that it all could have been much worse.

With sincerest thanks
and greeting,
FL

December 1, '76
Budapest

de Paganini transcendantes pour le piano," but Liszt deleted "transcendantes" in the proof stage. This version did bear the dedication to Clara.

6. Anna Mehlig-Falk (1843–1928), a pupil in Weimar beginning in 1869.

No 15/[July] 1878

Are the little events that involve you and Chopin true as told by Ch. Rollinat in "Le Temps," and which Krasowski includes in his book about Chopin?

If you are referring to the essay that appeared in several German newspapers a few years ago, then I declare they are untrue, because it would never occur to me to brag about myself in comparison with Chopin. I hardly read the French version of Rollinat's essay.[1]

And in what year did the game with the echo take place at Nohant? 1837? Or was it in the '40s?

I can't remember any "echo game."[2]

After '37, I didn't go to Nohant any more, and only seldom met Mme Sand.

Don't get caught up in too many details. My biography is more to be imagined than to be described.

---

1. Charles Rollinat (1810–77) was the brother of François Rollinat (1806–67), George Sand's lawyer. Both were frequent visitors to Sand's estate at Nohant, and became well acquainted with Liszt, Marie d'Agoult, the singer Pauline Viardot (1821–1910); and Chopin. Rollinat's essay, "Souvenir de Nohant," appeared in *Le Temps* 1 September 1874, some thirty years after the events, and contained stories about Chopin that were debunked subsequently by one of his early biographers, Friedrich Niecks (*Frederick Chopin as a Man and Musician* [London: 1888–1902]), as a result of personal conversations with both Liszt and Viardot. Rollinat's tale involved Liszt and Chopin supposedly arguing after Liszt took "liberties" with a Chopin piece at the keyboard. In his article, Rollinat offered the later frequently reproduced vignette of Liszt replacing Chopin at the keyboard in a darkened room, amazing those in attendance with his ability to emulate Chopin's style and touch. In the course of researching his own Chopin biography, Niecks spoke at length with Liszt in Weimar when the second edition of Liszt's own *Frédéric Chopin* was published (*La France musicale*, 1851; book form, Escudier, 1852), but Liszt remembered no such events. While it is true that Liszt's recollections could be faulty, in this case, Niecks's further investigations, especially his interviews with Pauline Viardot, substantiated Liszt's denial. See Adam Harasowski, "An Early Destroyer of Legends: *Frederick Chopin as a Man and Musician* by Frederick Niecks," in *The Skein of Legends Around Chopin* (Glasgow: 1967), pp. 96–99.

2. The "echo" effect was also first described by Rollinat in *Le Temps* as part of his spurious description of the composition of the D-flat section of the *Fantaisie impromptu*, op. 66, which purportedly took place on the terrace at George Sand's chalet at Nohant in the presence of Liszt and Viardot. According to Rollinat, the performers—Chopin, Liszt, and Viardot—all took advantage of the sylvan setting in which their keyboard and vocal renditions were answered by echoes. In fact, op. 66 was completed in 1834, some three years before Liszt ever visited Nohant.

No. 16/[March] 1880

When we touched on Schumann's music one day during a discussion, you named several of his compositions which you felt were "enduring." Have I made any mistakes if I record the following?

   The B major symphony,
   The C major [symphony],
   The string-quartets,
   The quintet (for piano),
   The piano trio No. 2,
   The music for "Manfred,"
   "Das Paradies und die Peri,"
   The Fantasy for Piano, dedicated to you, and several collections of Lieder?[1]

Schumann's piano works from his early period remain my favorites: the F-sharp Minor Sonata, Symphonic Etudes, Carneval,[2] the Fantasy (dedicated to me), Noveletten, Fantasiestücke, etc.; later the "Manfred" overture, and many fragments of the symphonic and vocal works. If I had to write a treatise on the influence of Schumann's genius upon his famous followers, they would gain no satisfaction from it.[3]

A number of things are in a bad way.

1. Symphony no. 1 in B-flat Major ("Spring"), op. 38; Symphony no. 2 in C Major, op. 61; most likely the String Quartet in E-flat Major, op. 47 (the only other published string quartets Liszt might have known are three that were dedicated to Mendelssohn, op. 41); Piano Quintet in E-flat Major, op. 44; Piano Trio no. 2 in F Major, op. 80; op. 115—Liszt conducted the first complete, staged performance of *Manfred* from manuscript in Weimar on 13 June 1852, to great acclaim, though Schumann was unable to attend because of a severe attack of rheumatism (see Margit McCorkle, *Robert Schumann: Thematisch-Bibliogaphisches Werkverzeichnis* [München: 2003], pp. 485–88); Fantaisie in C Major, op. 17, dedicated to Liszt 14 January 1839. Fourteen years later, Liszt dedicated the B Minor Sonata to Schumann (LW A179). Liszt's dedication page, reproduced in Bory (*Franz Liszt*, p. 158) is lost. Schumann was by that point too ill to respond, and Clara was soon to take umbrage at Liszt's every action, including his letter of condolence on Robert's death in 1856.
It is impossible to know to which Lieder Ramann was referring: apart from "Widmung" (LW A133), the first song in *Myrthen*, op. 25, transcribed and published as *Liebeslied* in 1848 with Kistner, Liszt never transcribed any Schumann songs while the composer was still alive. His other Schumann transcriptions are the *Zwei Lieder von R. Schumann* (LW A212/1, 2), the "Provençalisches Minnelied" from Schumann's *Des Sängers Fluch*, op. 139/4 (LW A306), and seven of the ten songs in Liszt's *Lieder von Robert und Clara Schumann* (LW 264a, b). Of all the works listed here, Schumann's *Szenen aus Goethes Faust* (WoO 3) is conspicuous by Liszt's omission, since he conducted it from manuscript with great success 29 August 1849 on the second day of the Weimar centenary Goethe celebration.
2. Sonata in F-sharp Minor, op. 11; *Études symphoniques,* op. 13; *Carnaval,* op. 9 (misspelled by Liszt). Liszt gave the first, albeit abridged, public performance of *Carnaval* on 30 March 1840 at the Gewandhaus in Leipzig. Following Schumann's instructions from a letter dated 24 December 1839, he played "Préambule," "Eusebius," "Florestan," "Coquette," "Réplique," "Chopin," "Pantalon et Colombine," "Reconnaissance," "Promenade," and the "Marche des 'Davidsbündler' contre les Philistins."
3. Liszt's remark was prophetic and struck close to home. One might understand this as an oblique reference to Johannes Brahms, Clara Schumann, and Joseph Joachim (1831–1907,

At the top of your Manchester concert program from 1825 it states:	Indeed. Since there was nothing to it, nothing came of it. Composers both young and old have to expect this lot. It's best when the manuscript goes missing before it's printed.
A new Grand Overture Composed by the celebrated Master Liszt, Will be performed by the Full Orchestra etc.	

FL

What happened to this overture? Was it perhaps from "Don Sancho"?

Liszt's concertmaster for the Weimar orchestra from 1850–52), who, with Eduard Hanslick, spearheaded an anti-Liszt faction dating from the late 1850s. The difficulties Liszt's new symphonic idiom had encountered in performance in Vienna extended well beyond that city to Leipzig, where the mostly conservative school championed by Clara Schumann and the disciples of her recently departed husband found themselves in staunch opposition to the workings of Liszt and his New German School—a cabal had firmly coalesced. This was borne out by the publication in May 1860 in the *Berliner Musik-Zeitung Echo* of what came to be called the "Brahms-Joachim Manifesto," a statement condemning the "Music of the Future" and, implicitly, Liszt's New German School. While never mentioning Liszt or Wagner by name, it stated: "The undersigned have long followed with regret the activities of a party whose organ is Brendel's *Neue Zeitschrift für Musik*." Written by Joachim, who now appeared to be firmly antagonistic toward Liszt's music and was openly leading the cabal, the Manifesto was later signed by Brahms as well. The debate had been fueled by Wagner's polemics, sent from his exile in Switzerland in the 1850s, especially *Opera and Drama* (1851), which set out premises for the "Music of the Future" that seemed at odds with the compositional efforts of anyone save Wagner, Liszt, and Berlioz. But the apparent misuse of the journal to promote the works of composers reviled by Clara and her cohorts led directly to the publication of the Manifesto. Coming on the heels of Liszt's precipitous departure from the podium at Weimar (December 1858), after a debacle involving the music of his pupil Peter Cornelius at the premiere of his opera, *Der Barbier von Bagdad*, it is no wonder that Liszt began to retreat from active conducting and urged his students to refrain from programming his works.

What were the names of the men who accompanied Pius IX when he visited you at Monte Mario?

The high prelates who accompanied Pius IX during his visit to Monte Mario,[4] where I had my apartment at the time, "Madonna del Rosario," were:

> Monsignor Hohenlohe (two years later he was elevated to the rank of cardinal)
> Monsignor de Mérode—and also some officials of the Papal Court.[5]

4. The visit took place 11 July 1863, after Liszt had been in residence three weeks. Liszt's report on the visit is found in his letter to Franz Brendel of 18 July 1863 (see *Briefe*, vol. 2, pp. 44–46).

5. Prince Cardinal Gustav Adolf von Hohenlohe-Schillingsfürst (1823–96) was the brother of Prince Konstantin von Hohenlohe-Schillingsfürst (1828–96). In 1859, Konstantin married Marie Sayn-Wittgenstein (1837–1920), the daughter of Princess Carolyne. Elevated to the College of Cardinals in 1866, Gustav played a crucial role in the intrigue that prevented Liszt's marriage in 1861. Frédéric-François-Xavier Ghislain de Mérode (1820–74), a confidant of Pope Pius IX, succeeded Cardinal Hohenlohe as papal almoner. Mérode's family claimed ancestral individuals such as Saint Elisabeth of Hungary, and Liszt's work on his oratorio, *Die Legende von der heiligen Elisabeth* (LW I4), which occupied the composer during his early years in Rome, may have benefited from Mérode's hagiographical insight.

No. 17/1881 [answered April 6, 1881]
[Liszt's Symphonic Poems]
[Lost]

PART III

CRITICISM AND RECEPTION

Fétis's Review of the Transcendental Etudes

INTRODUCED AND TRANSLATED BY PETER BLOOM

The world of music in nineteenth-century Paris, as in many other periods and places, was highly politicized. Reviews in the daily and weekly French press, which underwent tremendous development in what is commonly referred to as the Romantic era, were conditioned by alliances and enmities of a sort still well-known to today's readers and listeners. One of the conspicuous artistic friendships that developed in the early 1830s was between the brilliant young virtuoso Franz Liszt and the fiery young composer Hector Berlioz. And one of the more heated squabbles at the time occurred between that same revolutionary Berlioz and the old-school composer-historian-theorist François-Joseph Fétis, who in 1827 had founded the first serious periodical uniquely devoted to music, the *Revue musicale*, and would long contribute seminal articles to its distinguished successor, the *Revue et Gazette musicale de Paris*. No one would have been surprised to find Fétis expressing suspicion of a "friend of Hector's," or to find him greeting with pleasure, for example, the arrival in the French capital of Frédéric Chopin—for the Polish pianist's accomplishments, with all of their inspired inventiveness, were couched in recognizable forms of modest proportion.

Despite such a tendentious atmosphere, it was probably more by coincidence than by design that, one week before publishing the article by Fétis translated here, which was prompted by Liszt's new etudes for solo piano, the *Revue et Gazette musicale* printed Liszt's own review of the concert that Chopin gave in Paris on 26 April 1841, thus putting before the day's musically literate public some deeply penetrating thoughts on the two greatest pianists of the age. In Chopin, Liszt discovers a "poet—elegiac, profound, wistful, and pure." He also discovers a pianist of only limited renown, which causes him to set down a question that reveals the conflict by which he, Liszt, had begun to be tormented: "Is it not the case that the most noble and the most sincere kind of satisfaction an artist can experience is that of feeling above and beyond his established celebrity, superior to his acknowledged success, and even greater than his widely recognized achievement?"[1]

Liszt, at the time nearing the apex of the astonishing period of his career, which had begun with his first public recital in 1820 and which clearly had among its goals the domination of all rivals in the arena of the piano, was only beginning to come to terms with the affirmative answer to this question that would, before the decade was out, cause him to withdraw from the virtuoso stage. And yet, try as he might to elevate what one might call the virtuosity of art above the art of virtuosity, he could not yet free himself, in 1841, from the unfailingly successful dazzle to which Fétis alludes in his article by mentioning the sparkling new *Réminiscences de Robert le diable*. Liszt was compelled by popular demand to perform it—"Je suis le serviteur du public; cela va sans dire!"—at the otherwise all-Beethoven concert he gave with Berlioz on 25 April 1841 for the purpose of raising funds for the Beethoven monument in Bonn.[2]

Fétis displays more the historian than the critic, more the writer of the *Biographie universelle des musiciens* than the editor of the *Revue musicale* in his article. He begins by offering a historical overview of keyboard compositions from those of C. P. E. Bach through those of Haydn, Mozart, and Beethoven and on to those of certain contemporary composers, most notably Liszt's rival, Sigismond Thalberg. Quite evident is Fétis's role as author (together with Ignaz Moscheles) of the freshly minted *Méthode des méthodes de piano*, that avowedly eclectic treatise founded on the principle of extracting from past teachings—regarding hand placement, articulation, sound production, and fingering—only the best of the best techniques.[3] The article displays its author as an enemy of "progress": *not* because he rejected modern invention, but because he saw such invention as the result of a process he preferred to call *transformation*. "L'art ne progresse pas, il se transforme": this was his motto and his credo; it had the excellent effect of promoting the aesthetic validity and the appreciation of music both past and present. Fétis thus surveys the various styles and schools of pianism that have led to what he is now constrained to admit, given Liszt's new work, is a highly advanced state of art. In doing so he distinguishes music whose goal is sheer virtuosity from music whose goal is of a higher order, thus taking up a subject that concerned many at the time, including Richard Wagner, whose own variation on the theme appeared in this very same journal.[4]

In fact, Fétis pays so little attention to the ostensible subject of the article, new etudes by Liszt, that we cannot be sure what actually prompted it. Was it the publication of the work we know in its definitive version as the *Études d'exécution transcendante*? Liszt's studies under that conspicuous title were not published until 1852 (by Breitkopf & Härtel, in Leipzig). Their earlier incarnations were published, first, in 1827, under the title of *Étude pour le piano en quarante-huit exercices*, and second, in 1839, as *24 Grandes Études pour le piano*.[5] The latter printing was issued simultaneously in Vienna by Tobias Haslinger, in Milan by Giovanni Ricordi, and in Paris by Maurice Schlesinger, the owner of the *Revue et Gazette musicale*, who first advertised a collection called *24 Grandes Études* on 14 April 1839—a collection he continued to advertise under that title through 1842.[6]

Was it therefore Fétis, deploying the crucial word *transcendant,* who first suggested the definitive title for the *Grandes Études*, eleven years *avant la lettre*? Or did Fétis rather have in hand Liszt's *Études d'exécution transcendante d'après Paganini*, published in Paris by Georges Schonenberger in late 1840 and advertised in the *Revue et Gazette musicale* on 14 February 1841, only three months before the appearance of the article in question?[7] We simply cannot be sure; we know only that Fétis had earlier associated Liszt with "une école *transcendante* du piano,"[8] and that in the present article he finally expresses admiration for Liszt the composer as well as the pianist.[9] It may seem surprising that the Paganini *Études*, essentially arrangements of preexisting works, should have inspired such a long and thoughtful article. But it would be even more remarkable if the *Transcendental Etudes* had in fact been given their ultimate title by François-Joseph Fétis.

Fétis favors speaking of history in terms of "schools" and "systems," just as he favors speaking of his own thinking in terms of "doctrines" and "philosophies." History for him is "an *abstraction* made from the individual lives and works" of those who lived it, "men of genius . . . who, as a result of their powerful independence, break the bonds that restrain their contemporaries and cause their art to forge ahead."[10] Fétis's preference for generic purity and his desire to incorporate all musical phenomena into larger logical categories can thus come into conflict with his recognition of the uniqueness of certain observable facts, just as his insistence on speaking of *transformation* rather than *progress* can inhibit his perfectly normal desire to assert that one new practice might be *better* than another.

It was surely this "conservative" tendency that led him initially to favor the now lesser-known virtuoso in the Liszt-Thalberg "duel" which took place on 31 March 1837 in the Parisian salons of the Princess Belgiojoso. In a general sense, what was at issue here, before an elite audience of artists, writers, and politicians, was the determination to prove who was the greatest pianist of the day and, more subtly, what constituted great playing. Thalberg's particular novelty—readily graspable—was to attribute a principal melodic line to the middle register of the keyboard in such a way as to give the impression that it was magically played by a "third hand." Liszt's pyrotechnical improvisations, no less remarkable, were surely less easy for a lexicographer like Fétis to label. In his article, Fétis criticizes Liszt for somehow failing to infuse his earlier music with the mysterious element that in fact founds a "school" that is susceptible to transformation, that leads to imitation; and he asserts that precisely this sort of element—a "system," the joining together of the "bravura" school of piano playing with the "singing" school, as he put it elsewhere—was responsible for Thalberg's meteoric rise to the top.

Here Fétis speaks about the interior turmoil that Liszt suffered because of Thalberg's success. How does he know about this? It is reasonable to suppose—since Fétis relates Liszt's having played for him privately—that the younger man actually confided in the fatherly fifty-seven-old "sage of Brussels," whose acquaintance Liszt may well have made as a boy, Fétis's neighbor in the rue Montholon, and whose lectures on the future of harmony Liszt had indeed attended in the summer of 1832, as Fétis self-importantly recalls in his article.[11] It was in one of those lectures that Fétis advanced the notion of the *ordre omnitonique*—in essence a prescient if apprehensive description of the possibilities of post-Wagnerian chromaticism—which apparently caused Liszt to sketch a work, long since lost, called *Prélude omnitonique*.[12] Although they had clashed in 1837 over Thalberg, the two men, after 1840, had clearly restored what became a mutually respectful relationship for many years to come. Liszt would have come to understand that Fétis had a conviction about where the art of music ought to go—toward the same sort of eclectic ideal he preached in the *Méthode des méthodes de piano,* that Fétis was inclined to judge new music on the basis of the historical tendency it represented, and that Fétis particularly approved of those tendencies on which he had lectured and sermonized himself.

In a letter dated 17 May 1841, Liszt generously responded to Fétis's article: "Reading it, I felt that sincere gratification, that noble satisfaction (so rarely experienced!) that you have on being understood and judged by a man who has the right to judge you and by whom it is well worth-while being understood."[13]

FRANÇOIS-JOSEPH FÉTIS

Études d'exécution transcendante
pour le piano, par F. Liszt

Revue et Gazette musicale de Paris, 9 May 1841

Just as there are periods of tranquility for societies, so too are there periods of tranquility for artists, periods in which they live on the basis of an idea or form which they polish, develop, enlarge, or reduce to its essentials, an idea or form that serves them throughout their career, because, as its progenitors, they have ample time to consider all of its possible resources and manifestations. Art, after all, still pure, can be transformed only slowly; the least flight of the imagination becomes an event that can occupy an entire generation. Originality is not even a necessary condition for success; perfect workmanship can by itself do the trick. Consider the case of Clementi, that master of the elegant and brilliant school of pianism, that embodiment of proper technique, of naïve and spirited thinking, of the rounded musical phrase. Reflect upon the fact that he captured the attention of his contemporaries by imposing his work as a model and by molding the classic shape of the "brilliant" sonata just as Haydn had molded the shape of the "harmonic" sonata. Looking at his magisterial authority, at his universal reputation, and at all the keyboard artists of his day who felt it necessary to imitate him, you would take Clementi for a great inventor. And yet what he really knew how to do was to perfect the ideas of others, thus establishing himself as a man endowed more with good taste than with inner genius. The truly great inventor was Carl Philipp Emanuel Bach, who, with his inexhaustible imagination, endowed Germany with some sixty concertos and more than three hundred sonatas, but who became well-known only to the Germans, because in his day communications took place essentially via armies and ambassadors. Emanuel Bach invented both the "harmonic" sonata and the "brilliant" sonata. Haydn would develop the former; Clementi would develop the latter. The great designs of Emanuel Bach were created before 1740; sixty years later they were still not exhausted, as one may observe in the works of Dussek, Cramer, and Steibelt, all followers of Clementi, albeit with eminently personal characteristics of their own.

Art, precisely because of the works of these extraordinary men, existed in the realm of the gentle pleasures: to caress the ear, to touch the heart—those were its goals. Not aiming at stirring strong emotions, music did not make full use of the feelings it aroused. The very quality of these feelings resulted in keeping as they were the forms of composition that inspired those gentle pleasures in the first place.

A new order of forms and ideas was born when Mozart introduced into instrumental music the expressive qualities of drama and passion. The potentially disturbing aspects of this development were not immediately understood, and it encountered resistance from those who preferred the traditionally more soothing conventions; the agitation mixed with pleasure that Mozart's development produced found more detractors than supporters. Post-Mozartian piano music, with its richly expressive accents and incisive harmonies, had therefore to contend for some time with the light, elegant, and charming school of Clementi. But Beethoven's daring imagination came to its support, and the number of admirers of the new way began slowly but surely to grow. That same powerful thinker supplied the first examples of the formal instability that became inevitable in this newly expressive era. Because he was immediately seduced by the sheer splendor that characterized the products of Mozart's inventive genius, Beethoven at first merely followed the path that had been traced by his illustrious predecessor. But he soon began to contrive structures that were more robust and more adventurous; he replaced brilliant passagework with tonal development; he sought out harmonic richness with particular care and introduced into it a profusion of dissonance; and he did not hesitate to formulate associations between chords that were at the time totally unfamiliar and yet appear to us today as effortless and natural.

A new kind of fingering was the inevitable consequence of these developments, and this new fingering met with criticism from the students of Clementi and Cramer. But the Viennese school nonetheless adopted and presented the new system as the most advanced fingering available to the art of playing the piano. And the dynamic energies that have over the last forty years moved pianism to its current state of development were in fact derived from that Viennese school. Still, the works of Beethoven, considered by pianists as too weighty for the larger public, remained reserved for performance in intimate surroundings, and artists of great technical prowess continued to seek more brilliant if superficial success by playing the works from the "school of pianism" properly speaking, until Hummel arrived and furnished them with new objects of study embodying yet another transformation of music for the piano. In his day a virtuoso of the first rank, Hummel was also a highly gifted composer. His music was not the equivalent of Beethoven's in terms of boldness and originality, but it showed the composer to be a man of learning and of good taste. With remarkable dexterity, Hummel knew how to lend musical interest to virtuoso passages, and to play them in a way never encountered before. His approach gave rise to a host of imitators.

Note that we are only in 1807, that only fifteen years have elapsed since the death of Mozart, and that we have already witnessed the birth of three new and different movements promulgated by that great man. The style of Hummel fulfilled its mission for the next ten years. During this period, Carl Maria von Weber appeared on the scene with his own unique artistic gifts, putting forth a quite remarkable variant of the dramatically expressive genre as applied to the piano. But at that time Weber was in fact what others have sometimes pretentiously and mistakenly considered themselves to be: a misunderstood genius. Rejected equally by artists and amateurs, his piano music led publishers to fear financial ruin. It took nothing less than the overwhelming success of *Der Freischütz* to recover his piano music from the total obscurity into which it had fallen.

The year 1817 saw the appearance of another pianist-composer of superior talent, another man born to put his own stamp upon the art of his day. I am speaking here, obviously, of Ignaz Moscheles. More vigorous and more dazzling than Hummel in inventing virtuoso pieces, Moscheles infused them with many elegant innovations; the variations of his *Marche d'Alexandre* served some of the most gifted pianists as a model for this type of music. Somewhat later the composer broadened and elevated his style in the *Souvenirs d'Irlande*. No less distinguished a composer in his more serious works, Moscheles demonstrated in his piano concertos a profound knowledge of harmony and dramatic sentiment, and this became progressively more intense in his concertos known as the *Fantastique* and the *Pathétique*, both works remarkable for their emotional qualities, their inventiveness, and their craftsmanship. The piano *étude* as invented by Cramer was further developed by Moscheles, and the highly muscular forms in which he cast them became the seeds from which grew the work that is the principal object of this article.

Moscheles was at the peak of his career when there arrived in Paris a frail boy, phenomenally gifted but of limited technical prowess. That boy was Liszt, "Little Liszt," as we said at the time, and as we continued to say even after his capacities proved that he was not "little" at all.[14] I have written elsewhere of the moment at which these capacities, fully developed, took on the qualities of grandeur that have now elevated Liszt to the highest ranks of the pianists.[15] I spoke of the tremendous efforts that are responsible for the development of his prodigious technique and for the supremacy of his playing that now stupefies the entire world (a world that has now become his public). But even after this supremacy was established as unassailable, Liszt still had something to learn: this was to add to his magnificently distinctive musical personality some element that could be transmissible, which could serve as the foundation of a school that would remain in the history of art as a self-contained phase. Liszt's earliest compositions had no such distinguishing feature: the difficulty of their execution was the sole sign of their author's distinctive personality, but that difficulty in itself had no palpable form and led to no "system" susceptible to transformation.

All of a sudden Thalberg appeared in Paris and caused a sensation such as had never before been seen—not because the power of his playing was superior to Liszt's, or even equal to it, for that matter, but because the source of his great flair derived from a felicitous and readily graspable idea: to wit, filling in the empty space traditionally left in the middle range of the keyboard during the playing of virtuoso lines by employing the fingers normally unused during those rapid passages to play the melodies for which they provided nothing more than accompaniment. The magical effect associated with this novelty, the artist's facility in making the most of this technique, the lovely sonority he obtained from the instrument, and the lyrical quality he was able to lend to those interior lines via the use of the pedals, which no one ever exploited more adroitly than he—all of these things, I repeat, were responsible for and justified Thalberg's great success. More recently Thalberg has been attacked for his innovations by those who say that they do not originate with him, that they occur earlier in the sonatas of Beethoven. It has further been suggested that these innovations are useless in the creation of serious music, that Thalberg himself tends to overuse them, and that they lend to his music a regrettable uniformity of sound and effect. To refute these criticisms would take me too far from the subject at hand. Let me simply say, first, that Thalberg's system succeeds only when employed in the manner that *he* invented (which will guarantee his proprietary rights to it), and, second, that the system is so likely to lead to success that other extremely well-known artists have been led, whether by chance or by design, to imitate it, at least in certain ways, something that proves its practical value.

Liszt was away from Paris at the time of Thalberg's great triumphs. But it was not long before the exasperating news of his success reached Liszt's ears and caused him sleepless nights. Let us peer for a moment into the soul of an artist who—confidently aware of his powers, confidently aware of his lack of real rivals—suddenly finds himself displaced and, worse, outstripped in the public's opinion by another. This is cruel punishment indeed! If it is inflicted upon an artist when he is nearing the end of his career, he only becomes morose and cantankerous. If it is inflicted upon him when he is still young, however, then he rather becomes mortified and angry. It was thus anger that began to boil in Liszt's blood when, as fast as his horses could carry him, he arrived from Geneva in Paris.

Thalberg was no longer there. I do not care to recall the circumstances surrounding this trip, nor the polemical arguments that followed upon its heels. I prefer to follow the great artist in his peregrinations to Milan and to Lake Como.[16] There he becomes for us the object of highly interesting study; there we see him looking inward and saying to himself:

"I now have a rival! This rival has produced something that is now stunning the musical world. This something, I believe and I say, has been overvalued. But be this as it may, I can neither deny nor conceal its success—and success is always a historical fact. This something is thus a reality, or at least it has the reality of a form. But really, is this the last word in art? Is my career now over? And am I now destined forever to work with the old forms, or to become an imitator of the person against whom I am now pitted? Was I not also born to create new forms? And did not nature endow me with the facility to be the single most astonishing interpreter of the creations of others?"

What came after this interior monologue was silence—silence for some three years, interrupted only from time to time by the reverberation of the name of Liszt, thrown into space like a bolt of lightning. The life of a powerful man sometimes does indeed offer us an example of this sort of sublime silence, during which he is able to revitalize himself. Precisely what Liszt did during this period remains known only to a few, despite the widespread approval he has met with since putting an end to it, because the charming *Réminiscences de Lucia di Lammermoor* and the admirably varied *Réminiscences de Robert le diable* give only a very incomplete idea of his accomplishments.[17] Those who, at the concert he gave in Liège, heard him improvise, as I did, a marvelous caprice upon apparently incompatible themes suggested by members of the audience; those who saw him read at sight music laced with death-defying technical difficulties and hastily set down in all but unreadable hands, playing at speeds that surprised even the authors, with such effortlessness as to suggest the performance of mere bagatelles; those, finally, who know that all music of any value whatsoever is stored away in Liszt's mind in such a way that he is able instantaneously to perform whatever piece by whatever celebrated pianist or composer that one might care to name—those persons, I say, know that Liszt is the most complete musician of our time as well as the most accomplished virtuoso.[18] And yet those same persons remain ignorant of the revolution that took place in his creative imagination during the several years he spent in "retirement."[19]

Permit me to recall, in order to explain this revolution, that in one of the meetings of the course on the philosophy of music that I gave in Paris in 1832, I spoke of the future of harmony and of tonality, whose final stage ought to be the establishment of relationships among all the keys, major and minor, and as a consequence, the establishment of harmonic progressions heretofore unheard of—an artistic phenomenon to which I have given the name *ordre omnitonique*. Liszt was present at this lecture; he was struck by the novelty of my idea and, later on, he accepted it as a kind of incontrovertible truth. He then determined he would try to apply the idea to piano music. Accordingly, by combining in newly composed works the new modulatory procedures he had discovered in the transformations effected by Thalberg and now considered compositional necessities, and the new effects and processes of transcendental execution available only to someone of Liszt's spectacular technique, he created a genre of piano music that belongs only to himself, and that answers in the affirmative the question that has so often been posed: *Will Liszt become a distinguished composer?*

A colossal unpublished composition, whose various parts combine to form some twelve to fifteen hundred pages of music, and whose title is, I believe, *Trois années de pèlerinage* or *de pérégrinations*, is the work into which Liszt has poured his artistic thinking in its newest guises. The first part includes his recollections of Switzerland; the second, his recollections of Italy; the last, his recollections of Germany.[20]

The celebrated pianist played some excerpts from this work for me and I had to render justice to him by saying that he had now assumed a preeminent position in the field of music.[21] Perhaps, once this work is published, some will say that the composer has woven too much of the orchestra into traditional keyboard music rather than contenting himself with the piano; but it may well be that this commentary will turn out to be more of a compliment than a criticism.

Be that as it may, wishing in no way to anticipate the judgments that will eventually be made by the virtuosos, I limit myself here to expressing my feelings based on my first impressions. To speak only of what is today known to artists, I will mention solely the *Études d'exécution transcendante*, which are the subject, or rather the impetus, of this article, and whose new forms have rendered necessary my long preamble, because to analyze this kind of work in detail is at this point not even conceivable. There is far too much originality in its details for one to be able to comprehend the forms without hearing them construed by the powerful hands of their composer. Let us simply say this: one need only cast his eyes upon this music to be persuaded it represents the most advanced state of the art in terms of piano performance and it offers at the same time conceptions that are both daring and bold.

—Fétis père
Directeur du Conservatoire de Bruxelles

NOTES

1. "La plus noble et la plus légitime satisfaction que puisse éprouver l'artiste n'est-elle pas de se sentir au-dessus de sa renommée, supérieur même à son succès, plus grand encore que sa gloire?" *Revue et Gazette musicale,* 2 May 1841.

2. Liszt's exclamation—"I am the servant of the public, that's for sure!"— is quoted in French in Richard Wagner's report on the concert that appeared in the *Dresdener Abendzeitung* of 14 June 1841.

3. The full title of this treatise, which officially appeared on 15 November 1840, is sufficient to describe its intent: *Méthode des méthodes de piano ou Traité de l'art de jouer de cet instrument basé sur l'analyse des meilleurs ouvrages qui ont été faits à ce sujet et particulièrement des méthodes de Ch. P. E. Bach, Marpurg, Türk, A. E. Müller, Dussek, Clementi, Hummel, MM. Adam, Kalkbrenner et A. Schmidt, ainsi que sur la comparaison et l'appréciation des différents systèmes d'exécution et de doigter de quelques virtuoses célèbres tels que MM. Chopin, Cramer, Döhler, Henselt, Liszt, Moscheles, Thalberg* (Paris: 1840). The second part of the treatise is made up of *études de perfectionnement,* all expressly composed for this volume (testifying to the wide network of personal relationships maintained in the musical world by the two authors), by Julius Benedict, Frédéric Chopin (the *Trois nouvelles études*), Theodor Döhler, Stephen Heller, Adolf Henselt, Franz Liszt (a *morceau de salon* later published as *Ab irato*), Felix Mendelssohn, Amédée Méreaux, Ignaz Moscheles, Jacques Rosenhain, Sigismond Thalberg, and Édouard Wolff.

4. Wagner, "Du métier de virtuose et de l'indépendance des compositeurs," *Revue et Gazette musicale,* 28 October 1840.

5. The collection, marked "œuvre 6," was published in that year by Boisselot in Marseilles and by Dufaut et Dubois in Paris. Friedrich Hofmeister in Leipzig reissued this work—which, despite its title, contained only twelve *exercices*—as *Études pour le piano en douze exercices, œuvre 1,* apparently in 1839; a facsimile of the title page may be found in Ernst Burger, *Franz Liszt: A Chronicle of His Life in Pictures and Documents,* trans. Stewart Spencer (Princeton, N.J.: 1989), p. 46.

6. A facsimile of the title page of the Haslinger edition is given in Burger, *Franz Liszt,* p. 119. Schlesinger's advertisements of the same work appeared in the issues of the *Revue et Gazette musicale* of 14 April 1839; 2 May 1839; 20 October 1839; 26 April 1840; 25 October 1840; 4 April 1841; 28 November 1841; 5 June 1842; and beyond. These prove that the word *transcendant* was not publicly applied to the *Grandes Études* in the 1830s or early 1840s. (Schlesinger had first advertised this work, on 4 April 1839, as *Vingt-Cinq Grandes Études brillantes*; he corrected the title in the advertisement of 14 April.)

7. The *Études d'exécution transcendante d'après Paganini* were subsequently issued, in 1851, by Breitkopf & Härtel, as the *Grandes Études de Paganini.* The word *transcendant,* common in French at the time, must not be confused with *transcendental,* rare in French and sometimes associated with the philosophy of Kant. It has, of course, been argued that Liszt's mature thinking was influenced by Kantian aesthetics. See, for example, Jim Samson, *Virtuosity and the Musical Work* (Cambridge, Eng.: 2003), pp. 194–95. But Liszt presumably understood the word to mean, as did the *Dictionaire de l'Académie française* from the seventeenth through twentieth century, "élevé, sublime, qui excelle en son genre" (lofty, superior, advanced in its class). The word *transcendant* is sometimes (as in the *New Liszt Edition*) rendered as "in increasing degree of difficulty." This is not the case for the *études* by Liszt, but may be the sense of the word as first found in the *Revue musicale,* when the *Praktische Orgel-Schul* (Darmstadt: 1819–21) of Johann Christian Heinrich Rinck was reviewed by Fétis in the issue of October 1828 (vol. 4, p. 305) in the translation by Alexandre Choron: *L'École pratique d'orgue, méthode transcendante formée de la reunion de plusieurs recueils offrant une série graduée de tout genre propre à l'étude de cet instrument.*

8. In the *Revue et Gazette musicale* of 25 April 1837, Fétis, chastising Liszt for having openly criticized Thalberg (in an article for that magazine of 8 January 1837), suggests that Liszt's friends should have said to him: "Vous êtes l'homme *transcendant* de l'école qui finit et qui n'a plus rien à faire, mais vous n'êtes pas celui d'une école nouvelle. Thalberg est cet homme: voilà toute la différence entre vous deux." (You are the transcendent figure of the school that is coming to an end and that has nothing more to say, but you are not the transcendent figure of a new school. That figure is Thalberg. That is the difference between the two of you.) This is the article to which Liszt himself made a virulent rebuttal in the issue of 14 May 1837, excoriating Fétis for his ignorance and arrogance yet stating that the dispute was "much ado about nothing." Fétis concluded the exchange with a more neutral response in the issue of 21 May 1837.

Rapid summaries of this famous quarrel (there have been many) cannot do it justice, for both men cast light as well as aspersions. It should be noted that Liszt was writing with the editorial assistance of Marie d'Agoult, in a letter to whom he speaks "de mon (*ou de notre*) article sur Thalberg"—of my (*or our*) article on Thalberg. *Correspondance de Liszt et de Madame d'Agoult*, ed. Daniel Ollivier, 2 vols. (Paris: 1933–34), vol. 1, p. 187 (my emphasis). In the same letter, dated 13 February 1837, he notes how Chopin had told him that Fétis's positive view of Thalberg was paid for by Thalberg's father, Count Moritz Dietrichstein.

9. Joseph d'Ortigue, long an admirer of Liszt, was apparently surprised by the positive tone of Fétis's article, as Marie d'Agoult reported to Liszt on 18 May 1841. *Correspondance de Liszt et de Madame d'Agoult*, vol. 2, p. 138.

10. *Revue musicale*, 7 December 1834 and 3 December 1831.

11. In a letter of 1852 Liszt mentions his talks "of the rue Montholon" with Wilhelm von Lenz, in Paris in 1828. See Liszt, *Selected Letters*, trans. and ed. Adrian Williams (Oxford, Eng.: 1998), p. 335. It is conceivable that some of those talks included Fétis. Fétis left Paris in May 1833, when he became director of the Conservatoire in Brussels and Maître de chapelle for King Léopold I.

12. "If [the *Prélude*, last seen in a London exhibition of 1904] ever turns up again, historians may have some serious rethinking to do." See Alan Walker, "Liszt and the Twentieth Century," in *Franz Liszt: The Man and His Music*, ed. Alan Walker (London: 1970), p. 362.

13. See Julien Tiersot, *Lettres de musiciens écrites en français du XVe au XXe siècle*, (Turin: 1924), vol. 2, p. 362. This letter may have prompted the offer from Fétis to appoint Liszt to a post at the Conservatoire in Brussels, to which Marie d'Agoult alludes in a letter of June 1841, *Correspondance de Liszt et de Madame d'Agoult*, vol. 2, pp. 156, 164.

14. The Liszt family arrived in Paris on 11 December 1823.

15. Fétis refers to the article on Liszt in volume 6 of the first edition of the *Biographie universelle des musiciens* (Paris: 1840).

16. Liszt went to Lake Como and to Milan in the period from August 1837 to March 1838, *after* the "duel" with Thalberg (31 March 1837) that provoked the polemics Fétis, his chronology defective, prefers not to rehearse here. The last word on the contest was probably the Princess Belgiojoso's, who said something to the effect that Thalberg was the "greatest" pianist and that Liszt was the "only" pianist. See also note 8.

17. Composed and published (by Maurice Schlesinger, in Paris) in 1841.

18. Liszt played in Liège on 13 February 1841.

19. In order to enliven his narrative, Fétis seems to have invented the notion of Liszt's years "passées dans la retraite": the pianist may not have appeared in Paris, but in the later 1830s he was performing and composing extensively, including arrangements that were crucial to the rediscovery of Franz Schubert.

20. The definitive title would be *Années de pèlerinage* (sometimes appears as *pélerinage* or *pélérinage*). The first of these appeared in the summer of 1841, when Simon Richault published seven fascicles under the title *Année de pélerinage* [*sic*]. See György Kroo, "Années de Pélerinage—Première Année: Versions and Variants," *Studia Musicologica Academiae Scientarum Hungaricae* 34 (1992): 13. The third part of the *Années de pèlerinage*, published years later, in 1877, would not consist of "recollections of Germany," although Fétis's intriguing remark, reflected nowhere else in the literature, suggests that this may have been Liszt's original intention—something that would counter Dolores Pesce's hypothesis that Liszt "may indeed have conceived Book 3 with his native Hungary in mind." See Pesce, "Liszt's *Années de Pèlerinage*, Book 3: A 'Hungarian' Cycle?" *19th-Century Music* 13 (1990): 208.

21. Liszt played at a private concert organized by Fétis on 11 February 1841. The next day he wrote to Marie d'Agoult: "J'ai joué hier soir chez Fétis; il y avait 150 personnes. Après mon premier morceau Fétis s'est crié: 'Voilà la création du piano. On ne savait pas ce que c'était jusqu'ici'." (Last night I played at Fétis's; there were 150 people in attendance. After the first piece, Fétis cried out: 'There you have it—the creation of the piano. We didn't know what it was until now.') See *Correspondance de Liszt et de Madame d'Agoult*, vol. 2, p. 120.

Heinrich Heine on Liszt

SELECTED AND INTRODUCED BY RAINER KLEINERTZ
TRANSLATED BY SUSAN GILLESPIE

Heinrich Heine was one of the most important German poets in lyrics and prose. He was born into a Jewish family in Düsseldorf on 13 December 1797. The French occupation of the Rhine area and Napoleon Bonaparte's solemn entry into Düsseldorf (1811) made a strong impression on him. Later, after a fruitless attempt to enter the business of his uncle Salomon Heine in Hamburg (a successful banker), he studied law at the universities of Bonn, Göttingen, and Berlin, where he heard Georg Wilhelm Friedrich Hegel and attended the premiere of Carl Maria von Weber's *Der Freischütz* in 1821. In 1825 he converted from Judaism to Protestantism to prepare for a career as a civil servant in Prussia. Unsuccessful in his attempts to obtain a secure living, and feeling uncomfortable in Germany between its restoration government and nationalist opposition, he decided in 1831—soon after the July Revolution of 1830—to move to Paris, where he lived until his death in 1856. Apart from poems and narrative prose, Heine wrote a considerable number of articles for German newspapers that give a lively account of the political and cultural life in Paris. In 1854 he published these articles in two volumes titled *Lutetia,* certainly the most brilliant and witty mirror of his epoch. Contrary to his promise to leave all the articles unchanged, Heine made considerable changes in them. Some of these changes—which were one of his best guarded secrets—concerned contemporary musicians portrayed by him for posterity, such as Felix Mendelssohn-Bartholdy, Giacomo Meyerbeer, and . . . Franz Liszt.

Although Heine made several disparaging remarks about Liszt in his articles and poems, he and Liszt were friends.[1] They first met in June 1831, soon after Heine's arrival in Paris. In spite of a considerable age difference— Heine was fourteen years older—their relationship was quite cordial. Both attended the Saint-Simonian meetings in the Rue Taitbout, and through

Liszt Heine made the acquaintance of Parisian artists such as George Sand, his "dear cousin." In his essay "On the Situation of Artists" (1835) Liszt referred to Heine as "the most spirited and Parisian of Germans," and in 1837 he addressed the seventh installment of his *Lettres d'un bachelier ès musique* to Heine.[2] Their personal contact was interrupted in 1835, when Liszt left Paris with his mistress Marie d'Agoult for Geneva. But when Heine traveled to Marseilles in 1836 and heard about Liszt's projected Italian journey, he asked him in a warmhearted letter to describe his plans and expressed a wish to meet him in Italy.[3]

The Italian journey had to be postponed due to an outbreak of cholera in Italy, and at the end of 1836 both Heine and Liszt returned to Paris. It was this same winter that Liszt encountered, for the first and only time of his life, a serious rival on the piano: Sigismund Thalberg. Indeed, the "duel" between Liszt and Thalberg would become the most interesting event of the musical season 1837.[4] Liszt's strategy was to present himself as a composer and interpreter in the tradition of Beethoven and to belittle Thalberg as a mere piano virtuoso. He started with a vehement attack on Thalberg's compositions in the *Revue et Gazette musicale de Paris*, which was answered by Fétis in the same journal.[5] Heine echoed Liszt's strategy in the first of the three essays he eventually published on Liszt, from the series "Confidential Letters" (because this text is included in Charles Suttoni's *An Artist's Journey*, it is not included here).[6] Despite some mockery about Liszt's "philosophical hobbyhorses," the message of this letter was clear: while the preceding "Confidential Letter" had been dedicated to Rossini and Meyerbeer as the most important opera composers of their time, this letter presented Liszt, along with Berlioz and Chopin, as the most remarkable composers of instrumental music. Just as Heine proposed Meyerbeer as the modern "dramatic" opera composer, though his personal taste inclined more toward the older Rossini with his "beautiful" melodies, so he propagated Liszt as the truly modern pianist, though he enjoyed more the "romantic" music of Chopin. Chopin was the favorite of an aristocratic elite, his homeland "the land of poetry," "the land of Mozart, Raphael, and Goethe."[7] Liszt, however, was "a child of his times," a man who was tormented over the interests of humanity, worried about the future of mankind, no "placid pianist to entertain peaceable citizens and sensible cotton bonnets." When Heine confesses that "despite my friendship for Liszt, his music does not affect my feelings in an agreeable way," he asserts nothing else than the modernity of Liszt's music.

Liszt spent the following years in Italy, and in 1839 he started his virtuoso tours through all of Europe. When he returned to Paris in 1841, Heine was stupefied by the sovereignty of his piano playing and recorded it in his article "Musical Season in Paris" of 20 April 1841, published below in English translation. Heine compared Liszt not only with Lord Byron, "with whom Liszt has many similarities," but also with Beethoven, the musical genius *par excellence*. What Liszt had intended since 1837 with his transcriptions of Beethoven's symphonies and of Schubert's Lieder for the piano, with his own compositions such as *Lyon* and his first Lieder, became reality in Heine's prose: Liszt was a musical genius worthy of being named in the same breath as Lord Byron and Beethoven![8]

For Heine this was not just propaganda, but part of his concept of history, which was rooted in the philosophy of Hegel, especially the *Aesthetics*. In the introduction to his second essay, Heine presents a history of the arts in relation to the "gradual spiritualization of the human race." The final point of art would be "the dissolution of the entire material world," and so "music may be the last word of art, as death is the last word of life." Only in this philosophical context are Heine's *aesthetic* reservations about Beethoven and Liszt comprehensible. When he remarks in his report of 1841 that "Liszt's playing sometimes seems to me like a melodic agony of the world of appearances," and when he adds, upon announcement of Liszt's concert for the benefit of the Beethoven monument, that "this composer must in fact be the most appealing to the genius of a Liszt," he is saying nothing less than that for him, Heine, Liszt's music is, like Beethoven's late works, the expression of the "intensified spirituality" that marks the "end of the artistic phase."[9] The uncanny in Liszt's playing and compositions is thus at the same time the guarantor of its modernity. Liszt was quite pleased with the article, even proposing in a letter to Marie d'Agoult that it be translated and published in *Le Monde musical*.[10]

Heine's most notorious lines on Liszt are found in his third article on Liszt, the "Musical Season in Paris" of 1844, translated and presented here in two versions. In the *Lutetia* version of this article—which is the generally known version, though published by Heine a decade later—Liszt is ridiculed as a *parvenu*, "the errant knight of all possible orders, the Hohenzollern-Hechingen court councilor, the doctor of philosophy and miracle doctor of music." His incredible successes as a traveling virtuoso, or "Lisztomania"—a word coined by Heine—are explained by the fact that "no one in this world knows how to organize his successes, or rather the *mise en scène* of them, as well as our Franz Liszt." Heine insinuates that "the hour will soon strike when the titan of music will perhaps shrivel up into a municipal musician of very short stature," alluding in a faint prophecy to Liszt's settling in Weimar in 1848.

The ad hominem attacks in this article figure in an apocryphal story about a supposed attempt by Heine to blackmail Liszt, a story that has been repeated uncritically even in recent Liszt monographs.[11] True, Heine asked Liszt to meet him in person in April of 1844 to discuss an article that contained things that might not please him.[12] However, that article could not have been the one containing the insulting phrases about Liszt, since Heine wrote them much later. Few scholars seem to know that no less than three substantially different versions of "Musical Season in Paris" (1844) exist. The version most commonly reproduced, and the only one that contains the insulting insinuations, is that of *Lutetia*, published in 1854. The considerable changes made in this later edition were one of Heine's best-guarded secrets.

Thus, all the suspicions of Heine's blackmailing in 1844 refer to a text that did not exist then. The reason for Heine's later insults clearly had nothing to do with Liszt refusing to pay him off, and everything to do with Liszt's position at the court of Weimar, which he had held since 1848, the year of the revolution of 1848–49. Liszt's patron there, the Grand Duchess of Weimar, was a sister of the Russian czar who had cruelly suppressed the Hungarian uprising, and her daughter was married to the Prussian prince royal. Heine was not the only one in Paris who regarded Liszt's behavior as treason to his former ideals.[13] In his poem "Im Oktober 1849" Heine had already ridiculed the "Knight Liszt" whose sabre—the "Sabre of Honor" presented to him in Hungary 1839—was kept in the chest while Hungary bled to death.

It should be emphasized that—apart from Heine's usual mockery—the two original versions of this article were completely free of such attacks. In the first version, the "draft" (not reproduced here), a certain reservation about Liszt's enormous successes in Berlin is still perceptible (the Prussian court was Heine's principal political enemy). But then Heine hears—or rather "experiences"—Liszt's first concert in the Théâtre Italien and has to admit that Liszt "at this moment has generated, not only in all Paris, but even in the otherwise so calm writer of these pages, an excitement that cannot be denied." For Heine Liszt's concert was a unique experience: "The electric effect of a demonic nature on a crowd that is all pressed together, the infectious power of ecstasy, and perhaps the magnetism of the music itself, this spiritualistic illness of the age, which vibrates in almost all of us—I have never encountered these phenomena so distinctly and so frighteningly as in the concert by Liszt." For the newspaper publication of this article he added an entirely new paragraph (namely, from "Earlier, when I heard of the swoon that befell Germany, and specifically Berlin, when Liszt appeared there" until "I have never encountered these phenomena so distinctly and so frighteningly as in the concert by Liszt.") In that paragraph Liszt again appears as the enforcer of the Hegelian "Weltgeist." In Liszt *art* becomes *truth* revealing the spiritual illness of the age.

If neither the sketch nor the 1844 version of this article gives cause for any suspicion of successful or unsuccessful blackmailing, nor evidence of a revenge for nonpayment, or of a reward for payment, the question is: Who invented the story of Heine's blackmailing? The first to disseminate this legend was apparently Lina Ramann in her biography: "Liszt often spoke to me about Heine . . . expressing that his character did not attract him, and that his 'extortions could not earn him any taste.' During Liszt's concerts in Paris (1844, I believe) he received from Heine a merchant's bill for some thousands of francs, which he did *not* accept. 'I was neither able nor willing to pay for bought recognition,' were Liszt's exact words."[14]

Not only is the year 1844 her own supposition, but the whole seems to be based on a report of Princess Carolyne von Sayn-Wittgenstein, Liszt's mistress since 1847, who had lived in Russia previously. Ramann visited her in 1876 in Rome to learn more about Liszt's life. There, on 21 June 1876, after a conversation with the princess, she wrote the following sentences in her diary: "Heine had written favorably of Liszt at the beginning of the 30s [!] (see his comparison 'Paganini and Liszt').[15] When he printed it, he sent Liszt a bill for 1,000 francs. Liszt refused it with the remark 'that he has no money and would not pay for reviews of this kind.' From this moment forward date Heine's attacks on Liszt.— With Meyerbeer Heine had better luck. The articles in support of an artist, namely, were raised by Meyerbeer's wealth to enormous heights."[16]

It was these claims from Liszt's former companion that formed the basis of the corresponding lines in Ramann's biography of Liszt, which were in turn taken up by other authors and which, as Michael Mann has shown, were then linked concretely with the *Lutetia* text "Musical Season of the Year 1844."[17] What Heine originally published, which was neither so negative as to serve as revenge for non-payment, nor so positive as to be the result of a payment by Liszt, fell into oblivion. Here, as in many other cases, it can be seen that the last version is not always the best or the most authentic one.

NOTES TO THE INTRODUCTION

1. For a detailed discussion of the relationship between Liszt and Heine see Rainer Kleinertz, "'Wie sehr ich auch Liszt liebe, so wirkt doch seine Musik nicht angenehm auf mein Gemüt'—Freundschaft und Entfremdung zwischen Heine und Liszt," *Heine-Jahrbuch* 37 (1998): 107–39.

2. "De la situation des artistes et de leur condition dans la société," in Franz Liszt, *Frühe Schriften,* ed. Rainer Kleinertz (Wiesbaden et al.: 2000), vol. 1, p. 26.

3. "Before my departure from Paris I was told, dear Liszt, that you were still in Geneva, and would only later travel to Italy. I'm writing to you today in hopes of learning somewhat more about your visit and travel plans. I would be unspeakably pleased if I could meet up with you somewhere. . . . I was happy to hear that during your absence you have developed to the most astonishing degree. This absence was certainly healing—you needed this pause more than anyone; I always feared that your life in Paris, with the outer and inner turmoil in which I always saw you, might wear you out; you are an extraordinarily noble person, and I love you as a brother." Heine to Liszt, 12 October 1836, in Heine, *Werke, Briefwechsel, Lebenszeugnisse: Säkularausgabe* (Berlin and Paris: 1970), vol. 21, p. 163. Alongside the affirmation of his brotherly affection, Heine mentions a characteristic of Liszt that apparently had disturbed him: his physical and spiritual restlessness, a sort of overexcitement noted not only by Heine, but also by many contemporaries who regarded Liszt with much less sympathy.

4. See Dana Gooley, *The Virtuoso Liszt* (Cambridge, Eng.: 2004), pp. 18ff.; Rainer Kleinertz, "Subjektivität und Öffentlichkeit: Liszts Rivalität mit Thalberg und ihre Folgen," in *Der junge Liszt, Referate des 4. Europäischen Liszt-Symposions Wien 1991,* ed. Gottfried Scholz (Munich and Salzburg: 1993), pp. 58–67.

5. The texts of this polemic are published and commented in Liszt, *Frühe Schriften.*

6. The letter was published in German as number 10 of Heine's *Über die französische Bühne: Vertraute Briefe an August Lewald,* in August Lewald's *Allgemeine Theater-Revue* (Stuttgart and Tübingen) of 1837. A French translation is found in "Lettres confidentielles II," *Revue et Gazette musicale de Paris,* 4 February 1838, and is reproduced in Liszt, *Frühe Schriften,* pp. 442–47. For an English translation of this version see Liszt, *An Artist's Journey,* ed. Charles Suttoni (Chicago and London: 1989), pp. 219–26.

7. See Liszt, *An Artist's Journey,* p. 224.

8. Liszt's first Lied on a text by Heine was the 1840 "Im Rhein, im schönen Strome."

9. Regarding the comparison to Beethoven: In the manuscript sketch Heine writes, "It is this composer whose genius most resembles Liszt's and who deserves praise." In the book version (*Lutetia,* 1854), the word *genius* is replaced with *taste.* As for Heine and Hegel, see Willi Oelmüller, "Hegels Satz vom Ende der Kunst und das Problem der Philosophie der Kunst nach Hegel," *Philosophisches Jahrbuch* 73 (1965): 75–94; and the chapter "Das Ende der Kunstperiode—Aspekte der literarischen Revolution bei Heine, Hugo und Stendhal," in Hans Robert Jauß, *Literaturgeschichte als Provokation* (Frankfurt am Main: 1970), pp. 107–43.

10. "Would you be willing to translate Heine's article and give it to the *Monde musical?* It would only be necessary to add a couple of sentences before it, such as these: 'We borrow from the *Gazette universelle* of Augsburg the following article, in which we believe we recognize the pen of one of the most eminent poet-writers of Germany. Without taking any responsibility for the opinions of the famous critic, we believe we can please our readers in conveying to them these so ingeniously wise aperçus, which possess an ironic impartiality.' Do with it what you think best (without signing it of course) and give me notice afterward so I can write to Lireux." To Marie d'Agoult, Boulogne, 6 May 1841, in *Correspondance Franz Liszt, Marie d'Agoult,* ed. Serge Gut and Jacqueline Bellas (Paris: 2001), p. 792.

11. Alan Walker, for instance, tells the following story: "In April 1844 Heine wrote to Liszt warning him that he had prepared a newspaper article for publication *before* Liszt's second concert, and since there were things in it that might not please him, he offered to let him read it in advance . . . Liszt quite rightly ignored this veiled threat, and Heine's article duly appeared on April 25 in *Musikalische Berichte aus Paris*. It attributed Liszt's success to lavish expenditures on bouquets and to the wild behavior of his hysterical female 'fans.' After reading the offensive article Liszt broke off relations with Heine." Alan Walker, *Franz Liszt: The Virtuoso Years, 1811–1847,* 2nd ed. (Ithaca, N.Y.: 1987), p. 164.

12. Before Liszt's second concert, which also took place at the Théâtre-Italien on 25 April 1844, Heine tried to contact him: "I would like you, my dear, to visit me tomorrow between 2 and 3 o'clock. I have already written a 1st article that I would like to send off before your 2nd concert, and there might be something in it that may not please you; for this reason it is quite appropriate that I first talk with you. Your friend H. Heine" (Heine, *Säkularausgabe,* vol. 22, p. 102). A first version, written before Liszt's first concert, had been turned down by the editor of the *Allgemeine Zeitung,* because of its personal attacks ("How can you not yourself laugh . . . when you, in your musical reports, seriously favor Ernst over Mendelssohn and Thalberg over Liszt; you can't be serious!" (Heine, *Säkularausgabe,* vol. 26, p. 99). When he heard Liszt's first concert Heine was overwhelmed and changed his opinion on Liszt. So in Heine's invitation one would have to see first and foremost the hope of acquiring Liszt's approval for the revised version, in spite of its barbs. See Heinrich Heine, *Historisch-kritische Gesamtausgabe der Werke (Düsseldorfer Ausgabe),* ed. Volkmar Hansen (Hamburg: 1988), vol. 13, p. 387.

13. With the title "Voici M. Liszt" the satirical journal *Le Charivari* published an article on Liszt's activities in Weimar: "Ever since Goethe lived here, this town has aspired always to have a great man. It is now Liszt who is about to provide this service. Since the February revolution, I am amazed at the silence of Liszt. Where is he? what is he doing? why is he hiding? It's here or never for the invention of socialist music." *Le Charivari,* 18–19 May 1849.

14. Lina Ramann, *Franz Liszt als Künstler und Mensch,* 3 vols. (Leipzig: 1880–94). The statements on Heine are in vol. 2, part 1 (p. 43, n. 1), which appeared just after Liszt's death.

15. No article with this title or any corresponding content is known.

16. Lina Ramann, *Lisztiana: Erinnerungen an Franz Liszt in Tagebuchblättern, Briefen und Dokumenten aus den Jahren 1873–1886/87,* ed. Friedrich Schnapp (Mainz et al.: 1983), p. 80.

17. Michael Mann, *Heinrich Heines Musikkritiken* (Hamburg: 1971), pp. 107–10, 113.

HEINRICH HEINE

Musical Season in Paris

Supplement to the *Allgemeine Zeitung* (Augsburg)
29 April 1841

Paris, April 20.[1] This year's salon revealed nothing but a many-hued paralysis.[2] One might almost think that the renewed flowering of the visual arts here is at an end; it was no new springtime, but a disagreeable old Indian summer. Painting and sculpture, even architecture, enjoyed a joyful resurgence soon after the July Revolution, but the wings were merely tacked on from the outside, and the forced flight was followed by a most pathetic fall. Only the young sister art, music, had lifted herself up with authentic, particular strength. Has she already reached her shining summit? Will she be able to maintain her position there for long? Or will she quickly sink back down again? These are questions only a later generation can answer. But, in any case, it seems that in the annals of art our contemporary era could preferably be recorded as the age of music. The arts, too, are keeping pace with the gradual spiritualization of the human race. In the most ancient period, architecture necessarily had to emerge alone, glorifying unconscious, raw greatness with its masses, as we can observe, for example, among the Egyptians. Later on, among the Greeks, we see the period of the flowering of sculpture, and the latter already testifies to an external dominance over the material—intelligence chiseled a sense of expectant musing into the stone. But the spirit nevertheless found the stone much too hard for its growing need for revelation, and it chose paint, colored shadows, to represent a transfigured and twilit world of love and suffering. Then arose the great age of painting, which unfolded brilliantly at the end of the Middle Ages. With the development of the life of the conscious mind, all talent for the plastic arts diminishes among humans; and finally even the sense of color, which is, after all, always tied to specific drawing, disappears, and heightened spirituality, abstract thought, reaches for sounds and tones in order to express a babbling enthusiasm that is perhaps nothing but the dissolution of the entire material world— music may be the last word of art, as death is the last word of life.

I have prefaced my comments with these brief remarks in order to suggest why the musical season arouses in me more anxiety than joy. That one practically drowns in music here, that there is in Paris almost no single home in which one can take refuge, as in an ark, from this aural flood, that the noble art of music engulfs our whole life—this is for me a worrisome sign, and on this account I am sometimes gripped by an ill humor that even degenerates into the most irritable injustice toward our great maestros and virtuosi. Under these circumstances one can expect no all-too-cheerful song of praise from me for the man whom the musical world here adores at this moment with an almost insane enthusiasm, and who in fact is one of the most remarkable representatives of music. I am speaking of Franz Liszt, the pianist of genius, whose playing sometimes seems to me like a melodic agony of the world of appearances. Yes, Franz Liszt is here again and gives concerts that exert a magic that borders on the fabulous. Compared with him, all piano players are nothing—with the exception of one, Chopin, that Raphael of the fortepiano. Indeed, with this one exception, all other piano players, whom we heard this year in innumerable concerts, are nothing but piano players, they excel through the skill with which they manipulate the strung wood; whereas with Liszt, one no longer thinks of triumphed-over difficulties—the piano disappears and what is revealed is music. In this respect Liszt has made the most marvelous progress since the last time we heard him. With this advantage he combines a calm that we previously missed. For example, when he played a thunderstorm on the fortepiano, we saw the lightning bolts flicker over his face, his limbs shook as if in a gale, and his long tresses seemed to drip, as it were, from the downpour that was represented. Now, when he plays even the most powerful thunderstorm, he rises above it like the traveler who stands on the summit of a mountain while thunder rolls in the valley. The clouds lie far below him, the lightning bolts slither around his feet like snakes, he lifts his head, smiling, into the pure ether. Despite his genius, Liszt encounters an opposition here in Paris that may be a result of that very genius. This quality is in certain eyes an enormous crime that cannot be sufficiently punished. "Talent is quickly pardoned, but genius is unforgivable!" Thus once spake the late lamented Lord Byron, with whom Liszt shares many similarities.

Liszt has already given two concerts in which, contrary to all conventions, he played without other musical collaborators, entirely alone. He is now preparing a third concert for the benefit of the Beethoven monument.[3] This composer must be the most appealing to the genius of a Liszt. Beethoven, in particular, drives the spiritualist art to the point of that destruction of nature that fills me with a horror I have no desire to conceal, though my friends may shake their heads over it. For me it is a very significant circumstance that Beethoven, at the end of his life, became deaf and even the invisible world of tones no longer had any sounding reality for him. His tones had become mere memories of a tone, ghosts of sounds that had died away, and his last productions bear an uncanny mark of death on their brow.

Less gruesome than Beethoven's music for me was the friend of Beethoven, *l'ami de Beethoven,* as he ubiquitously presented himself here, I believe even on visiting cards—a black-haired beanpole with a dreadfully white cravat and a mournful expression.[4] Was this friend of Beethoven's really his Pylades?[5] Or was he one of those casual acquaintances with whom a man of genius occasionally surrounds himself all the more, the more insignificant they are and the more prosaic their blabber, which affords the genius relaxation after tiring poetic flights of fancy? In any case, we saw here a new kind of exploitation of genius, and the little journals made not a little fun of the *ami de Beethoven.* "How could the great artist stand such an un-uplifting, spiritually impoverished friend!" cried the French, who lost all patience when faced with the monotonous blather of that tiresome guest. They were not thinking of the fact that Beethoven was deaf.

The number of concert-givers during this year's season was legion, and there was no lack of mediocre pianists who were hailed as miracles in the papers. Most of them are young people who either modestly themselves, or through some modest brother, provide these panegyrics to the press. The self-deifications of this sort, the so-called *réclames,* make for extremely entertaining reading. One *réclame,* which was recently contained in the *Gazette musicale,* reported from Marseilles that the famous Döhler charmed all hearts there, too, and claimed the special attention of high society with his interesting pallor, the consequence of an illness he had suffered. The famous Döhler has meanwhile returned to Paris and has given several concerts; he also played in the concert of Mr. Schlesinger's *Gazette musicale,* which rewarded him most liberally with laurels. *France musicale* also holds him in high esteem, with equal objectivity; this journal is inspired by a blind enmity against Liszt, and in order to irritate this lion indirectly, it praises the little rabbit. What significance, however, does the real worth of the famed Döhler possess? Some say he is the last of the pianists of second rank; others claim he is the first among the pianists of third rank! In fact, he plays prettily, neatly, and attractively. His interpretation is most pleasing, reveals an astonishing digital skill, but shows neither strength nor spirit. Decorative weakness, elegant paralysis, interesting pallor.

NOTES TO "MUSICAL SEASON IN PARIS," 1841

1. Source: Heinrich Heine, *Säkularausgabe,* vol. 10, ed. Lucienne Netter, pp. 92–102.

2. The "Salon" was the annual exposition of paintings and sculptures in the Louvre. In 1841 it opened on 15 March.

3. The first concert took place in the Salle Erard on 27 March 1841, the second on 13 April. The third concert on 25 April with orchestra was for the benefit of the Beethoven monument in Bonn. The program included only works by Beethoven.

4. Heine refers to Anton Schindler (1796–1866), Beethoven's secretary and factotum since 1820. In 1840 he published the first edition of his Beethoven biography. Schindler tried to present himself as a close friend of Beethoven. To maintain this image he destroyed about two-thirds of Beethoven's conversation books and falsified entries in those he preserved.

5. In Greek mythology Pylades was the friend of Orestes.

Musical Season in Paris

Supplement to the *Allgemeine Zeitung* (Augsburg)
8 May 1844

EDITORS' NOTE ON THE TEXTS ON THIS AND FACING PAGES

Below and on the opposite pages are the two published versions of Heine's "Musical Season" articles about Paris in 1844. To facilitate comparison, we offer the two articles line for line on facing pages, with text that appears only in one version or the other enclosed by brackets ⟨. . .⟩. Due to this method of presentation, artificial gaps appear in the texts of both versions.

Paris, April 25.[1]

A tout seigneur tout honneur.[2] We begin today with Berlioz, whose first concert opened the musical season and could be regarded, so to speak, as the overture of the same. The more or less new pieces that were presented to the public here found the applause they deserved, and even the most sluggish hearts were swept away by the power of the genius that is revealed in all creations of the great Master. Here is a wing-beat that reveals no ordinary songbird, it is a colossal nightingale, a thrush the size of an eagle, of the sort that are said to have existed in prehistoric times. Indeed, for me, Berlioz's music as a whole has something prehistoric, if not antediluvian, about it; it reminds me of extinct animal species, of fabulous kingdoms and sins, of piled-up impossibilities: of Babylon, of the hanging gardens of Semiramis, of Nineveh, of the wonders of Mizraim, such as we see in the paintings of the Englishman Martin.[3] Indeed, if we look around for an analogy in the art of painting, we find the most elective affinity[4] between Berlioz and the mad Briton—the same feeling for the uncanny, the gigantic, for material immeasurability. In the one, the harsh effects of light and shadow, in the other screeching instrumentation; in the one, little melody, in the other, little color; in both, little beauty and no sensibility at all. Their works are neither ancient nor romantic, they recall neither Greece nor the Catholic Middle Ages; instead, they reach up much higher, to the Assyrian-Babylonian-Egyptian period of architecture, and to the massive passion that was expressed in it.

What a properly modern man, in contrast, is our Felix Mendelssohn-Bartholdy, the much celebrated compatriot, whom we mention first of all, today, on account of the symphony that was given by him in the concert hall of the Conservatory.[5] We have the active zeal of his friends and

Musical Season of the Year 1844
First Report

From *Lutetia: Berichte über Politik, Kunst und populäres Leben,* 1854

Paris, 25 April 1844[1]

A tout seigneur tout honneur. We begin today with Berlioz, whose first concert opened the musical season and could be regarded, so to speak, as the overture of the same. The more or less new pieces that were presented to the public here found the applause they deserved, and even the most sluggish hearts were swept away by the power of the genius that is revealed in all creations of the great Master. Here is a wing-beat that reveals no ordinary songbird, it is a colossal nightingale, a thrush the size of an eagle, of the sort that are said to have existed in prehistoric times. Indeed, for me, Berlioz's music as a whole has something prehistoric, if not antediluvian, about it; it reminds me of extinct animal species, of fabulous kingdoms and sins, of piled-up impossibilities: of Babylon, of the hanging gardens of Semiramis, of Nineveh, of the wonders of Mizraim, such as we see in the paintings of the Englishman Martin. Indeed, if we look around for an analogy in the art of painting, we find the most elective affinity between Berlioz and the mad Briton—the same feeling for the uncanny, the gigantic, for material immeasurability. In the one, the harsh effects of light and shadow, in the other screeching instrumentation; in the one, little melody, in the other, little color; in both, little beauty and no sensibility at all. Their works are neither ancient nor romantic, they recall neither Greece nor the Catholic Middle Ages; instead, they reach up much higher, to the Assyrian-Babylonian-Egyptian period of architecture, and to the massive passion that was expressed in it.

What a properly modern man, in contrast, is our Felix Mendelssohn-Bartholdy, the much celebrated compatriot, whom we mention first of all, today, on account of the symphony that was given by him in the concert hall of the Conservatory. We have the active zeal of his friends and sponsors here to thank for this pleasure. Although the reception of this symphony of Mendelssohn's in the Conservatory was very frosty, ⟨indeed offensively cold,⟩ it nevertheless deserves the recognition of all true connoisseurs of art. ⟨The second movement (*scherzo* in F major) and the third; Adagio in A major, in particular, are full of character, with passages of genuine beauty. The instrumentation is excellent and the entire symphony is⟩ among Mendelssohn's best works. ⟨But⟩ how does it happen that, following the performance of *Paulus* that was imposed on the public here, no laurel wreath wants to bloom on French soil for this so worthy and highly talented artist? How does it happen, here, that all efforts come to naught, and the last desperate measure of the Odeon Theatre, the performance of the choruses from *Antigone,* ⟨will also produce⟩ only a pathetic result? Mendelssohn always gives us an opportunity to reflect on the loftiest problems of aesthetics. Specifically, we are usually reminded, in his case, of the great question: what is the difference between art and ⟨labor⟩? We admire this Master's great talent for form, for style, his gift for appropriating the most extraordinary things, his charmingly beautiful construction, his fine lizard's ear, his tender antennae, and his earnest, I would almost like to say passionate indifference. If we search for an analogous phenomenon in a sister art, we will find it this time in poetry, and its name is Ludwig Tieck. This Master, too, always knew how to reproduce the most excellent things, whether writing or reading, he even understood how to make something naïve, and yet never created anything that was compelling to the masses and lived on in their hearts. ⟨Particular to both is the most fervid wish for dramatic accomplishment, and Mendelssohn, too, will perhaps grow old and ill-tempered without having brought anything truly great to the stage. He will probably try, but must fail in the attempt, for here truth and passion are what is sought above all.⟩

Besides Mendelssohn's symphony, we heard at the Conservatory, with great interest, a symphony by the late lamented Mozart, and a no less talented composition ⟨from an oratorio⟩ by Handel. They were received with great applause. ⟨These two, Mozart and Handel, have finally managed to attract the attention of the French, something that, admittedly, took considerable time, since no propaganda of diplomats, Pietists, and bankers was active on their behalf.⟩

sponsors here to thank for this pleasure. Although the reception of this symphony of Mendelssohn's in the Conservatory was very frosty,

it nevertheless deserves the recognition of all true connoisseurs of art. ⟨It is of genuine beauty and belongs⟩

among Mendelssohn's best works. How does it happen that, following the performance of *Paulus* that was imposed on the public here, no laurel wreath wants to bloom on French soil for this so worthy and highly talented artist? How does it happen, here, that all efforts come to naught, and the last desperate measure of the Odeon Theatre, the performance of the choruses from *Antigone*, ⟨also produced⟩ only a pathetic result? Mendelssohn always gives us an opportunity to reflect on the loftiest problems of aesthetics. Specifically, we are usually reminded, in his case, of the great question: what is the difference between art and ⟨a lie⟩? We admire this Master's great talent for form, for style, his gift for appropriating the most extraordinary things, his charmingly beautiful construction, his fine lizard's ear, his tender antennae, and his earnest, I would almost like to say passionate indifference. If we search for an analogous phenomenon in a sister art, we will find it this time in poetry, and its name is Ludwig Tieck. This Master, too, always knew how to reproduce the most excellent things, whether writing or reading, he even understood how to make something naïve, and yet never created anything that was compelling to the masses and lived on in their hearts. ⟨Mendelssohn, as the more talented of the two, would find it easier to create something everlasting, but not where truth and passion are immediately demanded, on the stage; Ludwig Tieck, in spite of his most fervid desires, was never able to achieve a dramatic accomplishment either.⟩

Besides Mendelssohn's symphony, we heard at the Conservatoire, with great interest, a symphony of the late lamented Mozart, and a no less talented composition   by Handel. They were received with great applause.

⟨However great the names that we have just mentioned, our excellent countryman Ferdinand Hiller enjoys too much recognition among true connoisseurs of art for us not to name him, too, among those composers whose works found well-deserved recognition at the Conservatoire. Hiller is more a thinking than a feeling musician, and furthermore he is accused of having too great a scholarly bent. Intellect and academic knowledge may, admittedly, seem a bit chilling at times in the compositions of this doctrinaire man, but nonetheless his works are always graceful, charming, and beautiful. Here is no trace of twisted-mouth eccentricity; Hiller possesses

There was no lack of concert-giving pianists this year either. In particular, the Ides of March were very remarkable days in this regard. They all start tinkling away and are desirous of being listened to, or at least to appear to be listened to, so that on the other side of the Parisian barrier they can behave like great celebrities. These artistic apprentices know the proper way to exploit every scrap of praise that they have begged or swindled from the *feuilletons*, especially in Germany, and consequently the advertisements there announce that the famous genius, the great Rudolf W.,[6] has arrived, the rival of Liszt and Thalberg, the pianistic hero who aroused such excitement in Paris and was even praised by the critic Jules Janin, hosanna! Whoever has come across such a poor creature in Paris, and, in general, knows how little notice is taken here of much more significant personages, finds the credulity of the public very amusing and the crude shamelessness of the virtuosos very disgusting. But the evil lies much deeper, namely in the condition of our daily press, and this, again, is only a result of even more fateful circumstances. I must come back again and again to the fact that there are only three pianists who deserve serious consideration, namely: Chopin, the beauteous composer, who, however, was unfortunately very ill and little visible this winter; then Thalberg, the ⟨noble figure⟩ who would not even have to play the piano in order to be greeted everywhere as a beautiful phenomenon, and who really seems to regard his talent as a mere *appanage*; and then our Liszt, who despite all the wrong-headedness and rough edges still remains our dear Liszt, and at this moment has ⟨generated not only in all Paris, but even in the otherwise so calm writer of these pages, an excitement that cannot be denied.⟩ Yes, he is here, the great agitator, our Franz Liszt, the errant knight of all possible orders,

the Hohenzollern-Hechingen court councilor, the doctor of philosophy and miracle doctor of music, the resurrected Pied Piper of Hamlin, the new Faust always followed by a poodle in the form of Belloni,[7] ⟨the Hungarian sword of honor of his century,⟩ the knighted and   noble Franz Liszt! He is here, the modern Amphion, who by sounding his strings during the construction of the Cologne cathedral made the stones move until they fit themselves together like the fabled walls of Thebes!

an artistic elective affinity with his compatriot Wolfgang Goethe. Like Goethe, Hiller was also born in Frankfurt, where I saw his paternal house the last time I passed through. It is called "At the Green Frog," and the image of a frog can be observed above the front door. But Hiller's compositions never make one think of such an unmusical beast, only of nightingales, larks, and other springtime birds.⟩

There was no lack of concert-giving pianists this year either. In particular, the Ides of March were very remarkable days in this regard. They all start tinkling away and are desirous of being listened to, or at least to appear to be listened to, so that on the other side of the Parisian barrier they can behave like great celebrities. These artistic apprentices know the proper way to exploit every scrap of praise that they have begged or swindled from the *feuilletons*, especially in Germany, and consequently the advertisements there announce that the famous genius, the great Rudolf W., has arrived, the rival of Liszt and Thalberg, the pianistic hero who aroused such excitement in Paris and was even praised by the critic Jules Janin, hosanna! Whoever has come across such a poor creature in Paris, and, in general, knows how little notice is taken here of much more significant personages, finds the credulity of the public very amusing and the crude shamelessness of the virtuosos very disgusting. But the evil lies much deeper, namely in the condition of our daily press, and this, again, is only a result of even more fateful circumstances. I must come back again and again to the fact that there are only three pianists who deserve serious consideration, namely: Chopin, the beauteous composer, who, however, was unfortunately very ill and little visible this winter; then Thalberg, the ⟨musical gentleman⟩ who would not even have to play the piano in order to be greeted everywhere as a beautiful phenomenon, and who really seems to regard his talent as a mere *appanage*; and then our Liszt, who despite all the wrong-headedness and rough edges still remains our dear Liszt, and at this moment has ⟨again generated great excitement among the Parisian *beau monde*.⟩

Yes, he is here, the great agitator, our Franz Liszt, the errant knight of all possible orders ⟨with exception of the French Legion of Honor, which Louis-Philippe does not wish to give to a virtuoso); he is here⟩, the Hohenzollern-Hechingen court councilor, the doctor of philosophy and miracle doctor of music, the resurrected Pied Piper of Hamlin, the new Faust always followed by a poodle in the form of Belloni, the knighted and ⟨yet⟩ noble Franz Liszt! He is here, the modern Amphion, who by sounding his strings during the construction of the Cologne cathedral made the stones move until they fit themselves together like the fabled walls of Thebes!

He is here, the modern-day Homer, whom Germany, Hungary, and France, the three greatest nations, advertise as their native son, while the singer of the *Iliad* was only claimed by seven little provincial cities! He is here, the Attila, the Scourge of God of all Erard pianos, which already trembled at the mere news of his coming and which now, under his hand, twitch, bleed, and whimper in such fashion that the humane society ought to take an interest in them! He is here, the mad, beautiful, ugly, mysterious, fateful and sometimes very childish child of his times, ⟨the today hale and hearty, tomorrow once again very ill Franz Liszt, whose magic power compels us, whose genius delights us, whose madness confuses even our senses, and whom we—in any case want to do justice to!⟩[8]⟩

Earlier, when I heard of the swoon that befell Germany, and specifically Berlin, when Liszt appeared there, I shrugged my shoulders sympathetically and thought: Quiet, Sabbath-like Germany doesn't want to miss the opportunity for a little bit of allowable activity, it wants to bestir its sleep-drunk limbs a little, and my Abderites[9] on the Spree like to tickle themselves into an available enthusiasm and declaim one after another: "Amor, ruler of men and gods!"[10] The spectacle, for them, is a matter of the spectacle itself, the spectacle *an sich,* whatever name the occasion bears, be it Herwegh, ⟨Saphir,⟩ Liszt, or Fanny Elssler;[11] if Herwegh is forbidden, they make do with Liszt, who is harmless and uncompromising. Thus I thought, thus I explained the Lisztomania to myself, and I took it for a characteristic of the ⟨political⟩ situation on the far side of the Rhine. But I was wrong, after all, and I noticed that last week in the Italian Opera House, where Liszt gave his first concert in front of a gathering that one could well call the flower of local society.[12] In any case, it was sharp-eyed Parisians, people familiar with the most elevated phenomena of the present, who had lived for a more or less long time through the great drama of the period, among them so many invalids of all artistic pleasures, the most exhausted men of action, women who were also very tired after having danced the polka all winter long, a large number of busy and blasé souls—it was truly no German-sentimental, Berlin-over-sensibilitized public that Liszt played before, all alone, or rather accompanied only by his genius. And yet, how powerful, how shattering was the effect of his mere appearance! How riotous was the

He is here, the modern-day Homer, whom Germany, Hungary, and France, the three greatest nations, advertise as their native son, while the singer of the *Iliad* was only claimed by seven little provincial cities! He is here, the Attila, the Scourge of God of all Erard pianos, which already trembled at the mere news of his coming and which now, under his hand, twitch, bleed, and whimper in such fashion that the humane society ought to take an interest in them! He is here, the mad, beautiful, ugly, mysterious, fateful and sometimes very childish child of his times, ⟨the gigantic midget, the raving Roland with the Hungarian sword of honor, the inspired Hans the Fool, whose madness confounds even our senses, and for whom we, in any case, do the loyal service of calling public attention to the public furor that he incites here. We affirm the fact of his enormous *succès* without equivocation; how we interpret this fact in our private musings, and whether we privately give or withhold our acclaim for the celebrated virtuoso, is likely of no concern to the latter, since ours is merely an individual voice and our authority in regard to the musical art is of no particular significance.⟩

Earlier, when I heard of the swoon that befell Germany, and specifically Berlin, when Liszt appeared there, I shrugged my shoulders sympathetically and thought: Quiet, Sabbath-like Germany doesn't want to miss the opportunity for a little bit of allowable activity, it wants to bestir its sleepdrunk limbs a little, and my Abderites on the Spree like to tickle themselves into an available enthusiasm and declaim one after another: "Amor, ruler of men and gods!" The spectacle, for them, is a matter of the spectacle itself, the spectacle *an sich,* whatever name the occasion bears, be it ⟨Georg⟩ Herwegh, ⟨Franz⟩ Liszt, or Fanny Elssler; if Herwegh is forbidden, they make do with Liszt, who is harmless and uncompromising. Thus I thought, thus I explained the Lisztomania to myself, and I took it for a characteristic of the ⟨politically unfree⟩ situation on the far side of the Rhine. But I was wrong, after all, and I noticed that last week in the Italian Opera House, where Liszt gave his first concert in front of a gathering that one could well call the flower of local society. In any case, it was sharp-eyed Parisians, people familiar with the most elevated phenomena of the present, who had lived for a more or less long time through the great drama of the period, among them so many invalids of all artistic pleasures, the most exhausted men of action, women who were also very tired after having danced the polka all winter long, a large number of busy and blasé souls—it was truly no German-sentimental, Berlin-over-sensibilitized public that Liszt played before, all alone, or rather accompanied only by his genius. And yet, how powerful, how shattering was the effect of his mere appearance! How riotous was the

applause, ⟨and how long-lasting! All week long I had to hear how grandiose the calm was with which the conqueror⟩
allowed the bouquets to rain down upon him, and

stuck a red camellia, which he plucked from one such bouquet, on his breast! ⟨I heard this again yesterday evening,⟩ in the presence of young soldiers just back from Africa, where they saw not flowers, but lead bullets rain down upon them, and their breast was decorated with the red camellias of their own heroic blood, without anyone here or there taking particular notice. Strange, I thought, these Parisians, who have seen Napoleon, who had to deliver one battle after another in order to capture their attention, now they are celebrating our Franz Liszt. And what a celebration! A true madness, unheard of in the annals of furor! But what is the reason for this phenomenon? The answer to this question may belong more to pathology than to aesthetics. ⟨The electric effect of a demonic nature on a crowd that is all pressed together, the infectious power of ecstasy, and perhaps the magnetism of music itself, this spiritualistic illness of the age, which vibrates in almost all of us—I have never encountered these phenomena so distinctly and so frighteningly as in the concert by Liszt.⟩

applause ⟨that was clapped in his direction! Bouquets, too, were thrown at his feet! It was a noble scene, the way the conquering hero calmly⟩ allowed the bouquets to rain down upon him, and ⟨finally, with a gracious smile,⟩ stuck a red camellia, which he pulled from one such bouquet, on his breast. ⟨And he did this⟩ in the presence of ⟨several⟩ young soldiers just back from Africa, where they saw not flowers, but lead bullets rain down upon them, and their breast was decorated with the red camellias of their own heroic blood, without anyone here or there taking particular notice. Strange, I thought, these Parisians, who have seen Napoleon, who had to deliver one battle after another in order to capture their attention, now they are celebrating our Franz Liszt! And what a celebration! A true madness, un-heard of in the annals of furor! But what is the reason for this phenomenon? The answer to this question may belong more to pathology than to aesthetics. ⟨A doctor whose specialty is female ailments, and whom I asked about the spell that Liszt casts over his audience, gave me a most peculiar smile and told me all kinds of things about magnetism, galvanism, electricity, about the contagion of a sultry hall filled with innumerable wax candles and several hundred perfumed and sweating human beings, about Histrionalepilepsy,[2] the phenomenon of tickling, musical cantharides[3] and other scabrous things, which, I believe, bear some relation to the mysteries of the *bona dea*.[4] But perhaps the answer to the question is not to be found in such adventurous depths, but rather on a very prosaic surface. Sometimes it will seem to me as if the whole witchery could be explained by the fact that no one in this world knows how to organize his successes, or rather the *mise en scène* of them, as well as our Franz Liszt. In this art, he is a genius, a Philadelphia, a Bosco, indeed a very Meyerbeer.[5] The most elevated personages serve as his *compères*, and his paid enthusiasts are trained in exemplary fashion. Popping champagne bottles and the reputation of wasteful generosity, trumpeted by the most reputable journals, is something that lures recruits in any city. Nevertheless, it may be the case that our Franz Liszt really is by nature very munificent and free of stinginess, a squalid vice that adheres to so many virtuosos, specifically the Italians, and that we have found even in the sweet-voiced Rubini, whose miserliness has become the subject of an anecdote that is very funny in every respect. Namely, the famous singer had undertaken an artistic tour in collaboration with Franz Liszt, at shared expense, with the profit from the concerts that they were to give in various cities to be divided between them. On this occasion, the great pianist, who takes the general manager of his fame, the above-mentioned Signor Belloni, along everywhere, gave the latter responsibility for all their business affairs. But when, at the end of

The transition from lion to rabbit is rather abrupt. Nevertheless, I must not leave unmentioned those tamer piano players who distinguished themselves in the current season. We cannot all be great prophets, and there must also be lesser prophets of whom twelve make up a dozen. As the greatest among the lesser, we here name Theodor Döhler. His playing is nice, pretty, pleasing, sensitive, and he has a very particular manner of touching the keys with his hand extended horizontally, through the bent fingertips alone. After Döhler, H—é deserves special mention among the lesser ⟨figures⟩; he is ⟨more or less one of those whom even a whale cannot abide and has to spit out again.[13]⟩

I cannot forbear to mention Herr Schad ⟨here, as well; he is a kind of Habakuk[14] and earns quite a good deal of applause. Herr Antoine de Kontski, a young Pole of respectable talent who has also already attained his celebrity, gave a quite outstanding concert. Among the remarkable phenomena of the season was the debut of the young Matthias, a talent of eminent standing. The older Pharaohs are left behind more completely with every passing day and are sinking into dejected darkness.⟩

the tour, Signor Belloni handed in his bill, Rubini noticed with horror that among the shared expenses was a significant sum for laurel wreaths, bouquets of flowers, hymns of praise, and other ovation costs. The naïve singer had imagined that people had thrown him these signs of approbation on account of his beautiful voice. Now he flew into a rage and did not, by any means, want to pay for the bouquets, among which the most costly camellias may have been found. If I were a musician, this quarrel would offer the very best subject for a comic opera.

⟨But, ach! Let us not examine all too closely the reverences that were paid to the famous virtuosos. The day of their vain fame is after all very short, and the hour will soon strike when the titan of music will perhaps shrivel up into a municipal musician of very short stature, who regales the regulars in his coffee house and tells them, on his honor, how people once tossed him bouquets of flowers with the most beautiful camellias, and how once two Hungarian countesses, in order to get hold of his handkerchief, even fell to the floor and fought until they drew blood! The fleeting reputation of the virtuosos evaporates and echoes away, desolate, leaving no trace, like the wind of a camel in the desert.⟩

The transition from lion to rabbit is rather abrupt. Nevertheless, I must not leave unmentioned those tamer piano players who distinguished themselves in the current season. We cannot all be great prophets, and there must also be lesser prophets of whom twelve make up a dozen. As the greatest among the lesser, we here name Theodor Döhler. His playing is nice, pretty, pleasing, sensitive, and he has a very particular manner of touching the keys with his hand extended horizontally, through the bent fingertips alone. After Döhler, Hallé deserves special mention among the lesser ⟨prophets⟩; he is ⟨a Habakuk whose merit is as modest as it is real. In addition,⟩

I cannot forbear to mention Herr Schad, ⟨who among the piano players is perhaps to be accorded the same rank as Jonas among the prophets; may he never be swallowed by a whale!⟩

NOTES TO THE 1844 VERSION

1. Source: Heinrich Heine, *Säkularausgabe*, vol. 10, ed. Lucienne Netter (Berlin, Akademie-Verlag, and Paris, Éditions du CNRS, 1979), pp. 229–33

2. "Honor to whom honor is due." French proverb.

3. Heine mentions the hanging gardens of the Assyrian queen Semiramis in Babylon; Nineveh, the capital of the Assyrian empire; Mizraim, the biblical name for Egypt. The English painter John Martin (1789–1854) was famous for his large-scale paintings with disastrous scenes, such as *The Fall of Babylon* (1819) and *The Fall of Ninevah* (1828).

4. This is a reference to Goethe's novel *Die Wahlverwandtschaften (Elective Affinities)*.

5. Mendelssohn's Symphony no. 3 in A Minor ("Scottish") had been performed on 14 January 1844 at the concert of the Société des concerts du Conservatoire.

6. The pianist Heinrich Rudolph Willmers (1821–78).

7. Gaëtano Belloni was Liszt's secretary since 1841 and accompanied him on his concert tours until 1847. In Goethe's *Faust* (part I), Mephistopheles follows Faust in the form of a poodle.

8. In the first version, which Heine sent to the editor of the *Allgemeine Zeitung* before Liszt's first concert, the entire passage on Liszt reads: "And then our Liszt, whom we must name here and who despite all his unpleasantnesses always remains our Liszt! As we write this, we hear that he is here in Paris, has rented the Salle Ventadour for four evenings, and will thus be giving four concerts. Yes, he is here, our Franz Liszt, the knighted and yet noble Franz Liszt, the great court councilor of Hechingen and extraordinary member of the Cologne Carnival Society, the knight of all possible orders (except for the *Legion d'honneur* that he would like to have), the sword-of-honor-bearing Franz of Hungary, the Attila, the Scourge of God of all Erard pianos, which already tremble and whimper at the word of his coming. —He is here, the modern Amphion, who by sounding his strings during the construction of the Cologne cathedral made the stones move until they fit themselves together like the fabled walls of Thebes! He is here, the Homer of the piano, whom Germany, Hungary, and France, the three greatest countries, advertise as their native son, while the Homer of the Iliad, instead, was only claimed by some cities! He is here, the splendid, generous Franz Liszt, the Maecenas of talented princes, the man who spends the most considerable sums on the costs of advertising his philanthropy and yet is capable of letting you feel that he once gave a breakfast for you—the Ariel-Caliban who can sometimes be as ugly as Pixis and then again as celestially beautiful as Panofka—the Napoleon-Scapin, as the Archbishop of Malines, who died a few days past, would call him. —I am nevertheless happy to see him again—and despite my aversion to pianos I am looking forward to his first concert, which, as I hear, he will give for the benefit of Queen Pommare." The following paragraph from "Earlier" until "as in the concert by Liszt" is missing completely.

Here is the German: "Und dann unser Liszt, den wir hier nennen müssen und der trotz all seiner Unannehmlichkeiten immer unser Liszt bleibt! Während wir dieses schreiben, hören wir dass er hier in Paris sey, die Salle Ventatur für vier Abende gemietet habe und also vier Konzerte geben wird. Ja, er ist hier, unser Franz Liszt, der geadelte und dennoch edle Franz Liszt, der grosse hechingsche Hofrath und ausserordentliches Mitglied des Kölner Karnevalvereins, der Ritter aller möglichen Orden mit Ausnahme der Legion d'honneur die er gern haben möchte, der ungarische Ehrensäbelfranz, der Attila, die Geissel Gottes aller Erardschen Pianos, welche schon bey der Nachricht seiner Ankunft erzittern und wimmern. —Er ist hier, der moderne Amphion, der durch die Töne seines Saitenspiels beim Kölner Dombau die Steine in Bewegung setzt, dass sie sich zusammen fügen wie einst die Mauern von Theben! Er ist hier, der Homer des Claviers, den Deutschland, Ungarn und Frankreich die drey größten Länder als Landeskind reklamieren, statt dass der Homer der Ilias nur von einigen Städten in Anspruch genommen ward! Er ist hier, der prächtige, freigebige Franz Liszt, der Mäzen talentvoller Fürsten, der Mann der allein für die Inserationskosten seiner Wohltätigkeit die größten Summen ausgibt, und doch im Stande ist es dir fühlen zu lassen dass er dir mal ein Frühstück gegeben—der Ariel-Kaliban, der manchmal so häßlich seyn kann wie Pixis und dann wieder so himmlisch schön wie Panofka—der Napoleon-Scapin wie ihn der Erzbischof von Malines nennen würde, der vor einigen Tagen gestorben ist. —Ich bin dennoch froh ihn wieder zu sehen—und trotz meiner Klavierscheu freue ich mich auf sein erstes Konzert, welches er, wie ich höre, zum Besten der Königin Pommare geben wird."

9. The inhabitants of the Greek city of Abdera in Christoph Martin Wieland's novel *Die Abderiten* (1774), decribed there as dull-witted fools.

10. Sophocles, *Antigone,* chorus in act 3, scene 2.

11. Georg Herwegh (1817–75), German socialist poet who had been exiled from Prussia in 1842; Moritz Gottlieb Saphir (1795–1858), writer and critic, editor of the review *Der Humorist;* Fanny Elssler (1810–84), famous prima ballerina.

12. Liszt's first concert (of four) took place in the Théâtre Italien (Salle Ventadour) on 16 April 1844. Heine had received two tickets from Liszt and attended the concert accompanied by his wife.

13. Charles Hallé (1819–95), English pianist and conductor of German birth. Heine alludes to the story of the prophet Jonas who was swallowed and spit out again by a whale.

14. One of the lesser prophets of the Old Testament.

NOTES TO THE 1854 VERSION

1. Source: Heinrich Heine, *Historisch-kritische Gesamtausgabe der Werke (Düsseldorfer Ausgabe),* ed. Volkmar Hansen (Hamburg: Hoffmann und Campe, 1990), vol. 14, pp. 127–33. The original book, *Lutetia,* was published by Hoffmann und Campe in 1854.

2. In German "Histrionalepilepsis," a word coined by Heine.

3. Medication and aphrodisiac made from Spanish flies.

4. The "good goddess" of ancient Rome, revered by women. Her feast on 1 May became an occasion for sexual excesses.

5. In his *Lutetia,* Heine repeatedly reproaches the opera composer Giacomo Meyerbeer (1791–1864) for owing his fame mainly to money and relations, though what Heine most resented was Meyerbeer's close relationship to the Prussian court. Heine compares him and Liszt here with the English "magician" Jakob Philadelphia and the Italian conjurer Bartolommeo Bosco.

"Even His Critics Must Concede"

Press Accounts of Liszt at the Bonn Beethoven Festival

SELECTED, INTRODUCED, AND TRANSLATED
BY JOSÉ ANTONIO BOWEN

The concerts of the Beethoven Bonn Festival in 1845 are perhaps the most completely documented performances of the nineteenth century before Bayreuth. The importance of the occasion drew musical guests such as Ignaz Moscheles, Jenny Lind, Marie Pleyel, Meyerbeer, Berlioz, and Louis Spohr, well-known writers about music such as George Smart, Charles Hallé, and Anton Schindler, and legions of the musical press including Maurice Schlesinger, Léon Kreutzer, and Jules Janin from France, François-Joseph Fétis from Belgium, and from Germany, Ludwig Rellstab and Karl Schorn. With Queen Victoria and Prince Albert making their first trip to the continent since her accession to the throne, and King Friedrich Wilhelm IV of Prussia and his wife, Queen Elizabeth, playing host, the festival had royal news value and nearly the entire London music press corps was sent.[1]

The following documentation presents a selection of articles and reviews from the English, German, and French press about the celebration. Most of these reports include both concert reviews and social news, everything from what happened at the parties to what was thought of the Beethoven statue, the unveiling of which was the main stimulus for the festival. Many of the papers ran additional stories on the queen. This sample focuses on recollections and reviews of the concert on the main day of the festival, at four o'clock on Tuesday, 12 August 1845, and specifically on Liszt's performances as both soloist and conductor. Most German, Italian, and French newspapers published advance notices or reports on what was performed, but these are not included here.[2] General information about conditions at the festival, the rehearsals on Sunday, 10 August, and the hall are covered extensively in the review by George Hogarth, placed first. Since the English reports are the most numerous, substantially longer, and more detailed, they are generally quoted at greater length.

The press was prepared to be hostile to Liszt. The festival committee, headed by local musician Professor H. K. Breidenstein, had underestimated the magnitude of the event and was unprepared for the five thousand guests, the many celebrities, and the two royal families. Liszt had been raising money for the festival through benefit concerts for six years, but when he arrived in Bonn in July and discovered that no suitable concert hall was available, he offered to build one, paid for out of his own pocket with 10,000 francs. Although the concert hall was completed in time, the city was unprepared, overcrowded and suffering from a heat wave. Perhaps because he bore some of the blame for the poor planning, and was further accused of putting himself at the center of the festival, Liszt asked Spohr to do most of the conducting and participated in only three works. He performed the piano solo in Beethoven's E-flat Concerto and conducted the Fifth Symphony on 12 August and his own *Festival Cantata*, written specifically for this occasion, on 13 August. In spite of this, many thought Liszt, as a virtuoso, was poorly suited for such a prominent role, and both he and the organization were condemned even before the festival began. In June, Schindler publicly proclaimed that Liszt did not have the necessary experience to conduct.[3] Ferdinand Hiller, Mendelssohn, and Schumann (the core of the conservative Leipzig establishment that would remain at odds with Liszt for the rest of his life) stayed away from the event entirely, and the *Morning Post* famously called it the "Beethoven Festival in honor of Liszt."[4] According to J. W. Davison, some thought Beethoven would be "desecrated" by contact with the "romantic" Liszt.[5] Under the circumstances, it would have been remarkable for Liszt to receive any kind words at all.

While I have attempted to limit these samples to 12 August, some descriptions of the general circumstances appear, as these are critical for understanding how, despite the desire to find fault with everything Lisztian, many critics were still persuaded by his performances. Liszt's conducting of Beethoven's Fifth Symphony, for instance, received mostly positive reviews, surprising both his critics and "even his warmest admirers."[6] With the eighty-three-year-old Domenico Dragonetti leading the basses, Liszt was able to conduct the daunting trio in the third movement as written (rather than with only one bass, as was the custom). Virtually every review praises the fidelity and spirit of the performance where most were expecting disaster. But we should not overstate the positive reactions. Many qualifications to the effect that "even his critics must concede" and "the orchestra was not in the least distracted by his unusual manner of conducting" suggest that Liszt's conducting was generally controversial and less then entirely successful.[7] Yet this performance was at least successful enough to overcome the bad publicity of his earlier conducting reputation and the poor management of the festival.

Even this triumph, however, was overshadowed by his performance of the "Emperor" Concerto with Spohr conducting. Where critics were again expecting the virtuoso Liszt, they were astonished by what was perceived as a different style of playing. The reviews praise Liszt, but are notable for the almost universal descriptions of his "unusual calm" and the "lack of liberties."[8] "Instead of altering and exaggerating *almost every passage*," a surprised critic wrote, "he altered but few, and exaggerated none."[9] For another critic, Liszt's playing "from book" was an unusual and welcome deviation.[10] Schindler himself, so ill-disposed toward Liszt, had to acknowledge that the performance "might have completely satisfied the composer himself."[11] Did the knowledge that Schindler and other Beethoven arch-conservatives were in the audience alter Liszt's usual style or did Beethoven simply require a different approach? On another occasion, a concert in London in 1841, Moscheles concluded that Liszt altered his style to fit that of the audience.

> When he [Liszt] came forward to play in Hummel's Septet, one was prepared to be staggered, but only heard the well-known piece which he plays with the most perfect execution, storming occasionally like a Titan, but still, in the main, free from extravagance; for the distinguishing mark of Liszt's mind and genius is that he knows perfectly the locality, the audience, and uses his powers, which are equal to everything, merely as a means of eliciting the most varied kinds of effects.[12]

Perhaps to make the same point, Liszt was reported to have "played from *book*" at this performance.[13] Whatever the cause, critical praise for this performance (even as a deviation) was almost unanimous and, more important, consistent, with only Morris Barnett accusing Liszt of taking "liberties" with Beethoven. Practically the only musical performance Barnett was happy with was a fantasia on airs from Weber by violinist Carl Möser. In fact, Barnett was responsible for the much-quoted joke calling the events in Bonn "The Beethoven Festival in honor of Liszt!" He is quoted at greater length below to make clear his anti-Liszt agenda.

Given the expectation of "liberties" or the "altering and exaggerating *almost every passage*," to say nothing of the blame heaped on Liszt for the disorganized management of the festival, most critics were prepared to echo Barnett in condemning Liszt's performances. But Liszt had a heightened reverence for Beethoven that was well-noted by his students.

Amy Fay wrote:

> He always teaches Beethoven with notes, which shows how scrupulous he is about him, for of course he knows all the sonatas by heart. He has Bülow's edition, which he opens and lays on the end of the grand piano. Then as he walks up and down he can stop and refer to it and point passages, as they are being played, to the rest of the class.[14]

Liszt was a showman who never missed an opportunity to make a visual impression, thus surely he understood the impression that using a score would have upon his students or the audience at the Beethoven Festival. These reviews, however, give the impression that Liszt's scrupulousness about the text was combined with a serious approach to the deep poetic feeling of Beethoven—again, something at odds with the virtuoso's reputation for mere surface effects. Berlioz's comment that Liszt's performance was "poetic and yet always faithful" was echoed by others.[15] The critic at the *Literary Gazette*, for example, noted the combination of "great passion" and an unusual "feeling for classical music."[16]

The Beethoven Festival provided Liszt with an opportunity to demonstrate a combination of deeper feeling and adherence to the text that would become standard in Beethoven interpretation. The reviews offered below demonstrate a remarkable unity of expectations between Liszt and the critics about how to play Beethoven. Such unity would even be remarkable if the performer had been, say, the conservative Mendelssohn. That Liszt, a virtuoso with a reputation for stunning effects and liberties with the text, should be praised at all for his performances of Beethoven in Bonn reflects a growing consensus about Beethoven interpretation that continues to this day.

Programs

Most reviews of this period included a concert program. The example below is adapted from the *Musical World*. The Beethoven Festival opened on Sunday, 10 August, with Louis Spohr conducting the *Missa Solennis* and the Ninth Symphony. The next day a new steamboat (the *Ludwig van Beethoven*, of course) was launched and there was a public ball. Tuesday morning began in the cathedral with the Mass in C, followed by the unveiling of the statue and an afternoon concert at four. After parties in the evening, the festival concluded on Wednesday with an "Artist's Concert" that featured Liszt's *Festival Cantata*. A rowdy party, where fighting broke out, followed at the Golden Star Hotel.

Tuesday, 12 August, four o'clock

FIRST PART.

CONDUCTOR	Dr. Spohr	
OVERTURE, *Coriolanus*		Beethoven
CANON (from *Fidelio*)		Beethoven
CONCERTO in E-flat—pianoforte—Dr. Liszt		Beethoven
INTRODUCTION, 1 & 2 from *Mount of Olives*		Beethoven

SECOND PART.

CONDUCTOR	Dr. Liszt	
SYMPHONY in C Minor		Beethoven
STRING QUARTET in E-flat, no. 10—		Beethoven
Herren Hartman, Derkum, Weber, and Breuer		
FINALE to the second act of *Fidelio*		Beethoven

Excerpts from Reviews

The Morning Chronicle (London), 13 August 1845
(George Hogarth)

Bonn, Friday afternoon, August 8.
I have spent a considerable portion of today at a rehearsal, in the new concert room, erected for this special occasion. Its history is somewhat remarkable, and throws additional luster on the character of a man already distinguished, independently of his fame as an artist, for noble and generous actions. It was intended by the managers of the *fête* that the performances should take place in a military *manège*, or riding school, and this was announced in the program which appeared in all the journals. But Liszt, when he came to Bonn to take a leading part in the arrangements, insisted on a place being prepared which should not be unworthy of such an occasion. He had already subscribed 10,000F. toward the expenses of the *fête*, and he instantly put down 10,000F. more toward the erection of a fitting concert room. The consequence was that only last week

its erection was begun, and it was completed in eleven days. It is, of course, a wooden building; but of magnitude sufficient to contain at least two thousand persons, besides an orchestra of several hundreds. It is somewhat low in the roof, and long in proportion to its breadth, but is really a noble room, and when brilliantly lit up (as it will be) must have a superb effect. It will be, too, a good room for sound: Staudigl, after the rehearsal today, expressed great satisfaction, particularly with the absence of echo. The orchestra is differently disposed from ours in England. Its front is raised not above five feet from the level of the room, the principal singers are in the middle of the front: the whole of the female choristers are drawn up on each side of the principals, in rows of two or three deep, with the tenors and bases immediately behind them. The whole of the instrumental orchestra are thus placed behind the chorus, with the exception of a few principal instruments, which are brought forward so as to be close to the principal singers. The effect of this arrangement I thought admirable; it greatly contributed to the singularly full and rich effect of the chorus, particularly of the female voices. In England, the chorus, be the performance what it may, is always overpowered by the instruments. This fault, to be sure, arises in part from the manner in which the instruments are played, but it also arises from the relative positions of the orchestra and the chorus. I hear much fault found, by some English critics, with this disposition of the performers, probably because it is different from what they have been accustomed to; for my part, I entirely dissented from them. The lowness of the orchestra in front, however, is really a fault; and there was another thing which seemed to be condemned unanimously. In front of the orchestra there is a pulpit or desk, exactly like an enormous beer barrel placed on end—a most clumsy and unsightly object, which completely hides a portion of the performers from the greatest part of the audience. It is ten times uglier than the pulpit of Mr. Surman, the worthy conductor at Exeter Hall; and even Spohr himself would have looked ridiculous in it, had not all sense of ridicule been excluded by his high reputation, his dignified aspect and demeanor, and the quiet yet powerful control which his baton exercised over the orchestra.

The pieces rehearsed today were Beethoven's Ninth, or Choral Symphony; his second Mass, in D, and his pianoforte concerto in E-flat, which was performed by Liszt. The rehearsal was in some measure public, for any person was admitted for payment of a few *groschen*, and there was consequently a considerable audience. The first two pieces had been carefully rehearsed before, and, notwithstanding their enormous difficulty, went on, with few interruptions on the part of the conductor. Of the four principal singers in the Symphony and Mass, the names of three are unknown in England. Though I heard them in the room, they have escaped me at this moment, and no programs of the performers have as yet appeared. The fourth was Staudigl. Of these singers, as well as pieces, I shall have more to say hereafter; but I found that even the Philharmonic Society have yet to learn how to perform the Ninth Symphony. As to the Mass, it has not been even attempted in England. I am at length convinced that the alleged *incomprehensibility* of Beethoven's latest works is more apparent than real; arising, not so much from the incapacity of the public to understand them, as from the inability of the performers to execute them so as to express their meaning and produce their effect.

Bonn is in a ferment; and enthusiasm for the memory of their illustrious townsman seems to pervade all classes of its inhabitants. They boast of him with well-founded pride, and point with veneration to the house in which he drew his earliest breath—a humble dwelling, but kept in good preservation. There is a concourse of strangers from all parts of Europe; many of our countrymen and countrywomen, of course.

I have just seen the English Ambassador at the Court of Berlin, the Earl of Westmoreland, so long known, under his late title of Lord Burghersh, as a most distinguished amateur and patron of the art. His lordship is waiting the arrival of our Queen Victoria at the chateau of Bruhl, near Cologne, where the King of Prussia now is, and will attend our Sovereign, when, with their Prussian Majestics, she comes here to "assist" at the inaguration [*sic*] of Beethoven's statue on Tuesday next. This solemnity was to have taken place on Monday, but, on the above account, has been postponed till the following day. In place of it, it is said, there is to be a great performance of wind instruments, by an assemblage of military bands, in the park of the Chateau of Bruhl, to which the public will be admitted. In that case there will, I suppose, be a general rush from Bonn. I trust it will take place; for, to know what military music is, we must hear it in Germany.

At present I can only mention a few of the musical notabilités who are here. Of ours, the principal is Sir George Smart, who was specially invited. Mr. T. Cooke, Mr. Neath, and Mr. Moscheles were also invited, but they are not here, though the last-named is expected. Spohr and Liszt I have mentioned already. Spohr, as usual, is quiet, plain, and pleasingly benevolent in his manners: Liszt all ardor and energy—he is the life of everything, and is worshipped wherever he goes. His forthcoming cantata is exciting intense expectation. It is said to be sublime, and will apparently raise his name higher than ever. Schindler, the friend of Beethoven, and the author of the well-known life of the composer, is here—a modest, agreeable man, whose conversation is full of matter. He has just published a Supplement to his Life of Beethoven, which seems to contain many important particulars respecting his life and compositions. M. Fetis, director of the Conservatoire of Brussels, the celebrated musical historian and critic, is another of the distinguished persons I have met— also Felicien David, the author of the *Désert,* which has created so great a sensation in Paris and London—a very young man, of most interesting appearance and manners. He is at present engaged in the composition of an oratorio, which I doubt not will be a work of genius. He speaks of visiting London next season. Among the visitors there are likewise Mr. Gardiner, of Leicester, who has brought with him all his intelligent enthusiasm for the memory of a man whose genius he was among the very first to proclaim in England; M. and Madame Dulcken; M. and Madame Oury; and though last, not least, Meyerbeer. Mendelssohn is *not* here.

Times (London), Saturday, 16 August 1845 (Charles Kenney)

At the beginning of this report Kenney describes the entire day from six A.M., including the preparations, the parade, the mass, and the unveiling of the statue, about which he notes: "The only fault to be found with the statue is that its vigor approaches too much coarseness and that its appearance is somewhat squatty."

The concert went off with the utmost brilliancy, the room being still more crowded, if possible, than on the first occasion. Liszt's execution of the concerto was in his best style, full of expression and fire, and the last movement was tumultuously encored. After the selection from the *Mount of Olives,* one of the ladies of the chorus came forward and placed a crown of laurels on the head of Dr. Spohr—a compliment which evidently took the great and venerable composer by surprise. He soon, however, recovered his usual undisturbed equanimity, and retired bowing with simple dignity to the applauding audience. With this concerto concluded the day's proceedings, with the exception of a general illumination in the town, and serenading in the Markt-platz.

Athenaeum (London), 16 August 1845 (Henry Chorley)

I wrote the above [part of the article] after the morning's rehearsal; at which Beethoven's C Minor Symphony and Liszt's own Cantata were played, directed by himself. So many persons had resolved, beforehand, that this great artist should not be able to conduct, owing to the superabundant animation of his pianoforte playing and his tendency to "grace" the music under his care, that I suppose I may, for once, have put faith in the character which was a mere prophecy, and felt a little nervous. I need not: his conducting is the union, to a wish, of spirit and steadiness, of musical science and the power to inspire confidence. But having stated this, because it will surprise some in England, I will not dwell further on the rehearsal.

Athenaeum (London), 23 August 1845 (Henry Chorley)

After the Overture to "Coriolan," (scarcely heard, owing to the noise) Liszt played the Pianoforte Concerto in E-flat, possibly as it has never been played before—occasion, audience, orchestra and artists taken into account. I must not be considered as partial or partisan in pronouncing it the most superb pianoforte performance I have ever heard. Without a trace of those liberties in the shape of super-animation, change of passage, and the like, which all honest persons must have perceived, after a week's acquaintance, were accidents merely—not essentials—to his playing.

The Morning Chronicle (London), 14 August 1845 (George Hogarth)

Bonn, Sunday, August 10.
At ten o'clock there was another rehearsal at the Concert Hall. The pieces rehearsed were Beethoven's Symphony in C Minor, and Liszt's Inauguration Cantata, for the third time; both under Liszt's direction. He conducts an orchestra as he does every thing else, with extraordinary fire and energy; endeavoring, with great vehemence and exuberance of action to convey to the band the expression and effect of every passage, and to bring their feelings into a state of sympathy with his own. More coolness, and a more methodical system of beating time, would carry an orchestra more readily through the first performance of a very complicated piece of music; and, in this respect, I am disposed greatly to prefer the conducting of Spohr and Mendelssohn; but Liszt certainly has, in a pre-eminent degree, the power of rousing and stimulating his performers—of throwing among them some sparks of his own fire. His Cantata is evidently a work of very high genius; but it is of great difficulty in performance, and he interrupted it so incessantly as to obscure its general effect, though the grandeur and beauty of many parts were sufficiently perceptible. He has done homage to Beethoven by introducing into it one of the great master's

most beautiful instrumental adagios, converted into a choral movement; but more of this Cantata afterward.

The Morning Chronicle (London), 16 August 1845 (George Hogarth)

Bonn, Wednesday, August 13.

I like Liszt so much, that I am grieved that I cannot like his music and his performance better. I had this feeling while he played Beethoven's concerto last evening, and still more strongly this morning; and I am unwillingly convinced that he never will acquire a permanent reputation either as a classical pianist or composer.

Musical World (London), 2 October 1845 (J. W. Davison)

When I arrived at the Beethoven Hall Spohr had already mounted the conductor's *rostrum*, saluted by a grand flourish of drums and trumpets from the orchestra and the general acclamations of the audience. It is quite true (if not quite just) that, as Janin observes in his second letter, the orchestra seemed impatient of other control than Spohr's, and threw as many stumbling blocks in the way of Liszt as they could possibly do without giving direct offence to the fiery Hungarian.[17] Nevertheless, to the surprise of many, Liszt winked at the evident discourtesy, and by quietude and resolution accomplished his duties as conductor so admirably as to surprise even his warmest admirers, who had no more idea of his possessing the peculiar talent of directing an orchestra than of his displaying so thorough a knowledge of instrumentation as is evinced in the scoring of his Cantata, which, I can assure you, astonished me and others not a little. . . .

The Concerto in E-flat, the *cheval de bataille* of all the Beethoven pianists, fared nobly in the hands of Liszt. It is almost as superogatory to speak now of the merits of Liszt's pianoforte playing as of the beauties of the composition he interpreted. I shall merely, in answer to the abuses of sundry of his quondam friends, who feasted and lived at his expense (not for the first time), give a direct denial to their statements in regard to his manner of rendering the concerto on this occasion. Instead of altering and exaggerating *almost every passage,* he altered but few, and exaggerated none. Instead of giving way to gestures and affectations of manner, he was remarkably quiet and unassuming. In short, I never heard him play a better style—with more of the air of a master and less of the grimace of an *étudiant*. There were a few instances of what, in my humble opinion, might be called mistakes of the composer's meaning, but these were totally eclipsed by the bold, animated, brilliant, and musician-like style of the general performance, which, at the end of each solo, and at its final close, was applauded with enthusiasm, and the pianist was recalled three times to receive new plaudits. The only thing that surprised me was that Liszt—a thing unusual with him—played from *book*—yet when we reflect on the turmoil and fatigue to which he had been exposed, day after day, by the blunders of the committee and the importunity of visitors and applicants for favors of every kind, it is matter for admiration that he could play at all—much more that he could play with energy and *aplomb*. However, Liszt may laugh at his detractors. In the estimation of those who think rightly and without prejudice he has covered himself with honor by his exertions in aid of the Beethoven Festival, which but for him might never have taken place. I attempt not to defend his faults, if he have any—which, since he is human and has been much flattered, is not impossible—but where praise can be so justly given it is unfair to withhold it. The question whether Liszt was the proper person to play so conspicuous a part in the proceedings at Bonn cannot be separated from the fact of his having been the chief promoter of them—and you might as well forbid an artist to play at his own concert, on the score of incapability, as forbid Liszt to figure at his own festival, on the score of unclassicality. Many who did not give a penny toward the proceedings (nor care, perhaps, much more for the memory of Beethoven) cried out in a fit of classical indignation— "And so, forsooth, because I give ten thousand francs, &c. I have a right to play at the Beethoven Festival—at which rate *anybody* who gives ten thousand francs may play—faugh!—that the *great dead* should be thus desecrated!" But the danger was easily avoided, for *nobody* except Liszt gave ten thousand francs, and as Liszt happens to be a tolerable pianist the desecration to the "great dead" was not so terrible after all. The boobies! Why a seat in Parliament has been bought for less money than Liszt gave toward the Beethoven fund, and he who sat in the seat was a fool. Liszt, who purchased his seat *at the piano* so dearly, will hardly be called a fool even by his enemies.

. . . The Symphony in C Minor was, on the whole, an excellent performance. Liszt conducted with spirit, and a manifest comprehension of the score—which as he knows the symphony by heart is not to be wondered at. The *tempi* of the various movements, however, appeared to me to be taken too slow, especially in the *Finale*—but Spohr, Moscheles, and Sir George Smart (three excellent authorities) assured me that I was wrong, and that I had been accustomed to hear them in London too fast—to which as my opinion was based purely on feeling I had nothing to reply.

The Morning Post (London), 18 August 1845 (Morris Barnett)

Wednesday, August 13.
The concert of yesterday, despite the promise of its program, came but lamely off—the truth is that, with few exceptions, the artistes procured have not been of the first order. Not a single tenor has been engaged, or, with the exception of Staudigl, a bass who could be considered worthy to give expression to the music of Beethoven. Madame Tuczek, the principal soprano, has musical feeling, extended register, and considerable energy, but she sadly lacks refinement. Mdlle Schloss, who *débuted* last season at the Ancient Concerts, has sung remarkably well, but the *ensemble* has been course and slovenly. The chorus, particularly the female voices, is beyond praise—they combine the nicest precision with immense power. Their hearts were ardently in the cause—the band has been selected from all parts, and, taking into consideration their strangeness to each other, went through their difficult task respectably. The ninth symphony of Beethoven, however, is the solitary work to which we can award a verdict of entire satisfaction. The concert was conducted by Spohr and Liszt; the latter, though a distinguished pianist, is, without exception, the vilest conductor we have seen; the most perfect orchestra and the most accomplished instrumentalists must have suffered from his indecision, and want of knowledge of orchestral exigencies. The following is the program:

[Program listed here]

The hall was intensely crowded at an early hour. The Overture to *Coriolan* was feebly rendered—its stately grandeur and grand combinations were ignobly interpreted, and it was accordingly, but coldly received. The Canon from *Fidelio* was effectively given—the deep tones and classic style of Staudigl, and the fine quality of Madame Tuczek's voice, ministered essentially to this charming *morceau*. The *cheval de bataille* of the night was Liszt's performance of the celebrated Concerto in E-flat. Since I heard him in England his style has not improved: his powers of execution remain unimpaired, but much of the pleasure elicited by his really fine talent is marred by his coxcombry of manner and exaggerated action. Considering that Liszt himself has, with many, established a reputation for his poetical interpretations of the music of Beethoven, the many liberties he took with the text were evidence of no reverential feeling for the composer. The entire concerto seemed rather a glorification of self, than the heart-feeling of the loving disciple. He was, of course, much applauded, for here he is considered as the *instar omnium* of the festival. The selections from *The Mount of Olives*, from which much pleasure was anticipated, turned out to be but an air for the soprano and a single chorus. This was a sad breaking of faith. The Symphony in C Minor went smoothly, in consequence of the band never by any chance looking at Liszt, who conducted. In the scherzo so many changes were made in the time, that the feeling was entirely at variance with its intention—the exquisite movement was given totteringly, and the very reverse of the fine rendering when conducted by Spohr and Mendelssohn. The splendid triumphal march gained in dignity, from the more retarded manner in which it was taken, than has been customary at our Philharmonic Society. Nothing more splendid than this symphony can be conceived—its entire design is colossal, and the various phases of passion are expressed with poetical fervor and enthusiasm. The quartet for stringed instruments was played with delicacy, but lacked energy and simultaneity, and was far behind the similar performances in London.

The third and last concert took place this morning. It will seem by the following program how inconsiderate has been the haste with which all the proceedings have been mismanaged:

Nine in the Morning
[Program listed here]

The cantata composed by Dr. Liszt is wholly worthless in design and execution. It is *rechauffée* of the opening of Mendelssohn's *Walpurgis Nacht,* and a minuet of Beethoven. It is patchy, and went raggedly. The uncertainty of the composer's baton deranged the time and confused the singers. The Queen, Prince Albert, the King and Queen of Prussia, and their suites, entered the Beethoven-hall just as this feeble work was finished; it was then repeated, I hear, at the desire of Prince Albert. The only other items of the programme which call for especial notice is the pianoforte playing of the celebrated Madame Pleyel. She is one of the finest performers in Europe. Her touch is firm and delicate, and the most extraordinary difficulties are achieved with marvelous facility. I believe she will visit London during the next season. A young man named Möser, *élève* of De Beriot, executed a fantasia from airs of Weber, with great purity of tone and command of bow; and Herr Ganz created a marked sensation in a solo on the violincello.

There was a grand dinner at the Goldnen Stern after the concert, at which above five hundred and sixty persons assisted. The affair was wound up with a riot, occasioned by a gentleman persisting to make speeches, despite the yells and sibillations of the company.

The entire arrangement of the Beethoven Festival has been marked with singular failure—socially and musically. Foreign artists of distinction have been treated with neglect, and the committee have earned for themselves anything but an enviable renown. The grand ball of tonight will close the festivities. I may sum up by saying, that it would have been more honest to have styled the affair "THE BEETHOVEN FESTIVAL IN HONOR OF LISZT!"

Allgemeine musikalische Zeitung (Leipzig), August 1845

At the conclusion of the concert came the C Minor Symphony under Liszt's direction and the finale from *Fidelio*. To judge from the rehearsal, where Liszt's intention was to render the details of this composition according to his own intentions, here accelerated and there broadened, an unsettled representation of this work was to be feared. Fortunately, this was deceptive. Liszt conducted the orchestra indeed energetically but with calm, and left the performance to his intermittent signals, trusting the moment and the alert mind of the orchestra, and so this ingenious work enjoyed a thoroughly worthy, genuine, and lively presentation. Liszt indeed emotes with overflowing warmth, but always properly and truthfully; only the degree of feeling is limited by his changing mood. Liszt is, however, through and through an artist and, without wanting to ignore his weaknesses, it must be conceded that without Liszt's gifted energy, and without the serenity provided by Spohr standing beside him, the festival would not have made the worthy and enthusiastic impression that it now enjoys in the greatest measure.[18]

Illustrirte Zeitung (Leipzig), 20 September 1845

The concert in the evening presented again only works by Beethoven: 1) The C-Minor Symphony, conducted boisterously by Mr. Liszt, for the improvised conductor has called the usual manner of conducting an orchestra "rococo."[19] Really! The orchestra, which already knows this wonderful work from memory, performed it all so well as if a rococo-conductor had been on the podium. The orchestra was not in the least distracted by his unusual manner of conducting. 2) The E-flat Concerto for pianoforte, performed by Mr. Liszt with unusual calm and deliberation. If other connoisseurs were not in agreement, one could blame the remarkable coquettishness with the *pianissimo* and other such effects which, due to the large hall, ought to have been omitted, but which I, for my part, thank Mr. Liszt for having controlled.[20]

Frankfurter Konversations-Blatt, 24 August 1845

Liszt conducted very well, as even his critics must concede. He also performed the piano concerto in E-flat by Beethoven, and enchanted the world with his playing, for many who lack all trust in this unique musician to perform a Beethoven concerto in the right spirit, as one says, were completely converted.

Grands Festivals de Bonn
Revue et Gazette musicale de Paris, 17 August 1845 (Léon Kreutzer)

The concerto was performed by Liszt. One can easily imagine the success. Spohr led the orchestra. As for the other pieces, Liszt conducted them, and in a truly sovereign way. I had heard the finale of *Fidelio* at the last concert of the Conservatory; but the execution was so poor that I could not judge this work myself. . . .

Concerning the symphony, an artist whose opinion has much weight pointed out that Liszt took the movement of the *andante* a little more quickly than usual. I must say that Liszt satisfied me perfectly and I think I have guessed his intention. The Symphony in C Minor never enters the field of soft ideas and melancholic persons; it is somber, austere, violent. Allowing the charm of the first motive of this *andante* to come out spoils the effect of the energetic phrase that follows it; the slow execution takes the work out of its frame; it is, so to speak, like the change of color on the palette of a grand master. Perhaps the section gains from this, but the whole piece undoubtedly loses. As for the sound quality of string instruments performing in a 200-foot long hall, it is certainly the most unfortunate imaginable idea.

Fêtes musicales de Bonn
Journal des débats, 22 August and 3 September 1845
(Hector Berlioz)

To say that Liszt played it [the Beethoven Concerto] and that he played it in a grandiose, fine, poetic and yet always faithful manner, is to utter a veritable tautology; there was a storm of applause and orchestral fanfares that must have been audible even outside the hall. Then Liszt, mounting the conductor's podium, directed the performance of the Symphony in C Minor, of which he let us hear the *scherzo* just as Beethoven wrote it, without cutting out the double basses at the beginning, as has been done for so long at the Paris Conservatory, and the finale with the repeat indicated by Beethoven, a repeat which is even today allowed to be omitted at the concerts of the same Conservatory.[21]

NOTES

1. Although many articles are unsigned, other sources allow us to determine the authors and where their reports appeared: Charles Kenney, *Times;* George Hogarth, *Morning Chronicle* and *Illustrated London News* (the latter with drawings by Robertson); Morris Barnett, *Morning Post;* Mr. Feeney, *Morning Herald;* Henry Chorley, *Athenaeum;* J. W. Davison, *Musical World;* French Flowers, reported, probably incorrectly, to be writing for *London Gazette;* and Charles Gruneison, *Britannia.* These attributions to journals are mine, largely based upon Davison and other reports. Charles Gruneison was the music critic of the *Post* until 1846, but it appears that he wrote reports of the Beethoven Festival for the *Britannia.* Davison, in the *Musical World,* says that Morris Barnett (who would succeed Gruneison as music editor at the *Post*) wrote them for the *Post.* See *Musical World* 20, no. 35, 28 August 1845. For an extended list of musical editors and contributors to London papers in the mid-nineteenth century, see the Reviewer index in José Antonio Bowen, "The Conductor and the Score: A History of the Relationship Between Interpreter and Text in the Generation of Mendelssohn, Berlioz, and Wagner," Ph.D. diss., Stanford University, 1994, vol. 3.

2. My investigation of new sources continues and I hope to publish all of the accounts of the complete festival soon.

3. *Kölnische Zeitung,* no. 179 (June 1845).

4. *The Morning Post* (London), 18 August 1845. All further references are cited in context below.

5. *Musical World* 20, no. 40 (2 October 1845).

6. Ibid.

7. *Frankfurter Konversations-Blatt,* no. 233 (24 August 1845); and *Illustrirte Zeitung* (Leipzig), no. 116 (20 September 1845). For more on Liszt's conducting, see José Antonio Bowen, "The Missing Link: Franz Liszt the Conductor," *Basler Jahrbuch für Historische Musikpraxis* 24 (2000): 125–50.

8. *Illustrirte Zeitung* (Leipzig), no. 116 (20 Sept. 1845); and *Athenaeum* (London), 23 August 1845.

9. *Musical World* 20, no. 40 (2 October 1845).

10. Ibid. Davison thought it "a thing unusual with him," but excused it on account of the turmoil and fatigue of recent weeks.

11 Anton Schindler, *Beethoven as I Knew Him,* trans. Constance S. Jolly, annot. Donald W. MacArdle, based on 3rd ed., 1860 (Chapel Hill, N.C.: 1966), p. 433. Schindler blames Czerny for corrupting Liszt's "divine spark" with training in the "bravura style." See pp. 416 and 432.

12. This edited version of Moscheles's diaries, appears in Charlotte Moscheles, *Life of Moscheles, with Selections from His Diaries and Correspondence,* trans. A. D. Coleridge (London: 1873), vol. 2, p. 88.

13 *Musical World* 20, no. 40 (2 October 1845).

14. Amy Fay, *Music Study in Germany from the Home Correspondence of Amy Fay,* ed. Mrs. Fay Pierce (Chicago: Jansen, McClurg & Co., 1880; repr. New York: Da Capo Press, 1979), with intro. by Edward Downes and index by Roy Chemus, p. 238. Other students confirm this was not his usual practice. See José Antonio Bowen, "Liszt the Teacher," *Journal of the American Liszt Society* 52/53 (Fall 2002/Spring 2003): 1–63; includes "An Annotated Bibliography of Students and Observers of Liszt's Teaching," with E. Douglas Bomberger, pp. 44–63.

15. [Hector Berlioz], "Fêtes musicales de Bonn," *Journal des débats* (22 August 1845 and 3 September 1845). See note 21 below for full citation.

16. *Literary Gazette and Journal of the Belles Lettres, Arts, Sciences &c.* (London), no. 1495 (6 September 1845).

17. Janin is the French critic Jules Janin, who wrote feuilletons for the *Journal des débats* of Paris.

18. This and the following four new translations from German periodicals are greatly indebted to Richard Green, whose poetic English translations so surpassed my own crude ones that I adopted his suggestions in almost every case.

19. This article was reprinted in *Allgemeine musikalische Zeitung* (Leipzig), 12 September 1845.

20. This is the "press report on a concert given as part of the Beethoven Memorial Festival" from the *Allgemeine musikalische Zeitung* in Ernst Burger, *Franz Liszt: A Chronicle of his Life in Pictures and Documents,* trans. Stewart Spencer (Princeton, N.J.: 1989), p. 156.

21. This was reprinted in Berlioz, *Les Soirées dans l'orchestre* (Paris: 1852). The English translation is *Evenings in the Orchestra,* ed. and trans. Jacques Barzun (New York: 1956; repr. Chicago: 1973), pp. 333–34. Cited here from a new translation by Kevin Bazzana, *The Beethoven Newsletter* 6/1 (Spring 1991), 6.

Defending Liszt: Felix Draeseke on the

Symphonic Poems

INTRODUCED AND EDITED BY JAMES DEAVILLE

TRANSLATED BY SUSAN HOHL

Of the young men and women most associated with Liszt's cause during the late 1840s and the 1850s, none could rival Felix Draeseke (1835–1913) in terms of analytical perspicacity and compositional audacity. That he later distanced himself from the progressive path of Liszt and colleagues does not diminish his "young radical" role among the so-called New Germans between 1855 and 1862.[1] Within that movement Draeseke was something of an anomaly, since even though he served as a leading representative of the avant-garde, he never resided in Weimar, Liszt's base of operations for many years. In April of 1852, the teenaged Draeseke relocated from Coburg to Leipzig, in order to study music at the conservatory there. Within months of his arrival, he traveled to Weimar to attend Liszt's performances of Wagner's *Lohengrin*, which proved decisive for his aesthetic development. At the conservatory, he attended the lectures of (among others) Franz Brendel, the progenitor of New German ideology, who developed so much confidence in the young progressive that he entrusted to him the 1855–56 Leipzig concert reviews for his journal, *Neue Zeitschrift für Musik*. Draeseke had the opportunity a few years later to write an extended essay about Liszt's symphonic poems for another of Brendel's Leipzig journals, *Anregungen für Kunst, Leben und Wissenschaft*. Originally presented in thirteen installments (six sections) between 1857 and 1859, the first two are translated into English here for the first time.

Even though Liszt had been conducting some of his symphonic poems since 1849, it was not until the publication of six of them in 1856, in two-piano arrangements, and nine of them in full score the following year, that they received serious attention. These works were Liszt's musical contribution to the dispute over program music, about which he had written in 1855 in a lengthy essay on Berlioz's *Harold in Italy*.[2] Once these orchestral works appeared in print they became the new battleground for progressive and conservative musical parties.[3] When the newspaper *Niederrheinische Musik-Zeitung* published unfavorable reviews in 1856 and 1857, including Eduard Hanslick's polemic against *Les Préludes*, the New Germans responded with a strong defense: Brendel, Draeseke, and Richard Pohl all contributed an extended article series about the symphonic poems, and even Wagner entered the fray with his important, if also unclear, open letter about the works.[4]

The *Anregungen* was a fit place for Draeseke's series, since it tended to publish longer articles devoted to controversial issues. Indeed, Brendel established the journal in 1856 as an "organ which could freely debate and further develop the artistic questions inspired by Richard Wagner."[5] As such, it was the first journal specifically created to represent the principles of the progressive party, the fruits of several years of discussion among Brendel, Wagner, and Liszt.[6] Wagner, however, was the focus: Draeseke's article was only one of three larger essays devoted to Liszt, compared with over twelve about Wagner (see list of articles at end of this introduction). Draeseke's series of articles resonated powerfully within Liszt's circle. In various contexts, including letters to Draeseke, Liszt himself approved the contents of the unfolding publication, even encouraging Draeseke to publish his full text as an independent brochure.[7] Liszt's biographer Lina Ramann records the composer's support for Draeseke's reading of the poetic basis for *Ce qu'on entend sur la montagne*, while Hans von Bülow felt that the article about *Les Préludes* was a "masterpiece and an exemplary piece of work."[8] The series may have invited comparison with Liszt's essay on *Harold in Italy*, but Draeseke provides a level of analytical detail absent from the *Harold* essay.

Draeseke wrote only about the nine symphonic poems that were extant at the time of his first installment (fall 1857), even though *Die Ideale* appeared in 1858 (before the series concluded), and he would have also been aware of the first performances of *Hunnenschlacht* and *Hamlet*, in 1857 and 1858 respectively. Helmut Loos speculates that Draeseke's reluctance to expand the cycle had to do with his positioning of the nine symphonic poems as the legacy of Beethoven's symphonic oeuvre.[9] Another possibility is that without the score he could not write about the works, since his analysis was so detailed. Finally, Draeseke may simply have not wanted to disrupt the groupings of the works that he had already laid out in the first two introductory articles from 1857. Whatever the case, the budding analyst divided the nine works into three groups, using the program as the prime criterion. The ever-popular *Les Préludes*, part of the first group, was treated first and at length. The other symphonic poems were clustered as follows: *Orpheus, Héroïde funèbre*, and *Festklänge*; *Prometheus, Tasso*, and *Mazeppa*; and *Hungaria* and *Ce qu'on entend sur la montagne*. He justifies these divisions and linkages through form and content. The first group of four, he argues, are objective in choice of subject and musical elaboration, not letting us hear Liszt's personality. The next three express Liszt's deep subjectivity, the Faustian character of his inner being, the struggle of genius with "epimetheic" (i.e., reactionary) forces. *Hungaria* and *Ce qu'on entend sur la montagne* also reveal to Draeseke struggles, but those of a nation and humanity rather than of heroic individuals.

The first two installments, translated here, are preliminary articles that provide the background for Draeseke's analyses. They first discuss the rationale behind such a detailed examination of the symphonic poems, and then look one by one at the stylistic and formal elements of the symphonic poems: melody, rhythm, harmony, instrumentation, form, and program. In the first article, Draeseke expresses his hope of using analytical means to dispel the misapprehension that has arisen around Liszt's symphonic works. He places Liszt in the musical party of Berlioz and Wagner (though they are not named), as a fellow genius in a triumvirate. He argues that while the symphonic poems appear to be new in style and thus offer special challenges to the casual listener, much of what Liszt accomplishes in them can be traced back to Beethoven, whose later works still were not understood or imitated. Here we find Draeseke caught in one of the more interesting ironies surrounding the progressive party of the 1850s: in order to establish the validity of Liszt's new music, they had to prove its basis in historical practices, especially those of Beethoven, who serves as a guiding star for Liszt throughout Draeseke's series.[10]

The second article sustains the historicist argument, whether justifying Liszt's orchestration through that of Beethoven, or highlighting Liszt's use of traditional sonata and "march" forms. Unusual and possibly unique in the literature is his association of Liszt with Mozart, which rests on the fusion of national styles. The most original and important observations in the second article, however, relate to harmony and thematic material. Drawing upon the ideas of Carl Friedrich Weitzmann, the chief theorist from the New German camp, Draeseke argues for what he calls "the modern enharmonic tonal system." According to this system, the composer can place in sequence any two consonant chords, as long as the individual notes move stepwise or the chords share a common tone, and the same principles apply to the resolution of any dissonant chord.[11] At this point in the essay, Draeseke creates his own examples, but later in the article series he will use the principle to justify Liszt's progression, in *Les Préludes* (mm. 85–89), from a G-sharp major chord to a C major chord, and the chromatically descending sequence of chords in the trombones at the coda of *Héroïde funèbre*. For Draeseke, such harmonic audacities were acceptable on the basis of the "modern enharmonic tonal system" in service of the poetic idea.

Draeseke also recognized Liszt's innovation in the area of formal cohesion through "the application of thematic art" (now called thematic transformation), which gives a unity to program music that might otherwise become a series of unrelated pictorial episodes. Even in the overview Draeseke praised Liszt's specific transformations of themes in *Tasso, Les Préludes*, and *Festklänge*, which he would develop at greater length in the following articles. Toward the end of the second article, he skilfully brings together thematic work, formal structure, and poetic content to justify Liszt's symphonic poems both individually and corporately. In doing so, he carefully distinguishes between Liszt's approach to the new genre, whereby the poetic idea determines the musical elements, and other examples of program music, called "materialistic," that musically evoke every detail of a narrative. Berlioz, in Draeseke's view, engages in the latter to the point of excess, a critique of the *Symphonie fantastique* typical of the New German camp.[12]

The rest of Draeseke's articles, not translated here, develop these ideas for individual works, with *Les Préludes* receiving the most detailed treatment. In general, after introductory remarks, these analyses lead the reader through the individual symphonic poem, evaluating the work's position in and relation to Liszt's orchestral oeuvre, pointing out along the way interesting, original musical details in the context of the work's general expressive intention. They incorporate an unusually high number of musical examples, and not just for the themes and their transformations. Many of Draeseke's observations have stood the test of time, such as the tripartite analysis of *Mazeppa* and *Héroïde funèbre*, the general outlines of his program to *Hungaria* (drawing upon the *topoi* within the music), and his identification of thematic unity, not only in *Les Préludes*, but also in *Tasso* and *Festklänge*.[13] That Draeseke did not identify any particular form in *Prometheus*, and failed to observe the tonal sequence in *Mazeppa*, cannot be blamed on him, since such matters have remained open to debate even among scholars of the twentieth and twenty-first centuries. Draeseke's tendency to overinterpret poetic programs in musical terms is a result of the analytical thought of the times in which he lived. Still, his separate discussions of form and other musical elements reveal that he was capable of addressing the symphonic poem from a purely musical standpoint, which was one of his goals.[14]

To translate, or even review, the individual analyses from the series of articles would exceed space limitations, but Draeseke's introductory pair of articles gives a clear indication of the surprisingly advanced analytical abilities and powers of perception of this twenty-two-year-old Liszt advocate. He stands out impressively within the Liszt circle as a theorist and apologist for musical progress. "Franz Liszt's Nine Symphonic Poems" refutes the tired argument that the New Germans were unable to mount a justification of their position that matched the level of analytical and aesthetic sophistication observed in their opponent Hanslick.[15] As such, it also represents a departure from the polemics that had emanated from Liszt's Weimar in the hands of such confrontational apologists as Bülow and Pohl. The change in strategy, by which Draeseke even felt free to exercise modest criticism of Liszt, may not have won many supporters from the opposing camp, but it did place the New German movement on a firmer footing in the face of its detractors.

Major Articles on Liszt and Wagner in
Anregungen für Kunst, Leben und Wissenschaft (1856–61)

Liszt

Peter Cornelius, "Franz Liszt in Leipzig," 2 (1857): 166–70.

Felix Draeseke, "Franz Liszt's neun symphonische Dichtungen," q.v.

Peter Lohmann, "Franz Liszt als Liedercomponist," 5 (1860): 3–11.

Wagner (Selection)

Anonymous, "Richard Wagner's Operndichtungen," 1 (1856): 121–28.

Franz Brendel, "Die Melodie der Sprache," 1 (1856): 10–28.

Louis Köhler, "Friedliche Kontroverse. Zur Wagnerliteratur," 1 (1856): 140–47.

Eduard Kulke, "Über *Den fliegenden Holländer* von Richard Wagner," 6 (1961): 4–11.

Eduard Kulke, "*Semele* und *Lohengrin*. Eine Parallele," 6 (1861): 41–46, 77–90.

Franz Müller, "R. Wagner's *Ring des Nibelungen*," 6 (1861): 319–29, 349–74.

Richard Pohl, "Richard Wagner und seine Stellung zur Vergangenheit und Zukunft, von Dr. Fr. Meyer," 4 (1859): 276–80.

Arnold Schloenbach, "Richard Wagner's Operntexte vom Standpuncte des Dramas aus betrachtet," 1 (1856): 68–77.

F. F. Weber, "R. Wagner's Textbuch zu *Tristan und Isolde*," 5 (1860): 337–54, 377–87, 413–23.

FELIX DRAESEKE

Franz Liszt's Nine Symphonic Poems
First Article

Anregungen für Kunst, Leben und Wissenschaft
Volume 2, Issue 5, Leipzig, 1857

Now that, with the publication of the first, eighth, and ninth symphonic poems of Franz Liszt, the whole collection of these mighty musical creations has appeared in its entirety, the appearance of a thorough, objective discussion of this body of work is justified. Indeed, until now the public has received reports only about individual works from this collection, according to the opportunities for their performances, while a complete musical analysis has had to wait for a later time and for the available means to a general perspective for considering these works as a whole—a course of action that, under the given circumstances, revealed itself to be the only practical one, and certainly the most appropriate. Therefore it is with particular joy that we greet the essays from St. Gall and Leipzig, to which we primarily refer in speaking of such discussions, in that they appear as completely ideal examples of the dignified fashion in which the public can be prepared to enjoy these great compositions.[16] We could hardly have taken more pleasure in the fact that these voices of recognition, which took up a lance on the great man's behalf, were joined by the weighty words of Richard Wagner, and that through the publication of his private letter, all of musical Germany learned how greatly its most celebrated composer esteemed the works of his friend.[17] This critically important document would have discouraged us from the attempted discussion begun here if it did not intentionally leave aside a purely musical analysis in favor of placing in brilliant and wonderfully clear perspective the epoch-making nature of the entire Liszt phenomenon. Wagner, of course, finds a dry, purely analytical style of musical discourse reprehensible and esteems, as is understandable in the poet, only that which is written in poetic terms. That being said, the following essay may demonstrate the advantages of just such a thorough analysis of the individual aesthetic elements in the works in question, since it is perhaps in this manner that the most effective antidote can be found for the boundless and in part fatuous skepticism with which the greater part of the musical world has observed Liszt the composer since the beginning of this splendid new phase of his career.

This skepticism is undeniably so very widespread among professional musicians and amateurs alike that a more exact account of its bases seems necessary. Some of these can merely be mentioned and then immediately dismissed as entirely platitudinous; others, however, require closer examination before they can be laid aside. We would place in the first category such ridiculous remarks as: "Liszt could not possibly have been born a composer, let alone a master of the first degree, since only in recent years did he discover in himself the drive to create"; "Liszt is a foreigner and therefore, due to his lack of understanding of its inwardness and depths, it is obvious that the German people's musical character is and must remain unknown to him"; and more of the same, which we have since forgotten. To the second category belongs the assumption that Liszt's inclusion among the ranks of great composers is merely the doing of his party of followers *[Partei]*. This assumption, which forms the basis for so much skepticism, deserves more attention. First of all, we cannot deny that only this party of followers, of whom he is the cofounder, has up to now actively worked for Liszt's recognition by all the means of acknowledgment commonly used in Germany with respect to geniuses, and that it will continue to work for him for a long time to come, even if only to gain the visible support of a few. Yet, we must hasten to add that it is through this party of followers that all the notable composers of recent years such as Schumann, Wagner, and Berlioz attained either full or incipient recognition; furthermore, to return to generalities, this party works primarily toward the end that the delights they alone currently enjoy can someday be tasted by all, and that the riches they alone now possess may presently become common property. To this end, it has been only the hostility and ignorance of an opposing majority that has forced these followers to adopt the position of an organized camp of support. One may ask if it is really necessary for this party to summon yet another new composer when Berlioz and Wagner, two geniuses of the first order, already swell their ranks. Or will an artist of equal merit be offended if Liszt's fame is proclaimed and he is named as Beethoven's successor in symphonic composition? Schumann is dead, and like Berlioz and Wagner still stands unimpeachable in his rights; men like Ferdinand Hiller and others who feed off of the scraps of a Mendelssohn or a Meyerbeer, could hardly be called geniuses with any justification whatsoever![18]

Liszt, however, has through his playing proven to all the world that he is a genius. That he truly possesses an urgent creative drive, not to mention great creative powers, has been proven almost hourly through the astounding, tireless productivity he has manifested in recent years and into the present day. An artist who is not suited to composing on a large scale certainly does not have the command of such a prodigious number of poetic ideas. Craftsmanship creates more slowly and economically—genius alone is capable of carelessly throwing about such a wealth of ideas. And should Liszt, who had reason during his earlier career to absorb the very essence of the entire body of musical literature, and then bring it forth once again as a unique creation; should he whose earlier virtuoso compositions, which, it goes without saying, will always be associated with this tasteful and sensitive artist and serve as proof of his elegant musical technique, so often shot through with flashes of inspiration—should Liszt not feel the need to create ever so much more after he has made composition his primary pursuit, and find such varied inspiration through the friendship of both of his great contemporary geniuses? And should the party that has so often successfully fought on behalf of great men at least deserve credibility, here where it hails Liszt as the third of the three remaining stars lighting the musical heavens? Should not so many brilliant examples of the Epimethean community shy away from a new disgrace?[19] It is earnestly to be desired that this time the useless struggle will be eased, yet it can hardly be hoped that the "art-loving" world might for once abandon its usual path.

In any case, one can claim that the *Partei* by now has more members who perhaps earlier felt themselves drawn to Wagner or Berlioz, and still showed themselves skeptical of Liszt's compositions, and later, after a single experience of listening to a Lisztian orchestral work, became enthusiastic supporters, and that these same people do not consider Liszt a great composer because they belong to his party of followers, but rather the reverse: the supporters first formed a party after they learned to marvel at Liszt as a composer. In the interests of the present discussion, which with hope will gain credibility through the following confession, the writer of these lines wishes to state that he himself once belonged to this above-mentioned group of people who were initially filled with general skepticism, and who, despite reading through some of the scores (which is recommended as a means of becoming more closely acquainted with Liszt's works), could not manage to gain a vivid sense of them. He was able to peruse long, inspired passages in his score reading, but in general he was expecting only intellectual discourse and lively interest; he did not expect to warm up to them. A single performance of Liszt's *Les Préludes* was sufficient not only to warm the writer, but indeed so set him afire that it took him weeks to fully master and digest the powerful impression it made. However, this writer is not the only one who has had such an experience with the symphonic poems; he could name many of his artistic friends in whom they produced the same effect. One can only hope, therefore, that performances of these powerful compositions of Liszt's will best promote their recognition. Unfortunately, only a very few people, even among professional musicians, have had an opportunity to be present at a performance. True artists, on the other hand, harbor enough interest in these works at least to gain a closer knowledge of the published scores. The majority have failed, however, to develop a clear picture of them through such a reading, and furthermore, have not begun with the works that are most ideal for this purpose. Thus besides the more common opinions, such as those mentioned above which we have sought to set aside, there are also those specifically musical ones, to which we cannot avoid giving more precise consideration.

Among these: that the symphonic poems are nothing more than a collection of bizarre, breakneck modulations, ear-splitting dissonances, formless piles of phrases, and deafening orchestral effects—opinions which until recently the majority of musicians were still united in holding, even though these opinions were indeed almost always based on a firm prejudice that could not be killed off immediately by a superficial study of the works. In addition, it cannot be denied that the formal structure, the massed instrumentation, the many harmonic novelties, and indeed even the treatment of the melodic and rhythmic elements seem at first glimpse to justify all the implied objections above. Liszt's way of composing for the orchestra is so new in every detail, and especially for the musician of the old Mozart-Mendelssohnian school so striking, that in order to arrive at any understanding of a composition, it is necessary to arrive first at a new perspective from which to judge better the handling of the various musical elements. This is not necessary, however, for the artist who has studied Beethoven's last works and made them a part of his own flesh and blood: the artist will perhaps stumble sometimes, but will find the proper standard by which to understand the whole. The majority of modern composers has unfortunately not yet reached this point; if in fact they nominally pay homage to Beethoven's Ninth Symphony and the *Missa Solemnis*, they nonetheless prove with their own compositions that these works in no way represent for them the norm, but rather the exception. Especially for them, and for the general public, the story of Liszt's uniqueness may now be written, as we wish to attempt here without the suggestion of hidden motives, which is imperative for the discussion of these brilliant works.

Second Article

Anregungen für Kunst, Leben und Wissenschaft
Volume 2, Issue 6, Leipzig, 1857

The first step must be to confront the seemingly common prejudice stating "there are no melodies in the symphonic poems," an assumption that in any case can only accompany ignorance of the works. Quite to the contrary, we can state that it is precisely the abundance of melody in these compositions that reveals the master's greatest achievement, and which alone would suffice to secure the popularity of his works with the concert-going public, just as Wagner's *Tannhäuser* has become popular with operagoers during the past few years. We are even more convinced of this because Liszt is the first composer in some time to reintroduce singable melody to symphonic music, from which it had been completely banned, largely through the efforts of the Schumann school. In fact, Schumann himself created a large number of fresh and fiery themes, but they were almost completely unsingable, and slavishly dependent on their harmonic attire; indeed, in some of his great orchestral works one is no longer even aware of melodies, in the normal sense of the word. Since the master offered such magnificent harmonies, such profound musical-poetic ideas, it was easy for any aesthetic taste to overlook this deficiency. In the end, his school came to look for everything in a brooding haze of harmony, and even the so-called singing passages are distinguishable only through the melodically empty phrases that Mendelssohn and his disciples created and not, as one could have wished, through expressive cantilenas with long melodic lines. Furthermore, this school was not distinguished for its profundity, and abused the clumsiness and timidity that lay in Schumann's nature as much as it could, looking down with holy horror on any melodious music, and made, despite its "uniquely German inwardness," such a frightful impression that it is hardly surprising that the general public went over to the side of the Italians and Flotow.[20]

The music-loving public, however, has relied so heavily on melody in the past that one can hardly believe this will change in the future, even if a basic musical education becomes the common property of the entire art-loving laity, and melody, as a result, is no longer the only attraction. Even if an impulse such as this were completely justified, melody may be so little removed from music as color is from painting, and only a sad ascetic error of the recent past would want to see it as a sign of the superficial and trivial, to be entirely banned from the realm of "serious music." Of course, it is undeniable that the songlike creations of the so-called melodious opera composers of recent years have been the cause of the above-mentioned one-sided conclusion that these artists, in their obsession with melody at the expense of all other artistic requirements, had in any case become very trivial and insipid. In particular modern Italian opera, because of this unhealthy melodiousness, offers a sorry perspective. But that in no way justifies throwing out the baby with the bathwater and doing away with melody in and of itself. On the contrary, a composer who strives to provide his works with a melodic interest in order to appeal to the tastes of the masses is to be esteemed when, like Liszt, he brings harmonic, rhythmic, descriptive, and contrapuntal elements equally to bear; in a word, he knows how to satisfy all the responsibilities of art. Even the Italian singing style, in fact precisely this, may be welcomed with pleasure under these circumstances, in that it certainly distinguishes itself from all others through ardor, passion, and a particular sensual magic. And why should a composer, whose works strive for the greatest possible brilliance, voluntarily reject these beautiful means? Indeed, why should not these admirable characteristics of Italian melody be separated from the superficiality and triviality that have been their result? Liszt may well have reached a similar conclusion in his own thinking about this question, which moved him to allow Italian melody to enter symphonic composition. In any case, his works have not been damaged by absorbing these elements, in that an overall ingenious, refined harmonization not only elevates but truly ennobles the works' magic, transforming them according to their own most intimate character, and through the quintessentially Germanic artistic creations of the great master, into an outwardly shining brilliance that could well be envied by many of his colleagues.

At the very least, the attacks Liszt has had to endure from the ascetic quarter because of his so-called Italianism can also be ignored by him with complete indifference, all the more so in that Liszt's collected melodies do not so much call Italy their home as reflect their variety of sources, all of which come together only in his works, where a sensual magic and a glowing passion are determined by the idea to be expressed. Some are born out of a truly German inwardness and sincerity, others out of a lovable, flirtatious coquettery, and still others out of the composer's own national originality, and all of them attest to the flexible musical intelligence and general intellectual diversity of their creator. Here we wish to be allowed to make reference to another work of the same genre, which, although of recent origin, has risen to epochal significance: we mean the broad, chorale-like melody that has gained such sudden and deservedly widespread popularity through Wagner's *Tannhäuser* Overture, the effect of which (provided that the melody is used in a fitting context) can be considered as wholly artistic. Suddenly it is possible to express in melody that which is magnificent, sublime, deeply serious, and majestic, and to present it to the masses in graphic vividness. The public, which is not accustomed to considering the main theme of a particularly melodic work if it is moving and forceful, even when it is clearly marked, and which only with the second, so-called lyrical theme allows a transfigured smile to steal upon its face—this public may now hear something other than tender, sentimental feelings in melodic form greeting its ears, and can accustom itself to extending its limited understanding of melody and allow greater consideration of powerful, energetic, sublime, and profound passages, and in this fashion steadily approach a more worthy relationship with art and its disciples. This is why the great, broad, orchestral chorale-melody is so heartily welcomed, and why Liszt especially receives our greatest thanks for introducing it into the concert repertoire. As has already been pointed out, the honor of this innovation belongs to the dramatic composers. Meyerbeer and Berlioz were its instigators, while Wagner immediately took up and developed this new invention, elevating its use to that of a guiding principle in his treatment of orchestral melody in opera. Liszt understood its importance immediately, and used it to best effect in symphonic form. He had the greatest right to do so, of course. Those who would raise the point here that the same elements that can be used to great effect in dramatic music are often out of place in music for the concert hall should consider that we are speaking of general musical innovation in both realms, without which neither can prosper, and should remember, furthermore, that without the strengthening mutual support provided by these dramatic and symphonic innovations, such great progress in so short a time would have been impossible in either genre.

If on the one hand, dramatic composition, stimulated by the advances of recent composers, has significantly acquired harmonic refinement and orchestral perfection, then on the other the elements of melody, description, and rhythm, which are privileged in operatic music, have had an enormous positive influence on orchestral composers. To consider briefly the progress made just with respect to rhythm, we must state that unfortunately it is precisely the German artists who can claim the least credit, since the French have conquered the field in this area and, in comparison with the brilliant inventions of the likes of Berlioz, the Germans clearly lag behind. Notable if also isolated exceptions can admittedly be found in the masterworks of Beethoven, Schubert, Franz, and others, but for the most part one cannot deny the presence of a certain awkward monotony that grips the rhythmic elements of even the most recent German composers.[21] One of the weaknesses native to the German artistic nature, without which it would be able to celebrate twice as many victories as currently, seems to reveal itself as the basis for this monotony. German composers, particularly contemporary ones, are so fixed on harmony and so overly concerned with the inner intensity of art that they have notably neglected this expressive element, as it seemed to them unimportant; they have ignored it in the same way in which they once ignored melody. They stitched together one four-beat measure after another, were endlessly perplexed when, against their best efforts, the goodness of fate placed a few triple-metered rhythms in their pen, cogitated about whether these will destroy the balance of the whole structure, and when finally, according to their suspicions, they discovered the 5- or 7-beat measures to be traitorous beyond all doubt, usually did not rest until, through the addition of a filled-in, meaningless beat they achieved a full 6 or 8 counts, creating the intended monotony and boredom.

A study of Berlioz's works, which have been available to the esteemed German musicians for the last twenty years, might have impressed upon them the empty thoughtlessness of their efforts, since these elements appear in the works of no other master with such epoch-making brilliance as they do in his; up to the present day, however, there has unfortunately been no such study undertaken by any but a very few of our worthy colleagues. While none dare any longer attempt to diminish the respect due to this great man, most of them still cannot bring themselves to trust this strange, foreign titan.[22] They comment only that Berlioz is "a highly interesting personality," and hope in this way to dismiss somehow this great force of nature entirely. While it is true that through his occasionally daredevil experiments, be they harmonic, instrumental, or rhythmic in nature, Berlioz has created no small amount of difficulty for himself in his relationship with the German public and German artists. This is due to the fact that both of these parties demanded unified, self-contained works of art and at the same time did not possess a broad enough perspective to understand the necessary achievements accomplished by these experiments, choosing rather to view them as proof of Berlioz's bizarre nature. This type of loophole, through which "healthy human understanding" sometimes tries against its own will to distance itself from its own nascent sense of wonder, may be more or less closed in the case of Liszt's creations. Liszt does not experiment—he produces unified, self-contained works of art. Within them however, as one of their intrinsic features, rhythm functions with a freedom and vivacity that returns to the land of the living any musician's heart that was ever martyred and deadened by the endless accumulation of four-beat measures. True, the Philistines will turn even this advantage into its opposite, and try to see animation as distortion and piquancy as frivolity, but why rob them of their fun? Why should we not smile indulgently at the harmless naïveté that sees the subdivision of the beat as an integral musical component, even though in fact only rhythm claims this role, while the former has only as much meaning for music as the grid lines of a map have for geography? And now we must add, not without malice, that in our view Liszt has not yet dared enough in these new symphonic poems of his! We are able and willing to tolerate far more, and also hope, following Franz Brendel in his remarks concerning the *Faust* Symphony in his "Report from Weimar" in the *Zeitschrift für Musik*, to see one day the longed-for ideal of rhythmic freedom and independence achieved in all its beauty.[23]

Let us turn now to the shaping of the harmonic element in Liszt's works, and consider his masterful achievements in the realm of composition most frequented by German artists. Liszt could, if he wished, boldly claim to be German in terms of the intelligence, refinement and audacity of his harmonization, and could also, because of this, expect the friendly approach of his artistic colleagues from this quarter—that is, if he were not too bold for their tastes. Even the foundation, which he continues to build on, is so new and unusual for the majority of them that they would be constantly dizzied at the sight of it if they were to use the guiding principles of the ordinary harmonic catechism as a measure for his progressions. Experts and understanding admirers of Berlioz and Wagner are in any case better prepared, but they too will find that Liszt dares far more than his predecessors with respect to this element, and writes individual harmonies that are for the moment exceptionally striking and thought provoking. In spite of this, I find in these new large-scale works only a few instances with which I would quibble with any justification; the great majority of striking harmonic passages seem to be by the book, understandable and in most cases (especially in view of the poetic subject) entirely natural, as long as one understands precisely the previously mentioned innovative foundations for them, and explains the risky business of genius. The establishment of this new foundation was necessary, however, since evidence of the shortcomings of the existing one can be seen through the efforts of all newer masters who work to introduce just such a reorganization. Not only do the works of Beethoven, Schubert, Schumann, Berlioz, and Wagner provide the proof of this, but even the arch-conservatives Mozart and Mendelssohn have given us notable examples of a disloyal harmonic sensibility, which could be mentioned here. We find, for example, the powerful succession of G major seventh and E-flat sixth chords, which is used repeatedly by every innovator and possesses the distinction of being an "invention of the future," already present in Mozart's great C Minor Fantasy for piano, and the even more aggressive progressions from A minor to F-sharp minor, and from

G-sharp major to B minor are already present in Mendelssohn's technically so very brilliant Third Symphony—let those who are astounded read the music themselves.

In the case of the aforementioned new masters such examples are naturally available in significantly large numbers; in Berlioz's works especially, these passages accumulate so frequently that they hardly count any longer as exceptions, and seem to be placed together with the textbook examples in a single category. This is true to an even greater degree in Liszt. In the first place, he has gathered all the exceptional, bold innovations of earlier masters (which are not really exceptional in that they were used by later composers and thus became part of tradition), arranged them cheek-by-jowl with more conventional means, and used them almost as extensively as the other previous methods. At the same time he also recognized the deepest fundamental rules of these harmonies, found and ordered similar analogous instances in great number, yet was still quite dissatisfied with them; so, like every epoch-making artist he discovered through the free and uninhibited choice of his own genius new combinations and among these some seem experimental, but others so brilliantly beautiful and moving that because of the latter one willingly accepts the former—which may perhaps yet prove justified in the future. Liszt is also fully within his rights in all these efforts, and the premature judgment of a know-it-all is just as out of place here as it was earlier with respect to Beethoven, who also gathered together the available harmonic materials of his time and, using them as a foundation, built upon them according to the direction of his own genius. And as far as the collecting of harmonic inventions by new masters and the equal rights of these vis-à-vis conventional textbook methods is concerned, it is (indeed always is) such that theory follows in the footsteps of practice, and is presently happy to ignore the now no longer usable, purely diatonic system and to feel its way instead toward the foundation of an up-to-date enharmonic system, according to the natural laws that lie at the heart of most innovations which have since become traditional or rule-bound, and thus to extend significantly the entire basis of harmony.

In his book *Die Wagnerfrage*, Joachim Raff has already referred to Weitzmann's theoretical works, and we here will do likewise, for in them, one finds two principles that contain the solutions to the above-mentioned problem.[24] They may also contain the central notion that is ideal for the building of a completely new system of harmonic instruction. The first of these can be expressed in the following way: any consonant chord can follow any other consonant chord if the progression of the individual intervals is stepwise or the intervals are common to both triads. In order to understand better the meaning of this rule, let us take as an example the C major triad, which can be followed not only by all the harmonies that lie within this key but also by, among others, the C-sharp minor triad (with which the E is common), the E-flat major and minor chords, the A major and indeed the A-flat and F-sharp minor triads, chords whose individual intervals either already exist in the previous chord, or are separated by only a step from that one. It goes without saying that, in any case that would result in a succession of fifths, the composer must avoid the triads in question through transposition. The use of this rule in practice offers the attentive researcher, in addition to the above, any number of interesting cases to consider, especially if he chooses, in this context, the more productive minor triad as the object of his study. Many striking progressions, which had earlier perhaps seemed to him unreasonable risks, will now, from this new perspective, tell a completely different story and certainly gain his approval. We number among these in particular the previously mentioned direct connection of the C- and E-flat major or A-major triad, which is beloved of all new masters without exception, after the progressions that are separated from one another by a major third (C–E–A-flat major), but have lost their element of surprise through overuse. Also this first combination, which earlier was all too quickly and all too often treated with hostility and harshly judged, is now beautified and redeemed because of the new rule.

However, enough of this first principle of Weitzmann's theory, for although it opens a large, wide field for new harmonic combinations, this field is not so extended as the one created by the second principle, whose main point is, briefly put: any dissonant chord can resolve to any consonant chord whose intervals are separated from its own by one step or are partly contained within it, with the obvious caveat that no interval of the dissonance can move to a tone belonging to the harmony of the same dissonance. A single example will suffice, we hope, to render this unclear-sounding sentence more understandable. If we begin by taking as the point of departure for this investigation the 6/4/2 chord, F–G–B–D (together with the reservation of the enharmonic exchange of its individual components), we can find for it no fewer than twenty possible resolutions allowed by this second rule, in that the minor and major triads formed by the scale degrees C, C♯, D, E♭, F, F♯, A♭, A, and B can all follow that chord, and some of these progressions in spite of their striking originality create not only a surprising, but also a truly beautiful effect. We would place in this category, for example, the until now very seldom used but highly commendable progression of the A-flat minor 6/4 chord or the E-flat major triad. The latter must be written, by the way, so that the third occurs in the upper voice, but this will then create a very fresh-sounding harmony. But no more of that!

The preceding provides enough information so that the musically literate reader will now be in a position to prepare his own analogous resolutions for whatever dissonant chords he desires, and likewise to test at last the actual legitimacy of today's inventions, which were sanctified by tradition but are still considered bold strokes. In any case, Liszt's customary harmonic spelling may be a great deal clearer to the reader with the knowledge of the two primary rules mentioned, since the progressions of dissonant sounds to others are achieved through suspensions, or are similar to those ordinarily used until now, or lastly, may be determined by one of the two analogous rules. But this is still not the main point of Lisztian innovation in this area. The most striking element of his harmonic progressions consists in the immediate connection between distant triads, and if we can accustom ourselves to these juxtapositions, recognize their legality and especially, in my opinion, overthrow the outdated notion of a despotic, exclusive principal key area, then we will be in large part acquainted and on good terms with Liszt's treatment of the musical elements under discussion. Although we do not have enough space here to go into the details, which in spite of this are likely to cause displeasure, we will perhaps find the opportunity in the specifically musical analysis of the symphonic poems to justify and defend these details, and thus set aside the doubts they may raise. It is worth taking the time now to remark that the rules of Weitzmann mentioned above were determined exclusively in light of strict counterpoint and do not, therefore, forbid these or any other exceptions. Indeed, it was Beethoven who demonstrated how genius reveals itself at its most powerful in just such a contravention of the rules! In my opinion at least, why should Liszt not be allowed such a splendidly remarkable venture?

We turn now to yet another chapter in this story, since the previous one has already become disproportionately extended! Modern instrumentation, the magnificent clothing of all Lisztian orchestral works, which has been reproached for being heavy with as much impertinence as lack of justification, deserves in any case a closer examination and defense. We could simply repeat everything we have already mentioned almost two years ago in the *Neue Zeitschrift für Musik* with regards to Wagnerian instrumentation, but we wish instead to refer to these remarks only briefly, and to present several new points of consideration that will be of greater effect than those used previously to justify the practice of orchestration on a grand scale.[25] The earlier remarks were for the most part limited to proving that all great masters have added to the means of expression available to them; for example, when Mozart introduced the trombone into the opera and Beethoven did likewise in the symphony, when Meyerbeer first used the ophicleide in the theater and Mendelssohn brought the same instrument into the concert hall.[26] Thus the saying expressed with such contempt by the reactionaries—the greatest triumph of art is to achieve much with little—cannot possibly be that on which the guiding principle of artistic progress could be developed, since the great masters of former ages have always used the largest known ensembles, and therefore had as much reproach heaped upon them in their day as is presently heaped upon their major successors. At the same time, we wish to point out at the beginning of our discussion that this kind of an increase in means could continue on without any particular end. Still, a boundary will quickly become apparent, one that may have already been crossed by some composers and must remain in the sights of any artist blessed with aesthetic feeling, though Liszt's compositions all still fall on this side of the boundary. Such a boundary also does not run dead-straight, but rather can be likened to a continuously winding path, which narrowly restricts the composer for the instrumentation of a simple song and retreats into the invisible distance when the artist seeks to bind the thunder of Judgment Day to his manuscript paper. The work of instrumental music in particular has taken on such a completely elevated nature in recent years it is no wonder that an artist could not see himself in a position to realize his ideas through the available means, and thus form a new combination for mass effects that allows him the desired colors with which to paint his more complex compositions.

Let it be said often: program music is the mother of the entire modern approach to instrumentation, at least insofar as the latter has claimed a place in the concert repertoire. With the *Eroica*, Beethoven opened the door for the use of a third horn in the orchestral configuration of his day, and with the C Minor Symphony he brought together almost all the forces of what we now consider the modern orchestra. In his great Mass he wrote a part for a second pair of horns which, as is well-known, is used commonly today, and in the Ninth Symphony even Turkish musical effects found their representation. The orchestra used by Beethoven in the latter work is also that used by Liszt, increased only by a pair of bells, cymbals, one or two trumpets, the newly added woodwinds (English horn and bass clarinet), and harp. The goal of this increased ensemble in large-scale effects was not an increase in sound dynamic, as can be seen in the fact that Liszt seldom uses the cymbals in forte, the increased number of trumpets is used in only four of the symphonic poems, and the other instruments mentioned are not powerful ones. Any complaints about too loud a noise must therefore be directed not only at Liszt, but also at Beethoven. The considerable respect commanded by the latter does not allow for the expression of such (truth be told) unfounded criticism, and therefore it cannot be leveled with any fairness or justification at the recent master, either. We call such criticism unfounded because there can be no question of "noise" with respect to either Beethoven's or Liszt's orchestration. The poetic subjects of both composers demand the accumulation of mass effects at the appropriate passages, and without the same would not have been able to find the right musical expression. Indeed, in those places that require a tender, simple orchestral treatment, both masters have always demonstrated real artistic insight, neither of them using any thicker coloration than was required or appropriate. In particular with regard to Liszt, musicians may look for examples with which to justify our claims in many passages from *Festklänge, Orpheus,* and *Les Préludes.* Let us look, rather, for the reasons why the use of larger ensembles for program music was necessary from the start, and here we must be allowed to begin by casting our glance toward opera, the development of which likewise necessitated a richer palette of coloration, for the same reasons.

As long as the lyrical elements remained in the foreground in musical drama—the dramatic life of a work freely revealed only in the longer recitatives, and the story itself taken from everyday life, unburdened by either romanticism or pomp—then the existing instrumental forces were completely sufficient. As we know, the dramatic element gained increasing prominence, the arias, duets, and small ensembles no longer played such a large part in the total picture, the recitatives appeared less strictly differentiated from lyrical passages, the subjects required more magnificent and more romantic settings. At the same time, the demands made on the powerfully developed, expressive orchestra became both more various and more meaningful. The orchestra should no longer figure simply as the accompaniment to the voices, but rather should perform alone from time to time, to create atmosphere and context, to color various situations, to support cogently the dramatic effects and lend a hand at major climaxes. However, its existing abilities were no longer sufficient to these demands. New colors and new combinations had to be found, larger-scale effects had to be reinforced, and the tender passages had to be rendered more delicately, more meltingly. The romantic, the magical and fairy-like, the sinister and the demonic would now be portrayed, certain individual dramatic passages received characterizing coloration, and the entire orchestra was overhauled and enlarged with this goal in mind. In this manner modern operatic instrumentation developed. In concert music it gained unrestricted dominance only later, because until the present day, the question of the necessity of program music has gone undecided and, in our view, only this artistic direction was in the position to bring about an increase in materials and an enrichment of colorative techniques. As long as instrumental music limited itself merely to sketching feelings, remaining the lyrical expression of a subjectivity, the existing materials were likewise sufficient. A fortissimo in the trumpets and timpani was enough to represent the grip of powerful feeling, and an espressivo in the woodwinds or string section could reveal romantic longing, melancholy, and other tender emotions of the heart. For the contents of an *Eroica*, however, the existing orchestra was already too feeble; a material increase here seems not only fitting, but necessary. I for one have always had the feeling, upon listening to this titanic work, as if the orchestra, laboring so considerably under Beethoven's demands, which require efforts beyond its natural strength, were nearly breaking itself to pieces as it tried to bring forth new powers with which to conquer the awesome musical ideas. In order to attain the resolution of a C Minor Symphony, in which from the very beginning all the available resources of an ensemble are used to the utmost of their abilities, a dynamic intensification was unavoidable; the storm of the *Pastoral* Symphony required tuba, the march in the Ninth demanded Turkish musical effects. Mazeppa's ride will finally be resplendently rendered in even more vivid colors, as is entirely proper. The unwilling snorting and neighing of the steed as it almost flies from the earth in its wild racing, while its hooves so thunder with rage that sparks fly from them, and the youth who is tied upon the steed, who arches and writhes in inexpressible terror, trying to tear loose his bound limbs—while we hear all around them the ghostly chorus of wolves and ravens hurrying after their certain prey—who would want to paint all this with an orchestra possessed of only a single powerful means of coloration?

By these examples we hope to have successfully justified the use of large ensembles. Clearly, they serve a higher purpose and are not merely to be used for their own sake. It seems to us equally obvious and incontrovertible, however, that even if a composer voluntarily limits himself to using a smaller orchestra of reduced coloristic means, the limitation may betray him. The greatest and most difficult task, of course, is to be able to use this large ensemble to actual effect, to work with it economically when called for, moreover, to find the appropriate color, to create the desired mood; and above all to achieve the greatest possible degree of melodious sound through the beautiful, measured use of it. With good conscience and the best certainty we can assure all our readers that Liszt has given evidence of his brilliance in an unusually magnificent way by the completion of this task. In tone-painting alone he belongs among the greatest masters, and if he cannot in fact claim his place as first among equals, it may be that Berlioz possesses a more comprehensive intelligence, a more substantial virtuosity; it is in any case undeniable that his natural proclivity to experimentation has often overtaken him, and caused him to allow particular characteristics to shine forth at the expense of the total impression. For Liszt, on the other hand, the total impression is the main point, and from this perspective his method of instrumentation seems to be the best, insofar as it is the most artistic. His colorations are distinctive and re-create a mood in such powerful fashion that we no longer hear, but rather believe that we actually see what is happening. They beam forth with a blinding glory and are never base. Even in the luridly colored *Mazeppa* I found no passage deserving of this name, or in which the euphony was at risk. By the way, Liszt's intelligence in this area is understandably extensive; few combinations of truly beautiful effect remain unknown to and unused by him. With a sure and practiced eye he measures all the materials compiled by the great artists of the past, and selects only the best for his own use. As may be expected in one so brilliant, he does not stop at considering solely the artistic combinations currently on offer, but rather takes an active role as an innovator, and through his experiments, which are always undertaken with a refined sensibility and accompanied by brilliant successes, he provides endless inspiration for further discoveries. We hope to address what this means for his instrumental discoveries through a discussion of his individual works.

At this point we will allow ourselves a look at the formal structure of the symphonic poems, about which we can with good conscience refrain from any defensive arguments, since eloquent and weighty voices have disproved the accusations of so-called formlessness that have been leveled at our master. "Breaking with clichés" has become the motto of our entire party and, in the special individual case, "breaking with the usual symphonic form" seemed therefore necessary for our modern instrumental composers. The insights provided by a precise and loving study of the works in question will quickly demonstrate that not one of them has thrown himself into the arms of actual formlessness. On the contrary, Liszt in particular (as Franz Brendel recently expressed it in a discussion of the *Faust* Symphony) always demonstrates a refined sense of form, knows what kind of container will best hold the large, rich contents of his works, and despite its frequently complicated nature, always polishes form artistically and makes it understandable to the critical observer.[27] Though the poetic kernel nestles so exactly and intimately within this container, and is presented to us in such a variety of forms and with such diverse subjects, that we never fail to grasp the relationship, the artistic unity, the flow, and the necessity of what follows—we always grasp the artistic structure and logic of his conception. The formal structure of the symphonic poems is also not so foreign that analogies to its main features cannot be found among the works of earlier masters. On the contrary, not a few are in sonata form, and some (*Orpheus, Héroïde funèbre*) actually harken back to the even simpler form of the march.

We will not be remiss in providing proof for these observations when we take the opportunity to offer a specific musical analysis of the works in question. Here, where our purpose is to illuminate only the primary characteristics of Liszt's compositions, we will emphasize instead another of our master's merits, which has more than a little to do with the above-mentioned formal clarity of his creations and because it falls upon him, a newcomer and an innovator, to have to emphasize it with redoubled vigor, in opposition to Zion's guardians of art. We have in mind his well-known and, among all experts, undebated mastery of thematic formation and development. This characteristic is, of course, known to be found in all competent symphonists and should therefore not simply be presented as some original trait of Liszt's. Only because of our opponents, who, through the occasionally peculiar methods of thematic development in Berlioz's works and the complete lack of them in Wagner's creations, have been seduced into believing that the "musicians of the future" want nothing more to do with it, as a "superseded historical position"; we have to make assurances that it is not so, and that from our party's standpoint the rejection of so essential a requirement in instrumental music would never be considered.[28] It is true that Wagner earlier let slip a few remarks that could have been interpreted in this way; however, his letter on the creations of his friend proves that he has since changed his outlook (if in fact it was ever really his), and that a useless or indeed positively damaging sweeping away of completely justified and unchangeable rules of composition was never in question.

In any case, Berlioz's thoroughly imposing creations, with regard to their artistic technique, have already provided proof that thematic work and polyphony can be easily reconciled with the essence of program music. Liszt's works allow us to realize how these two elements can be used for the purposes of a new plastic, characteristic art, and for this reason deserve to be assiduously practiced now and in the future by all young symphonic composers. It is not even in debate that without some sort of specifically musical balance, compositions of program music easily run the danger of throwing out every basis, every unity, and as a result, of racking up various unrelated themes one after the other that will only confuse the senses of the listener. This evil can best be avoided through the use of thematic art. A talented composer can easily accomplish this by means of the latter, by presenting from one thought new and diverse motives capable of expressing the most varied emotions, while always allowing for the recognition of their common source. A composer working in this way would require only a relatively small number of themes in order to produce the richest poetic musical materials and a large number of various moods all flowing from one source, which he makes perceptible through artistic changes and revisions of a single musical thought. Let us note as an example Liszt's *Tasso*, a rather extended tone-painting that is rich in variety yet has main themes taken completely and specifically from a Venetian gondola song; let us further consider the first tender motive of *Les Préludes*, a melody full of romantic longing, which later develops into a war cry, complete with force and fire, and let us think finally about the main theme of *Festklänge*, by turns fluttering, light, boisterous, merry, serious and inward, imposing and majestic, each time according to its respective garb.

Thus we will be forced to conclude that though on the one hand the characterizing plastic element and with it the true reflection of the poetic subject does not in the least fall short, on the other hand the particular tone-painting, as a piece of music in and of itself, maintains an inner foundation, a positive unity, an artistic completeness and technical interest, the least of which would be rich enough to lastingly captivate even the opponents of program music. It is well-known that there are more than enough of these opponents. Most of them are also hateful and ignorant in their opposition, yet in spite of this an unprejudiced, unbiased view of the path taken by recent artistic events must bring them to a single perspective, and cause them to blush with shame. (They have that much more cause for shame in that even Beethoven, the founder of this new path, could not escape their damnation, if consistency and fearlessness prevailed.) In any case, one may not tire of calling out to these people: "History will judge in matters of Art as well." At a time when any new production that is missing a poetic subject is viewed as leftover scraps of something that has been better said already, and so often that no more interest can be paid to it, and which, as we have been taught by experience, even the general public has lost interest in—at a time when, simultaneously, musical creation also longs for programs, and the opportunity of its production stirs the noblest, most brilliant minds of this age to grant spiritual life in its expression—at such a time it must be said, regarding the justification for this new path: it is a necessity, this plastic direction; let there be no doubt about it. However, to preach caution to certain people is to speak to deaf ears, or to make Berliners enthusiastic—and so here, in the knowledge of the victory that will soon be fully achieved, we will not unnecessarily tire ourselves further. Only those among the opponents of program music who do not dismiss out of hand everything that bears this name, but rather still hesitate to give their complete acknowledgment to this art form because of well-founded considerations, may credit the following words of understanding. Namely, there is—and we do not seek any argument whatsoever in this—an aberration in program music composition that can be called materialistic, which seeks to express every detail and give every note a meaning. Unfortunately, we cannot deny that in spite of our boundless respect for Berlioz's genius, this great mind indeed sometimes leans dubiously in a materialistic direction. It could hardly have been possible in any other fashion, as long as he wished to be true to his splendidly completed mission to cultivate and let blossom external things. In view of Liszt's works, however, this kind of reservation is unfounded. A mere glance at the given program for each is enough to see how general these are, how much space remains for the purely musical presentation, and how much the principal characteristic of our art, which is to say that which words cannot, is held in honor in spite of any program.

Further, a glance at the topics of the nine symphonic poems will also demonstrate that it is impossible for any of the crass superficiality of materialism to find a place in them. The poetic subjects that Liszt chose for musical presentation are of an ideal nature through and through, and contain a deeper, inwardly spiritual context even where it seems that only the actions of the narrative are given (as, for example, in *Mazeppa*). The poet Victor Hugo has given his sensually rich and wonderful interpretation of the youth, threatened with an ignominious martyr's death and later elevated to the status of prince, an allegorical meaning, wherein Mazeppa signifies the genius who strains against his bonds, who "defies death with every step" and finally "rises, a king." Anyone who has ever listened to this piece will recognize in Liszt's music the reflection of this poetic allegory. Just as there will be no doubts among art lovers and the enlightened that the tone-paintings *Tasso* and *Prometheus* also paint a portrait of a genius in chains, each naturally in its own way. The son of Greece is cloaked in a harsh and rough garment that calls to mind antiquity, and Tasso suffers and triumphs under the smiling skies, among the carefree people of Italy. Thus we can see in three large tone-paintings various solutions to one and the same task: the externals of the program—the scenery and coloring of the poetic painting—determined the externals of the music, above all the characteristic mood; yet the inner kernel remained in large part the same, aside from the modifications also made here. We are completely certain that this procedure, which Liszt and only Liszt principally used, will be decisive for the whole future of program music. All purely external topics and prosaic materialism aside, it is music that on the one hand is able to express the most sublime, ideal, and poetic thought, while on the other hand it is also able to present the most varied, magnificent pictures, within the vividness of which those abstractions are given life. The composer is thus in a position to express all the demands of reality, without in any way ignoring the striving toward the elevated and ideal.

It is hoped that these words are sufficient to allow the above-mentioned intelligent opponents of program music to drop or at least to mitigate their fears concerning its degeneration, and also to cause them, bearing this in mind, to be more fair in their criticism of Liszt's compositions. We hope they, and indeed together with them, all sympathetic readers of this publication, will realize that after all our expressed opinions we respect our master not just as an individual, legitimately artistic personality, not merely as a deeply meaningful talent, but rather as a genius, whose works for the present and long into the future will build a wondrous monument worthy of admiration and honor. All the most moving elements of our time have their musical expression in the symphonic poems, and must in light of this create a congenial effect on every educated, advanced person. Their poetic bases are also truly full of poetry, humanity, and the ideal sublime—they represent purely human nature, and are therefore understandable and accessible to all. All of these available musical materials are furthermore assembled by the composer, who where necessary has brushed away the cinders and used them to an imposing overall effect.

Liszt has at this time, when national chauvinism has led either to superficiality or to Philistinism and partisanship, and in either incarnation has proven itself damaging to the development of art, done the great deed and created an international music. Born a Hungarian, and familiar since his childhood with a fiery, still vital folk music tradition; French in his upbringing, and thus no stranger to the elements of grace, ease, deftness, and outward polish; and finally a transplanted German, who has lived long enough with these people to learn to love their earnestness, their depth of feeling, their inwardness and distrust of superficiality, and who furthermore is ingenious enough to absorb these same qualities, he seems to be exactly the right man both to dare and to achieve such a great undertaking. One artist, Meyerbeer, already attempted this in recent years with his operas, and one could declare, on account of their widespread, enormous effect on Europe, that he has achieved this goal, were it not for the hindering presence of a single giant "but. . . ." Meyerbeer possessed an uncommon, at times brilliant talent, was remarkably clever in using it, and knew how to marvelously dupe the great masses. But it is well-known that he had an unfortunate lack of artistic purity, and did not possess the drive toward that which is most elevated in art, and rejected the purity of creation as inimical to him. He sought to catch and satisfy the majority of the public, but not to win the applause of the noblest and highest spirits.

Until the present day, it has been given to only one genius to succeed at both, and also to reach this goal unconsciously and in complete naiveté, and that was Mozart. Indeed, his great successor Beethoven, who surpassed him in so many ways, described him as having a specifically Germanic nature, the value of which could never be fully appreciated by foreigners and could also never be congenial to them, in the full sense of that word. The thoroughly German Wagner also seems destined to share this fate. Liszt, however, has inherited Mozart's legacy, and like this master, who seventy years before found a common expression for the musical feeling of all creative nations in his operas, has now in the nine symphonic poems laid out a new, powerful musical language accessible to the whole educated world, the fundamental power and freshness of which completely silences any thought of simple eclecticism. One cannot possibly interpret Liszt's achievement in assembling the various musical elements to a great overall effect as resulting in the potpourri-cookery style of Meyerbeerian opera, in which a passage of German music always mingles with others full of French or Italian music. Rather, one can compare it with a chemical bonding, in which the combination of two or more types of materials form a new, independent whole according to the various orders of the day of its creator. Furthermore, this combining has not remained Liszt's only task; on the contrary, his powerful nature continually urges him to other innovations, including the harmonic, structural, and instrumental elements upon which we have already commented in this discussion. Even if his sole innovation was the already prepared—like all epoch-making deeds—discovery of the "symphonic poem," through which he paved the smooth future path of program music, which had until then raged between lawlessness and overdetermination; this would be enough to secure him a place of honor in the history of music. If we remember in their totality all the other great characteristics of the composer, which until now we have sought to illuminate individually, there can be no more doubt that Liszt is justified in taking his place as an epoch-making genius among the most preeminent masters.

We believe this all the more firmly, and can speak it with all the more assurance, since according to all reports we cannot consider even the sublime, colossal culmination point of the current tone-paintings, the symphonic poem *Ce qu'on entend sur la montagne*, which in the truest sense of the word is a mountain of a creation towering over the other symphonic works of the present, to be Liszt's greatest work, but rather expect that we may find in his as yet unknown *Faust* Symphony a still more significant rival. And so we hope accordingly to greet in this great man not the close of a powerful artistic period, but rather the blossoming of a new one. In any case, we shortly expect to see a great school arise around this firmly pronounced artistic personality, a school that, as the result of the versatility and brilliance of its master, will not lose itself in petty mannerism and monotony, but will do much to establish and promote its much-maligned leader's recognition in the widest possible circles. That it will soon be achieved, we wish from our hearts, and greet it therefore in advance with the motto: *Vivat, crescat, floreat.*[29]

NOTES

1. A term coined by Franz Brendel in 1859, "New German" designates Liszt, Wagner, and the musicians who shared their musical and aesthetic principles. Another term applied to these musicians was the "progressive" party or movement in music. Draeseke spent the years between 1862 and 1876 in Switzerland, and after his return to Germany became increasingly alienated from the progressive cause in music.

2. Franz Liszt, "Berlioz und seine Haroldsymphonie," *Neue Zeitschrift für Musik* 43 (1855): 25–32, 37–46, 49–55, 77–84, and 89–97.

3. Until this point, Wagner's early "Romantic" operas *(Tannhäuser and Lohengrin)* and his writings about music (especially *Oper und Drama*) had served as the primary objects of anti-progressive criticism.

4. Eduard Hanslick's polemic: "Les Préludes . . . ," reprinted in *Niederrheinische Musik-Zeitung* 5 (1857): 89–94. Franz Brendel's response: "F. Liszt's symphonische Dichtungen," *Neue Zeitschrift für Musik* 49 (1858): 73–76, 85–88, 97–100, 109–12, 121–23, 133–36, and 141–43. Pohl did not publish his articles until later, because of the surplus of publications on the symphonic poems at the time. They eventually appeared as "Liszts symphonische Dichtungen: Ihre Entstehung, Wirkung und Gegnerschaft (1859)," in *Franz Liszt: Studien und Erinnerungen* (Leipzig: 1883), pp. 199–228. Wagner's contribution to the debate came in: "Ein Brief von Richard Wagner über Franz Liszt," *Neue Zeitschrift für Musik* 46 (1857): 157–63. Reprinted as "Über Franz Liszt's Symphonische Dichtungen," in *Richard Wagner: Gesammelte Schriften und Dichtungen,* 2rd ed., vol. 5 (Leipzig: 1887), pp. 182–98. Because of Wagner's personal belief that the future of music did not reside in the instrumental realm, the letter's position on the symphonic poems is far from unequivocally supportive, and in fact it can also be read as a veiled critique. Regarding the problematic nature of Wagner's letter, see for example Thomas Grey, *Wagner's Musical Prose: Texts and Contexts* (Cambridge: 1995), pp. 1–4, 306–14.

5. Franz Brendel and Richard Pohl, "Beim Beginn des zweiten Bandes," in *Anregungen für Kunst, Leben und Wissenschaft* 2 (1857): 1.

6. Wagner's article "Über musikalische Kritik: Brief an den Herausgeber der Neuen Zeitschrift für Musik," *Neue Zeitschrift für Musik* 19 (1852): 57–63, started the discussions about an alternative journal—Wagner quickly dismissed the idea, based on what he considered to be Brendel's inability to understand his aesthetic ideas. Liszt continued corresponding with Brendel about the journal, which led to the eventual establishment of the *Anregungen* in 1856. On the history of the journal, see James Deaville, *"Anregungen für Kunst, Leben und Wissenschaft:* An Introduction and Index," *Periodica Musica* 2 (1984): 1–5.

7. Regarding Liszt's approval, see Helmut Loos, "Einleitung: Die Wagner- und Liszt-Aufsätze," in *Felix Draeseke: Schriften 1855-1861,* ed. Martella Gutiérrez-Denhoff and Helmut Loos (Bonn: 1987), p. xxii. Liszt's letter to Draeseke: Weimar, 30 December 1860; *Letters of Franz Liszt,* ed. La Mara, trans. Constance Bache (Leipzig: 1894), vol. 1, p. 460.

8. Regarding Ramann, see the letter from Liszt to Lina Ramann, dated Rome, 27 November 1874; Lina Ramann, *Lisztiana: Erinnerungen an Franz Liszt . . . ,* ed. Arthur Seidl, rev. Friedrich Schnapp (Mainz: 1983), 41. For Bülow, see "Ein Meister- und Musterwerk." This clever play on words, typical for Bülow, disappears in translation. The passage, from a letter of Bülow to Draeseke from early 1858, appears in Erich Roeder, *Felix Draeseke: Der Lebens- und Leidensweg eines deutschen Meisters,* vol. 1 (Dresden: 1932), p. 88.

9. Loos, "Einleitung," p. 23.

10. James Deaville, "The Controversy Surrounding Liszt's Conception of Programme Music:" in *Nineteenth-Century Music: Selected Proceedings of the Tenth International Conference,*

ed. Jim Samson and Bennett Zon (Aldershot: 2002), pp. 98–124. On Beethoven's legacy in Liszt's Weimar, see above all Axel Schröter, *"Der Name Beethoven ist heilig in der Kunst": Studien zu Liszts Beethoven-Rezeption*, 2 vols. (Sinzig: 1999).

11. William Kinderman, "Introduction" to *The Second Practice of Nineteenth-Century Tonality*, ed. William Kinderman and Harald Krebs (Lincoln, Nebr.: 1996), p. 2; and Jim Samson, *Virtuosity and the Musical Work: The "Transcendental Studies" of Liszt* (Cambridge: 2003), p. 162.

12. Fritz Reckow, "'Wirkung' und 'Effekt': Über einige Voraussetzungen, Tendenzen und Probleme der deutschen Berlioz-Kritik," *Die Musikforschung* 33 (1980): 1–36. Once the German commentators moved away from the *Symphonie fantastique*, the "materialistic" problems of Berlioz tended to disappear, which is why Liszt could write his article series about *Harold in Italy* with a clear conscience and impunity from his New German colleagues. Not all of the critics from the progressive movement were as careful and selective in their Berlioz critique as Liszt was.

13. See Keith Johns, *The Symphonic Poems of Franz Liszt*, ed. Michael Saffle (Stuyvesant, N.Y.: 1997), pp. 10–45 for a discussion of how topoi function in Liszt's symphonic poems, and pp. 72–74 for his views on topoi in *Hungaria*.

14. The conservative opposition wished to deprive Liszt's works of musicality. See Deaville, "Controversy."

15. Alan Walker, *Franz Liszt: The Weimar Years 1848–1861* (New York: 1989), 363–67.

16. Draeseke is referring to favorable reviews in the *Neue Zeitschrift für Musik* of concerts of Liszt's symphonic poems in St. Gall, Switzerland, on 23 November 1856 and in Leipzig on 26 February 1857. See the anonymous review "Musikalische Briefe aus der Schweiz. Franz Liszt und Richard Wagner . . . ," *Neue Zeitschrift für Musik* 47 (1857): 83–85, and Franz Brendel's extended review-essay "Franz Liszt in Weimar," *Neue Zeitschrift für Musik* 47 (1857): 101–05.

17. "Ein Brief von Richard Wagner über Franz Liszt," *Neue Zeitschrift für Musik* 46 (1857): 157–63; reprinted as "Über Franz Liszt's Symphonische Dichtungen," in *Richard Wagner: Gesammelte Schriften und Dichtungen*, 2nd ed. (Leipzig: 1887), vol. 5, pp. 182–98. This publication was originally a private letter from Wagner to Marie von Sayn-Wittgenstein, Zürich, February 1857.

18. Ferdinand Hiller (1811–85) was a conductor, composer and critic whose activity centered on the Middle Rhine region, especially Cologne. Strongly influenced by his friend Mendelssohn, Hiller revealed his conservatism above all in his bitter polemics leveled against Wagner and Liszt in local newspapers and in music journals.

19. Translator's note: "Epimethean" is a reference to the Prometheus/Epimetheus dichotomy, based in Greek mythology. Prometheus and Epimetheus were two Titan brothers, whose names mean "forward-looking" and "backward-looking," respectively.

20. Friedrich von Flotow (1812–83) was a German opera composer whose works revealed a strong affinity with French opera.

21. Robert Franz (1815–92) counts among the most gifted Lied composers of the mid-nineteenth century. Liszt himself wrote an extended essay about Franz in 1855.

22. Translator's note: The phrase "dieser unheimlichen Grösse" is uncommonly difficult to translate. The adjective *unheimlich* refers to something sinister, eerie, and/or strange. It can also be broken down etymologically as "not home-like," hence "foreign." Draeseke, here discussing Berlioz, may be drawing attention to Berlioz's "outsiderness" in relation to the German symphonic tradition, as well as his eccentricity.

23. (Karl) Franz Brendel (1811–68) was Schumann's successor as editor of the *Neue Zeitschrift für Musik*, and there served as the staunchest literary supporter of Liszt and Wagner during the 1850s and 1860s. The report in question is actually entitled "F. Liszt's neueste Werke und die gegenwärtige Parteistellung: I. Das Concert in Weimar das 5 September,"

which appeared in the *Neue Zeitschrift für Musik* 47 (1857): 121–24. The occasion was the premiere of Liszt's *Faust* Symphony.

24. Joachim Raff's *Die Wagnerfrage: Kritisch beleuchtet* (Brauschweig: 1854) caused a stir within the progressive party, since in his analysis of *Lohengrin*, he freely juxtaposed praise with criticism. Regarding the harmonic theories of Carl Friedrich Weitzmann (1808–80), see R. Larry Todd, "Franz Liszt, Carl Friedrich Weitzmann, and the Augmented Triad," in *The Second Practice of Nineteenth-Century Tonality*, Kinderman and Krebs, eds., pp. 153–61.

25. Draeseke must be referring to his article "Richard Wagner, der Componist: Eine Betrachtung vom rein musikalischen Standpuncte aus," *Neue Zeitschrift für Musik* 44 (1856): 133–36, 145–47, 157–60, 169–70, and 177–80. It is the fourth installment (pp. 169–70) that deals with the issue of instrumentation.

26. The ophicleide is a low brass instrument known for its appearances in the *Symphonie fantastique* of Berlioz, operas by Meyerbeer (e.g., *Robert le diable* of 1831), and the incidental music to Mendelssohn's *A Midsummer Night's Dream*. It was eventually replaced by the tuba.

27. Draeseke is referring once again to Brendel's "Report from Weimar," about Liszt's concert there on 5 September 1857, an article which appeared, as mentioned above, in the *Neue Zeitschrift für Musik* 47.

28. The phrase "superseded historical position" (überwundener Standpunkt) is a Hegelian term associated with Brendel.

29.Translator's note: Latin phrase for "May it live, create, and flourish."

PART IV

REFLECTIONS ON FRANZ LISZT

A Mirror to the Nineteenth Century:

Reflections on Franz Liszt

LEON BOTSTEIN

I. Liszt and History

Virtuoso (homo plebi admirabilis) Thrives in civilized Europe and in the nineteenth century, loves laurels and Friedrich d'ors and won't refuse even guineas; knows how to manipulate ten fingers and exploit the attentive audience; understands the weak strings in the souls of the masses better than the strong strings of the piano; purchases fame from journalism and finds himself in a state of absolute immortality.[1]

This entry in the 1893 edition of the leading satirical German-language lexicon of the nineteenth century, written a half-century earlier by the legendary Hungarian-born Jewish humorist Moritz Saphir (who made his career first in Vienna and then in Berlin), offers a glimpse of the place of public concert life in nineteenth-century culture. Saphir touched a raw nerve: the suspicion that virtuosi made careers and achieved fame on less than admirable grounds. Saphir's derisive mocking of virtuosity was contingent on his readers' recognition of their own conceits. A society that embraced concert attendance could consider itself "civilized." By placing the manipulative aspect of the virtuoso's stardom in the foreground, Saphir rendered the vanity and venality of virtuosi less troublesome than the public's vulnerability and gullibility in thinking that it was responding to something noble—art perhaps.

Saphir's "attentive audience" for public music making was neither trivial in size nor socially insignificant. The astonishing reach of concert music in the European nineteenth century had rendered the virtuoso a man (or, as in the case of Jenny Lind, a woman) admired by the plebs.[2] Franz Liszt's career charted the path for this mass appeal.[3] His fame, fueled by a journalism which by the mid-nineteenth century had embraced concert music, extended well beyond an elite. Liszt, the nineteenth century's most versatile, eclectic, famous, and long-lived musician, offers an ideal prism through which to reconsider the character of that century.[4]

We have come to accept the concept of a "long" nineteenth century. The idea derives its allure from the argument that 1789 and the French Revolution, not 1800, marked the end of a period—a metaphorical century—in which the ideas of the Enlightenment held sway and the aristocracy, with its attendant privileges, was predominant in setting cultural mores and tastes. The year 1789 set into motion a process of radical social and political change that altered the map of Europe as well as distinctions of class and nation. At the other end of the century, 1914 or perhaps 1918 (World War I)—not 1900—closed the era that began with 1789. The year 1918 marked another fundamental redrawing of the map and a decisive blow to the roles of the monarchy and the landed elite. Within this extended nineteenth century, there was one clear watershed year, 1848, the end point of the post-Napoleonic period of restoration and reaction and the starting point of the age of nationalism.

This plausible periodization is justified by the history of politics. The economic and social change surrounding sharply delineated political shifts was more gradual and evolutionary, blurring even the extended boundaries of the nineteenth century.[5] The history of culture, ideas, and the arts, when treated as reflective of politics and economics, and therefore as causally subsidiary, further complicates the defining of periods, since changes are hard to characterize and pinpoint. Furthermore, the arts, and music in particular, have been treated frequently as self-referential, with autopoetic logic independent of economic and political history. Even when the arts are deemed to be responsive reflections of political and social change, not as engines of history, their connection to other forms of life is often vague at best. No one seriously believes that the causes of the Revolution of 1830 can be found in the music of Daniel-François-Esprit Auber's 1828 *La Muette de Portici,* even though, as one venerable textbook put it, a performance in Brussels on 25 August 1830, "triggered a revolution." The inspiring link, if any, was the libretto by Eugène Scribe and Germain Delavigne with its overt challenge to the power of tyrants.[6]

What might be learned about the nineteenth century from the study of music and musical life does not strictly concern causes in history. By the same token, given how central music was, we might learn something other than how music and musical culture reflect historical generalizations formulated without insights from the study of music history. From the perspective of music, for example, the "long" nineteenth century may be less persuasive. The classical style of the eighteenth century underwent a decisive change only after 1815. Twentieth-century modernism can be located closer to 1900, or between 1906 and 1913, before the outbreak of World War I.

Liszt was born before the fall of Napoleon and died after the Congress of Berlin. His presence and influence traversed all of Europe, from Madrid and London to Odessa and Istanbul. He was at one and the same time a celebrated public figure among the Hungarians, the French, and the Germans. His pupils and protégés constituted a nearly complete set of leading figures in late-nineteenth-century national schools of composition. As pedagogue and mentor, Liszt's influence stretched from the United States (Daniel Gregory Mason, Amy Fay, and Edward MacDowell) to Russia (Borodin and Balakirev). Even Liszt's posthumous influence has been unusual. He died in 1886, resigned to the poor reception his compositions had received. Yet his compositional strategies were crucial to two fin-de-siècle masters of the modern: Richard Strauss and Gustav Mahler. Mahler died in 1911, the date of Strauss's *Der Rosenkavalier,* a work that has long been regarded (mistakenly) as marking the end of that composer's avant-garde period, arguably Strauss's most Lisztian.[7]

The coincidence between Liszt's aesthetic project and the nineteenth century has a dialectical dynamic. He absorbed contemporary trends but transcended them. His reputation for originality as a composer has rested primarily on his mid-career turn toward orchestra music. Yet in retrospect Liszt has gained enormously in stature as a precursor of aspects of twentieth-century musical aesthetics. The posthumous publication in the 1920s of much of Liszt's very late music gives this notion its own peculiar twist. Liszt's primary role in the mid-nineteenth century—his formulation of the connection between music and poetry and narrative—has now been supplemented by the seemingly prophetic qualities of his last works.[8] Yet many of these were not known by composers in the twentieth century in whose music Liszt's influence seems to be audible.[9] Liszt indeed distilled musical rhetoric at the end of his career, attenuated harmonic connections, reduced sonorities, gambled with abrupt juxtaposition and silence, cultivated simplicity, and highlighted the fragmentary. Late Liszt has forced us to rethink the sources of twentieth-century developments such as minimalism, harmonic experimentation, and the redefinition of pitch relationships. Liszt's spiritualist persuasion and the static surface of the very late music inspire a reconsideration of reductive contrasts between twentieth-century modernism and late nineteenth-century Romanticism.

In Arnold Schoenberg's awkward and convoluted 1911 centennial tribute to Liszt, in which he repeated the conventional misgivings about the quality of Liszt's music, Liszt is praised generically on account of his advocacy of the new, his faith in God and ideals, "the personality, the true artist-being, that draws from direct vision."[10] For Schoenberg, "Liszt created an art form which our time necessarily regards as a mistake."[11] At the same time, Schoenberg had the foresight to predict the possibility that his own reaction against Liszt's "mistranslation" of the connection between poetry and music into music that was "secondhand poetry" would in turn be rejected.[12] Schoenberg conceded that "a later time will perhaps again see exclusively the genius's insight," suggesting the late twentieth-century trends that echo Liszt's music.[13] A return to program music did not take place, but an evocation of Liszt's faith in God and spiritualist minimalism did.[14]

Liszt was heralded in his lifetime for his support of others and his uncanny capacity to mirror his environment and adapt and absorb influences. Liszt's first biographer, Joseph d'Ortigue, observed about Liszt while the artist was still in his twenties that "we do not believe that any contemporary has drawn more broadly from the common reservoir of his time or has reflected its diverse characteristics as fully."[15] This note was struck again by Liszt's countryman Béla Bartók, also writing in 1911. Equally astonishing and repellent were Liszt's "many-sidedness, his eclecticism, his over-susceptibility to all musical sensations, from the most commonplace to the most rare. Everything he had experienced in music, whether trivial or sublime, left a lasting imprint upon his work. Even as a man he showed an amazing variety of characteristics."[16] For Bartók, however, Liszt was no chameleon, despite his mastery of imitation. Rather, his musical mind worked as a highly discriminating filter, curious but generous, open to all influences. Liszt's extensions and reformulations of the ideas of others—d'Ortigue's "common reservoir"—were original and pathbreaking, as his development of the model of the symphonic poem out of the encounter with Berlioz's music makes plain.

II. Out of the Shadow of Mozart:
Aristocracy, Sentiment, and Realism

In terms of chronology, the first characteristics and influences Liszt drew from the "common reservoir" mirrored premises that cast the very young Liszt in the role of a latter-day Mozart. In 1826, the *Allgemeine musikalische Zeitung* cited a contemporary Parisian journalist's view that Liszt "was the miracle that is the Mozart of our age."[17] The comparison to Mozart was the consequence of an explicit strategy on the part of Liszt's father, Adam. But the comparison left a lifelong imprint on Liszt that highlights continuities, not divisions, between the eighteenth and nineteenth centuries. One of Liszt's first popular biographers, writing in 1887, explored striking parallels between Adam Liszt and Leopold Mozart, particularly with respect to their furthering of their sons' ambitions to achieve long-lasting fame as composers.[18] That comparison suggests more than shared generic qualities of career management and parental pressure; similar aesthetic prejudices and ideals were transmitted to the young Liszt.

Retracing the path of Mozart meant acknowledging, if not embracing, aristocratic patronage and judgment. For Adam Liszt, the key to success and fame depended not only on the financial support of the landed aristocracy but also on deference to its aesthetic tastes and expectations. Because of the international standing and solidarity of the European aristocracy, Adam Liszt assumed that local success, even in the 1820s, could be parlayed into a European career centered in royal capitals—Vienna, London, Paris, and Berlin. The starting point for Liszt, as for Mozart, was provincial. But the gap between the tastes and mores of Liszt's birthplace (in the shadow of the Esterházys) and the Vienna of the early 1820s, was wider than that between Salzburg and Vienna circa 1760.

The Vienna of 1822 and 1823 in which Liszt studied stood in marked contrast, culturally and politically, not only to the Vienna of Mozart, but to the Vienna in which Beethoven made his career in the 1790s, a fact that troubled Beethoven himself in the early 1820s. Adam Liszt's embrace of the Mozart model had the aspect of an anachronism. Nonetheless, both the aesthetic and social values reflective of that anachronistic imitation of Mozart would flourish in Liszt's self-definition, just as the emulation of Mozart would persist in the music of a contemporary from Poland, Frédéric Chopin. Chopin came from a region that was comparably coherent to Liszt's part of Hungary in terms of language, lack of political independence, and "peripheral" status in early-nineteenth-century Europe.[19] Among the values characteristic of Mozart's age were a complex and ambivalent attachment between musician and aristocracy, and an allegiance to the forms and rhetoric of classicism. Mozart's greatness lay partly in how he complicated classicism with a resistant, rebellious, and proto-Romantic expressive originality. Liszt's friendship with and devotion to Felix von Lichnowsky, the nephew of Beethoven's patron, reflects a lingering deference on the part of the musician-artist to the refined aristocratic patron. Liszt, like Mozart (and to an even greater extent Beethoven), cherished the capacity of musical fame to generate a social platform on which an aristocracy of merit could hold its own alongside the aristocracy of birth.

The legacy of aristocratic patronage and culture in music had not been entirely undone by the thirty years of political transformation that began in 1789. The influence of the court and noble families continued in Vienna after 1815 and in Paris after the Revolution of 1830, and in both cities—to a rapidly declining degree—after 1848. But as the founding of the Gesellschaft der Musikfreunde in 1812 suggests, in Vienna, as in London and Berlin, a new untitled and literate public, able and willing to buy instruments, seek music instruction, purchase sheet music, and read journals that covered musical life had emerged out of the wars and chaos created by Napoleon. They spearheaded and benefited from the ensuing rapid economic transformation.[20] Voluntary clubs and societies were formed in which the old aristocracy and a new elite mingled and shared in participation and leadership. The marked difference between the Vienna of Mozart and that of Liszt (and the last decade of Beethoven's life) was the breaking of the aristocratic monopoly on active connoisseurship. The leading amateurs in the era between 1820 and 1848 were not primarily aristocrats, as they had been in Mozart's lifetime. Indeed, the post-Napoleonic age marked the start of a precipitous decline of the old aristocracy as the arbiters of taste in the arts.[21]

Furthermore, by the time Liszt arrived in Vienna, a tension had developed between new and old tastes and styles, framed in part by the success of Weber in Vienna in 1821 with *Der Freischütz*, the Rossini craze, the new theater of farce, and a demand for a music of domesticated intimacy with a distinctly non-aristocratic pedigree, one that offered vehicles of emotional response to the politically repressive stability of the 1820s. Paganini's phenomenal success in 1828 in Vienna deepened that tension. Schubert's output of Lieder and chamber music was the highlight of the emergence from Viennese classicism of a new aesthetic. Schubert's career stood in stark contrast with Mozart's (and Liszt's) by its absence of both virtuosity and noble patronage. By being labeled as the new Mozart and seeking to gain Beethoven's blessing in the city as child prodigy (kiss or no kiss and Anton Schindler's machinations notwithstanding), Liszt started on a career path less akin to Schubert's, or even Schumann's, than to an older type, defined by his father against the grain of the historical moment.[22]

Although celebrated as emblems of a distinctly nineteenth-century trend, Liszt's later theories of the connection between music and language, and between the poetic and the musical, owed more to the eighteenth-century conception of the link between sentiment and the musical experience of listening than is often realized. Liszt's appropriation, during his virtuoso years, of eighteenth-century fashions regarding the display of emotional susceptibility, enthusiasm, and refined feeling for music contains echoes of his debut as the latterday Mozart. They are less the behavioral habits of early Romanticism than extensions to a new public of rituals and responses identified with the aristocratic salon and imperial household.[23]

The complex intersection of old and new in aesthetic tastes in music in the European 1820s also derived from the connection between politics and aesthetics. Eighteenth-century notions of musical meaning ranged from the theory of sensibilities and sentiments to the use of musical rhetoric as illustration. That type of illustration was quite distinct from later notions of program music—music defined by a poetic or narrative structure or idea.[24] The *Pastoral* Symphony of Beethoven, as the composer's own prefatory remarks explained, pointed to a complex link between real-time events and the subjective, reflective response. But the work, as the storm sequence indicates, also contained conventional elements of pure illustration, as did *Wellington's Victory*, a work that has a more central place in Beethoven's oeuvre than subsequent Beethoven reception has usually conceded. Works of characteristic instrumental music—the battle symphony, for instance—were still popular in the 1820s. In such works, unlike Beethoven's, music was used reductively, employing simplifications that re-created visual impressions. Nineteenth-century program music, as Liszt defined it in his prefaces to the symphonic poems, can be seen as a novel extension of Beethoven's practice. Liszt's idea, like Chopin's reformulation of Mozart's lyricism, nonetheless revealed debts to eighteenth-century precedents. Liszt, following Beethoven and Mozart (as mediated through Chopin), utilized music to generate a sensibility regarding the subjective alteration of the external. External events such as storms and battles remained in a rhetorical, quasi-illustrative usage, structured to evoke internal responses and feelings.

Liszt's fantasies and improvisations on themes became a crucial component of the incredible fame he achieved after moving to Paris with his father in the mid-1820s. The highly complex later versions, particularly those based on melodic material from the operatic stage, rejected the formal frame employed by Mozart and Beethoven that utilized an elaborate system of musical parallelisms linking sentiment, sound, and language. In the case of Mozart, Beethoven, and notably Haydn, the extramusical significance of keys and the rhetorical implications of thematic materials reflected normative notions of beauty that justified criteria of proportion and form. The composer, the amateur performer, and the listener shared and assumed a literacy of musical practice that permitted a discourse through music that stood apart from real-time experience. Illustration and elementary correspondences with external events had been transcended by Viennese classicism. The recognition of beauty and refined aesthetic judgment became connected to the capacity for sentiment in response to elaborate musical forms. Sentiment emerged from the recognition of meaning defined by structural procedures. That recognition became an emblem of aristocratic judgment and taste. This art of musical contemplation demanded that the patron acquire active musical skills, an achievement that lent high social prestige to musical understanding.

The phenomenon of an enlarged, new, non-aristocratic audience for music after 1815 inspired a deviation from the achievement of Viennese classicism in instrumental music. Liszt became a pioneer of that variation on classicism. The new aesthetic demanded the abandonment of traditional structures and their procedures, such as contrasting tonal frameworks and the elaborate development of multiple themes and symmetries marked by, for example, expositions and recapitulations. In the place of the expectation of formal structure came a new strategy for inspiring sentiment: the sequential dramatization of extraordinary feeling in the musical time of performance for spectators. The eighteenth-century heritage of a link between sentiment and music was adapted to define instrumental music as the medium through which the self-consciousness of one's imagination and a condensed but realistic emotional journey could be triggered.

The young composer-improviser Liszt adapted the authorial voice of the nineteenth-century novel in which the awareness of form and artificiality, even the voice of the author, became muted. The author's presence in the text is acknowledged but subordinated by the reader, who is drawn into an illusion of realism.[25] In the real time of reading, the reader of novels by Sand, Austen, Balzac, and Stendhal believes that he or she encounters, sympathetically, the experiences and emotions of life cast in a narrative that acts as a surrogate for the extensive elapse of time. The illusion of realism is not complete, for the early-nineteenth-century novel maintained the eighteenth-century framework of a moral argument—a thinly visible, self-contained, didactic structure that justified the evocation of reality through storytelling.[26] The instrumental music from the first half of the nineteenth century, including Schumann's Fantasy in C, op. 17 (dedicated to Liszt); Berlioz's two major orchestral works, *Symphonie fantastique* and *Harold en Italie*, Liszt's numerous fantasies on operatic themes, and even the B Minor

Piano Sonata; and distilled miniatures—Chopin's nocturnes, for example—
sought to create the conscious impression of a coherent musical reflection
or argument. However, in the service of a new aesthetics of emotional
realism, these works adapted the semantic practices of classicism without
its traditional structure. The syntax and semantics of inherited musical
expectations were manipulated in a manner that attenuated the formal
framework of classicism. The underlying ambition was to create an aural
analogue to the experience of reading fiction. Hence the popularity in
piano music of episodic forms or sequences of shorter, chapter-like units.
These units received headings, some suggestive of landscapes and texts
and literary forms, while others retained identifying musical markings of a
traditional type.[27]

The striking advantage and allure of music, owing to the traditions of
eighteenth-century musical aesthetics with respect to the task of generating sympathetic sentiment (radically extended by Mozart and Beethoven),
lay in the compact and distilled flexibility of musical rhetoric. Inherited traditional formal structures were no longer essential to define for the listener
the ways in which meaning could be attributed and anticipated in the
elapsed time of music. And the eighteenth-century habit of artificial parallelisms and associations between sound and experience made possible the
subordination of evident illustration, despite its persistence, notably in
Berlioz's music and in some of Liszt's mid-career symphonic poems. But
listening to instrumental music became an intense species of seemingly
open-ended, individualized, sequential real-life daydreaming. That internal journey for the listener as spectator was guided by performance, as in
the theater. It was not a solitary act akin to reading, except for the performer.

Liszt learned music's syntax from classical models, along with its suggestion of meaning. Although both musical syntax and grammar appeared
removed from external reality, through classical forms music assumed
the status of a language with meaning. Liszt and his contemporaries
reemployed and removed that language from its traditional frameworks
to suggest the emotional sensibility of real-time experience. The use of
operatic themes or songs made that extension, the illusion of an emotional
realism within instrumental music, easier. But the debt to an eighteenth-
century culture of the sympathetic creation of sensibility through music
was profound.

A telling analogy can be made with the transformation in the aesthetics of acting in eighteenth-century England, away from a refined artifice
of classical rhetorical style to one of feeling, in which the body could be
"impelled by the Will" to imitate qualities "proper to a passion," to be a
"soul touched" by emotions: joy, anger, pity, hatred, wonder, love, grief,

fear, scorn, and jealousy. The new theatrical techniques associated with Aaron Hill and David Garrick set a pattern and precedent followed by Liszt and his contemporary virtuosi in performance, improvisation, and composition.[28] Ultimately, in music as in acting, rhetorical devices were disguised and reconfigured to provide the means to stimulate and expand naturalistic sensibilities—to distill and heighten, albeit by artifice, the spectator's sense of authentic human imagination and emotional experience.[29] For Liszt in the 1830s, however, the recognition and response were still contingent on an aristocracy of highly cultivated taste analogous to the eighteenth-century landed aristocracy that had been music's connoisseur patrons, its classically literate public.

III. Tradition and the Audience

Conservative critics during the mid-nineteenth century derided the way in which new instrumental music approximated the realist illusionism of the early-nineteenth-century novel. The theatrical adaptation of musical semantics into a narrative of feeling and intimate experience, like virtuosity as a self-contained object of admiration, was deemed exploitative of a declining level of musical literacy. That species of cultural criticism—the argument of lost standards—mirrored doubt about the post-1815 social transformation that enabled the spread of musical education and literacy. The price paid for the expansion of culture included a reductive trivialization of the inherent meaning, power, and complexity of music that in the era of classicism required an appreciation of traditional formal procedures and structures.[30]

The growing numbers of educated, urban, non-aristocratic elites sought to emulate directly the cultural habits of the old aristocracy. The new elite of wealth, whether or not ennobled prior to 1848 by the Habsburgs or Louis Philippe, created salons imitative of the traditions of eighteenth-century court entertainment that were all too familiar to Haydn during his employment in the Esterházy household.[31] The new reading and listening public recognized musical culture as an arena in which one's standing and status could be affirmed; the demonstration of taste and sentimental response to music (and thereby its meaning) were antidotes to the social insecurity that wealth alone could not mitigate. Benchmarks of social approval derived from the image, reality, and memory of the eighteenth-century landed aristocracy persisted among the urban bourgeoisie well into midcentury. At the same time, the consequences of the transformation of political and economic life—the expansion of public space spurred by the extension of literacy and the attendant reformulation of time, work, and leisure—generated, particularly in the new audience, a demand for new modes and vehicles of musical expression. A new urban culture defined the terms of fashion in the arts.

Liszt betrayed a consistent ambivalence about this historical process. On the one hand, he craved popularity. On the other, as his eventual retirement from the stage indicated, he never shed the eighteenth-century attachment to the linkage between aesthetic connoisseurship and aristocracy. The market for reading material helped propel the development of a new form of fiction, the contemporary novel. In music, the audience that sought an immediacy and intensity of meaning in the presence of music spurred a transformation of inherited aristocratic aesthetic practices in the direction of realist evocations of intimate experience. For all of Liszt's later innovations, throughout his life his music was indebted to the early model of the novel—Hugo and Balzac, rather than Flaubert and Zola. Although realist in its surface, Liszt's early narrative music, like Balzac's prose, presumed a logic reminiscent of eighteenth-century practices. The difference lay in a structure that was didactic rather than formal, in the sense of sonata form (even in the B Minor Piano Sonata). Balzac, the "master storyteller," for example, employed a language that "was expository, declarative, abounding in rhetorical balance and antithesis . . . insisting on thematic unities . . . executed with brilliance and energy." The same terms could describe Liszt's paraphrases and improvisations and much of his early piano music, all directed at a new audience: "the curious, perhaps disinterested, purposeless observer of teeming urban variety, the spectator connoisseur."[32] For Balzac, classical rhetoric allowed him to cast social criticism in the form of realism. For Liszt, musical structure was determined by his desire to evoke through instrumental music the logic of spiritual, religious, and philosophical ideas contained in literary and poetic narratives.[33]

The most widespread contemporary cultural form to benefit from the social transformation of urban Europe and the evolution of a new audience after 1815 was the theater. Predictably, the new forms of theater and opera were critiqued as symptoms of cultural decline and vulgarity just as intensely as was instrumental virtuosity. Like the taste for instrumental music on stage and in the home, the popularity of theater and opera in the three decades after 1815, particularly in Liszt's Paris (as documented so eloquently by Balzac), thrived, ironically, on the recognition of the aristocratic provenance of these art forms.[34] In the eighteenth century, opera had been practically and symbolically identified with the monarchy and highest aristocracy. Like public concerts, opera and theater functioned as primary public venues during the first half of the nineteenth century that brought distinct social classes into one shared space.[35]

But the theatricality and fame of Liszt the virtuoso in the 1830s was not merely an extension of the enthusiasm accorded singers and actors. He and, in a more muted manner Chopin, translated the experience of the real-time parallels, narratives, and illusions possible on stage and in the opera, and intensified them as experiences of intimacy through music alone. Using miniaturization, music generated emotion and memory by indirect allusion to image and word. The family resemblance between the new emotionalist musical rhetoric and late eighteenth-century practices in acting, the novel, the opera, and the play was disguised by the density of musical syntax, not by the personality or showmanship of the performers. Like the actor, the instrumentalist became the vehicle of a believable experience of recollection and illusion. In the case of music, the spectator experienced self-recognition through the encounter with emotions that exceeded those available within the boundaries of quotidian work and routine. Music's realism was not dependent on observable syntactic correspondences with reality. At the same time, music's realism was rendered more believable because the response it triggered was private, intimate, and intense, and had no comparable source in the public sphere.

The severe criticism of these simulated and altered extensions of eighteenth-century musical traditions as evidence of a decline in standards and taste came not only from expert observers but also from Beethoven. When Adam Liszt brought his son to Vienna to make his debut, he arranged for Liszt to be taught by Czerny and Salieri on account of his own allegiance to the aesthetic premises of the classicism of Haydn. The residue of Liszt's encounter with Vienna forged in him a unique and unstable amalgam of competing trends. Czerny's influence is not to be underestimated.[36] Liszt's advocacy of Beethoven became focused on the later work, such as the *Hammerklavier* Sonata, op. 106, dismissed as incomprehensible and reflective of the composer's declining health and advancing age by all but the composer's closest colleagues and aristocratic patrons. The new audience, dazzled first by Rossini and later Paganini, was simply not interested in late Beethoven. But late Beethoven seemed to prefigure for Liszt a new ethereal interiority.[37]

Liszt also embraced Schubert, who generated the most compelling symbiosis between eighteenth-century classical ideals of artistic beauty and sentiment and the newer demands for narrative illusionism focused on intensity, reflection, and emotion.[38] Schubert's ambition and frustration concentrated on trying to succeed in the burgeoning genre of opera.

Liszt, the novice composer, tried his hand at opera as well. The shift from Vienna to Paris was testimony to his need to succeed with a contemporary public whose expectations and judgments were moving away from the tastes of the traditional aristocracy. Despite the local rage for the new in opera, theater, and instrumental music, Vienna was still more backward and conservative in economic and political life than Paris. But despite Liszt's recognition of shifting tastes and his ambition, the classical legacy, the image and model of Beethoven, remained.

The voices of cultural decline notwithstanding, Liszt understood that the new audience with its particular musical expectations would appropriate Beethoven and Mozart far more readily than Haydn. For the new public, Chopin transformed Mozartian lyricism by integrating Bellini-inspired evocations of bel canto. Ludwig Rellstab permanently recast the first movement of the Piano Sonata in C-sharp Minor, op. 27, no. 2, as the "Moonlight," and Berlioz reinterpreted the meaning of Beethoven's symphonies. Liszt's paraphrases and transcriptions, notably of Schubert's music, highlighted suggestive meanings in the heritage of musical classicism and made them comprehensible to the new spectator public. Using virtuosity and performance as re-creation, he found a way of making sense of tradition within the changing aesthetic criteria of the early nineteenth century. As the criticism of E. T. A. Hoffmann (and Berlioz and later Wagner) reveals, Mozart and Beethoven were routinely invoked as inspirations to Romanticism, even though Hoffmann's 1816 *Undine* and Berlioz's 1830 *Symphonie fantastique* display fewer overt debts than the rhetoric their authors utilized in their critical writings might suggest. These musical works traded on thematic and structural simplification, sequential narration, and novelistic illusion and emotionalism quite distant from Mozart and Beethoven. As his critics suggested, Liszt engaged in a comparable form of simplification, thereby rendering tradition accessible. The classical masters quickly came to be understood as historic inspirations and prophetic voices, not as end points or culminations of a high-water mark in the history of music. Liszt's historicism was overt, but not reactionary.

What distinguished Liszt's lifelong effort to reconcile the legacy of Mozart and Beethoven with a new context for musical life was his belief in the logic and necessity of historical progress. Yet Liszt, more than Chopin and Wagner, wavered between disciplined respect and creative appropriation. He played and interpreted more musical history than his contemporaries. Like every performance, the Lisztian transcription was an act of both authentic re-creation and modernization. Indeed, rewriting the music of the masters, improvising on it, quoting it, and personalizing its expressive power were acts of devotion. Liszt, more than Berlioz, employed the rhetoric of normative ideals of beauty and truth evocative of eighteenth-century philosophy. And Liszt, far more than Wagner, stressed not only continuities between past and present in music history but also the legitimacy of inconsistency and eclecticism within his own historical era. Wagner's self-serving account of history privileged a single direction as authentic and progressive. Liszt favored competing continuities in musical practice.

Nonetheless, Liszt's use of history as inspiration for discontinuity and change in musical compositional practice—his justifications of his own music as well as Chopin's and Berlioz's—brought him into direct conflict with those who used history as normative, reflective of a conservative, anti-progressive aesthetic that required defense in the context of an endangered standard of musical literacy defined in eighteenth-century terms. In the later 1850s, Beethoven and Mozart became central in the split between the New German school, the Lisztians, and those who cast their lot with the signers of the infamous 1860 manifesto against Liszt and Wagner. The timing of this open conflict was not arbitrary. After 1848, contemporaries observed a further shift away from the elite musical culture of the eighteenth century, in the direction set in the 1820s. The tradition of high-quality, active amateurism in public and private performance apart from choral singing had receded, giving way to a musical life that thrived on the radical separation of a large-scale, non-aristocratic public of spectator-listeners and a cadre of highly skilled professional composer-performers, of whom Liszt quickly became the pan-European model.

In this process of segregation, the musical skills expected of and achieved by the majority of listeners changed. The world of listeners was no longer made up of amateur players and composers. The vast expansion of music education was made possible by the development of the piano into an afford-able, pitch-stable consumer item. The midcentury public became divided between an elite of old-style connoisseurs, a self-styled aristocracy of cul-tivation, not birth, and the broad public. Insofar as a modern composer's task could be defined as analogous to a writer's and construed, as was the case in Liszt's connection to the Hungarian cause, as politically significant and even populist (in the context of post-1848 nationalism), the immedi-ate, easy, and wide accessibility of music as an experience of meaning and translatable significance became a priority for composers.

For those who stuck to an idealized definition of literate musical culture, the path away from classicism charted by Liszt's generation of composers was little more than an irresponsible act of pandering, a debasement of an ideal form of life. Liszt's defense of Wagner was located in the imagi-nation and genius of the music, not in its appeal to the large public that, despite its innovations, relied on Wagner's use of repetition and dependence on the theatrical. Liszt never seriously tried to enter the field of opera. He sought in instrumental music a way to square the circle and circumvent an ideological choice between past and present. Liszt searched for a legitimate reconciliation between the claims of eighteenth-century normative ideals of music alone and the contemporary audience's demands for a realist illusion linking external experience and interior emotion.

Liszt's aesthetic innovations—those from his Weimar years—would be appropriated by Wagner and Tchaikovsky in ways that would lead each to achieve a mass popularity that eluded Liszt himself. They took from Liszt compositional strategies that responded to the growing demand to experience music, as a listener, as a real-time distillation of the reading, not of the early-nineteenth-century novel, but of the massive and complex realist novel of the mid-nineteenth century. In their music, formal traditions and the techniques of classical composition became more attenuated and subordinated. The authorial voice became curiously hidden in the context of a constructed illusion of time and space. Yet it was Liszt, in his orchestral music, who pioneered the use of evident repetition, the intensification of sonic variety, the emphasis on sequences, harmonic color, monothematic transformation, rhetorical gesture, and direct symbolic analogues between sound and language (as in the opening of the *Dante* Symphony), and ultimately the evident presence of a narrative framework derived from the linguistic and the visual.[39]

Liszt, however, remained recalcitrantly conflicted about the transition of instrumental music from an elite art form that utilized sound self-referentially and was evocative of aristocracy, to a middle-class, bourgeois enterprise contingent on the visible and theatrical. Despite his capacity to mesmerize and dazzle crowds by using the theater of performance and personal style, he might have sympathized with the twenty-seven-year-old Sigmund Freud, who proudly resisted the temptation to become one of the crowd as it was swept away by an 1883 performance of Bizet's *Carmen*.[40]

IV. The Sublime, Politics, Gender, and Religion

The symbiosis between Liszt's advocacy of aesthetic innovation and his self-image as carrier of the classical tradition to a new audience can be understood in terms of the philosophical currents of the early nineteenth century, particularly the aesthetic theory of Edmund Burke. Burke's primary historical significance derives from his 1790 critique of the French Revolution and rationalist claims concerning the interplay between theories of political rights and the actual course of history. His critique helped outline the philosophical basis of the reaction against the Enlightenment. For Burke, politics needed to be grounded in an understanding of the limitations inherent in history, the dynamics between tradition and change, and the rational and irrational in human nature. Tradition was legitimately only subject to gradual change over the course of time. The Terror only seemed to confirm as prescient Burke's critique of the revolution.

The presumption of an organic gradualism in history suggests a persuasive framework through which to consider Liszt's aesthetics. In 1757, Burke published *A Philosophical Enquiry into the Origin of Our Ideas of the Sublime and Beautiful*. By associating the sublime with pain, danger, and terror, Burke embraced in a radical manner an essential component of what would become the aesthetic taste of the nineteenth century's new audience.[41] The sublime, the territory of the vast, produced the strongest emotions the mind was capable of. Beauty, in contrast, was construed as being based on pleasure. It resided in the small scale and revealed that which is not obscure, but the "smooth and polished."[42] From this perspective, the astounding virtuosity that brought Mozart fame in the 1760s and early 1770s, as well as the music of his maturity, could be framed as essentially beautiful. The evocations of the sublime, as nineteenth-century Mozart reception revealed, were located in a few late concerti, the last symphonies, *Don Giovanni*, and the Requiem.

The balance between the sublime and the beautiful shifted in the dominant musical taste of the first half of the nineteenth century. The identification with the sublime deepened. The astonishment Mozart aroused in his contemporaries, amateurs of noble birth, was based on his dexterity and his imitation and formal invention of beauty. By the time Liszt played to the public, virtuosity and precocity demanded a more overt and intense character. Liszt's public expected not only technical prowess and polished elegance but also the capacity to excite, through improvisation and performance, the sensibility of danger, fear, and terror in Burke's sense of the sublime. The recognition of beauty and the pleasure of refined entertainment had been complicated by a search for emotional intensity.

Prefiguring later Romantic poets and theorists, Burke's project was reactionary, placing the imagination at the service of restraining the revolutionary in politics but encouraging the compensatory personal sense of fantasy, including the extremes of emotion accessible through the aesthetic. This transfer of sensibility from the public sphere to the interior of the self, however, had the ironic aspect of sustaining traditions of the aristocratic culture of aesthetic judgment. Burke's aesthetics anticipated Romanticism in a manner that coincided with Liszt's debts to pre-Romantic ideals regarding music and its public.

In the Vienna of the early 1820s, audience demand for a different sort of experience from music can be understood in terms of the experience of the sublime. Hearing Rossini, Weber, and Schubert evoked precisely what qualified, in Burke's formulation, as the sublime, even though the eighteenth-century contrast between the beautiful and the sublime was not explicitly invoked. The terrifying immediacy and intensity in the new music appealed to a public blocked from active political life, free discourse, and public speculation. The ambitions of the audience and their self-conceptions as individuals had been symbolically shaped—if ever so slightly—by the fear and awe accorded the quintessential self-made hero, Napoleon. The arena for heroic action between 1789 and 1815 had been politics. After 1815, art supplanted politics.

The demand for interior fantasy as evocation of the power of the individual was fulfilled by the role of the individual as spectator. That shift was contingent on the political limitations of the Biedermeier and Vormärz politics of Metternich. The frustrated emotions associated with the dream of self-realization in the arena of politics and the cult of the hero were transferred to silent observation, the realm of the imagination, the stage, the picture gallery, and the private sphere. The search for the experience of the sublime through music became widespread in part because the response to music was both public and private. The effect of music was subject to concealment, to an arena of secrecy. Music inspired an internal emotional sojourn. It traded in an illusion of realism that was ideally suited to the age. Music, like the theater of farce, was at once overtly artificial and public and the arena of a camouflaged personal expression of the actual, the dangerous, and the subversive.[43] The politically repressed audience sought out music that could inspire an active emotional recognition of reality, an echo of the deepest emotions of fear and terror.

Liszt's love-hate relationship with virtuosity and the theatrical aspects of performing on the piano can be understood as a response to the initially lukewarm reaction to his very first appearances. As Liszt realized during his first years in Paris, he would have to revise and augment the contained and idealized canons of musical form and beauty in order to equal Mozart in the contemporary social and political context. Virtuosity needed to be cultivated not as a mere skill, but through improvisation, as a vehicle of a theatrical narration that satisfied the need to simulate the danger, terror, and pain his audience had experienced as consequences of war and revolution. The memory of and associations to events between 1789 and 1815 took on a transmuted aesthetic function. They were translated into a realm of virtual pantomime, the artificial realm of the theatrical. Liszt shaped virtuosity into a persuasive surrogate for the sense of astonishment once derived from the vast expanse of revolutionary political action and conquest. To gain notice, even in the hands of a child, virtuosity needed to approximate the Napoleonic, to startle with the sublime.[44]

In recent years, scholarship on Liszt's reception history—his phenomenal early success in Paris and London and his subsequent international fame and reputation—has forced a consideration of the role of sexuality and gender in nineteenth-century art and politics. Within this literature on virtuosity and Liszt's explosive public popularity during the late 1820s and '30s is the claim that gender identity in Liszt's case was destabilized, particularly since the keyboard was defined as being understood as "commonly" if not "universally" feminine.[45] Linked to this line of investigation is the extensive speculation concerning Liszt's personal life, particularly his relationships with women. One need not go beyond the novel *Nelida* by Marie d'Agoult, with whom he had three children. This thinly veiled account of their affair portrays Liszt's competing ambitions, including the desire to be both an idealized creative artist in the eighteenth-century aristocratic tradition (albeit still dependent) and the more contemporary goal to be celebrated as a quasi-political symbol for the wider public: the artist as surrogate conqueror, not only in the public square, but also in the bedroom.[46]

The idea that musical performance and listening suggest metaphors of sexuality and gender relations is not new. Liszt's career in the years following his initial period of childhood fame—as a public presence representing raw masculinity in command of an uncommon (and, aesthetically speaking, sublime) form of seduction—can be read as a variant of the myths and reality that surrounded Beethoven. In the context of the strict delineations of class in the 1790s, the visual and aural intensity of Beethoven's performance did not shock morals or challenge respectability. Unlike Liszt, Beethoven did not demolish pianos in the act of performing.[47] The exclusive circle of the aristocracy did not regard themselves as subject to bourgeois propriety in terms of sexual behavior. The image of Beethoven as an exotic, nearly savage possessor of genius and unrequited sexual desire represents a conservative, post-Napoleonic biographical construct. It expressed, ambivalently, the need to acknowledge a restrictive bourgeois morality and also concede to the artist an exception, but only to the extent of his genius.

Indeed, it was only after 1848, in the provincial midcentury bourgeois environment of Weimar, that Liszt encountered any sustained social stigma regarding his private life. And his patron, the Grand Duchess Maria Pavlovna, true to eighteenth-century aristocratic mores, protected him, as a genius, from the petty disapprovals of the local citizenry. Insofar as Liszt sought to defend artists as a socially progressive elite, exempt (much like the aristocrat) from the strictures of bourgeois propriety, he encountered an extreme fascination that drew part of its strength from the envy, criticism, and resistance of the new bourgeois audience. As a member of the aristocracy, Marie d'Agoult sacrificed her position and security by leaving her husband, not by having an affair or bearing the children of a great artist. Liszt had no status to lose; his behavior caused only wonderment, not emulation. The displacement of ambition from politics to spectator of the arts encouraged within the public a passivity and acceptance of regulation congruent with early-nineteenth-century political reaction.

The widespread reputations Paganini and Liszt cultivated point to a key difference from the legends and aura surrounding Beethoven and, to a lesser extent, Haydn and Mozart. Beethoven was singularly unsuccessful as a Lothario or Don Juan in breaking into the aristocratic circles in which he sought acceptance. Liszt, in contrast, excelled at crossing class barriers. Seduction through the use of celebrity was evidence of the formation of a public for the arts in which the achievement of aristocratic status remained prized but not tied to wealth or birth. The new social context permitted the aristocracy of merit to contest successfully with the aristocracy of birth, an ambition that Liszt explicitly attempted to realize. Both were exempt from social convention.

Nonetheless, in the pre-1848 years, Liszt sought to lend his aesthetic ambitions a moral dimension, as his essay on the death of Paganini demonstrates. He believed the artist's role was essential to an agenda of utopian social and cultural reform.[48] The public performance of music and its composition (for domestic use) assumed an idealized ethical and moral purpose: the Rousseau-like celebration of human capacity, imagination, sensitivity, and empathy. Music was not mere entertainment but a quasi-religious and spiritual experience. In contrast to the moral argument of fiction (as in Balzac's works, for instance), music's task was not cynical recognition, but elevated fantasy. It should evoke tragedy, not venality; hope, not despair. The realist aspect in virtuosic performance and composition that

Liszt aspired to realize using a calculated self-presentation and an emotional expressiveness conveyed by a phenomenal athleticism, was a concentrated evocation of the extremities of the sublime. The spectator was inspired and entertained; the artist who could suggest the power of the human imagination was privileged and therefore permitted the transgression of seduction.

Liszt shared Beethoven's insecurity of class. Both were drawn to women of the aristocracy. Beethoven, for his part, was haunted by his social status and engaged in an awkward masquerade, a direct pretense to aristocracy, that has its analogue in Liszt's self-representation.[49] Beethoven's response to the aristocracy ranged wildly from resentment and superiority to emulation and the demand for recognition. Liszt's dependence on aristocratic patronage was welcome as an antidote to commerce and modern fame and yet resented as servitude. The artist as aristocrat admired and envied the freedom in mores and style afforded those with titles. Liszt, like Beethoven, openly sought the company of the wellborn and cherished the access fame and art gave them to an exclusive world. His resentment was, however, less pronounced.

Furthermore, Liszt's justification of the social role of the artist in his Paris years elevated the artist beyond mere social equivalence. The notion of genius, derived in part from Beethoven's image, legitimated the notion of the aristocracy of the spirit as a quasi-religious order, a priesthood of utopia. Beethoven demonstrated, through the inherent progressive innovation and resistance in his art, its function as prophecy. Given the necessity to confront the struggle, limits, and pain of human existence, sublime vision in art took precedence. The calling to evoke the sense of human capacity, signalling an equivalence between talent and noble birth, gave the artist an ethical valence. As musical culture increasingly took on the aspect of a middle-class enterprise over the course of the century (particularly after 1848, when the older aristocracy abandoned the field of high culture as a field of leisure), Liszt's reactionary self-regard, the idea that an artist possessed a moral status equal to high nobility, led him to associate with an even more resilient hierarchy—organized religion.

From the 1830s on, Liszt shared with many of his contemporaries the post-1789 conviction that religion was a human and historical necessity in the sense argued by Joseph de Maistre: as an antidote both to suffering and the arrogance of reason alone.[50] Liszt's self-reinvention as Abbé Liszt was, however, more than the result of a gradually conservative shift in his social views and the influence of Carolyne von Sayn-Wittgenstein, his second long-term mistress. Catholicism offered the structure required to sustain Liszt's need to remain above the crowd in a manner that transcended mere fame and provided a surrogate response to the residues of late-eighteenth-century social ambitions. The experience of faith also could inspire the feeling of the sublime. In the context of the 1860s, Catholicism provided a lasting didactic framework superior but comparable to the semi-religious utopian speculations fashionable during the frustrating politics of the 1830s and '40s, in which art assumed a central role.

The enthusiasm for music in the decades following 1848 took on a less universal, egalitarian political implication and a more pointed, nationalist political meaning. Liszt, however, did not follow this trajectory. He did not abandon the application of eighteenth-century normative premises or the philosophical idealism of the 1830s in his aesthetics. The transnational framework of Catholicism combined the ideal and the universal. It secured Liszt's early reputation as an international European figure in a world of incipient and divisive modern nationalism. In his later years, Liszt brilliantly sustained his superior European status in society by assuming the dignity afforded the wearer of clerical garb.

Liszt's fascination with the social attraction and seductive potential of virtuosity decreased with the expansion of musical culture and the proliferation of virtuosi in the generations that followed him. His status as an abbé sustained and solidified his reputation as a legendary personality, an idealist, and a disavower of the commercial concert world. Liszt's demand for social equivalence, even superiority, and solidarity with the traditional elite demonstrated a resistance to the markedly expanded European world of commerce and the marketplace. Liszt harbored an old-fashioned prejudice against the radical modernization of musical life in the nineteenth century, visible in the growth of music publishing, instrument manufacture, concert management, and music education after 1848. His public embrace of religion permitted him to sustain the notion of art as an elevated sphere, beyond commerce, tied only to the true and good. With the demise of utopian socialism as a movement, the church offered a context in which contemporary art could subsist without sacrifice to cherished premodern classical traditions. In it, the artist could sustain a noble public status as a thinly disguised priest.

Liszt's public image as male hero and seducer of women, his vague religiosity notwithstanding, had first been protected by his status as an artist. His taking of orders extended that image. In the economically transformative context of post-1789 Europe, social change altered the intersection of gender and class. In the social dynamics on the Continent in the 1820s and '30s, gender and sexuality became means by which to differentiate wealth and mitigate and obscure the residual power of traditional distinctions in status.[51] Liszt's career mirrors the lingering power of eighteenth-century status distinctions as well as the gradual break-down of those barriers. The creation of a non-aristocratic class defined by money brought with it not only a distinct bourgeois morality but also an emphasis on gender as a means to defend the new radical class distinctions created by modern commerce. The construction of new forms of gender distinctions in turn recalibrated the ideal of sensibility, the potential for extreme sentiments, the susceptibility to the arousal by theater and music, and the response to the sublime. A bourgeois moral skepticism vis-à-vis the arts took on gendered meanings. Protecting respectability, particularly as acting and virtuosity called for a masculine use of the body as expressive instrument, emerged as a bourgeois virtue. As the economic function of the aristocracy declined in the second half of the nineteenth century, the construction of gender within the public life of the arts, notably in music, became for the middle class a contested arena of status differentiation.

Liszt played a leading role in the support of women as public artists.[52] Liszt's relationship with Agnes Street-Klindworth has been properly understood as reflecting his gradual emergence from the Beethovenian aristocratic obsession.[53] Liszt had his first powerful emotional disappointment in love when confronted with his unacceptable status as a suitor to his beloved Caroline de Saint-Cricq.[54] The relationships with Marie d'Agoult and Carolyne Sayn-Wittgenstein were realizations of a successful breaking of class barriers. As his affection for Carolyne cooled, his attention turned more visibly to women without aristocratic provenance, not only in his romantic attachments, such as Agnes, but also in his selection of pupils such as Sophie Menter, Amy Fay, and Lina Schmalhausen. As he expressed in his correspondence to Agnes, he retained the antibourgeois but aristocratic presumption of sexual freedom. The wellborn libertine of the eighteenth century had become an object of derision (as the operas of Mozart make plain), not so much on mid-nineteenth-century grounds of sexual immorality, but as an example of the abuse of freedoms and privileges held exclusively but illegitimately by the aristocracy.

As gender relations in the nineteenth century became dominated by standards of legal and formal propriety, Liszt retained the idealized rhetoric of love and passion as universal spiritual attributes analogous to those generated by music, qualities that could not be contained by bourgeois rules. Although his liaisons with Marie and Carolyne were officially shunned, at the same time they were tacitly accepted and their impropriety circumvented. Carolyne could not be received at court, and in an earlier era Marie sacrificed some dimension of respectability. Liszt's role in their lives, meanwhile, secured his self-presentation as an equal of the landed aristocracy, for whom libertine and extramarital behavior were presumed as distasteful perhaps, but appropriate. Nonetheless, as Marie's post-Liszt career (under the pen name of Daniel Stern) suggests, and as Carolyne's massive intellectual output makes plain, Liszt was drawn to the emancipated woman as artist and professional, albeit with some ambivalence.[55]

In the era of Liszt's concert career, from the 1820s to 1848, the priority of status persisted alongside the reformulation of class and gender. The assertion that the keyboard was in some fashion identified with the feminine, circa 1830, is a notion inappropriately displaced backward in time. Before 1789, male monarchs played keyboard instruments as markers of aristocratic status. The traditions of the eighteenth-century aristocracy in no way linked the keyboard with the feminine. The great figures of organ virtuosity in the eighteenth century were male. What gives credibility to the notion that the keyboard can be understood as feminine is the piano's eventual fate as a piece of domestic furniture in the decades after 1830. The violin, in contrast, maintained an unchallenged status as masculine well into the nineteenth century. It was readily transportable; its use demanded a mobility denied women, particularly in the urban marketplace morality of post-1815 Europe. The keyboard, on the other hand, was ideally suited to domesticity. Unlike the violin, its literature was freestanding; music for the unaccompanied violin represented only a small part of the repertoire. The piano justified isolation and solitude and demanded less collaboration; it was singularly appropriate for women. Women were restricted in social mobility and membership in societies and private organizations, with the partial exception of vocal and choral participation (amateur chorus life, well into the nineteenth century, remained segregated by gender).[56] These restrictions limited the opportunity for women to attain proficiency on instruments used in amateur ensembles other than the piano. Music education for women focused of necessity on the keyboard and the voice. Both were construed by midcentury as compatible with modesty and domesticity.[57]

Only over the course of the later nineteenth century can one identify a marked increase in the number of professional women violinists. In Liszt's lifetime they remained exceptional, as in the case of Arma Senkrah, who is remembered through her association with Liszt.[58] Women cellists played sidesaddle into the twentieth century. However, the moral sanction applied to female access to musical culture through the medium of the keyboard, even in the eighteenth century for women of noble birth, did not render the keyboard feminine. Female access to piano instruction only strengthened the power of music and virtuosity as instruments of seduction.

Men continued to control access to music as teachers. In Liszt's career, as in Paganini's, there is no evidence of the blurring of gender identity. Liszt's and Sigismond Thalberg's achievements as performers did not assist in shifting the gendered symbolism of the piano from masculine to feminine.[59]

The piano became a universal, self-sufficient medium for music education in a mid-nineteenth-century world dominated and defined by men. Given the comfort and immobility associated with the piano's place in the furniture of the home, the woman as public performer on the piano became acceptable only gradually, as Clara Schumann's career suggests. The piano's sustained function as a marker of masculinity, notably in the case of Liszt, is further underscored by the aesthetics of piano playing and sound.

From the very beginning of his career as a virtuoso, Liszt distinguished himself from his competitors by being uniquely able to make the piano approximate orchestral sound. In its mannerisms and character, his pianism represented masculine rather than feminine power. Particularly after his encounter with Thalberg, Liszt sought to command the full range of emotional narration at the piano and all its facets of sound, including the legendary third-hand effect. His capacity to evoke stillness and quiet mystery was described as magical. The pianist was a sorcerer: a male image. But the most persistent commentary on his piano playing remained the repeated analogy to the power and range of the orchestra.

In Liszt's generation, partly through Liszt, the piano became a virtual orchestra, the central medium of compositional imagination. Economically and strategically, the piano was a viable means for the spread of a public musical culture defined increasingly by the theater of orchestral performance. Command of the piano could give individuals access to the entire range of musical expression in the home, even opera and symphonic music. The feminine in music, insofar as it became linked to the piano, was a later nineteenth-century differentiation. This concept, in the hands of Otto Weininger's generation, became codified as pejorative, inferior, and subordinate to the quintessentially masculine Wagnerian ideal.[60] In contrast, the musical aesthetics that Liszt advocated in piano playing and developed in his own compositions were understood as a universal vocabulary adequate to both genders and all classes. A universality vis-à-vis aesthetic refinement, in gender terms, derived from the age of Mozart and Beethoven, constituted a stable premise within Liszt's call for a progressive new tradition of contemporary instrumental music.

V. Fashion

The drama of Liszt's reconciliation of classicist aesthetics and the philosophical idealism of the eighteenth century with the ideological and spiritual currents of the era in which he lived, particularly with respect to gender, group, and national identity, can be gleaned not only from his musical project, but also from something as mundane as his physical self-representation. The visual self-representation of few musicians in history has been so carefully documented in painting, lithography, caricature, and photography. Liszt himself, and not only under Carolyne's influence, made a strong distinction between fashion and taste. Nonetheless, Liszt was conscious of his physical appearance, particularly during his virtuoso years. The visual theater of his presence at the piano was an essential and carefully managed dimension.

At the beginning of the so-called long nineteenth century, aristocratic male attire was designed to reveal class. As a 1790 illustration (figure 1) suggests, the legacy of eighteenth-century aristocratic fashion—what would later be associated with dandyism—had not vanished. The variety of colors in the dress for men, the walking stick (the residue of the limited privilege of wearing a sword), the elaborate hair, and a slender figure were prized, narrowing the differentiation between men and women (figure 2). By the early nineteenth century (figure 3), male attire became increasingly simplified and far less decorative.[61] From the early 1830s on, Liszt adapted to this more modern, clearly male attire, one that eschewed pastel colors and tightly fitted clothes. The new male dress included long pants, vest, frock coat, and tie (figure 4). The color was increasingly restricted to black, a color wealthy non-aristocrats used to signal affluence. The aristocracy in the post-revolutionary period sought to diminish visible signs of their status. Consider the shift by the brilliant watchmaker Abraham-Louis Breguet from making sounding pocket repeaters to the repetition *à toc*, a dead sound that suppressed the exclusivity linked with the carrying of a fine watch. Dress became a signifier of manliness and wealth, not status.

Male dress became increasingly nondecorative, and facial hair and weight became far more popular. Muted residues of eighteenth-century dandyism (figures 5 and 6) remained in the 1830s and '40s.[62] Liszt's particular deviations from this gender simplification in costume were his sporting of the Hungarian national costume (figure 9), which was equally an assertion of his national identity and status as an aristocrat. The Hungarian nation was for him a nation of Magyar aristocracy. His membership in that exclusive club was symbolized most famously by his receipt of a sword. Liszt cherished that sword, as he did his extensive network of Hungarian

Figure 1. 1790, *Journal des Dames*.

Figure 2. 1830, *La Mode*.

Figure 3. 1810, *The Repository*.

Figure 4. Mid 1850s.

Figure 5. Devéria, *Quarelling Couple*.

Figure 6. 1844, *Les Modes parisiennes*.

Figure 7. Male attire, 1830s.

Figure 8. 1839, *Parade*.

Figure 9. Liszt in Hungarian
gala uniform, 1838.

Figure 10. Liszt, 1873.

Figure 11. Liszt in his abbé's frock.

aristocratic friends. Furthermore, Liszt was noted, not always in a flatter-
ing manner, for his delight in attaching his many medals and decorations
to his clothing (figure 10).

In the end, Liszt abandoned the fashionable visible symbols of wealth
and gender that remained in place at the end of the 1830s (figure 8) and
even the most aggressive, distinctly masculine dress (figure 7) of the midcentury, opting ultimately for the striking and uniquely male costume, the
frock (figure 11).[63] The cloak of the abbé transcended nation and class but
was unmistakably masculine. It referenced Catholicism, which unlike
Protestantism privileged the male as sacred vessel. The frock also camouflaged the humble class origins or status of the wearer. The theatrical
exclusivity Liszt achieved as a virtuoso found its later analogue in his
unmistakable and unique presence in the enlarged social world of busi-
nessmen and aristocrats as a servant of the Church. Through his garb as
artist-teacher, as worldly priest, he found a way to transcend fashion and
remain modern in terms of gender role and evoke his place in historical
continuity, which connected him not only with the era of Mozart and
Beethoven (whose patrons and friends included the wellborn Catholic
clergy) but also the long trajectory of history, notably the Renaissance, in
line with his contemporaries, the painters of the Nazarene movement.[64]

VI. Performance and Composition

Liszt's dissatisfaction with his virtuoso career was the result of his extensive internal musings regarding the inadequacy of performance alone as
realizing the higher calling of the artist and the elevation of the new public's taste. When Liszt retired from the concert stage and devoted himself
to composition, conducting, and teaching, one of his ambitions was to sustain the eighteenth-century link between performance and composition.
He witnessed in his lifetime the rapid growth of a class of performers whose
ambitions and talents in composition were meager. A concert life centered on performance skills revealed an unwelcome contrast with the
classical era. Liszt's effort to restore Weimar to the glories of its classical
past through music represented a belief in the necessity of retaining the
traditional integration of composition and performance. His derision of
conservatory education was in part derived from the poverty of its role
in producing performers who were genuine creators. Their failure was
also the result of an overemphasis on mechanical technique, and the
absence of an intellectual basis apart from music for inspired re-creation
in performance, much less the writing of new music.

The piano (as well as the organ) was ideally suited to a form of improvisation that suggested a complete musical argument as real-time expressive narration. Liszt's experience with improvisation pointed the way for his experiments in musical expression and style using the orchestra. Composition, like improvisation, had to frame the new within an audible trajectory of history. For Liszt, improvisation and *preludieren*, new and old, were dialectically linked.[65] Liszt added to Weber's *Konzertstück*, embellished passages in Beethoven's sonatas, and, more important, improvised long introductions to his performances of the great works of the past, even Beethoven's *Hammerklavier* Sonata. Musical expression was an organic, progressive phenomenon whose transformation into the contemporary was evolutionary, not revolutionary and arbitrarily calculated.

Liszt's foray into composition and his ambition to leave a body of work that would stand the test of time was both ambivalent and unique. No other composer in the nineteenth century wrote with so clear an allegiance to the experience of concert performance. Chopin, whose music was formulated through keyboard improvisation, was revered as a performer, but had neither the ambition nor the constitution to rival Liszt or Thalberg as a performing artist. Musical composition for Liszt began and remained tied to the musical event as a performative experience, even after his retirement from the concert stage. Not the text, but the momentary temporal experience of playing music for a group of listeners defined the musical ideal. The goal represented by a fully worked-out, permanent composition did not sit well with Liszt, whose habits and experience as a performer led him to appreciate the wide divergences in the actual perception of and response to music. Liszt constantly revised his music and updated it. Liszt's fusion of performance and composition suggest that his written texts cannot be seen so much as a stable account of authorial claims but rather as a script whose full realization in the moment of performance demanded, for him, adaptation, revision, and extension, all in accord with the novelty and uniqueness of the historical moment.[66]

The philosophical origins of Liszt's model for novelty in the arts were not indebted to Newton, Locke, or Kant, but rather to late and post-Enlightenment thought that placed the theory of history and the differentiation in nature at the center of the nineteenth-century intellectual agenda.[67] The fascination with the organic and the differentiated that marked a shift from the eighteenth to the nineteenth centuries influenced the politics of identity. The eighteenth century was dominated by ideas of universal human nature that provided the underpinnings of social compact and democratic theory. Whether in Rousseau's, Locke's, or, for that matter, Jefferson's formulation, the notion that at birth there is an equality that can be construed logically as interchangeable made matters of economic and political inequality (and therefore class) primary obsessions for Henri de Saint-Simon and Félicité Robert de Lamennais. Hegel and Marx continued that utopian obsession within the framework of a theory of historical change. The challenge to this trajectory came in the writings of Herder and Fichte, who sought to explain shifts in the human condition as a function of the evolutionary expression of an overarching logic of history and a nearly mystical sense of the power of nature. Hegel, although decisive to Marx, and in key respects sympathetic with the rationalist universal ideals of the French Revolution, also employed the logic of historical development as an argument against radical political action designed to create, artificially, against history, a utopian world.[68] The intellectual reaction to the Enlightenment and the revolution in German-speaking Europe, in poetry and philosophy, focused on the evolution of history, groups, and languages and customs. Identity became prized not as universally human and marked by economic privilege or political status. Rather, one was a member of a specific subgroup that had developed its unique character, language, and culture over time. The variegation within the plant and animal world provided the key metaphor.

Liszt fashioned his own personal philosophical outlook within this transformative early-nineteenth-century intellectual context. Utopianism, religion, and a pre-Romantic universalism were the foundation on which Liszt cultivated his appreciation for the culturally unique and the historically distinctive. This allowed him a creative synthesis that sought to elude radical contradictions. In Liszt's music from the Weimar period, the universal and the differentiated found a plausible coherence. Despite valid national differences music, like religion, retained its universality. The musician's task was to craft a language of expression and interior reflection that merged the particular with the universal. The vehicle of program music, by connecting the musical experience with both the visual and the literary, provided a new formal logic for instrumental music through which the particular could be rendered universal, as in the *Hunnenschlacht*. Instrumental music could express specificities such as national and ethnic distinctions. But in turn, just as with the music of Mozart, the seemingly nationalist music of a Smetana, Sgambati, or Grieg could also be appropriated by an Englishman and a Frenchman, just as the Wagnerian had been turned into an object of French enthusiasm by Baudelaire. Liszt's Hungarian patriotism never assumed a late-nineteenth-century stridency. Liszt, to the end of his life, was therefore able to appreciate diverse constructs of national identity as part of a universal human fabric.

This merger of the universal and particular enabled Liszt to reconcile Hungarian patriotism with monarchist loyalty and Catholic orthodoxy; it permitted him as a composer to replace the classical formal structure of instrumental music in a manner adequate to modernity. The legacy of his early piano works, made up of shorter episodes or reflective of sequential improvisations, was transformed with an ambition to create a new basis for large-scale essays of instrumental music. A new structural symphonic framework for the elaboration of meaning, the intensity of the sublime, and the inspiration of the individual could equal the classical masters and yet pay them homage.[69]

VII. Modernity and Meaning

Before 1848, music and theater were protected and unique arenas of public action for the literate urban public. After 1848 Liszt regarded the political situation differently, despite the collapse of the Hungarian resistance and coup d'état of Napoleon III.[70] In the decades after 1848, an even larger urban public rekindled a direct connection to politics. Liszt regarded the ear as more sensitive and more nervous than sight, and more emotionally powerful. In Liszt's view, the extension of aesthetic feeling to this widening public in the years after 1848 carried with it the potential of inspiring spiritual recognition and adjustment to a modernity that demanded a Burke-like equilibrium between progress and tradition. In the post-1848 context, Liszt sought to inspire the older ideas of universality, not the new rhetoric of nationalism.

The examples of Chopin and Berlioz remained most persuasive to Liszt. They succeeded even though, in Liszt's view, taste in music, precisely because of music's unique emotional effect on human beings, was more recalcitrant. Even an elite of connoisseurs was loath to welcome change in music, more so than in the other arts. Chopin had created new harmonies. His construct of melody with its fluctuating patterns and breathlessness realized a new communicative potential in music. It approximated the inner yearning and intensity of emotion that Liszt understood was characteristic of his contemporaries who had displaced the ferment unleashed by the events of 1789 to the interior of their lives. But despite its novelty, Chopin's music sustained traditional values: it was learned, disciplined, clear, and elegant; it revealed depth beneath grace, skill beneath charm. It had no excess of baroque eccentricity. Liszt understood Chopin's ideal to have been Mozart, the supreme poet in music.[71]

Berlioz, in contrast, elevated the dramatic, the poetic, and the epic—the program—as the bases of instrumental music. He realized the sublime in extending the use of scale, sonority, and the grotesque to achieve the grandeur of a massive fresco. At stake, for Liszt, was whether music would atrophy into a mere game, an abstract field of nearly mathematical calculation, or realize its power to evoke in the contemporary public the full range of the sufferings and ecstasies of the spirit. Berlioz, by basing instrumental music on narrative, transcended the conservatism in taste from which music suffered. The example of sculpture, which functioned as an embodiment of pure form and meaning, was instructive for the future of instrumental music. Progress was not defined purely by the traditions of form. Ethical and spiritual education, in the spirit of Alexander von Humboldt, could be furthered by making a new kind of public art using modified tradition that would shield civilization from the threat of a corrupt modernity driven by war and greed.[72]

Both Chopin and Berlioz had been utterly contemporary, and yet indebted to tradition. Chopin's audience was a new aristocracy of spirit, in Joseph de Maistre's sense, distinct from a regressive aristocracy, the masses, and the parvenus, the world of business and fashion. His Poland, like Liszt's Hungary, was a nation of nobles. Their freedom—not the independence of the masses—was Chopin's dream. Berlioz's music, by its very scale, was directed to the larger citizenry. But its linkage between sound and word pointed to a legitimate response to the altered musical literacy of the now expanded public. Chopin was an inventor of a new musical discourse of intimacy and subjectivity (and solidarity with his people). Chopin's achievements bridged the rational, the geometric, and the mathematical with the emotional and infinite. But he had little faith in democracy. Berlioz was seen by Liszt as a revolutionary who extended the power of art to the whole of mankind, as an artist who invented new means of enlightening the larger public. Berlioz's accomplishment was achieved not arbitrarily or artificially, but organically within the framework of history, as a timely outgrowth of the past. For Berlioz the model had been Beethoven.

Ultimately Liszt realized that it was Wagner, not Chopin and Berlioz, who created music that could bridge the gap between the artist true to the spirit of his age and the tastes of the new public. Caught in his own ambivalence between the elegant, miniature expressiveness of Chopin and the dramatic, epic design of Berlioz, Liszt formulated his post-1848 project: creating the musical means that would realize the modern possibilities of musical expression alone. The symphonic poem became a medium of reconciliation between the traditional and the new public. Wagner's example was rejected not because it was grandiose, but because it challenged the historic validity of instrumental music. Therefore Liszt's ambitions in the 1850s veered more in the direction set by Berlioz.[73] Symphonic music could inspire enlightenment and progress. The perils of democracy, as Chopin understood them, would be mitigated.

Art would educate modernity by legitimating the authority of the spirit, by extending the richness of feeling and idealistic ambition to a new elite, larger in scale than the audience of the 1820s and '30s but ever more threatened by the allure of fashion, fame, and materialism. Musical culture, properly spread throughout the expanding newspaper-reading and concert-going public, could mitigate the extreme dangers of modern politics of violence and abrupt change. Liszt's allegiances mirrored a Stendhalian nostalgia for the hero. If in literature that hero was represented by Faust (to which Berlioz introduced him) or the Byronic figures of Manfred and Harold, or by writers like Dante, Shakespeare, Goethe, or Hugo, the lasting image of the hero in politics was Napoleon's. Napoleon had come and gone, but his example in the arts would linger.

The means Liszt cultivated after 1848 were shaped by the limitations he identified in Chopin and Berlioz. Liszt integrated Chopin's expressive rhetoric of the intimate with Berlioz's massive theatrical scale. Underlying this achievement was a startling refinement of the relationship of literary program to musical form. The use of program furthered a radical rethinking of musical time. Liszt fashioned a truly accessible strategy of musical communication that engaged the listener in precisely the sympathetic manner he had sought as a pianist, but now over an extended experience and on a grand scale. The solution included the compositional practices of simplified thematic transformation and a redefinition of how music works sequentially by employing repetition, digression, and elongation as instruments of recollection and recognition. Symbolism of meaning was attached to traditional rhetorical expectations in the form of mottos and interrelated gestures. Wagner is clearly indebted to Liszt's evocation of meaning, space, mood, and harmonic usage over long periods.

Liszt, for all the rhetoric of innovation and courage, and his praise of Berlioz, Chopin, and later Wagner, worked within decisively conservative frameworks beginning in 1848 and after the 1860s. He chose to avoid the radical nationalist and populist political consequences of the revolutionary new aesthetic vanguard that followed Wagner. Wagner's popularity as a composer, in contrast to Liszt's failure, exposed how the New German school emerged only rhetorically in conflict with established taste and institutions; Wagner represented a new, popular, potent nationalist cultural force. Liszt increasingly portrayed himself as a victim, particularly at the hands of the press, an example of the perilous place of the artist in post-1848 modernity. After 1848, the limits of working within a tradition of musical communication established in the eighteenth century became more pronounced. Liszt's attachment to Weimar echoed a pre-nationalist ideological element in modern music. The ambition to equal the achievement of Goethe and Schiller implied the need for culture to bolster a new form of enlightened monarchy, a political system grounded in humane leadership counseled by an aristocracy of the spirit in which the great artists could play a heroic role.[74]

The potential political radicalism of Liszt's innovations regarding the narrative and symbolism associated with instrumental music was limited by Liszt's engagement with the Roman Catholic Church, whose political significance was anything but revolutionary.[75] Liszt's grand protestations of Hungarian patriotism notwithstanding, his work to generate an infrastructure in Budapest after 1867 was part of an effort by the Hungarian aristocracy to generate within the urban middle class a balance between national pride and deference to the Habsburg monarchy. Culture need not encourage a sharp nationalism from below that challenged aristocracy and monarchy. Liszt's allegiance as a Hungarian was to the aristocratic class (as all his friendships suggest), and his patriotism had little in common with either the antidemocratic populist nationalism of the fin de siècle or the radical nationalist movements of the twentieth century.[76]

Liszt's development of a musical strategy and form within orchestral music constituted the most powerful model of how musical communication could be extended to the wider audience of the mid-nineteenth century. In doing so, Liszt ran afoul not only of musical conservatives who took issue with his claims regarding the connection between the logic of music and the meaning of language. By creating an accessible orchestral experience for a large public, he undercut the monopoly on judgment asserted by arbiters of learning, defenders of a more traditional species of musical literacy. The spread of the piano, as publishers in the early and mid-nineteenth century realized, generated a wide audience not only for simplified repertoire at home—selections from concert repertoire, piano reductions of orchestral music, and potpourris from the musical theater— but also for reductions, scores, and copies of the elaborate music played by virtuosi, which were bought merely as souvenirs and collectibles.

Liszt's extensive touring convinced him of the dynamic, progressive potential in the public's literacy, urbanization, and affluence. At the same time, it would be difficult to maintain the high level of amateur skill and discernment that was common in aristocratic circles before 1815, and still remarkable in cities such as Leipzig, Vienna, and Berlin (and even in smaller towns such as Düsseldorf, where the numbers of choral societies, amateur orchestral associations, and chamber music had increased). This new generation of music lovers may have been more limited than their predecessors in purely musical skills, but after 1848 they were broadly educated. They were readers of literature, philosophy, and poetry.

The intersection of higher levels of general literacy and education with simplified musical literacy, made possible by the modern piano for which the creation of true pitch by the individual (as required in singing or on a string instrument) was unnecessary, defined the contemporary challenge to instrumental music. Opera's increasing popularity was understandable, since spectacle, action, and words combined with music to hold the attention of the audience. The transference of the allure of the theater into large-scale instrumental music—a path initially suggested by Berlioz's example—required more than a revival of the characteristic symphony of the eighteenth century. Yet if the eighteenth-century aesthetics of sentiment, which allied tonality with emotion, required too much musical discernment, then the reductive illustrative tradition demanded too little.

Liszt found a way to integrate four key elements to generate a new form of musical narrative and experience that circumvented the seemingly autonomous logic of music "as tonally moving forms," in Eduard Hanslick's 1854 formulation.[77] As Felix Draeseke observed in 1857, the first element was Liszt's focus on melody. An instrumental work had to possess clear unity through melody: "melodic interest in order to appeal to the tastes of the masses."[78] The nature of the melody was not derived from the example of Beethoven's music, but Chopin's. Symphonic music, in Draeseke's terms, required singable melody. That Liszt achieved. No doubt Liszt also employed, as constituents of that melody, fragments that were reminiscent of Beethovenian mottos and motives. But at the heart of the matter was the need to find an opera-like tune, a song, in the sense of Liszt's beloved Schubert, that could function as the basis of an orchestral essay, not only on account of its sonic allure but also because of its semantic significance to the listener.[79] That melody, in contrast to the dynamic transformation of multiple themes in sonata form, altered and unaltered, had to frame the work. Hence Liszt's formulation of a monothematic strategy. Melody unified the work.

Second, the melody had to adapt well-recognized rhetorical associations and conventions. In its musical construction, the melody had to function symbolically. The so-called tropes of significance in Liszt's tone poems reveal patterns of musical gesture that run parallel to ideas of lament, landscape, love, war, and loss. Melody was an explicit instrument of extramusical symbolism. It functioned much as a character in a novel. Music did not merely describe a character, in the sense of illustration, but revealed its essence. And the character's sojourn through the work required a theatrical analogue of mood (background), plot, and dramatic trajectory.

The centrality of melody in musical form and the explicit exploitation of symbolic associations created the groundwork for Liszt's method of harmonic transformation and extension.[80] Despite those who would seek echoes of classical procedure in Liszt's symphonic poems, involving expositions, developments, and recapitulations, these works are marked by sequential harmonic alteration, where one moment seems to emerge from the previous, seamlessly. Using repetition and digression, Liszt crafted a musical analog to the experience of following an argument and observing the course of events. Unlike the early piano music, the parallel was no longer with solitary reading. Listening needed to be a collective experience that for each individual was, from the outset, open-ended, but pointed to a goal, capable of tangents and sudden exploratory moves. A form of realism located in dramatic form as well as poetic metaphor defined the structural logic. Composition was no longer derivative of musical improvisation alone. Using his inventiveness in harmonic change, Liszt created a musical equivalent to the experience of an internal dialogue where association, recollection, memory, and distraction follow unexpectedly. As each listener's mind runs free, the return to dramatic form is signaled in the music's constant connection to a constructed time and imagined place. In this context, Liszt created a structure in which musical syntax and vocabulary could approximate the widest range of human emotions, from the sense of space (nature) to the attribution of meaning and experiences such as foreboding and triumph.[81]

Liszt found a way to expand musical time, so that the musical experience of listening could more closely approximate not only the experience of reading, but also the actual memory of reading.[82] The text no longer needed to be contemporary or a work of fiction. The illusion of descriptive realism was supplanted by the act of retrospective textual interpretation. The listener could compare his memory and reading with the composer's. In this expanded time frame, the third of Liszt's contributions to the aesthetics of instrumental music takes on singular importance: the expansion in the variety and scale of sonority. Again, Berlioz was the inspiration. But Liszt, with his extensive experience of making the piano sound as varied and as imposing as an orchestra, developed new ways to use instruments, orchestral combinations, registration, and massive sonorities such as unisons and sharp contrasts in texture to expand the range of meanings associated with instrumental sound. Instrumentation helped underscore musical symbolic equivalents.[83]

The visual in Liszt's music was highlighted in the use of instrumentation. Although only two of the symphonic poems are directly tied to visual objects—*Hunnenschlacht* and *From the Cradle to the Grave*—visualization is implied in all the orchestral works, both on the part of the composer and the listener. Whether in the *Dante* Symphony, *Tasso*, or the *Bergsymphonie*, the dramatic techniques Liszt developed at the keyboard were adapted to suggest mental images and pictures. Music as a means of visual evocation, especially when generated sequentially, was among Liszt's most powerful and successful tools. The form his symphonic poems took enabled music to generate a visual narrative, a sequence of frames in the mind's eye, something—in contrast to contemporary elaborations of classical symphonic usage, notably by Brahms—late nineteenth-century conservative symphonic usage was not explicitly designed to do. Liszt's tastes in art centered on contemporary historical schools of painting and the Romantic evocations of Renaissance models. Since Liszt eschewed simple illustration, the content and character of images generated by music remained personal for each listener. Music was not tied, as in opera, to a shared visual reality. Liszt's music made for a powerful experience of listening because of its ready adaptability, not to linguistic explanation but to visual memory. His strategy reinforced the subjective interpretive capacity and artistic imagination within the listener by inspiring a coherent translation from musical sound to mental image.

Fourth and most notorious was Liszt's advocacy of literary and poetic programs as framing foundations. The idea that reading and writing should become the basis of musical form and experience was the indispensable precondition for the successful use of melody, harmonic change, symbolic association, complex sonority, and visual parallelism. However, as in opera, the listener had to know the basic argument before the music began. That argument was written in language. It was this bold assertion that divided the New Germans from their detractors.[84] For Brahms and his allies, an argument had to be made with musical means, independent of expectations generated by language prior to listening. Music had to formulate its own logic and structure. If a piece of music suggested parallel nonmusical significance, that effect was at best temporary, supplemental, and purely an act of personal attribution. Liszt demanded an overt nonmusical premise that enabled him to construe listening to symphonic music in public as a didactic experience.

For Liszt, instrumental music had to be framed, albeit loosely, by a shared human experience, understandable in language, that music then elaborated. How the music succeeded was not defined, but the opening gambit pointed the way. Therefore, the framing material needed to be profound and grand, not trivial: the tragic, the heroic, the communal, the epic, the divine, nature, and the towering masterpieces of literature. In this way, Liszt, not Wagner, created the basis for the wide popularity of concert and classical music for instruments in the culture of the second half of the nineteenth century.[85] Liszt's literary appropriations account for the widely divergent and eclectic character of his music. It is no surprise that Bartók, who took notice of this, eventually came to value the B Minor Sonata most of all.[86] But the most characteristic and influential body of Liszt's music for the wider public, apart from the religious works, was crafted to fit, albeit using a shared rhetoric of musical symbolism, an eclectic and diverse set of familiar narratives that ranged widely over history and literature.

The centrality of the frame—the narrative, visual, philosophical, or poetical argument—was the element that took hold most quickly among Liszt's Russian devotees, including Tchaikovsky and Borodin, and his other protégés, including Smetana, Saint-Saëns, and Grieg. Liszt enabled instrumental music to become a sought-after experience within a vast educated public that lacked an eighteenth-century form of musical sophistication. Ironically, it paved the way for the use of music at odds with Liszt's own ideals—as an instrument of nationalist politics (Bartók's *Kossuth*, for example). Liszt's legacy in the twentieth century, however, was most important in the response against his procedures by the most skilled composer of symphonic poems: Richard Strauss. Despite Strauss's evident debt to Liszt's example, he chose two strategies in direct conflict with Lisztian aesthetics. First, he reveled in radical illustrative realism (as in *Don Quixote* and the *Sinfonia domestica*), intent on his revisionist project of stripping instrumental music of its didactic, idealist, and philosophical pretensions. Second he reintegrated, as in *Don Juan*, strategies of musical development and transformation characteristic of sonata form. Strauss's tone poems therefore work on two levels, the narrative and the formal, capable of making a persuasive argument independent of any hint of the philosophy, poetry, or story line with which the music appears to be linked.[87]

Strauss persists in the repertoire while Liszt's symphonic works do not because the twenty-first century no longer seeks a framework for visual and mental daydreaming in real time. The motion picture and video screen more than meet this demand, forcing us to judge Liszt's orchestral music either against film or, more conservatively, against classical standards of the autonomous musical argument that may or may not inspire either intentional or conventional allusions. Strauss, keenly aware of modernity's engagement with the complex realism exemplified by photography, made sure that, as with Beethoven, his works of instrumental music could survive without the assistance of programs. It is for this same reason that Mahler abandoned the Lisztian model and ceased including programs to help define the logic of his music.[88] Liszt's music, however, retained a debt to reading. In the twenty-first century it faces a comparative disadvantage, since for the greater part of the audience Dante, Faust, and Tasso—much less Hugo, Schiller, and the Huns of the *Hunnenschlacht*—signify little or nothing.

From the very start of Liszt's career, the making of music took on universal meanings larger than any particularistic definition. That meaning was consistently vague and spiritual, akin to Liszt's flexible view of doctrine, his status as a devoted Catholic and abbé notwithstanding. Music became the public instrument of the creation of community and the medium by which the nonrational and passionate aspects of human nature could be underscored without rendering the hope of social progress entirely implausible in a Hobbesian way. Music contained the tension between freedom and regulation. Insofar as art and love were linked, as the very word *Romanticism* sometimes suggests, the Janus face of music in Liszt's hands had its parallel in the conduct of his personal life. Like music, love and passion remain infinite and irrational, not easily contained by conventional and rational rules such as marriage.

But at the core of Liszt's quest was the centrality of music in human existence and its unique capacity as a spiritual medium. Although his Paris years demonstrate Liszt's affinity with elaborate theories about the role of the artist as builder of communities, this utopian, communitarian streak remained for him a thin veil over the primary spiritual transaction that music enables for the individual alone. As Liszt's career developed, his religious and spiritual instincts led him to address the assembled group of listeners alongside the elite individual. It is important to note that his enthusiasm for the Hungarian cause and his support of Wagner and Wagner's followers (the German nationalists) coincided with his symbolic affiliation with religion. The resolution of the individual and the community within religion provided Liszt with a model for construing nationhood. His thoughts about the origins of distinctive musical styles within the Roma, his construct of the Hungarian nation, and his idealized picture of what the Russians, Scandinavians, Italians, and Czechs (and for that matter, his later French contemporaries) were achieving for their respective national cultures, are little more than variants of his thinking about the role of art in the formation of human community as a whole, ideas with which he flirted in the 1830s under the influence of Saint-Simon and Lamennais.[89]

This subordination of the particular to the universal distinguishes Liszt's view of the nation from Wagner's and from later nineteenth-century nationalisms. Just as individual differentiation could, through art, thrive nondestructively within a utopian spiritual community, so could nations persist as distinct entities within sovereign frameworks framed by monarchy and aristocracy. This framework, for example, justifies the view that Liszt was not an anti-Semite in the modern sense. His views on the Jewish question can be contrasted with Wagner's. Liszt's anti-Semitism was of a more ordinary nineteenth-century social character, akin to Schumann's and Max Bruch's. Liszt's anti-Semitism is perhaps best expressed in his relief that Sophie Menter chose not to marry a Jew. This reflected less racialist thinking than concern for potential conflict in terms of mutual understanding and social status. Jewish identity seemed a historical barrier to the task of transcending the barriers of birth through art, an unnecessary and unwelcome social stigma for the non-Jew.[90]

It was Carolyne, not Liszt, who made the intellectual transition to modern anti-Semitism in a manner reminiscent not only of Wagner but also of Liszt's own daughter, Cosima. Liszt's anti-Semitism is reflective of an eighteenth-century variant that despised the Jew as socially disfigured but redeemable. In post-emancipation Christian thought, conversion and assimilation were instruments of redemption. Liszt, influenced by early-nineteenth-century theories of cultural and historical development, went more in the direction of George Eliot, whom he oddly enough understood to be Jewish. In a manner not too far from the argument in Eliot's *Daniel Deronda*, he believed that the redemption of the Jew required the loss of pariah status in political terms through the return to Palestine.[91] In this proto-Zionist vision, the disfigurement of the Jews would come to an end and their aesthetic abilities would no longer be limited, for the range of their emotions would be enlarged and normalized. Liszt's anti-Semitism and yet sympathetic account of Salomon Sulzer in Vienna form a picture of his intellectual formation as linked more to late-eighteenth-century than late-nineteenth-century ideologies, distant from the determinist racialist approaches to national identity and destiny associated with Houston Stewart Chamberlain and Arthur de Gobineau (despite Liszt's admiration for the latter).[92]

Liszt's career and work reveal an evolutionary shift from the eighteenth-century conception of the musician as elite craftsman and servant to the later nineteenth-century view of the artist as spiritual guide and professional and national spokesperson. Liszt's lifelong campaign was against the segmentation of music as apart from life, learning, community, and culture in modernity. He sought to harness music's spiritual and emotional content for his contemporaries all over the world. His voracious quest for learning and his belief in music's significance in building community justified his link between the musical and the so-called extramusical. To realize music's power required ideas. A musical imagination was philosophical and literary and, in Goethe's sense, tied to vision as a means of human expression.

Paradoxically, Liszt was perhaps the single most gifted individual in the nineteenth century in his capacity to think and act purely musically. There was nothing he could not do in music. At the same time he believed in the integration of music with all modes of human thought and expression. His eclecticism and his synthesis of the past and present mirrored his faith in the universality and unique power of musical expression to redeem the noble in humanity. But for music to realize its power, it demanded bold re-creation, at once contemporary and connected to its history. The poignant irony in Liszt's case is that ideologically, his connection to the trajectory of nineteenth-century history was one of idealistic resistance.

NOTES

1. M. G. Saphir, *Konversations-Lexikon für Geist, Witz und Humor*, vol. 4, 2nd ed. (Berlin: 1893), p. 293. The entry dates most likely from the early 1850s. This text was taken from the expanded four-volume edition published in 1893 with Adolf Glassbrenner as co-editor. On Saphir (1795–1858) in pre-1848 Vienna, where he started his career, see Eduard Castle et al., *Deutsch-Österreichische Literaturgeschichte*, vol. 2: *Von 1750 bis 1848* (Vienna: 1914), pp. 887–88. Saphir was a great admirer of Liszt. They had considerable contact in the years 1838–40. In 1839 Liszt participated in a program of readings of humor at the Josefstadt Theatre organized by Saphir. See Deszö Legány, *Franz Liszt: Unbekannte Presse und Briefe aus Wien* (Vienna: 1984), pp. 27 and 75. In 1838 Saphir, with only slight touches of irony, pointed to the extraordinary character of Liszt's playing, his music, his personality, his uniqueness. See "Franz Liszt," in *Der Humorist* 2, no. 64, pp. 253–54. I thank Christopher Gibbs for bringing this text to my attention. Saphir comments on Liszt's capacity to evoke the extremes of response and to use music to penetrate the secrets of the riches of the soul, pushing the sublime to the limits of the baroque, all without rules or a sense of form in the conventional sense.

2. Lind (1820–87), called the "Swedish Nightingale," had a popular following rivaling Liszt's. She, unlike Liszt, went on a spectacular tour of America, in 1850.

3. See for example, Dana Gooley, *The Virtuoso Liszt* (Cambridge, Eng.: 2004); Paul Metzner, *Crescendo of the Virtuoso: Spectacle, Skill, and Self-Promotion in Paris during the Age of Revolution* (Berkeley and Los Angeles: 1998); and Susan Bernstein, *Virtuosity of the Nineteenth Century: Performing Music and Language in Heine, Liszt, and Baudelaire* (Stanford, Calif.: 1998). I thank Dana Gooley for his helpful comments on this essay.

4. This essay is indebted to the massive Liszt biographical literature, for example: Alan Walker's three-volume biography, *Franz Liszt* (Ithaca, N.Y.: 1987–97); Serge Gut, *Franz Liszt* (Paris: 1989); Wolfgang Dömling, *Franz Liszt und seine Zeit* (Laaber: 1985); Manfred Wagner, *Franz Liszt: Werk und Leben* (Vienna: 2000); and two important collections, *The Cambridge Companion to Liszt*, ed. Kenneth Hamilton (Cambridge, Eng.: 2005), and *The Liszt Companion*, ed. Ben Arnold (Westport, Conn.: 2002).

5. For a discussion of the lasting imprint of pre-1789 values, see Arno J. Mayer, *The Persistence of the Old Regime* (New York: 1981).

6. See Donald J. Grout, *A Short History of Opera* (New York and London: 1965), p. 317.

7. This was the period, from the composition of *Aus Italien* (1886) and *Macbeth* (begun in 1887, published in final form only in 1891) when Strauss produced all the tone poems, including the later *Sinfonia domestica* (1904) and *Alpine Symphony* (1911). The extent of Liszt's influence on Strauss (communicated in part by Alexander Ritter) has been a source of controversy. However, the notion of a poetic, dramatic, or visual narrative as a basis for symphonic music derives from Liszt, even though Strauss's compositional methods are, curiously, more indebted to formal classical procedures of development and the explicit use of musical means in mischievous, starkly realistic, and illustrative ways. See Charles Youmans, *Richard Strauss's Orchestral Music and the German Intellectual Tradition: The Philosophical Roots of Musical Modernism* (Bloomington, Ind.: 2005), esp. p. 170; and Walter Werbeck, *Die Tondichtungen von Richard Strauss* (Tutzing: 1996), pp. 15–44, 89–94.

8. On late Liszt, see Bence Szabolcsi, *The Twilight of Ferenc Liszt*, trans. András Deák (Budapest: 1959).

9. See Norbert Nagler, "Die verspätete Zukunftsmusik" and "Das Liszt-Bild—ein wirkungsgeschichtliches Missverständnis?" in *Franz Liszt* (Musik-Konzepte, vol. 12), ed. Heinz-Klaus Metzger and Rainer Riehn (Munich: 1980), pp. 4–41, 115–27.

10. Arnold Schoenberg, "Franz Liszt's Work and Being" (1911), in *Style and Idea*, ed. Leonard Stein, trans. Leo Black (London: 1975), pp. 442–47.

11. Ibid.

12. Ibid.

13. Ibid.

14. Ibid.

15. See Joseph d'Ortigue's biography, reprinted in this volume.

16. Béla Bartók, *Essays*, selected and ed. Benjamin Suchoff (Lincoln, Neb.: 1992), p. 451.

17. *Allgemeine musikalische Zeitung* 28, no. 5 (February 1826), p. 87.

18. Raphael Ledos de Beaufort, *Franz Liszt: The Story of His Life* (Boston: 1887), pp. 49, 55.

19. The linguistic coherence in early-nineteenth-century Hungary and Poland refers to the majority of the population, not the landed aristocratic classes, who spoke multiple languages, including French and German. Nonetheless, for Chopin, the Polish language was crucial in his identification as a Pole. Liszt, in contrast, spoke no Hungarian, which would isolate him after 1848 even from avid proponents of an aristocratic national definition. Both nations celebrated their national identity in the nineteenth century as a nation of nobles. The term "peripheral" is employed here with a pointed irony explicitly evocative of the German-centered prejudices of Theodor W. Adorno, exemplified by his views on, for example, Tchaikovsky.

20. See the two exhibition catalogs *Biedermeiers Glück und Ende: . . . die gestörte Idylle 1815–1848*, ed. Hanns Ottomeyer with Ulrike Laufer (Munich: 1987); and *Wien 1815–1848: Bürgersinn und Aufbegehren—Die Zeit des Biedermeier und Vormärz*, ed. Robert Waissenberger (Vienna: 1986).

21. See Alice M. Hanson, *Die zensurierte Muse: Musikleben im Wiener Biedermeier* (Vienna and Cologne: 1987); and Hannes Stekl, *Österreichs Aristokratie im Vormärz* (Vienna: 1973).

22. On the legend of the kiss allegedly bestowed on Liszt, see Allan Keiler, "Liszt and Beethoven: The Creation of a Personal Myth," *19th-Century Music* 12, no. 2 (Fall 1988): 116–31.

23. See Paul Goring, *The Rhetoric of Sensibility in Eighteenth-Century Culture* (Cambridge, Eng.: 2004).

24. See Wolfram Steinbeck, *Romantische und nationale Symphonik*, part 1 of *Die Symphonie im 19. und 20. Jahrhundert*, ed. Steinbeck and Christoph von Blumröder, *Handbuch der musikalischen Gattungen*, vol. 3/I (Laaber: 2002), pp. 24–29; Richard James Will, *The Characteristic Symphony in the Age of Haydn and Beethoven* (Cambridge, Eng.: 2002); also Frederick Niecks, *Programme Music in the Last Four Centuries* (London: 1906), pp. 46–113; and Carl Dahlhaus's critique of the simplistic association of realism with program music as well as his discussion of Wagner's analysis of Liszt's later symphonic poems in Dahlhaus, *Gesammelte Schriften*, ed. Hermann Danuser, 10 vols. (Laaber: 2000–), vol. 4: *19. Jahrhundert I*, pp. 160–63; and vol. 5: *19. Jahrhundert II*, pp. 772–78.

25. Schumann is discussed extensively as a composer who was influenced by literary practice. However, the role of contemporary literature and reading habits in shaping Liszt's music not only in the 1850s, but before 1848, is less frequently examined.

26. An example is Jane Austen's *Mansfield Park* (1813). These trends account as well for the decline in popularity of the epistolary form, in which it is harder to accomplish the manipulation of duration—elapsed time—through narration.

27. Consider Liszt's *Album d'un voyageur* (1835–36) and the first two volumes of *Années de pèlerinage* (1835–39). See Peter Raabe, *Liszts Schaffen* (Tutzing: 1968), pp. 244–45.

28. Aaron Hill, quoted in Goring, *The Rhetoric of Sensibility*, pp. 127–41.

29. The nineteenth-century debt to the eighteenth century included a shift in focus to the imagination, particularly in the manner in which Coleridge—inspired in part by Herder—understood it. See John Whale, *Imagination Under Pressure 1789–1832: Aesthetics, Politics, and Utility* (Cambridge, Eng.: 2000), esp. pp. 166–75.

30. Axel Beer, *Musik zwischen Komponist, Verlag und Publikum* (Tutzing: 2000), pp. 134, 396–403. See also James Deaville's article in this volume.

31. On the nineteenth-century salon, see Ernst Siebel, *Der grossbürgerliche Salon 1850–1918* (Berlin: 1999), particularly the section on the period 1785–1850, pp. 32–36.

32. See Robert Alter, *Imagined Cities: Urban Experience and the Language of the Novel* (New Haven and London: 2005), pp. 7–9.

33. Liszt's historicism appeared as well in the later religious music, where, in a manner almost comparable to Mendelssohn, the evocative tone painting of Bach was emulated. In 1869, Liszt made a present to himself of editions of the choral music of Bach, whom he called the "St. Thomas Aquinas of music." The B Minor Mass was for him the "Mont Blanc of church music." *Franz Liszt: Selected Letters*, ed. and trans. Adrian Williams, (Oxford, Eng.: 1998), p. 709. See also the related argument about Liszt's relationship to Handel by W. Rackwitz, "Liszts Verhältnis zur Musik Georg Friedrich Händels," in *Bartók-Liszt*, Report of the Second International Musicological Conference Budapest 1961 (Budapest: 1963), pp. 267–75.

34. See William G. Atwood, *The Parisian Worlds of Frédéric Chopin* (New Haven and London: 1999).

35. No doubt there were distinct differentiations in audiences and the social mix within the public, depending on the genre. Singspiel—even the *Magic Flute* at the Theater auf der Wieden—or opéra comique in pre-1848 Paris were directed to and linked with differing audiences, but in all cases, particularly public concerts, these events were utilized by members of classes otherwise segregated socially.

36. Jim Samson, *Virtuosity and the Musical Work: The "Transcendental Studies" of Liszt* (Cambridge, Eng.: 2003), pp. 14–18.

37. Berlioz's 1836 account of Liszt's performance of op. 106 (one of many accounts of Liszt's playing) reveals the link between classicism and the new aesthetics. The work is viewed as a "sublime poem." Liszt solved "the riddle of the Sphinx" and "proved that he is the pianist of the future." Quoted from the *Revue et gazette musicale*, 12 June 1836, in Adrian Williams, *Portrait of Liszt* (Oxford, Eng.: 1990), pp. 77–78. It is also interesting to consider the influence of Beethoven on the dramatic musical rhetoric employed by Donizetti.

38. See, for example, the extraordinary praise given to Liszt's Schubert song transcriptions by G. W. Fink in the *Allgemeine musikalische Zeitung* 40, no. 48 (November 1838), pp. 795–96. Schumann also commented on these publications, noting that Liszt made changes and additions, suggesting that the songs were transformed into character pieces more akin to the Schubert impromptus, whose publication (by Diabelli) Schumann was reviewing. Schumann's praise is muted, restrained by the fear that Liszt's example might be followed by mediocre, destructive "bunglers." In *Neue Zeitschrift für Musik* 9, no. 48 (14 December 1838): 192–93. The English version can be found in Schumann, *On Music and Musicians*, ed. Konrad Wolff, trans. Paul Rosenfeld (New York: 1946), pp. 154–53.

39. The influence of Liszt on Tchaikovsky can be understood in terms of the emphasis on single symbolic themes in the Tchaikovsky tone poems, such as *Romeo and Juliet*, *The Tempest*, and *Hamlet*, the emulation of Liszt's poetic sources (Dante and Shakespeare), the theatrical use of the orchestra (consider the example of Liszt's *Mazeppa*), and the subordination of musical form to a poetic narrative structure. In literature, the phenomena parallel to Wagner and Tchaikovsky, despite their evident differences, might be Flaubert, Dickens, Fontane, and later Thomas Mann. In Flaubert's narrative, for example, the authorial voice seems totally camouflaged, as in Wagner, in a complex utilization of memory, allusion, and anticipation. See Alter, *Imagined Cities*.

40. Ludwig Marcuse, *Sigmund Freud* (Zurich: 1972), p. 174. See the letter from Liszt to Agnes Street-Klindworth, dated 14 February 1867: "At the risk of seeming intolerably

arrogant, I believe that truly *hearing* certain music requires a higher intelligence, and a more elevated, more educated, and more refined moral sense than is encountered generally among artists and audiences. The predominance of coarse practices, prejudices, and every kind of ineptitude and ill will, in the most varied forms (pedantic, trite, puffed-up, or scatterbrained) is still far too common in the musical world. Perhaps it will decline little by little, and perhaps I shall then find *my* audience. I am not seeking it and barely have any more time to wait for it." *Franz Liszt and Agnes Street-Klindworth: A Correspondence 1854–1886*, introd., trans., and ed. Pauline Pocknell, Franz Liszt Studies, (Hillsdale, N.Y.: 2000), p. 254

41. On Burke, see Whale, *Imagination Under Pressure*, pp. 19–41.

42. It is significant in this context to point out that in addition to the currency Burke's treatise had in the second half of the eighteenth century, it had considerable influence in the early nineteenth, as the popularity of a "new" edition published in 1812 indicates. See Edmund Burke, *Philosophical Enquiry into the Origin of Our Ideas of the Sublime and Beautiful* (London: 1812; fac. repr., Charlottesville, Va.: n.d.), pp. 50–60, 65–68, 95–96, 237–41.

43. The great work on pre-1848 Viennese theater remains Roger Bauer, *La Réalité royaume de Dieu* (Munich: 1965).

44. See Gooley, *The Virtuoso Liszt*.

45. James Deaville, "Liszt and the Twentieth Century," in *The Cambridge Companion to Liszt*, p. 44; and Richard Leppert and Stephen Zank, "The Concert and the Virtuoso," in *Piano Roles: Three Hundred Years of Life with the Piano*, ed. James Parakilas et al. (New Haven and London: 1999), p. 279. The source cited by Leppert for this claim is a work by Foucault (see p. 426).

46. As Marie d'Agoult's *Nelida* (trans. Lynn Hoggard [Albany, N.Y.: 2003]) makes plain— and Liszt's career indicates—the idealization of an aristocracy of merit in the arena of music existed side by side with its opposite: the unambiguous and often humiliating public display of the monopoly on aristocratic status by the possessors by birth of aristocratic status. Liszt adored his Weimar patrons and also suffered at their hands. He gained the reputation of challenging the czar, but was deferential to the landed aristocracy of Hungary. In *Nelida*, the protagonist is humiliated by his noble employer, who refuses to seat the artist at his own table as an equal. *Nelida* is less significant as a source of biographical insight into Liszt than as a source of d'Agoult's account of the shifting mores and social attitudes regarding the function of art. Daniel Stern, despite her social status, would not drift from the social idealism of her youth as did Liszt, a commoner who ended his career admiring Napoleon III and deferential to the authority and social influence of the Church and the nobility in Hungary. Consider Liszt's response to the execution of Maximilian, the Austrian archduke and briefly emperor of Mexico. See Williams, *Selected Letters*, p. 665.

47. For Boesendorfer on the piano epidemic, see Leon Botstein, "Music and Its Public," Ph.D. diss., Harvard University, 1985, vol. 3.

48. Liszt's article on Paganini, in *Gesammelte Schriften*, 6 vols. (Hildesheim and New York: 1978), vol. 2, pp. 108–13.

49. See Maynard Solomon, "The Nobility Pretense," in *Beethoven Essays* (Cambridge, Mass.: 1988), pp. 43–55.

50. On de Maistre's influence in the nineteenth century, see Sheldon S. Wollin, *Politics and Vision: Continuity and Innovation in Western Political Thought* (Boston: 1960), pp. 358–99.

51. Consider, for example, this issue in the first European country to experience the Industrial Revolution, England, in the second half of the eighteenth century. In the 1778 novel *Evelina* (by Francis Burney, Charles Burney's daughter), a prostitute is mistaken for a lady of the aristocracy. Over the course of the nineteenth century, gender-specific markers would become highlighted in the demarcation of class and wealth.

52. See the list of pupils in Alan Walker, *Franz Liszt: The Final Years, 1861–1886* (Ithaca, N.Y.: 1997), pp. 249–52.

53. See the commentary by Pauline Pocknell in *Franz Liszt and Agnes Street-Klindworth*.

54. Williams, *Selected Letters*, p. 4.

55. One can contrast Liszt's behavior with the attitude of Schumann, whose relationship to Clara's career was at best ambivalent.

56. The best sources are the institutional histories usually published on the anniversaries of their founding by the choral societies, particularly in major cities. One of Johannes Brahms's first professional roles was as a conductor of a women's chorus in Hamburg.

57. That did not, however, prevent the power of music making at the keyboard from being viewed as a source of danger for women. The manner in which George Eliot utilized the many-sided dimension of music making in *Middlemarch* is a case in point. See also Ruth A. Solie, *Music in Other Words: Victorian Conversations* (Berkeley and Los Angeles: 2004).

58. See the photographs in Ernst Burger's volumes, *Franz Liszt in der Photographie seiner Zeit: 260 Portraits 1843–1886* (Munich: 2003); and *Franz Liszt: A Chronicle of His Life in Pictures and Documents*, trans. Stewart Spencer, foreword by Alfred Brendel (Princeton, N.J.: 1989).

59. For example, Saphir, in his 1838 article cited earlier, stresses the masculine aspect of Liszt's virtuosity.

60. On Weininger, see Jacques le Rider, *Der Fall Otto Weininger* (Vienna: 1985).

61. See Norbert Stern, *Mode und Kultur*, 2 vols. (Leipzig: 1915); and Oskar Fischel and Max von Boehn, *Die Mode: Menschen and Moden im Neunzehnten Jahrhundert nach Bildern und Kupfern der Zeit*, 3 vols. (Munich: 1907–08).

62. Ibid.

63. Ibid.

64. Consider his great admiration for Johann Friedrich Overbeck; see letter to Carolyne, 7 July 1868, in Williams, *Selected Letters*, p. 681. There is also his relationship to Wilhelm von Kaulbach, whom Liszt considered exceptional within the historical school; see letter to Carolyne, 21 July 1855, in Williams, *Selected Letters*, pp. 380–81. Liszt also admired Peter von Cornelius, the painter, and shared the traditional nineteenth-century awe of Raphael.

65. See the accounts in August Stradhal, *Erinnerungen an Franz Liszt* (Bern: 1929); and *The Piano Master Classes of Franz Liszt 1884–1886: Diary Notes of August Göllerich*, trans. and ed. Richard Louis Zimdars (Bloomington, Ind.: 1996). A good example is the recollection of Wendelin Wessheimer from 1857 in Williams, *Portrait of Liszt*, pp. 342–43. See also Uli Molsen, *Die Geschichte des Klavierspiels in historischen Zitaten* (Balingen: 1982), pp. 144–59.

66. The persistent disappointment with Liszt's music can in part be explained by this notion. The printed text, realized without a performer's own emendations, may not succeed as well as cases where composers have been intent on writing music that can make its point no matter the performer. During the nineteenth century, composition increasingly took on the aspect of the writing of literature, where the performer was more like a reader. Realization in real time demanded adherence to the text. Response, not alteration, revision, or addition was expected.

67. See Charles C. Gillespie, *The Edge of Objectivity* (Princeton, N.J.: 1960).

68. The most influential writings of Johann Gottfried Herder (1744–1803) were written in the last third of the eighteenth century. He had a strong interest in music, particularly the folk song. Kant reviewed, critically, Herder's influential essay on history, the "Reflections on the Philosophy of History of Mankind," in 1785. Hegel's most important work for this context is *The Philosophy of Right*, first published in 1821. See Joachim Ritter, *Hegel and the French Revolution: Essays on "The Philosophy of Right,"* trans. Richard Dien Winfield (Cambridge, Mass.: 1982). Fichte's 1807 *Reden an die deutsche Nation* was also critical to

German Romanticism. The key figures included Schelling, Schlegel, Novalis, Jean Paul Richter, and Tieck. See the two-volume collection, with interpretive essays, edited by Gerhard Stenzel, *Die deutschen Romantiker* (Salzburg: n.d.). See also Frank E. Manuel and Fritzie P. Manuel, *Utopian Thought in the Western World* (Cambridge, Mass.: 1979), pts. 4–6; and Terry Pinkard, *German Philosophy 1760–1860: The Legacy of Idealism* (Cambridge, Eng.: 2002). Herder played a significant role in Liszt's essay on *Lohengrin* on the occasion of its premiere in Weimar in 1850, an event that coincided with a Herder festival; see Liszt, *Gesammelte Schriften*, vol. 3, pp. 63–81. Liszt's attitude toward nationalism has persistently made it hard for nationalists in the modern sense to appropriate him. On the Hungarian side, see Bartók's 1936 reflections on Liszt's national identity in *Essays*, pp. 508–10. See also the curious Nazi-era publication *Franz Liszt: Ein Künstlerleben in Wort und Bild* by Werner Füssmann and Béla Mátéka (Berlin and Leipzig) from 1936, precisely when Bartók sought to resist the rising tide of Hungarian right-wing nationalism. This publication was a joint effort under Peter Raabe's supervision between the Germans and the Hungarians. The weight was placed on Liszt's status as a part of German culture.

69. Religious music also provided Liszt with a traditional option, as the *Gran Mass* indicates. Liszt's large sacred oratorio projects were reminiscent of an early-nineteenth-century genre that persisted after Mendelssohn. Although employed by Dvořák and Max Bruch, the oratorio was limited in its reach, despite the extensive network of choral societies in German-speaking Europe. The limitation was greater in Catholic Europe. In religion, beauty and the sublime could coexist together with reason and passion. Liszt's claims, and those of his first biographers, that he wavered early in his life between the career of artist or priest suggest the internal consistency that religion provided within the three main phases of his career: before 1848, in Weimar, and the last period, split among Rome, Budapest, and Weimar. Although the religious revival in Europe after 1815 is understood as a reaction to the revolutionary and Napoleonic eras, in Liszt's case we can see how religion, in its nineteenth-century incarnation, was construed by him as a means to sustain an aesthetic continuity dating back before 1789. Liszt's energetic pursuit of non-musical studies led him to enthusiasms that revealed a spiritual synthesis of political utopianism and piety. He therefore did not turn to scientific socialism, in Marx's definition. Religion permitted him to reconcile notions of authority with universal social justice. Liszt's delight in honors bestowed by the old aristocracy, the Church, and monarchy, and his defense of Napoleon III, much to Marie d'Agoult's later dismay, have their source in this romance with religion. His reaction to suppression of the Hungarian resistance after 1848 was ultimately modulated into a deference to the moderate 1867 compromise and the resolution of Hungarian aspirations within Habsburg rule. Consider the opinion dating from 1851 of the historian Theodor von Bernhardi on the conservative shift in Liszt's political outlook. See Williams, *Portrait of Liszt*, p. 278.

70. See Richard Bolster, *Marie d'Agoult: The Rebel Countess* (New Haven and London: 2000), p. 238; and Phyllis Stock-Morton, *The Life of Marie d'Agoult alias Daniel Stern* (Baltimore and London: 2000), pp. 190–91. Liszt's acceptance of the 1867 compromise is best understood by the *Coronation Mass*. See his 1867 letters to Archbishop Haynald and Count Festetics; in *Franz Liszt: Briefe aus ungarischen Sammlungen, 1835–1886*, ed. Margit Prahács (Kassel: 1966), p. 129.

71. See Liszt, *Friedrich Chopin*, trans. La Mara (Leipzig: 1880), esp. p. 228.

72. It is interesting in this regard to consult Liszt's essay on Mozart from 1856, in *Gesammelte Schriften*, vol. 3, p. 151. On Liszt's relationship to Humboldt, see Williams, *Portrait of Liszt*, pp. 176 and 522.

73. For Liszt on Berlioz, see Liszt's 1855 essay, "Berlioz und seine Harold Symphonie," in *Gesammelte Schriften*, vol. 4, esp. pp. 42–50.

74. Consider, for example, the symphonic poem *Die Ideale*, based on Schiller, as well as, of course, the writings on the Goethe Stiftung. See the essay collection *Liszt und die*

Weimarer Klassik, ed. Detlef Altenburg (Laaber: 1997), esp. Altenburg's essay "Franz Liszt und das Erbe der Klassik," pp. 9–32; and Christian Berger's "Die Musik der Zukunft: Liszts Symphonische Dichtung *Die Ideale*," pp. 101–14.

75. Ironically, Wagner, as *Parsifal* makes plain, veered away from his early political radicalism.

76. The best source for understanding Liszt's network of Hungarian colleagues and his construct of the Hungarian nation are the two volumes by Deszö Legány, *Ferenc Liszt and His Country, 1869–1873* (Budapest: 1983); and *Liszt and His Country 1874–1886* (Budapest: 1992).

77. On Hanslick and Liszt, see the essay by Markus Gärtner, "Der Hörer im Visier: Hanslicks und Liszts Prinzipienstreit über die wahre Art, Musik zu verstehen," in *Eduard Hanslick: Sämtliche Schriften*, vol. 1/5: *(Aufsätze und Rezensionen)*, ed. Dietmar Strauss (Vienna: 2005), pp. 457–68.

78. See "Defending Liszt: Felix Draeseke on the Symphonic Poems," the translation of Felix Draeseke's essay in this volume, pp. 485–511.

79. Ibid.; and Keith T. Johns, *The Symphonic Poems of Franz Liszt*, rev. and ed. Michael Saffle (Stuyvesant, N.Y.: 1997), esp. pp. 1–82. See also Arthur Hahn, *Franz Liszt: Symphonische Dichtungen*, with a foreword by A. Pochhammer (Vienna: n.d.).

80. See I. Szelény, "Der unbekannte Liszt," in *Liszt-Bartók*, pp. 311–31.

81. Johns, *The Symphonic Poems*, pp. 18–20.

82. See Alan Richardson, *Literature, Education, and Romanticism: Reading as Social Practice 1780–1832* (Cambridge, Eng.: 1994).

83. Niecks, *Programme Music*, pp. 295–316.

84. In the writing of history, the aesthetic quarrels and rivalries of the past can become too exaggerated, not in terms of the distaste and enmity between the protagonists, but in terms of the actual aesthetic differences. Consider the place of Robert Schumann, once a Liszt colleague, who was later appropriated by the enemies of Liszt and Wagner as a proponent of the "absolute" non-programmatic approach to instrumental music. Schumann's last symphony, in terms of chronology, not numbering, was the "Rhenish," op. 97 in E-flat. In its original form it contained a subtitle for the fourth movement "In the character of an accompaniment to a solemn ceremony." Although the title was probably given by violinist and Schumann biographer Wilhelm Joseph von Wasielewski, Schumann himself described the work to his publisher as reflecting "something of Rhenish life here and there." And there is the disputed connection between the work and the revolution of 1848 and its subsequent suppression (in the allusions to Beethoven's E-flat *Eroica* Symphony). Furthermore, regarding the programmatic aspects of the work, one must consider the supposition that the nationalist symbolism of the rebuilding of the Cologne Cathedral inspired the fourth movement. The symphony was finished in late 1850, at a time when Schumann was not regarded as representing a conservative alternative to Liszt or young Wagner. Indeed, some sort of program and perhaps narrative is at work in this unusual five-movement work, despite its use of an overtly classical form. See Joachim Draheim, "Preface," in Robert Schumann, *Symphony no. 3, op. 97* (Breitkopf & Härtel no. 5263; Wiesbaden: 2001). See also Ernst Lichtenhahn, "Sinfonie als Dichtung," in *Schumanns Werke: Texte und Interpretation: 16 Studien*, ed. Akio Mayeda and Klaus W. Niemöller (Mainz and London: 1987), pp. 17–27.

85. In the two largest works, the *Dante* Symphony and the *Faust* Symphony, sung texts appear, but they play a minor though dramatic role that does not detract from the overriding character of the compositions as instrumental essays

86. For Bartók on the B Minor Sonata, see Bartók, *Essays*, pp. 453–54. Pianist Piers Lane has pointed out striking similarities between Alkan's "Quasi-Faust" (from his op. 33,

Grande Sonate: Les Quatre Ages, from 1848) and the musical materials of the B Minor Sonata, suggesting the continuity in Liszt's instrumental music of framing literary ideas.

87. See Youmans, *Richard Strauss's Orchestral Music*; also the essays by Stephen E. Hefling and James Hepokoski in *Richard Strauss: New Perspectives*, ed. Bryan Gilliam (Durham, N.C.: 1992), pp. 41–53, 135–175; and Hepokoski's essay on *Macbeth*, in *Richard Strauss and His World*, ed. Bryan Gilliam (Princeton, N.J.: 1992), pp. 67–89.

88. Constantin Floros, *Gustav Mahler: Mahler und die Symphonik des 19. Jahrhunderts in neuer Deutung*, vol. 2 (Wiesbaden: 1977), see esp. pp. 59–106.

89. Liszt's attitude to the question of national identity and culture was most extensively expressed in *Des Bohémiens et de leur musique en Hongrie*, best known in its revised edition published in November 1881. The German version, somewhat toned down, was translated by Lina Ramann and appeared in 1883. See Walker, *Liszt: The Final Years*, pp. 405–9, 411. But equally telling is his letter to Baron Anthal August on the subject of patriotism in Williams, *Portrait of Liszt*, pp. 363–64.

90. See Liszt's letter to Baron August, 20 September 1871, where he comments on Sophie Menter's mother's despair at the idea that her daughter would marry a Jew. Liszt's response is mild. Another reference, from 1883, is Liszt's delight upon hearing that Alexander Siloti had broken up with his Jewish girlfriend. See Williams, *Selected Letters*, p. 734; and Williams, *Portrait of Liszt*, p. 620. For Bruch's attitude, see Christopher Fifield, *Max Bruch: His Life and Work* (New York: 1988), p. 318.

91. See Solie on George Eliot, in *Music in Other Words*, pp. 153–86.

92. Compare the text of the 1859 edition *Des Bohémiens et de leur musique en Hongrie* to the German 1883 version, *Die Zigeuner und ihre Musik in Ungarn*. See also Rainer Riehn, "Wider die Verunglimpfung des Andenkens Verstorbener: Liszt soll Antisemit gewesen sein," in Metzger and Riehn, *Franz Liszt*, pp. 100–14; Gut, *Franz Liszt*, pp. 205–12. On Liszt's impression that Eliot was Jewish, see his letter to the *Gazette d'hongrie* of 6 February 1883, in Williams, *Liszt: Selected Letters*, p. 897. On Eliot's attitude to proto-Semitism and the Wissenschaft des Judentums movement, see Stephen Graham, "George Eliot's Dialogue with History," Ph.D. diss. Columbia University (2004), chap. 4.

INDEX

Index

Index of Liszt's Musical Works

Note: Page numbers followed by *n* indicate notes; *italicized* page numbers indicate musical examples.

Subject Index

Page numbers followed by *n* indicate
notes; *italicized* page numbers indicate
material in tables, figures, or musical
examples. Also *see* separate Index to
List of Works.

Notes on the Contributors

Peter Bloom's research since his doctoral dissertation on François-Joseph Fétis has focused on the life and work of Hector Berlioz. He is the editor of volumes 7 and 24 of the *New Berlioz Edition* and of four collections of articles on Berlioz and his era: *Music in Paris in the Eighteen-Thirties* (1987), *Berlioz Studies* (1992), *The Cambridge Companion to Berlioz* (2000), and *Berlioz Past, Present, Future* (2003); he is also coeditor of the *Dictionnaire Berlioz* (2003). His *Life of Berlioz* was published by Cambridge University Press in 1998. Currently at work on a new critical edition of the *Mémoires d'Hector Berlioz*, Bloom is the Grace Jarcho Ross Professor of Humanities at Smith College, where he has been teaching since 1970.

Leon Botstein is president and Leon Levy Professor in the Arts and Humanities at Bard College. He is the author of *Judentum und Modernität* (1991) and *Jefferson's Children: Education and the Promise of American Culture* (1997). He is the editor of *The Compleat Brahms* (1999) and *The Musical Quarterly*, as well as coeditor, with Werner Hanak, of *Vienna: Jews and the City of Music, 1870–1938* (2004). The music director of the American and the Jerusalem symphony orchestras, he has recorded works by, among others, Szymanowski, Hartmann, Bruch, Toch, Dohnányi, Bruckner, Chausson, Richard Strauss, Mendelssohn, Popov, Shostakovich, and Liszt for Telarc, CRI, Koch, Arabesque, and New World Records.

José Antonio Bowen is dean of the School of Fine Arts and a professor of music at Miami University. He has degrees in chemistry, music, and humanities, and a joint Ph.D. in musicology and humanities from Stanford. He has written over 100 scholarly articles, is the editor of the *Cambridge Companion to Conducting* and is currently working on the *Smithsonian Anthology of Jazz*. As a jazz performer, he has appeared in Europe, Israel and the United States with Stan Getz, Dizzy Gillespie, Bobby McFerrin, Dave Brubeck, Hubert Laws, Liberace, and many others. He has written a symphony (nominated for the Pulitzer Prize), a film score, and music for Jerry Garcia, and appears on numerous recordings. He received a NEH fellowship, is a fellow of the Royal Society of Arts (FRSA) in England, and is on the National Preservations Recording Board for the Library of Congress.

Anna Harwell Celenza holds the Caestecker Chair in Music at Georgetown University. She is the author of *The Early Works of Niels W. Gade: In Search of the Poetic* (2001); *Hans Christian Andersen and Music: The Nightingale Revealed* (2005); and several articles on Liszt, the most recent of which have appeared in *19th-Century Music* and *The Cambridge Companion to Liszt*. In addition to her scholarly work, she has authored a series of award-winning children's books about music and is a regular writer for NPR's "Performance Today."

James Deaville is associate professor and director of graduate studies in the School of the Arts of McMaster University. He has lectured and published about Wagner, Mahler, Strauss, Reger, Liszt and his circle in Weimar, music criticism, music and gender, television and film music, and music and race. The editor of the Bayreuth memoirs of Wagner's ballet master Richard Fricke (1997), his writings have appeared in the *New Grove Dictionary of Music and Musicians*, the *New Grove Dictionary of Opera*, the *Norton/New Grove Dictionary of Women Composers*, *Studies in American Music*, *Notes*, *Hamburger Jahrbuch für Musikwissenschaft*, *Studien zur Wertungsforschung*, the *Cambridge Companion to Liszt*, and the *Cambridge Companion to the Lied*, among others. He coedited *Criticus musicus* and is currently English-language editor of the *Canadian University Music Review*. He is writing the first scholarly study of the Allgemeiner deutscher Musikverein.

Christopher H. Gibbs is James H. Ottaway Jr. Professor of Music at Bard College, coartistic director of the Bard Music Festival, and associate editor of *The Musical Quarterly*. He edited *The Cambridge Companion to Schubert* (1997) and is the author of *The Life of Schubert* (2000), which has been translated into three languages. Since 2000 he has written the program notes for the Philadelphia Orchestra.

Susan H. Gillespie is vice president for Special Global Initiatives at Bard College, and Founding Director of Bard's Institute for International Liberal Education. Her published translations include novels, non-fiction works, poems, and works on musicology and philosophy including numerous essays by German philosopher Theodor Wiesengrund Adorno.

Vincent Giroud is currently professor of history at Bard College, having previously taught at Johns Hopkins, Vassar, and Yale, where he also served as curator of modern books and manuscripts. Among his most recent publications are *St Petersburg: A Portrait of a Great City* and *The World of*

Witold Gombrowicz, as well as a volume of essays on Isabelle de Charrière, coedited with Janet Whatley; he also contributed to the volume of Paul Morand's novels published in the Bibliothèque de la Pléiade (2005). His current projects include *A Short History of French Opera* for Yale University Press and, in collaboration with Jean-Christophe Branger, a catalogue of the works of Jules Massenet.

Dana Gooley is assistant professor of music at Brown University. He received his Ph.D. in musicology from Princeton University, and subsequently taught at Harvard University, Amherst College, and Case Western Reserve University. His book *The Virtuoso Liszt* (2004) examines Liszt's performing career in relation to the social and cultural currents of the 1830s and '40s.

Susan Hohl is completing her doctoral studies at the University of Chicago in comparative literature and music, and is writing a dissertation about Liszt as both reader and songwriter. She is also active as a singer, dramaturge, and acting coach.

Allan Keiler is professor of music at Brandeis University. He has a Ph.D. in linguistics from Harvard University, where he studied with Roman Jakobson. He did his graduate work in musicology and music theory at the Universities of Michigan and Chicago, and did a lay traineeship at the Boston Psychoanalytic Institute. His work in semiotics, the history of music theory, and Liszt has appeared in many journals and collections including *Journal of Music Theory*, *19th-Century Music*, *Music and Perception*, *Musical Quarterly*, *Perspectives in New Music*, *Studia Musicologica*, *Music Theory: Special Topics*, and *The Sign in Music and Literature*. His biography *Marian Anderson: A Singer's Journey*, was published by Scribner in 2000. He is working on a biography of Liszt.

Rainer Kleinertz is professor of musicology at Regensburg University. He studied music (viola and harpsichord) at the Hochschule für Musik Detmold, and musicology and German and Romance literature at Paderborn University. He was visiting professor at Salamanca University (1992–94), and visiting fellow at Oxford University (2000–01). His main areas of research are the music and writings of Franz Liszt and Richard Wagner, and Spanish music theater. Among other publications, he is coeditor of the *Complete Writings of Franz Liszt* (1989–) and author of *Grundzüge des spanischen Musiktheaters im 18. Jahrhundert* (2 vols, 2003).

Ralph P. Locke is professor of musicology at the Eastman School of Music (University of Rochester). He is the author of *Music, Musicians, and the Saint-Simonians* (1986) and co-editor (with Cyrilla Barr) of *Cultivating Music in America: Women Patrons and Activists since 1860* (1997). He is senior editor of *Eastman Studies in Music* (a series from the University of Rochester Press). Five of his articles have received the ASCAP-Deems Taylor Award. He has recently published articles on Aaron Copland (two interviews from the early 1970s), Virgil Thomson, and Leonard Bernstein, and is currently working on a book about the role of the exotic in Western art music from the sixteenth century to the present. His writings have been published also in French, German, Italian, Spanish, Czech, and Japanese.

Ryan Minor is assistant professor of music at SUNY Stony Brook. He recently received his Ph.D. from the University of Chicago, and has published on Wagner and Brahms. He is currently working on a book exploring the music and politics of the chorus in nineteenth-century Germany.

Rena Charnin Mueller teaches in the Department of Music at New York University, Faculty of Arts and Science. A specialist in nineteenth-century music, her article on the Liszt/Wagner reception history in New York is forthcoming in *Importing Culture: European Music and Musicians in New York City, 1840–1890* (University of Rochester Press); and her chapter on the Liszt Lieder appeared in the *Cambridge Companion to the Lied* (2004). She has published source-critical editions of Listz's *Les Préludes*, the *Trois Études de Concert*, and the two *Ballades*. Her edition of the recently-discovered Liszt *Walse* was published by Thorpe Music, Boston. With Mária Eckhardt, she is the author of the Franz Liszt "List of Works" for the *New Grove of Music and Musicians* (2001), and together they are preparing a complete thematic catalog of Liszt's music.

Benjamin Walton is lecturer in music at the University of Bristol. His work on French musical culture in the 1820s and '30s has appeared in *19th-Century Music*, the *Cambridge Opera Journal*, the *Blackwell Companion to European Romanticism*, and the *Cambridge Companion to Rossini*. He has recently completed a book on Rossini and 1820s Paris, which will be published by Cambridge University Press.

Susan Youens is J. W. Van Gorkom Professor at the University of Notre Dame, where she has taught since 1984. She is the author of numerous scholarly articles and eight books on nineteenth-century song, including *Schubert's Late Lieder: Beyond the Song Cycles* and *Hugo Wolf and his Mörike Songs* (both from Cambridge University Press, 2000 and 2002). Her current project, *Heinrich Heine and the Lied: The Early Years*, is forthcoming from Cambridge University Press in late 2006.